Lecture Notes in Computer Science 3947

Commenced Publication in 1973
Founding and Former Series Editors:
Gerhard Goos, Juris Hartmanis, and Jan van Leeuwen

Yeh-Ching Chung   José E. Moreira (Eds.)

Advances in Grid and Pervasive Computing

First International Conference, GPC 2006
Taichung, Taiwan, May 3-5, 2006
Proceedings

 Springer

Volume Editors

Yeh-Ching Chung
National Tsing Hua University
Department of Computer Science
Hsin-Chu, Taiwan 300, ROC
E-mail: ychung@cs.nthu.edu.tw

José E. Moreira
IBM Systems & Technology Group
Blue Gene Software Systems
Rochester, MN 55901, USA
E-mail: jmoreira@us.ibm.com

Library of Congress Control Number: 2006924367

CR Subject Classification (1998): F.1, F.2, D.1, D.2, D.4, C.2, C.4, H.4, K.6

LNCS Sublibrary: SL 1 – Theoretical Computer Science and General Issues

ISSN	0302-9743
ISBN-10	3-540-33809-8 Springer Berlin Heidelberg New York
ISBN-13	978-3-540-33809-3 Springer Berlin Heidelberg New York

Springer is a part of Springer Science+Business Media

springer.com

© Springer-Verlag Berlin Heidelberg 2006
Printed in Germany

Typesetting: Camera-ready by author, data conversion by Scientific Publishing Services, Chennai, India
Printed on acid-free paper   SPIN: 11745693   06/3142   5 4 3 2 1 0

Message from the General Chairs

It is our great pleasure to welcome you to the beautiful campus of Tunghai University, Taiwan, and the first annual event of the International Conference on Grid and Pervasive Computing (GPC). Grid computing addresses the needs for coordinating and sharing large-scale heterogeneous resources for problem solving in dynamic, multi-institutional virtual organizations. Extending the resource concept into our physical surroundings and everyday objects, it is not hard to see the overlapping of grid and pervasive computing. It is with this view that GPC 2006 was established to serve as the premier forum covering the emerging research and development on blending and extending grid and pervasive technologies.

An international conference of this scale requires the support of many people. First of all, we would like to thank the Steering Committee Chair, Hai Jin, and the committee members for nourishing the conference and guiding its course. We also like to express our sincere appreciation to the Program Chairs, Yeh-Ching Chung and Jose Moreira, who, together with the exceptional Program Committee members, put together a highly selective and very exciting technical program. We are also indebted to the members of the Organizing Committee. Particularly, we thank Chao-Tung Yang, Kuan-Ching Li, Cho-Li Wang and Ching-Hsien Hsu for their devotions and efforts to make this conference a real success. Our heartfelt gratitude also goes to the Honorary General Chair, President of Tunghai University, Haydn H.D. Chen for his full support of this conference. Finally, we would like to take this opportunity to thank all the authors, reviewers and participants for their contributions to making GPC 2006 a grand success.

It has been an honor for us to serve as General Chairs for the first event of this great conference and to work with a group of dedicated and capable people. We trust that you will enjoy the proceedings of GPC 2006.

May 2006 — Sajal K. Das and Chung-Ta King, General Co-chairs

Message from the Program Co-chairs

We are proud to present the proceedings of the First International Conference on Grid and Pervasive Computing 2006, held at Tunghai University during May 3-5.

Grid and Pervasive Computing (GPC) is an annual international conference on the emerging areas of merging grid computing and pervasive computing, aimed at providing an exciting platform and paradigm for all the time, everywhere services. This emergence is a natural outcome of the advances in cluster computing, high-performance computing, utility computing, service-oriented computing, peer-to-peer computing, mobile computing, sensor networks, and smart devices technologies. The aim of GPC 2006 was to be the premier event on grid and pervasive computing, focusing on all aspects of grid and pervasive computing and providing a high-profile, leading edge forum for researchers and engineers alike to present their latest research.

In order to guarantee high-quality proceedings, we put extensive effort into reviewing the scientific papers and processing the proceedings. We received 267 papers from 24 countries. All submissions were peer reviewed by three or four program or technical committee members or external reviewers. It was extremely difficult to select the presentations for the conference because there were so many excellent and interesting ones. In order to include as many papers as possible and keep the high quality of the conference, we finally decided to accept 64 papers for oral presentations. We believe all of these papers and topics will not only provide novel ideas, new results, work in progress and state-of-the-art techniques in this field, but will also stimulate future research activities in the area of grid and pervasive computing with applications.

This conference would not have been possible without the support of many people and organizations that helped in various ways to make it a success. The exciting program for this conference was the result of the hard and excellent work of many people. We would like to express our sincere thanks to the invited speakers who delivered such high-quality lectures at GPC 2006 and all authors for their valuable contributions. We thank the Program Committee members for their excellent job of reviewing the submissions and thus guaranteeing the quality of the conference and the proceedings under a very tight schedule.

May 2006

Yeh-Ching Chung and Jose E. Moreira
Program Co-chairs

Organization

Conference Committees

Honorary General Chair

Haydn H.D. Chen, Tunghai University, Taiwan

Steering Committee Chair

Hai Jin, Huazhong University of Science and Technology, China

Steering Committee Members

Jean-Luc Gaudiot, University of California - Irvine, USA
Chung-Ta King, National Tsing Hua University, Taiwan
Jysoo Lee, KISTI, Korea
Kuan-Ching Li, Providence University, Taiwan
Satoshi Sekiguchi, AIST, Japan
Cho-Li Wang, The University of Hong Kong, China
Chao-Tung Yang, Tunghai University, Taiwan
Albert Y. Zomaya, The University of Sydney, Australia

General Co-chairs

Sajal K. Das, The University of Texas at Arlington, USA
Chung-Ta King, National Tsing Hua University, Taiwan

Program Committee Co-chairs

Jose E. Moreira, IBM Systems and Technology Group, USA
Yeh-Ching Chung, National Tsing Hua University, Taiwan

Publicity Co-chairs

Hao-Hua Chu, National Taiwan University, Taiwan
Kuan-Ching Li, Providence University, Taiwan

Publication Co-chairs

Cho-Li Wang, The University of Hong Kong, China
Ching-Hsien Hsu, Chung Hua University, Taiwan

Finance Co-chairs

Chao-Tung Yang, Tunghai University, Taiwan
Wen-Chung Chiang, Hsiuping Institute of Technology, Taiwan

Registration Co-chairs

Liang-Teh Lee, Tatung University, Taiwan
Kun-Ming Yu, Chung Hua University, Taiwan

Local Arrangement Co-chairs

Chu-Hsing Lin, Tunghai University, Taiwan
Hsiao-Hsi Wang, Providence University, Taiwan

Best Paper Award Committee Chair

Jemal Abawajy, Deakin University, Australia

Best Paper Award Committee

Yong-Kee Jun, Gyeongsang National University, Korea
Wang-Chien Lee, Penn State University, USA
Ivan Stojmenovic, University of Ottawa, Canada

International Program Committee

Jemal Abawajy, Deakin University, Australia
Jose Nelson Amaral, University of Alberta, Canada
Hamid R. Arabnia, University of Georgia, USA
Mark Baker, University of Portsmouth, UK
Rajkumar Buyya, University of Melbourne, Australia
Jiannong Cao, Hong Kong Polytechnic University, China
Christophe Cerin, Universite de Paris XIII, France
Jerry Hsi-Ya Chang, NCHC, Taiwan
Ruay-Shiung Chang, National Dong Hwa University, Taiwan
Wenguang Chen, Tsinghua University, China
Hao-Hua Chu, National Taiwan University, Taiwan
Walfredo Cirne, UFCG, Brazil
Toni Cortes, Universitat Politecnica de Catalunya, Spain

Cho-Li Wang, University of Hong Kong, China
Frank Zhigang Wang, Cranfield University, UK
Sheng-De Wang, National Taiwan University, Taiwan
Andrew Wendelborn, University of Adelaide, Australia
Weng Fai Wong, National University of Singapore, Singapore
Jingling Xue, University of New South Wales, Australia
Chao-Tung Yang, Tunghai University, Taiwan
Guangwen Yang, Tsinghua University, China
Laurence T. Yang, St. Francis Xavier University, Canada

Table of Contents

Session 4: Web/Grid Services

Session 5: High Performance Computing

Session 6: Ad Hoc Networks

Session 7: Wireless Sensor Networks

Session 8: Grid Applications 1

Session 9: Data Grid

Session 10: Pervasive Applications 1

Session 11: Semantic Web / Semantic Grid

Session 12: Grid Load Balancing

Session 13: Wireless Ad Hoc/Sensor Networks

Session 14: Grid Applications 2

Session 15: Mobile Computing

Session 16: Pervasive Applications 2

Optimizing Server Placement in Hierarchical Grid Environments

Chien-Min Wang[1], Chun-Chen Hsu[1], Pangfeng Liu[2],
Hsi-Min Chen[3], and Jan-Jan Wu[1]

[1] Institute of Information Science, Academia Sinica, Taipei, Taiwan
{cmwang, tk, wuj}@iis.sinica.edu.tw
[2] Department of Computer Science and Information Engineering,
National Taiwan University, Taipei, Taiwan
pangfeng@csie.ntu.edu.tw
[3] Department of Computer Science and Information Engineering,
National Central University, Taoyuan, Taiwan
seeme@selab.csie.ncu.edu.tw

Abstract. In this paper, we address some problems related to server placement in Grid environments. Given a hierarchical network with requests from clients and constraints on server capability, the minimum server placement problem attempts to place the minimum number of servers that satisfy clients requests. Instead of using a heuristic approach, we propose an optimal algorithm based on dynamic programming to solve the problem. We also consider the balanced server placement problem, which tries to place a given number of servers appropriately so that their workloads are as balanced as possible. We prove that an optimal server placement can be achieved by combining the above algorithm with a binary search of workloads. We extend this approach to deal with constrains on network capability. The simulation results clearly show an improvement in the number of servers and the maximum workload. Furthermore, as the maximum workload is reduced, the waiting times are reduced accordingly.

1   Introduction

Grid technologies, which enable scientific applications to utilize a wide variety of distributed computing and data resources, classified into two categories: Computing Grids and Data Grids [1, 2]. A Data Grid is a distributed storage infrastructure that integrates distributed, independently managed data resources. It addresses the problems of storage and data management, data transfers and data access optimization, while maintaining high reliability and availability of the data. In recent years, a number of Data Grid projects have emerged in various disciplines, for instance, EU Data Grid [3], PPDG [4], iVDGL [5], GriPhyN [6] and BIRN [7].

One way of solving the data access optimization problems is to distribute multiple copies of a file across different server sites in the grid system. It has

Y.-C. Chung and J.E. Moreira (Eds.): GPC 2006, LNCS 3947, pp. 1–11, 2006.

been shown that file replication can improve the performance of the applications [8, 9, 10, 11]. The existing works focus on how to distribute the file replicas in a data grid in order to optimize different criteria such as I/O operation costs [11], response time and bandwidth consumption [9].

In this paper, we focus on some server placement problems in Data Grid environments. Given a hierarchical network with requests from clients and constraints on server capability, the solution to minimum server placement problem attempts to place the minimum number of servers that can satisfy clients requests. Instead of using a heuristic approach, we propose an optimal algorithm based on dynamic programming to solve this problem. We also consider the balanced server placement problem, which tries to place a given number of servers appropriately so that their workloads are as balanced as possible. We prove that an optimal server placement can be achieved by combining the above algorithm with a binary search on workloads. We extend this approach to deal with constrains on network capability. The experiment results clearly show the improvement in the number of servers and the maximum workload. Furthermore, as the maximum workload is reduced, waiting times are also reduced.

2 Background

In this paper, we use a hierarchical Grid model, one of the most common architectures in current use [8, 9, 12, 13, 14]. Consider Fig. 1 as an example. Leaf nodes represent client sites that send out I/O requests. The root node is assumed to be the I/O server that stores the master copies of all files. Without loss of generality, we assume that root node is the site 0. Intermediate nodes can be either routers for network communications or I/O servers that store file replicas. Edges represent communication channels between nodes. We further assume that, initially, only one copy (i.e., the master copy) of a file exists at the root site, as in [9, 13].

Associated with each client site i, there is a parameter r_i that represents the arrival rate of read requests for client site i. A data request travels upward from a client site and passes through routers until it reach an I/O server on the path.

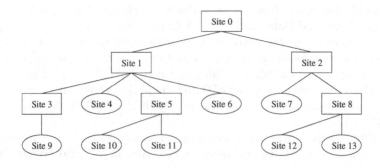

Fig. 1. The hierarchical Grid model

Upon receiving the request, the I/O server sends data back to the client site if it owns a copy of the requested file. Otherwise, it forwards the request to its parent server. This process continues up the hierarchy recursively until a node that has the requested file is encountered or the root node is reached. The root server might update the contents of the file. For each update, corresponding update requests are sent to the other I/O servers to maintain file consistency. Let u be the arrival rate of update requests from the root server.

Associated with each server site j, there is a parameter λ_j that represents the arrival rate of I/O requests; λ_j can be written as: $\lambda_j = \sum_{i \in C_j} r_i + u$, where C_j is the set of clients served by server site j. The first term represents the read requests generated by clients in C_j. The second term denotes the update requests that will be sent to server site j. We can further generalize this model so that each edge has its own connectivity bandwidth constraints.

In the absence of file replicas, all I/O requests must be served by the roots node. However, the request arrival rate is usually much higher than the service rate of the root node so that clients have to wait indefinitely for service. By placing I/O servers between client sites and the root node, some of I/O requests can be served by these I/O servers thereby alleviating the workload on the root node. According to Queueing Theory, the workload of I/O servers is the dominant factor in the waiting time of I/O requests. Therefore, to benefit from file replicas, it is important to place I/O servers at appropriate locations in a hierarchical Grid system.

3   The Minimum Server Placement Problem

I/O requests generated by client sites and data transfer requests served by server sites can be modeled as queueing systems. According to Queueing Theory, the queue length and the waiting time of a queueing system will eventually reach infinity if the arrival rate of data is greater than the service rate. Hence, there is a hard constraint on the arrival rate of each I/O server in a Grid system. File replicas present a natural solution to this problem. By placing the replicas with more I/O servers, it is possible to share I/O requests along servers and balance their workload. However, it is quite expensive to set up I/O servers in a Grid system, as having more servers usually lead to lower utilization, which means a waste of the systems resources and increased maintenance costs. Therefore, our first problem is to place the minimum number of I/O servers that will balance the workload of I/O requests.

Definition 1. Given the network topology, request arrival rates and I/O service rates, the *minimum server placement problem* tries to place the minimum number of I/O servers such that the arrival rate of requests that reach each I/O server isless than its service rate.

To solve this problem, we intuitively employ a greedy method, similar to that in [12], by placing I/O servers one by one until all the servers including the root server meet their constraints. Although this algorithm is rather fast and easy to implement, we found that it did not always generate the minimum number of servers in our experiments. Therefore, instead of employing a heuristic approach, we try to find an optimal algorithm based on the dynamic programming approach as shown in the remainder of this section.

Definition 2. Let $L(i, m)$ be the minimum arrival rate of *leakage requests* that pass through node i when at most m servers are placed in the sub-tree rooted at node i, and the arrival rate of requests that reach each I/O server is less than its service rate.

Leakage requests that pass through node i are requests generated by leaf nodes in the sub-tree rooted at node i, but not served by the I/O servers in that sub-tree. Such requests must be serviced by an I/O server above node i in the hierarchy. Hence, it is desirable to minimize the arrival rate of these leakage requests. Depending on the server placement, the arrival rate of the leakage requests may change. $L(i, m)$ represents the minimum arrival rate of leakage requests among all possible placements of at most m servers. Let n be the number of nodes in the Grid system. Based on the following theorems, such a minimum arrival rate can be computed in a recursive manner.

Theorem 1. $L(i, m + 1) \leq L(i, m)$ for any node i and $m \geq 0$.

Theorem 2. If node i is a leaf node, then $L(i, m) = \lambda_j$ for $0 \leq m \leq n$.

Proof. Since a leaf node cannot be an I/O server, all I/O requests generated by a client site will travel up the tree to the leaf nodes parent. By Definition, $L(i, m) = \lambda_j$ for $0 \leq m \leq n$.   □

Theorem 3. For an intermediate node i with two child nodes j and k, we can derive:

$$L(i, m) = 0 \text{ if } min_{0 \leq r \leq m-1}\{L(j, r) + L(k, m - r - 1)\} \leq \mu_i$$

$$L(i, m) = min_{0 \leq r \leq m}\{L(j, r) + L(k, m - r)\}, \text{ otherwise}$$

Proof. Case 1: A server is placed on node i. Consequently, at most, $m - 1$ servers are placed on sub-trees rooted at node j and node k. This happen if and only if $min_{0 \leq r \leq m-1}\{L(j, r) + L(k, m - r - 1)\} \leq \mu_i$. The "if" part can be proved as follows. Suppose that the minimum can be obtained when there are p servers on the sub-tree rooted at node j and q servers on the sub-tree rooted at node k as shown in Fig. 2(a). By Definition, the minimum arrival rate of leakage requests that pass through node j and node k will be $L(j, p)$ and $L(k, q)$ respectively. Since node i has only two child nodes, j and k, the arrival rate of I/O requests that reach node i must be the sum $L(j, p) + L(k, q)$. Accordingly, we can derive:

$$L(j, p) + L(k, q) = min_{0 \leq r \leq m-1}\{L(j, r) + L(k, m - r - 1)\} \leq \mu_i$$

Hence, a server can be placed on node i. In this case, $L(i, m) = 0$ and must be optimal. The "only if" part can be proved similarly. Suppose that, in an optimal

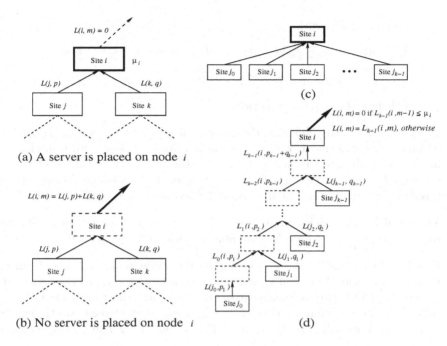

Fig. 2. (a). (b) Illustrate two possible server placements on node i. (c). (d) Illustrate the basic concept of Theorem 4.

server placement, there are p servers on the sub-tree rooted at node j and q servers on the sub-tree rooted at node k. Obviously, we have the inequalities $0 \leq p,q \leq m-1$ and $p+q \leq m-1$. Since node i has only two child nodes, j and k, the arrival rate of I/O requests that reach node i must be the sum $L(j,p)+L(k,q)$ and must meet the constraint $L(j,p)+L(k,q) \leq \mu_i$. According to Theorem 1, we can derive: $\mu_i \geq L(j,p)+L(k,q) \geq L(j,p)+L(k,m-1-p) \geq min_{0 \leq r \leq m-1}\{L(j,r)+L(k,m-r-1)\}$. This completes the proof of case 1.

Case 2: No server is placed on node i. Consequently, at most m servers are placed on sub-trees rooted at nodes, j and k. Suppose that, in an optimal server placement, there are p servers on the sub-tree rooted at node j and q servers on the sub-tree rooted at node k, as shown in Fig. 2(b). Obviously, we have the inequalities $0 \leq p,q \leq m$ and $p+q \leq m$. Since node i has only two child nodes, j and k, the arrival rate of I/O requests that reach and pass through node i can be computed as: $L(i,m) = L(j,p)+L(k,q) \geq L(j,p)+L(k,m-p) \geq min_{0 \leq r \leq m}\{L(j,r)+L(k,m-r)\}$. According to above the assumption, this is an optimal server placement. Hence, all the equalities must hold. This completes the proof of case 2.   □

Theorem 4. For an intermediate node i with k child nodes $j_0, j_1, \ldots, j_{k-1}$, the minimum arrival rate of leakage requests that pass through node i can be computed iteratively as follows:

$$L_0(i, m) = L(j_0, m),$$

$$L_q(i, m) = min_{0 \leq r \leq m}\{L_{q-1}(i, r) + L(j_q, m - r)\}, 1 \leq q \leq k - 1,$$

$$L(i, m) = 0 \text{ if } L_{k-1}(i, m - 1) \leq \mu_i; \text{ and}$$

$$L(i, m) = L_{k-1}(i, m), \text{ otherwise.}$$

Proof. Fig. 2(c), 2(d) illustrate the basic concept of this theorem. To find an optimal server placement, we can view an intermediate node with k child nodes in Fig. 2(c) as the sub-tree in Fig. 2(d). Then, the minimum arrival rate of leakage requests, $L(i, m)$, can be computed recursively along the sub-tree. As the detailed proof of this theorem is similar to that of Theorem 3, it is omitted here.   □

Theorem 5. The minimum number of I/O servers that meet their constraints can be obtained by finding the minimum m such that $L(0, m) = 0$.

Based on Theorems 2 to 4, we can compute the minimum arrival rate of leakage requests that start from leaf nodes and work toward the root node. After the minimum arrival rate of leakage requests that reach the root node has been computed, the minimum number of I/O servers that meet their constraints can be computed according to Theorem 5. The proposed algorithm is presented in Fig. 3.

Algorithm Minimum_Leakage
Input: 1. the arrival rate λ_i for all leaf nodes.
              2. the service rate μ_i for all intermediate nodes.
Output: the minimum arrival rate $L(i, m)$ for $0 \leq i, m \leq n$.
Procedure:
    1.   sort all nodes according to their distance to the root node in decreasing order.
    2.   for each node i do
    3.   if node i is a leaf node then
    4.   compute $L(i, m) = \lambda_i$ for $0 \leq m \leq n$
    5.   else
    6.   Let the child nodes of node i be nodes $j_0, \ldots, j_{k-1}$
    7.   compute $L_0(i, m) = L(j_0, m)$ for $0 \leq m \leq n$
    8.   for q from 1 to $k - 1$ do
    9.   compute $L_q(i, m) = min_{0 \leq r \leq m}\{L_{q-1}(i, r) + L(j_q, m - r)\}$ for $0 \leq m \leq n$
    10.   endfor
    11.   for m from 0 to n do
    12.   if $L_{k-1}(i, m - 1) \leq \mu_i$ then $L(i, m) = 0$ else $L(i, m) = L_{k-1}(i, m)$ endif
    13.   endfor
    14.   endif
    15.   endfor

Fig. 3. An optimal algorithm for the minimum server placement problem

In the first line of the algorithm, we sort all nodes according to their distances to the root node in decreasing order. This ensures that child nodes will be computed before their parents so that Theorems 2 to 4 can be correctly applied. The execution time of this step is $O(n \log n)$. The loop in line 2 iterates over every node in the system. For each leaf node, it takes $O(n)$ execution time in line 4. For an intermediate node that has k child nodes, it takes $O(n^2)$ execution time in line 9, and iterates $k-1$ times in line 8. This results in $O(kn^2)$ execution time for lines 8 to 10. Lines 11 to 13 also take $O(n)$ execution time. Consequently, the complexity of lines 3 to 13 is $O(kn^2)$; and the complexity of the whole algorithm is $O(n^3)$, where n is the number of nodes in the Grid system.

4   The Balanced Server Placement Problem

As mentioned in section 2 (the last paragraph), a major factor in the performance of a queuing system is the workload of the servers. Since each server may have a different capability, a servers workload is defined as the ratio of the arrival rate over the service rate. The minimum server problem sets a lower bound on the number of I/O servers. However, usually we would like to set up more I/O servers to reduce the workload. In this case, we are concerned with the maximum workloads of the I/O servers. In other words, we try to place a given number of servers appropriately so that the workload of the servers is as balanced as possible. We call this the *balanced server placement problem*.

Definition 3. The workload of a server i, denoted by ρ_i, is defined as the ratio of its arrival rate over its service rate: $\rho_i = \lambda_i/\mu_i$.

Definition 4. The maximum workload of a system is defined as the maximum workload among all servers in the system.

Definition 5. Given the network topology, request arrival rates and I/O service rates, the *balanced server placement problem* is: How to place a given number of I/O servers such that the maximum workload of the grid system is minimized?

Let m_0 represent the lower bound on the number of I/O servers, assume there are $m \geq m_0$ servers to be placed. Our goal is to place at most m servers such that the maximum workload is minimized. First, we present an algorithm to find a server placement when the maximum workload is known. Instead of solving this problem directly, we transform it into a minimum server placement problem discussed in section 3.

Theorem 6. There exists a placement of at most m servers such that $max\{\frac{\lambda_i}{\mu_i}\}$ $\leq \rho$ if and only if the minimum number of servers needed for arrival rates λ_i and service rates $\mu'_i = \rho \cdot \mu_i$ is less than or equal to m.

Proof. First, suppose that the minimum number of servers needed for arrival rates λ_i and service rates $\mu'_i = \rho \cdot \mu_i$ is less than or equal to m. By Definition, there must exist a placement of at most m servers such that $\lambda_i \leq \mu'_i = \rho \cdot \mu_i$ for all server nodes i. Thus, $\lambda_i/\mu_i \leq \rho$ for all server nodes i. Accordingly, we can derive $max\{\lambda_i/\mu_i\} \leq \rho$. This completes the proof of the "if" part.

Next, suppose there exists a placement of at most m servers such that $max\{\lambda_i/\mu_i\} \leq \rho$. We can derive $\lambda_i/\mu_i \leq \rho_i$ and $\lambda_i \leq \rho \cdot \mu_i$ for all server nodes i. Therefore, the minimum number of servers needed for arrival rates λ_i and service rates $\mu'_i = \rho \cdot \mu_i$ must be less than or equal to m. This completes the proof of the only if part. $\square$

Theorem 7. If there is no placement of at most m servers such that $max\{\lambda_i/\mu_i\}$ $\leq \rho$ and $\rho' \leq \rho$, then there cannot be a placement of at most m servers such that $max\{\lambda_i/\mu_i\} \leq \rho'$.

Proof. We prove this theorem by contradiction. Assume that there is no placement of at most m servers such that $max\{\lambda_i/\mu_i\} \leq \rho$ and $\rho' \leq \rho$, there exists a placement of at most m servers such that $max\{\lambda_i/\mu_i\} \leq \rho'$. Accordingly, we can derive that there must exist a placement of at most m servers such that $max\{\lambda_i/\mu_i\} \leq \rho' \leq \rho$. However, this contradicts the assumption. Therefore, there cannot be a placement of at most m servers such that $max\{\lambda_i/\mu_i\} \leq \rho'$.   □

According to Theorem 6, we can determine if there exists a placement of at most m servers such that $max\{\lambda_i/\mu_i\} \leq \rho$ by using the algorithm for the minimum server placement problem in section 3. The main difficulty with this approach is that we do not know the optimal value of the maximum workload yet. Fortunately, Theorem 7 provides a foundation for searching the optimal value of the maximum workload. It implies that if there is no server placement for a maximum workload ρ, then the optimal value must be greater than ρ. On the other hand, if there is a server placement for a maximum workload ρ, then it is possible to further minimize the value of the maximum workload. Combining Theorem 6 and 7 allows us to find the optimal value through a binary search of the maximum workload.

Before applying a binary search, however, we have to determine an upper bound and a lower bound. It is rather easy to get an upper bound and a lower bound on the maximum workload. So long as $m \geq m_0$, there always exists an upper bound of 1 on the maximum workload. A lower bound can be computed by assuming that the fastest m servers are chosen and I/O requests are distributed to these servers evenly. Next, we can combine a binary search of the maximum workload and the algorithm for the minimum server placement problem to find the optimal value of the maximum workload. Because the upper bound of the binary search is a constant and the lower bound is a function of the input parameters, the workload-balance algorithm is strongly polynomial.

Our algorithm can be further generalized to consider network bandwidth. Take Fig. 2(a) and 2(b) as examples. The arrival rate of I/O requests that pass through the communication channel between node j and node i is denoted as $L(j,p)$. Let μ_{ji} be the service rate of this communication channel. To meet the constraint of the communication channel, it is desirable that $L(j,p) \leq \mu_{ji}$ in the minimum server placement problem and $L(j,p) \leq \rho \cdot \mu_{ji}$ in the balanced server placement problem.

5   Experimental Results

To evaluate the performance of the proposed algorithms, we conducted several experiments in which 1000 test cases based on the proposed Grid model are randomly generated. The number of nodes in each case is approximately 1000. The arrival rates for the leaf nodes and the service rates for intermediate nodes

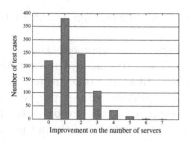

Fig. 4. Performance comparison for the minimum server problem

are generated from a negative exponential distribution. We also implemented a heuristic-based greedy method similar to that proposed in [12] as a reference.

The experimental results for the minimum server placement problem, shown in Fig. 4, compare the performance of the proposed optimal algorithm with the heuristic-based greedy method. The performance metric is the difference in the number of servers by the proposed optimal algorithm and the greedy method. The vertical axis shows the number of test cases, while the horizontal axis shows the difference in the number of servers used by the two methods.

According to the experimental results, the greedy method can only generate an optimal solution for 22.1% of the test cases. The optimal solution generated by our algorithm uses one less server than the greedy method in 38% of the test cases and two or less servers than the greedy method in 39.9% of test cases. Based on the results in Fig. 4, we classified the 1000 test cases into seven sets for use in the following experiments. Thus, test set S_i contains those test cases in which our algorithm uses i less servers than the greedy method.

Fig. 5(a) shows the workloads of the greedy method and the optimal algorithm. For each test set, the optimal algorithm and the greedy method use the same number of servers, and we take the average of maximum workloads of the optimal algorithm and the greedy method as the performace metric in this experiment. It is obvious that the the difference of the workloads becomes larger when the difference of the minimum numbers of servers required by the two algorithms increases. This means that, when using the same number of I/O servers, the optimal algorithm can actually reduce the maximum workload of

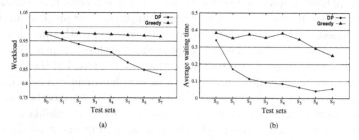

Fig. 5. (a) The workloads of the optimal algorithm and the greedy method (b) The average waiting times of different test sets

the I/O servers and therefore balance their workload better than the greedy method.

Next, we compare the average waiting times of the two algorithms. The results are shown in the Fig. 5(b). This experiment demonstrates the major benefit of our optimal algorithm. The results show that, using the same number of servers as the greedy method, our algorithm reduces the average waiting time of the grid system dramatically compared to the greedy method.

Fig. 6(a) shows the maximum workload of the optimal algorithm as the number of I/O servers increases, where m_0 is the lower bound on the number of I/O servers for test cases in S_0. It is clear that the maximum workload decreases as the number of I/O servers increases. This data can help us determine an appropriate number of servers in a grid system. Fig. 6(b) also shows the average waiting time of the optimal algorithm as the number of I/O servers increases. It can also help us to determine an appropriate number of servers in a grid system when the average waiting time is the major concern.

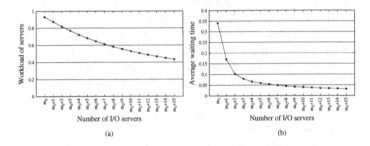

Fig. 6. The workload and the average waiting time versus the number of I/O servers

6   Conclusions

In this paper, we focus on some server placement problems in Data Grid environments. Given a hierarchical network with requests from clients and constraints on server capability, the minimum server placement problem attempts to place the minimum number of servers that can deal with clients requests. As our model allows servers have different I/O capabilities, it is more general than similar work in the literatures. Instead of using a heuristic approach, we propose an optimal algorithm based on dynamic programming as a solution to this problem.

Next, we consider the balanced server placement problem, which tries to place a given number of servers appropriately so that the workload of the servers is as balanced as possible. We show that optimal server placement can be achieved by combining the above algorithm with a binary search of workloads. Finally, we extend the above approach so that constraints on network capability can also be dealt with. The experiment results clearly show an improvement on the number of servers and the maximum workload. As the maximum workload is reduced, the waiting time is also reduced.

Acknowledgments

The authors would like to thank the anonymous referees for their helpful suggestions. The authors also acknowledge the National Center for High-performance Computing in providing resources under the national project, "Taiwan Knowledge Innovation National Grid". This research is supported in part by the National Science Council, Republic of China, under Grant NSC 94-2213-E-001-023.

References

1. Foster, I.T., Kesselman, C., Tuecke, S.: The Anatomy of the Grid : Enabling Scalable Virtual Organizations. The International J. of High Performance Computing **15**(3) (2001)
2. Johnston, W.E.: Computational and data Grids in large-scale science and engineering. Future Generation Computer Systems. **18**(8) (2002) 1085–1100
3. EU DataGrid. (http://www.edg.org)
4. PPDG: Particle Physics Data Grid. (http://www.ppdg.net)
5. iVDGL: International Virtual Data Grid Laboratory. (http://www.ivdgl.org)
6. Deelman, E., Kesselman, C., Mehta, G., Meshkat, L., Pearlman, L., Blackburn, K., Ehrens, P., Lazzarini, A., Williams, R., Koranda, S.: GriPhyN and LIGO, Building a Virtual Data Grid for Gravitational Wave Scientists. In: HPDC 2002. (2002)
7. BIRN: The Biomedical Informatics Research Network. (http://www.nbirn.net)
8. Hoschek, W., Jaén-Martínez, F.J., Samar, A., Stockinger, H., Stockinger, K.: Data Management in an International Data Grid Project. In: GRID 2000. (2000) 77–90
9. Ranganathan, K., Foster, I.T.: Identifying Dynamic Replication Strategies for a High-Performance Data Grid. In: GRID 2001. (2001) 75–86
10. Chervenak, A., Foster, I., Kesselman, C., Salisbury, C., Tuecke, S.: The Data Grid: Towards an architecture for the distributed management and analysis of large scientific datasets. Journal of Network and Computer Applications **23**(3) (2000) 187–200
11. Lamehamedi, H., Shentu, Z., Szymanski, B.K., Deelman, E.: Simulation of Dynamic Data Replication Strategies in Data Grids. In: IPDPS 2003. (2003) 100
12. Abawajy, J.H.: Placement of File Replicas in Data Grid Environments. In: International Conference on Computational Science. (2004) 66–73
13. Bell, W.H., Cameron, D.G., Carvajal-Schiaffino, R., Millar, A.P., Stockinger, K., Zini, F.: Evaluation of an Economy-Based File Replication Strategy for a Data Grid. In: International Workshop on Agent based Cluster and Grid Computing at CCGrid 2003. (2003) 120–126
14. Grid Physics Network (GriphyN). (http://www.griphyn.org)

Using OGRO and CertiVeR to Improve OCSP Validation for Grids

Jesus Luna[1], Manel Medina[1], and Oscar Manso[2]

[1] Polytechnic University of Catalonia, Computer Architecture Department,
Jordi Girona 1-3 08034 Barcelona, Spain
{jluna, medina}@ac.upc.edu
[2] CertiVeR, Technical Director,
Diputacion 238 08007 Barcelona, Spain
o.manso@certiver.com

Abstract. Authentication and authorization in many distributed systems rely on the use of cryptographic credentials that in most of the cases have a defined lifetime. This feature mandates the use of mechanisms able to determine whether a particular credential can be trusted at a given moment. This process is commonly named *validation*. Among available validation mechanisms, the Online Certificate Status Protocol (OCSP) stands out due to its ability to carry near real time certificate status information. Despite its importance for security, OCSP faces considerable challenges in the computational Grid (i.e. Proxy Certificate's validation) that are being studied at the Global Grid Forum's CA Operations Work Group (CAOPS-WG). As members of this group, we have implemented an OCSP validation infrastructure for the Globus Toolkit 4, composed of the CertiVeR Validation Service and our Open GRid Ocsp (OGRO) client library, which introduced the *Grid Validation Policy*. This paper summarizes our experiences on that work and the results obtained up to now. Furthermore we introduce the *pre-validation* concept, a mechanism analogous to the Authorization Push-Model, capable of improving OCSP validation performance in Grids. This paper also reports the results obtained with OGRO's pre-validation rules for Grid Services as a proof of concept.

1 Introduction

Many distributed environments (i.e. the computational Grid, Web services, etc.) base their authentication and authorization mechanisms on the life cycle management of cryptographic electronic credentials, with special focus on the issuing and revocation processes. Let us take for example the X.509 digital certificates [1] which may open the door to a distributed system for its owner only when he is authorized to process the operation being requested. In order to do so, at a very basic security level the system verifies the credential (i.e. issuer's digital signature, validity period, etc.) together with the purpose by which such credential was issued (i.e. roles and attributes). However, this mechanism is not enough to ensure complete security. If a higher level of security has to be reached the system should also *validate* the credential. Through this paper we will use the term "validation" as the process in charge of verifying that the

Y.-C. Chung and J.E. Moreira (Eds.): GPC 2006, LNCS 3947, pp. 12–21, 2006.

credential has not been reported by its owner as stolen, lost or compromised. In most of the cases the entity issuing the credentials – in a PKI such entity is named Certification Authority (CA) – is in charge of providing such validation information to any relying party requesting it. On top of that, it is also necessary to iteratively validate the issuer's credentials until a trust anchor has been found; this process is often called Certificate Path Validation. The validation process is traditionally done via the placement of Certificate Revocation Lists (CRL[1]) on a public directory accessible through protocols like HTTP, LDAP and FTP. However this solution tends to be cumbersome for both the CA and the application. In terms of the CA it is difficult to manage because it involves providing revocation information efficiently (in some scenarios near real time notification is a must). Also on the client side such a solution penalizes efficiency, because it becomes forced to periodically download and parse the whole list of revoked certificates – which can be extremely large –in order to perform the validation process. In consequence, more efficient mechanisms to allow for the provision of real time certificate status information to relying parties have begun to be adopted in some demanding environments, where highly efficient and secure solutions are required.

Proposed in 1999 on RFC 2560 [2], the Online Certificate Status Protocol (OCSP) is one such mechanisms. In this paper we will focus our analysis into one distributed system, which due to its special features poses strong security and performance challenges on OCSP: the computational Grid. Take for example the Globus Toolkit 4 (GT4) [3], which uses Proxy Certificates (defined in RFC3820 [4]) as short-lived cryptographic authentication credentials, acting on behalf of their issuer (typically the user itself) and implementing mechanisms that provide a secure framework for Grid's relying parties. Integration of OCSP into GT4 requires not only the implementation of special mechanisms not available in other distributed systems (i.e. Proxy Certificate validation), but also tailored and efficient solutions for others particular issues (i.e. OCSP Responder discovery, fault tolerance, high performance, etc.). This problem has been considered so important that communities like the Global Grid Forum (GGF) are actively studying the adoption of OCSP into the Grid very closely. Precisely, as members of the GGF's CA Operations Workgroup (CAOPS-WG) and co-authors of the document "OCSP Requirements for Grids" [5] we have designed - based on the guidelines of such document- and developed the *Open GRid Ocsp (OGRO)* Java API, which provides OCSP support for Grid relying parties through a set of customizable validation rules, named the *Grid Validation Policy*.

Based in that work this paper proposes a completely functional OCSP validation infrastructure for Grids that uses OGRO and the CertiVeR OCSP service [6]. Furthermore, we also introduce a new mechanism called *pre-validation,* consisting of OGRO-enabled Grid clients embedding the OCSP Response received from CertiVeR into a non-critical extension from the Proxy certificate, in such a way that while OCSP security level is kept, the overall validation performance is greatly improved.

This paper presents our proposal in the following manner: section 2 explains and shows the results obtained with our first proposal on the use of CertiVeR and OGRO

---

[1] Files digitally signed by a CA, containing the serial numbers of those certificates which have been revoked, cancelled or suspended in the PKI.

to provide a validation infrastructure for the Grid. Next section 3 mentions and also presents the results of a further OCSP validation improvement by introducing OGRO's pre-validation mechanism. The related work can be seen in section 4 and finally section 5 contains our conclusions and planned future work with OGRO and CertiVeR.

2   Using CertiVeR and OGRO to Provide an OCSP Infrastructure for Grids

In this section we will introduce an OCSP infrastructure for the Grid, based on the CertiVeR service for the Trusted Responder and the OGRO Java API integrated into the GT4 client.

2.1   CertiVeR

CertiVeR is an EU funded project that offers a comprehensive validation service that, on top of providing validation information of a X.509 certificate in real time through the Online Certificate Status Protocol –OCSP- it also implements a CRL Updater module, which is in charge of retrieving revocation information directly from the CA's CRL through protocols like LDAP and HTTP. This information is stored in a local cache.

A DeltaCRL connector has been also developed, which is used by the CRL Updater modules to remotely push any new revocation information from the remote CA into the Cert Status DB. Support for proxy certificate validation has been also implemented in such a way that the Grid client may decide to securely revoke such credential. Through a customizable set of extensions on the OCSP response CertiVeR can report information at several levels, such as technological – e.g. the reliability of the degree of trust in the issuing authority of the certificate- or commercial – e.g. information provided by the Chambers of Commerce about a company-. Such type of information may dramatically increase security and e-Trust.

For each organization member of the Grid's VO, CertiVeR OCSP responder can be configured in trusted or authorized mode as defined in [2]. Finally fault tolerance (through replication techniques, backup sites and load balancers) and high performance (using cryptographic hardware) are also provided for those organizations requiring them.

2.2   The Open GRid OCSP (OGRO): An Open Source OCSP Library for GT4

In previous work [7] we introduced the basis of an OCSP client for GT4, able to use CertiVeR for proxy certificate's OCSP path validation and also to request authorization information in OCSP extensions from such service. This client has evolved since then and now it has been published as open source, with the name of OGRO -Open GRid OCSP– [8]. OGRO implements the *one-message proxy certificate validation*, a mechanism able to validate the whole Proxy Certificate Path with just one OCSP Request/Response pair. Furthermore by being Open Source and 100% Java, OGRO is suitable for integration into Grid applications, also it is easily configurable through the so-called *Grid Validation Policy* which has been defined as a flexible set of XML rules. The next section covers in detail this feature.

2.2.1 Customizing OGRO: The Grid Validation Policy

OGRO is configured through a set of rules -written in XML- called the Grid Validation Policy, which customizes relying parties' validation behavior. Figure 1 shows the DTD of such policy.

```
1  <?xml version="1.0" encoding="UTF-8" ?>
2  <!ELEMENT ocsppolicy ( issuerdn+ ) >
3  <!ELEMENT issuerdn ( source?,unknownstatus?,
     errorhandler?,request?,proxycert? ) >
4  <!ATTLIST issuerdn dn CDATA #REQUIRED>
5  <!ATTLIST issuerdn name CDATA #REQUIRED >
6  <!ATTLIST issuerdn hash CDATA #REQUIRED >
7  <!ELEMENT revsources ( source+ ) >
8  <!ELEMENT source EMPTY >
9  <!ATTLIST source order CDATA #REQUIRED >
10 <!ATTLIST source signingcert CDATA #IMPLIED >
11 <!ATTLIST source location CDATA #REQUIRED >
12 <!ATTLIST source  type (trusted|authorized) "trusted" >
13 <!ATTLIST source timeout CDATA #IMPLIED >
14 <!ELEMENT unknownstatus EMPTY >
15 <!ATTLIST unknownstatus action (good|revoked) "revoked">
16 <!ELEMENT errorhandler ( action+ ) >
17 <!ELEMENT action EMPTY >
18 <!ATTLIST action order CDATA #REQUIRED >
19 <!ATTLIST action type
     (tryLater|setFinalResp)"setFinalResp">
20 <!ATTLIST action value (good|revoked) "revoked" >
21 <!ATTLIST action maxRetries CDATA #IMPLIED >
22 <!ELEMENT request ( signreq?, usenonce?, prot?, ext* ) >
23 <!ELEMENT signreq EMPTY >
24 <!ATTLIST signreq value (true|false) "false" >
25 <!ELEMENT usenonce EMPTY >
26 <!ATTLIST usenonce value (true|false) "true" >
27 <!ELEMENT prot EMPTY >
28 <!ATTLIST prot value (http|https) "http" >
29 <!ELEMENT ext EMPTY >
30 <!ATTLIST ext order CDATA #REQUIRED >
31 <!ATTLIST ext oid CDATA #REQUIRED >
32 <!ATTLIST ext value CDATA #REQUIRED >
33 <!ELEMENT proxycert ( unknownstatus, prevalidation ) >
34 <!ELEMENT prevalidation EMPTY>
35 <!ATTLIST prevalidation value (true|false) "false" >
36 <!ATTLIST prevalidation noprevalinfo (ocsp|ommit) "ocsp" >
```

Fig. 1. DTD of OGRO's Grid Validation Policy

From previous figure we can observe at line 2 that the OGRO's policy allows per issuer validation rules customization or even the option to configure a *default* issuer, that is, rules applying to any user whose issuer is not referenced anywhere else in the policy.

A set of revocation sources (lines 8-13) can be also defined, which means that the relying party may be able to consult more than one OCSP Responder thus providing fault tolerance and high availability. Moreover a customizable meaning of the "Unknown" OCSP status –line 15- can be defined for any certificate on the path (Proxy or non-Proxy). Also at lines 16-19, error handling mechanisms may be declared to take a certain action if for example an OCSP Responder could not be contacted. The current set of error handlers can be extended to fulfill special requirements of VOs.

Customization of OCSP Requests (i.e. use of signatures and nonces) is provided also by OGRO –lines 22 to 32- .

Important to note are Proxy Certificate's pre-validation rules (lines 34-36), which will be explained in the next section.

More than being a set of configuration directives, OGRO's Grid Validation Policy represents a mechanism to tailor validation process' security level. For example a VO may decide to use only a defined set of internal OCSP Trusted Responders benefiting performance (i.e. not using digital signatures, nonces nor HTTPS), while other VO may use external OCSP Authorized Responders but compelling its clients to use strong OCSP Requests (i.e. digitally signed, using a nonce and HTTPS).

The following section compares several Grid Validation Policies for an OCSP infrastructure based in CertiVeR and OGRO, with the purpose to help potential users in deciding which policy best fits their security requirements.

2.3 Performance Results Obtained for the Globus Toolkit 4 with CertiVeR and OGRO

In this section we show our results for a validation architecture based on the CertiVeR Service and the OGRO client implemented into the Globus Toolkit 4. The setup used for the tests is described next:

- CertiVeR Validation Service configured as Trusted Responder at http://ta-car.certiver.com and http://globus-grid.certiver.com:
  - Installed on a server with one Xeon processor @2.9 GHz, 1.5 Gb RAM and Windows 2000. An Oracle database is being used by the Responder.
  - No cryptographic hardware is being used in the Responder.
  - One OCSP extension is being handled: the "CA_RATING_EXTENSION" (registered with the OID "1.3.6.1.4.1.4710.2.454.10.1.1").
  - Proxy certificate revocation was not configured to simulate a typical OCSP service. Also no precomputed OCSP Responses were used.
- OGRO client:
  - Integrated into the ProxyPathValidator class of the Java CoG version 4 [9], so that it could be used with the ProxyInit class from the same package. Remember that the same classes are used by the Globus Toolkit 4 (Java Core).
  - Apache Ant's script to run 50 Grid clients concurrently (each one under a different instance of the Java Virtual Machine) in a server with 4 Xeon processors using RedHat Linux 7.2.
  - OGRO always verifies the OCSP Response's nonce and digital signature.

Before the tests we were expecting to identify a policy with the best performance (presumably the *NoNonce-NoSign-HTTP* which generates OCSP Requests without nonce, not being signed and using HTTP) and also the most secure policy (in theory the *Nonce-Signed-HTTPS* generating OCSP Requests with nonce, digitally signed and using HTTPS). However from the results obtained we found that on the client-side there is really *no big difference among any of them* (in fact only a 2%-6% of variation was observed). It is also interesting to note that the use of HTTPS did not imply a visible overhead neither in OGRO nor CertiVeR. A policy commonly used by relying parties in environments like Web Services is the *Nonce-NoSign-HTTP* (which protects against replay attacks, does not identify the client to the OCSP Responder and goes over clear-text HTTP), which resulted in a fair balance between security and performance. Figure 2 shows obtained results over HTTP, even though the use of HTTPS produced similar conclusions.

From a performance point of view, the use of nonces in the OCSP Request is almost irrelevant and it would be advisable only if CertiVeR was using precomputed Responses. Otherwise, for security reasons, it should be enabled.

Similar to the above observation is the use of digital signatures on the OCSP Request (its use is only advisable if a special reason to justify it exists –i.e. service accountability or access control purposes-).

On the OCSP service-side we observe that CertiVeR kept sustained response times for all the clients. In other words, no bottlenecks were evident even though all OCSP Requests were launched in parallel.

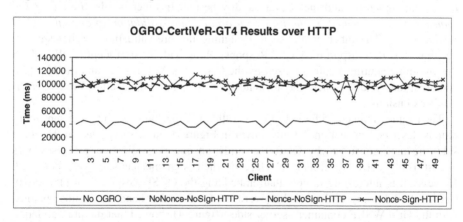

Fig. 2. Proxy Cert initialization with CertiVeR and different OGRO Policies over HTTP

We have to notice that the use of OGRO is more time-expensive for Grid clients, than when OCSP validation is not performed at all because obviously more processing is required (i.e. Grid Validation Policy parsing, cryptographic operations for the OCSP message, disk access and response validation just to name a few). Further research in OCSP validation performance took us to find that important improvements could be done through a mechanism named *pre-validation*, which is explained next.

3 Improving OCSP Validation: Pre-validating with OGRO

3.1 The Problem

As mentioned in previous section, Grid Validation Policies created with different Request rules (in particular combining the digital signature, nonce and protocol parameters) kept similar performances in OGRO and GT4. Although the OCSP validation overhead on the server-side represents approximately 30% (i.e. when the `CounterService` Grid Service is invoked) it becomes far more critical for overall performance. Such conclusion raised the following question: are we able to sacrifice client's performance *prior to invoking a Grid Service* to benefit WSRF Container's overall performance? Our novel pre-validation mechanism in OGRO took this direction to provide a secure and high-performance OCSP validation solution for Grid environments.

3.2 Introducing OCSP Pre-validation

When we faced the challenge of improving the performance of OCSP validation in Grids without affecting its overall security, a concept from the authorization area [10] came to our mind: *the push model. Here we use the OCSP Response itself as a validation ticket to be exchanged between the user and the service.* The rationale behind this is very simple given the fact that such message is authenticated (digitally signed by the OCSP Responder which is a trusted third party), tamper protected (again thanks to the digital signature) and includes a validity period. In other words, *the OCSP Response can be presented by the user as a proof of pre-validation to any other Grid relying party.* The other challenge in designing the pre-validation mechanism was deciding how to transport the OCSP Response along with the user identity. We solved this by implementing a solution used by the CAS [11], VOMS [12] and PRIMA [13] authorization systems, where the attributes assertions are embedded as Proxy Certificate's extensions.

The results obtained with OGRO's pre-validation mechanism, under the same conditions described in section 2.3 are shown in Figure 3. Just as expected in the client side, the time consumed by OGRO's validation and pre-validation processes, was almost 100% above the time that elapsed when such mechanisms were not used. However it is interesting to note that embedding the OCSP Response into the Proxy Certificate did not result in a visible overhead. On the other hand, the results obtained with the Grid WSRF container –server side- (figure 4) showed that the pre-validation process reduced in little more than 30% the time required to validate with OCSP a Proxy Certificate. Even more important to note is that the pre-validation checking at the server side did not introduce a visible overhead (in fact less than 1%). On the other hand, even though a bottleneck at the WSRF Container itself was noticeable as the number of concurrent invocations increased (around the 9th invocation in figure 4), again it does not deny the fact that pre-validating improves OCSP performance and in the best of the cases (if no bottleneck was generated at the WSRF Container) the gap between the `OCSP No Prevalidated` and `OCSP Prevalidated` series (figure 4) could be reduced, but would never be the same.

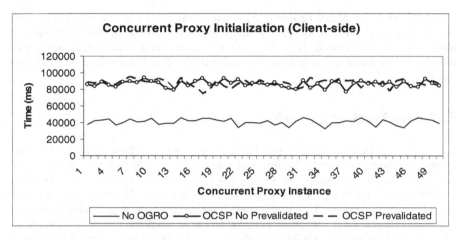

Fig. 3. Results obtained with the Grid client when creating the Proxy Certificate

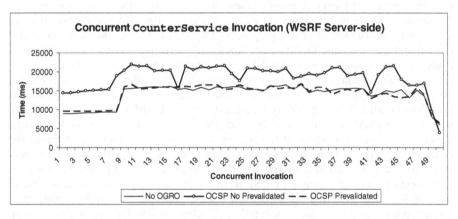

Fig. 4. Results obtained with the WSRF Container when validating the Proxy Certificate

4 Related Work

Even though there are several standalone OCSP clients currently available (maybe one of the most commonly used is the OpenSSL [14], which also includes a set of C libraries), as far as we know OGRO is the first one adapted for the Globus Toolkit (and very likely for any other Grid software) and thus the only client providing a pre-validation mechanism as presented in this paper. However, there are a couple of solutions that, even if they do not provide OCSP validation, make use of *fresh* CRLs to validate certificates: the first one is MyProxy [15] which implements a remote service that stores user certificates automatically populated from a CA. The second implementation is the Data Grid's edg-fetch-crl [16] script which can be scheduled to periodically download remote CRLs. Regarding pre-validation we have to mention that the idea of embedding information into Proxy Certificate's extensions is not new, and in fact it has been used by solutions implemented in the Authorization field like

CAS [11], VOMS [12] and PRIMA [13]. In the OCSP service-side it is worth to mention Sytrust's OpenValidation [17] which implements several of the functionalities also presented in CertiVeR. However, it does not support the Authorized Responder mode with the same cryptographic key-pair nor the Proxy Certificate's revocation service.

5 Future Work and Conclusions

This paper has introduced the Open GRid Ocsp –OGRO– client API which implements the requirements of OCSP infrastructures in order to be suitable for Grid environments, just as proposed by the GGF's CA Operations Workgroup (CAOPS-WG). OGRO's functionality can be easily customized by a set of XML rules in the form of a Grid Validation Policy. To provide some insight into the security and performance effects of different Grid Validation Policies, an OCSP infrastructure based in the CertiVeR Validation Service, OGRO and the Globus Toolkit 4 was setup. We observed that the overall response time of the policies was pretty much the same, therefore from the client's performance point of view there is no big difference if nonces, digital signatures or secure channels are used when connecting to a service like the one we have tested (which does not preprocess OCSP responses). Our tests have also show that the architecture OGRO-CertiVeR greatly improves Grid security, but overloads such environments with the delay generated by the OCSP validation mechanism. For this reason was introduced the concept of pre-validation as a mechanism capable of improving OCSP validation performance in Grid environments. This has been done by embedding the OCSP Request in a Proxy Certificate extension in such a way that the overhead introduced by traditional OCSP has been moved from the server to the client. In doing so the overall system security is not affected, because the Grid server is enforced to perform a series of security verifications over the pre-validated data contained in the Proxy Certificate to ensure its correctness (verification of Responder's digital signature, OCSP Response's validity period, etc.). As a proof concept we have modified the Open GRid Ocsp –OGRO– client to support pre-validation through a new rule introduced in the client's Grid Validation Policy being defined. This API was then tested with the Globus Toolkit 4 in such a way that pre-validation is performed by the Grid user when creating a Proxy Certificate, and then enforced at the WSRF Container when a Grid Service was being invoked through the secure messaging mechanism. Results showed that important improvements could be obtained at the Grid server without any extra overhead introduced at the client's OCSP validation process. Even though obtained results were affected by external factors (the throughput of the OCSP validation service being accessed, the WSRF Container, and OGRO itself –policy parsing-) we believe that general conclusions about the overall advantages of the pre-validation mechanism were not influenced by them and moreover future work will be aimed to enhance performance by using new algorithms (i.e. use of precomputed OCSP Responses in CertiVeR and inclusion of an OCSP cache in OGRO) and cryptographic hardware.

We expect that the use of OCSP in Grids will be very common in the near future. In consequence, the practical experience that the Grid community will acquire with software like OGRO and services like CertiVeR may prove very useful in building OCSP architectures fully optimized for such environments. Current research on Grid OCSP in general and the CertiVeR-OGRO-GT4 architecture in particular, will continue over topics like future uses of OCSP extensions as we have also begun a new research line using the concepts of pre-validation and the OGRO API to build the Unified AAI introduced in [7], by conveying not only the OCSP Response but also Authorization information into the Proxy Certificate's extensions.

Finally it is worth highlighting that OGRO is in the process of being integrated into the next release of the Globus Toolkit, which may bring further improvements as a result of the Grid community's testing and comments.

References

1. "RFC 3280: Internet X.509 Public Key Infrastructure Certificate and Certificate Revocation List (CRL) Profile". Housley R, et. al., April 2002.
2. "RFC 2560: X.509 Internet Public Key Infrastructure, Online Certificate Status Protocol – OCSP". Myers M, et. al. June 1999.
3. "The Globus Toolkit 4". http://www.globus.org
4. "RFC 3820: Internet X.509 Public Key Infrastructure (PKI), Proxy Certificate Profile". Tuecke S, et. al. June 2004.
5. "OCSP Requirements for Grids". Global Grid Forum, CA Operations Work Group. Working Document. May 2005. https://forge.gridforum.org/projects/caops-wg
6. "CertiVeR: Certificate Revocation and Validation Service". http://www.certiver.com
7. "Towards a Unified Authentication and Authorization Infrastructure for Grid Services: Implementing an enhanced OCSP Service Provider into GT4". Luna J., Manso O., Medina M., 2nd EuroPKI 2005 Workshop. To be published in the Proceedings by Springer in Lecture Notes in Computer Science series. July 2005. http://sec.cs.kent.ac.uk/europki2005/
8. "OGRO - The Open GRid Ocsp client API". http://grid-globus.certiver.com/info/ogro
9. "A Java Commodity Grid Kit" Gregor von Laszewski, Ian Foster, Jarek Gawor, and Peter Lane, Concurrency and Computation: Practice and Experience, vol. 13, no. 8-9, pp. 643-662, 2001, http:/www.cogkit.org/
10. "RFC 2904: AAA Authorization Framework". Vollbrecht J, et. al. August 2000.
11. "A Community Authorization Service for Group Collaboration". L. Pearlman, et.al. IEEE 3rd International Workshop on Policies for Distributed Systems and Networks, 2002.
12. "VOMS, an Authorization System for Virtual Organizations". R. Alfieri,. et. al. Presented at the 1st European Across Grids Conference, Santiago de Compostela, Spain. February 2003. http://infnforge.cnaf.infn.it/voms/VOMS-Santiago.pdf
13. "The PRIMA Grid Authorization System". M. Lorch and Dennis Kafura. Journal of Grid Computing, 2004, Vol. 2, Pages 279-298
14. "The OpenSSL software". http://www.openssl.org
15. "An online credential repository for the Grid: MyProxy". V. Welch, et. al. In 10th IEEE International Symposium on High Performance Distributed Computing. San Francisco, CA. IEEE Computer Society Press, Los Alamitos, CA, 2001.
16. "Data Grid: Security for the RLS". http://edg-wp2.web.cern.ch
17. "The Openvalidation service". http://www.openvalidation.org

Efficient Target Detection for RNA Interference

Shibin Qiu[1], Cundong Yang[2], and Terran Lane[1]

[1] Dept. Computer Science, University of New Mexico, Albuquerque, NM, 87131
{sqiu, terran}@cs.unm.edu
[2] Dept. Electrical and Computer Eng., University of New Mexico, USA
cundongyang@ece.unm.edu

Abstract. RNA interference (RNAi) is a posttranscriptional gene silencing mechanism used to study gene functions, inhibit viral activities, and treat diseases. Due to the nonspecific effects of RNAi, target validation through target detection is crucial for the success of RNAi experiments. Since target detection involves large amounts of transcriptome-wide searches, computational efficiency is critical. To efficiently detect targets for RNAi design, we develop both sequential and parallel search algorithms using RNA string kernels, which model mismatches, G-U wobbles, and bulges between siRNAs and target mRNAs. Based on tests in *S. pombe*, *C. elegans*, and human, our algorithms achieved speedups of 6 orders of magnitude over a baseline implementation. Our design strategy also leads to a framework for efficient, flexible, and portable string search algorithms.

1 Introduction

RNAi is an intracellular mechanism for posttranscriptional gene silencing used to study gene functions, inhibit viral activities, and treat diseases therapeutically [1, 2, 3, 4]. RNAi is initiated by short interfering RNA (siRNA) of about 21 nucleotides (nt) long, either generated from a dsRNA by the enzyme Dicer, or directly transfected. Associating with a silencing complex (RISC), siRNA targets complimentary mRNA molecules for destruction, preventing expression of the associated proteins. RNAi has been regarded as a highly effective means of gene repression[2, 5]. However, its effectiveness can be compromised by nonspecific, or off-target knockdown, which is the unintentional silencing of a gene other than the target. In this paper, we develop efficient algorithms searching whole transcriptomes to detect targets of siRNA and dsRNA for target validation.

Although RNAi is predominantly considered highly specific [5], significant nonspecific gene knockdowns have been reported [6, 7, 8]. Experiments in human cells found silencing of nontarget genes containing only 11 nt identity to the siRNA [6]. A computational study reported that using dsRNA of length 200 nt, there existed a 30% chance of silencing incorrect genes in human by permitting exact matches only [8]. If mismatches of 3 nt were allowed, more than 50% chance of false positive knockdown existed. This level of off-target error rate suggested that silencing one gene would silence at least one nontarget gene. Because RNAi specificity is critical [3, 4], it is important to detect and verify the targets of a dsRNA or siRNA before it is used in a biological experiment.

Y.-C. Chung and J.E. Moreira (Eds.): GPC 2006, LNCS 3947, pp. 22–31, 2006.
© Springer-Verlag Berlin Heidelberg 2006

The recommended procedure for target validation is BLAST [9, 10]. However, BLAST misses targets in some cases, and is not suitable for accurate sequence matching, such as RNAi [11]. The sequence binding between an siRNA and its target allows for mismatches, G-U wobbles, and bulges[7]. Though BLAST allows for deletion, insertion and substitution, it cannot control the exact patterns of imperfect matches encountered in RNAi. Due to their quadratic complexity, algorithms based on dynamic programming are not feasible for large scale searching. Alignment algorithms align the input sequences into whatever pattern needed to get an optimal score based on a cost model and do not guarantee generating the desired patterns[12, 13]. To simulate siRNA-target binding, we develop search algorithms based on string kernels that accurately control matching patterns by adjusting the length and position of the patterns. To search for imperfectly matched targets, we develop algorithms using search trees constructed with reverse strings and shuffled strings. Furthermore, we exploit parallelism in our algorithms for parallel target detection. Our algorithms have demonstrated superior quality in target detection and achieved substantial speedups.

Related to RNAi, computational methods exist to predict microRNA genes and targets[14], and putative RNAi[15]. An algorithm for string searches with single letter mismatch was developed[16]. However, single-length mismatch is not enough for RNAi. A multiple instruction stream-single data stream (MISD) architecture was developed for fast sequence matching[17]. But this hardware solution is not flexible and its proprietary architecture is expensive. String kernels provide flexibilities for evaluating the similarity between the sequences based on input patterns[18, 19]. But these string kernels were not specifically designed for RNA biology and their computational performances were unsatisfactory. Previously, we have developed the RNA string kernels and used them for RNAi off-target studies focusing on computational models and biological implications[8, 20]. In this work, we use the RNA string kernels to allow flexible imperfect matches, focusing on high performance sequential and parallel implementations. We develop a series algorithms of increasing sophistication for computing the kernels to efficiently detect targets of a dsRNA or siRNA for RNA interference.

2   Target Detection by RNA String Kernels

We formulate a computational representation for RNAi using the RNA string kernels including mismatches, bulges, and G-U wobbles[8, 20]. The destruction of an mRNA is caused by hybridization between the binding strand of the siRNA and the target, which can be modelled by sequence matching between the sense stand and the target [5]. Thus, a sequence matching signifies a gene knockdown.

2.1   Target Search by Exact Match String Kernel

We describe each gene by its contiguous subsequences of length n (~ 21 nt), called n-mers, or n-grams, representing siRNAs. A gene, g_x, represented in the input space $\mathcal{X}$, consisting of sequences drawn from the alphabet $\mathcal{A} = \{A, C, G, U\}$, is mapped into an n-gram feature space $\mathbb{R}^{4^n}$ by the feature map of exact match

$$\Phi^{ex}(g_x) = (\phi_a(g_x))_{a \in \mathcal{A}^n}, \tag{1}$$

where $\phi_a(g_x)$ is the number of times n-gram a occurs in g_x[8]. Therefore, the image of g_x is the coordinates in the feature space indexed by the number of occurrences of its constituent n-mers.

A dsRNA d matches g_x if the following condition is met,

$$K(d, g_x) = \langle \Phi^{ex}(d), \Phi^{ex}(g_x) \rangle \geq T, \tag{2}$$

for a threshold T, where $\langle ., . \rangle$ is the standard inner product. The similarity measure $K(d, g_y)$ in (2) defines a kernel as used for a support vector machine classifier [21]. Instead of classifying, we use this kernel to match a dsRNA and its target. Since any match between an siRNA from a dsRNA and an mRNA will silence the gene, we choose $T = 1$.

2.2   String Kernels of Mismatches, Bulges, and Wobbles

An siRNA is able to silence its target despite the presence of a limited number of mismatches, bulges, and wobbles[6, 7]. To detect the targets when imperfect matches exist, we use string kernels defined through the notion of similarity neighborhoods. Since these imperfect matches frequently exist in RNA biology, these kernels are called RNA string kernels. The RNA kernels first define contiguous imperfect match patterns and parameterize their positions, then permute the positions, so that imperfect matches occur everywhere[20].

For an n-mer a from an alphabet $\mathcal{A}$, we define its mismatch neighborhood, $N_{m,p}^{mis}(a)$, as the set of n-mers γ from $\mathcal{A}$ that differ from a by at most m contiguous mismatches starting at position p in a. And we define the mismatch feature map of a as $\Phi_{m,p}^{mis}(a) = (\phi_\gamma(a))_{\gamma \in \mathcal{A}^n}$, where $\phi_\gamma(a) = 1$ if $\gamma \in N_{m,p}^{mis}(a)$, and $\phi_\gamma(a) = 0$, otherwise. The feature map of a gene g_x is defined as the sum of the feature maps of its n-mers,

$$\Phi_{m,p}^{mis}(g_x) = \sum_{a \in g_x} \Phi_{m,p}^{mis}(a). \tag{3}$$

The bulge neighborhood $N_{b,q}^{bulge}(a)$ for n-mer a is defined as all $(n + b)$-mers γ from the target that match a exactly everywhere except by a bulge of b nt long starting at position q on γ. And the bulge feature map of a is defined as $\Phi_{b,q}^{bulge}(a) = (\phi_\gamma(a))_{\gamma \in \mathcal{A}^{n+b}}$, where $\phi_\gamma(a) = 1$ if $\gamma \in N_{b,q}^{bulge}(a)$, and $\phi_\gamma(a) = 0$, otherwise. The feature map of g_x is defined as the sum of the feature maps of its n-mers,

$$\Phi_{b,q}^{bulge}(g_x) = \sum_{a \in g_x} \Phi_{b,q}^{bulge}(a). \tag{4}$$

The wobble feature map $\Phi_{w,r}^{wobble}(.)$ is defined similarly to $\Phi_{m,p}^{mis}(.)$ in (3), except only G-U wobbles exist in its neighborhood. By defining the similarity neighborhood for the combination of mismatches, bulges, and wobbles as the union of the separate neighborhoods, we can define the feature map of simultaneous mismatches, bulges and wobbles $\Phi_{m,p,b,q,w,r}^{mbw}(.)$ accordingly. Thus to evaluate the

RNA string kernel between a dsRNA d and a gene g_x, we calculate the inner product using the above feature maps,

$$K(d, g_x) = \langle \Phi^{mbw}_{m,p,b,q,w,r}(d), \Phi^{mbw}_{m,p,b,q,w,r}(g_x) \rangle. \tag{5}$$

To allow imperfect matches to exist at all possible positions, we sum up over all positions within the strings, as done for the mismatch feature map below.

$$K_m(d, g_x) = \sum_{p=1}^{n-m+1} \langle \Phi^{mis}_{m,p}(d), \Phi^{mis}_{m,p}(g_x) \rangle. \tag{6}$$

3 Efficient Implementations for RNA String Kernels

The RNA string kernels defined above characterize imperfect match patterns in RNAi. However, since these kernels need substantial processing and target validation requires large scale scan, we develop their efficient implementations.

3.1 Computing the Exact Match String Kernel

Calculating the similarity of (2) directly in a vector space requires $O(DF4^n)$ time, where F is the number of n-grams in the genome (40×10^6 for *C. elegans* and 60×10^6 for human) and $D = |d| - n + 1$ is the number of n-mers in the dsRNA of length $|d|$. For whole genome searches, this computing time is prohibitive and can be improved by taking advantage of the sparsity of the feature space. We use an *inverted file* where the n-mers serve as identifiers and their gene names serve as attributes. In the inverted file, the records for g_x contains the pairs (a_1, g_x), (a_2, g_x),...,(a_{k_x}, g_x), where a_j, $1 \leq j \leq k_x$, is the jth n-gram of g_x, and $k_x = |g_x| - n + 1$ is the number of n-mers in g_x. The inverted file for a genome is the collection of the pairs of its genes. To speed up computation, we sort the inverted file on the n-mer field using a binary search tree (BST).

The exact match similarity $K(d, g_x)$ in (2) can be computed using the SS0 algorithm in Algorithm 1. After the BST T_1 is built, the matched genes are collected in C at Step 2. $K(d, g_x)$ is the number of occurrences of g_x among the matched genes. Each search in the BST takes $O(\log F)$ time, resulting in an $O(D \log F)$ time for computing $K(d, g_y)$. An alignment algorithm would need $O(n^2 DF)$ time. SS0 gains a speedup of $O(n^2 F / \log F)$.

Algorithm 1	Algorithm 2
Search by Exact Match, SS0(d)	Single Tree Search, SS1(d, m)
Input: dsRNA d, BST T built for the inverted file using n-mers.	**Input:** dsRNA d, length of mismatch m, BST T built for the inverted file using n-mers.
Output: Target genes matched by d.	**Output:** Target genes matched by d.
1: **for each** n-mer s_j in d **do**	1: **for each** n-mer s_j in d **do**
2: $C \leftarrow C \bigcup$ matched nodes in T	2: **for each** $p \in [1, n - m + 1]$ **do**
3: **end for**	3: $R \leftarrow p - 1$ leading range of s_j from T
4: Return C	4: $C \leftarrow C \bigcup$ nodes in R satisfying ending criterion
	5: **end for**
	6: **end for**
	7: Return C

3.2   Target Search Using Reverse Strings

Since mismatches dominate off-target chances among the imperfect matches and the wobble and bulge kernels can similarly be implemented, we focus on implementing mismatch kernels[20]. First, we need some notation.

For a BST populated with strings from a set $S = \{s_1, s_2...s_N\}$ of strings of length k drawn from an alphabet $\mathcal{A}$, we define a u ($u < k$) *leading range* of a string $s \in S$ searched in the BST as the set of nodes returned by a search that only matches the first u letters of s. The u leading range of a string s_0 can be searched from a BST by first finding s_0, followed by retrieving the nodes among the neighbors of s_0 (equivalently along the sorted array) as long as the first u letters are matched. If s_0 is not found, the closest location returned by a binary search is used as the center point of the neighborhood.

The SS1 algorithm in Algorithm 2 performs target detection with mismatches. In the loop starting at Step 2, targets are searched allowing mismatches at all positions. At Step 4, the *ending criterion* collects those genes in C whose n-mers in R are matched with s_j at the last $n - m - p + 1$ positions. However, the search in SS1 is not always efficient. At Step 3, the size of the neighborhood subtree for the leading range is $O(4^{n-m-p+1})$ if the tree is fully populated. It is small if the mismatch is at the end of the sequence, and gets exponentially larger as the mismatch moves to the beginning of the string. Its worst case size is $O(4^{n-m})$. Therefore, SS1 uses $O(pD4^{n-m} \log F)$ time. However, if we can keep the mismatches at the end of the strings, then our searches are always fast.

Suppose string $s_i = a_1...a_k$ has reverse string $\overline{s_i} = a_k...a_1$. We define a *mirrored tree* of a BST populated with strings from S as the BST populated with

---

| **Algorithm 3** | **Algorithm 4** |
Search by Reverse String, SS2(d,m)	Search by Shuffled String, SS3(d,m)
Input: dsRNA d, length of mismatch m, BST T_1 and mirrored BST T_2 for the inverted files using n-mers.	**Input:** dsRNA d, length of mismatch m, BST T_R built with s, T_L with $\overline{s}$, and T_M with s_M using n-mers.
Output: Target matched by d.	**Output:** Target matched by d.
1: **for each** $p \in [1, n-m+1]$ **do**	1: **for each** $p \in [1, n-m+1]$ **do**
2: **for each** n-mer s_j in d **do**	2: **for each** n-mer s_j in d **do**
3: **if** $p \geq \lceil n/2 \rceil$ **then**	3: **if** $p \geq 2\lfloor n/3 \rfloor$ **then**
4: $R \leftarrow p - 1$ leading range of s_j from T_1	4: $R \leftarrow p - 1$ leading range of s_j from T_R
5: **else**	5: **else if** $p \leq \lceil n/3 \rceil$ **then**
6: $R \leftarrow n - m - p + 1$ leading range of $\overline{s_j}$ from T_2	6: $R \leftarrow n - m - p + 1$ leading range of $\overline{s_j}$ from T_L
7: **end if**	7: **else**
8: $C \leftarrow C \bigcup$ nodes in R satisfying ending criterion	8: $R \leftarrow \lceil n/3 \rceil + p - 1$ leading range of s_M from T_M
9: **end for**	9: **end if**
10: **end for**	10: $C \leftarrow C \bigcup$ nodes in R satisfying ending criterion
11: Return C	11: **end for**
	12: **end for**
	13: Return C

reverse strings $\overline{s_1},...,\overline{s_N}$. The SS2 algorithm in Algorithm 3 first builds BST T_1 and a mirrored BST T_2. If the mismatch is in the ending half of the string, T_1 is queried in Step 4 to obtain the leading range. If it is in the beginning half, T_2 is searched using its reverse string in Step 6. Since the sizes of the subtrees used to retrieve the leading ranges are bounded by $O(4^{n/2-m})$, SS2 takes $O(pD4^{n/2-m}\log F)$ time. The speedup of SS2 over SS1 (baseline) is $O(4^{n/2})$.

3.3 Target Search Using Shuffled Strings

We can further improve search performance by dividing the string into three segments and shuffling the mismatches to the end of the sequences. SS3 in Algorithm 4 shows this implementation by building three trees. Let $s=s_1+s_2+s_3$, where s_1, s_2, and s_3 are the left, middle and right substrings. Each of them has a length of about one third of s. The tree T_R is inserted with s, and facilitates searches with mismatches at the end. Tree T_L is inserted with the inverse sequences $\overline{s}$ for searches with mismatches at the beginning. T_M is inserted with the shuffled sequence $s_M=s_3+s_1+s_2$ for searches with mismatches in the middle.

In Algorithm 4, if a mismatch is at the right end, $p \geq 2\lfloor n/3 \rfloor$, then R collects the leading range of s_j searched in T_R. If the mismatch is on the left, then R collects the leading range of $\overline{s_j}$ searched in T_L. Otherwise, the mismatch is in the middle and R stores the leading range of s_M searched in T_M. Since the sizes of the subtrees used to retrieve the leading ranges (Steps 4, 6, and 8) are bounded by $O(4^{n/3-m})$, SS3 takes $O(pD4^{n/3-m}\log F)$ time. SS3's speedup over SS2 is $O(4^{n/6})$. Its speedup over SS1 is $O(4^{2n/3})$. However, SS2 and SS3 use more memory space than SS1.

Although we only implemented up to SS3, it is not difficult to construct $\rho = n/m$ trees, so that each search is exactly at the end of the string. This extension yields a time complexity of $O(pD\log F)$ and a speedup of $O(4^{n-m})$ over SS1, achieving speedups of more than 8 orders of magnitude for human genome. Thus our design strategy provides a framework for fast searching algorithms with easy extensions. This extended design will benefit special purpose software and hardware architectures that pursue extremely fast target detection.

3.4 Parallel Target Detection

Due to the popularity and cost decline of parallel computers, improving computational performance through parallelism becomes practical. In this section, we parallelize our algorithms to further enhance the speed of target detection and prepare them for large throughput searches required by a server.

To parallelize SS3 using an input partition scheme on a shared memory machine, we first build the trees T_R, T_L, and T_M for a organism. We then share these trees among the processors during the search stage. Assuming there are P processors, we partition the dsRNA into P parts and assign one part to each processor for searching. The output targets are the union of the targets returned by each processor. We can also partition the transcriptome into P parts and assign one part to each processor, which in turn builds three trees. In the search stage, each processor searches its own shuffled trees for the entire input sequence.

4   Experiments

We test our algorithms for dsRNA target detection in *S. pombe*, *C. elegans*, and *H. sapiens*.

4.1   Performance of Target Detection

We searched targets for dsRNAs of 500 nt long from genes SPAC664.06, F52C9.8b, and Kua-UEV (gi|40806189) in *S. pombe*, *C. elegans*, and *H. sapiens*, respectively. Fig. 1 (a) shows that the number of targets increased dramatically with mismatches. In the case of human, when only exact match was allowed, the dsRNA targeted 3 variants of the ubiquitin-conjugating enzymes (gi|40806189, gi|40806191, and gi|40806192). When one mismatch existed at every position in the siRNAs (21 nt), it matched 6 genes, additional targets being FLJ20512, AZI1, and KIAA1984. Fig. 1 (a) also suggests that larger genomes (human and *C. elegans*) yielded more targets than smaller ones (*S. pombe*).

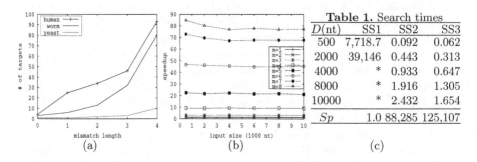

Fig. 1. Performance comparison. (a) Number of targets increases with m in *S. pombe*, *C. elegans*, and *H. sapiens* ($D = 500$ nt, $m = 0 - 4$ nt). (b) Speedups of SS3 over SS2 for $D = 500 - 10000$ nt, $m = 1 - 8$, $n = 21$ nt in *C. elegans*. (c) Comparison of search times (in seconds) in *C. elegans*. D=500–10000 nt, $m = 2$, $n = 21$ nt, $*$ unavailable (too long). Speedup Sp is relative to SS1, for D=2000 nt.

To handle high throughput required by a server, we tested SS1, SS2, and SS3 for dsRNAs of 10,000 nt long, although < 1000 nt dsRNAs are commonly used in biological experiments. We used a computer with a 1.6GHZ CPU and an 8GB RAM. Table 1 in panel (c) of Fig. 1 shows that SS2 and SS3 gained speedups of 88,285 and more than 10^5 folds over SS1 respectively, for the case of $D = 2000$ nt, $m = 2$, and $n = 21$, in *C. elegans*. As the table shows, for dsRNAs of 500–10000 nt long, SS3 found the targets in 0.06–1.7 seconds. For the same input sets, BLAST took 21–121 seconds. SS1 took hours to finish, but faster than alignment searching (time not shown). Fig. 1 (b) shows that SS3 gained a speedup of about 80 fold over SS2 and this speedup increased with m. The speedup's increase with m is because that the number of possible mismatch positions is $n - m + 1$ and larger m yields fewer positions to search and less overhead for the partition and combining. The figure also indicates that the speedups did not change much with the input size (D), suggesting that the algorithms are scalable.

We noticed that the speedup of SS3 over SS2 was lower than its theoretical estimation $O(4^{n/6})$. This is because real genomes are much smaller than 4^n. It was also related to the overhead in SS3 incurred by dividing the strings and combining the results. In addition, more trees caused more memory segmentation, which slowed down memory accesses. While our algorithms used BSTs and were written in C++ language, they can also be implemented using B-Trees in database tables. Our web tool for target detection, using the search strategy of SS2 and two MySQL database tables, works with reasonably fast response (`http://rnai.cs.unm.edu/projects/`).

4.2   Parallel Speedups

Our parallel experiments were conducted on a Sun E4500 shared-memory machine with 14 Ultra SPARC II 400MHz CPUs, each having 16KB L1 cache and 4MB L2 cache. Programs were written in C++ using p–threads. Fig. 2 displays SS3's speedups using input-partition, indicating that more than 8 fold speedups were achieved. However, the speedups were less than linear and even decreased with more processors in some cases. This decrease of speedup is attributed to the drawbacks of the computer architecture. Since our BSTs were shared by all processors, bus contention and deep cache hierarchy deteriorate performance greatly with the increase of processors. The figures also show that more speedups were achieved for longer mismatches. This is because longer mismatches yielded fewer possible mismatch positions in the siRNAs and fewer searches, which reduced the chances of bus contentions and undesirable cache behaviors. Although the speedups dropped with more processors for short mismatches, this drop was not serious in human as shown in Fig. 2 (c), suggesting that our parallel implementations were more efficient for larger genomes. Parallelizing SS3 with genome-partition gained only 3 fold speedups, due to large amount of cache misses and bus contentions incurred when more trees were accessed.

Combining the parallel speedup and that gained by SS3 $(> 10^5)$, a total speedup of 6 orders of magnitude over SS1 was achieved. If the strings are shuffled into more segments using more trees SS3, higher speedups can be achieved.

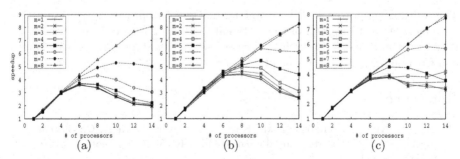

Fig. 2. Parallel speedups. (a) *S. pombe*, $D = 10000$ nt. (b) *C. elegans*, $D = 5000$ nt. (c) *H. sapiens*, $D = 5000$ nt. $n = 21$, $m = 1 - 8$ nt.

5 Conclusions

Target detection in RNAi must meet the requirements of the similarity model and computational efficiency. To ensure the quality of target detection and capture the matching patterns in RNAi, we used RNA string kernels characterizing sequence similarity, allowing for mismatches, G-U wobbles, and bulges. We developed algorithms of increasing sophistication for performance improvement. First, we used searches based on sorted inverted files as a baseline implementation. We then introduced searches using reverse strings and mirrored trees, which improved search times dramatically, especially when mismatches are present. Furthermore, we developed searching algorithms using shuffled strings that yielded better performance. Finally, we used parallel processing and made target detection even faster.

We have analyzed, compared, and tested the algorithms extensively for different scenarios. Experiments in the genomes of *S. pombe*, *C. elegans*, and human demonstrated that our algorithms achieved speedups of 6 orders of magnitude over the baseline implementation. They were faster than BLAST and detected targets that were otherwise missed by BLAST. They are flexible and can be implemented using database tables. The parallel implementations are portable and practical for commonly used multiprocessor systems. Moreover, our design strategy provides a framework of fast searching algorithms, which makes it easy to extend the algorithm beyond what we have tested (SS3) for even better performance.

We need to point out that the multiprocessor system we used to test our parallel implementations was made many years ago. On today's multiprocessor systems using high-speed switches, parallel performance can be improved substantially. On commonly used, low cost, small multiprocessor computers (<8 processors), we expect the parallel speedups will be close to linear. Although the genome-partition scheme did not achieve the expected speedup on this system, it might work well on a cluster of workstations, where memory accesses are independent on each node. In the future, we will combine the two partition schemes for better efficiency on a cluster and investigate load balancing issues.

Acknowledgement

This work is supported by NIH grant P20RR18754 from the Institutional Development Award Program of the National Center for Research Resource. The authors thank David A. Bader for giving accesses to the shared-memory machine, and Coenraad M. Adema for helpful suggestions.

References

1. Fire, A., Xu, S., Montgomery, M., Kostas, S., Driver, S., Mello, C.: Potent and specific genetic interference by double-stranded RNA in *C. elegans*. Nature **391** (1998) 806–811
2. Elbashir, S.M., Harborth, J., Weber, K., Tuschl, T.: Analysis of gene function in somatic mammalian cells using small interfering RNAs. Methods **26** (2002) 199–213

3. Check, E.: Hopes rise for RNA therapy as mouse study hits target. Nature **432** (2004) 136
4. Dillin, A.: The specifics of small interfering RNA specificity. Proc. Natl. Acad. Sci. USA **100** (2003) 6289–6291
5. Tuschl, T., Zamore, P.D., Lehmann, R., Bartel, D.P., Sharp, P.A.: Targeted mRNA degradation by double-stranded RNA *in vitro*. Genes Dev. **13** (1999) 3191–3197
6. Jackson, A., Bartz, S., Schelter, J., Kobayashi, S., Burchard, J., Mao, M., Li, B., Cavet, G., Linsley, P.: Expression profiling reveals off-target gene regulation by RNAi. Nature Biotechnology **21** (2003) 635–637
7. Saxena, S., Jonsson, Z.O., Dutta, A.: Small RNAs with imperfect match to endogenous mRNA repress translation. J. Bio. Chemistry **278**(45) (2003) 44312–44319
8. Qiu, S., Adema, C., Lane, T.: A computational study of off-target effects of RNA interference. Nucleic Acids Research **33** (2005) 1834–1847
9. Altschul, S.F., Gish, W., Miller, W., Myers, E.W., Lipman, D.J.: Basic local alignment search tool. J. Mol. Biol. **215** (1990) 403–410
10. Khvorova, A., Reynolds, A., Jayasena, S.: Functional siRNAs and miRNAs exhibit strand bias. Cell **115** (2003) 209
11. Ola Snøve, J., Holen, T.: Many commonly used siRNA risks off-target activity. Biochemical and Biophysical Research Communications **319** (2004) 256–263
12. Needleman, S.B., Wunsch, C.D. J. Mol. Biol. **48** (1970) 443–453
13. Smith, T.F., Waterman, M.S. Journal Molecular Biology **147**(1) (1981) 195–197
14. Lim, L.P., Glasner, M.E., Yekta, S., Burge, C.B., Bartel, D.P.: Vertebrate microRNA genes. Science **299** (2003) 1540
15. Horesh, Y., Amir, A., Michaeli, S., Unger, R.: A rapid method for detection of putative RNAi target genes in genomic data. Bioinformatics **19** (2003) ii73–ii80 Suppl. 2.
16. Amir, A., Landau, G., Keselman, D., Lewenstein, M., Lewenstein, N., Rodeh, M.: Text indexing and dictionary matching with one error. J. Algorithms **37** (2000) 309–325
17. Halaas, A., Svingen, B., Nedland, M., S.ætrom, P., O. Snøve, J., Birkeland, O.: A recursive MISD architecture for pattern matching. IEEE Trans. Very Large Scale Integr. Syst. **12**(7) (2004) 727–734
18. Leslie, C., Eskin, E., Cohen, A., Weston, J., Noble, W.S.: Mismatch string kernels for discriminative protein classification. Bioinformatics **1**(1) (2003) 1–10
19. Lodhi, H., Saunders, C., Shawe-Taylor, J., Cristianini, N., Watkins, C.: Text classification using string kernels. Journal of machine learning research **2** (2002) 419–444
20. Qiu, S., Lane, T.: String kernels of imperfect matches for off-target detection in RNA interferance. In Sunderam, V., et al., eds.: Proc. 5th Int'l Conf. Computational Sci., Atlanta, GA, USA, LNCS 3515, Springer-Verlag (2005) 894–902
21. Vapnik, V.N.: Statistical Learning Theory. John Wiley & Sons, New York (1998)

Smart Instant Messenger in Pervasive Computing Environments*

Chun-Fai Law, Xiaolei Zhang, Sung-Ming Chan, and Cho-Li Wang

Department of Computer Science,
The University of Hong Kong,
Pokfulam Road, Hong Kong

Abstract. In this paper, we explore the potential of extrapolating the instant messaging paradigm into pervasive computing environments. Under this vision, an instant messenger is regarded as a unified interface for all communications among human, software services and various devices. To meet the demands, we introduce a novel instant messenger system i.e., *Smart Instant Messenger*, with original features of context-aware presence management, dynamic grouping, and resource buddy services. This system is built atop a context-aware supporting middleware, which adopts an ontology-based context model and handles the chore of retrieving and managing context information. Jabber protocol is exploited as the underlying message exchange format for extensibility. The system prototype is implemented and evaluated with respect to the responsiveness of queries and memory usage of the middleware.

1 Introduction

Instant messaging (IM) has been booming since its birth and gradually becoming the most popular communication tool [15]. IM is characteristic of instantaneous message delivery and presence awareness. In particular, presence awareness differentiates IM from other communication paradigms. We believe such features fit natually into pervasive computing environments, where communication and awareness are essential. Under this vision, "chat" would no longer be the privilege of human; rather, interactions between human-software, software-device and device-device could freely take place. We envision the potential of extrapolating IM paradigm as a unified interface for all communications. Aiming this, we have identified several new design concepts including context-aware presence management, resource buddy services and dynamic grouping.

Presence information shows a user's responsive status, i.e., availability to be involved in a conversation. Current IM products predefine a set of options such as online, busy, and away. This coarse-grained categorization of user status, however, is incompetent under the pervasive vision. We propose a context-aware presence management approach and introduce improvements from three aspects: (1) Context should be used as presence information. Apparently, when a user is

---

* This research is supported in part by a CERG grant (HKU 7146/04E) from the Hong Kong Government.

Y.-C. Chung and J.E. Moreira (Eds.): GPC 2006, LNCS 3947, pp. 32–41, 2006.

aware of the other's situation such as her location, activity, security level and mood, they could communicate more appropriately. An imperative case is the mobile IM system, where showing "online" is meaningless if the user just keeps the connected device in pocket. (2) Presence information should be disseminated in a context-aware manner. Current IM products show the same status of a user to all her buddies. In reality, however, a user's availability is affected not only by her own situation, but also by the relationship with the corresponding buddy. For example, we ought to be "online" among the discussion members, yet appear "busy" to the outliers. (3) Presence information should be set automatically by the system. Nowadays an IM user needs to manually change her status, which tends to be burdensome and fallible. For a mobile user, things would be even more intractable, as her status might change frequently and in an arbitrary way. It is therefore appropriate for the system to handle this task, provided that the presence information can be automatically induced.

In pervasive computing environments, all smart artifacts can "talk" with you. Should they each adopt their own "dialects", a human user would be obliged to master a multitude and burdened in shifting the "language" to and fro. Also, it would involve a great deal of human attention to monitor, control and utilize various resources. Reflecting on the success of IM, we borrow the idea of "buddy" and view human, software and all sorts of devices uniformly as parties of communication. We also propose to use IM as the unified interface. Via IM, a user may include all usable resources in her contact list and "talk" with them in a personalized way. Another advantage of this approach is that, the user and the resource buddies could mutually stay aware of each other's status. The user can quickly tell which resource is near and ready for use, and select a "best" buddy to serve her purpose. Vice versa, the resource buddies could observe the user's situation and decide on the most appropriate way to interact with the user. For example, a notification service could choose to call the user's office phone if she is there, or email a reminder if she is temporarily away.

Grouping mechanism is commonly adopted in IM products to organize the buddy list for the user. In current situation, strategies for grouping are typically framed by the producer and remain unchanged after distribution. Groups are set by the user once for all. In real life senarios, however, human relationships might be temporary, impromptu and varying. We devise a novel dynamic grouping mechanism so that: (1) Grouping should be adaptive i.e., able to change automatically according to the real situation; (2) Grouping should pertain to the user's requirement. For example, grouping the buddies by their locations can help a user "bump into" an acquaintance in a crowded hall, and grouping the relevant members of the same task can speed up the collaboration efficiency.

In this paper, we present our Smart Instant Messenger (SIM) system which fulfills the new concepts listed above. Section 2 overviews the SIM system design, elaborates on how the new features are realized and then introduces the context-aware supporting middleware, which underlies the SIM framework. Details of system implementation and experimental results are given in Section 3, followed

by a comparison with related work in Section 4. The paper is concluded with a
discussion and outlook on future work.

2   System Design

2.1   System Overview

We have designed and prototyped the Smart Instant Messenger (SIM) system to
extrapolate the IM paradigm into pervasive computing environments. This is approached from two layers. The IM Framework layer extends the existing Jabber
[8] Instant Messaging platform and prepares for incorporating the new features.
The context-aware supporting middleware (CASM) underlies the IM framework
and handles the chore of context provision, including retrieving context information from various context providers, interpreting and reasoning over context,
and monitoring the context changes on behalf of applications. The main components of SIM system and their interactions are shown in Figure 1. Inside the SIM
client, the *Instant Message* module provides the basic message exchange functions. The *roster* module is extended to include the presence, dynamic grouping
and resource buddy features. The *context interface* module interacts with the
context-aware supporting middleware either by direct query or by subscription
to interested events. It also monitors the user's conversational behavior, collects

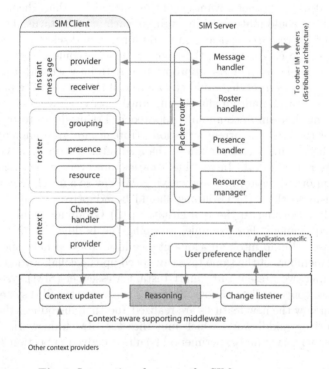

Fig. 1. Interactions between the SIM components

the IM context (i.e., context inferred from chatting and typing) and supplies this information to CASM.

The Jabber message protocols are extended. Three types of messages are defined including chat message, presence update message and context message. The SIM server adds three message handlers to handle them respectively, i.e., the *instant message handler* module, the *presence handler* module and the *context handler* module. A *resource manager* module is also included for resource buddy registration.

2.2 Realizing the Features

SIM supports two types of presence information. The first follows conventional status options i.e., "online, away, busy". However, the status is distributed adaptively. A user's availability displayed to a specific buddy is inferred from both her situation and their relationship. Different buddies might, therefore, observe different status of the same user. This inherently considers the user's preferences and enables fine control over how a user's availability is distributed. Figure 2 shows the adaptive presence notification process. Upon initialization, the SIM client first registers user preference rules to the CASM describing the condition under which the presence should be updated. It also prescribes the different status that should be displayed to different groups of buddies. When the relevant events happen, the change handler in SIM client is notified and dispatches the updated presence to the SIM server, which in turn broadcasts the presence to the buddies.

The second type of presence information embodies the subset of a user's context which she is willing to disclose, including for example her current activity, location and the people nearby. This is enabled by CASM, which actively collects

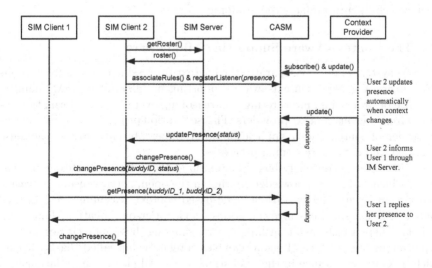

Fig. 2. Sequence diagram showing adaptive presence notification process

user context on behalf of applications. When a user's context is inquired by a buddy as presence information, her context is encapsulated in an XML-formatted message, routed to the buddy's client, parsed and displayed on the roster.

In SIM, human users and resource buddies are conceptually identical. One slight difference is that, upon initialization, the resource client uses its resource module to register to the local SIM server, while the user client performs service discovery on whenever necessary. There are two ways to communicate with the resource buddy. One is to use the original chat window and type the user-defined commands; the other is to download a UI from the resource, which is described in an XML DataForm format. According to devices' configurations and users' preferences, the UI may be rendered in different customized ways.

The SIM system provides an extensible set of grouping mechanisms, including location, activity, hobby and relationship. In the current stage, we specifically investigate the location-based grouping and activity-based grouping. Location-based grouping retrieves from CASM the most updated user locations and groups the buddies of the same location. This is especially useful to help a mobile user, when entering a place, to "bump into" an acquaintance and to initiate a serendipitous interaction. It will also keep the user informed of the surrounding resources. Activity-based grouping reflects on the "distraction-free" tenet, aiming at facilitating the user's activity (or task) by grouping the relevant people, materials and resources together. For example, suppose a user is involved in preparing a project presentation, SIM will dynamically group the project memebers, documents, applications, printer and projector in her buddy list, forming a virtual collaboration environment, so that she could easily reach what she needs to contact or utilize. Current implementation assumes the user's activity can be inferred and the relevant information are stored in the context knowledge base. Upon request, CASM will retrieve the information of all possible buddies (human as well as resources) and return the result to the roster module in the SIM client, which in turn updates the grouping.

2.3   The Context-Aware Supporting Middleware

The SIM system explicitly separates the context processing routines from application logic. A generic context-aware supporting middleware (CASM) handles the chore of processing, interpreting and reasoning over context information retrieved from various context providers. This separation principle not only relieves the burden of context-aware application programmers, but also fosters the reuse of context and context reasoning processes.

CASM centers an ontology-based context model for a formal context representation, which facilitates knowledge sharing in the open, heterogeneous pervasive environments, and enables various logic-based context reasoning mechanisms. Contexts are classified into five categories: Device, Person, Location, Time, and Activity. There are also relationship properties among these main classes. For example, an instance of class "Person" can have a relationship called "hasLocation" which links to an instance in the "Location" class. All classes and relationships can be added or removed as needed.

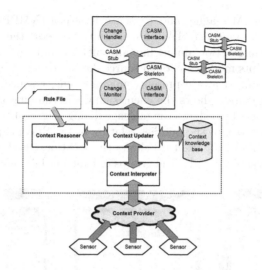

Fig. 3. Detailed design of context-aware middleware

Figure 3 shows the detailed design of CASM. The *Context Interpreter* translates the context from heterogeneous sources to form an OWL instance data, which stores all the dynamic context information (e.g. location, time, current activity) in OWL files. The *Context Updater* directly manipulates the context model. When the context model is first created, the schema file will be parsed and data type of the domain and range for each property are specified. The *Context Updater* validates the data type for that particular context statement each time an add/remove request is received. Upon a context query, it inquires the context model and formulates the answer in a regular format that can be used by the client side easily. The *Context Reasoner* provides two kinds of reasoning over the context ontology, i.e. the transitive reasoning and the rule-based reasoning. The former is used to store and traverse class and property lattices. The latter supports user-defined rule set. Depends on the schema and domain of the ontology bound to the context model, rules can be written to derive the existence of some implicit information or map information to a standard format for applications.

CASM also provides a set of standard methods for application developers to update, query and register context event listeners to the middleware. An application registers interested context events to CASM, and relies on the latter to monitor the environment on its behalf. Notifications will be fired when the events happen, and the *Change handler* module in the application will invoke the corresponding event handling methods.

3   Implementation and Experiments

We have implemented SIM server and two versions (PC and PDA) of SIM clients. The SIM server uses and extends the Jabber open source server. We extends

Jabber's Extensible Messaging and Presence Protocol (XMPP), which is currently an Internet Engineering TAsk Force draft, to report the state of buddies and to handle the interaction among human, software and devices through XML messages. SIM clients modify the open source Jabber client program "JBother" [9] to introduce context-aware presence management, resouce buddy and dynamic grouping. Figure 4 shows the client-side GUIs running on the PDA (HP iPAQ H5500). Figure 4 (a) shows the message dialog, Figure 4 (b) illustrates the SIM's roster, which groups the buddies relating to the SIM project, including 6 members and a printer. Figure 4 (c) shows the location-based grouping, where the buddies are organized under the groups of canteen, lab and office.

(a) Message Dialog   (b) Group by activity   (c) Group by location

Fig. 4. Client-side GUI

We built up several ontologies for pervasive computing environments. Figure 5 shows one ontology used for modeling the basic concepts of campus life. The Web Ontology Language (OWL) has been selected as the ontology language for its expressivity and standardization. Reasoning and inference over the context models are based on the Jena [10] framework. A set of rules has been developed to infer high-level context from low-level facts.

We notice the major time-consuming part of the system (wireless delay excluded) is related to operations on CASM middleware. As more context instances are added into the context knowledge base, the overhead of the middleware grows accordingly. To test the performance, we evaluate the responsiveness and memory consumption with the increase of the number of instances. The experiment proceeds as follows. A PC (Intel Pentium4 2.26GHz, 512MB memory, Linux FC 3.0) which runs Jena version 2.2. A typical sequence of operations is compiled as a sample test, including 2 add (adding instance data into the ontology), 1 remove (removal of instance data), 1 class query and 1 instance query. We increase the instance at the number of 300, 700, 1000 and 1800. At each stage, the sampling sequence is performed and the total processing time and memory

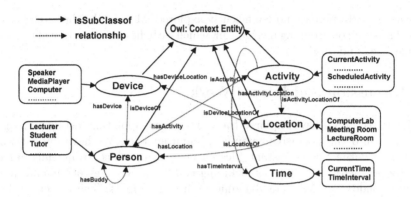

Fig. 5. Diagrammatic view of the campus ontology model

usage are measured. The result reports an approximately linear growth of memory usage varying from 17MB to 22MB and an average processing time of 3.4s with variations within 0.2s. The performance of the system is tolerable for non-crisis scenarios and the increase of instance will not cause much degradation.

4   Related Work

The idea of combining awareness with communication originates in computer supported cooperative work (CSCW) and human-computer interaction (HCI). Researchers in media space research [1][18] and awareness systems [3][6] have identified the importance of shared context to facilitate conversation. For example, social awareness has been explored in [7] and [14]. However, this stream of research mainly targets an efficient group collaboration among human users. Our work, on the other hand, considers all types of interactions including human, software and hardware resources.

The distinctive features of IM have been gaining more attention in recent years. Nardi [12] suggested that, beyond information exchange, IM could implicitly be used to negotiate availability, maintaining the sense of social connection and switching media. There've also been several research projects on extending IM with context-aware features. They could be broadly categorized into two groups. The first exploits context for conditional message delivery. For example, CybreMinder [2] allows users to associate the contextual information with to-do items and delivers them upon pre-defined condition. This can be viewed as a special type of context-aware one-way message delivery. Similarly, a handheld IM system descibed in [11] also empowers users to specify a set of situations that must be met before the system delivers the message. The second group explicitly uses context information to broaden the communication spectrum. ConChat [16], for example, supports two conversational parties to exchange or query each other's context. The AwareNex [17] system from Sun Laboratories displays location and activity information of the users on the contact list. Similar to SIM, these projects emphasize more on the "outeraction" [12] functionality of IM. However, the issues of contextual presence and context-aware presence distribution are not sufficiently explored. Meanwhile, there tends to be little discussion on grouping mechanism, which we believe is also a tool of potential yet has been underused.

5   Discussion and Future Work

In this research, we have explored the vision of extrapolating instant messaging paradigm into the pervasive computing environments. We have designed and implemented the Smart Instant Messenger system, which transcends current IM products with new features including context-aware presence management, resource buddy services and dynamic grouping support. The system is built on top of a context-aware supporting middleware, which centers an ontology-based context modeling approach. Though at the prototype stage, it has already demonstrated the advantages for being used in pervasive computing environments. Experiments on performance evaluation also suggest its feasibility.

Our design fulfilled the following principles: *Separation of context provision from context consumption.* The chore of retrieving and managing context should not be directly integrated in an application; rather, a separate middleware layer or the systems infrastructure should be responsible for providing context information. SIM adopts a context-aware supporting middleware approach. It not only relieves the burdens of programmers and the small devices; the generic middleware could potentially support more applications.

Design for extensibility. Extensibility is essential in pervasive environments as users, applications, devices and sensors might all come and go dynamically. Also, the users' requirements might change over time. SIM chooses the Jabber protocol for its extensibility consideration, adopts a distributed architecture, and exploits an ontology-based context modeling solution to facilitate the re-use and integration of knowledge.

Prototype for real life usage. Pervasive computing is still in the germinal stage. We believe live applications will stimulate and inspire the research. Therefore this version of SIM is designed for using on campus, with resources, users and use cases rich enough for a real system.

We believe such an attempt is of great potential, both in practical usage and in research. Future work includes supporting user-level mobility of instant messenger among different devices, improving the performance of context-aware supporting middleware and exploring the SIM usage in hospital scenarios.

References

1. S. Bly, S. Harrison and S. Irwin. Media spaces: Bring people together in a video, audio and computing environment. Communications of the ACM, 36 (1), 28-46, 1993.
2. A. K. Dey and G. D. Abowd. CybreMinder: a context-aware system for supporting reminders. In 2nd International Symposium on Handheld and Ubiquitous Computing, volume 1927 of Lecture Notes in Computer Science, 172-186. Springer, 2000.

3. P. Dourish, S. Bly. Portholes: supporting awareness in a distributed work group. Proceedings of CHI'93 Human Factors in Computing Systems, 541-547, New York: ACM Press.
4. J. Fogarty, J. Lai and J. Christensen. Presence versus availability: the design and evaluation of a context-aware communication client. International Journal of Human-Computer Studies (IJHCS), Vol. 61, No. 3, September 2004, pp. 299-317.
5. D. Greene and D. O'Mahony. Instant messaging and presence management in mobile ad-hoc networks. Proceedings of the Second IEEE Annual Conference on Pervasive Computing and Communications Workshops. March 14-17, Orlando, Florida, pp. 55-59, 2004.
6. C. Gutwin, S. Greenberg. Design for individuals, design for groups: Trade-offs betwwn power and workspace awareness. In Proceedings of CSCW96 Conference on Computer Supported Cooperative Work, 207-216, New York: ACM Press.
7. S. E. Hudson and I. Smith. Techniques for addressing fundamental privacy and disruption tradeoffs in awareness support systems. Proc. Comp. Supported Cooperative Work, 1996, pp. 248C57.
8. Jabber Instant Messaging. Online resource. http://www.jabber.org/
9. JBother Homepage. Online resource. http://www.jbother.org/
10. Jena: a semantic Web framework for Java. Online resource. http://jena.sourceforge.net/
11. Miguel A. Munoz, Marcela Rodriguez, Jesus Favela, Ana I. Martinez-Garcia, Victor M. Gonzalez. Context-aware mobile communication in hospitals. IEEE Computer, vol. 36, no. 9, pp. 38-46, Sept., 2003.
12. B. Nardi, S. Whittaker, E. Bradner. Interaction and outeraction: instant messaging in action. In Proceedings of ACM 2000 Conference on Computer Supported Cooperative Work, 2000.
13. A.J.H. Peddemors, M.M. Lankhorst, J. de Heer. Presence, location and instant messaging in a context-aware application framework. 4th International Conference on Mobile Data Management (MDM2003), Melbourne, Australia, Jan 2003.
14. E. R. Pedersen and T. Sokoler. AROMA: abstract representation of presence supporting mutual awareness. Proc. SIGCHI Conf. Human Factors in Comp. Sys. , Atlanta, GA, Mar. 22C27, 1997, pp. 51C58.
15. Pew Internet & American Life Project. How americans use instant messaging, Sept 2004. Online resource.
http://www.pewinternet.org/pdfs/PIP_Instantmessage_Report.pdf
16. A.Ranganathan, Roy H. Campbell, A. Ravi, and A. Mahajan. ConChat: a context-aware chat program. Pervasive Computing, 1(3):51-57, July-September 2002.
17. J.Tang, N. Yankelovich et al. ConNexus to AwareNex: extending awareness to mobile users. Proc. SIGCHI Conf. Human Factors in Comp. Sys., Apr. 1998, pp. 566-73.
18. S. Whittaker, G. Swanson, J. Kucan and C. Sidner. Telenotes: managing lightweight interactions in the desktop. Transactions on Computer Human Interaction, 4(2):137-168, 1997.

Negotiation Strategies for Grid Scheduling

Jiadao Li and Ramin Yahyapour*

Institute for Robotics Research - Information Technologies,
University Dortmund, 44221 Dortmund, Germany
{jiadao.li, ramin.yahyapour}@udo.edu

Abstract. Grid computing is considered the next step of distributed computing architectures. For such Service Oriented Architectures (SOAs) resource management is an important component that has to cope with the challenges of heterogeneous, decentralized and autonomous resources. The use of agreements is expected to become a key technology for the reliable interaction between resource providers and consumers. Negotiation is the process of creating agreements in which the different and typically conflicting objectives of the negotiation parties are taken into account. For the broad proliferation of Grids and the efficient use of Grids, this negotiation process must be automated and should only require minimal interaction from the actual providers and users. To this end, strategic negotiation models are required that can be used to perform this task. In this paper, a strategic negotiation model is proposed for Grid computing. Discrete event based simulation is used to evaluate this model. The simulation results demonstrate that it is suitable and effective for Grid environments.

1 Introduction

Grid computing [1, 2] is considered a cornerstone of next generation distributed computing, as it tackles many issues to dynamically interact between autonomous and decentralized resources from different providers. It is the infrastructure model which is typically envisioned as a Service Oriented Architecture (SOA [3, 4]), in which resources are virtualized into services. In this scenario, a resource user typically expects a certain service quality given by a service provider. As in Grids usually autonomous and independent parties interact, the a priori information of quality of service (QoS) prior to using the resource is becoming a crucial requirement for Grid resource management; here, agreement based resource management [5] is generally considered as a suitable means to the problem. Prior to service usage the parties have to negotiate towards service level agreements (SLA) that define what kind of services will be provided and what the obligations of the user will be.

Of course, the resource providers and the resource consumers have typically conflicting objectives which need to be considered during the negotiation. The whole task of negotiation is challenging as the resources are heterogeneous and the service provisioning is not a standardized good but depends on the individual requirements and preferences of the user for a particular task. During the negotiation process, the conflicts of the different objectives and policies between the resource users and resource

---

* Member of CoreGRID.

Y.-C. Chung and J.E. Moreira (Eds.): GPC 2006, LNCS 3947, pp. 42–52, 2006.

providers must be reconciled. However, this process must be automated as it cannot be expected that the actual service/resource consumer and the corresponding provider personally perform this task. For efficient Grid computing, this task must be frequently be performed. Here, suitable negotiation models are required that take the different policies and objectives into account and produce suitable service level agreements in reasonable time with minimized or even no user and provider interference. In this paper, such negotiation models and strategies for agreement negotiation are considered. Currently, there are no mature and accepted negotiation models nor infrastructures available for the Grid computing scenario.

However, there are efforts for a general Grid architecture like the *Open Grid Services Architecture (OGSA)* by the Global Grid Forum [6]. There are also first steps towards core protocols that can be used for agreement management, like the "WS-Agreement" [7] draft proposed by the GRAAP working group in the GGF. This protocol can be used as a simple negotiation protocol. But in the current WS-Agreement proposal, the negotiation process is a one-shot approach in which negotiation parties can only accept or reject opponent's proposals. This one-shot negotiation process can be quite unsatisfying for actual implementations as the negotiating parties have not means to steer a negotiation towards an agreement if the first proposal is unacceptable [8]. In order to make negotiation efficiently, the process should be *multi-rounded*. (Some discussion on creating negotiation frameworks have been given by Dash et.al.[9].)

In this paper, we focus only on the negotiation process in which a user agent negotiates with a set of resource providers. This is considered the *one to many* negotiation type. Usually, this negotiation type can be treated as reversed auctioning. However, there are some drawbacks of using auction mechanisms, for instance, there is no flexible way of exercising different strategies with different negotiation opponents. Moreover, auctions do not support bidirectional offers with counter offers between the parties. We propose a strategic negotiation model which includes utility functions /preferences for the negotiation parties. Moreover, we propose and evaluate first negotiation strategies for Grids. This paper is organized as follows: In Section 2, the related work in the area of resource management in Grid computing is reviewed. In Section 3, the strategic negotiation model which includes the bilateral negotiation model and the concurrent bilateral model in the Grid computing environment is explained. The simulation configuration and the simulation results are presented and analyzed in Section 4. Conclusions and information on future works are given in Section 5.

2 Strategic Negotiation Model

There are many approaches proposed for the Grid resource management problems, for example, economic method and matchmaking approach. Economic methods for computational tasks in Grids have been subject of research for some time. An overview of such models is, for example, given by Buyya et.al. in [10] or Ernemann et.al. in [11], or Wolski et.al. in [12]. Matchmaking approach is adopted in the Condor project [13]. The matchmaker performs scheduling in a Condor pool, resource requests and offers are described in the Condor classified language and the matchmaker is responsible for finding suitable resources to satisfy the needs of the job users. To this end, a lot of efforts have been made on the Grid resource management considering the Service level agreement (SLA), e.g. in paper [14], a Grid resource usage SLA broker called GRU-BER is presented and evaluated in a real grid, GRID3; in paper [15], an architecture for specifying, monitoring and validating Service Level Agreements (SLA) for use in Grid environments is presented.

However, strategies for conducting the negotiation between the participating parties are not yet well understood. There have been several efforts in discipline of economics which are not yet well analyzed to the Grid scenario. Here, additional work in regards of the influences of the strategies is required. In our work we selected the bilateral negotiation model as a suitable the building block for concurrent negotiation model. Therefore we will briefly introduce these in the following.

2.1 Bilateral Negotiation Model

There are three parts in the bilateral negotiation model that have to be considered, [16]: 1) the negotiation protocol, 2) the used utility/preference functions for the negotiating parties, and 3) the negotiation strategy that is applied during the negotiation process. In our approach, we adopted and modified Rubinstein's sequential alternating offer protocol for Grids, see [17].

In Rubinstein's alternating offers bilateral negotiation protocol, the bargaining procedure is as follows: The players can take actions only at certain times in the (infinite) set $T = \{1, 2, 3, ...t\}$. In each period $t \in T$, one of the players, say i, proposes an agreement, and the other player j either accepts the offer or rejects it. If the offer is accepted, then the bargaining ends, and the agreement is implemented. If the offer is rejected, then the process passes to period $t + 1$; in this period player j proposes an agreement, which player i may accept or reject. The negotiation process will go on in this way.

In the Grid resource management scenario, time plays an important role as every negotiation party has only limited negotiation time available. Therefore, the number of the negotiation rounds is limited. In our scenario, the above time set T is finite. In the negotiation process, when either one negotiation side times out or an agreement is created, the negotiation process will end. An offer is assumed to be valid until a counter offer is received. Therefore the consistent state problem between the negotiation parities can be avoided.

As mentioned before, we support utility functions to express the objectives of the users; preferences relationships are used to indicate the preferences of resource providers. Usually, the objectives of the user request minimizing the job waiting time or to get cheaper resources; on the other side, the resource providers expect to gain higher profit and higher utilization. However, the real weighting of the utility factors depend on the individual user or resource provider. In real Grid systems, there can be many different negotiation objectives, that are interdependent and should be dealt simultaneously which yields to a multi-criteria optimization problem [18]. Depending on the specific application domain, cost for service/resource usage can be supported.

In the following we consider as first examples the expected waiting time of the jobs and the expected cost per cpu time as the negotiation issues. However, the model can be applied and extended to other criteria as well. In this model, $U_{price}(P_c^t)$ (E.q.1) is the job's utility function of the price and $U_{time}(T_c^t)$ (E.q.2) is job's utility function of the waiting time.

$$U_{price}(P_c^t) = \frac{P_c^{max} - P_c^t}{P_c^{max} - P_c^{min}} \tag{1}$$

$$U_{time}(T_c^t) = \frac{T_c^{max} - T_c^t}{T_c^{max} - T_c^{min}} \tag{2}$$

The variables are explained as follows: W_{price} is the weight of the price utility. W_{time} is the weight of the time utility. P_c^{max} (P_c^{min}) is the maximum (minimum) acceptable price of the user offered by the negotiation opponent at the time t. T_c^{max} (T_c^{min}) is the maximum (minimum) acceptable waiting time of the user.

This leads to the following aggregate utility function of the job user:

$$U_{job} = W_{price} * U_{price} + W_{time} * U_{time} \tag{3}$$

Because the negotiation time in this scenario is usually short, the utilities in this scenario are not discounted as negotiation time goes on. The weights of different negotiation issues are normalized, so we assume that $\sum_{j=1}^{n} w_j = 1$ if the number of the negotiation issues is n. In the negotiation process, an agent can change its preference for an issue by changing the weight associated to that issue. Different agents can have quite different preferences over different issues.

For the resource providers, there are also two corresponding negotiation issues which are: the expected waiting time of the job $T_s^t(Job)$, and the expected price $P_s^t(Job)$. The expected waiting time for the newly incoming job can be obtained from the current resource status and the future schedule plan considering the created agreements which have to be fulfilled. The expected price will be obtained via the negotiation process.

The *zone of possible agreement* denotes the overlap in the negotiation issues between the participating parties [19]. If there is no zone of possible agreement, an agreement can not be achieved. For the negotiation issue j, the acceptable value range of the job is $[C_{min}^j, C_{max}^j]$, the acceptable value range of the resource provider is $[S_{min}^j, S_{max}^j]$. If $C_{max}^j > S_{min}^j$ and $C_{min}^j < S_{max}^j$, then the agreement zone exists.

In the negotiation process, our negotiating parties act rationally. Disagreement is treated as the worst outcome, therefore the negotiation party always avoids opting out of the negotiation process. One of the principles of good-faith bargaining is that once a concession is made, it is usually not easily reversed [19]. On the basis of the initial values, successive offers by sellers are monotonically decreasing while successive offers by the buyers are monotonically increasing. It is important that the negotiating parties provide suitable initial values for the negotiation issues.

In the negotiation model, the negotiation parties must not know the opponents' private reservation information and their preferences/utility functions. Without this restriction, the parties could exploit the condition of the corresponding negotiating partners. That means, a negotiation scenario with *incomplete information* is considered. In the negotiation process, the negotiation parties should make reasonable reservation values of different negotiation issues in order to make sure that it is possible to create agreements.

2.2 Negotiation Strategies

In the strategic negotiation model there are no rules that bind the negotiation parties to any specific strategy. The essence of the negotiation strategy for the negotiation party is to create suitable offers in its acceptable value range of specific negotiation issue in order to create the agreement and make its utility as much as possible at the same time. There already exist several general negotiation strategies, for example [8], argumentation based approach, game theoretic models, heuristics approaches in the agent community. These different strategies have advantages and disadvantages and they can be applied in several scenarios. As shown before, the negotiation parties do not know the reservation values and the utility functions/preferences of the opponents in our scenario. Therefore, *heuristic based negotiation strategies* are adopted for this paper. The negotiation process in the Grid computing domain is time-limited, the strategies of the negotiation parties are considered to change dynamically based on the remaining available negotiation time. Typically, a user will not negotiate and wait for the negotiation result for a long time, if he/she has a very urgent job needed to be executed. To this end, we limit our scope on *time dependent negotiation strategies* [20]. However, note that there are also other negotiation strategies available which are based on other assumptions, for example, if there are many resources available for a job, then the job user may become very tough during the negotiation process.

We assume that V_j is the utility function of the negotiation party which associates with the negotiation issue j and the $x_{a \to b}^t[t]$ is the offer provided by one party (denoted by a) to another negotiation party (denoted by b).

If V_j is decreasing:

$$x_{a \to b}^t[t] = min_j^a + \alpha_j^a(t)(max_j^a - min_j^a), \tag{4}$$

if V_j is increasing:

$$x_{a \to b}^t[t] = min_j^a + (1 - \alpha_j^a(t))(max_j^a - min_j^a), \tag{5}$$

Equations (4) and (5) represents the job user's strategy and the resource provider's strategy respectively.

There are many ways of defining the function for $\alpha_j^a(t)$. For the initial bargaining value k_j^a is used, for which the following relation holds $0 \le k_j^a \le 1$.

We use the following function for $\alpha_j^a(t)$:

$$\alpha_j^a(t) = k_j^a + (1 - k_j^a)(\frac{t}{t_{max}^a})^{1/\beta}, \tag{6}$$

where t_{max}^a is the deadline of the negotiation party a for the completion of negotiation, t denotes the current time instant in the negotiation time set, the parameter β is the degree of convexity that determines the type of the negotiation party in the time dependent strategy. Different β values yield different negotiation strategies.

There are three typical strategies for different negotiation parties [20]. When $0 < \beta < 1$, the negotiator will be tough (Boulware), which means that he will maintain the offered value longer until the time is almost exhausted. Close to the deadline he will concede up to the reservation value. In contrast, for $\beta > 1$ the negotiator will be the type of Conceder and will concede to its reservation value very quickly at the beginning of the negotiation, while its concession rate become flattened as the time limits approached. For $\beta = 1$, the negotiator will linearly concede to its reservation value.

2.3 Concurrent Bilateral Negotiation Model

To this end, in the Grid environment, it is assumed that after a resource discovery phase there are a number of available resources which are capable of fulfilling the constraints of the job. These constraints include, e.g., the required number of CPU nodes, the needed memory capacity, etc. The user or a corresponding scheduling component will contact different resource providers and initiate the negotiation process for the actual resource allocation.

We just assume that the negotiation process is started by the user, more precisely by the job agent, who contacts different resource providers and begins the negotiation process. In the concurrent negotiation threads in which the same user is involved, the reservation values of the negotiation issues and preferences of the user are the same. However, the user may adopt different strategies with respect to different negotiation opponents. Furthermore, they might change the negotiation strategies during the negotiation process according to the types of opponents and their behavior. Because these negotiation threads are progressed concurrently, it is very difficult to predict whether the user might achieve a better offer from another negotiation thread if there is already a suitable offer found that could be committed to an agreement. For now we assume that once there is an agreement available, the agreement is made. This limitation will be reviewed in future work.

3   Evaluation

For a first analysis of the approach we use discrete event simulation. Currently, there is no real data from the Grid computing environments that include suitable information for negotiation models. Therefore, we use high performance computing workload traces from actual machine installations. However, negotiation information are not included in this data as none of the real system supported negotiation models. To this end, the missing information can only be modeled based on first assumptions. Note, that the presented results may vary for practical implementations with different workloads. The impact of the workload and the verification of modeling assumption will be part of the future work. In the following the simulation configuration is described and the simulation results are analyzed.

3.1   Simulation Configuration

We use the exploratory studies method introduced in the book [21]. In the simulation, we investigated different negotiation parameters which possibly has some kind of influence in the negotiation result. In the beginning of the negotiation, the negotiation parties will always make the offers which are most favorable to themselves, at the first assumption, we assume that the initial values of k_j of all the negotiation parties are 0. We assume that the negotiation interval between every negotiation round is 1s. In the following we describe the modeling of the user and the resource providers.

User Model. In our simulation we consider parallel batch jobs in an online scenario. We assume types of user behavior are quite different. For our simulation, we just assume that there are two different kinds of user objectives: time-optimization and cost-optimization. Other user preference will be subject of future research. Below are the parameters of the user modeling which have been applied for the simulation.

- Negotiation span is uniformly distributed in $[0, 30]$s.
- Maximum price of the different job user is uniformly distributed in $[4.0, 9.0]$.
- Acceptable waiting time for the job users are uniformly distributed in $[0, 36000]$s.
- For the tough negotiator, β value is uniformly distributed in $[0.02, 0.2]$.
- For the conceder negotiator, β value is uniformly distributed in $[20, 40]$.
- Weights of waiting time and price for the time-optimization are 0.8 and 0.2, while the weights of the time and price for the cost-optimization are 0.2 and 0.8.

Resource Provider Model. Currently there are many local resource management systems available. Here, we use the common FCFS scheduling strategy with backfilling [22]. There is no preemption allowed. In this evaluation we do not yet consider the co-allocation and combination of different agreements from different providers. For the moment, the resources are considered to be homogeneous only differing in the number of available CPU nodes at each site. We assume that the job users will contact with the resource providers in a Round Robin fashion. The simulated Grid configurations for the resource providers are consistent with the actual configurations of the systems from which the real traces originated. In this paper, we used traces from the Cornell Theory Center [23] which had 512 CPU nodes. In our simulation we assumed a Grid scenario with 6 different machines and therefore 6 resource providers. However, to stay consistent with the available workload from the CTC traces, the number of nodes for all simulated machines is again 512 nodes. The number of nodes on each machine is given below. The following list also includes the negotiation parameters for each resource provider in this scenario.

- The numbers of the CPU nodes are $\{384, 64, 16, 16, 16, 16\}$.
- Their different maximum prices per CPU time are $\{8.2, 8.0, 7.5, 7.6, 7.4, 7.5\}$.
- Their different minimum prices per CPU time are $\{2.4, 2.3, 2.0, 1.95, 1.90, 1.80\}$.
- Negotiation deadlines of different resource providers are all 30s, which means that usually the resource provider will not opt out of the negotiation once the negotiation thread is created.
- For the tough negotiator, β value is $\{32, 35, 34, 38, 40, 40\}$.
- For the conceding negotiator, β value is $\{0.03, 0.05, 0.04, 0.10, 0.05, 0.06\}$

3.2   Evaluation Remarks

Without a reference benchmark for negotiation-based Grid scenarios, it is difficult to compare and analyze the quantitative and qualitative output of such a scheduling model. In the following we provide some first simulation results which give some information about the performance of the model. The actual quality will have to be verified with better workload models and in real implementations.

We use the following criteria for evaluation:

- Comparison between the negotiation result and the reference point [19], which is the middle of the agreement zone of user and resource provider: $[C_j^{max}, S_j^{min}]$. The reference point is computed by the following function:

$$U_j^{ref} = \frac{C_j^{max} + S_j^{min}}{2} \qquad (7)$$

- The rate of successfully created agreement for all jobs.
- The negotiation overhead to create the agreement measured by the time taken to create the agreement. In our case, we use the final negotiation rounds which represents the required number of messages exchanged. The actual network overhead will depend on the actual network speed for this message exchange.
- In the Grid computing environment, the users will concern about the job response time and the waiting time; while for the resource providers the utilization and the profit will probably be the main objectives. We also compare these criteria to get some feedback about the feasibility of the negotiation model.

3.3   Simulation Results

We used 5000 jobs from the CTC workload traces [23] to do our simulation. As mentioned before, the negotiation parties use different negotiation strategies and they have different reservation values and utility functions/preferences. In the result figures we use the following abbreviations: T, L, C denote the tough, linear, and conceding strategies respectively. T-T means both parties act tough, T-C means that the job users are tough, while the resource providers are conceding. We compared four different scenarios for our simulations: L-L, C-C, T-C, T-T. Every simulation scenario is represented by every group bar as shown in every result figure. Note, that, in every group bar of the result figure except the first figure, there are six bars which represent the result of resource one to resource six separately. We compare the on average required number of negotiation rounds for successfully creating the agreements. In addition, we consider the rate of successfully created the agreement in comparison to the total number of job requests. Other criteria are the average weighted response time (AWRT), the average weighted wait time (AWWT), the average price difference between the agreement price and the reference price. For the weight in AWRT and AWWT we used the job resource consumption [24].

In Figure 1, we can see that the C-C scenario provides the highest number of successfully created agreements, as well as the highest resource utilization. However, also the AWWT and AWRT are high. This indicates that the conceding partners usually reach

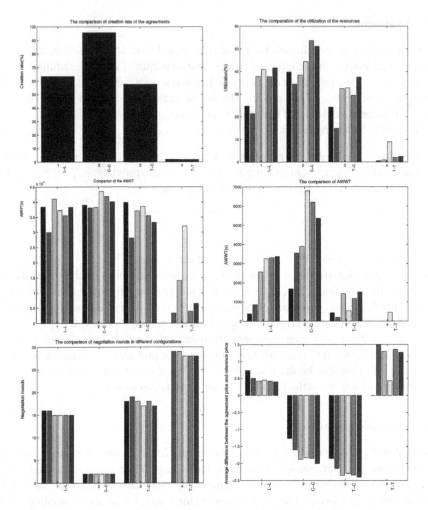

Fig. 1. Comparison between different negotiation scenarios including the results for the individual six resources were appropriate

an agreement for this strategy, while the service quality for the user is relatively low as jobs are delayed. In the T-C scenario, the succeeding rate of the created agreement is not so high, but the job users get on average cheaper offers from the resource providers. In the L-L case, negotiation results are in the middle compared to the other cases. In the T-T case, there are a very few number of successfully created agreements and the job users still have to pay higher cost and incurred much communication cost, as shown in the picture, the agreement can only be created at end of the user's negotiation span.

In the time dependent negotiation strategies, the negotiation span can also influence the result of negotiation strategies. For example, in the C-C case, if we change the time span for negotiation for the resource providers to 20, the number of the successfully created agreements are the same while the agreement prices are lower as the provider concedes faster to his reservation value. Similarly, the resulting price is higher if the user has less time for negotiation. More simulations have been conducted, however due to limited available space we present only these excerpts of the results which show the feasibility of the model. From these simulations, we see that just insistent on using a single strategy for the whole negotiation, may not necessarily provide a higher utility. In order to get the most out of the negotiation, the negotiation parties will have to change their strategies dynamically during the process which will be part of our future work.

4 Conclusions and Future Work

In this paper, we discussed the use of strategic negotiation model which includes utility functions, preference relationships and time dependent negotiation strategies. This model is reviewed for practical use in automatic job scheduling. The current research in Grid computing shows that there is a trend for future resource management systems to include automatic management features for quality of service and cost consideration. As we can see from our experiments, the user can obtain quality of service and reliable agreement for the Grid jobs by applying the presented negotiation strategies. In our scenario, the expected waiting time is guaranteed by the resource provider. The simulation results shows that the model can be used in the Grid scheduling environment. The presented results can be seen as first steps in analyzing the features and requirements for automatic negotiation strategies. They indicate that the negotiation overhead in terms of exchanged messages is manageable for practical application. The obtained agreement results can also be considered to be good enough for real world scenarios. Future work will include further investigation in different negotiation strategies and a broader basis for evaluation results. Also the extension to more sophisticated negotiation features like co-allocation are foreseen.

References

1. Foster, I., Kesselman, C., Tuecke, S.: The anatomy of the Grid: Enabling scalable virtual organizations. Lecture Notes in Computer Science **2150** (2001)
2. Foster, I., Kesselman, C.: The Grid: Blueprint for a New Computing Infrastructure. Morgan Kaufmann (2003)
3. The w3c web services architecture working wroup public draft (2004) http://www.w3.org/TR/ws-arch/.
4. Czajkowski, K., Foster, I., Kesselman, C.: Resource and service management. In Foster, I., Kesselman, C., eds.: The Grid: Blueprint for a New Computing Infrastructure. Morgan Kaufmann (2003)
5. Czajkowski, K., I.Foster, C.Kesselman: Agreement-based resource management. Proceedings of the IEEE **93**(3) (2005) 631–643
6. The open grid services architecture, version 1.0 (2005) https://forge.gridforum.org/projects/ogsa-wg.
7. Web services agreement specification (2005) https://forge.gridforum.org/projects/graap-wg.
8. Jennings, N.R., Faratin, P., Lomuscio, A.R., Parsons, S., Sierra, C., Wooldridge, M.: Automated negotiation: Prospects, methods and challenges. Int. J. of Group Decision and Negotiation 10 (2) 199-215. **2**(10) (2001) 199–215
9. R.K.Dash, N.R.Jennings, D.C.Parkes: Computational mechanism design: A call to arms. IEEE Intelligent Systems **18**(6) (2003) 40–47

10. Buyya, R.: Economic-based Distributed Resource Management and Scheduling for Grid Computing. PhD thesis, Monash University, Melbourne, Australia (2002)
11. Ernemann, C., Yahyapour, R.: "Applying Economic Scheduling Methods to Grid Environments". In: "Grid Resource Management - State of the Art and Future Trends". Kluwer Academic Publishers (2003) 491–506
12. Wolski, R., Plank, J.S., Brevik, J., Bryan, T.: Analyzing market-based resource allocation strategies for the computational grid. International Journal of High Performance Computing Applications **15**(3) (2001) 258–281
13. Raman, R.: Matchmaking Frameworks for Distributed Resource Management. PhD thesis, University of Wisconsin-Madison (2000)
14. Dumitrescu, C., Foster, I.T.: Gruber: A grid resource usage sla broker. In: Euro-Par. (2005) 465–474
15. Padgett, J., Djemame, K., Dew, P.M.: Grid-based sla management. In: EGC. (2005) 1076–1085
16. Kraus., S.: Strategic Negotiation in Multi-Agent Environments. MIT Press, Cambridge, USA, (2001)
17. Rubinstein, A.: Perfect equilibrium in a bargaining model. Econometrica **50** (1982) 97–110
18. Kurowski, K., Nabrzyski, J., Oleksiak, A., Weglarz, J.: "Multicriteria Aspects of Grid Resource Management". In: "Grid Resource Management - State of the Art and Future Trends". Kluwer Academic Publishers (2003) 271–295
19. Raiffa, H.: The Art and Science of Negotiation. Harvard Universtiy Press (1982)
20. Faratin, P.: Automated Service Negotiation Between Autonomous Computational Agents. PhD thesis, Department of Electronic Engineering, Queen Mary College, University of London, UK (2000)
21. Cohen, P.R.: Empirical Methods for Artificial Intelligence. MIT Press (1995) Cambridge, Massachusetts.
22. Lifka, D.: The ANL/IBM SP scheduling system. In Feitelson, D.G., Rudolph, L., eds.: Job Scheduling Strategies for Parallel Processing. Springer-Verlag (1995) 295–303 Lect. Notes Comput. Sci. vol. 949.
23. Standard workload format (2005) http://www.cs.huji.ac.il/labs/parallel/workload/index.html.
24. Schwiegelshohn, U., Yahyapour, R.: Analysis of first-come-first- serve parallel job scheduling. In: Proceedings of the 9th SIAM Symposium on Discrete Algorithms. (1998) 629–638

An Enhanced Grid Scheduling with Job Priority and Equitable Interval Job Distribution

HyoYoung Lee, DongWoo Lee, and R.S. Ramakrishna

Department of Information and Communications,
Gwangju Institute of Science and Technology,
1 Oryong-dong Buk-gu, Gwangju 500-712, Republic of Korea
{hyylee, leepro, rsr}@gist.ac.kr

Abstract. The scheduling service is an important component of large scale computing environments. In this paper, we take a local and grid-wise look at the scheduling problem. First an advance backfilling algorithm based on the job square with a wide job priority is presented. Experimental results show that the priority scheduler reduces the mean waiting time to an extent that depends on the proportion of narrow jobs within a workload. Subsequently, we consider a load sharing technique that selects the site in the Grid that is executing the least number of jobs of similar size as that of the current job. The adaptive sharing scheme offers significant benefits in terms of the average weighted waiting time.

1 Introduction

Grid computing - a new paradigm involving distributed computing environments - is a technology that allows the users and application programs to access a large scale IT domain. Grid scheduling is a general middleware service and it determines the order in which the jobs assigned to the distributed system are processed. Job scheduling strategies that rely on load sharing have been proposed as the core technique for grid services.

Job scheduling aims to optimize the performance of the computing environment. The performance is measured by the response time and the number of processed jobs. We focus on a couple of scheduling issues in this paper. First, we present a variant of the backfilling scheme, a well known general mechanism for scheduling parallel supercomputers, considering the job set amenable to execution at once. The product of the number of (needed) nodes and the user's estimated runtime is used in this regard. In addition, a wide job is given a priority with a view to avoid long waiting time. Second, we propose a new load sharing technique to be executed by the global dispatcher in the grid environment. Our motivation is based on the fact that the entire system performance can be strongly influenced by the distribution of the prevailing job size. Under this arrangement, the global dispatcher collects the system information and derives a stable distribution of jobs on the basis of size-level interval of the processor capacity. These two schemes improve scheduling performance in comparison with the traditional approaches.

Y.-C. Chung and J.E. Moreira (Eds.): GPC 2006, LNCS 3947, pp. 53–62, 2006.
© Springer-Verlag Berlin Heidelberg 2006

The remainder of this paper is organized as follows. Section 2 describes related work about job scheduling schemes in large-scale multiprocessors. Section 3 addresses the model and configurations of the simulations. In Section 4, we evaluate the results in the light of the proposed methodology. Section 5 contains conclusions.

2 Related Work

2.1 Enhanced Backfilling Algorithms as a Job Scheduling

The backfilling algorithm was introduced by Lifka [7]. It adopted non-FCFS strategy to increase system utilization for parallel job scheduling. The algorithm has received widespread attention in the research community. These studies addressed differential policies that allow certain job priority and reservation under an established backfilling rule. There are two common variations to backfilling - *conservative* and *EASY*. The results showed that the performance depends on the workload and the selected metric [9, 13]. There is considerable work on time priority. Sorting the waiting jobs by estimated execution times [18]; assignment of the requested jobs to a multiple job queue based on projected execution time [6] may be mentioned here. Speculative approaches based on execution-time have also been considered [10]. The results of average slowdown and response time show an improved scheduling performance. Other approaches to backfilling scheduling can be included in the job feature. A scheduler which assigns differential priorities to jobs based on the characteristic of each job has been proposed in [14]. A high priority job can bypass a low priority job thereby improving the system efficiency [12].

2.2 Enriched Approaches to the Grid Scheduling

Dynamic load sharing has already been considered in distributed systems. Tan et al. [15] propose a load distribution that is proportional to the processing capacity of servers. The mean waiting time is reduced by penalizing the large task. In grid computing, the main focus is on scheduling with a global backfilling scheduler. The proposals presented in [1, 17] emphasize the importance of job sharing in the grid environment and provide a global scheduler that uses a snapshot that carries the scheduling information of every cluster. In addition, the impact of the global resources encompassing different time zones has also been investigated [2]. These proposals indicated that the overall system performance can be enhanced with a judicious job sharing strategy.

3 The Backfilling Scheme with Wide Job Priority

In this section, we present the workload characteristics and the simulation model. The simulation was performed under the open systems environment with real workload traces for modeling an actual parallel and distributed system.

3.1   Workload Model

Feitelson [5] showed that the characteristics of the workload influence the evaluation of system performance. Therefore, to understand the effect of the proposed algorithm with regard to the workload, we performed experiments using four distinct workload traces which were collected over a year from real workloads in large scale computer systems [19]. The arrival time, the requested number of nodes, the runtime, and the estimated runtime demanded by each user are represented in the workload trace. The workloads used in the simulation are summarized in Table 1.

Table 1. Description of Workload Traces

Workload Name	Max Nodes	Number of Jobs	Period	
			Start Time	End Time
CTC	512	79267	Jul. 1996	May 1997
KTH	100	26456	Oct. 1996	Jul. 1997
SDSC-SP2	128	37178	May 1998	Apr. 1999
SDSC-BLUE	1152	90492	Jan. 2001	Dec. 2001

3.2   Proposed Scheduling Scheme

EASY backfilling allows a short job to execute ahead as long as it does not delay the job (reserved) at the head of the queue. Most scheduling models have employed job partition in accordance with the required number of processors and the estimated runtime and the jobs have been divided into narrow and wide jobs based on processor size [13]. However, there are mainly two limitations to the backfilling algorithm:

(1) The relatively long delay before a wide job makes a reservation.
(2) The unreliability of the user's estimated runtime [9].

We intend to address the above issues. We have to take into account two factors affecting the backfilling scheduling. The first refers to the ability to backfill with narrow jobs which is the main reason for improved performance. The other is concerned with shortening the waiting time of wide jobs.

The main characteristics of the proposed algorithm are described below.

- *The creation of the job-set*
  We consider the square of a job to decide its order (of execution) for efficient scheduling. Besides, to improve the system performance, the genetic algorithm is employed to discover an optimal job-set that leaves as small a number of idle nodes as possible at schedule time. Here the job set is composed of jobs capable of backfill at schedule time.
- *Differential priorities to wide jobs*
  The backfilling algorithm favors narrow jobs. Wide jobs wait for a relatively longer time than do narrow jobs. For this reason, we distinguish the wide job from among current jobs for prioritization. When creating a job-set, we

evaluate the maximum waiting time of the first wide job in the queue. Thereafter, if there are enough idle nodes capable of handling that job whose waiting
time exceeds the specified maximum waiting time, it can be executed right-
away. More specifically, we define the availability condition by the equation

$$j \in W_j \text{ and } T_{w_j} \geq (\ EstimatedTime_j + (\ EstimatedTime_j \times \mathcal{R}\ ))$$

where W_j is a wide job , T_{w_j} is the waiting time of job j and $\mathcal{R}$ is the priority
proportion for maximum waiting time. The parameters are described below.

- *Criterion of a wide job.* This depends on the system characteristics such
  as system capacity and the general use of power-of-two nodes [3]. A wide
  job satisfies the inequality

$$W_j > 2^{\lfloor \frac{log_2 N}{2} \rfloor}$$

where N is the system capacity.
- *Setting up maximum waiting time.* In queueing theory, jobs arrive at an
  average rate of λ at a single processor CPU where they are served. It
  has been shown [8] that the workload profile at a given site tends to
  be fairly stable over time. So, we calculate the maximum waiting time
  using the priority proportion, $\mathcal{R}$, based on the historical information
  and assign adaptive time to various jobs in each workload. When the
  number of arriving jobs is large enough, the effect of a wide job priority
  has to be reduced by increasing $\mathcal{R}$. In contrast, if the proportion of wide
  jobs is large (with the same λ), the value of $\mathcal{R}$ has to be reduced in
  order to prevent long delay for a wide job. For example, suppose two
  workloads have 20% wide jobs. Let the first and the second workload
  have 20 wide jobs out of 100 jobs and 200 wide jobs out of 1000 jobs
  respectively. Here the priority for a wide job of the second workload has
  to be reduced because it has relatively many narrow jobs. In the end,
  the priority ratio $\mathcal{R}$ is directly proportional to λ of a given site and is
  inversely proportional to the ratio of wide jobs. That is, the equation is
  formulated as follows.

$$\mathcal{R} = \frac{\lambda}{proportion\_of\_wide\_jobs} \times 100$$

4   Extensions to the Grid

There have been many attempts to extend the major features of parallel and
distributed systems to grid computing. The computational grid tries to enhance
the computing speed by capitalizing on the resources available all over the world.

4.1   Model Description

We carried out simulations with independent jobs to look for effective distribution in regard to job requests of diverse users. The grid architecture model used
here is shown in Figure 1. The synthetic workload was created by combining the
workloads mentioned above with due regard to job's submission time.

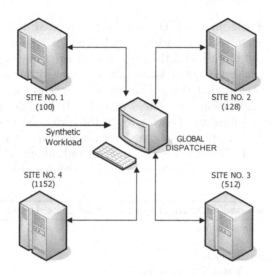

Fig. 1. A Simple Architecture for Grid Simulation

4.2   Impact of Load Sharing Based on the Job Size-Level Interval

The workload characteristic at an arbitrary site is quite involved. To illustrate, Figure 2(a) shows an irregular job distribution of the above workloads in a real system. Note that CTC and SDSC_SP2 workloads represent extreme cases.

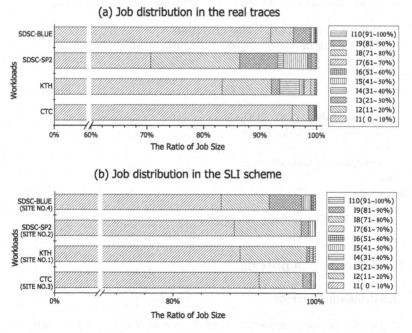

Fig. 2. Comparison of job distributions under real and SLI scheme

More than 95% of jobs in the CTC workload requested only 0 to 51 nodes (within 10% of system capacity) while merely 70% of jobs in the SDSC_SP2 workload requested 0 to 13 nodes(the same percentage as before). That is, the job distributions of the two workloads are quite different with respect to size-level interval. Thus, it is clear that the job has to be assigned to the proper system by taking into consideration the system capacity. It is uniformly distributed to the same size-level interval of each site. In this proposed model, the global dispatcher finds a target site that has the least proportion of busy nodes among all the available sites for a given size-level interval and submits the requested job to the local queue of that site. The load sharing algorithm is given in Algorithm1.

Algorithm 1. The Load Sharing Based on the Size-Level Interval

Require: $S \leftarrow Number of Sites$

1: **while** Global Dispatcher is up **do**
2:     $r_j \leftarrow$ *Number of Nodes the Job Requests*
3:     $c_s \leftarrow$ *Site Capacity*
4:     $m_s \leftarrow$ *Minimum Site Capacity Among Sites That r_j can be Executed*
5:     $i \leftarrow$ *Interval of Involving r_j When m_s Capacity is Divided into 10 Ranges*
6:     $R_s \leftarrow$ *Ratio of the Interval i of Site s*
7:     $C_{ul}, C_{ol} \leftarrow \infty$
8:
9:     **while** termination condition not met **do**
10:        **if** $r_j \leq c_s$ and idle nodes $\geq r_j$ **then**
11:            underloadedSite = s having the least ratio satisfied ($R_s \leq C_{ul}$)
12:            $C_{ul} = R_s$
13:        **else if** $r_j \leq c_s$ and idle nodes $< r_j$ **then**
14:            overloadedSite = s having the least ratio satisfied ($R_s \leq C_{ol}$)
15:            $C_{ol} = R_s$
16:        **end if**
17:     **end while**
18:
19:     **if** underloadedSite is found **then**
20:        targetSite = underloadedSite
21:     **else**
22:        targetSite = overloadedSite
23:     **end if**
24: **end while**

---

5   Performance Analysis

5.1   Evaluation Metrics

The metrics for performance evaluation depend on the type of simulation. The implemented simulation is the open online system and the scheduling system aims to ensure user satisfaction by reducing the waiting time. Hence, the user-centric metrics - the waiting time and bounded slowdown [4] - have been used in order to measure system performance. The metrics are defined as follows:

$$WaitingTime_j = StartTime_j - SubmitTime_j$$

$$Bounded\_Slowdown_j = \frac{WaitingTime_j + RunTime_j}{Max(RunTime_j, 10)}$$

In the same way, the metric used for estimating performance in the grid environment is the average weighted waiting time(AWWT) [11]. The amount of resources consumed is indicated by the product of the number of nodes assigned to the job and the execution time of the job:

$$Resource\_Consumption_j = (number\_of\_nodes_j \times execution\_time_j)$$

The AWWT is defined by,

$$AWWT = \frac{\sum_{j \in Jobs}(Resource\_Consumption_j \times Waiting\_Time_j)}{\sum_{j \in Jobs}(Resource\_Consumption_j)}$$

The weighted waiting time is proportional to the resource consumption and this formula gives an identical waiting time for the needed resources.

5.2   Backfilling Based on Wide Job Priority

Figure 3 depicts the overall waiting time and bounded slowdown of expanded backfilling with a wide job priority in relation to four workloads. The system load in the simulation environment is dealt with by multiplying the submit time by a certain factor [9]. The simulation results indicate not only that the proposed algorithm has better performance than that of traditional backfilling, but also that the extent of performance improvement varies with the workload.

To understand the sensitivity of performance to workload characteristics, we have to note that the workload presents anomalous distribution in job size, as shown in Figure 2(a). Indeed, the performance with regard to the four workloads improves on an average as follows:

$$CTC(19\%) > SDSC\_BLUE(12\%) > KTH(8\%) > SDSC\_SP2(1\%)$$

It is seen that the performance is closely connected with the proportion of narrow jobs. This is due to two main reasons. Firstly, an unexpected slow down of narrow jobs brought about by wide jobs is largely reduced owing to the job-set that is ready for execution. Secondly, even when we consider wide job priority, the scheduling scheme based on the square can penalize wide jobs in the workload. Therefore, the workload having a larger proportion of narrow jobs shows a greater improvement.

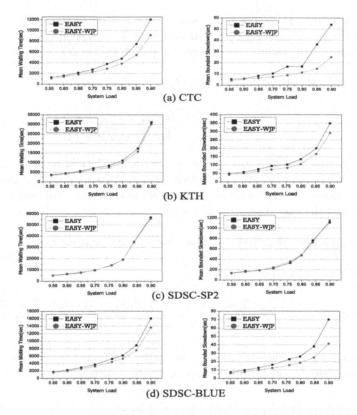

Fig. 3. Performance comparison of backfilling scheme for four workloads : EASY vs. EASY with wide job priority

5.3   Load Sharing Performance Under a Job Size-Level Interval

This subsection compares the load sharing technique for choosing the target site that will process a job in the grid. The simulation tests were conducted without regard to migration or costs of communication. The results of simulation of the proposed load sharing algorithm are presented in Figure 4. A comparison with the LLF [16] approach, which assigns requested jobs to the server with the least amount of work remaining(LWR), and SLI(Size-Level Interval) is depicted in the figure. The SLI determines the target site with the least proportion of jobs in the same interval. An improvement by about 65% is effected by the simple SLI scheme over the LLF approach. Furthermore, the SLI based on the new backfilling scheme with the local scheduler shows a slight improvement by 6% over traditional backfilling. The reason why the performance is enhanced can be understood from Figure 2(b). As shown in this figure, we find that jobs are distributed nearly with the same proportion in each SLI of the participant sites. To conclude, a regular distribution of jobs on the system has a major impact on the performance.

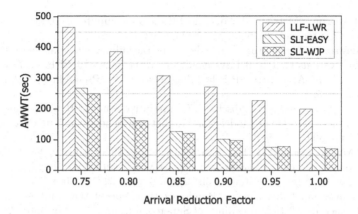

Fig. 4. Comparison of AWWT based on the load sharing scheme

6 Conclusions

The scheduling service plays a very important role in computing systems. Indeed it decides the number of jobs the system eventually processes. In our work, we focused on two schemes with a view to improve the scheduling performance. First, we devised a new variant of backfilling by considering the job square based on backfilling scheduling principle at a local system scheduler. We grant priority to wide jobs because they can significantly affect the overall waiting time. By simulation studies, we found that the performance is better than that of traditional EASY backfilling. The extent of improvement depends on the characteristics of the workload, especially the proportion of narrow jobs. Second, we presented the results on the impact of job sharing, wherein the global dispatcher assigns the requested jobs to the proper site by comparing the proportion of jobs at the same size-level interval at the participant sites. By doing so, we showed that a fairly uniform distribution of jobs at the sites is possible and it has a considerable impact on the performance.

References

1. C. Ernemann, V. Hamscher, U. Schwiegelshohn, A. Streit, and R. Yahyapour, "On Advantages of Grid Computing for Parallel Job Scheduling," Proc. of 2nd IEEE Int'l Symposium on Cluster Computing and the Grid (CC-GRID 2002), Berlin, Germany, IEEE ComputerSociety Press, pp. 39-46, 2002.
2. C. Ernemann, V. Hamscher, and R. Yahyapour., "Benefits of global grid computing for job scheduling," Proc. of 5th IEEE/ACM Int'l Workshop on Grid Computing, in Conjunction with SuperComputing 2004, GRID 2004, IEEE Computer Society, pp. 374-379, November 2004.
3. D.G. Feitelson, "Packing Schemes for Gang Scheduling," In Proceedings of JSSPP, pp. 89-110, 1996.
4. D.G. Feitelson, L. Rudolph, U. Schweigelshohn, K.C. Sevcik and P. Wong, "Theory and Practice in Parallel Job Scheduling," In Proceedings of JSSPP, pp.1-34, 1997.

5. D.G. Feitelson, "Metric and Workload Effects on Computer Systems Evaluation," IEEE Computer, vol. 36, no.9, pp. 18-25, 2003.
6. B.G. Lawson and E. Smirni, "Multiple-Queue Backfilling Scheduling with Priorities and Reservations for Parallel Systems," In Proceedings of JSSPP, pp.72-87, 2002.
7. D. Lifka, "The ANL/IBM SP Scheduling System," In Proceedings of JSSPP, pp. 295-303, 1995.
8. V. Lo, J. Mache, and K.Windisch, "A Comparative Study of Real Workload Traces and Synthetic Workload Models for Parallel Job Scheduling," In Proceedings of JSSPP, pp. 309-314, 1998.
9. A.W. Mu'alem and D.G. Feitelson, "Utilization, Predictability, Workloads, and User Runtime Estimates in Scheduling the IBM SP2 with Backfilling," IEEE Trans. Parallel & Distributed Systems, vol. 12, no. 6, pp. 529-543, 2001.
10. D. Perkovic and P.J. Keleher, "Randomization, Speculation, and Adaptation in Batch Schedulers," In Proceedings of Supercomputing 2000, November 2000.
11. U. Schwiegelshohn and R. Yahyapour, "Analysis of First-Come-First-Serve Parallel Job Scheduling," Proc. of 9th SIAM Symposium on Discrete Algorithms, pp. 629-638, 1998.
12. Q.O. Snell, M.J. Clement and D.B. Jackson,"Preemption Based Backfill," In Proceedings of JSSPP, pp. 24-37, 2002.
13. S. Srinivasan, R. Kettimuthu, V. Subramani and P. Sadayappan, "Characterization of Backfilling Strategies for Parallel Job Scheduling," In Proceedings of 2002 Intl. Workshops on Parallel Processing, 2002.
14. D. Talby and D.G. Feitelson, "Supporting Priorities and Improving Utilization of the IBM SP Scheduler Using Slack-Based Backfilling," Proc. of 13th Int'l Parallel Processing Symp., pp. 513-517, 1999.
15. L. Tan and Z. Tari, "Dynamic Task Assignment in Server Farm : Better Performance by Task Grouping," In Proc. of IEEE Computers and Communication, pp. 175-180, 2002.
16. Z.Tari, J. Broberg, A.Y. Zomaya, and R. Baldoni, "A least flow-time first load sharing approach for distributed server farm," Journal of Parallel and Distributed Computing, vol. 65, no. 7, pp. 832-842, 2005.
17. J. Yue, "Global Backfilling Scheduling in Multiclusters," In Asian Applied Computing Conference (AACC 2004), pp. 232-239, 2004.
18. D. Zotkin and P.J. Keleher, "Job-Length Estimation and Performance in Backfilling Schedulers," Proc. of 8th Int'l Symp. High-Performance Distributed Computin, IEEE CS Press, pp. 39-46, 1999.
19. Parallel Workloads Archive, http://www.cs.huji.ac.il/labs/parallel/workload/.

Average Schedule Length and Resource Selection Policies on Computational Grids

Uei-Ren Chen[1,2], Chien-Hsun Wang[1], and Woei Lin[1]

[1] Department of Computer Science, National Chung Hsing University,
250, Kuo Kuang Road, Taiwan, R.O.C.
{s9356033, wlin}@cs.nchu.edu.tw
[2] Department of Electrical Engineering, Hsiuping Institute of Technology,
11, Gungye Rd., Dali City, Taiwan, R.O.C.
urchen@mail.hit.edu.tw

Abstract. The computational grid provides many resources with powerful computational ability; however, we need to select appropriate resources for resolving the problem. In this paper, several simple and fast resource selection policies are presented. Under varying types of resource topologies and problems, the efficiency of these resource selection policies is compared. The contribution of this research is following. To solve the undetermined resource problem in the grid computing, the bottom level equation is modified in the list scheduling algorithm. Average Schedule Length (ASL) is presented to approximate the schedule length of the improved list scheduling method, and simulation result shows the accuracy of this approximation. The bounded number of the resources is found by performing the FindAlpha algorithm. Simulation result shows that selection policies can achieve minimal schedule length efficiently by choosing the limited number of the resources.

1 Introduction

The resources in the computational grid [1] are different in types and administrated by their owners. A grid network topology is typically large in scale, and the communication is varied in speed. Resource selection (or node selection) policy is a mechanism to select a number of suitable computing nodes from multiple available candidates. Task scheduling is an assignment of a set of tasks to a certain number of resources, and its goal is to minimize the schedule length. Task scheduling problem has been proved to be NP-hard [2]. A resource selection policy should be able to reduce the complexity of task scheduling. The traditional list scheduling algorithm is adopted in the parallel processing system [3]. However, it can not be used directly in the grid environment. The improved bottom level method in the list scheduling is proposed to resolve this problem.

Some related resource selection schemes are summarized as follows. (1) *Usage Pattern Based*: The node selection mechanism based on the usage pattern of computational nodes on Campus Grid is proposed [4]. The node usage pattern is represented by a history of CPU load. The length of the usage pattern is a critical problem in this scheme. (2) *Communication Pattern Based*: The method selects resources by

Y.-C. Chung and J.E. Moreira (Eds.): GPC 2006, LNCS 3947, pp. 63–72, 2006.
© Springer-Verlag Berlin Heidelberg 2006

analyzing network status and communication pattern used by the application [5]. The drawback is that the method depends on the accuracy of network status information is measured and future performance is predicted. (3) *Mapping Strategy Based*: The Resource Selector Service (RSS) [6] selects a resource set that satisfies the requirements by adopting a mapping strategy. The problem is that an efficient general mapping algorithm suitable for all applications is difficult to find. (4) *Random Based*: Resources are selected by a random policy. It is simple but hard to analyze. (5) *Genetic Algorithm (GA)*: A resource selection agent uses a genetic algorithm is developed [7]. The generating time of a genetic algorithm is an issue for resource selection. (6) *Multi-site Resource Selection*: A clustering-based grid resource selection algorithm is proposed by adopting multiple sites [8]. There is a critical issue that accuracy of predicted execution time will determine the correctness of the algorithm. (7) *Pull-Based*: A resource broker called Surfer [9] is implemented for resource selection and ranking resources to meet constraints.

This paper is organized as follows. In Section 2, the system model is defined. Section 3 discusses the performance criteria used in this research. Section 4 evaluates the performance of these resource selection policies in different types of resource topologies. Our paper ends with a brief conclusion and future work in Section 5.

2   System Model

The system consists of five components. The *grid resource model* is represented by a resource topology with resource information. The *problem model* is represented by a directed acyclic graph (DAG) of tasks. Selected computational nodes are the resources selected by means of *resource selection policy* from resource topology. The *routing model* can provide the information about routing path to the scheduling model. *Scheduling model* performs task assignment in the problem model to the selected computational nodes.

2.1   Grid Resource Model

The computational grid includes a set of resources $R = \{r_C, r_R \mid r_C, r_R \in R\}$ and network links $L = \{l_{i,j}, l_{i,j} \in L\}$ used to connect these resources. The computational grid can be modeled as an undirected connected graph $G = (R, L)$ with two elements, the resource set R and the link set L.

Resource: There are three types of resource nodes in the grid resource model, computational node, switching node and original node.

- *Computational node*: It is the border term logically that may be a supercomputer, a cluster of workstations or other computing devices practically. The computational node $r_C(i) \in R$, is specified by a triple, $r_C(i) = \langle P_C, P_M, P_T \rangle$, where P_C is the computational ability, P_M is the memory size, and P_T is the data transfer ability, respectively. In this research, the memory size is assumed to be sufficient.
- *Routing node*: It is a routing device for its computational node. $r_R \in R$.

- *Original node*: It is s special computing node that issues sub-problems to other computational nodes after performing problem decomposition, and the original node is denoted as $r_O \in R$.

Network Link: The link $l_{i,j} \in L$ is full duplex and used to connect two switching nodes of computational node $r_C(i)$ and $r_C(j)$. The link is defined as $l_{i,j} = \langle P_B, P_L \rangle$, where the parameter P_B is the link capacity (or bandwidth) and P_L is the length of link.

2.2 Problem Model

In this research, we assume that a problem can be divided into sub-problems called tasks. A task is a basic job that is executed in a computational node.

A problem p is represented as a directed acyclic graph (DAG), $D_p = (T, E)$, where T is a finite set of tasks $t_i \in T$, and E is a finite set of directed edges. Each directed edge $e_{i,j} \in E$ expresses the execution order of adjoint tasks t_i and t_j, and task t_i must be finished before task t_j. The task $t_i \in T$, can be defined as $t_i = \langle V_C(t_i),$ $V_M(t_i) \rangle$, where $V_C(t_i)$ is the *computational volume* of task t_i, and $V_M(t_i)$ is the *message volume* of task t_i.

2.3 Resource Selection Policy

Several simple selection policies are proposed as follows:

1. *Fast Node First* (FNF) *Policy*: The top n fast computing nodes are selected form m available nodes in the topology, and m is greater than n. A computing node A that has higher value of computational ability than a computational node B is assumed to be faster than B in computing speed.
2. *Near Node First* (NNF) *Policy*: The top n near computational nodes are selected from m available nodes in a resource model, where m is greater than n. A computing node A is nearer than B, if the communicational cost of A is lower than B.
3. *Fast Among Near* (FAN) *Policy*: We select r nodes using NNF policy, Then we select top n fast nodes from r nodes, where r is greater than n.
4. *Near Among Fast* (NAF) *Policy*: We select r nodes using FNF policy. Then we select top n near nodes from r nodes, where r is greater than n.
5. *Random Selection Policy*: Select randomly n computing nodes from m available nodes in the topology, where m is greater than n.

2.4 Routing Model

The routing model is used to determine the path form the source computational node to the destination. We use the well-defined routing methods by Floyd-Warshall [10] in the routing model. The method determines a path with the minimal communication cost.

A *critical link*, denoted as $\ell_{s,d}$ is the link with the minimal bandwidth in a routing path. The critical link can be defined as follows. $\Re P_{s,d}$ is the routing path from the source computational node $r_C(s)$ to the destination $r_C(d)$.

$$P_B(\ell_{s,d}) = \min\{P_B(l_{i,j}), \forall l_{i,j} \in \Re P_{s,d}\} \tag{1}$$

2.5 Scheduling Model

The list scheduling algorithm can achieve reasonable worst-case performance bound in grid environments with large applications and the schedule length does not impacted significantly by the heterogeneous communication [11]. The schedule length *SL* of the list scheduling algorithm is the maximal execution time that is needed for all selected computational nodes to finish their assigned tasks [12]. It can be defined as follows:

$$SL = \max\{SL[r_C(i)], \forall r_C(i) \in R_s\} \tag{2}$$

The *bottom level* is used in the list scheduling algorithm to set the priority of the tasks in the DAG. However, there is a problem that computational cost and communicational cost are undetermined until each task is assigned to the computational nodes in the computational grid environment. Our solution is to define these two parameters before task scheduling is performed.

Computational Cost: After performing the node selection, there are N_S computational nodes selected from the grid resource model. The computational cost for each task t_i is defined as follows.

$$C_{comp}(t_i) = V_C(t_i) \Big/ \left(\frac{1}{N_S} \sum_{\forall r_C(j) \in R_S} P_C[r_C(j)] \right) \tag{3}$$

Communicational Cost: After N_S nodes are selected, the communicational cost for each directed edge $e_{s,d}$ from task t_s to the task t_d in a DAG is defined as:

$$C_{comm}(e_{s,d}) = V_M(t_s) \times d_{out}(t_s) \Big/ \left(\frac{1}{N_S^2} \times \sum_{\forall r_C(i), r_C(j) \in R_S} P_B(\ell_{i,j}) \right) \tag{4}$$

$d_{out}(t_s)$ is the outgoing degree of the task t_s, and it is equal to the number of its successors. $P_B(\ell_{i,j})$ is the bandwidth of the critical link in the path $\Re P_{i,j}$. The path $\Re P_{i,j}$ is from the selected computational node $r_C(i)$ to the selected node $r_C(j)$. The communicational cost at the same computational node is neglected.

The bottom level $BL(t_s)$ of task t_s can be obtained by substituting $C_{comp}(t_s)$ and $C_{comm}(e_{s,d})$ into the bottom level equation recursively, where the task t_d is the successor of the task t_s:

$$BL(t_s) = C_{comp}(t_s) + \max\{C_{comm}(e_{s,d}) + BL(t_d)\}$$

(5)

We found that the number of resources needed to resolve a problem is bound by the number of the independent tasks in a DAG. The maximal number of tasks could be executed at the same time in the DAG is defined as the factor α referred to as *assignable factor*, and $1 \leq \alpha \leq N_t$. The algorithm of finding the factor α for a DAG is given below.

FindAlpha Algorithm
Begin
Input: A directed acyclic graph (DAG) with N_t tasks;
Output: Assignable factor α;
Generate all combinations of r tasks form N_t tasks in the DAG $(1 \leq r \leq N_t)$;
For (each combination of task Cb_i)
  For (any two tasks and t_i and t_j in the Cb_i, and $t_i \neq t_j$)
    If not exist a path between tasks t_i and t_j, **then**
      Add this Cb_i into the DisjGroup DG;
    End If
  End For
End For
For (each combination Cb_i in the DG)
  Count the number of tasks $N(Cb_i)$ for this Cb_i;
End For
Factor α is assigned the largest for all $N(Cb_i)$;
Return α;
End

The complexity of FindAlpha algorithm increases exponentially with number of tasks because it is required to generate all tasks combinations in the DAG. Our research effort attempts to reduce the complexity of FindAlpha algorithm in the future.

The proposed Average Schedule Length (ASL) is a theoretical model used to approximate the schedule length of the improved list scheduling algorithm. The ASL is derived by discussing the following two cases. Let N_e be the number of edges in the DAG. Assume that tasks t_i and t_j are assigned to the computational node $r_C(s)$, and is $r_C(d)$ respectively after performing task scheduling. Let $\ell_{s,d}$ denote the link that has the minimal bandwidth in the routing path $\mathfrak{R}P_{s,d}$ from the source computational node $r_C(s)$ to the destination $r_C(d)$. The outgoing degree $d_{out}(t_s)$ of the task t_s is equal to the number of its outgoing edges.

Case 1: If $1 \leq N_s \leq \alpha$, then *ASL* is derived by calculating the sum of three terms, average computational cost C_{comp}, average communication cost C_{comm} and average idle cost C_{idle}, and the equations are given as follows.

$$C_{comp} = \left(\frac{1}{N_t} \times \sum_{\forall t_i \in T} V_C(t_i)\right) \bigg/ \left(\frac{1}{N_S} \times \sum_{\forall r_C(j) \in R_S} P_C[r_C(j)]\right) \qquad (6)$$

$$C_{comm} = \frac{1}{N_e} \times \sum_{\forall t_i \in T, \, \forall e_{i,j} \in E} \left[(V_M(t_i) \times d_{out}(t_i))/\ell_{s,d}\right] \qquad (7)$$

$$C_{idle} = \mu \times (C_{comp} + C_{comm}) \qquad (8)$$

The idle factor μ of task t_i is the ratio of number of dependent edges from the task t_i to the $N_t - 1$ edges of other tasks in the DAG. Pr_{edge}^D is edge probability.

$$\mu = (N_t - 1) \times Pr_{edge}^D / (N_t - 1) = Pr_{edge}^D \qquad (9)$$

In this case, the ASL is represented as:

$$ASL = (N_t/N_S) \times (C_{comp} + C_{comm} + C_{idle}) \qquad (10)$$

Case 2: If $N_S > \alpha$, then the ASL is expressed as follows:

$$ASL = (N_t/\alpha) \times (C_{comp} + C_{comm} + C_{idle}) \qquad (11)$$

In Case 2, the schedule length becomes convergent while N_S is near to α and the additional selected computational nodes does not help reduce the schedule length, because of the limit of independent tasks in the DAG is reached.

3 Performance Criteria

There are four types of resource topologies defined as follows, where the average computational volume of the problem $\bar{V}_C = 1/N_t \times \sum_{\forall t_i \in T} V_C(t_i)$, and the average message volume of the problem $\bar{V}_M = 1/N_t \times \sum_{\forall t_i \in T} V_M(t_i)$.

1. *Low Computation and Low Communication*: If the average computational ability of the resource topology is smaller than the average computational volume of the problem $\bar{P}_C < \bar{V}_C$ and the average link capacity of the resource topology is smaller than the average message volume of the problem $\bar{P}_B < \bar{V}_M$.
2. *High Computation and Low Communication*: If $\bar{P}_C \geq \bar{V}_C$ and $\bar{P}_B < \bar{V}_M$.
3. *Low Computation and High Communication*: If $\bar{P}_C < \bar{V}_C$, $\bar{P}_B \geq \bar{V}_M$.
4. *High Computation and High Communication*: If $\bar{P}_C \geq \bar{V}_C$ and $\bar{P}_B \geq \bar{V}_M$.

In this paper, the type of a problem can be defined as follows:

1. *Computation-oriented Problem*: The total computational volume for a problem is great than the total message volume. $\hat{V}_C > \hat{V}_M$, where $\hat{V}_C = \sum_{\forall t_i \in T} V_C(t_i)$, $\hat{V}_M = \sum_{\forall t_i \in T} V_M(t_i)$, and T is the set of tasks in the problem.

2. *Message-oriented Problem*: The total computational volume in a problem is less than the total message volume, $\hat{V}_C < \hat{V}_M$.

3. *Equivalent Problem*: The total computational volume in a problem is equal to the total message volume, $\hat{V}_C = \hat{V}_M$.

4 Experimental Performance Evaluation

To reduce the system complexity, we make a number of simplifying assumptions as follows: (1) resource selection mechanism can get the information needed form all computing nodes, (2) no congestion in the network, (3) no conflict on the resources, (4) communication is reliable and no data will be lost, (5) all elements are fault-free, (6) resources are sufficient to tasks, and (7) no switching or routing delay.

Our simulator is coded in Java. The resource topology is generated by GT-ITM [13]. The resource topology is modified by adding proposed resource parameters. Problem models are generated by the DAG generator [14] with required task parameters. The combination algorithm is quoted from [15].

Efficiency Analysis of Resource *Selection Policies*. In Fig. 1, the schedule length is convergent while the number of selected resources for selection policies increases. The schedule length decreases more than 90% in the resource number range from 0 to α. This means that more selected resources do not help reduce the schedule length. The average assignable factor of all DAGs is 5.2 in this simulation. In Fig. 1, the FNF policy is most outstanding; and the Random and NNF policy is worse than others in this case.

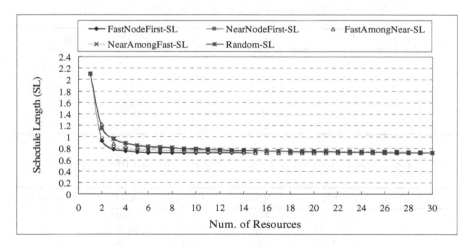

Fig. 1. Schedule Length for Resource Selection Policies

Accuracy Analysis of ASL. In Fig. 2, because the schedule length decreases rapidly, the average difference of ASL and SL is greater than 40% while the number of resources is 2. These two measurements differ by less than 10% while the resource number is equal to α, less than 14% while resource number is from α to 10, and less than 10% in the resource number range from 10 to 30.

Comparison of Selection Policies. Form Tables 1 to 4, five resource selection policies are performed in four types of resource topologies, and problems with different computation-message ratio $(\log(\hat{V}_C/\hat{V}_M) = x, -3 \le x \le 3)$ are studied. The schedule lengths of these selection policies are compared. From Table 1 to 4, the FNF policy produces smallest schedule length, if the problem is computation-oriented. Table 2 indicates that if the problem is highly message-oriented $(\log(\hat{V}_C/\hat{V}_M) < -2)$, and the type of

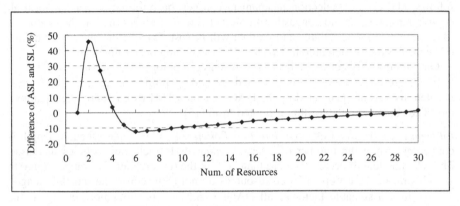

Fig. 2. Average Difference of ASL and SL

Table 1. Low Comp. and Comm. ($10 \le P_C \le 10^2$, and $10 \le P_L \le 10^2$)

$\log(\hat{V}_C/\hat{V}_M)$	FNF	NNF	FAN	NAF	Random
-3	137.31	141.48	144.31	147.00	143.31
-2	17.94	18.48	18.69	18.47	18.54
-1	2.39	2.52	2.51	2.48	2.59
0	0.69	0.78	0.73	0.72	0.79
1	6.41	7.35	6.95	6.78	7.47
2	59.03	68.54	64.17	62.35	70.10
3	634.12	734.43	690.26	671.70	748.62

Table 2. High Comp. and Low Comm. ($10^3 \le P_C \le 10^4$, and $10 \le P_L \le 10^2$)

$\log(\hat{V}_C/\hat{V}_M)$	FNF	NNF	FAN	NAF	Random
-3	142.75	140.92	147.04	149.95	140.26
-2	16.94	17.93	18.41	18.39	17.59
-1	1.63	1.66	1.75	1.76	1.68
0	0.15	0.15	0.16	0.16	0.16
1	0.21	0.23	0.22	0.22	0.23
2	0.76	0.93	0.84	0.82	0.89
3	6.17	7.75	6.91	6.72	7.47

resource topology is high computation and low communication, then the NNF selection policy outperforms others. Table 3 and 4 shows that if the resource topology is high communicational, the NNF policy performs the worst. Overall, the schedule length of random policy is worse. The schedule lengths of FAN and NAF policies perform between those of FNF and NNF in the computation-oriented problem.

Table 3. Low Comp. and High Comm. ($10 \leq P_C \leq 10^2$, and $10^3 \leq P_L \leq 10^4$)

$\log(\hat{V}_C/\hat{V}_M)$	FNF	NNF	FAN	NAF	Random
-3	2.20	2.44	2.27	2.21	2.40
-2	0.83	0.97	0.89	0.85	0.96
-1	0.52	0.63	0.58	0.54	0.62
0	0.47	0.56	0.51	0.49	0.55
1	6.23	7.36	6.77	6.44	7.19
2	58.07	69.35	63.56	60.24	67.99
3	624.15	745.45	682.54	648.00	726.47

Table 4. High Comp. and Comm. ($10^3 \leq P_C \leq 10^4$, and $10^3 \leq P_L \leq 10^4$)

$\log(\hat{V}_C/\hat{V}_M)$	FNF	NNF	FAN	NAF	Random
-3	1.42	1.48	1.44	1.38	1.40
-2	0.19	0.19	0.18	0.18	0.18
-1	0.02	0.03	0.02	0.02	0.03
0	0.01	0.01	0.01	0.01	0.01
1	0.06	0.07	0.07	0.06	0.07
2	0.56	0.70	0.62	0.58	0.69
3	5.97	7.46	6.65	6.18	7.34

5   Conclusion and Future Work

Conclusions of this paper are drawn as follows. The grid resource model and problem model are established with resource and task parameters respectively. Several simple and fast resource selection policies are proposed and studied in this paper. The number of selected resources can be found by adopting the FindAlpha Algorithm, and using these resources can achieve the bound of schedule length above 90%. The Average Schedule Length is proposed to approximate the schedule length of improved list scheduling algorithm. The accuracy of the Average Schedule Length is evaluated. The maximal variation to schedule length drops below 14%, if the number of the selected resources is greater than or equal to the assignable factor α. The performance of resource selection policies is compared in four types of resource topologies with a variety of problems distinguished by the ratio of computation to message volume.

There are a number of directions for future research: (1) consider the background loading in the gird resource model, (2) perform multiple problems in the computational gird simulation, (3) improve the FindAlpha algorithm and reduce its complexity, (4) establish the model of the communication congestion and routing delay, (5) compare the communicational cost of different routing methods, (6) adopt other task scheduling algorithms, and evaluate their performance, (7) compare with other selection policy, such as usage pattern and genetic algorithm, and (8) improve the efficiency of the resource selection policy.

References

1. Foster, I., and Kesselman, C.: The Grid: Blueprint for a New Computing Infrastructure, Morgan Kaufmann, San Francisco, CA, (1999)
2. Ulman, J. D.: NP-Complete Scheduling Problems, Journal of Computing System Science, 10 (1975)
3. Adam, T. L., Chandy, K. M., and Dickson, J. R.: Comparison of List Schedule for Parallel Processing Systems, Communications of the ACM, 17 (1974)
4. Arikawa, H., Fujikawa, K., and Sunahara, H.: A Node Selection Mechanism based on the Node Usage Pattern on Campus Grid, IEEE Pacific Rim Conference on Communications, Computers and Signal Processing, (2003)
5. Goteti, S., and Subhlok, J.: Communication Pattern Based Node Selection for Shared Networks, Proceedings of the Autonomic Computing Workshop, (2003)
6. Liu, C., Yang, L., Foster, I., and Angulo, D.: Design and Evaluation of a Resource Selection Framework for Grid Applications, Proceedings of the 11th IEEE International Symposium on High Performance Distributed Computing HPDC-11, (2002)
7. Lee, H., Chung, K., Chin, S., Lee, J., Lee, D., Park, S., and Yu, H.: A Resource Management and Fault Tolerance Services in Grid Computing, Journal of Parallel and Distributed Computing, 65 (2005)
8. Zhang, W., Fang, B., He, H., Zhang, H., and Hu, M.: Multisite Resource Selection and Scheduling Algorithm on Computational Grid, Proceedings of the 18th International Parallel and Distributed Processing Symposium, (2004)
9. Kolano, P. Z.: Surfer: An Extensible Pull-Based Framework for Resource Selection and Ranking, IEEE International Symposium on Cluster Computing and the Grid, (2004)
10. Cormen, T. H., Leiserson, C. E., and Rivest, R. L.: Introduction to Algorithms, The MIT Press, (1990)
11. Li, K.: Job Scheduling for Grid Computing on Metacomputers, Proceedings of the 19th IEEE International Parallel and Distributed Processing Symposium (2005)
12. Sinnen, O., and Sousa, L. A.: Communication Contention in Task Scheduling, IEEE Transactions on Parallel and Distributed Systems, 16 (2005)
13. GT-ITM project. http://www.cc.gatech.edu/projects/gtitm/.
14. Lloyd Allison's web site. http://www.csse.monash.edu.au/~lloyd/tildeAlgDS/Graph/ DAG/.
15. Parberry, I., and Gasarch, W.: Problems on Algorithms, Second Edition, (2002)

A Performance-Based Approach to Dynamic Workload Distribution for Master-Slave Applications on Grid Environments

Wen-Chung Shih[1], Chao-Tung Yang[2,*], and Shian-Shyong Tseng[1,3]

[1] Department of Computer and Information Science,
National Chiao Tung University,
Hsinchu 30010, Taiwan, R.O.C.
{gis90805, sstseng}@cis.nctu.edu.tw
[2] High-Performance Computing Laboratory,
Department of Computer Science and Information Engineering,
Tunghai University,
Taichung 40704, Taiwan, R.O.C.
ctyang@thu.edu.tw
[3] Department of Information Science and Applications,
Asia University,
Taichung 41354, Taiwan, R.O.C.
sstseng@asia.edu.tw

Abstract. Effective workload distribution techniques can significantly reduce the total completion time of a program on grid computing environments. In this paper, we propose a dynamic performance-based workload partition approach for master-slave types of applications on grids. Furthermore, we implement two types of applications and conduct the experimentations on our grid testbed. Experimental results showed that our method could execute more efficiently than traditional schemes.

Keywords: Workload distribution, master-slave paradigm, grid computing, parallel loop scheduling, data mining, Globus, NWS.

1 Introduction

As inexpensive personal computers and Internet access become available, much attention has been directed to grid computing [2, 3, 4, 8, 9, 14, 21, 22, 23, 24, 25, 33]. The basic idea of grid computing is to share the computing and storage resources all over the world via Wide Area Networks. In this way, computational jobs can be distributed to idle computers far away, probably in other countries. Moreover, remote data can be accessed for large-scale analysis.

Master-slave paradigms are commonly utilized to model the task dispatching processes in parallel and distributed computing environments [38]. This model designates one computing node as the master, which holds a pool of tasks to be dispatched to other slave nodes. Divisible Load Theory (DLT) [1, 16, 17, 30] addresses

---

[*] Corresponding author.

Y.-C. Chung and J.E. Moreira (Eds.): GPC 2006, LNCS 3947, pp. 73–82, 2006.
© Springer-Verlag Berlin Heidelberg 2006

the case where the total workload can be partitioned into any number of independent subjobs. This problem has been discussed in the past decade, and a good review can be found in [15]. In [19], a data distribution method was proposed for host-client type of applications. Their method was an analytic technique, and only verified on homogeneous and heterogeneous cluster computing platforms. In [20], an exact method for divisible load was proposed, which was not from a dynamic and pragmatic viewpoint as ours.

In this paper, we focus on the problem of dynamic distribution of workload for master-slave applications on grids. We implement two types of applications, Parallel Loop Self-Scheduling [18, 27, 34, 35, 36] and Association Rule Data Mining, with MPI directives, and execute them on our grid testbed. Experimental results show that effective workload partitioning can significantly reduce the total completion time.

Our major contributions can be summarized as follows. First, this paper proposes a new performance-based algorithm to solve this dynamic workload distribution problem. Second, we implement the algorithm and apply it to both loop self-scheduling and data mining applications on our grid testbed. Consequently, experimental results show the obvious effectiveness of our approach. To the best of our knowledge, this is the first paper to consider dynamic workload distribution within a program on grid environments.

Our previous work [31, 32] presents different heuristics to the parallel loop self-scheduling problem. This paper generalizes their main idea and proposes to solve the dynamic workload distribution problem. This approach is applied to both the parallel loop self-scheduling application and the association rule mining application. There have been a lot of researches of parallel and distributed data mining [12, 13, 26, 37]. However, this paper focuses on workload distribution, instead of proposing a new data mining algorithm.

The rest of this paper is organized as follows. Our approach is proposed in Section 2. Then, Section 3 shows the experimental results on our grid testbeds. Finally, we conclude this paper in Section 4.

2 Our Approach

Our performance-based approach is based on the estimated performance of each slave node and each link to distribute the corresponding workload. In this section, the system model and the concept of performance ratio are explained first. Then, we present the heuristics which the algorithm is based on. Finally, the algorithm is described.

2.1 System Model

Our system model and cost model are extended from the framework in [15]. The master-slave model for a grid is represented by a star graph $G = \{P_0, P_1,..., P_n\}$, as shown in Figure 1. In this graph, P_0 is the master node and the other n nodes, P_1, ..., P_n, are slave nodes. In addition, there is a virtual communication link L_i connecting the master node and the slave node P_i.

In our cost model, each node P_i is associated with a computing capacity C_i, a memory capacity M_i, and a disk storage capacity D_i. Furthermore, each link L_i is also associated with a transmission capacity T_i. In our linear cost model, it takes $W \times C_i$ time units for the slave node P_i to conduct computation on W units of data. Besides, it takes $W \times T_i$ time units for link L_i to transmit W units of data. In this model, we assume that the master can only communicate with one slave node at the same time.

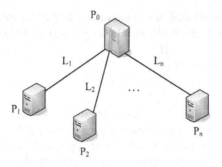

Fig. 1. The system model

2.2 Performance Functions and Performance Ratio

We propose to partition the workload according to the performance ratio of all slave nodes. Therefore, the effectiveness of this approach depends on the accuracy of estimating the performance ratio. To estimate the performance of each slave node, we define a Performance Function (*PF*) for a slave node j as

$$PF_j (V_1, V_2, ..., V_M) \tag{1}$$

where V_i, $1 \le i \le M$, is a parameter of the performance function. In more detail, the parameters could include CPU speed, networking bandwidth, memory capacity, etc. In this paper, our *PF* for node *j* is defined as

$$PF_j = w_1 \times \frac{1/t_j}{\sum\limits_{\forall node_i \in S} 1/t_i} + w_2 \times \frac{B_j}{\sum\limits_{\forall node_i \in S} B_i} \tag{2}$$

where

- *S* is the set of all slave nodes.
- t_i is the execution time (sec.) of node *i* for some benchmark application program, such as matrix multiplication.
- B_i is the bandwidth (Mbps) between node *i* and the master node.
- w_1 is the weight of the first term.
- w_2 is the weight of the second term.

The Performance Ratio (*PR*) is defined to be the ratio of all performance functions. For instance, assume the *PF*s of three nodes are 1/2, 1/3 and 1/4, respectively. Then, the *PR* is 1/2 : 1/3 : 1/4; i.e., the *PR* of the three nodes is 6 : 4 : 3. In other words, if there are 13 transactions to be processed, 6 transactions will be assigned to the first node, 4 transactions will be assigned to the second node, and 3 transactions will be assigned to the last one.

2.3 Performance-Based Algorithms

Our algorithm is based on two heuristics to dispatch workload to slave nodes.

1. The total workload is divided in n chunks according to the *PR* of the *n* slave nodes.
2. Send the data chunk to the node with faster network bandwidth first. The network bandwidth is estimated by $\dfrac{B_j}{\sum\limits_{\forall node_i \in S} B_i}$.

In this paper, B_j is obtained from NWS (Network Weather Service) statistics [7]. Specifically, our network bandwidth estimation is extracted directed from [11].

Our algorithm is also a master-slave type of application. In the MASTER module, the total workload is divided according to the PR of slaves, and the partitioned workload is transmitted accordingly. In the SLAVE module, the workload is computed. The algorithm of our approach is described as follows.

Module MASTER

```
1. Initialization
2. Calculate performance ratio of all slave nodes
3. Partition the total workload according to the PR
4. Get network bandwidth B_i of the link to node i
5. Send data to slaves in non-increasing order of B_i
6. //Master could does its own computation work here
7. Gather results from all slave nodes
8. Print the results
9. Finalization
END MASTER
```

Module SLAVE

```
1. Receive workload from the master node
2. Conduct computation on its local workload
3. Send the result to the master
END SLAVE
```

Without loss of generality, we assume the master node does not participate in computation in our algorithm. However, the algorithm can be modified to utilize the computing power of the master node by remove the comment notation (*//*) in line 6.

3   Experimental Results

To verify our approach, a grid testbed is built, and two types of application programs are implemented with MPI (Message Passing Interface) to be executed on this testbed. This grid testbed consists of one master and three domains. We have built this grid testbed by the following middleware:

- Globus Toolkit 3.0.2 [10]
- Mpich library 1.2.6 [5, 6]

In this experiment, the performance function and the performance ratio are the same as those defined Section 2. Specifically, w_1 is assigned as 1 and w_2 is assigned as 0.5, suggested by our experiences in this testbed. Furthermore, T_i for node i is obtained by executing Matrix Multiplication, for input size 512×512, while B_i for node i is obtained by NWS statistics [7, 11]. The resulting performance ratio is shown in Figure 2. For example, node 4 and node 5 have the same CPU speed. However, our method assigns higher PR to node 4 because of its higher network bandwidth. In addition, the execution time is an average of five repetitive measurements.

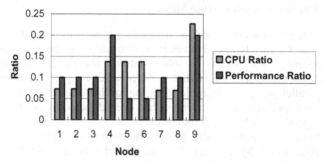

Fig. 2. Performance ratio of 9 slave nodes for our grid testbed

3.1   Application 1: Parallel Loop Self-scheduling for Matrix Multiplication

We have implemented a series of application programs in C language, with message passing interface (MPI) directives for parallelizing code segments to be processed by multiple CPU's. In this paper, the scheduling parameter   is set to be 50 for all hybrid schemes, except for the schemes by [36], of which   is dynamically adjustable according to cluster heterogeneity.

First, execution time on the grid for GSS [29] group is investigated. Figure 3(a) illustrates execution time of static [28], dynamic [29] and our scheme, with input matrix size 512×512, 1024×1024 and 1536×1536 respectively. Experimental results show that our performance-based scheduling scheme got better performance than static and dynamic ones. In this case, our scheme for input size 1536×1536 got 39% and 23% performance improvement over the static one and the dynamic one respectively.

Figure 3(b) illustrates execution time of previous schemes (ngss [35] and ngss2 [36]) and our scheme, with input matrix size 512×512, 1024×1024 and 1536×1536

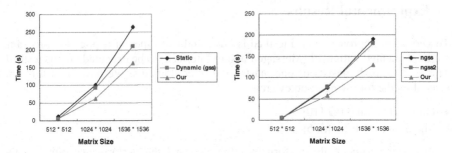

Fig. 3. Matrix multiplication execution time on the grid for GSS group schemes. (a) Static, dynamic (gss) and our scheme; (b) ngss, ngss2 and our scheme.

respectively. Experimental results show that our performance-based scheduling scheme got better performance than static and dynamic ones. In this case, our scheme for input size 1536×1536 got 32% and 28% performance improvement over the ngss and the ngss2 respectively.

3.2   Application 2: Association Rule Mining

Traditional parallel data mining work assumes data is partitioned and transmitted to the computing nodes in advance. However, it is usually the case in which a large database is generated and stored in some station. Therefore, it is important to efficiently partition and distribute the data to other nodes for parallel computation. As the rising of parallel processing, parallel data mining have been well investigated in the past decade. Especially, much attention has been directed to parallel association rule mining. A good survey can be found in [37].

In this section, we implement the Apriori algorithm, and apply our approach to conduct data distribution. Specifically, the parallelized version of Apriori we adopt is Count Distribution (CD) [12, 13, 26].

In this experiment, "cd_eq" means to distribute the workload to slaves equally, and "cd_cpu" means to distribute the workload to slaves according to the ratio of CPU speed values of slaves. And, cd_our is our scheme. Our datasets are generated by the tool as in [13]. The parameters of the synthetic datasets are described in Table 1.

Table 1. Description of our dataset

Dataset	Number of Transactions	Average Transaction Length	Number of Items
D10KT5I10	10,000	5	10
D50KT5I10	50,000	5	10
D100KT5I10	100,000	5	10

3.2.1   Relative Performance for Different Dataset Sizes

First, execution time on the grid for the three schemes is investigated. Figure 4 illustrates execution time of cd_eq, cd_cpu and our scheme, with input size 10K, 50K and 100K transactions respectively. Experimental results show that our scheme got

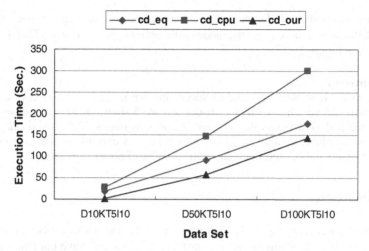

Fig. 4. Performance of data partition schemes for different datasets

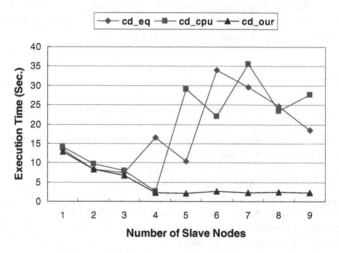

Fig. 5. Speedup performance of data partition schemes

better performance than cd_eq and cd_cpu. In this case, our scheme for input size 100K transactions got 18% and 52% performance improvement over cd_eq and cd_cpu respectively.

From this experiment, we can see the significant influence of partition schemes on the total response time. In grid environments, network bandwidth is an important criterion to evaluate the performance of a slave node. Cd_eq and cd_cpu are static data partition schemes. Therefore, they can not adapt to the practical network status. When communication cost becomes a major factor, our scheme would be well adaptive to the network environment.

Moreover, the reason why cd_cpu got the worst performance can be contributed to the inappropriate estimation of node performance. In grid computing environments,

CPU speed is not the only factor to determine the node performance. A node with the fastest CPU is not necessary the node with optimal performance. This has been illustrated in Figure 2.

3.2.2 Speedup

In order to see how well our scheme speeds up, we keep the dataset constant to be D10KT5I10 and vary the number of nodes. Figure 5 shows that the response time of our scheme is decreasing as the number of nodes increases. This means our scheme can choose available computing power to optimize its execution time. However, the curves of cd_eq and cd_cpu fluctuate as the number of nodes increases.

4 Conclusions

In this paper, we have proposed a performance-based approach to solve the dynamic workload partition problem for master-slave applications, and have implemented it on our grid testbeds. In each case, our approach can obtain performance improvement on other schemes. In our future work, we will implement more types of application programs to verify our approach. Furthermore, we hope to study theoretical analysis to find better solutions, and consider more status information.

References

1. Divisible Load Theory, http://www.ee.sunysb.edu/~tom/MATBE/index.html
2. Global Grid Forum, http://www.ggf.org/
3. Introduction to Grid Computing with Globus, http://www.ibm.com/redbooks
4. KISTI Grid Testbed, http://Gridtest.hpcnet.ne.kr/
5. MPICH, http://www-unix.mcs.anl.gov/mpi/mpich/
6. MPICH-G2, http://www.hpclab.niu.edu/mpi/
7. Network Weather Service, http://nws.cs.ucsb.edu/
8. Sun ONE Grid Engine, http://wwws.sun.com/software/Gridware/
9. TeraGrid, http://www.teraGrid.org/
10. The Globus Project, http://www.globus.org/
11. THU Bandwidth Statistics GUI, http://monitor.hpc.csie.thu.edu.tw/tiger/
12. R. Agrawal and J. C. Shafer, "Parallel Mining of Association Rules," IEEE Transactions on Knowledge and Data Engineering, vol. 8, no. 6, pp. 962-969, Dec. 1996.
13. R. Agrawal and R. Srikant, "Fast algorithms for Mining Association Rules," Proc. 20th Very Large Data Bases Conf., pp. 487-499, 1994.
14. Mark A. Baker and Geoffery C. Fox. "Metacomputing: Harnessing Informal Supercomputers." High Performance Cluster Computing. Prentice-Hall, May 1999. ISBN 0-13-013784-7.
15. O. Beaumont, H. Casanova, A. Legrand, Y. Robert and Y. Yang, "Scheduling Divisible Loads on Star and Tree Networks: Results and Open Problems," IEEE Transactions on Parallel and Distributed Systems, Vol. 16, No. 3, pp. 207-218, Mar. 2005.
16. V. Bharadwaj, D. Ghose, V. Mani, and T.G. Robertazzi, Scheduling Divisible Loads in Parallel and Distributed Systems, IEEE Press, 1996.

17. V. Bharadwaj, D. Ghose and T.G. Robertazzi, "Divisible Load Theory: A New Paradigm for Load Scheduling in Distributed Systems," Cluster Computing, vol. 6, no. 1, pp. 7-18, Jan. 2003.
18. Kuan-Wei Cheng, Chao-Tung Yang, Chuan-Lin Lai, and Shun-Chyi Chang, "A Parallel Loop Self-Scheduling on Grid Computing Environments," Proceedings of the 2004 IEEE International Symposium on Parallel Architectures, Algorithms and Networks, pp. 409-414, KH, China, May 2004.
19. N. Comino and V. L. Narasimhan, "A Novel Data Distribution Technique for Host-Client Type Parallel Applications," IEEE Transactions on Parallel and Distributed Systems, Vol. 13, No. 2, pp. 97-110, Feb. 2002.
20. Maciej Drozdowski and Marcin Lawenda, "On Optimum Multi-installment Divisible Load Processing in Heterogeneous Distributed Systems," Euro-Par 2005 Parallel Processing: 11th International Euro-Par Conference, Lecture Notes in Computer Science, vol. 3648, pp. 231-240, Springer-Verlag, August 2005.
21. I. Foster, N. Karonis, "A Grid-Enabled MPI: Message Passing in Heterogeneous Distributed Computing Systems." Proc. 1998 SC Conference, November, 1998.
22. I. Foster, C. Kesselman, S. Tuecke, "The Anatomy of the Grid: Enabling Scalable Virtual Organizations," International J. Supercomputer Applications, 15(3), 2001.
23. I. Foster, C. Kesselman., "Globus: A Metacomputing Infrastructure Toolkit," International J. Supercomputer Applications, 11(2):115-128, 1997.
24. I. Foster, "The Grid: A New Infrastructure for 21st Century Science." Physics Today, 55(2):42-47, 2002.
25. I. Foster, C. Kesselman, eds., The Grid: Blueprint for a New Computing Infrastructure, Morgan Kaufmann; 1st edition (January 1999)
26. J. Han and M. Kamber, Data Mining: Concepts and Techniques, Morgan Kaufmann Publishers, 2001.
27. S. F. Hummel, E. Schonberg, and L. E. Flynn, "Factoring: a method scheme for scheduling parallel loops," Communications of the ACM, Vol. 35, 1992, pp. 90-101.
28. H. Li, S. Tandri, M. Stumm and K. C. Sevcik, "Locality and Loop Scheduling on NUMA Multiprocessors," Proceedings of the 1993 International Conference on Parallel Processing, vol. II, pp. 140-147, 1993.
29. C. D. Polychronopoulos and D. Kuck, "Guided Self-Scheduling: a Practical Scheduling Scheme for Parallel Supercomputers," IEEE Trans. on Computers, vol. 36, no. 12, pp 1425-1439, 1987.
30. T.G. Robertazzi, "Ten Reasons to Use Divisible Load Theory," Computer, vol. 36, no. 5, pp. 63-68, May 2003.
31. Wen-Chung Shih, Chao-Tung Yang, and Shian-Shyong Tseng, "A Performance-Based Parallel Loop Self-Scheduling on Grid Environments," Network and Parallel Computing: IFIP International Conference, NPC 2005, Lecture Notes in Computer Science, vol. 3779, pp. 48-55, Springer-Verlag, December 2005.
32. Wen-Chung Shih, Chao-Tung Yang, and Shian-Shyong Tseng, "A Hybrid Parallel Loop Scheduling Scheme on Grid Environments," Grid and Cooperative Computing: 4th International Conference, GCC 2005, Lecture Notes in Computer Science, vol. 3795, pp. 370-381, Springer-Verlag, December 2005.
33. Larry Smarr, C. Catlett, "Metacomputing," Communications of the ACM, vol. 35, no. 6, pp. 44-52, 1992.
34. T. H. Tzen and L. M. Ni, "Trapezoid self-scheduling: a practical scheduling scheme for parallel compilers," IEEE Transactions on Parallel and Distributed Systems, Vol. 4, 1993, pp. 87-98.

35. Chao-Tung Yang and Shun-Chyi Chang, "A Parallel Loop Self-Scheduling on Extremely Heterogeneous PC Clusters," Journal of Information Science and Engineering, vol. 20, no. 2, pp. 263-273, March 2004.
36. Chao-Tung Yang, Kuan-Wei Cheng, and Kuan-Ching Li, "An Efficient Parallel Loop Self-Scheduling on Grid Environments," NPC'2004 IFIP International Conference on Network and Parallel Computing, Lecture Notes in Computer Science, Springer-Verlag Heidelberg, Hai Jin, Guangrong Gao, Zhiwei Xu (Eds.), Oct. 2004.
37. M. J. Zaki, "Parallel and Distributed Association Mining: A Survey," IEEE Concurrency, vol. 7, no. 4, pp. 14-25, 1999.
38. C. Banino, O. Beaumont, L. Carter, J. Ferrante, A. Legrand, Y. Robert, "Scheduling strategies for master-slave tasking on heterogeneous processor platforms," IEEE Transactions on Parallel and Distributed Systems, Vol. 15, No. 4, pp. 319-330, Apr. 2004.

The Peering Problem in Tree-Based Master/Worker Overlays

Hung-Chang Hsiao and Hao Liao

Department of Computer Science and Information Engineering,
National Cheng Kung University, Tainan 701, Taiwan
hchsiao@csie.ncku.edu.tw

Abstract. Master-worker applications often demand high throughput.
A master-worker application consists of master and worker processes.
The master processes generate tasks, while the worker processes compute
the tasks. A peer can solely implement the master process, the worker
process, or both. A scalable implementation of master-worker applications is to form an overlay network in which masters deliver their tasks
to workers through their interconnect links, and workers either compute
received tasks or forward some of the tasks to other workers. Different overlay construction could result in various system throughputs. In
this work, we study the fundamental issue. That is, how the overlay is
structured to maximize the system throughput. We first propose a basic,
simple overlay formation algorithm to form an overlay. Then, we develop
a number of peering strategies. The simple overlay formation algorithm
is flexible to integrate these peering strategies, generating types of the
overlay. Our performance studies show that the overlays based on the
exploitation of network locality can perform better.

1 Introduction

Peer-to-peer (P2P) applications received widely attention, recently. These applications include distributed file sharing such as Napster [1] and Gnutella [2],
content distribution networks [3], multiplayer games [4], etc. One widely received
P2P application, namely the *master-worker application*, is constituted by task
sources (*master processes*) and sinks (*worker processes*), in which sources generate tasks and sinks perform computation for these tasks. The bag-of-tasks
computational application such as SETI@home [5] is the example. In such an
application, one peer acts as a master generates tasks, while others are workers
performing computation for these tasks.

Applications with the master-worker paradigm often demand high throughput. That is, the number of tasks completed per time unit is maximized. Maximizing the throughput denotes that the system can accommodate clients as much
as possible. The state-of-the-art master/worker interconnect such as SETI@home
in the Internet often is a star *overlay network* in which the root node implements
the master process while other workers are directly connected to the root. Such
an overlay requires that the root node is quite capable which can accept a very

Y.-C. Chung and J.E. Moreira (Eds.): GPC 2006, LNCS 3947, pp. 83–92, 2006.

large number of connections to workers. This thus leads to the performance bottleneck introduced to the root.

In contrast to the star interconnect, masters and workers may overlays such as trees, meshes and grids. In such overlays, the master continuously generates and sends tasks to workers that have overlay connections linked to the master. Upon receiving tasks, a worker performs computation for the task. If the worker cannot immediately process the task, then the worker either forwards the task to another worker that has an overlay link to the worker, or buffers the tasks for later computation.

Apparently, to maximize the through-put of a master-worker overlay depends on the design of the overlay system. Con-sider an example as shown in Figure 1. In Figure 1(a), four nodes form a star-based interconnect in which the root node A generates 100 tasks per time unit at most, and the worker nodes B, C and D can fin-ish 3, 1 and 6 tasks per time unit, respec-tively. A at most can respectively send 10, 5 and 1 tasks to B, C and D. Conse-quently, the star-shaped overlay can ac-

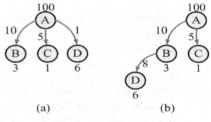

(a)   (b)

Fig. 1. Two overlays with four nodes, where (a) a star overlay and (b) a tree-shaped overlay

complish 5 tasks per time unit at most. However, the tree-shaped overlay shown in Figure 1(b) can finish 10 tasks per time unit if D is connected to B and B can send 8 tasks per time unit to D. This throughput is twice of that generated by the star-based overlay.

The issues of designing a master/worker overlay include at least as follows.

Task scheduling. As mentioned, a worker i may receive tasks from other workers (say $\mathcal{G}$). It forwards some of tasks it cannot accommodate to other workers in $\mathcal{G}$ that may be able to handle the tasks, where all the workers in $\mathcal{G}$ have the overlay links to i. Therefore, i needs to determine which of the workers in $\mathcal{G}$ are likely to perform the computations for the tasks it sends. To schedule tasks to the workers $j \in \mathcal{G}$ from i may depend on several parameters including the network bandwidth or the delay between i and j, the computation ability of j, the availability of j's receiving buffers, etc. "Given" an overlay network graph, previous studies [6] have proposed the scheduling algorithms for any workers in the overlay to schedule their tasks in hand.

Overlay network topology. Given a set of nodes, where each node in the set has a predefined maximum number of links (or bandwidth) that the node can be used to connect other nodes, there are many possible topologies that the overlay networks can be formed. Formatting the topology may require to consider the heterogeneity (e.g., computation speeds) of nodes involving the master-worker computation. In addition, communication bandwidths and delays among the nodes are unlikely equal. The heterogeneity is the nature of an overlay. Efficient and effective exploitation of heterogeneity of a master-worker overlay may help the scheduling algorithms adopted to further leverage the system throughput.

Allocation of master and worker processes. Typically, worker processes in a master/worker application are identical and there is no clear difference when they are deployed in different locations (i.e., nodes) in the overlay. However, when given a scheduling algorithm and an overlay network topology, different locations of the master process deployed may result in different overall system throughput. Shao *et al.* [7] provided a study of how to deploy the master process in order to maximize the system throughput.

This study devotes to the second challenge mentioned above and intends to understand how to have a good overlay that can improve the system throughput. Particularly, we study the tree-shaped overlay networks. This is because tree-shaped overlays are scalable and they are easy to be implemented. Second, there has existed a simple, heuristic localized scheduling algorithm [6] which can maximize the throughput for any given tree-shaped overlay without knowing the global knowledge including the capability of each node and the communication bandwidth between any two nodes.

Formatting an overlay suitable for applications based on the master/worker paradigm can have a number of design criteria. We first provide in this study a basic, generalized algorithm for tree-based overlay construction. The algorithm is flexible to include different peering strategies such that different types of overlays can be generated. We investigate how different tree-shaped overlays can affect the system throughput and discuss which of the designs can perform better.

To our best knowledge, few work studies the overlay formation issue for applications comprising of masters and workers regarding the system throughput, and the novelty of this study is to provide the design of master/worker overlay formation and to investigate the performance impact on system throughput using different peering strategies.

2   Preliminaries

System model. We consider a P2P overlay $G(V, E)$, where $V = \{p_1, p_2, p_3, \cdots, p_n\}$ is the set of peers and $E = \{ \overline{p_i p_j} | p_i, p_j \in V,$ and p_i and p_j have a link (or a connection) in the overlay $G \}$. For short, p_j is called the *neighbor* of p_i and vice versa. We assume that in this study an overlay link is bi-directional, that is, $\overline{p_i p_j} = \overline{p_j p_i}$ [1]. In G, each node can only have a constant number of neighbors [2]. The maximal degree of a node p_i is denoted as $deg_{max}(p_i)$, which is the maximal number of neighbors p_i can maintain. Consequently, $|E| \leq \frac{\sum_{k=1}^{n} deg_{max}(p_k)}{2}$.

In $G(V, E)$, an application designates a node $p_{\mathcal{M}} \in V$ as the master node which executes the master process. Each node $p_{\mathcal{S}} \in V - \{p_{\mathcal{M}}\}$ is thus a worker node responsible for performing the worker process. All worker processes are

---

[1] However, we believe that our idea proposed in this paper can also be simply extended to overlays with asymmetric communication links, i.e., $\overline{p_i p_j} \neq \overline{p_j p_i}$.

[2] We believe that the discussion in this paper can be simply applied to the case that each peer has a bandwidth constrain to connect to other peers.

identical. Since worker nodes may be heterogeneous in terms of their computational power, a worker node p_S is simply denoted to have the working rate
$\mathcal{WP}(p_S)$ equal to the maximal number of tasks completed (including to send
back the result to or towards the master node) by p_S per time unit. We note
that $\mathcal{WP}(p_M)$ is the maximum number of tasks generated and results manipulated, if required, by the master node p_M.

Each worker node $p_S \in V - \{p_M\}$ has two first-in-first-out buffers: one denoted
as $FIFO_{S(T)}$ is used to receive tasks and the other $FIFO_{S(R)}$ is used to buffer
the computation results. p_S can pick a task in $FIFO_{S(T)}$ and then remove the
task from $FIFO_{S(T)}$ to execute if it can accept the task without exceeding its
working rate. If p_S cannot process the tasks buffered in its task buffer locally,
it may forward those tasks to other worker nodes. If a task is forwarded, it is
removed from an associated task buffer. p_S stores the computation results in its
local $FIFO_{S(R)}$ that will be then returned "towards" the master node p_M. It
may help relay the computation results received from other workers towards p_M
by buffering their results in its $FIFO_{S(R)}$. Similarly, if a result is forwarded, it
is removed from $FIFO_{S(R)}$.

For the master node p_M, two buffers, namely $FIFO_{M(T)}$ and $FIFO_{M(R)}$,
are available to store tasks it generates and results received from workers, respectively. The master simply forwards tasks to worker nodes, which does *not* compute tasks it generates. However, it requires to process results in its $FIFO_{M(R)}$.
If a result is processed, it is removed from $FIFO_{M(R)}$.

We assume that either the master or any worker can simultaneously process
results and tasks in the result and tasks buffers, respectively. That is, a node
can perform computation and communication, concurrently.

Each overlay link $\overline{p_i p_j}$ also has a working rate $\mathcal{WL}(\overline{p_i p_j})$ that is the maximum
number of tasks transferred both from p_i to p_j (or p_j to p_i) per time unit over the link
$\overline{p_i p_j}$. Apparently, $\mathcal{WL}(\overline{p_i p_j})$ is proportional to the bandwidth between p_i and p_j.

Since master and workers nodes cooperatively serve an application, we assume
that they are willing to arbitrarily interconnect.

Problem Statement. In this paper, we intend to design a high-throughput
overlay $G(V, E)$ by formatting the overlay geometry structure. The high-
throughout overlay maximizes the working rate $\mathcal{W}^\star$ (i.e., to maximize the number of tasks completed per time unit) for the application running on top of G
subject to

$$|E| \leq \frac{\sum_{k=1}^{|V|} deg_{max}(p_k)}{2}. \tag{1}$$

Apparently, the throughput of the overlay G is constrained by the task generating rate at p_M, i.e., $\mathcal{W}^\star \leq \mathcal{WP}(p_M)$.

3   Basic Algorithm

Table 1 shows the notations used in this paper. We note that

- The total number of parent ($p_i.prt$) and child neighbors ($p_i.chd(k)$) of p_i is
  equal to $c(p_i)$, where $c(p_i) \leq deg_{max}(p_i)$.

Table 1. Notations used in the algorithms

Notation	Description
$G(V, E)$	V (E) includes all nodes (edges) in the system
$p_{\mathcal{M}}$, $p_{\mathcal{S}}$	the master and worker nodes, respectively
$\overline{p_i p_j}$	the overlay link with two end nodes p_i, $p_j \in V$
$deg_{max}(p_i)$	the maximal degree (number of overlay links) of p_i
$c(p_i)$	the number of links currently used by p_i
$\mathcal{W}^*$	the overall system throughput
$\mathcal{WP}(p_i)$	the maximal computation working rate of p_i
$\mathcal{WL}(e)$	the maximal communication working rate of $e \in E$
$FIFO_{p_i(\mathcal{T})}$	the buffer to store pending tasks in p_i
$FIFO_{p_i(\mathcal{R})}$	the buffer to store computation results in p_i
$p_i.prt$	the parent neighbor of p_i
$p_i.chd(k)$	the kth child neighbor of p_i
$\mathcal{F}(p_i)$	the naming value of p_i
$diff(p_i)$	the value of $\mathcal{F}(p_i) - \mathcal{F}(p_{\mathcal{M}})$

- $|E| = \frac{\sum_{i=1}^{|V|} c(p_i)}{2} \leq \frac{\sum_{i=1}^{|V|} deg_{max}(p_i)}{2}$.
- The initial value of $\mathcal{F}(p_i)$ will be discussed later.

3.1   Generalized Overlay Formation

When a node A intends to join (or rejoin [3]) the overlay, it first connects to the bootstrap node that provides an entry point, say a node B, of the overlay (we adopt the mechanism similar to Gnutella [2] that provides a bootstrap node for a node joining). In general, if $diff(A) < diff(B)$, B requires leaving and rejoining the overlay, and meanwhile it reports its parent ($B.prt$) to A (in this study we simply let B to rejoin the overlay by connecting to A if A has available connections to accept B as its child node). Upon receiving the network address of $B.prt$, A then iteratively performs the joining request by sending the request to $B.prt$. The joining process is proceeded until the joining request is forwarded to an ancestor node Q of $B.prt$ having the $diff(Q)$ such that $diff(Q) < diff(A)$.

A then connects to Q if Q has not reached its maximum number of connections (i.e., $c(Q) < deg_{max}(Q)$) and $diff(Q) < diff(A)$. Otherwise, Q either

- (i) forwards the joining request of A to one of its children nodes among $Q.chd(i)$ (where $i = 1, 2, 3, \cdots, k$) if $c(Q) = deg_{max}(Q)$, or
- (ii) forwards the joining request of A to the bootstrap node that in turn randomly picks a node to receive the joining request and this node is not a descendant node of Q if $diff(Q) \geq diff(A)$.

For choosing a child node (i.e., item (i)), each node maintains a *needle* value. That is, Q forwards the joining request to a child node $Q.chd(k')$, where

---

[3] A node rejoins if it detects the failure of its parent node.

$\sum_{i=1}^{k'-1} deg_{max}(Q.chd(i)) < needle < \sum_{i=1}^{k'+1}$. Meanwhile, Q increases its needle value as follows when forwarding a joining request every time

$$needle = (needle + 1) \ mod \ \sum_{i=1}^{k} deg_{max}(B.chd(i)). \tag{2}$$

We note that Q sorts its children nodes in decreasing order according to their $deg_{max}(\cdot)$ values. The idea is to let Q uniformly relay joining requests to its children nodes according to their maximum numbers of connections. To avoid generating cycles in the overlay, in our implementation once a joining request is forwarded downwards the overlay, the request cannot be sent towards the master node $p_{\mathcal{M}}$[4].

As we mentioned in Section 2, the system throughput $\mathcal{W}^{\star}$ is smaller than or equal to $\mathcal{WP}(p_{\mathcal{M}})$.

Theorem 1. The "ideal" system throughput $\mathcal{W}^{\star}$ of a given tree-shaped overlay $G(V, E)$ is

$$\mathcal{W}^{\star}(p_{\mathcal{M}}), \tag{3}$$

assuming that each node in G can effortlessly forward the tasks it cannot accommodate to its children nodes. And,

$$\mathcal{W}^{\star}(p_A) = \min \left(\mathcal{WP}(p_A), \sum_{\forall e \in \bigcup\{\overline{p_A p_B}\}} \min(\mathcal{WL}(e), \mathcal{W}^{\star}(p_B)) \right), \tag{4}$$

where p_B is a child node of p_A.

Proof. The proof is trivial. Given a tree-shaped overlay G, to find a maximum throughput of G is to recursively do the bottom-up traversal of the tree.

Figure 2 illustrates Theorem 1. Consider the node A that can send tasks to its left-hand (B) and right-hand (C) child nodes in the rates of $50 = \min(100, 50)$ and $10 = \min(10, 20)$ tasks per time unit, respectively. The resultant throughput for the sub-tree rooted at A is thus $90 = 30 + 50 + 10$. Similarly, we can calculate the throughput for other nodes. Consequently, we can have the overall system throughput $\mathcal{W}^{\star} = 55$.

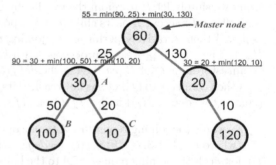

Fig. 2. The values denote the computation and communication overlay rates

---

[4] Due to space limitation, the details of the algorithm can be found in [8]. [8] also provides the maintenance and optimization for the overlay formation.

3.2   Task Computation and Dissemination

Conceptually, the above overlay formation algorithm is to form a tree-shaped overlay $G(V, E)$. To our best knowledge, given $G(V, E)$, the best scheduling algorithm without global knowledge is based on the *bandwidth-centric principle* [9], which lets a node A send a task to its child node according to the communication delay between the sending node and each of its children nodes if A is executing another task and its task buffer $FIFO_{A(T)}$ is not empty. More precisely, A prioritizes its children nodes according to the delay required of receiving a task sent by A. A child node B receives a task from A if B's task buffer ($FIFO_{B(T)}$) is not full. Otherwise, A selects the next child node C that has the smallest communication delay between A and C and that can accept the task sent by A. In this study, higher the working rate of an overlay link, say $\overline{AB}$, the higher priority to receiving a task sent by A is assigned to B. To control the buffer usage, we implement the heuristics proposed in [6].

When A completes a task, it pushes the associated computation result to its result buffer ($FIFO_{A(R)}$). A pushes the results stored in the result buffer back to its parent node $A.prt$ if $A.prt$'s result buffer ($FIFO_{A.prt(R)}$) is not full.

4   Peering Strategies

In this section, we discuss a number of overlay alternatives using the basic algorithm presented in Section 3. These alternatives depend on how we define the naming value for each peer, i.e., the peering strategies. As we will show, the basic algorithm is flexible to construct different types of overlays.

4.1   Degree-Centric

The *degree-centric* overlay (DC) is constructed by referring to the maximal number of connections a peer has. A previous study has shown that capable peers are often connected by a large number of peers [10]. Therefore, the number of overlay neighbors a peer can have implicitly implies the "capability" of a peer.

For formatting a degree-centric overlay (DC), we define the naming value $\mathcal{F}(p_S)$ for each worker node p_S as $\frac{1}{deg_{max}(p_S)}$. We note that in this type of overlays $\mathcal{F}(p_{\mathcal{M}}) = 0$ for the master node $p_{\mathcal{M}}$.

Apparently, if the naming function is defined as $\frac{1}{deg_{max}(\cdot)}$, then a degree-centric overlay organizes nodes that have relatively larger $deg_{max}(\cdot)$ close to $p_{\mathcal{M}}$. Nodes with less numbers of available connections are likely planted nearby the leaves of the overlay. Intuitively, this overlay will potentially have a low diameter in terms of the number of overlay hops.

4.2   Network Delay-Centric

In the *network delay-centric* overlay (NDC), the naming function $\mathcal{F}(p_S)$ is defined as the delay required to send a task from p_S to $p_{\mathcal{M}}$ for any $p_S \in V$. For simplifying the discussion, we assume the overlay link is symmetric, i.e., the delays of sending a task from p_S to p_M and from p_M to p_S are equal. Notably, $\mathcal{F}(p_M) = 0$.

Conceptually, the network delay-centric overlay is to structure nodes according to their network delays to the master. Nodes geographically close to the master join nearby the master. Nodes nearby the leaves of the overlay are distant from the overlay root. That is, the delay-centric overlay intends to match the underlying network topology.

It will be clear that the master node in a delay-centric overlay can rapidly disseminate its tasks to workers. However, this requires a node to measure the communication latency between the master and itself. If the node joins multiple applications, then the node will need to take considerable overhead to measure these delays. It becomes worse if the delays have high variance, and thus requires nodes to measure the delays often.

It is possible that a delay-centric overlay depends on the public network service such as the network positioning system [11] that provides the virtual coordinate of any node in the system. If so, we can simply estimate the communication delay between any two nodes by calculating the difference of their coordinates. However, this approach depends on the availability of the network coordinate service.

We note that in this study we measure the delay of an overlay link $e \in E$ as the value $\frac{task\ size}{\mathcal{WL}(e)}$.

4.3   Compute-Centric

The *compute-centric* overlay (*CC*) refers to the naming function $\mathcal{F}(p_S) = \frac{1}{\mathcal{WP}(p_S)}$. Here, $\mathcal{F}(p_M) = 0$. The heuristic of constructing such an overlay is to aggregate nodes that have high computation working rates $\mathcal{WP}(\cdot)$ nearby the master node. These nodes may efficiently accomplish tasks when compared with incapable ones.

Notably, nodes in a compute-centric overlay need to estimate their $\mathcal{WP}(\cdot)$ values. However, nodes can be heterogeneous and need to compare their naming values. Consequently, nodes require benchmarking their performance regarding a reference machine [12]. Clearly, this needs to have representative benchmark programs.

4.4   Synthetic

It is possible to synthesize several naming functions into a single one in order to generate a desirable overlay. That is, the naming function is defined as

$$\mathcal{F}(p_S) = f_1(p_S) \oplus_1 f_2(p_S) \oplus_2 \cdots \oplus_{k-1} f_k(p_S). \tag{5}$$

We discuss one possible type of overlay as follows.

$\frac{Delay}{Compute}$-**Centric.** One possible type of overlays is called the $\frac{Delay}{Compute}$-Centric overlay (denoted as $\frac{D}{C}$) by having $k = 2$, $\oplus_1$ as the division operator, $f_1(p_S)$ as the delay of sending a task from $p_{\mathcal{M}}$ to $p_{\mathcal{S}}$, $f_2(p_{\mathcal{S}}) = \mathcal{WP}(p_{\mathcal{S}})$, and $f_1(p_{\mathcal{M}}) \oplus f_2(p_{\mathcal{M}}) = 0$. This type of overlays is from the intuition that the master node is likely to send its tasks to nodes that are capable and also geographically nearby.

Clearly, when including more performance metrics to the naming function, the overheads to measure those metrics are increased, accordingly.

Hybrid of ID-, Degree-, Delay- and/or Computer-Centric. Basically, the ID-, degree-, delay- and compute-centric overlays are special types of synthetic overlays. They simply choose a single naming function such as the random hash, $\frac{1}{deg_{max}(\cdot)}$ and $\frac{1}{\mathcal{WP}(\cdot)}$. It is possible to study other synthetic overlays with different naming functions, though we only consider the $\frac{Delay}{Compute}$-centric in this paper.

5 Performance Results

We perform the detailed simulations [5]. We also perform the numerical analysis. However, due to space limitation, the readers who are interested in the analysis results can refer to [8]. The simulation results are shown in Figure 3. When $\frac{comm}{comp}$[6] decreases, the performance bottleneck appears in the overlay network links. This leads to DC, NDC, CC and $\frac{D}{C}$ have the nearly identical system throughput (see Figure 3(a)). However, when $\frac{comm}{comp}$ increases, NDC performs better than DC and CC (see Figure 3(c)). This is because NDC can exploit the network locality to improve the system throughput. However, $\frac{D}{C}$ has the performance results nearly identical to NDC. This does not confirm what we have estimated for $\frac{D}{C}$ [8]. This may be because we have not taken the estimation errors into our analysis. We will investigate this in the future.

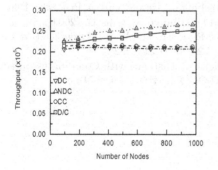 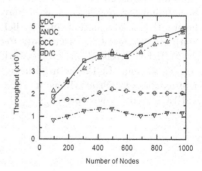

Fig. 3. Effects of varying $\frac{comm}{comp}$

---

[5] The details of the experimental setting are in [8].

[6] The $\frac{comm}{comp}$ ratio denotes the ratio of the communication working rate to the computation working rate.

6 Conclusions

We have presented an overlay formation algorithm which dynamically structures master and worker nodes as a tree-shaped master-worker overlay. The basic algorithm is flexible to include different peering strategies based on the number of connections, network delay, computation capability, etc. We investigate a number of different master-worker overlays, namely, DC, NDC, CC and $\frac{D}{C}$. Through numerical analysis and simulations, we conclude that NDC can perform better than DC, CC and $\frac{D}{C}$ in terms of the system throughput since it is designed with the exploitation of network locality in mind.

References

1. (Napster) http://www.napster.com/.
2. (Gnutella) http://rfc-gnutella.sourceforge.net/.
3. Verma, D.C.: Content Distribution Networks, An Engineering Approach. Wiley (2002)
4. Knutsson, B., Lu, H., Xu, W., Hopkins, B.: Peer-to-Peer Support for Massively Multiplayer Games. In: Proceedings of IEEE INFOCOM. (2004)
5. (SETI@home) http://setiathome.ssl.berkeley.edu/.
6. Kreaseck, B., Carter, L., Casanova, H., Ferrante, J.: Autonomous Protocols for Bandwidth-Centric Scheduling of Independent-task Applications. In: Proceedings of the International Parallel and Distributed Processing Symposium, IEEE Computer Society (2003) 26–35
7. Shao, G., Berman, F., Wolski, R.: Master/Slave Computing on the Grid. In: Proceedings of the Heterogeneous Computing Workshop, IEEE Computer Society (2000) 3–16
8. Hsiao, H.C., Liao, H.: The Peering Problem in Tree-based Master/Worker Overlays. Technical report, National Cheng-Kung University, Taiwan (2005)
9. Banino, C., Beaumont, O., Carter, L., Ferrante, J., Legrand, A., Robert, Y.: Scheduling Strategies for Master-Slave Tasking on Heterogeneous Processor Platforms. IEEE Transactions on Parallel and Distributed Systems 15 (2004) 319–330
10. Sen, S., Wang, J.: Analyzing Peer-to-Peer Traffic Across Large Networks. ACM/IEEE Transactions on Networking 12 (2004) 219–232
11. Ng, T., Zhang, H.: Predicting Internet Network Distance with Coordinates-Based Approaches. In: Proceedings of IEEE INFOCOM. (2002) 170–179
12. (SPEC) http://www.spec.org/.

MUREX: A Mutable Replica Control Scheme for Structured Peer-to-Peer Storage Systems

Jehn-Ruey Jiang[1], Chung-Ta King[2], and Chi-Hsiang Liao[2]

[1] Department of Computer Science and Information Engineering,
National Central University,
Jhongli, 320 Taiwan
jrjiang@csie.ncu.edu.tw
[2] Department of Computer Science, National Tsing Hua University,
Hsinchu, 300 Taiwan
king@cs.nthu.edu.tw, g926704@oz.nthu.edu.tw

Abstract. This paper proposes MUREX, a mutable replica control scheme, to keep one-copy equivalence for synchronous replication in structured P2P storage systems. For synchronous replication in P2P networks, it is proper to adopt crash-recovery as the fault model; that is, nodes are fail-stop and can recover and rejoin the system after synchronizing their state with other active nodes. In addition to the state synchronization problem, we identify other two problems to solve for synchronous replication in P2P storage systems. They are the replica acquisition and the replica migration problems. On the basis of multi-column read/write quorums, MUREX conquers the problems by the replica pointer, the on-demand replica regeneration, and the leased lock techniques.

1 Introduction

Peer-to-Peer (P2P) storage system has been an active research topic and many systems have been proposed [1, 3-6, 10, 12, 14, 16]. Some systems adopt the *unstructured P2P* approach [1, 3], in which there is no restriction on the interconnection of the nodes. Unstructured P2P storage systems are easy to build and maintain, but it is difficult to guarantee the quality in accessing the stored data [11]. Many P2P storage systems [4-6, 10, 12, 14, 16] are thus built on top of *structured P2P networks* [11, 13, 15].

Structured P2P storage systems rely on the concept of *distributed hash table* (DHT). Data objects and peer nodes use the same hash function to acquire their IDs. A data object with the hashed key k is published to and managed by the peer node whose hashed key (or ID) is "closest" to k. Any given key in the hashing space has a node to take charge of. Even after that node leaves, the underlying routing scheme will always send requests for that key to the node currently having the closest ID to the key. In this way, the leaving node is substituted and the keys managed by it are taken over by the substituting node. Please refer to Fig. 1 for such a scenario (node p substitutes leaving node q). Similarly, when a node newly joins the network, it will partially substitute a certain node to manage the keys that are now closest to its ID. Please refer to Fig. 1 for such a scenario (newly joining node u partially substitutes node v).

Y.-C. Chung and J.E. Moreira (Eds.): GPC 2006, LNCS 3947, pp. 93–102, 2006.
© Springer-Verlag Berlin Heidelberg 2006

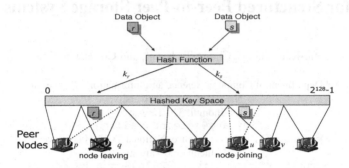

Fig. 1. The scenarios of node joining and leaving

Although the underlying P2P routing can adapt to dynamic node joining and leaving, there is a problem that the data object stored in nodes will be lost when nodes fail or leave. A common solution to this problem is to replicate the data objects among nodes to provide high data availability. If the data objects are read-only (or non-mutable), then the P2P storage system will only need to consider where to replicate the data objects [4-6]. The system becomes much complicated if the data objects are mutable [10, 12, 14, 16]. In this paper, we concentrate on mutable P2P storage systems because they are desirable by most practical applications.

In mutable P2P storage systems, data replication must obey the criteria of one-copy equivalence to ensure data consistency. There are two types of mechanisms to achieve such a criterion: synchronous replication and asynchronous replication. The former requires that each write operation should finish updating all replicas before the next write operation proceeds. The latter regards a local write operation as complete once data object is written to the local replica; data object is then asynchronously written to other replicas. The synchronous replication can ensure data consistency strictly, but may have long operation latency. On the other hand, the asynchronous replication may violate data consistency, but has shorter latency. However, when data inconsistency occurs, complex log-based mechanisms should be invoked to roll back the system to a consistent state. In this paper, we adopt synchronous replication since we take data consistency as the most significant factor and we regard that there may not be available storage for storing logs for system roll-back in asynchronous replication.

For synchronous replication in P2P networks, it is proper to adopt crash-recovery as the fault model. In a crash-recovery system, nodes are fail-stop and can recover and rejoin the system after synchronizing their state with other active nodes. In addition to the *state synchronization problem*, we have two more problems to solve for synchronous replication in P2P storage systems. First, in P2P environments, an active node p may substitute some failing/leaving node q in the recovery process. Thus, node p must acquire the replicas hosted by node q somehow. Below, we call this the *replica acquisition problem*. Second, a newly joining node u will partially substitute an active node v to share v's load by hosting part of v's replicas. Thus, part of v's replicas should be migrated to node u. Below, we call this the *replica migration problem*.

In this paper, we propose MUREX, a mutable replica control scheme, to keep one-copy equivalence for synchronous replication in structured P2P storage systems. On the basis of multi-column read/write quorums, MUREX conquers the problems mentioned by the *replica pointer*, the *on-demand replica regeneration*, and the *leased lock* techniques. We will analyze and simulate MUREX in terms of communication cost and operation success rate.

The rest of the paper is organized as follows. Preliminaries are given in Section 2. In Section 3, we discuss the problems encountered in realizing synchronous replication for P2P mutable storage systems. We then in Section 4 show how MUREX solves the problems, and simulate MUREX in Section 5. Concluding remarks are drawn in Section 6.

2 Preliminaries

As a replica control scheme, MUREX needs to ensure data consistency. In this paper, we adopt the *one-copy equivalence* consistency criteria [8], which states that the set of replicas must behave as if there were only a single copy. Conditions to ensure one-copy equivalence are

(1) no pair of write operations can proceed at the same time,
(2) no pair of a read operation and a write operation can proceed at the same time,
(3) a read operation always returns the replica that the last write operation writes.

Quorum-based schemes are popular mechanisms to enforce one-copy equivalence for synchronous replication since they render relatively high data availability and low communication cost. The basic concept of such schemes is described as follows. Each data object has n replicas, each of which is associated with a version number. A read operation should read-lock and access a read quorum of replicas and return the replica owning the largest version number. On the other hand, a write operation should write-lock and access a write quorum of replicas and then updates them with the new version number, which is one more than the largest version number just encountered. If we restrict the write-write exclusion and the write-read lock exclusion, and restrict that any pair of a read quorum and a write quorum, and any two write quorums have a non-empty intersection, then one-copy equivalence is guaranteed.

MUREX adopts the multi-column quorums, which have the smallest quorums (constant-sized quorums in the best case) among the mechanisms. It is noted that smaller quorums imply few accesses of replicas, which in turn imply lower communication cost. Furthermore, as shown in [8], multi-column quorums are candidates to achieve the highest availability, which is the probability for a quorum to be formed in an error-prone environment.

Multi-column quorums are constructed with the aid of the *multi-column structure* $MC(m) \equiv (C_1, ..., C_m)$, which is a list of pairwise disjoint sets of replicas. Each set C_i is called a *column* and must satisfy $|C_i| > 1$ for $1 \leq i \leq m$.

By organizing data replicas as multi-column structure $MC(m) \equiv (C_1, ..., C_m)$, the write and the read quorums are defined as follows:

A *write quorum* under $MC(m)$ is a set that contains all replicas of some column C_i, $1 \le i \le m$ (note that $i=1$ is <u>included</u>), and one replica of each of the columns $C_{i+1},...,C_m$.
A *read quorum* under $MC(m)$ is either
Type-1: a set that contains one replica of each of the columns $C_1,...,C_m$.
Or
Type-2: a set that contains all replicas of some column C_i, $1 < i \le m$ (note that $i=1$ is <u>excluded</u>), and one replica of each of the columns $C_{i+1},...,C_m$.

3   The Problems

In this section, we identify three problems encountered in enforcing synchronous replication for structured P2P storage systems. The three problems are replica migration, replica acquisition, and state synchronization. Below, we elaborate the problems one by one.

- *Replica Migration*: When a node u newly joins the system and partially substitutes another node v to host some replicas, node v should transfer the replicas to u immediately. However, in a constantly changing P2P environment, the cost of transferring replicas may be too high. We need an efficient mechanism to allow replicas to migrate from substituted node to substituting node.
- *Replica Acquisition*: When an active node p substitutes a failing/leaving node q, node p needs to acquire all replicas hosted by q. The problem is that node q has no idea about which replicas are hosted by p. Thus, we need a mechanism to make node p know which replicas are hosted by node q and to acquire the replicas efficiently.
- *State Synchronization*: Suppose an active node p substitutes a failing/leaving node q, and p has acquired a replica r hosted by q previously. To make replica r effective, we have to synchronize r's state, i.e., to ensure that all the participating nodes have the same view with respect to r's states. We must ensure the acquired replica r is an up-to-date copy. Furthermore, since there may be a node that has locked replica r to make r in the locked state, we need a mechanism to ensure that the locked state is not violated after p acquires replica r.

4   The Proposed Scheme – MUREX

4.1   Overview

For a data object, there are n replicas with hashed keys $k_1,...,k_n$, where $k_1=HASH_1$(data object name), ..., $k_n=HASH_n$(data object name). The replicas are disseminated to the nodes whose hashed ID are nearest to $k_1,...,k_n$, respectively. Please refer to Fig. 2 for the illustration of the replica dissemination. Each replica has a version number which is 0 initially and will increase gradually. MUREX organizes the n replicas into a multi-column structure to help form read and write quorums. MUREX provides the following operations:

- ***publish***(CON, DON): to place n replicas at the nodes associated with $k_1,...,k_n$ for the object of name DON (standing for Data Object Name) with content CON (standing for CONtent) and version number 0.
- ***read***(DON): to acquire the up-to-date replica of the object of name DON by locking all replicas of a read quorum.
- ***write***(CON, DON): to update all the replicas of a write quorum with content CON for the object of name DON.

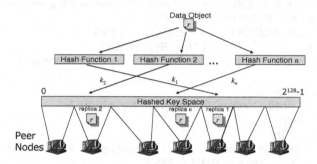

Fig. 2. The dissemination of n replicas of a data object

4.2 Read/Write Quorum Construction

Initially, a data object owner publishes the data object of name DON with content CON by calling ***publish***(CON, DON). Afterwards, any participant can call ***read*** (or ***write***) operation to read (or write) the data object by issuing RLOCK (or WLOCK) messages. With the help of the DHT and the multi-column structure, the messages will reach all members of a read (or write) quorum. The two functions *Get_Read_Quorum* and *Get_Write_Quorum* in Fig. 3 try to issue RLOCK and WLOCK messages to nodes in a last-to-first column-wise manner to return respectively the read and the write quorums under a multi-column structure. It is noted that below we use the words "node" and "replica" interchangeably since a replica must be hosted by a node. Below, we also use LOCK messages to stand for WLOCK messages or RLOCK messages.

When a node receives a LOCK message to request for locking a data object, it sends a MISS message to the requester if it does not own a replica of the data object. As we will show, the MISS message will cause the requester to send an up-to-date replica of the data object later. It is noted that a node has at most one pending MISS message for each replica. A MISS message is said to be pending if there is no replica sent in response to it. When a node has a pending MISS message for a replica and further receives a LOCK message for locking the replica, it will send a WAIT message to the requester. On the other hand, if the node owns the replica when it receives a LOCK message for a data object, it then checks if there is a lock conflict. We say that there is a lock conflict if a read-locked replica receives a write-lock request, or if a write-locked replica receives a write-lock or a read-lock request. If there is no lock conflict, the node locks the replica and then replies with an OK message containing the replica version number. On the contrary, if there is a lock conflict, the node replies with a WAIT message.

```
Function Get_Write_Quorum(($C_1$,...,$C_m$): MC Structure): Set;
  Var $R = \emptyset$: Set;
  For ($i = m$,...,1) Do
    Send WLOCK to all nodes in $C_i$ and enter "wait period" for getting replies;
    If all nodes in $C_i$ reply with WAIT or MISS
      Then {Send UNLOCK to nodes in $C_1 \cup ... \cup C_i$; Exit;}
    If all nodes in $C_i$ reply with OK Then Return $R \cup C_i$;
    Else If a node $u$ replies OK Then $R = R \cup \{u\}$; //note: NO Return here
  EndFor
End Get_Write_Quorum
Function Get_Read_Quorum(($C_1$,...,$C_m$): MC Structure): Set;
  Var $R = \emptyset$: Set;
  For ($i = m$,...,1) Do
    Send RLOCK to all nodes in $C_i$ and enter "wait period" for getting replies;
    If all nodes in $C_i$ reply with WAIT or MISS
      Then {Send UNLOCK to nodes in $C_1 \cup ... \cup C_i$; Exit;}
    If $i \neq 1$ and all nodes in $C_i$ reply with OK Then Return $R \cup C_i$;
    Else If $i \neq 1$ and a node $u$ replies with OK Then $R = R \cup \{u\}$; //note: NO Return here
    Else If $i = 1$ and a node $u$ replies with OK Then Return $R \cup \{u\}$;
  EndFor
End Get_Read_Quorum
```

Fig. 3. Two functions that can properly return a read and a write quorum, respectively

After sending LOCK messages, a node enters the "wait period", which is of the length of a turn-around time. During the wait period, if a node has got any WAIT message, it can conclude that there is lock contention. For such a case, the node sends UNLOCK messages to all the nodes that it has sent LOCK messages. Only after a random backoff time, can the node start over again to send LOCK messages for locking replicas of a quorum. The random backoff concept is borrowed from Ethernet [2]. It is used to avoid continuous conflicts among contending nodes.

After *Get_Write_Quorum* or *Get_Read_Quorum* function returns a write quorum or a read quorum, it means that all replicas in the quorum have been locked. The node calling the function can then execute the desired operation. After the operation is finished, a node sends UNLOCK messages to all nodes that it has sent LOCK messages to unlock the replicas. A read operation in MUREX reads the replica of the largest version number from the read quorum. On the other hand, a write operation always writes all replicas of a write quorum with the version number one more than those ever encountered.

4.3 Replica Pointers

When a node u newly join the system to share part of the load of node v by managing replicas of keys from k to k', the replicas of keys from k to k' should migrate from

v to u. To reduce the cost of transferring all the replicas, MUREX transfers replica pointers instead of the actual replicas. A *replica pointer* is a five-tuple of the form: <hashed key, data object name, version number, lock state, actual storing location>.

It is produced when a replica is generated and can be used to locate the actual replica. When node v owns the replica pointer of replica r, it is regarded as r's host, which can reply to the lock request for r. On the other hand, when node v sends out the replica pointer of replica r, it is no more the host of r and cannot reply to the lock request for r (even if it stores the actual replica of r).

The replica pointer is a lightweight mechanism for transferring replicas; it can be propagated from node to node in a very low cost. When a node u owing the replica pointer of r receives a lock request for r, it should check whether the node actually storing r is still alive. If so, u can behave as host of r. Otherwise, u regards itself as having no replica r. It is noted that every transfer of replica pointer between two nodes, say from v to u, should be recorded locally by v so that later messages, such as UNLOCK messages, destined to v for replica r can be sent to the last node having the replica pointer.

4.4 On-Demand Replica Regeneration

When a node q fails/leaves and another node p substitutes node q, it is needed for node p to acquire all replicas hosted by q. However, we have the problem that node p has no idea about which replicas are hosted by q. Below, we show how the replicas can be acquired in an on-demand manner. The term "on-demand" means that node p only acquire requested replicas. When node p receives a LOCK message from node u for locking a replica, it should send a MISS message if it does not own the replica. Node p is assumed to have no replica r if the following conditions hold:

1. p does not have the replica pointer of r
2. p has the replica pointer of r and the pointer indicates that w stores r, but w is not alive.

After obtaining (resp., generating) the newest replica by executing a read (resp., write) operation, node u should send the replica to node p. It is noted that a node has at most one pending MISS message for a replica. Furthermore, when a node has a pending MISS message for a replica and further receives a lock request for the replica, it will send a WAIT message to the requester. In such a manner, we can ensure that a node will only receive one replica in response to a MISS message.

By the on-demand replica regeneration technique, node p passively acquires replicas only when the replicas are requested. For the replicas never requested, there is no need to acquire them to keep the overhead as low as possible. However, the number of replicas of a data object may decrease gradually and influence the persistency of the data object. Fortunately, the bad influence does not occur for replicas that are accessed frequently. Moreover, we can allow the publisher of a data object to periodically perform the "dummy read operation" for the data object, which will be described later. We even can demand each participating node to periodically perform the dummy read operation for rarely-accessed data object replica hosted by it. When a replica of a data object is not accessed for a specific period of time, the dummy read operation is performed once. The dummy read operation is similar to the read operation and plays the role of checking if replicas of the data object are still alive; it does not read the replica in practice and thus only incurs little overhead. When some replicas of the data object are missed, the node initiating the dummy read operation can re-disseminate the replica to the proper node. The persistency of the data object can thus be ensured.

4.5 Leased Locks

When a replica r of a data object is re-disseminated to some node, we must ensure that all participating nodes have the same view with respect to the replica. We first need to ensure the replica is up-to-date. If the replica is re-disseminated due to a node's receiving a MISS message, the replica is surely up-to-date. This is because a node re-disseminates the replica only after it has executed the read (or write) operation to acquire (or generate) the up-to-date replica. On the other hand, if the replica is re-disseminated due to a node's performing a dummy read operation, the node is demanded to first obtain the up-to-date replica and then to re-disseminate the replica.

The second thing for all participating nodes to agree with is the state of replica r. Since there may be some node that has locked replica r to make r in the lock state, we need to ensure that the lock state is not violated. To achieve this, each lock is assumed to be a *leased lock* that has a leased period of L. That is to say, after a replica is locked, it becomes unlocked automatically after a period of L. Assume that the critical section (CS) of a read or a write operation takes C time to complete. A node should release any obtained lock if it still has no chance to enter the CS and $H>L-C-D$ holds, where H is the holding time of the lock and D is the propagation delay for transmitting the lock. Please see Fig. 4 for the relation of H, L, C and D. The condition of $H>L-C-D$ can ensure a node to complete the desired operation before any lock expires.

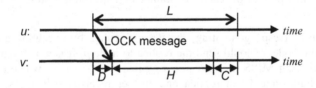

Fig. 4. The relation of H, L, C and D

When a node detects that a lock of a specific replica is expiring (i.e., $H>L-C-D$ is going to hold), it is possible that the locks of other replicas will also expire in the near future. Thus, we demand a node to release all locks and start over to acquire the locks again. In this manner, MUREX can avoid deadlock and starvation. Furthermore, we demand a node to wait for a random backoff time before acquiring the locks next time. This can alleviate the chance of repeatedly occurrence of contention-then-release-all-locks situation.

Now, we describe how to make all participating node have the same view for the lock state by the concept of leased locks. Suppose a node p substitutes a failing/leaving node q to host replica r, and node p has received the up-to-date replica of r at time T. After receiving the up-to-date replica, node p generates a replica pointer for r

and can start to reply to LOCK messages for locking r at time $T+L$, where L is the leased period of the lock. In this manner, all participating nodes have the same view with respect to r's lock state.

5 Simulation

We conduct a simulation for MUREX with regard to success rates of operations for the purpose of evaluating the influence of different multi-column quorums. An operation is considered to be successful if it can finish before any leased lock expires. The simulation assumes that the underlying DHT is Tornado [7]. We adopt four multi-column structures, namely MC(5, 3), MC(4, 3), MC(5, 2) and MC(4, 2), for the construction of read/write quorums. When we simulate the case for MC(m, s), the leased period is assumed to be $m\times$(turn-around time). We also assume that there are totally 2000 nodes in the system. There are three experiments in our simulation. For each experiment, we perform the simulation for 3000 seconds, during which 10000 operations are requested, half for reading and half for writing. Each request is assumed to be destined for a random file (data object); thus, when the number of files increases, the degree of contention decreases. We have plotted performance figures for the three experiments. However, due to the limitation of space, we do not include them here. Please refer to [9] for the figures.

In the first experiment, we assume there are 200 nodes that may join or leave the system randomly during the experiment. In this experiment, we observe that the success rate increases as the number of files increases. This is because the degree of contention decreases when there are more files. Among the four multi-column structures, we can see that MC(5, 3) achieve the best performance and MC(4, 2) achieves the worst, while MC(4, 3) and MC(5, 2) achieve in-between and resembling performances. From this experiment, we can check that lower contention renders higher success rates.

In the second experiment, we assume there are 250 files in the systems and 0, 50, 100 or 200 nodes may leave during the experiment. We observe that the success rate decreases as the number of leaving nodes increases. This is because more leaving nodes can cause more unsuccessful lock requests. Among the four multi-column structures, we can see that MC(5, 3) renders the best performance and MC(4, 2) renders the worst, while MC(4, 3) and MC(5, 2) render in-between and resembling performances. From this experiment, we can see that higher node leaving rates cause worse performances.

In the third experiment, we assume that no node joins or leaves. We observe that the success rate increases as the number of files increases. This is because the degree of contention decreases when there are more files. We can also see that the performances for the four multi-column structures are resembling. By this experiment, we can see that the degree of contention is a dominant factor in the success rate.

6 Conclusion

In this paper, we have identified three problems for synchronous replication in DHT-based mutable P2P storage systems. The problems are replica migration, replica acquisition and state synchronization. We have proposed MUREX, a mutable replica control scheme, to solve these problems by the concepts of multi-column read/write quorums, replica pointers, on-demand replica regeneration and leased locks. We have simulated MUREX to show that it has good operation success rates.

References

1. Bhagwan, R., Moore, D., Savage, S., Voelker G.: Replication Strategies for Highly Available Peer-to-peer Storage. In: Proc. of International Workshop on Future Directions in Distributed Computing. (2002)
2. Chockler, G., Malkhi, D., Reiter, M. K: Backoff Protocols for Distributed Mutual Exclusion and Ordering. In: Proc. of the 21st International Conference on Distributed Computing Systems. (2001) 11-20
3. Cohen, E., Shenker, S.: Replication Strategies in Unstructured Peer-to-peer Networks. In: Proc. of SIGCOMM. (2002)
4. Dabek, F., Kaashoek, M., Karger, D., Morris, R., Stoica, I.: Wide-area Cooperative Storage with CFS. In: Proc. of SOSP. (2001)
5. Druschel, P., Rowstron, A.: PAST: A large-scale, persistent peer-to-peer storage utility. In: Proc. of HotOS VIII. (2001)
6. Gopalakrishnan, V., Silaghi, B., Bhattacharjee, B., Keleher, P.: Adaptive Replication in Peer-to-peer Systems. In: Proc. of International Conference on Distributed Computing Systems. (2004)
7. Hsiao, H.-C., King, C.-T.: Tornado: A Capability-aware Peer-to-peer Storage Overlay. Journal of Parallel and Distributed Computing. 64 (2003) 747-758
8. Jiang, J.-R.: The Column Protocol: A High Availability and Low Message Cost Solution for Managing Replicated Data. International Journal of Information Systems. 20 (1995) 687-696
9. Jiang, J.-R., King, C.-T, Liao, C.-H.: MUREX: A Mutable Replica Control Scheme for Structured Peer-to-Peer Storage Systems. Technical Report. In: http://www.csie.ncu.edu. tw/ ~jrjiang/MUREX.pdf. (2006)
10. Muthitacharoen, A., Morris, R., Gil, T., Chen, B.: Ivy: A Read/write Peer-to-peer File System. In: Proc. of the Symposium on Operating Systems Design and Implementation. (2002)
11. Ratnasamy, S., Francis, P., Handley, M., Karp, R., Shenker, S.: A Scalable Content-Addressable Network. In: Proc. of ACM SIGCOMM. (2001)
12. Rodrig, M., Lamarca, A.: Decentralized Weighted Voting for P2P Data Management. In: Proc. of the 3rd ACM International Workshop on Data Engineering for Wireless and Mobile Access (2003) 85–92
13. Rowstron, A., Druschel, P.: Pastry: Scalable, Distributed Object Location and Routing for Large-Scale Peer-to-Peer Systems. In: Proc. of IFIP/ACM International Conference on Distributed Systems Platforms. (2001)
14. Stein, C., Tucker, M., Seltzer, M.: Building a Reliable Mutable File System on Peer-to-peer Storage. In: Proc. of 21st IEEE Symposium on Reliable Distributed Systems. (2002)
15. Stoica, I., Morris, R., Karger, D., Kaashoek, F., Balakrishnan, H.: Chord: A Scalable Peer-to-peer Lookup Service for Internet Applications. In: Proc. of ACM SIGCOMM. (2001)
16. Yu, H., Vahdat, A.: Consistent and Automatic Replica Regeneration. In: Proc. of First Symposium on Networked Systems Design and Implementation. (2004)

The Subscription-Cover Based Routing Algorithm in Content-Based Publish/Subscribe

HongLiang Yuan, ChangGuo Guo, and Peng Zou

School of Computer, National University of Defense Technology, ChangSha, China
hlyuan@nudt.edu.cn, cgguo@163.net, pzou@nudt.edu.cn

Abstract. Subscription-cover relationship has been proposed to reduce the size of routing-table in intermediate brokers in the publish/subscribe network. Existing researches neglect the extent that covering can be applied and don't give a simple approach to validate the correctness of routing-table when using subscription-cover. In this paper, we propose two routing algorithms based on subscription-cover, which are strict subscription-cover based routing (SSCBR) and relaxed subscription-cover based routing (RSCBR). The goal of the former is to maintain the least covered subscriptions. The latter maintains more covered subscriptions to balance in memory, time and network traffic. On the other hand, we propose a necessary and sufficient condition of correct routing-table configuration when applying SSCBR. We can easily validate the correctness of broker's routing-table through it. Experiments evaluate the ability of two algorithms in reducing the routing-table size of intermediate broker and the efficiency of SSCBR and RSCBR under different subscribing/unsubscribing distribution.

1 Introduction

Publish/Subscribe (P/S) paradigm provides asynchronous, anonymous and one-to-many communication, which has got great attention over the past few years. P/S decouples in time, space and control flow [3]. Subscribers specify their interests in certain event conditions, and will be notified afterwards of any event fired by a publisher that matches their registered interests. Especially content-based publish/subscribe provides filtering on notification's content, which has been widely used for selective data dissemination [1], P2P and pervasive computing [2], and so on.

The research emphasis has been on the architecture [6], matching algorithm [23, 24] and content-based routing [5, 11, 21]. For large scale P/S system, a great challenge is to manage amounts of subscriptions (interest of information consumer) and events. Most existing content-based P/S use subscription forwarding [6] to build route for events diffusing. Subscription-cover [5, 6, 11] has been proposed to reduce the routing table size of intermediate broker. But they all focus on how to efficiently manage and calculate subscription covering. All of them pay attention on the optimal subscription-cover, which is to reduce the routing table size as best as. But that may need much time to calculate the covering or covered relationship between subscriptions. Either of them doesn't distinguish the extent of applying

Y.-C. Chung and J.E. Moreira (Eds.): GPC 2006, LNCS 3947, pp. 103–114, 2006.

subscription-cover idea. Additionally, Either of them doesn't put forward a simple and efficient approach to validate the correctness of broker's routing table.

This paper focuses on the covering relationship between subscriptions when the broker topology is an acyclic graph. **Our contributions** are three folds. **First**, we distinguish the optimal and suboptimal subscription-cover. We propose two routing algorithms based on subscription-cover: strict subscription-cover based routing (SSCBR) and relaxed subscription-cover based routing (RSCBR). The former is the optimal subscription-cover as defined by other research effort [11]. The latter is suboptimal subscription-cover, which balances in memory, calculation time and network traffic. **Secondly**, We propose a necessary and sufficient condition of correct routing-table configuration when using SSCBR. We can easily validate the correctness of broker's routing table according to it. Furthermore, we prove the correctness of SSCBR and RSCBR algorithm implementation through that necessary and sufficient condition. **Thirdly**, we evaluate SSCBR and RSCBR in detail and compare their performances under different subscribing and unsubscribing operation distribution.

This paper is organized as follows. We first introduce the background and our contributions. Section 2 presents related works. Section 3 describes our subscription-cover based routing algorithm in detail. Section 4 is experiments. Section 5 concludes this paper and presents future works.

2   Related Works

Now there exist many publish/subscribe routing algorithms. They can approximately be divided into two categories [8], filter-based approach [5, 6, 7, 8, 9, 10, 11] and multicast-based approach [12, 13, 14, 15, 16, 17, 18]. In the multicast-based approach, event is mapped into the single appropriate group at the publisher side. Because only a limited number of multicast groups can be built, subscribers with different interests may be clustered into same group, and events may be sent to uninterested subscribers as well. The network efficiency of this approach is often highly sensitive to the distributions of events and subscriptions.

In the filter-based approach, events are filtered on its content at each hop in the transmission from publisher to subscriber, and only forwarded toward directions that lead to matching subscriptions. This approach can achieve high network efficiency, but at the cost of expensive subscription information management and event matching at every intermediate server. On the other hand, filter-based approach is highly affected by the publish/subscribe server topology. In order to avoid duplication, most system adopt acyclic (application layer) network topology, such as acyclic graph topology [5, 6, 7, 11], hierarchical topology [6, 9, 10]. Some others [19, 20, 21] use distributed hash approach to assign a subscription to one server, and send producing events to that server. If matching, events are directly sent to matching subscriber. Paper [22] presents a distance vector/dynamic receiver partitioning (DV/DRP) protocol for sensor network, supporting cyclic graph. However, this protocol is only suitable for the scenario that less node consume data and more node produce data.

In an acyclic graph topology, the simplest routing algorithm is forwarding each subscription to every broker unconditionally [7]. Because each subscription would appear in the routing table of every broker, the size of routing table will linearly increase with subscription number. So subscription-cover idea [5, 6, 11] is suggested to decrease the subscriptions of intermediate broker. But they don't distinguish the extent applying subscription-cover. They only consider the optimal covering. Additionally, paper [11] proposes a condition of correct routing-table configuration. But the condition presented by paper [11] is based on notification forwarding, not on subscription issuing. We cannot judge whether the configuration of routing table is correct just according to subscription information. On the contrary, our necessary and sufficient condition of correct routing-table configuration bases on subscription issuing information. So we can validate the correctness of routing-table configuration just basing on subscriptions knowledge.

3   Subscription-Cover Based Routing Algorithms

The routing based on undirected acyclic graph topology usually use subscription forwarding scheme [6], in which subscriber's subscription (named S) is sent to access broker, named SHB (Subscriber Hosting Broker), then SHB forwards subscriptions to neighbor brokers. All brokers compose a spanning tree about subscription S, rooted at SHB. Each broker's routing table is composed of (S, U) pairs, which indicates direction of broker U issues subscription S. When publisher produces events, events are sent to access broker, named PHB (Publisher Hosting Broker). PHB forwards events (Notification) to neighbor brokers, which directions have issued subscription matched by events. Events are forwarded from PHB to all SHBs hop-by-hop, eventually to all subscribers.

Let $N(S)$ denote the notification set of matching subscription S. For subscription S1 and S2, if $N(S1) \supseteq N(S2)$, then we say S1 covers S2, denoted by $S1 \supseteq S2$. If $N(S1) \equiv N(S2)$, then say S1 equals to S2, denoted by $S1 \equiv S2$. If $N(S1) \supset N(S2)$, then say S1 is a real cover of S2, denoted by $S1 \supset S2$. If subscription S1 covers S2, we only need forward S1 to neighbors, because S1 can stand for S2 to express interest to neighbor directions, which is the idea of subscription-cover. Subscription covered by other subscription needn't be forwarded to all brokers, which can reduce the size of broker's routing table and the time of notification matching in general.

In this paper, we assume that Broker network topology is undirected acyclic graph, message transition between brokers is FIFO and reliable, $sub(s)$ denotes producing a new subscription s, $unsub(s)$ denotes canceling subscription s, all the brokers denoted by B^i ($1 \le i \le N$, N is the broker number), $SHB(S)$ denotes the access broker of the client issuing subscription S. $SUB(B^i)$ denotes the subscription set issued by all the client accessed to broker B^i, RTB is the abbreviation of the routing table. We are only concerned about brokers, and ignore clients, because client is irrelevant to routing.

In order to facilitate discussion, we give some definitions.

Definition 1. *The configuration of RTB is correct iff notifications matching S will be forwarded from PHB to $SHB(S)$ except S is cancelled before notifications arrive $SHB(S)$.*

Definition 2. *The publish/subscribe system is stable iff no sub(s) or unsub(s) message are in transition over the broker network.*

Definition 3. *A publish/subscribe routing algorithm is correct iff when receiving subscription or unsubscription, through definite sequence sub(s) or unsub(s) forwarding, publish/subscribe system can be stable and the configuration of RTB is correct.*

Definition 4. *The edge between broker B^m and B^n is defined by $e^{m,n}$, then the path between B^i and B^j denoted by route(B^i, B^j) = $B^i e^{i,i'} B^{i'} e^{i',i''} B^{i''} \ldots\ldots B^j$.*

There is only one path between two brokers because an acyclic graph is a tree in fact.

Definition 5. *For subscription $S \in SUB(B^i)$, let $B(SUB \supset S) = \{B^j \mid \exists S' \in SUB(B^j), S' \supset S, 1 \leq j \leq N\}$, $B(SUB \equiv S) = \{B^j \mid \exists S' \in SUB(B^j), S' \equiv S, 1 \leq j \leq N\}$.*

$B(SUB \supset S)$ defines such brokers: the clients accessed to them issue subscriptions that cover S. $B(SUB \equiv S)$ defines the case of equivalence.

Definition 6. *For subscription $S \in SUB(B^i)$, let $B(\supset S) = \{B^m \mid \forall B^j \in B(SUB \supset S), B^m \in route(B^i, B^j), 1 \leq m \leq N\}$, $B(\equiv S) = \{B^m \mid \forall B^j \in B(SUB \equiv S), B^m \in route(B^i, B^j), 1 \leq m \leq N\}$.*

$B(\supset S)$ defines the common (overlapped) path of all the route($SHB(S)$, $SHB(S')$) ($S' \supset S$). If there is only one broker B^j in $B(SUB \supset S)$, then $B(\supset S)$ are all the brokers in route(B^i, B^j). If B^i is also in $B(SUB \supset S)$, then $B(\supset S)$ only contains B^i. $B(\equiv S)$ defines the case of equivalence. In Figure 1, the set of $B(\supset S5)$ contains {B5, B4, B2}.

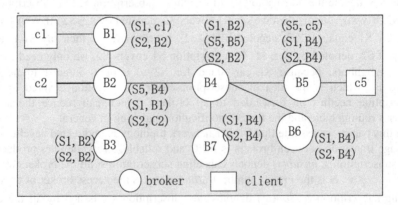

Fig. 1. Example of Strict Subscription-Cover Based Routing ($S1 \supset S5, S2 \supset S5$)

Below we give two routing ideas of subscription-cover, which differ in maintaining the count of covered subscriptions. A condition of correct RTB configuration basing on SSCBR is proposed. We prove the correctness of the routing algorithm implementation through this condition.

3.1 Strict Subscription-Cover Based Routing Idea

Definition 7. Except using subscription-forwarding scheme, a routing algorithm is called *Strict Subscription-Cover Based Routing (SSCBR)* if it uses below rules [11].

(1)   *A subscription is not forwarded to a neighbor if a subscription that covers the former was forwarded to that neighbor that has not been canceled.*

(2)   *If a subscription is forwarded, the receiving broker deletes all routing entries whose subscriptions are covered by the new subscription and that refer to the same destination as new subscription.*

(3)   *An unsubscription is not forwarded to a neighbor if there is a subscription of a local client or another neighbor that covers the former.*

(4)   *If an unsubscription is forwarded to a neighbor, the sending broker also forwards a possibly empty subset of subscriptions covered by former.*

SSCBR aims at deleting the entry of covered subscription as best as and maintaining the least covered subscriptions. According to SSCBR, there is no entry of S5 in broker B1, B3, B6 and B7 in Figure 1.

Theorem 1. *When applying SSCBR, the configuration of RTB is correct iff when publish/subscribe system is stable, for subscription $S \in SUB(B^i)$:*

(1)   *If there are only subscriptions that is real cover of S, then S is only contained in RTB of brokers in $B(\supset S)$, and there is no entry of S in other broker's RTB.*

(2)   *If there are only subscriptions that are equal to S, then RTB of brokers in $B(\equiv S)$ must contain entry of S, and other broker's RTB either contains S, or the equal subscription of S.*

(3)   *If the condition of (1) and (2) hold at the same time, then RTB of brokers in $B(\supset S)$ contains either S or the equal subscription of S, but there is no entry of S in other broker's RTB.*

(4)   *Otherwise, all the brokers' RTB contains entry of subscription S.*

Proof

The Necessity. For (1), (a). According to subscription forwarding scheme, we only need prove that if RTB of all the neighbor broker of $B(\supset S)$ (of course not including the neighbor broker that belongs to $B(\supset S)$) does not contain entry of S, then we can conclude that RTB of all the brokers except for $B(\supset S)$ do not contain entry of S. Consider $B^s(B^s \notin B(\supset S))$ that is the any neighbor of $B(\supset S)$, if entry of S is in B^s, then there is a broker $B^t \in B(\supset S)$, because S is diffused from $B(\supset S)$, and B^s contains (S, B^t). On the other hand, $\exists \ S' \in SUB(B^j)$ $(B^j \in B(SUB \supset S))$, S' is not covered by any other subscription, and B^s is not in route(B^i, B^j) because B^s is not in $B(\supset S)$, then B^s must contain (S', B^t) otherwise S' cannot be forwarded to B^s (there is only one path between two brokers). So entry (S, B^t) and (S', B^t) are both in RTB of B^s, according to SSCBR, (S, B^t) must be deleted, that is to say there is no entry of S in B^s.

(b). Consider the farthest broker from B^i in $B(\supset S)$ is B^t, then the brokers in $B(\supset S)$ are in route(B^i, B^t). Now we prove that the entry of S is certainly contained in RTB of brokers in route(B^i, B^t). Otherwise, don't lose universality, assume that (S, B^r)

is not in RTB(B^t), B^r is the neighbor broker of B^t. Because there is no $S' \supset S$ and (S', B^r) is in RTB(B^t), else indicate $\exists B^j \in B(SUB \supset S)$, s.t $B^t \notin$ route(B^i, B^j), which is not consistent with the definition of $B(\supset S)$. Then system cannot forward notifications matching subscription S to $SHB(S')$, which need traverse broker B^t, so it is illogical. Therefore the RTB of brokers in $B(\supset S)$ must contain entry of S.

According to (a) and (b), S is only contained in the RTB of brokers in $B(\supset S)$.

(2) can be proved in similar approach. (3) can be proved by colligating (1) and (2). (4) holds obviously. So far we complete necessity proof.

The Sufficiency. Assuming the PHB is B^p which published notification matching S. (a) If there is no subscriptions which are equal to or real cover of S, then notification can be forwarded to B^i ($SHB(S)$) along route(B^p, B^i) hop-by-hop. (b) If there are subscriptions which are real cover of S, assuming the farthest broker from B^i in $B(\supset S)$ is B^t, then there must exist $S' \supset S$, and notification can be forwarded to B^t along route(B^p, B^t) according to matching S' (if B^p cannot see S', then can prove in recursive method). Then notification can be forwarded to B^i ($SHB(S)$) along route(B^t, B^i) according to matching S or S'' ($S'' \equiv S$) if there exist. (c) If there are only subscriptions that are equal to S, then notification can be forwarded to B^i ($SHB(S)$) along route(B^p, B^i) according to matching S or S'' ($S'' \equiv S$) if there exist. Summing up (a), (b) and (c), we have proved that notification matching S can be forwarded from any PHB to $SHB(S)$. The sufficiency is proved.   □

Theorem 1 describes that covered subscription S would just exist in $B(\supset S)$. According to the property of graph, we can compute $B(\supset S)$ and $B(\equiv S)$ easily. Therefore, we can validate the correctness of SSCBR routing.

3.2 SSCBR Algorithm Implementation and Correctness Proof

In order to maintain subscription-cover relation, [6] proposes a POSET (Partially Ordered Set) method. We extend POSET and name it SCG (Subscription Covering Graph). SCG records every subscription and its sender (neighbor broker or local client). Each subscription/sender pair has two variables, named N_B-covering-degree and L_C-covering-degree, which denote neighbor directions and local clients whose subscription covers current subscription respectively. SCG supports two functions: s_add_SCG(S, sender) and s_delete_SCG(S, sender), in which S is a subscription, sender is the neighbor or local client issuing S. Function s_add_SCG and s_delete_SCG calculate the value of N_B-covering-degree and L_C-covering-degree. When broker receives a new subscription S, s_add_SCG adds "in" and "out" directed edges of S (from covering subscriptions to S and from S to subscriptions covered by S).

SSCBR algorithm implementation is in the left of figure 2.

Algorithm Correctness Proof
As long as we can prove SSCBR algorithm can make publish/subscribe system stable and the configuration of routing table satisfy the necessary and sufficient condition of theorem 1, then the SSCBR algorithm implementation is correct.

Assume for subscription $S \in SUB(B^i)$ and a set of subscription real covering S, named S^k, $S^k \in SUB(B^{j^k})$, $1 \le k \le n$, the cross point of $route(B^i, B^{j^1})$, ..., $route(B^i, B^{j^n})$ is B^t. According to definition 6 and the assumption, the brokers in $B(\supset S)$ are all in $route(B^i, B^t)$.

Subscription Forwarding. When $sub(S)$ is forwarded along $route(B^i, B^t)$ from broker B^i to B^t, for any broker B^c in $route(B^i, B^t)$, (1) if B^c hasn't received any one of $\{sub(S^k)\}$ yet, $sub(S)$ will be forwarded to all neighbors of B^c when B^c receives

```
// SSCBR algorithm
void ProcessSubMessage( Sender,sub(S) )
1.    {
2.      s_add_SCG(S,Sender);
3.      C1={(S1,u)|S1 ⊇ S,u ≠ Sender,(S1,u)∈ SCG};
4.      C2={(S2,u)|S ⊇ S2};
5.      if Sender∈ N_B then
6.        for (S2,Sender) ∈ C2 do
7.          s_delete_SCG(S2,Sender);
8.        end for
9.      end if
10.     if L_C-covering-degree of (S, Sender) >0 then
11.        return;
12.     end if
13.     switch N_B-covering-degree of (S,Sender)
14.        case 0: forward sub(S) to all neighbors
                   except Sender;
15.        case 1: only forward sub(S) to u,  (*,u) ∈ C1;
16.        default:(≥ 2) don't forward sub(S);
17.     end switch
18.    }
void ProcessUnsubMessage(Sender, unsub(S))
1.    {
2.      C1={(S1,u)|S1 ⊇ S,u ≠ Sender,(S1,u)∈ SCG};
3.      if L_C-covering-degree of (S,Sender) =0 then
4.        switch N_B-covering-degree of (S,Sender)
5.           case 0: forward unsub(S) to all neighbors;
6.           case 1: only forward unsub(S) to u,
                      (*,u) ∈ C1;
7.           default:(≥ 2) don't forward unsub(S);
8.        end switch
9.      end if
10.     s_delete_SCG(S,Sender);
11.     C2={(S2,u)|S ⊇ S2};
12.     for (S2,u) ∈ C2 do
13.        if L_C-covering-degree of (S2,u) =0 then
14.          C3={(S3,v)| S3 ⊇ S2,v ≠ u};
15.        switch N_B-covering-degree of (S2,u)
16.           case 0: forward sub(S2) to all neighbors ;
17.           case 1:only forward sub(S2) to v,(*,v)∈ C3;
18.           default:(≥ 2) don't forward sub(S2);
19.        end switch
20.        end if
21.     end for
22.    }
```

```
// RSCBR algorithm
void ProcessSubMessage( Sender,sub(S) )
1.    {
2.      s_add_SCG'(S,Sender);
3.      C1={(S1,u)|S1 ⊇ S,u ≠ Sender,(S1,u)∈ SCG};
4.      if L_C-covering-degree of (S, Sender) >0 then
5.        return;
6.      end if
7.      switch N_B-covering-degree of (S,Sender)
8.        case 0: forward sub(S) to all neighbors
                   except Sender;
9.        case 1: only forward sub(S) to u, (*,u) ∈ C1;
10.       default:(≥ 2) don't forward sub(S);
11.     end switch
12.     record the neighbors that S is forwarded to;
13.    }

void ProcessUnsubMessage(Sender, unsub(S))
1.    {
2.      if L_C-covering-degree of (S,Sender) =0 then
3.        if N_B-covering-degree of (S,Sender) = 0 then
4.          forward unsub(S) to all neighbors;
5.        else
6.          forward unsub(S) to neighbors that sub(S)
                   has been forwarded to;
7.        end if
8.      end if
9.      s_delete_SCG(S,Sender);
10.     C2={(S2,u)|S ⊇ S2};
11.     for (S2,u) ∈ C2 do
12.        if L_C-covering-degree of (S2,u) =0 then
13.          C3={(S3,v)| S3 ⊇ S2,v ≠ u};
14.        switch N_B-covering-degree of (S2,u)
15.           case 0: forward sub(S2) to neighbors that
                      sub(S2) has not been forwarded to;
16.           case 1:only forward sub(S2) to v,
                      (*,v)∈ C3 and if sub(S2) has not
                      been forwarded to v;
17.           default:(≥ 2) don't forward sub(S2);
18.        end switch
19.        end if
20.     record the neighbors that S is forwarded to;
21.     end for
22.    }
```

Fig. 2. SSCBR algorithm and RSCBR algorithm

sub(S). The line 5~9 of procedure **ProcessSubMessage** assures that the broker in the neighbor directions of B^c would delete the entry of S after it receives any one of *sub(S^k)*. (2) if B^c has received any one of {*sub(S^k)*}, the line 10~17 of procedure **ProcessSubMessage** assures that *sub(S)* will just be forwarded along route(B^i,B^t).

Combine (1) with (2), procedure **ProcessSubMessage** just keep the entry of S in route(B^i,B^t) and store the cover knowledge in route(B^i,B^t) (through SCG graph), which assures the necessary and sufficient condition of theorem 1 holds. If there are subscriptions equaling to S, then $B(\supset S)$ may keep the subscription that equals to S, which also satisfies the necessary and sufficient condition of theorem 1.

Due to acyclic graph assumption, procedure **ProcessSubMessage** assures that *sub* message would terminate in definite forwarding.

Unsubscription Forwarding. The line 3~9 of procedure **ProcessUnsubMessage** assures that *unsub(S)* would not be forwarded to a neighbor direction if an un-canceled subscription that covers S has been forwarded to that direction.

If any one of {S^k} is unsubscribed, we can divide two scenarios: (a). before *unsub(s^k)* is forwarded to B^t; (b). After *unsub(s^k)* is forwarded to B^t.

(1) For any broker B^l in route(B^t,B^k), when it process *unsub(s^k)*, if there is subscriptions in B^l that covers S, so B^l needn't re-forward S. Otherwise, there is no entry of S in B^l and no subscription covering S , that is to say another *unsub($s^{k'}$)* has already been processed by B^l, the proof can be merged into (2).

(2) If *unsub(s^k)* can be forwarded to B^t (there is no subscriptions covering S^k), for any direction of B^t, if there is no subscription covering S, The line 10~21 of procedure **ProcessUnsubMessage** assures that S can be re-forwarded. So S can be forwarded by procedure **ProcessSubMessage**. Therefore the necessary and sufficient condition of theorem 1 holds when using procedure **ProcessSubMessage.**

In one word, SSCBR algorithm implementation is correct.   □

3.3 Relaxed Subscription-Cover Based Routing Algorithm

In last section, we investigate the scenario of strict subscription-cover based routing. For subscription S1, S2 and $S1 \supset S2$, if *sub(S2)* and *sub(S1)* is received from the same neighbor direction, SSCBR algorithm deletes the entry of S2 if S2 is received first, which can reduce the size of broker's routing table. But if *unsub(S1)* is issued before *unsub(S2)*, then SSCBR will re-forward S2, the cost of earlier forwarding S2 is wasted in vain. So we propose a **Relaxed Subscription-Cover Based Routing** (**RSCBR**) algorithm:

(1)   A subscription is not forwarded to a neighbor if a subscription that covers the former was forwarded to that neighbor that has not been canceled.

(2)   An unsubscription is not forwarded to a neighbor if it never be forwarded to that neighbor (because there is a subscription that covers it).

(3)   If an unsubscription is forwarded to a neighbor, the sending broker also forwards a possibly empty subset of subscriptions that are covered by the former and never be forwarded to that neighbor.

The goal of SSCBR algorithm is to reduce the size of routing table as best as. RSCBR admits the fact that covered subscription has been forwarded. It doesn't consider whether current subscription covers earlier received subscriptions, which reduces the time of calculating subscription-cover and decreases the traffic of duplicate forwarding of covered subscriptions when covering subscriptions are first canceled. RSCBR and SSCBR is a trade-off between time/network-traffic and space.

RSCBR algorithm implementation is in the right of figure 2.

In RSCBR algorithm, the semantic of s_add_SCG is changing. So we rename it s_add_SCG'. s_add_SCG' only find the subscriptions that cover current subscription, and it doesn't calculate whether there are subscriptions covered by current subscription. That is to say s_add_SCG' only return in-edge of S.

RSCBR algorithm implementation would keep subscription-cover knowledge in $B(\supset S)$, so the correctness of it is obvious. Proof is omitted. Both SSCBR and RSCBR use subscription-cover idea, so they can reduce the size of routing table in intermediate broker. Compared with SSCBR, RSCBR maintains more covered subscription in intermediate broker. We will evaluate their behavior in reducing the size of routing table and network traffic through experiments.

4 Experiments

The goal of experiments is to evaluate the behavior of SSCBR and RSCBR in reducing the size of routing table, network traffic, etc. The metric of routing table size is the average subscription count of each broker. The metric of network traffic is the average **sub** and **unsub** message number of each subscription. We evaluate three routing algorithm SSCBR, RSCBR and N-CBR (routing without using subscription cover).

The experiments setup is as follows.

(1) There are 1000 brokers and broker network topology is undirected acyclic graph. The longest path (from one broker to another broker) is 15 brokers. All brokers distribute symmetrically as best as.

(2) For simplification, all the subscriptions contain three predicates on the same (attribute name) numeric type attribute, for example $length \in [100-l, 100+l]$, $width \in [80-w, 80+w]$, $height \in [50-h, 50+h]$. The subscription count issued by each broker (broker's client) is the same. Every broker first issues all the subscription, then issue unsubscription one by one after all subscription have be issued.

(3) The most important factor influencing the behavior of SSCBR and RSCBR is the cover ratio ρ. We define the cover ratio $\rho = \dfrac{\sum\limits_{i=1}^{N} C_i}{N}$, N is the active subscriptions count, C_i is the count of subscription that covers subscription S_i. The cover relation increases with ρ. The value of ρ can range from 0 to N/2. The most extreme scenario is that subscription S_1 is covered by $S_2, S_3, \ldots, S_N$, and S_2 is covered by $S_3, \ldots, S_N$, and so on. So $\rho = ((N-1)+(N-2)+\ldots+1+0)/N \approx N/2$.

We test SSCBR and RSCBR with $\rho = 0.5$ and $\rho = 0.8$ individually. From Figure 3(a), we find that both SSCBR and RSCBR can greatly reduce the size of routing table, and the size of routing table decrease with increasing ρ, which can be explained that the more covering relation, the less covered subscription would be forwarded. Under the same ρ, SSCBR can reduce more size of routing table than RSCBR.

In Figure 3(b), we set ρ =0.8. The **-R means random unsubscribing subscriptions. The **-FC means first unsubscribing covered subscriptions. The **-LC means last unsubscribing covered subscriptions. The average message count of N-CBR is approximately twice the count of brokers (2*N), which is not affected by the subscription count.

The traffic of SSCBR-LC is the most, which can be explained that because covered subscriptions are last unsubscribed, so SSCBR need re-forward them when covering subscriptions are unsubscribed. On the contrary, SSCBR-FC produces the least traffic. The traffic of RSCBR-FC is between SSCBR-FC and SSCBR-LC. The traffic of RSCBR-FC is more than SSCBR-FC is because RSCBR-FC need forward more *unsub* message of covered subscription than SSCBR-FC (because RSCBR store more covered subscription in intermediate brokers than SSCBR). However, the traffic of RSCBR-R, RSCBR-LC and RSCBR-FC is less than SSCBR-LC at any time because RSCBR algorithm maintains redundant covered subscriptions (which don't need to be re-forwarded when covering subscription are canceled) than SSCBR. In general, RCSBR-R, RSCBR-LC and RSCBR-FC produce less traffic than SSCBR-R.

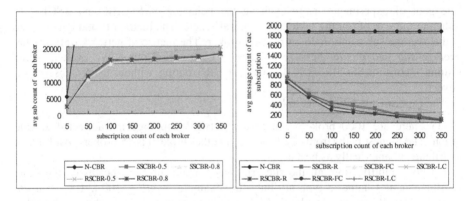

Fig. 3. (a) routing table size experiment. (b) traffic experiment.

We can't arbitrarily say that RSCBR would produce less traffic than SSCBR because the network traffic of RSCBR largely depends on subscribing/unsubscribing distribution. If covered subscriptions are first canceled, RSCBR still needs to forward those unsubscribing messages. But because RSCBR need calculate less subscription covering relationship than SSCBR, we can definitely say that RSCBR costs less calculating time than SSCBR, which is not illustrated by us.

5 Conclusions and Future Works

The necessary and sufficient condition of correct routing-table configuration proposed by us can be used to validate the correctness of SSCBR routing idea. The two subscription-cover routing (SSCBR and RSCBR) use different policy to maintain the count of covered subscriptions. They can find suitable scenarios for different subscriptions distribution individually.

We have compared SSCBR and RSCBR in network traffic through evaluations. But that is only primary. Further experiments are necessary to evaluate them in other performance metric. In addition, it is a great challenge to apply the idea of subscription-cover into cycled graph. For cycled graph, an alternate routing algorithm is DV-based [22] (distance/vector). In DV approach, for brokers in a circle, they may not forward matching events to the direction of covered subscription if that direction is not the shortest path for the covering subscriptions. However, we must find a method to solve this problem if we extend subscription-cover idea to cycled graph. We have tried several methods. It is believed that we would make a progress in the forthcoming future.

Acknowledgements

This paper is founded by the National Natural Science Foundation of China under Grant Nos. 90412011, and by the National High-Tech Research and Development Plan of China under Grant Nos. 2003AA115410, Nos. 2004AA112020.

Reference

1. C. Marchetti, M. Mecella, M. Scannapieco, and A. Virgillito. Enabling Data Quality Notification in Cooperative Information Systems through a Web-service based architecture, Proceedings of the 4th International Conference on Web Information Systems Engineering, Roma, Italy, 2003.
2. Simon Courtenage and Steven Williams. Automatic Hyperlink Creation Using P2P and Publish/Subscribe, In the Workshop on Peer-to-Peer and Agent Infrastructures for Knowledge Management (PAIKM), Apr 2005.
3. P. T. Eugster, P. Felber, R. Guerraoui, and A.-M. Kermarrec. The Many Faces of Publish/ Subscribe, ACM Journal Comput, Vol. 35, No. 2, page 114~131, March 2003.
4. Ying Liu, Beth Plale. Survey of Publish/Subscribe Event Systems, technical report, Department of Computer Science. (CSCI) at Indiana University, TR574, May 2003.
5. Guoli Li, Shuang Hou, Hans-Arno Jacobsen. A Unified Approach to Routing, Covering and Merging in Publish/Subscribe Systems Based on Modified Binary Decision Diagrams, In Proceedings of the 25th IEEE International Conference on Distributed Computing Systems (ICDCS'05), Pages 447-457, 2005.
6. Antonio Carzaniga, David S. Rosenblum, and Alexander L. Wolf. Design and evaluation of a wide-area event notification service, ACM Transactions on Computer Systems, 19(3): 332~383, 2001.
7. IBM Corporation. Gryphon: Publish/subscribe over public networks. Technical report, IBM T. J. Watson Research Center, 2001.
8. Fengyun Cao, Jaswinder Pal Singh. Efficient Event Routing in Content-based Publish-Subscribe Service Networks, In IEEE INFOCOM 2004.
9. G. Cugola, E. Di Nitto, and Fugetta. The JEDI event-based infrastructure and its application to the development of the OPSS WFMS, IEEE Transactions on Software Engineering 27, 9 (Sept.), 827~850, April 2001.

10. G. Cugola, E. Di Nitto, A. Fuggetta. Exploiting an event-based infrastructure to develop complex distributed systems, In Proceedings of the 20th International Conference on Software Engineering, Kyoto, Japan, April 1998.
11. Gero Muhl. Large-Scale Content-Based Publish/Subscribe Systems, PhD thesis, Technical University of Darmstadt, 2002.
12. L. Opyrchal, M. Astley, Joshua S. Auerbach, G.Banavar, R. E. Strom, and D. C. Sturman. Exploiting IP Multicast in Content-Based Publish-Subscribe Systems, In Proceedings of Middleware 2000, 2000.
13. Z. Ge, M. Adler, J. Kurose, D. Towsley and SteveZabele. Channelization problem in large-scale data dissemination, Technical report, University of Massachusetts at Amherst, 2001.
14. A. Riabov, Z. Liu, J. Wolf, P. Yu and L. Zhang. Clustering Algorithms for content-based publication-subscription systems, In Proceedings of IEEE International Conference on Distributed Computing Systems (ICDCS'02), 2002.
15. T. Wong, R. Katz, and S. Mc Canne. An evaluation of preference clustering in large scale multicast applications, In Proceedings of IEEE INFOCOM, March 2000.
16. G. Banavar, T. Chandra, B. Mukherjee, et al. An efficient multicast protocol for content-based publish-subscribe systems. In Proceedings of the 19th IEEE International Conference on Distributed Computing Systems, pages 262~272, 1999.
17. Xue T, Feng BQ. Research on routing algorithm and self-configuration in content-based publish-subscribe system. Journal of Software, 16(2): 251-259, 2005.
18. J.C. Lin and S. Paul. A reliable multicast transport protocol, In INFOCOM, pages 1414~1424, 1996.
19. Antony I. T. Rowstron, Anne-Marie Kermarrec, et al. SCRIBE: The design of a large-scale event notification infrastructure, In Networked Group Communication, pages 30~43, 2001.
20. S.Q. Zhuang, B.Y. Zhao, A.D. Joseph, R. Katz, and J. Kubiatowicz. Bayeux: An Architecture for Scalable and Fault-tolerant Wide-area Data Dissemination, In Proceedings of International Workshop on Network and Operating Systems Support for Digital Audio and Video NOSSDAV, 2001.
21. P. Triantafillou and I. Aekaterinidis. Content-Based Publish-Subscribe Over Structured P2P Networks, In International Workshop on Distributed Event-Based Systems (DEBS04), 2004.
22. C.P. Hall, A. Carzaniga, J. Rose, and A.L. Wolf. A Content-Based Networking Protocol For Sensor Networks, Technical Report, Department of Computer Science, University of Colorado, August 2004.
23. Aguilera, M. K., Strom, R. E., Sturman, D. C., Astley, M., and Chandra, T. D. Matching Events in a Content-based Subscription System, In Proceedings of ACM PODC, Atlanta, GA, Pages 53–61, 1999.
24. Fabret, F., Jacobsen, H., Llirbat, F., Pereira, J., Ross, K., and Shasha, D. Filtering Algorithms and Implementations for Very Fast Publish/Subscribe Systems, In Proceedings of ACM SIGMOD. Santa Barbara, California, Pages 115–126, 2001.

Alliatrust: A Trustable Reputation Management Scheme for Unstructured P2P Systems*

Jeffrey Gerard, Hailong Cai, and Jun Wang

Computer Science & Engineering, University of Nebraska–Lincoln
{jgerar, hcai, wang}@cse.unl.edu

Abstract. Content pollution and free-riders are increasingly threatening the utility and dependability of modern peer-to-peer systems. One common defense against these threats is to maintain a reputation for each peer in the network based on its prior behavior and contributions, which can help other users make informed decisions about future transactions. However, most current reputation schemes for unstructured P2P systems are prone to attack and therefore not very reliable. In response, we propose a trustable, distributed, reputation-management scheme called *Alliatrust* to combat content pollution and free-riders. Alliatrust demonstrates resilience against collusion by malicious peers by elegantly managing distributed copies of reputation data on a few homologous peers. Simulations show that Alliatrust is able to reduce undesirable transfers of polluted resources to good peers by up to 70%, while decreasing the success of queries issued by malicious peers and free-riders.

1 Introduction

Modern peer-to-peer (P2P) networks reach gigantic proportions with many users. While a large P2P community affords more benefits for each peer, a network of extensive scale necessarily incurs many unexpected incidents that harm the community. Anonymity opens the network to possible misuses and abuses, and P2P users cannot be assumed to exhibit inherit credibility or altruism.

Consequently, both free-riding and content pollution are prevalent in modern P2P networks. Free-riders are peers that consume system resources without sharing any of their own. One study of a Gnutella P2P network found 68% of all active peers to be free-riders [1]. Meanwhile, more than half of the copies of many popular songs in the KaZaA network are polluted, meaning they have corrupt data content or inaccurate associative metadata [2]. As such, a P2P system that does not consider peers' reputations may fall victim to threats such as dominance of free-riders, polluted content, and hacking.

---

* This work is supported in part by the US National Science Foundation under grants CNS-0509480 and CCF-0429995, the US Department of Energy Early Career Principal Investigator Award DE-FG02-05ER25687, and a University of Nebraska-Lincoln Undergraduate Creative Activities & Research Experiences grant.

Y.-C. Chung and J.E. Moreira (Eds.): GPC 2006, LNCS 3947, pp. 115–125, 2006.

1.1 Motivation

While trust metrics are useful in P2P systems, their efficacy relies on the ability to securely store and distribute reputation data. Existing reputation management schemes work well in structured networks [3, 4]. For example, the secure implementation of the EigenTrust reputation computation algorithm organizes data placement throughout the network using a distributed hash table, which makes it easy to attain homologous peers as candidate computation and storage agents. However, distributed hash tables require costly maintenance overhead to handle rapid node churn, and they limit the effectiveness of keyword-search queries. [5, 6].

Perhaps for these reasons, we observe a strong prevalence of unstructured networks in commercial P2P software [7, 8] and subsequently envision that reputation schemes for unstructured networks presently have greater pragmatic value. Without proper restraints on data placement, however, the design of reputation schemes for unstructured networks faces more challenges in enforcing symmetric functionality. Specifically, the security of schemes proposed thus far for use in unstructured environments is often unreliable. Most of these schemes store a single peer's reputation data on the peer itself, where it may easily be subjected to hacking attempts [8, 9, 10].

Unstructured, decentralized networks require a reliable reputation management scheme in which each user's reputation data is distributed among multiple homologous peers in the network. Only by asking multiple peers to be engaged in managing each peer's reputation can we trust these reputation values with confidence.

1.2 A Novel Solution

We propose *Alliatrust*, a trustable, distributed reputation-management scheme for unstructured, decentralized P2P systems. Alliatrust provides incentives for peers to share quality resources and is resilient against malicious nodes. In Alliatrust, each peer has multiple managers that maintain copies of its reputation value. We fashion a reputation overlay to create links between peers and their managers, so that managers can compute, maintain, and supply reputation values. New data to be used in updating a peer's reputation is always sent directly to the managers as it becomes available to prevent a peer from meddling with its own reputation value. As to not place undue emphasis on any particular peers, all peers in the network have approximately the same number of managers and comparable responsibilities to store reputation data for other users. We also develop a majority-voting policy that peers can use to resolve discrepancies of a reputation value that might arise in the presence of deceitful managers.

Experiments demonstrate Alliatrust's ability to impede uploads of polluted content by malicious peers and its capability to fail ten times as many queries issued by malicious peers and free-riders, compared with a baseline system. Whether malicious peers work independently, cooperate with others, or camouflage their motives by sharing authentic resources occasionally, they are generally unable to distribute large amounts of polluted content when our reputation scheme is activated.

1.3 Assumptions

In developing a new, highly reliable reputation scheme, we must make important assumptions regarding the nature of the network. To ensure a high degree of security, our scheme never assumes that any given node is trustworthy. We tackle this vulnerability, which is inherent to public, unsupervised networks, by avoiding intermediaries wherever possible and by always duplicating sensitive data. We also assume that each peer has an unique identifier that can be used to locate the peer in the network, such as an IP address.

Without a central authority, the accumulation of any distributed data in a network will ultimately reflect the testimony given by the majority of the users. For example, if all peers maintain individual opinions of each other, and most users find favor in unpolluted content, then the peers that share unpolluted resources will accrue high reputations, even though the network may contain peers with differing predilections. Thus, although we never presume any single peer is trustworthy, we must assume that more peers are trustable than are not.

2 Alliatrust

The Alliatrust system architecture consists of several components, including a reputation overlay, a way to propagate reputation updates, and a fault tolerance mechanism.

2.1 The Reputation Overlay

In our distributed reputation-management scheme, each node n has a number of peers called *managers* that store n's reputation value (n.RV); every node also stores a copy of its own reputation value locally to prevent data loss if all its managers should fail. Having multiple copies of n.RV helps combat node churn and protect integrity in the presence of untrustworthy peers. We propose, then, a reputation overlay that exists over all nodes in the P2P network. This overlay connects each of n's managers to n itself via connections referred to as *supervisor links*. Supervisor links are unidirectional to make corrupt arrangements difficult by hindering two nodes from controlling each other's reputation values [9].

While the host-manager relationship is unidirectional, node n does know about the role its managers have and maintains each of its managers' unique identifiers in a *manager list*, $M(n)$. The reputation overlay is defined such that each node n has a number of managers $|M(n)|$, which is the cardinality of its manager list. Not all nodes have exactly the same number of managers, but we restrict $|M(n)|$ such that $\mathbf{M_{min}} \leq |M(n)| \leq \mathbf{M_{max}}$ for all n. The lower and upper bounds of the number of managers for each node, $\mathbf{M_{min}}$ and $\mathbf{M_{max}}$ respectively, are constants throughout the network and should be fairly tight. As a result, nodes empirically have roughly the same number of managers, labeled $\mathbf{M_{\mu}}$.

When a new node n joins the network, it bootstraps onto an existing peer, which becomes n's first manager. Immediately, n builds its manager list by searching for peers in the network that are managers of fewer than $\mathbf{M}_{max}$ peers. Once n has a total number of managers $|M(n)| = \mathbf{M}_{min}$, n stops searching for new managers and distributes a message to all the managers it found, instructing them to initialize n.RV to the system's default starting reputation value.

Although a node initially seeks only $\mathbf{M}_{min}$ managers when it joins the network, it continues to passively enlist additional managers throughout its regular P2P activity. At the onset of occasional transactions, node n asks its client or server peer p if p can become n's manager. As before, n enlists p as a new manager if p manages fewer than $\mathbf{M}_{max}$ other peers. The frequency of these searches is determined by the number of managers that n has already: if $|M(n)|$ is close to $\mathbf{M}_{min}$, n will look for new managers more actively than if $|M(n)|$ is large. Because n and p are already involved in a transaction, p is temporarily storing a copy of $M(n)$ as will be specified in Section 2.3. By passively procuring new managers, n will usually have a sufficient number to endure one's departure. However, if $|M(n)|$ should ever drop below $\mathbf{M}_{min}$, n will immediately search out new managers in the same way that it did when it first joined the network.

2.2   Calculating Reputation Values

Alliatrust's primary purpose is to facilitate secure storage and retrieval of reputation data in an unstructured network, leaving the meticulous details of actually calculating reputation values to other research [3, 10]. Nevertheless, we must assume some basic attributes of the computation procedure. We adopt a condition common to many reputation schemes that a node's reputation value is updated whenever it is involved in a transaction with another peer, whether the node acts as a server or client. When a client node receives a resource, its reputation value is decreased to represent its debt to the network. Conversely, when a peer p serves a resource to a node n, p.RV is updated according to its contribution to the network. Upon completion of the transfer, n is allowed to rate the quality of the resource it received, based on criteria such as the accuracy of metadata and the degree of pollution. If n deems the resource to be of sufficient quality, p.RV is increased, but if n finds the resource to be polluted, p.RV is decreased as punishment for sharing polluted material in the network.

2.3   Distributing Reputation Updates

We assumed that a peer's reputation is updated after it completes a transaction. Any new information regarding the transaction should be distributed as soon as possible to provide the most accurate impression of a peer via its reputation value. To minimize the control a peer has over its own reputation value, the peers on both sides of a transaction notify each other's managers directly with this additional transaction information.

Following a transaction in which p serves a resource to n, both p's and n's reputation values should be updated. Before the actual resource transfer begins,

p and n exchange their manager lists, $M(p)$ and $M(n)$, during the underlying network's handshake process. This way, upon completion of the transfer, the peers can alert each other's managers to initiate an update of their reputation values. Server p tells n and n's managers that n received a resource, triggering all these nodes to independently calculate n's new reputation value using the same reputation calculation algorithm. Simultaneously, n rates the resource it received according to predefined criteria and sends its evaluation to p and the managers in $M(p)$.

However, the rating process that n performs on the resource it receives from p may be expensive to perform or require human interaction [11]. Thus, although p will notify n's managers to decrease n.RV immediately after the transaction, n may defer this rating interminably, or may not even do it at all. One possible solution is to initially assume that a transferred resource was of decent quality and update p.RV with a tentative positive rating. If the client n does rate the resource some time later, it can simply update p.RV via p's managers.

The overhead required in exchanging manager lists is low. The greatest strain on the network occurs when the peers notify each other's managers about the transaction. Both peers send messages to about $\mathbf{M}_\mu$ managers and to the other peer, generating a total of $2 \times (\mathbf{M}_\mu + 1)$ messages. This is 10 extra messages per transaction when $\mathbf{M}_\mu = 4$, as observed in our simulations described in Section 4.1.

2.4   Resolving Discrepancies

Reputation schemes allow a node to know at a glance which peers to favor in future transactions. With Alliatrust, the most secure way to obtain a peer's reputation value is to ask that peer's managers directly. There is no guarantee that any given manager is trustworthy, so a node ought to query multiple managers of a peer and independently resolve any discrepancies of the returned reputation values. A querying node does not necessarily have to query every manager of a peer, but rather the proportion of managers it asks should rely on the severity of any negative consequences resulting from inaccurate data. For simplicity, however, we will assume that the utmost available trust is always essential, so the nodes we describe here will always query every manager of the peer whose reputation value is desired.

After a node accumulates the responses from a peer's managers, it compares all the copies of reputation values and checks for any disagreement. If there is a disparity, our experiments show that there will likely remain a majority of managers exhibiting the correct value. Hence, the node can simply assume the statistical mode[1] of the set to be correct. If there is more than one mode, the node uses the arithmetic mean of these modes.

2.5   Tolerating Peer Departures and Failures

When node n leaves the network, either intentionally or as the result of a failure, it saves its own reputation and manager list locally, and its managers retain

---

[1] The mode is the value that occurs the most frequently in a set.

its reputation value for a specified duration after the departure. This duration should be long enough to survive most "round trips" of leaving and returning to the network [5, 12], but must be small enough so that managers do not become overwhelmed with reputation data about old peers. When n returns to the network later, it attempts to contact all the peers in its stored manager list. Any former managers still in the network continue as n's managers. Then, n seeks to replace any managers that had since departed from the network until it again has $\mathbf{M}_{\min}$ managers. If, however, none of n's former managers remain in the network, n's new managers will be forced to adopt n's local copy of $n.\mathrm{RV}$. This final scenario is unfavorable because of our assumption that n may not be trustable; fortunately, our experimental results show that this happens less than 5% of the time.

3   Using Reputation in Queries

Alliatrust can benefit P2P applications in a number of ways. We demonstrate two examples in which reputation data can improve search queries in the network, one of the most utilized services in current P2P systems. We offer one tactic peers can use and another that may be implemented by the P2P system itself.

3.1   Differentiated Quality of Service

For a reputation scheme to be beneficial, the P2P system must provide some manner of incentive for peers to increase their own reputations. Several approaches can differentiate the quality of service a peer receives, each with its own features and applications. One scheme allows users to download resources only from peers with equal or lesser reputation values than their own [13]. Other research recommends that peers forward search queries according to the reputation values of the querying users: queries from users with high reputations might receive a longer time-to-live, or forwarding peers might arrange incoming queries in a priority queue, serving those from highly-reputed users first [9, 13].

3.2   Selecting Quality Resources

Once a network has provided sufficient incentive for peers to foster their reputations by sharing their resources with others, the peers can use the reputation system to make informed decisions in their transactions.

If a peer p is able to fulfill a forwarded search query, p responds directly to the client n that issued the query. In addition to the typical information that p sends n as is implemented in the underlying P2P system, p also transmits its own reputation value and manager list. Over time, n collects this information from various peers that have the targeted resource. After a maximum amount of time has passed or a minimum number of peers have responded to the query, n can use these replies and their accompanying reputations to pick a trustworthy server peer.

The client n selects a peer q that sent a high reputation value along with its response to the query. To verify that q.RV is indeed what was claimed in the query response, n contacts one or more of q's managers. If the reputation value that q claimed to have is greater than the value of q.RV reported by q's managers, then n assumes q is untrustworthy and repeats this verification process using another responding peer. The client n will request the resource from the first peer it finds that did not inflate its reputation value.

4   Experimental Results

To evaluate Alliatrust's performance in combating free-riders and polluted content, we implement the reputation overlay on a large-scale network model. We simulate network activity under an assortment of threat models and compare the Alliatrust scheme with a baseline that has no reputation scheme in place.

4.1   Simulation Configuration

We construct a physical topology emulating a hierarchial Internet network using the Transit-Stub model [14] with the same parameters described in [15]. Of the 51,984 nodes that comprise the network model, we randomly choose 10,000 to be peers participating in the P2P system. Our logical network topology is modeled from a Gnutella network trace provided by the Limewire Organization [7]. Each peer in the P2P system shares a number of resources, following the distribution observed in a real Gnutella network [12]. Accordingly, 24% of all peers are free-riders, sharing no resources at all. The specific resources stored on the remaining peers are assigned according to a probabilistic content distribution model [16].

Peers disseminate queries to the system via the Gnutella overlay. In baseline networks, the time-to-live (TTL) for all queries is six hops. Alliatrust differentiates quality of service as summarized in Section 3.1. Specifically, it partitions the range of possible reputation values into five balanced segments, each with a corresponding TTL value. These five TTL values are 2, 3, 5, 7, and 8, providing longer TTLs to queries from peers with high reputations. For example, queries from brand new peers with a median reputation value live for five hops, while queries issued by well-behaved peers can live for seven or eight hops.

We assign a constraint that a peer must have at least $M_{min} = 3$ managers and may not have more than $M_{max} = 6$. In all our simulations, these bounds produce an average number of managers per peer $M_\mu = 4$. For simplicity, we choose an inelaborate reputation calculation algorithm in which reputation values may take on integers from 0 to 200 points. New peers start with the median reputation value of 100. The penalty for receiving a resource is 3 points, and a peer may gain or lose 5 points for serving a resource, depending on the rating it receives.

4.2   Peer Behaviors

Essentially, we consider three types of peers in the network: good peers, malicious peers, and free-riders. These groupings form disjoint subsets that partition the set of all peers. Free-riders do not share resources but do actively issue queries and, when the reputation scheme is in place, truthfully rate all resources they receive. Both good and malicious peers share resources and issue queries, but a specified ratio of all resources distributed by malicious peers are polluted. Furthermore, malicious peers try to attack Alliatrust's effectiveness by misrepresenting reputation values or rating resources unfittingly. We study a variety of such strategies, or *threat models*, that malicious peers might employ to thwart the reputation scheme. Good peers share quality resources 95% of the time, accounting for rare mistakes users might make in generating metadata or forgetting to remove a polluted resource from the shared folder.

Threat Models. In threat model A, malicious peers act individually, and endeavor to fill the network with polluted content. They always serve polluted resources and rate resources they receive as "quality" if they are polluted and "not quality" if they are not polluted. This is the opposite behavior of good peers. Malicious peers also attempt to thwart the reputation scheme to receive a privileged quality of service: when any peer asks a malicious peer p for its reputation value, p returns a value equal to 150% of p.RV's true value.

We conduct a series of simulations in which malicious peers behave according to threat model A. We assign a ratio of peers to be malicious such that they make up between 10% and 50% of all peers in the network. For each scenario, Figure 1 compares Alliatrust with a baseline system using the proportion of polluted resources received by good peers out of all resources received by good peers. Alliatrust reduces the number of accidental downloads of polluted resources as much as 70%, because malicious peers acquire low reputations, causing good peers to seldom choose them as servers. By contrast, malicious peers find no difficulty dispersing polluted content in the baseline system, and the fraction of polluted downloads actually exceeds the fraction of malicious peers in the network.

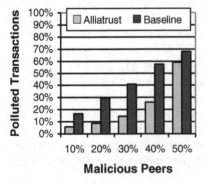

Fig. 1. Alliatrust helps good peers receive up to 70% more quality resources when malicious peers operate under threat model A

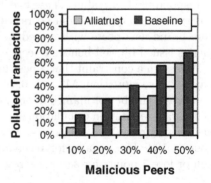

Fig. 2. Even when malicious peers form collectives under threat model B, Alliatrust decreases the polluted resources transferred to good peers

Figure 1 may seem unconvincing when half of the peers are malicious because such scenarios violate our assumption that trustable peers should outnumber malicious peers. For instance, when 40% of peers are malicious and 24% are free-riders, only 36% are good peers. Even so, Alliatrust noticeably reduces the number of polluted resource transfers in these harsh environments. Moreover, no reputation scheme in existence claims to completely abolish polluted resources.

Under threat model B, malicious peers can recognize each other and form collectives, allowing them to inflate their claims of each other's reputation values to good peers. As before, malicious peers only share polluted content, rate polluted content favorably, and multiply their own reputation values by 150%. In addition, if a malicious peer m manages another malicious peer p, and an outsider requests $p.RV$ from m, then m returns a value equal to 150% of the true $p.RV$. This is analogous to a single malevolent user creating numerous identities and using them to boost each other's reputation values [17].

As before, we test situations in which a malicious collective makes up between 10% and 50% of all peers, even though it is unlikely that a single collective could comprise half of a large-scale P2P network. Figure 2 portrays the fraction of polluted resources received by good peers for experiments in networks with and without Alliatrust. The formation of collectives scarcely increases malicious peers' attempts to circulate polluted content, and Alliatrust continues to reduce the number of polluted resources downloaded by good peers by up to 70%.

Unable to successfully thwart the Alliatrust reputation scheme by actively inflating each other's reputation values through collectives, malicious peers may try to increase their reputations by sharing some quality resources. Under threat model C, malicious peers inherit all the behaviors from threat model B, but they also share a certain fraction of quality resources to cloak their true intentions, thereby attempting to raise their reputation values.

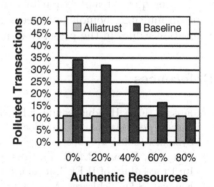

Authentic Resources

Fig. 3. Sharing a fraction of quality resources in an attempt to inflate their reputations does not help malicious peers disseminate polluted content

We run a series of simulations in which malicious peers act under threat model C, returning proportions of quality resources ranging from 0% to 80%. They comprise 25% of all peers. Figure 3 shows the fraction of polluted downloads by good peers when malicious peers share various fractions of authentic resources. With Alliatrust, malicious peers see almost no additional success by occasionally sharing authentic resources to thwart the scheme. Only about 11% of downloads by good peers are polluted in all cases.

Discouraging Free-Riders & Malicious Peers. In addition to reducing the polluted resources that good peers receive, Alliatrust deters bad peers by differentiating quality of service according to a peer's reputation. Without sharing any quality resources, free-riders' reputations should steadily fall as they issue queries to the system. Similarly, under the assumption that a peer's reputation value should decrease when it transfers a polluted resource, malicious peers' reputations should fall even more rapidly.

Having completed simulations under multiple threat models, we measure the failure rates of queries that were issued by malicious peers and free-riders. This is the only occasion we actually desire a high failure rate, because the poor quality of service that bad peers receive provides them with a strong motivation to increase their reputation values. Generally, Alliatrust causes ten times as many queries from bad peers to fail.

5   Conclusions

Alliatrust, a trustable, distributed reputation-management scheme for decentralized, unstructured P2P systems can successfully reduce the prevalence of polluted content by over 70% when malicious peers comprise 30% of the network. Even if peers form a malicious collective or camouflage their intentions by sharing quality resources, Alliatrust consistently and significantly cuts distribution of polluted content. The scheme also discourages free-riders and malicious peers by failing ten times as many of their queries, thereby providing bad peers with fewer query results than in a baseline network. By distributing reputations on multiple, homologous peers, Alliatrust can securely maintain accurate reputation values in the presence of malicious peers.

References

1. Fessant, F.L., Handurukande, S.B., Kermarrec, A.M., Massoulié, L.: Clustering in peer-to-peer file sharing workloads. In: International Workshop on Peer-to-Peer Systems. (2004) 217–226
2. Liang, J., Kumar, R., Xi, Y., Ross, K.W.: Pollution in P2P file sharing systems. In: Proceedings of IEEE Infocom. (2005)
3. Kamvar, S.D., Schlosser, M.T., Garcia-Molina, H.: The Eigentrust algorithm for reputation management in P2P networks. In: Proceedings of the 12th international conference on World Wide Web, New York, NY, USA, ACM Press (2003) 640–651
4. Xiong, L., Liu, L.: Peertrust: Supporting reputation-based trust for peer-to-peer electronic communities. In: IEEE Transactions on Knowledge and Data Engineering. (2004) 843–857
5. Cai, H., Wang, J., Li, D., Deogun, J.S.: A novel state cache scheme in structured P2P systems. Journal of Parallel and Distributed Computing 65 (2005) 154–168
6. Chawathe, Y., Ratnasamy, S., Breslau, L., Lanham, N., Shenker, S.: Making gnutella-like P2P systems scalable. In: SIGCOMM '03: Proceedings of the 2003 conference on Applications, technologies, architectures, and protocols for computer communications, New York, NY, USA, ACM Press (2003) 407–418
7. Limewire: (http://www.limewire.org/)
8. KaZaA: (http://www.kazaa.com/)

9. Dutta, D., Goel, A., Govindan, R., Zhang, H.: The design of a distributed rating scheme for peer-to-peer systems. In: Workshop on Economics of Peer-to-Peer Systems. (2003)
10. Gupta, M., Judge, P., Ammar, M.: A reputation system for peer-to-peer networks. In: Proceedings of the 13th international workshop on Network and operating systems support for digital audio and video, New York, NY, USA, ACM Press (2003) 144–152
11. Marti, S., Garcia-Molina, H.: Limited reputation sharing in P2P systems. In: Proceedings of the 5th ACM conference on Electronic commerce, New York, NY, USA, ACM Press (2004) 91–101
12. Saroiu, S., Gummadi, P.K., Gribble, S.D.: A measurement study of peer-to-peer file sharing systems. Technical Report UW-CSE-01-06-02, (University of Washington)
13. Ranganathan, K., Ripeanu, M., Sarin, A., Foster, I.: To share or not to share: An analysis of incentives to contribute in collaborative file sharing environments. In: Workshop on Economics of Peer-to-Peer Systems. (2003)
14. Zegura, E.W., Calvert, K.L., Bhattacharjee, S.: How to model an internetwork. In: Proceedings of IEEE Infocom. (1996) 594–602
15. Cai, H., Wang, J.: Foreseer: a novel, locality-aware peer-to-peer system architecture for keyword searches. In: Proceedings of the 5th ACM/IFIP/USENIX international conference on Middleware, New York, NY, USA (2004) 38–58
16. Schlosser, M.T., Condie, T.E., Kamvar, S.D.: Simulating a P2P file-sharing network. In: First Workshop on Semantics in P2P and Grid Computing. (2002)
17. Douceur, J.R.: The Sybil attack. In: First International Workshop on Peer-to-Peer Systems. Volume 1. (2002)

A Fault-Tolerant Distributed Scheme for Grid Information Services

Ming-Jeng Yang[1], Chin-Lin Kuo[2], Shih-Hsiang Lin[2], and Yao-Ming Yeh[2]

[1] Department of Information Technology, Takming College, Taipei, 114 Taiwan
mjyang@mail.takming.edu.tw
[2] Department of Information & Computer Education, National Taiwan Normal University,
Taipei, 106 Taiwan
{genemlsh178, virtualbow}@yahoo.com.tw, ymyeh@ice.ntnu.edu.tw

Abstract. The Grid Information Service (GIS), mainly used for resource discovery and monitoring, is a key component of grid system. The resource description and specification should be meditated for efficient search and access. In this paper, we propose a distributed system for grid information services, which deploys a number of registry servers at different regions of the world. A new scheme for registering, updating, querying, and deregistering a resource in registry servers is devised. For the purpose of fault-tolerance and load-balance, the meta-data, including description and specification, of each resource can be replicated and disseminated at some registry servers instead of reproducing resource itself for service discovery. In our scheme, the workload on each registry server is balanced and the faults of registry servers can be tolerated. Also, the user could obtain all resource information satisfied with the query conditions even some of registry servers crashed.

1 Introduction

Grid technology has increasing played an important role in scientific computing field. The resources of grid are scattered on numerous places or organizations and with distinct type, function or/and owner. The issues of resource information discovering, registering and securing become more and more important. In order to discover necessary resources as soon as possible, effective mechanism of information service, such as accessing interface, meaning of parameters and resource function, is strongly demanded. Hence, resource description and specification must be clear and efficient enough. In [1] the authors propose an XML-based grid resource specification language and its usage in Resource Registry Meta-Service.

Grid is considered as a service oriented architecture (SOA) system and could be accessed through services. So we still take grid as a different type of web service. But there are still many problems required to be conquered. For example, the centralized model of UDDI [2] which is the information center of web service architecture providing XML based service specification standardization is not appropriate for the grid environment. Web service inspection language (WSIL) [3] does not provide good implementation at distribution of services and is difficult to be used in grid. There are several related works about grid information service, which include GMA [4],

Y.-C. Chung and J.E. Moreira (Eds.): GPC 2006, LNCS 3947, pp. 126–136, 2006.
© Springer-Verlag Berlin Heidelberg 2006

Hawkeye [5] and MCS [6]. However these works are not open grid service infrastructure (OGSI) [7] compliant and therefore their ability of manipulating dynamic, heterogeneous, distributed information is profoundly limited.

The open grid service architecture (OGSA) [8] was developed to solve the challenges in such dynamic, heterogeneous and geographical grid environment. OGSA builds on the web service technology mechanisms to create, name and discover transient grid service instances with a uniform manner and it is a popular and a widely accepted architecture. Web services provide important machinery, but are lack of some important topics relevant to basic service semantics: how services are created, how long they live, how to manage faults, and how to handle long-lived state. These issues are addressed by the design of OGSI which defines essential building blocks for distributed systems. The OGSI is a formal and technical specification from OGSA. Using a combination of WSDL interface descriptions and human readable specifications, OGSI defines mechanisms for creating, naming, managing lifetime, monitoring, grouping, and exchanging information among grid services. OGSI also introduces standard factory and group registration interfaces for creating and discovering grid services. While developing a GIS system, the requirement and features of OGSA should be taken into consideration. The globus toolkit 3 [9], a reference implementation of the OGSI, provides a grid service-oriented information service.

In this paper, we present a quorum based grid fault-tolerant scheme for information service registering, updating and querying. In our scheme, based on the *Leg-Ring* system [10], the workload disseminated on each service node is balanced and the faults of service nodes can be tolerated. Meanwhile, by using the meta-data which describes and explains resource characteristics detailed, the service could provide efficient and accurate interface for searching, understanding and further processing.

The rest part of this paper is organized as follows: section 2 describes the architecture of the grid information service. Section 3 explicates *Legion* structure, quorum system and its application on this GIS. Section 4 describes these protocols that include registry, query, update and deregistry. Finally, in section 5, we draw conclusions based on our research.

2 Architecture Overview

In our design, the information service is based on the distributed architecture and the meta-data information of resources is stored at a number of service nodes. For the purpose of fault tolerance and load-balance, the meta-data, including description and specification, of each resource can be replicated and disseminated at some service nodes instead of reproducing resource itself for service discovery. Similar to meta-data based model in [11], each user in client terminal could issue a query with appropriate keywords to a server. Upon receiving the query, the local server forwards the message to some servers for discovering registered resources satisfied with the inquired conditions.

We call this information service "Quorum-based fault-tolerant information service (QFIS)". The architecture of QFIS consists of three layers: resource layer, control layer, and service layer, which are depicted in figure 1.

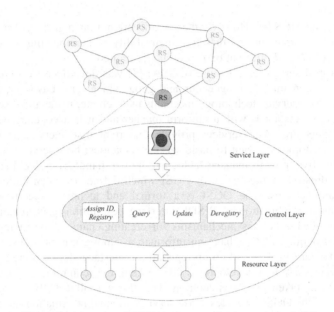

Fig. 1. Architecture of QFIS — three service layers in each RS

- **Resource layer** is composed of various grid service data (GSD) [12]. The creators or providers of GSD should provide detailed meta-data, including description and specification, and send the meta-data information to the registry mechanism of QFIS. The registry mechanism will assign a unique resource *id* about the resource.
- **Control layer** manages actions of resource meta-data, such as registration, generation of a unique *id*, query and deregistration. The operation of fault tolerance is implemented in this layer. After receiving the meta-data from lower layer, the control layer replicates the meta-data and then disseminates them to other registry nodes which are randomly selected from the quorum sets. The detailed selecting scheme will be described in later section.
- **Service layer** provides the user interface and aggregates these parameters from the control layer. Communicating with other registry servers is manipulated and included here. Since information service is a component of grid, a special web service, and SOAP is the basic communication protocol for web service, we adopt SOAP as the messages passing method in the process of registration, query and so on.

From the geographical view of global world, we separate the whole server nodes into *N* partitions. Each partition contains exactly one resource registry server (RS) and other server nodes. A partition is called a region and the number of server nodes in a region should be meditated when we program the region area. While there is a fault occurring on a RS, the leader election algorithm [13], [14] is launched among these server nodes in this region and a newly elected RS is generated, which maintains the functions of the fault RS.

3 Quorum Constructions for QFIS

In the QFIS system, all the resource registry servers (RSs) play the role of a fault-tolerant system. Based on a quorum-based scheme, the fault-tolerant system can tolerate the failures of RSs. In this section, in order to prove the correctness of quorum system for QFIS, we introduce some definitions and theories, such as quorum, set system [15], and *Legion* structure [10] of our previous work.

A set system [15] is composed of a number of quorums.

Definition 1. *A* **set system** $C = \{Q_1, Q_2,..., Q_n\}$, $1 \leq n$, *is a collection of nonempty subsets* $Q_i \subseteq U$ *of a finite universe U.*

Each element Q_i of C in Definition 1 is called a **quorum**.

Take the set $C = \{\{a,b,c\}, \{d,e\}, \{f,k,h\}\}$ as an example. C is a set system, and any element in C, for example, $\{f,k,h\}$ is a quorum.

In the following, we introduce a definition of *Legion* structure, which is our previous work [10]. A *Legion* is constructed from set systems.

Definition 2. *A* **Legion structure** $\{C_i, C_j\}$ *is a collection of two set systems that has the following properties:*

[I] $C_i = \{Q_1, Q_2,..., Q_n\}$ *and* $C_j = \{Q_1, Q_2,..., Q_m\}$ *are set systems.* $(1 \leq n, m)$
[II] *For any pair of quorums* $Q_s \in C_i$ *and* $Q_t \in C_j$, *there is* $Q_s \cap Q_t \neq \emptyset$. *That is,* Q_s *and* Q_t *have at least one common element.* $(1 \leq s \leq n, 1 \leq t \leq m)$

Claim 1. *The Legion structure* $\{C_i, C_j\}$ *defined in Definition 2 can be used as a mathematic model for quorum-based information service in QFIS system.*

According to the Definition 2, any two quorums of a pair (Q_s, Q_t) have at least one common element, where Q_s is a quorum in C_i and Q_t is a quorum in C_j. This structure can be applied to develop a quorum-based information service scheme for QFIS systems. In QFIS systems, if one of the servers requires information from the other, it suffices to query one server from an appropriate quorum. While using this quorum-based service scheme, we can assign quorums in C_i as registration-quorums, and quorums in C_j as query-quorums. According to the definition of *Legion*, the set of queried servers is bound to contain at least one server that belonged to the registration-quorum that received the registration information.   □

Based on the properties of *Legion* structure, we use ring-based approach to construct a quorum scheme called *LegRing* in order to manage location information. First, N registry servers (RSs) are arranged as a logical ring, denoted by N-*LegRing*. Every RS in the QFIS system is assigned a distinct number from 0 to N-1 and arranged by its number sequentially. In the following, some sequences of patterns in the N-*LegRing* are employed as Registration-quorum (R-quorum) and Query-quorum (Q-quorum).

Definition 3. *In an N-LegRing system, the Registration-set system (R-set) and Query-set system (Q-set) are defined as follow:*

$$R\text{-}set = \{\{n, (n+1) \bmod N, (n+2) \bmod N,..., (n+d-1) \bmod N\} \mid 0 \leq n \leq N\text{-}1\}$$

$$Q\text{-}set = \{\{n, (n+d) \bmod N, (n+2d) \bmod N, ..., (n+kd) \bmod N\} \mid 0 \leq n \leq N\text{-}1,$$

$$k=\lfloor (N-1)/d \rfloor \}$$

Where d $= \lceil \sqrt{N} \rceil$; n, k, and N are all integers.

Each element of R-set and Q-set is called an **R-quorum** and a **Q-quorum**, respectively.

Claim 2. *The R-set and Q-set of an N-LegRing system defined in Definition 3 satisfy the properties of Legion structure $\{C_i, C_j\}$.*

According to the Definition 2, the properties of *Legion* structure $\{R$-set, Q-set$\}$ are: (I) R-set and Q-set are set systems. (II) Any pair of R-quorum in R-set and Q-quorum in Q-set have joint elements. We need to prove these properties. First, according to Definition 3 and Definition 1, it is easy to see that R-set and Q-set are set systems. Second, we define the distance of ordered pair of registers v_1, v_2 in the N-LegRing system as $\text{Dist}(v_1, v_2)= v_2$-$v_1$, if $v_1 \leq v_2$; or v_2+N-v_1, if $v_1 > v_2$. We choose an arbitrary R-quorum $\{u_1, u_2, ..., u_d\}=\{n, (n+1) \bmod N, (n+2) \bmod N,..., (n+d-1) \bmod N\}$. It is obvious that this R-quorum are d consecutive registers in the N-LegRing system, since any tow adjacent registers of R-quorum have $\text{Dist}(u_i, u_{i+1})=1$, $1 \leq i \leq d$-1. Now we choose another arbitrary Q-quorum $\{v_1, v_2,..., v_{k+1}\}=\{n, (n+d) \bmod N, (n+2d) \bmod N, ..., (n+kd) \bmod N\}$. The distance of any two adjacent registers of Q-quorum is $\text{Dist}(v_i, v_{i+1})=d$ $(1 \leq i \leq k)$ and $\text{Dist}(v_{k+1}, v_1) \leq d$. Since $\text{Dist}(v_i, v_{i+1})=d$ for any two adjacent registers v_i, v_{i+1} and $\text{Dist}(v_{k+1}, v_L) \leq d$ in Q-quorum, and $u_1, u_2,..., u_d$ are d consecutive registers, we can conclude that at least one register v_i in Q-quorum intersects with one register u_j in R-quorum, i.e. $v_i = u_j$, for some j $(1 \leq j \leq d)$. This satisfies property (II). Hence, the R-set and Q-set of N-LegRing system satisfy the properties of *Legion* structure.   □

4 Quorum-Based Approach

In the information service system QFIS, there are mainly four mechanism including registry, query, update, and deregistry for a single resource. The resource provider creates a resource and its metadata which describes the name, location, functions, and other properties at the same time. First, the local RS will assign a global unique resource *id* for it. After generating the resource global *id*, the local RS forwards the registry message to the RSs in the registry quorum.

The data of resource registry is completely distributed. When demanding services, the user issues a query with keywords to local RS. Upon receiving the query, the RS selects the query quorum and sends a query message to all the RSs in this quorum. When a RS receives a query, it searches registry database for the satisfied resource information and replies back. The user could obtain all resource information satisfied with the query conditions. If a user queries with resource *id*, then exact one resource information is responded.

4.1 Data structures in a RS

To accomplish the QFIS system, the RSs maintain some data structures and algorithms. In our design, the system should be initialized and the registry and query set table should be kept in each RS. The following items are necessary for a RS.

➤ *RS ID*: Each RS has its own unique registry server *id*.

➤ *N-LegRing* system: including *R*-set and *Q*-set. The construction of this system should be initialized and the set table should be kept in each RS before launching the registry mechanism.

➤ *Registry database*: a space for storing the metadata information of registered resources. Each entry has the format (*G_id*, *metadata*), where metadata is an XML file of small size and includes all the needed attributes-- name, location, time, status etc.

4.2 Registry

When a service provider creates a new resource, the first step is to register on the information service system and the owner of this resource is the service provider. Naturally, the metadata, the description document (XML file), of the resource should be provided. Basically, the registry process is separated into two stages. The first stage randomly generates a new resource number *r_id* and checks the other existed *r_ids* in local RS to acknowledge that this new *r_id* is unique. Meanwhile, each RS was assigned an identical prefix *id*. Then the global unique *G_id* for this resource is "RS's *id*" + "this newly generated *r_id*". Such method of generating *G_id* can guarantee that each *G_id* is globally unique. Meanwhile, the resources can be found by using the *G_ids*.

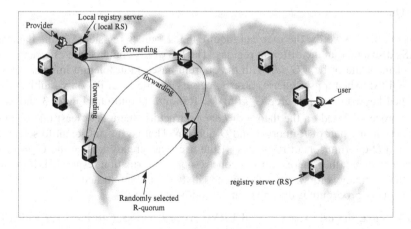

Fig. 2. The registry process -- local RS forwards REGISTRY (*G_id*, *metadata*) to all the RSs in the randomly selected *R*-quorum

After finishing the first registry stage, the registry process of local RS goes to the second stage and sends REGISTRY(G_id, *metadata*) messages to all the RSs in an *R*-quorum to enter the resource information into registry databases. Figure 2 shows the registry process.

The registry procedure is described in the following steps:

Step 1: The service provider sends the metadata of this resource to local RS and the RS generates a new random number r_no for it.

Step 2: The local RS compares this r_no with existed r_nos in registry database.

Step 3: If this r_no had existed , then discards it and randomly regenerate another one and goes step 2; else assign "the local RS's id" + "this newly generating r_no" as the global identification G_id of this resource; and appends the G_id to the metadata of this resource;

Step 4: The local RS forwards REGISTRY(G_id, *metadata*) to all the RSs in the randomly selected *R*-quorum.

Step 5: Upon receiving the REGISTRY(G_id, *metadata*), the RSs add the new information received in their caches and send the registry acknowledgement R_ACK messages back.

Step 6: If the local RS does not receive all the R_ACK messages from all the RSs in the quorum during a given period of time, then it randomly selects another *R*-quorum and sends REGISTRY(G_id, *metadata*) to all the RSs in this quorum and goes to step 5.

Step 7: After receiving all the R_ACK messages, the local RS sends R_DONE message to all the RSs in the *R*-quorum, stores the resource information FORWARD(G_id, *R*-quorum) in its database and replies R_COMPLETED (G_id) back to the resource provider.

Step 8: Upon receiving the R_DONE message, the RSs save the cached REGISTRY (G_id, *metadata*) information into their registry databases.

4.3 Query

By using the keywords, the user can inquire the resources registered in the databases of RSs distributed in the different regions. The keywords could be the different attributes of metadata or be a G_id. With the quorum-based fault-tolerant information service (QFIS), when a user queries a resource service, the local RS only multicasts the searched keywords or resource G_id to $\sqrt{N}$ RSs in a *Q*-quorum. Figure 3 shows the query process. Based on the theory of *Legion* structure, there is at least one common RS node in any pair of *R*-quorum and *Q*-quorum. That is, it's sufficient to search the RSs in a *Q*-quorum for all resources. If the user has already known the G_id of the queried resource, then there is exactly one resource information responded. If the user searches with keyword(s), many resources satisfied will be returned.

The query procedure is described in the following steps:

Step 1: First, the user sends the QUERY(*keyword*) message to local RS which forwards the message to all the RSs in the randomly selected *Q*-quorum.

Step 2: Upon receiving the QUERY(*keyword*) message, the RS, which has copies of the queried information, returns all REPLY(G_id, *metadata*) messages back.

Step 3: When all the REPLY messages from all the RSs in the quorum are received, the local RS forwards these available information to the user.

Step 4: If the local RS does not receive all the REPLY messages after a given period of time, then it randomly selects another Q-quorum, forwards the QUERY(*keyword*) message to all the RSs in this new quorum, and goes to step 2; Otherwise, the procedure stops.

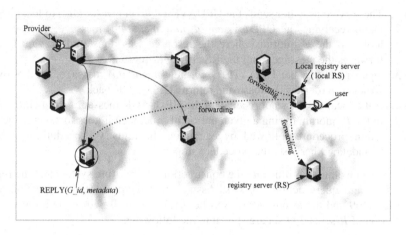

Fig. 3. The query process -- local RS forwards QUERY(*keyword*) to all the RSs in the randomly selected Q-quorum

4.4 Deregistry

When the resource provider would like to terminate the service, the procedure is invoked by the user to remove the resource information from the RSs. With the G_id, the following steps are performed.

Step 1: The service provider sends the DELETE(G_id) to local RS.

Step 2: Upon receiving the DELETE(G_id) message, the local RS looks up the R_quorum where the resource was registered previously and forwards the message to all the RSs in the R-quorum.

Step 3: Upon receiving the DELETE(G_id) message, the RS deletes the information registered by the provider previously and returns DEL_ACK back.

Step 4: If the local RS does not receive all the DEL_ACK messages from all the RSs in the R-quorum during a given period of time, then it sends the DELETE(G_id) message to the deletion pool of itself, which continues to handle the deletion processes until the crashed RSs recover their faults and call back.

Step 5: After receiving all the DEL_ACK messages from all the RSs in the R_quorum or transferring the DELETE(G_id) messages to the deletion pool, the local RS terminates the deletion procedure.

4.5 Update

When any attributes of metadata of resource are changed, the provider invokes the update procedure through the local RS. All the RSs of the dedicated update quorum are notified to modify the metadata with new information. The dedicated update quorum is the same as the registry quorum (R-quorum) which is the quorum that the resource registered previously. The procedure of update is performed as follows.

Step 1: The service provider sends the UPDATE(G_id, *new metadata*) to local RS.
Step 2: Upon receiving the UPDATE(G_id, *new metadata*) message, the local RS looks up the R_quorum where the resource was registered previously and forwards the message to all the RSs in the R-quorum.
Step 3: Upon receiving the UPDATE(G_id, *new metadata*) message, the RS overwrites it in registry database and returns UPD_ACK back.
Step 4: If the local RS does not receive all the UPD_ACK messages from all the RSs in the R-quorum during a given period of time, then it goes to execute the deletion procedure followed by executing the registry procedure with new metadata; Otherwise, the procedure stops.

We take an example to illustrate the construction of *Leg-Ring* system and the registry, update, and query actions of RSs. Assume that there are nine registry servers (RSs). Let $N=9$ and the *id* number of RSs be 0,1,2,......,8. Based on definition 3, the construction of R-set and Q-set are shown in the following.

R-set = {{0,1,2},{1,2,3},{2,3,4},{3,4,5},{4,5,6},{5,6,7},{6,7,8},{7,8,0},{8,0,1}}
Q-set = {{0,3,6},{1,4,7},{2,5,8},{3,6,0},{4,7,1},{5,8,2},{6,0,3},{7,1,4},{8,2,5}}

Obviously, every pair of R-quorum and Q-quorum contains at least one common element. When a provider wants to register a resource r_1, the local RS, for example, server 3, generates a G_id and forwards the REGISTRY(G_id, *metadata*) message to all the RSs, for example, servers 8, 0, and 1, of the R-quorum. Upon receiving the message, the RSs add the information in their caches and send the R_ACK back. If any RS, for example server 1, crashed, the local RS resends the REGISTRY(G_id, *metadata*) message to all the RSs, for example, servers 6, 7, and 8, of new randomly selected R-quorum. After receiving all the R_ACK messages, the local RS sends R_DONE and R_COMPLETED(G_id) messages to all the RSs in the R-quorum and the resource provider, respectively. Similarly, another provider could register a resource r_2 at servers 3, 4, and 5 of the R-quorum.

After a period of time, the provider invokes the update procedure through the local RS which forwards the UPDATE(G_id, *new metadata*) message to all the RSs, for example, servers 6, 7, and 8, in the R-quorum where the resource r_1 was registered previously. Upon receiving the UPDATE(G_id, *new metadata*) message, the RS overwrites it in registry database and returns UPD_ACK back. Hence, the servers 6, 7, and 8 have the newest registration information of resource r_1.

When a user wishes to get resource services, the user sends the QUERY(*keyword*) message to local RS which forwards the message to all the RSs, for example, servers 0, 3, and 6, in the randomly selected Q-quorum. If the keyword of query is included in the metadata of resources r_1 and r_2, then these registry information of resources should be inquired and delivered to the user. Therefore, through the intersected servers 6 and 3, the resource information of r_1 and r_2 could be retrieved, respectively.

Furthermore, assume that some of queried servers crashed, for example, servers 0 and 3, and the procedure requests other RSs, for example, servers 2, 5, and 8, in the randomly reselected Q-quorum for resource information. Therefore, through the intersected servers 8 and 5, the resource information of r_1 and r_2 could be retrieved, respectively.

5 Conclusion

Grid computing has becoming an important technology in many scientific fields needing huge computing work. For the dispersion of plentiful resources in the world, the information service of resources makes a challenging issue. Most of the related works design the architecture of information service as hierarchical levels. From the point of discovery view, hierarchical architecture can provide an effective method of discovery and appendage but it lacks the ability of fault tolerance. In this paper, we propose a distributed architecture for grid information service. Since the *Leg-Ring* system has the properties of symmetry, load balance and fault tolerance, our quorum-based information service provides absolutely distinct algorithms for resource registry, query, update and deregistry. In a region there is exactly one registry server (RS) selected to execute the information service. Every resource provider only sends the message to the local RS and then the local RS will complete the registry process. Based on the proposed mechanism and *Leg-Ring* system, the system for a resource service is effective enough, fault-tolerant, and load-balanced.

References

1. Huang, Z.C., Gu, L, Du, B., He, C.: Grid Resource Specification Language based on XML and its usage in Resource Registry Meta-Service. In: Proceedings of the 2004 IEEE International Conference on Service Computing (SCC'04), September (2004) 467-470
2. OASIS UDDI Specification TC: http://www.oasis-open.org/committees/tc_home. php? wg_abbrev =uddi-srec
3. Web Service Architecture: The W3C Web Service Architecture working group, public draft: http://www.w3.org/TR/2003/WD-ws-arch-20030808/, August (2003)
4. Tierney, B., Aydt, R. et al: A Grid Monitoring Architecture. In: The Global Grid Forum GWD-GP-16-2, January (2002)
5. Hawkeye: http://www.cs.wise.edu/condor/hawkeye
6. Singh, G., Bharathi, S. et al: A Metadata Catalog Service for Data Intensive Applications. SC2003, Nov. (2003)
7. Tuecke, S., Czajkowski, K., Foster, I. et al: Open Grid Services Infrastructure (OGSI) Version 1.0. Global Grid Forum Draft Recommendation, http://www-unix.gridforum.org/ mail_archive/ogsi-wg/2003/06/pdf00004.pdf (2003)
8. Foster, I., Kesselman, C., Nick, J., Tuecke, S.: The Physiology of the Grid: An Open Grid Services Architecture for Distributed Systems Integration. http://www.globus.org/research/ papers/ogsa. pdf, January (2002)
9. Globus Toolkit 3.0: http://www.globus.org/gt3

10. Yang, M.J., Yeh, Y.M., Cheng, Y.M.: Legion Structure for Quorum-Based Location Management in Mobile Computing. Journal of Information Science and Engineer, vol.20 (2004) 191-202
11. Zang, T., Jie, W., Hung, T., Lei, Z., Turner, S. J., Cai, W., Zhu, M., Katsinis, C.: An OGSI-compliant Grid Information Service-Its Architecture and Performance Study. High Performance Computing and Grid in Asia Pacific Region, 7th International Conference on (HPCAsia'04), July (2004) 63-71
12. Tuecke, S., Czajkowski, K., Foster, I., Frey, J. et al: Grid Service Specification. http://www. globus.org/ogsa
13. Chang, E., Roberts, R.: An improved algorithm for decentralized extrema-finding in circular configurations of processes. Communications of the ACM, vol.22(5), May (1979) 281-283
14. Lann, G. L.: Distributed systems-towards a formal approach. In: Bruce Gilchrist, editor, Information Processing 77; Proceedings of IFIP Congress, vol. 7, North-Holland, Amsterdam (1977) 155-160
15. Naor, M., Wool, A.: Access control and signatures via quorum secret sharing. IEEE Transactions on Parallel and Distributed Systems, vol. 9 (1998) 909-922

A Market-Oriented Model for Grid Service Management*

Huan Wang, Zhihui Du, Lei Wu, Suihui Zhu, and Erfan Shang

Department of Computer Science and Technology, Tsinghua University,
Beijing, 100084
Huan-wang03@mails.tsinghua.edu.cn

Abstract. Grid service management and trading is a complex undertaking as services are geographically distributed, heterogeneous and large-scale, owned by different organizations with their local policies. Each service provider needs flexible relationships between them, and each consumer joins Grid with the intention of getting its purchase requirements satisfied. To allow Grid to reduce the cost of e-business trading, to deal faster and to open up more new opportunities, a market-oriented architecture called GTM (Grid Trading Model) is proposed in order to establish a real-life Grid which provides a business mechanism for organizing users and services efficiently based on market economic rationale. GTM derives from an inherent similarity between typical networks and classical economic market structures based on Virtual Organization (VO) concept and the small-world theory. An emulated environment is presented to illustrate the model's economic feature, performance and cheap service trading cost.

1 Introduction

Grid provides an opportunity to integrate large numbers and various types of dynamic services owned by different individuals or organizations with their own policies in distributed environment [1]. Service management and trading in large-scale Grid is challenged due to Grid needs to organize users and services efficiently and let users find more trading opportunities, which is similar with the business problem in the real-life market. A market-oriented Grid environment can combine the advantages of traditional service providing systems, and integrate present network applications across distributed, heterogeneous, dynamic environments and communities, in order to organize services in various industries, facilitate service providers finding credible cooperation partners, establish efficient service trading platform between enterprises and consumers. How to operate business process in Grid based on service characteristic and the market economic rationale is the challenging problem which this paper tries to deal with.

The specific problem that underlies the market-oriented Grid is coordinated resource sharing and problem solving in dynamic, multi-institutional Virtual Organizations

---

* This paper is partly supported by National Natural Sciences Foundation of China (No.60503039), Beijing Natural Sciences Foundation(No.4042018) and China's National Fundamental Research 973 Program (No. 2004CB217903).

Y.-C. Chung and J.E. Moreira (Eds.): GPC 2006, LNCS 3947, pp. 137 – 146, 2006.

(VO) [2]. In real-life market economy, enterprises producing homologous products in the same industry form a "Product Group" [3]. In our market-oriented Grid model, Product Groups of different industries come to form corresponding industrial Virtual Organizations. Each VO in the model provides some distinct kinds of services in order to classify service provider and consumer groups by different service requirements and purchase interests.

To support service trading, The VO-based Grid model is focuses on market driven service management architecture, in which an essential base is the inherent symmetric relationship between typical networks architectures (including Client/Server, small-world and P2P) and classical economic market structures (including monopoly, oligopoly, monopolistic competition, perfect competition). By detailed description of network/market relationship, we expound that monopoly market fits in with Client/Server network; monopolistic competition market fits in with small-world network; and perfect competition market fits in with P2P network. Based on the most popular market type in e-business environment (monopolistic competition structure) and its corresponding network (small-world), we propose an architecture which can be employed in Grid market situation, and establish the Grid Trading Model (GTM).

2 Principles of Economics and the Small-World Phenomenon

2.1 Principles of Economics in GTM

Market structures are influenced by the number of sellers in the marketplace. With the number of enterprises increasing, the roles of product sellers, originally as price makers, are converted into price takers, and the product price is closer to its marginal cost [4]. A classification of markets is defined as the following four major types:

Monopoly: A single seller with complete control and the price maker over an industry in which each product has no close substitute, such as industries of water and CATV.**Oligopoly**: A market condition in which sellers are so few that the actions of any one of them will materially affect price and have a measurable impact on competitors, such as industries of tennis ball and base oil. **Monopolistic competition**: There are many sellers producing products that are close substitutes for one another. Sellers produce slightly differentiated products. It is popular in real-life economy; such as movies, books, PC games and music industries which are most popular contents of network market today. **Perfect Competition**: It is only an ideal market with many sellers and buyers in the market where sellers are price takers and price competition forces the price to marginal cost, such as industries of wheat and milk.

2.2 The Small-World Phenomenon

A social network exhibits the small-world phenomenon if, roughly speaking, any two individuals in the network are likely to be connected through a short sequence of intermediate acquaintances [5]. Recent work has suggested that the phenomenon is pervasive in a range of networks arising in nature and technology [6]. The GTM can be also demonstrated as a self-organized system based on small-world network.

Watts-Strogatz model [6] is one of the most refined models that were formulated in recent work. The edges of the model are divided into "local" and "long-range" contacts. Two characteristics distinguish the small-world networks: first, a small average path length, typical of random graphs (here 'path' means shortest node-to-node path); second, a large clustering coefficient C that is independent of network size. Suppose that a node v has k_v neighbors; then at most $k(k-1)/2$ edges can exist between them. Let C_v denote the fraction of the valid edges that actually exist. Define C as the average of C_v over all v [7]. C is less than 1 and it captures how many neighbors of a node are connected to each other.

3 Symmetric Relationship Between Market Structures and Typical Networks

[7] proposes a random rewiring procedure to interpolate between a regular ring lattice ($p=0$) and a random network ($p=1$), in which the edges of the network are divided into "local" and "long-range" contacts (Fig.1). It starts with a ring of N nodes, each connected to its k nearest neighbors by undirected edges. With probability p, it reconnects each edge to a node chosen uniformly at random over the entire ring, with duplicate edges forbidden and the process completes till each edge rewires.

[7] defines characteristic path length $L(p)$ and clustering coefficient $C(p)$ for the family of randomly rewiring graphs. When $L(p)$ is almost as small as $L(1)$ yet $C(p)$ remains almost constant at its value for the regular lattice and $C(p)>>C(1)$, the graph situation transform to the small-world.

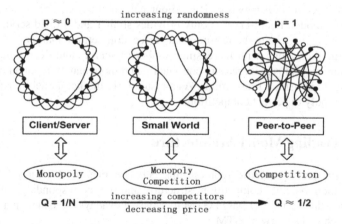

Fig. 1. Symmetric relationships between market structures and typical networks

With p increasing from 0 to 1, more and more nodes provide long-range edges. We define that the probability of one node being a server (white node in Fig.1) is $Q=(1-(P_k^k/P_{n-1}^k))\cdot p\cdot(1-p/2)$, i.e. one node that initiated a long-range edge has the probability of $(1-p/2)$ become a server which represents an enterprise in Grid market. Others are clients (black node in Fig.1) which represent consumers. Along with Q's increasing, different forms of network and market structures are homologous transformation.

Monopoly Vs C/S: When $p \approx 0$ and $Q=1/N$, only one node initiates a long-range edge which become the unique server, and the graph state is a typical Client/Server network. The single server who is a monopolist in its industry; the clients who have edges to the server become real consumers; other clients are only latent consumers still outside the market.

Monopolistic competition Vs small-world: When p is small (about $0.001<p<0.1$ in Fig.1), $p(1- p/2) \approx p$ and $Q \approx p$, some nodes become servers, and the graph state is transformed to the small world network which we will use in GTM. The nodes close to the servers cluster into sub graphs which connect with each other by long-range edges. Each sub graph represents a distinct industry's consumer group. Each server is an enterprise in this industry. If a client has no edge to any server, it doesn't enter the market yet. Some servers monopolize several industries together and compete against each other when they are so near that they have a large size of client intersection. When a server has no or few intersection with other servers, it means this server monopolize one industry alone. One or some enterprises monopolize some kind of services in their sub graphs, and they compete for the same industry's consumers. That is a typical monopolistic competition structure.

Perfect Competition Vs Peer-to-Peer: When p is close to 1, $(1-p/2) \approx 1/2$ and $Q \approx 1/2$, long-range edges are all over the graph; completely random graph is homologous with a Peer-to-Peer network in which each node may be a server. This situation accords with current P2P network in that free riders are ubiquity and demanders are unequally the suppliers of files in P2P networks [8]. About half of the nodes are designed to be servers in the model. Each server is only provides similar and limited services and no peer is larruping, which are the features of a perfect competition market.

In Grid market, along with increasing number of servers and decreasing services price, consumer surplus is increasing continually and more and more latent consumers will participate in market transactions. As a result, Grid market model transform from perfect monopoly to perfect competition.

4   Grid Trading Model Architecture

Based on [9] and symmetric relationships between market structures and typical networks, monopolistic competition structure and its corresponding small-world network are selected for VO-based GTM to satisfy nowadays e-business market. Fig.2 shows the schematic view of GTM.

GTM has four basic specifications:
```
Model ::= Service, VO, Relation, Edge
VO ::= VO server, General node
Relation ::= Client/Server, P2P, Complete connectivity
Edge ::= Local edge, Long-range
```

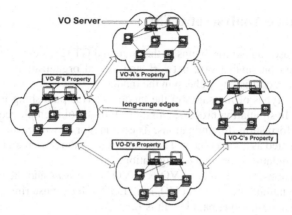

Fig. 2. The schematic view of Grid Trading Model

The model has four basic components: Service, VO, Relation and Edge. SV_i represents the ith type of service. VO is the basic unit of user and service management, represented by VO_i. VO contains VO server, General node. S represents the set of all the VO servers in GTM, S_i represents the set of all servers in VO_i, and S_{ij} represents server No.j in VO_i. Server S_{ij} is an enterprise which provides some types of services in Grid market. G represents a General node, or a consumer in GTM. G_{ik} represents General node No.k in VO_i. Relations between nodes inside VO involve Client/Server, P2P, and Complete connectivity. There are two kinds of edges between nodes: Local edge and Long-range. Local edge exists inside VO (between S_{ij} and S_{ik}, G_{ij} and G_{ik}, S_{ij} and G_{ik}, $j \neq k$); Long-range exists between different VOs (between S_{ij} and S_{km}, S_{ij} and G_{km}, G_{ij} and G_{km}, $i \neq k$).

VO_i is a node organization partitioned by service requirements and purchase interests. It provides $[SV_{im}, SV_{in}]$ types of services, where im and in are numerically close, and $im < in$, indicating that each VO provides some slightly differentiated types of services and VO_i is the product group of $[SV_{im}, SV_{in}]$. Enterprises establish servers actively by their profit needs, and accordingly organize an industry product group in a VO, and attract G to join their VOs. Generally, the number of servers in S_i and Long-range edges are both more than 1 in VO_i, not a single one in network models illustrated in Section 3. Some servers monopolize several kinds of services in their VO, and they compete in the same industry. That is a typical monopolistic competition feature. S is capable of running for a long time stably and reliably, so it dominates the topology of GTM. Complete connectivity among each VO's servers.

User's requirements and interests are seldom changed in a short term, for instance one user's most interested services are to download mp3, download movies and browse news at all times. So the model should not be stroked by user's behavior of frequently entering and exiting different VOs.

Three general e-business trading process modes in GTM are B2B, B2C and C2C, where B2B takes place between servers, B2C takes place between server and client, and C2C takes place between clients.

5 Performance Analysis of GTM

This section focuses on two problems in the emulated GTM system: (1) Proving GTM is certainly based on small-world network and virtual organization. (2) Proving the service transaction cost is fairly cheap in the model.

There are two types of messages in the model: service publishing information and service request. In simulation process, Gossip [10] protocol is employed here for those two kinds of information disseminations. The simulator is written in Java, and each node is implemented as a Java object. The simulation results presented in this paper are based on 100 simulations for each configuration.

In our simulations, the number of VO is n; VO_i's size is m_i and the total number of nodes is N. The number of server in VO_i is s_i. Let Model's clustering coefficient is C and the average node-to-node path length is L.

5.1 Small-World and VO Concept in GTM

5.1.1 Clustering Coefficient in GTM

$C_i(local)$ measures the clustering coefficient inside VO_i, calculating only local edges without long-range edges. Assume that all nodes had joined GTM before the first request was generated. The starting topology including two types of edges is constructed with two steps: *(I)* each node randomly selects k local nodes inside VO and l nodes in other VOs (long-range) to connect with. *(II)* adds edges between any two servers in local VOs to extend S_i to be a complete sub-graph; each server randomly selects k_l servers in other VOs to connect with. After connecting edges, the model graph is constructed by loosely connecting a set of almost complete sub-graphs, which can be pictured a typical Small World [7].

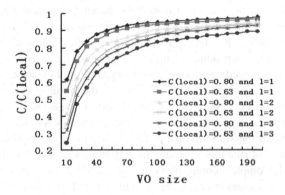

Fig. 3. Influence for $C/C(local)$ by long-range's emergence

A conclusion (1) can be drawn from the random node edge connection: the value of $C(local)$ is independent of the number of VO n and VO size m, and only decided by the value of k.

C is simulated in two situations to prove the model has a large clustering coefficient: 1) each VO has the same size m, the total number of nodes in the balanced distribution is $N=m*n$; 2) VO is divided into different sizes by uniform distribution and Gaussian distribution separately.

(1) Balanced Distribution of VO Size

$C/C(local)$ is simulated in $l=1,2,3$, and $k=0.8*m,0.5*m$ separately, described in Fig.3. Two large numbers of $C(local)$ with the value of 0.8 and 0.63 respectively are created according to different values of k. Long-range edge's emergence makes $C/C(local)$ decrease because long-range edges bring local nodes new neighbors, whereas the graph connectivity with new ones is looser. The simulation results suggest that it will influence the value of $C/C(local)$ when l is larger. When $l=3$ and VO size is 100, $C/C(local)$ drops to 81%. Fig.3 also reveals that influence of long-range edge's emergence for $C/C(local)$ falls by the increasing of VO's size. When VO's size is larger than 50 nodes and $l=1$, $C/C(local)>90\%$. So long-range edge brings small effect to C when VO is in rational sizes.

(2) Unbalanced Distribution of VO Size

Firstly, Gaussian distribution is adopted. Let $l=1$, $k=0.8*m$ and $n=100$. Suppose the network model is divided into 9 kinds of VOs ranging from 10 to 90, spacing out 10 nodes apart. The total number of nodes is about 5000. In Gaussian distribution, σ is from 0.1 to 1 and $\mu=0$, the clustering coefficient is named C_g. Most VOs' sizes are close to 50. When $C=0.677$, $m=50$, $n=100$ and $N=m*n=5000$. And C_g only decreases less than 10% with C. Similar result is gained from uniform distribution experiment. There are 10 sizes of VOs from 10 to 100 by 10 nodes apart, so $N=5500$, and the clustering coefficient is 93.4% of C.

Due to the small influence on $C/C(local)$ by long-range edge's emergence, after initialization of graph's two types of edges, regardless of the distribution type of VO size, the entire model's clustering coefficient C can follows large $C(local)$ inside VO so long as each node has enough local neighbors.

5.1.2   Short Average Node-to-Node Path Length

This model also has short average node-to-node path length L. L is calculated by Dijkstra arithmetic. L is simulated with VO sizes changing between 100 and 4000, shown in Fig.4. Simulation result reveals that after adding *(I) and (II)* edge, L is very small. L in larger scale isn't simulated, because Dijkstra arithmetic is not the practically used path length calculation method in GTM, which is detailed in next section.

Each node in the model holds a great deal of VO local information (local edges) and some other VOs' information (long-range). Each node has lots of local information to

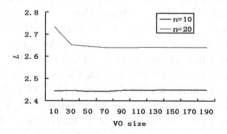

Fig. 4. The average node-to-node path length L in balanced distribution of VO size

make large C and short L. The emulated model for GTM is thus based on small world network and virtual organization.

5.2   Cheap Service Transaction cost

Transaction cost includes three main sorts: search and information costs, bargaining and decision costs, and policing and enforcement costs [4]. GTM is focus on solving the search and information costs of finding trading partners. For L is short in the model, one node can reach any other node through a small hops. So one search request will be fed back quickly in the model, and small L brings low service transaction cost.

Table 1. Relationship of $L(local)$ and $C(local)$

VO size	C(local)	L(local)	C(local)	L(local)	C(local)	L(local)
100	0.804	1.195	0.695	1.303	0.556	1.444
200	0.802	1.198	0.700	1.299	0.552	1.447
300	0.799	1.201	0.697	1.302	0.545	1.451

According to the local edge connection mode and conclusion (1), conclusion (2) is drawn as following.

$$C(local) + L(local) = 2 \qquad \text{conclusion (2)}$$

$L(local)$ measures average path length among nodes inside local VO. Conclusion (2) shows that large $C(local)$ is corresponding to the small $L(local)$, and is tenable when $k*N > \sqrt{N}$ at least. Table 1 also indicates that $L(local)$ and $C(local)$ are both independent of VO size.

The connection mode of *(II)* edge forms a set of complete sub-graphs connected by some long-range edges. Regarding each VO as one node, and long-range edges among servers is corresponding to local edge inside a VO; the connection mode of *(II)* edge is almost the same with a single VO. So the relationship among different VOs' servers obey conclusion (2) too.

Using Dijkstra arithmetic, with the number of VO n increasing, transaction cost is more and more expensive along with L's increasing continuously. In the model's trading process, including B2B, B2C and C2C, conclusion (2) is used practically to assure stably low transaction cost. This is because GTM distinguishes General node and VO server so that local information inside VO is able to disseminate efficiently abroad through long-range edges among servers. The clustering coefficient of edges connecting servers in different VOs is called $C(VO)$.

In B2B process, distance among local servers in same VO is 1. The model assumes that the shortest trading distance between any two enterprises is $(2-C(VO)+1)$ at most. Adding 1 is for dissemination among servers inside VO. In B2C process, client sends service request to local server directly, and then it is the same process with B2B. Therefore the model's maximum trading distance is $(2-C(VO)+1+1)$. In C2C process, the distance of service request disseminating in local VO_i is $(2-C_i(local))$. If the destination service provider is not in VO_i, local servers use $(2-C(VO))$ hops to send message to any other VO's server. In the destination VO_j, request also disseminates $(2-C_j(local))$ hops to any VO's node. That is to say, the appearance of VO server makes the average node-to-node path length in the graph of the model to be $(2 - C_i(local) + 2 - C(VO) + 2 - C_j(local))$, which is independent of the model size.

This conclusion brings cheap search and information costs, so it controls the Grid transaction costs efficiently.

6 Related Work

This architecture can be associated with super-peer [11]. The differences of the two systems are: each super-peer is a complete proxy of its clients who submit queries to their super-peer and receive results from it, and this query mode only takes place in GTM's B2C process. In GTM each client has its own long-range edges and many local edges, so each node has the ability of forwarding requests outside local organization.

Some present search protocols [12],[13] can be applied to GTM system, as the use of GTM and the choice of those are orthogonal issues so long as enterprises and consumers obey service and user organization policy of GTM. Market-based computational and resource trading system designs including some useful market models, which can also be employed seamlessly inside VO domain of GTM, which have been proposed in [14].

A few other systems such as GRACE [15] and JaWS [16] have built up market-oriented environments. However, they just try to solve idle computer resources reusing problems by renting computational power, storage, or special services, which is a different aspect of Grid economy problem from ours.

7 Conclusions and Future Work

GTM derives from an inherent similarity between typical networks and classical economic market structure. It is simulated based on graph model [7]. We expound that GTM may also turn out to be a useful model for "real-life economics".

GTM is a hybrid system which integrates C/S and P2P structure (P2P relation is among VOs; C/S and P2P are concurrence inside VO), so the architecture can adapt to different trading processes. The small-world feature of GTM brings system large clustering coefficient and short average node path length which are corresponding to the various close business relationships and cheap transaction cost. All of those system advantages make GTM fit in with monopolistic competition mode economy.

Some interesting directions of this work are still to come in future work. 1) Incentives for query forwarding: competition is a problem in P2P frameworks that rely on peers to forward queries, because a peer acting in its own best interests will not forward queries to potential competitors. 2) The tragedy of web services: If one company becomes dependent on many companies, it will be only a question of time until it is out-of-business because one of the companies that it depends on goes out-of-business. 3) GTM essentially thinks about service Qos, security and payment system, and considers preventing the illegal sharing of copyrighted files. 4) We will build a more practical Grid system to explore the integration of market economy and Grid. And more information search protocols will be applied to GTM to improve the trading efficiency.

References

1. Foster, C. Kesselman, J. Nick and S. Tuecke, "The Physiology of the Grid: An Open Grid Services Architecture for Distributed Systems Integration", Globus Project, 2002.
2. I. Foster, C. Kesselman and S. Tuecke, "The Anatomy of the Grid: Enabling Scalable Virtual Organizations.", International Journal of High Performance Computing Applications, 15 (3), 2001.
3. C.R. Mcconnell, S.L. Brue. Macroeconomics Principles, Problems, and Policies. McGraw-Hill Inc. New York, 2001.
4. G. Mankiw, "Principles of Economics", 3rd Edition, South Western College Publishing, USA, 2004
5. S. Milgram, "The small world problem.", Psychology Today, 22, 1967, pp. 61-67
6. J. Kleinberg, "The Small-World Phenomenon: An Algorithmic Perspective.", Tech. rep 99-1776, Cornell University, 1999
7. D. Watts, S. Strogatz, "Collective dynamics of 'small-world' networks.", Nature 393, 1998, pp. 440-442
8. E. Adar and B.A. Huberman, "Free Riding on Gnutella." Technical report, XeroxPARC, Aug, 2000
9. E.F. Shang and Z.H. Du, "Efficient grid service location mechanism based on virtual organization and the small-world theory", Journal of Computer Research and Development, Beijing, 40 (12), 2003, pp. 1743-1748.
10. A. Kermarrec, L. Massoulie, A. Ganesh, "Reliable probabilistic communication in large-scale information dissemination systems.", MSR-TR-2000-105, Microsoft Research Cambridge
11. B. Yang, H. Garcia-Molina, "Designing a Super-Peer Network", 19th International Conference on Data Engineering, Bangalore, India, March 2003, pp. 49-62
12. A. Crespo and H. Garcia-Molina, "Routing indices for peer-to-peer systems.", In Proc. of the 28th Intl. Conf. on Distributed Computing Systems, July 2002.
13. S. Ratnasamy, P. Francis, M. Handley, R. Karp, and S. Shenker, "A scalable content-addressable network.", In Proc. ACM SIGCOMM, August 2001.
14. M. Stonebraker, R. Devine, M. Kornacker, etc., "An Economic Paradigm for Query Processing and Data Migration in Mariposa", Proceedings of 3rd International Conference on Parallel and Distributed Information Systems, Austin, TX, USA, Sept. 1994.
15. R. Buyya, J. Giddy, D. Abramson, "An Economy Grid Architecture for Service-Oriented Grid Computing", 10th IEEE International Heterogeneous Computing Workshop (HCW 2001), In conjunction with IPDPS 2001, San Francisco, USA, April 2001.
16. S. Lalis and A. Karipidis, "An Open Market-Based Framework for Distributed Computing over the Internet", First IEEE/ACM International Workshop on Grid Computing (GRID 2000), Dec. 2000, Bangalore, India: Springer Verlag, Germany.

Pricing Web Services

Kevin Ho[1], John Sum[1,*], and Gilbert S. Young[2,**]

[1] Department of Information Management, Chung Shan Medical University,
Taichung, 402, Taiwan, ROC
`pfsum@csmu.edu.tw`
[2] Department of Computer Science, Cal State Poly Pomona CA, USA

Abstract. In this paper, a preliminary survey on the utilization of combinatorial auction as a mechanism for the allocation and the Gomory-Baumol price and the Shapley value as a pricing mechanism for web services is presented. It is shown that Gomory-Baumol price is in general unable to determine the prices for the individual service, even though the services can be optimally allocated. Except when the solution of the allocation problem is integral, the condition for which the Gomory-Baumol price could be determined is unclear. On the other hand, it is found that Shapley value could be applied to price individual service. By allowing the service providers setting reserve prices on their services, it can guarantee that the price is individual rational.

1 Introduction

Computing grid, *an infrastructure enabling the integrated, collaborative use of high-end computing systems, networks, data archives, and scientific instruments that multiple organization operate* (p.65 in [14]), has been one of the major research topics in recent years. While lots of works have been done on the technological advancement enabling the construction of such infrastructure [8, 14], only a few work have been done on the pricing of a resources being shared within the grid or P2P [7, 9, 10, 12, 17]. Unless the stakeholders (both services providers and consumers) of a grid are all from non-profit organizations, services should be priced and service consumers should pay for what they have been served. That should be the way for the sustainability of a grid.

A computational grid is essentially an online market for trading services (like web services) and resources (like Internet bandwidth). Providers publicize the services or resources they can supply, and then the consumers utilize the services or resources by paying service charge. As in a normal market, trading services could be accomplished by 4 different models. The simplest is that a buyer goes directly to a seller site to get the service and then pay for what he/she has got. Flea market is an example of this type. In the second to the forth type of market are shown in Figure 1.

---

* Corresponding author.
** The work is supported in part by US NSF Grant 0321333.

Y.-C. Chung and J.E. Moreira (Eds.): GPC 2006, LNCS 3947, pp. 147–156, 2006.

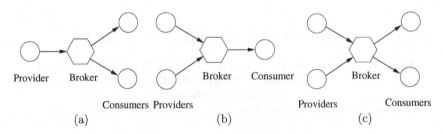

Fig. 1. Trading models: (a) Single supplier (provider) multiple buyers (consumers); (b) Multiple suppliers (providers) single buyer (consumer); (c) Multiple suppliers (providers) multiple buyers (consumers)

Amongst these four types of trading model, the complication lies in the fact that each consumer might want to buy products from more than one provider, and each provider might provide more than one product. In such case, the trading problem is essentially a combinatorial optimization problem. While the trading involves a large number of consumers/providers and the number of services for auction off is large, the problem is intractable (in the sense of computational complexity). Generally speaking, the fundamental problems to be solved in a trading market can be summarized as the following two problems.

Q1 Revenue maximization: How the services can be sold at their maximum market value ?

Q2 Services pricing: How the money being collected can effectively pay back to the suppliers[1] ?

Many studies have been reported in the literature [1, 2, 6, 11, 13] in regard to these problems. Basically, the solutions developed are problem depended. For many instance, problem Q2 have no need to be solved. In such case, trading problem is simply a revenue maximization problem.

For a market only one seller and multiple sellers (Figure 1a), like the FCC Spectrum auction or the airport landing slots allocation problems, one approach to solve problem could be accomplished by combinatorial auction [5]. As all the money collected will go directly to the government, the second problem Q2 does not exist. Similarly, for a market that consists of only one buyer and multiple suppliers bid for selling their services or product, Figure 1b, the second problem Q2 does not exist neither. When a market consists of more than one supplier, as shown in Figure 1c, the solution will no more be easy.

In this paper, our focus is on the market consists of multiple suppliers and multiple buyers. The difficulty of using combinatorial auction to price a web service will be presented. It is shown by example that combinatorial auction in general can allocate the resource to the buyers and get back the maximum revenue. Solution obtained by combinatorial auction does not help much in determining the price of

---

[1] In this paper, seller, supplier and provider are used interchangeably. All of them are referred to the one who provide services. Buyer and consumer are also used interchangeably. They are referred to the one who consume the services.

a service being sold. In [5], de Vries & Vohra have described how to use Gomory-Baumol integer price as a method to set the price of a commodity in combinatorial auction. Recently, in [16], Xia, Koehler and Whinston have also surveyed different approaches for setting the clearance price in combinatorial. In this short note, we would like to argue with example that computing Gomory-Baumol price is not easy. The so-called free good can be of non-zero price. Besides, we would like to add that Shapley value can in fact be a simple alternative pricing scheme for a combinatorial auction and show how Shapley value can be applied even in the case that the sellers have their own reserve prices.

2   Service Allocation by Combinatorial Auction

Considering the following auction problem with four bidders, $B1, B2, B3$ and $B4$, bidding for three commodities, A, B and C. Their bids and bid prices are depicted in the following table.

Bidders	A	B	C	Bid Price c_i
B_1	√	√	-	3K
B_2	-	√	√	3K
B_3	√	-	√	3K
B_4	√	√	√	4K

Solving the above allocation problem, one can formulate the problem as the following integer programming problem :

$$\text{Max. } z = 3x_1 + 3x_2 + 3x_3 + 4x_4$$
$$\text{s.t.} \begin{cases} x_1 + x_3 + x_4 \leq 1 \\ x_1 + x_2 + x_4 \leq 1 \\ x_2 + x_3 + x_4 \leq 1 \end{cases} \tag{1}$$
$$x_i \in \{0,1\} \ \forall i = 1, 2, 3, 4;$$

and then solve it by using Chavtal-Gomory Cutting Plane approach. By linear relaxing, i.e. setting the constraints on x_i be $0 \leq x_i \leq 1$, and adding slack varibles s_1, s_2 and s_3, the IP Problem (1) can be represented by the following tabular form.

x_1	x_2	x_3	x_4	s_1	s_2	s_3	z
3	3	3	4	0	0	0	0
1	0	1	1	1	0	0	1
1	1	0	1	0	1	0	1
0	1	1	1	0	0	1	1

Applying Dantzig's Simplex method [4], the optimal solution for the linear relaxed problem will be given by the following tabular form.

x_1	x_2	x_3	x_4	s_1	s_2	s_3	z
0	0	0	-0.5	-1.5	-1.5	-1.5	4.5
1	0	0	0.5	0.5	0.5	-0.5	0.5
0	1	0	0.5	-0.5	0.5	0.5	0.5
0	0	1	0.5	0.5	-0.5	0.5	0.5

The optimal z is 4.5 and the solution for (x_1, x_2, x_3, x_4) will be $(0.5, 0.5, 0.5, 0)$.

Since the table consists of non-integer elements, the following artificial constraint (considering the second row only) is added to the original problem.

$$0.5x_4 + 0.5s_1 + 0.5s_2 + 0.5s_3 \geq 0.5. \tag{2}$$

It can be re-written by adding a slack variable, $s_4 : 0.5x_4 + 0.5s_1 + 0.5s_2 + 0.5s_3 - s_4 = 0.5$. Again, applying Dantzig's Simplex method, the optimal solution of this new problem can be given by the following tabular form.

x_1	x_2	x_3	x_4	s_1	s_2	s_3	s_4	z
0	0	0	0	-1	-1	-1	-1	4
1	0	0	0	0	0	-1	1	0
0	1	0	0	-1	0	0	1	0
0	0	1	0	0	-1	0	1	0
0	0	0	1	1	1	1	-2	1

The optimal z is 4 and the solution for (x_1, x_2, x_3, x_4) will be $(0, 0, 0, 1)$. Since all the elements in the tabular form are integers, this is the optimal solution for the IP Problem (1).

That is to say, the auctioneer will allocate all the commodities A, B and C to bidder B_4 and get the optimal profit 4. Now it comes to another problem. Suppose commodities A, B and C are from three different suppliers. The auctioneer will need to impute the values of these three commodities and then pay back the amount to each supplier.

3   Gomory-Baumol Price

Ralph E. Gomory & William J. Baumol have suggested an algorithm for such imputation. First, the artificial constraint, Equation (2), is re-written by writing s_1, s_2 and s_3 in terms of x_1, x_2, x_3 and x_4, i.e.

$$0.5x_4 + 0.5(1 - x_1 - x_3 - x_4)$$
$$+0.5(1 - x_1 - x_2 - x_4)$$
$$+0.5(1 - x_2 - x_3 - x_4) \geq 0.5$$
$$x_1 + x_2 + x_3 + x_4 \leq 1. \tag{3}$$

Second, adding this artificial constraint to the Problem (1) and treating it as an artificial goods, the prices for A, B, C and this artificial goods can be obtained by solution the following constraint minimization problem.

$$\text{Min. } w = \pi_1 + \pi_2 + \pi_3 + \pi_4$$
$$\text{s.t.} \begin{cases} \pi_1 + \pi_2 + \pi_4 \geq 3 \\ \pi_2 + \pi_3 + \pi_4 \geq 3 \\ \pi_1 + \pi_3 + \pi_4 \geq 3 \\ \pi_1 + \pi_2 + \pi_3 + \pi_4 \geq 4 \end{cases} \tag{4}$$
$$\pi_i \geq 0; \ \forall i = 1, 2, 3, 4,$$

where π_1, π_2, π_3 and π_4 are the shadow prices for A, B, C and the artificial goods respectively. It is not difficult to solve the above problem by using Simplex method. The optimal w will be 4 and the solution for $(\pi_1, \pi_2, \pi_3, \pi_4)$ will be $(1, 1, 1, 1)$.

Since π_4 is the shadow price for an artificial goods, its value has to be re-distributed to the real goods, i.e. A, B and C. Gomory & Baumol suggested that the re-distribution can be accomplished by considering the relationship between the artificial constraint and the original constraints. Considering a general IP problem defined as follows:

$$\text{Max. } z = cx$$
$$\text{s.t. } \begin{cases} a_1 x \le b_1;\ a_2 x \le b_2;\ \cdots\ a_m x \le b_m \\ -x_1 \le 0;\ -x_2 \le 0;\ \cdots\ -x_n \le 0 \end{cases} \tag{5}$$

where x is a n-vector and $a_i = (a_{i1}, a_{i2}, \cdots, a_{in})$ corresponds to the coefficient vector in the ith constraint. Suppose there is only one artificial constraint being added for solving the problem and is denoted as follows : $a'x \le b'$. The essential idea of Gomory-Baumol algorithm is to find out the coefficients $\alpha_1, \alpha_2, \cdots, \alpha_{m+n}$ for the following equation:

$$a' = \alpha_1 a_1 + \cdots + \alpha_m a_m + \alpha_{m+1} e_1 + \cdots + \alpha_{m+n} e_n, \tag{6}$$

where e_k is an n-vector with the kth element -1 and other zeros. Let π_1, π_2 to π_{m+n+1} be the optimal prices evaluated based on solving the dual of the following problem.

$$\text{Max. } z = cx$$
$$\text{s.t. } \begin{cases} a_1 x \le b;\ a_2 x \le b_2;\ \cdots\ a_m x \le b_m \\ -x_1 \le 0;\ -x_2 \le 0;\ \cdots\ -x_n \le 0 \\ a'x \le b' \end{cases} \tag{7}$$

The price π_{m+n+1} can thus be distributed to the rest of the other goods by the following scheme:

$$\delta\pi_j = \begin{cases} \alpha_j \pi_{m+n+1} & \text{if } j = 1, \cdots, m+n \\ 0 & \text{if } j = m+n+1 \end{cases} \tag{8}$$

where $\delta\pi_j$ is the amount to be marked up for the unit price of the jth commodity. Therefore, the unit prices for the real goods (Alcaly and Klevorick in [1] called it Baumol-Gomory price), π'_js, can be defined as follows:

$$\pi'_j = \pi_j + \alpha_j \pi_{m+n+1} \tag{9}$$

for all $j = 1, \cdots, m+n$.

As noted by Alcaly and Klevorick in [1] and O'Neill et al in [11], Gomory-Baumol algorithm does not always can lead to a solution that the free good is of zero value. That is, $b_1\pi'_1 + \cdots b_m\pi'_m \neq z_{opt}$. Let us consider the auction problem (1) again. Its corresponding linear problem is given by the following problem.

$$\text{Max. } z = 3x_1 + 3x_2 + 3x_3 + 4x_4$$

$$\text{s.t.} \quad \begin{cases} x_1 + x_3 + x_4 \leq 1 \\ x_1 + x_2 + x_4 \leq 1 \\ x_2 + x_3 + x_4 \leq 1 \\ x_1 + x_2 + x_3 + x_4 \leq 1 \end{cases} \tag{10}$$

$$-x_i \leq 0 \; \forall i = 1, 2, 3, 4.$$

The dual problem will be given by

$$\text{Min. } w = \pi_1 + \pi_2 + \pi_3 + \pi_4 + 0\pi_5 + 0\pi_6 + 0\pi_7 + 0\pi_8$$

$$\text{s.t.} \quad \begin{cases} \pi_1 + \pi_2 + \pi_4 - \pi_5 \geq 3 \\ \pi_2 + \pi_3 + \pi_4 - \pi_6 \geq 3 \\ \pi_1 + \pi_3 + \pi_4 - \pi_7 \geq 3 \\ \pi_1 + \pi_2 + \pi_3 + \pi_4 - \pi_8 \geq 4. \end{cases} \tag{11}$$

Here π_5, π_6, π_7 and π_8 correspond to the unit price of the artificial goods in the constraints $-x_1 \leq 0$; $-x_2 \leq 0$; $-x_3 \leq 0$; $-x_4 \leq 0$. Solving the above problem using Simplex method, four solutions for π can be obtained.

π_1	π_2	π_3	π_4	π_5	π_6	π_7	π_8
1	1	1	1	0	0	0	0
0	1	1	2	0	1	0	0
1	0	1	2	0	0	1	0
1	1	0	2	1	0	0	0

In accordance with Gomory-Baumol approach, one possible coefficient vector of the artificial constraint is expressed as the following equation.

$$\begin{pmatrix} 1 \\ 1 \\ 1 \\ 1 \end{pmatrix}^T = 0.5 \begin{pmatrix} 1 \\ 0 \\ 1 \\ 1 \end{pmatrix}^T + 0.5 \begin{pmatrix} 1 \\ 1 \\ 0 \\ 1 \end{pmatrix}^T + 0.5 \begin{pmatrix} 0 \\ 1 \\ 1 \\ 1 \end{pmatrix}^T + 0.5 \begin{pmatrix} 0 \\ 0 \\ 0 \\ -1 \end{pmatrix}^T \tag{12}$$

The unit prices, π_1, π_2, π_3, π_5, π_6, π_7 and π_8.

π_1	π_2	π_3	π_4	π_5	π_6	π_7	π_8	$\sum_k \pi_k b_k$
1.5	1.5	1.5	0	0	0	0	0.5	4.5

Obviously the total amount that the sellers received is 4.5 which is larger than the revenue 4. An interesting point is about π_8. It is the shadow price of the constraint $-x_4 \leq 0$. It seems to be meaning something.

As a matter of fact, Equation (12) is only a possible linear expression for $(1, 1, 1, 1)$. There could be many alternatives. One example is

$$\begin{pmatrix} 1 \\ 1 \\ 1 \\ 1 \end{pmatrix}^T = \begin{pmatrix} 1 \\ 0 \\ 1 \\ 1 \end{pmatrix}^T + \begin{pmatrix} 1 \\ 1 \\ 0 \\ 1 \end{pmatrix}^T + \begin{pmatrix} -1 \\ 0 \\ 0 \\ 0 \end{pmatrix}^T + \begin{pmatrix} 0 \\ 0 \\ 0 \\ -1 \end{pmatrix}^T. \tag{13}$$

Similarly, there are four solution for the unit prices, $\pi_1, \pi_2, \pi_3, \pi_5, \pi_6, \pi_7$ and π_8.

π_1	π_2	π_3	π_4	π_5	π_6	π_7	π_8	$\sum_k \pi_k b_k$
2	2	1	0	1	0	0	1	5
1	2	1	0	1	1	0	1	4
2	1	1	0	1	0	1	1	4
2	2	0	0	2	0	0	1	4

Therefore, it comes up with a question about which linear expression used for imputation and which one is the most meaningful.

4 Shapley Value for Pricing

In 1953, Shapley proposed the Shapley value for the computation of the value of players in a cooperative game [15]. The definition of Shapley value is stated as follows. For a game with n players and the characteristic function for the coalition $S \subset N$ is denoted by $v(S)$, the value of the ith player, satisfies the conditions : (i) $v(\phi) = 0$, $v(S) \geq 0$ for all $S \subset N$ and (ii) $v(S \cup T) \geq v(S) + v(T)$ for any disjoint subsets $S, T \subset N$.

Condition (ii) is normally called superadditivity. The Shapley value is defined by the following equation.

$$\pi_i = \sum_{S \subset N \, i \in S} \frac{(n-s)!(s-1)!}{n!}(v(S) - v(S - \{i\})), \tag{14}$$

where s is the number of elements in the set S. Solution π implies the following properties: [P1] (Group rational) $\sum_{i=1}^{n} \pi_i = v(N)$, and [P2] (Individual rational) $\pi_i \geq v(\{i\})$ for all $i \in N$.

Bid prices are superadditive. Follow the same example and assume the revenue has been calculated by the cutting plane approach as before, the profit sharing problem can be formulated as a 3-persons game. In which $N = \{A, B, C\}$. The characteristic functions are thus be given by

$$v(ABC) = 4, v(AB) = 3, v(BC) = 3, v(AC) = 3,$$

$$v(A) = 0, v(B) = 0, v(C) = 0, v(\phi) = 0.$$

Here ϕ is the empty set. The reason why $v(A) = v(B) = v(C) = 0$ can be explained as no one interests in one single item. Single item values nothing. The Shapley value of commodity A, B and C can thus be computed. The price paid by the bidders and the profit gained by sellers could be defined as

$$\text{Price}(B_1) = 0 \quad \text{Price}(B_2) = 0 \quad \text{Price}(B_3) = 0 \quad \text{Price}(B_4) = 4$$
$$\text{Price}(A) = 4/3 \; \text{Price}(B) = 4/3 \; \text{Price}(C) = 4/3.$$

Bid prices are not superadditive. To apply the Shapley value equation, the characteristic function must be *superadditive*. But bid prices are usually not superadditive, like the example below.

Bidders	A	B	C	Bid Price
B_1	-	-	$\checkmark$	3K
B_2	$\checkmark$	$\checkmark$	$\checkmark$	4K

To apply Shapley value, one approach to define the characteristic function as the maximum revenues that can be gained instead of the bid prices. That is, for all $S \subset N$,

$$v(S) = \max\left\{c(S), \max_{T_S}\left\{\sum_{S' \subset T_S} v(S')\right\}\right\}, \tag{15}$$

where T is a partition of S and $c(S')$ is the bid price for subset $S' \subset S$. Therefore, the characteristic function could be defined as follows :

$$v(ABC) = 4, v(AB) = 0, v(BC) = 3, v(AC) = 3,$$

$$v(A) = 0, v(B) = 0, v(C) = 3, v(\phi) = 0.$$

Here $v(S)$ is the maximum revenue that can be gained whenever the subset S is allocated and ϕ is the empty set.

Ignoring the computational burden, the Shapley values for the commodities can thus be computed. Let π_1, π_2 and π_3 be the prices for commodities A, B and C respectively. $\pi_1 = 1/3$, $\pi_2 = 1/3$ and $\pi_3 = 10/3$.

Auction with reserve prices. As Shapley value is individually rational, it is able to modify the auction mechanism by allowing sellers to set a reserve price. In such case, the sellers are also treated as bidders. Suppose the reserve prices of the items are $1K, 2K$ and $2K$ respectively, the bid patterns can be tabulated as following table.

Bidders	A	B	C	Bid Price c_i
B_1	-	-	$\checkmark$	3K
B_2	$\checkmark$	$\checkmark$	$\checkmark$	4K
B_4	$\checkmark$	-	-	1K
B_5	-	$\checkmark$	-	2K
B_6	-	-	$\checkmark$	2K

Solving the above combinatorial auction, one will see that the commodities will eventually be allocated to B_4, B_5 and B_1. That is to say, commodities A and B are not sold. Only C will be sold to B_1 at a price of $3K$. To compute the Shapley values for these commodities after auction, one can tabulate the characteristic functions as follows :

$$v(ABC) = 6, v(AB) = 3, v(BC) = 5, v(AC) = 4,$$

$$v(A) = 1, v(B) = 2, v(C) = 3, v(\phi) = 0.$$

The corresponding Shapley values for A, B and C will be $1, 2$ and 3 respectively. As C is the only one being sold, seller C can get $3K$.

Remark on reserve price. It should be noted that the idea of reserve price cannot be extended by allowing sellers to form coalitions and set reserve price for the commodities they sell. It is because Shapley value cannot ensure the condition that

$$\sum_{i \in S} \pi_i \geq v(S).$$

This situation can be observed from a simple example. Suppose there are two bidders B_1 and B_2 bidding for commodities A, B and C.

Bidders	A	B	C	Bid Price c_i
B_1	√	√	√	6K
B_2	√	-	√	4K
B_3	√	√	-	7K
B_4	-	√	-	3K

Sellers A and B form a coalition and set the reserve price for $\{A, B\}$ to be $7K$. Seller B furthermore set the reserve price for B to be $3K$. The characteristic functions for the above auction will be given by

$$v(ABC) = 7, v(AB) = 7, v(BC) = 3, v(AC) = 4,$$

$$v(A) = 0, v(B) = 3, v(C) = 0, v(\phi) = 0.$$

Let π_1, π_2 and π_3 be the prices for commodities A, B and C respectively. $\pi_1 = 8/3$, $\pi_2 = 11/3$ and $\pi_3 = 2/3$. Obviously, $\pi_1 + \pi_2 = 19/3 < 7$. That means, sellers A and B have to pay the auctioneer $2/3$ even though their commodities have not been sold. It seems to be rather odd. Therefore, it is necessary to restrict the setting of reserve price in order to apply Shapley value. Each seller can only set the reserve price for his/her own commodity.

5   Conclusion

In this paper, two approaches for pricing web services, namely Gomory-Baumol price and Shapley value, have been presented, The incapability of determining Gomory-Baumol price for an web service has been shown by an example. In view of the limitation of using Gomory-Baumol pricing mechanism, we have suggested to use Shapley value in return. By slightly modifying the auction mechanism by allowing providers setting reserved prices, it can ensure that the price for a service is no less than the reserved price if the service can be sold successfully. Unfortunately, as the calculation of Shapley values is NP complete [3], Shapley value approach can only be suitable for a small size problem. Parallel algorithm for computing Shapley value and establishing rules of making a reserved price for each web service in a composited web services market seem to be a valuable future work for further investigation.

References

[1] R.E. Alcaly and A.K. Klevorick, A notes on the dual prices of integer programs, *Econometrica*, Vol.34, 206-214, 1966.

[2] S. Bikhchandani, S. de Vries, J. Schummer, and R.V. Vohra. Linear programming and Vickrey auctions *Mathematics of the Internet: E-Auction and Markets*, IMA Volumes in Mathematics and its Apllications Vol. 127, p.75-116, 2001.

[3] V. Conitzer and T. Sandholm, Complexity of determining nonemptiness of the core. *Proceedings IJCAI-03*, pp. 613-618, 2003

[4] G.B. Dantzig, *Linear Programming and Extensions*, Princeton University Press, 1963.

[5] S. de Vries and R. Vohra, Combinatorial auction: A survey, *INFORMS Journal of Computing*, Vol.15, 284-309, 2003.

[6] R.E. Gomory & W.J. Baumol, Integer programming and pricing, *Econometrica*, Vol.28, 512-550, 1960.

[7] D. Hausheer, N.C. Liebau, A. Mauthe, R. Steinmetz and B. Stiller, Token-based accounting and distributed pricing to introduce market mechanisms in a peer-to-peer file sharing scenario, *Proceedings of P2P'03*, 2003.

[8] M.N. Huhns and M.P. Singh, Service-oriented computing: Key concepts and principles, *IEEE Internet Computing*, Vol.9(1), 75-81, 2005.

[9] R. Jain, *Efficient Market Mechanisms and Simulation-based Learning for Multi-Agent Systems*, UC Berkeley EECS PhD Dissertation, Dec 2004.

[10] R. Jurca and B. Faltings, Reputation-based pricing of P2P services, *SIG-COMM'05*, August 22-26, 2005.

[11] R.P. O'Neill, P.M. Totkiewicz, B.F. Hobbs, Michael H. Rothkopf and William R. Stewart, Jr., Equlibrium prices in markets with nonconvexities, submitted to *American Economic Reivew*, 2001.

[12] J. Ostwald and V. Lesser, Combinatorial auctions for resource allocation in a distributed sensor network, UMass Computer Science Tecchnical Report 04-72, August 31, 2004.

[13] D.C. Parkes, J. Kalagnanam and M. Eso, Achieving budget-balance with Vickrey-based payment schemes in exchanges. *Proceedings IJCAI-01*, 2001.

[14] D.A. Reed, Grids, the TeraGrid and beyond, *IEEE Cpmputer*, 62-68, Jan. 2003.

[15] L.S. Shapley, A value of n-person games, *Contributions to the Theory of Games II*, 307-317, Princeton University Press, 1953.

[16] M. Xia, G.J. Koehler and A.B. Whinston, Pricing combinatorial auctions, *European Journal of Operational Research*, Vol. 154, 251-270, 2004.

[17] J. Sum, J. Wu and C.S. Leung, On profit density based greedy algorithm for a resource allocation problem in web services, to appear in *International Journal of Computers & Applications*.

A Performance Improvement of Web Service System Based on the Probability Distribution Characteristics

Il Seok Ko[1] and Yun Ji Na[2]

[1] School of E-Commerce, Chungbuk Provincial University, 40 Gumgu-ri, Okchon-eup,
Okchon-gun, Chungbuk 373-807, South Korea
isko@ctech.ac.kr
[2] School of Internet Software, Honam University, 59-1 Seobong-dong, Gwangsan-gu,
Gwangju 506-714, South Korea
yjna@honam.ac.kr

Abstract. A web caching technology, which analyzes and reflects the reference characteristics of users, is required to effectively operate an electronic commerce system, because the reference characteristics of web objects becomes a major factor in decreasing the performance of an electronic commerce system. Therefore, it is necessary to study the increase in the performance of web caching based on the probability distribution of the object reference characteristics in order to increase the performance of an electronic commerce system. This paper proposes a web caching method based on the probability distribution of the object reference.

Keywords: web object & web caching, probability distribution characteristics.

1 Introduction

Web caching can effectively deal with requirements of the user of an electronic commerce system, and improve the performance of Internet. The performance of web caching depends on the effective management of a limited storage scope of the web cache. In order to achieve this performance, studies on replacement methods to maintain the frequently used web objects in the storage scope of web cache have been largely conducted [4, 5]. A replacement method for web cache should reflect the characteristics of web objects. The user reference characteristics in an electronic commerce system can be summarized as follows [1, 2, 6].

The referenced web object has a reference locality according to the time and region. These reference characteristics can be varied according to the passage of time, and this will be a major factor decreasing the performance of the existing caching method.

- The user reference characteristics, such as users' age, level of skill in Internet usage, education level, and various other conditions, affect the reference characteristics.
- Types and characteristics of web services affect the reference characteristics of the user.

Y.-C. Chung and J.E. Moreira (Eds.): GPC 2006, LNCS 3947, pp. 157–164, 2006.
© Springer-Verlag Berlin Heidelberg 2006

- The variability of the reference characteristics increases the deviation of the object-hit ratio.
- The variability of the reference characteristics occur not periodically.

The change in the variable web object reference characteristics of the user of an electronic commerce decreases the performance of web caching, and that becomes a major factor decreasing the performance of an electronic commerce system. However, the existing web caching method fails to effectively reflect the characteristics of the user of an electronic commerce system. This is because the existing web caching related studies have been focused mainly on the improvement of the object-hit ratio and caching costs [2, 3, 7]. Therefore, studies in this field are required.

This study proposes a new web caching method based on the analysis of the reference probability distribution characteristics of the user of web service system. In addition, this study increases the performance of web caching through the analysis of the characteristics of the probability distribution of the reference characteristics and a structural approach for a caching system, rather than that of the study of caching itself, such as an object-hit ratio.

2 Related Studies

An effective cache algorithm is used to estimate the reference possibility for the object existing in the cache, and then stores objects, which have a high possibility of referencing the near future, in the storage scope of cache. There are two leading characteristics that affect the predisposition of the reference of web objects: temporal locality and reference popularity. A replacement algorithm should be decided by reflecting on the past record of the related object for these two characteristics.

① Temporal locality

Temporal locality means that a currently referenced object has a high possibility of being referenced. From the aspect of this temporal locality, most algorithms are used just before the reference time of objects. However, the LNC-R algorithm uses the past k_{th} reference time. This algorithm uses the LRU-K algorithm, which is a type of buffer caching method, to fit a caching method for heterogeneity objects.

② Reference popularity

The reference popularity means that an object, which has a large number of references, has a high possibility to be referenced. From the aspect of this reference popularity, certain algorithms use a number of object references. In addition to this, certain methods add an aging mechanism to protect against cache pollution.

③ Estimation of the reference possibility using a mixed method

The currently used algorithm estimates the reference possibility by considering both temporal locality and reference popularity. The LRV and MIX algorithms estimate the reference possibility by considering the prior reference time and reference numbers of objects. The past k_{th} reference time used in the LNC-R algorithm is a type of coupled method, which uses both temporal locality and reference popularity. In addition, there are some studies on the coupling method, which couples the reference popularity with the GD-SIZE algorithm based on the temporal locality. In the LUV algorithm, almost all records of the past reference are used to estimate the reference possibility of objects. The LUV algorithm is a type of generalized method of the LRFU algorithm, which is studied in buffer caching, to fit it to the characteristics of web cache.

These web caching related studies have only focused on the improvement of the performance of caching itself, and they don't reflect the probability distribution characteristics of the object reference characteristics for the user of web service system, which is the major focus of this study.

3 Proposed Method

3.1 Changes in Cache-Hit Ratio

Fig. 1 presents the change in cache-hit ratios acquired using a data smoothing method according to the change of the reference characteristics of the user of an electronic commerce system. The actual object-hit ration doesn't appear as a smoothen state as presented in Fig. 1, but it appears with undulations and outliers. It is necessary to conduct a preprocess using a certain smoothing process in order to present these data in a more smooth state as presented in Fig. 1. A smoothing process is a type of data purification that changes average data into smooth data by removing non-similarity from an original set. This study applies a smoothing method with bin means, which replaces data as a mean value of bins. As described in Chapter 1, there are many changes in the user of an electronic commerce system due to various factors. These changes also bring changes in cache-hit ratios as illustrated in Fig. 1.

Almost all the existing studies related to the web caching have focused on the improvement of the performance of caching methods through an increase in the object-hit ratio of y-axis. However, the objective of this study is to increase the caching capability by reducing the widths of $\Delta t1$, $\Delta t2$, $\Delta w1$, and $\Delta w2$, which are generated from the results as presented in Fig. 1. In order to achieve this objective, it is necessary to investigate the probability distribution characteristics of the object reference characteristics, and structural approach for a caching system rather than conduct an investigation of the caching itself, such as object-hit ratio.

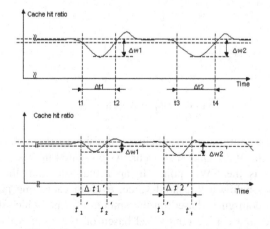

Fig. 1. Reference characteristics variation graph

As shown in Fig. 1, a rapid decrease in the object-hit ratio between t1 and t3 causes a decrease in the object-hit ratio below the mean value. In addition, a rapid increase in the object-hit ratio between t2 and t4 maintains the object-hit ratio as the mean value. These results can be caused largely by the characteristics of changes in the surfing type noted as follows.

▷ Changes in the user's preference
▷ Changes in the user's web surfing type
▷ Changes in the user: terminating the use of the existing user, starting the use of a new user.

In the graph, using a decrease in the width of $\Delta t1$ between t1 and t2, and in the width of $\Delta t2$ between t3 and t4, the performance of web caching can be increased. It is evident that the decrease in $\Delta t1 \rightarrow \Delta t1'$, $\Delta t2 \rightarrow \Delta t2'$, $\Delta w1 \rightarrow \Delta w1'$, and $\Delta w2 \rightarrow \Delta w2'$ increases the performance of web caching.

3.2 Cache Wear Out (CWO)

Definition 1 presents the definition of an OWS (Object Working Set). The item of OWS (i) is a set of web objects to maintain the object-hit ratio more than a threshold value in a time period (i) of cache.

<Definition 1> OWS (i)
OWS (i)=$\{O_1, O_2, ..., O_n\}$, where $O_1, O_2, ..., O_n$ is the objects to maintain the object-hit ratio more than a threshold value in a time period (i).

Fig. 2 presents the OWS in the time period of (i-1), (i), and (i+1).

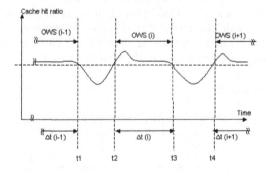

Fig. 2. Object Working Set

When the cache-hit ratio decreases below a threshold value, which configures an OWS, a CWO (Cache Wear Out) will occur. As presented in Fig. 3, the time period between t1 and t3 is the CWO point. In an actual situation, the cache-hit ratio frequently decreases below a threshold value, even in each time period. Thus, the CWO point can be configured based on the amount of time, which decreases below the threshold value, and can be configured based on the point where the object-hit ratio decreases a specific object-hit ratio based on the mean object-hit ratio for each time period. Moreover, this paper configures the CWO point using a probability distribution function of the object reference. This will be mentioned in Chapter 4.

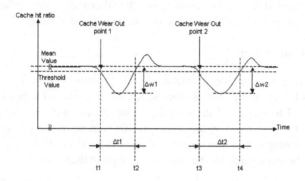

Fig. 3. Cache Wear Out

A correspondence cache empties a cache, and stores a new object when the CWO occurs. Then, the cache will be filled with the new cache until a new OWS, which reflects the reference characteristics of new objects, is configured in order to increase the object-hit ratio. In this case, there may occur a sudden decrease in the object-hit ratio due to the CWO. In order to compensate for this decrease, a double structured cache, which will be presented in the next chapter, will be used. In the proposed method, the CWO will occur based on the object reference distribution characteristics, and this method has an adaptability to changes in the object reference characteristics due to the configuration of a new OWS. Using this proposed method, it is possible to decrease the time to manage a cache, object replacement time, object search time, and verification time. In addition, it is possible to decrease the delay time and costs according to the increase in the cache-hit ratio.

3.3   Cache Structure

A sudden decrease in the cache-hit ratio before the cache is to be totally empted, and is fully filled again by new objects can be complemented using a double structured cache, as illustrated in Fig. 4. In a time period, which has a stable object-hit ratio, one

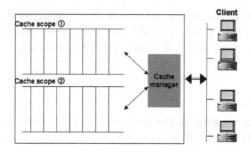

Fig. 4. Cache structure

side of the cache scope can be totally empted when CWO occurred, while two caches are used as a single scope. Then, the empted scope is filled with new incoming objects. When the empted scope is filled with new objects, and the cache-miss occurs, a replacement method can be applied as a not empted scope, or a single scope. After the passage of time, if the CWO occurs again, the other side of the cache scope can be totally empted, and then the cache operation can be performed again.

3.4 Mean-Life of Object

Web objects have a mean life in cache. Fig. 5 presents an object, which has four different items based on the size of objects, according to the reference characteristics of web objects. The section of item 1 can be configured by the object size less than 5K, item 2 can be configured by the object size from more than 5K to less than 100K, item 3 can be configured by the object size from more than 100K to less than 400K, and item 4 can be configured by the object size of more than 400K.

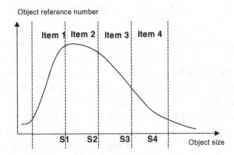

Fig. 5. Classification for object items

Four items (S1, S2, S3, S4) will be tested simultaneously. Cache-miss frequency in each division is as follows.

S1 = 75,123
S2 = 315,634
S3 = 67,473
S4 = 13,935

This is the number of object-misses for each object period until the object-hit ratio decrease below 36% from the total of 90% when the object-hit ratio was configured by 40%. The mean life parameter (θ) can be described as follows.

$$\hat{\theta} = \frac{T}{r}$$

T = Total test time accumulated on all items
r = Total number of cache-miss

We can get the mean-life through the value of chi-square (χ^2) distribution as follow.

$$P\left[\chi^2_{1-\alpha/2,2r} \leq \frac{2r\hat{\theta}}{\theta} \leq \chi^2_{\alpha/2,2r}\right] = 1-\alpha$$

We can get Mean-life as follow.

Mean-life = 472,165/4 = 118,041

Getting the 95% two-sided confidence interval on mean-life, we can get the proper test value of the chi-square as follow.

$$\hat{\theta} = \frac{\sum_{i=1}^{4} x_i}{4} = \frac{472,165}{4} = 118,041$$

$$\chi^2_{0.975,8} = 2.180$$

$$\chi^2_{0.025,8} = 17.535$$

$$13,464 \leq \theta \leq 108,295$$

Therefore, the mean life of objects for the experiment, which has a Chi-square distribution, presents as the minimum and maximum values of 13,464 and 108,295 times, respectively. This method can be generally used to obtain the mean life of products [15]. The section between the maximum value and the minimum value can be recognized as the mean life of products, and the product is to approach the fault state in this section. When a product reaches the fault state, it can be changed, or renewed. From the viewpoint of cache, the performance can be improved through this renewal using the CWO.

3.5 CWO Policy Using Aging Techniques

This paper uses the object reference distribution characteristics for the issue of when a cache wears out. The CWO adaptively occurs using an aging technique in the range of the minimum value$\leq \theta \leq$the maximum value (that is the mean life parameter) based on the mean life of objects. The CWO policy can be noted as follows.

Policy 1: Wear out based on the maximum value
In the case of frequently used objects, an object-miss will frequently occur. In this case, the time to approach the fault state will be shortened in each item section of the object. If the item approaches the fault state in cache, the CWO will frequently occur when a single CWO policy is used. Therefore, the CWO point can be decided using the maximum value used in this case.

Policy 2: Wear out based on the minimum value

In the case of rarely used objects, a cache-miss will slowly occur. In this case, the CWO can be generated using the minimum value in the mean life section.

4 Conclusions

If the proposed system applies in an electronic commerce system, which presents a fast change in the user reference characteristics, this system will satisfy the customer's loyalty and satisfaction through an increase in the user response speed. In addition, this will increase the competitiveness of an e-business company.

Studies on modeling techniques for the reference characteristics in a preprocessing, which smooth out the reference characteristics of web objects, will be continuously conducted. In addition, we would like to attempt to increase the performance of a web caching system through future studies on the reference characteristics using continuous log analysis materials.

References

[1] Il Seok Ko, Choon Seong Leem, "An Improvement of Response Time for Electronic Commerce System," Information Systems Frontiers, vol6, no4, pp.313-323, 2004.

[2] Il Seok Ko, Yun Ji Na, Choon Seong Leem, "ACASH: An Adaptive Web Caching Method with Heterogeneity of Web Object and Reference Characteristics," Journal of KISS: Information networking, vol.31, no.3, pp.305-313, 2004.

[3] Yun Ji Na, Il Seok Ko, Gun Heui Han, "An Adaptive Web Caching Method based on the Heterogeneity of Web Object," LNCS3758, pp.853-858, 2005.

[4] L. Rizzo, L. Vicisano, "Replacement Polices for a Proxy Cache," IEEE/ACM Trans. Networking, vol.8, no.2, pp.158-170, 2000.

[5] H. Bahn, S. Noh, S. L. Min, and K. Koh, "Efficient Replacement of Nonuniform Objects in Web Caches," IEEE Computer, vol.35, No.6, pp.65-73, June 2002.

[6] Jia Wang, "A Survey of Web Caching Schemes for the Internet," ACM Computer Communication Review, 29(5), pp.36□46, 1999.

[7] S. Williams, M. Abrams, C. R. Standridge, G. Abhulla and E. A. Fox, "Removal Policies in Network Caches for World Wide Web Objects," Proc. 1996 ACM Sigcomm, pp.293-304, 1996.

An Optimal Scheduling Algorithm for an Agent-Based Multicast Strategy on Irregular Networks

Yi-Fang Lin[1,2], Zhe-Hao Kang[1], Pangfeng Liu[1], and Jan-Jan Wu[2]

[1] Department of Computer Science and Information Engineering,
National Taiwan University, Taipei, Taiwan
[2] Institute of Information Science, Academia Sinica, Taipei, Taiwan

Abstract. This paper describes an agent-based approach for scheduling multiple multicast on switch-based networks with irregular topologies. Our approach assigns an agent to each subtree of switches such that the agents can exchange information efficiently and independently. The entire multicast problem is then recursively solved with each agent sending message to those switches that it is responsible for. In this way, communication is localized by the assignment of agents to subtrees. This idea can be easily generalized to multiple multicast since the order of message passing among agents can be interleaved for different multicasts. The key to the performance of this agent-based approach is the message-passing scheduling between agents and the destination processors. We propose an optimal scheduling algorithm, called *ForwardInSwitch* to solve this problem.

We conduct experiments to demonstrate the efficiency of our approach by comparing the results with SPCCO, a highly efficient multicast algorithm. We found that SPCCO suffers link contention when the number of simultaneous multiple multicast becomes large. On the other hand, our agent-based approach achieves better performance in large cases.

1 Introduction

Multicast/broadcast is commonly used in many scientific, industrial, and commercial applications. Distributed-memory parallel systems, such as cluster systems, require efficient implementations of multicast and broadcast operations in order to support various applications. In a multicast, the source node sends the same data to an arbitrary number of destination nodes. When multiple multicast operations occur at the same time, it is very likely that some messages may travel through the same network link at the same time and thus content with each other, if they are not scheduled properly.

Minimizing contention in collective communication has been extensively studied for systems with regular network topologies, such as mesh, torus and hypercubes [1, 2, 3, 4, 5, 6, 7]. Cluster networks, especially switch-based clusters, on the other hand, typically have irregular topologies to allow the construction of scalable systems with incremental expansion capability. These irregular topologies

Y.-C. Chung and J.E. Moreira (Eds.): GPC 2006, LNCS 3947, pp. 165–174, 2006.

lack many of the attractive mathematical properties of the regular topologies. This makes routing on such systems quite complicated. In the past few years, several routing algorithms have been proposed in the literature for irregular networks [8, 9, 10, 11]. These routing algorithms are quite complex and thus make implementation of contention-free multicast operations very difficult.

The goal of this paper is to develop efficient (multiple) multicast algorithms for irregular switch-based networks. In [12], Fan and King proposed an unicast-based implementation of single multicast operation based on *Eulerian trail* routing. In this paper, we consider the widely used, commercially available routing strategy called "up-down" routing. The best known results on multicast on irregular networks are the *Partial-Order-Chain*-based algorithms proposed by Kesavan and Panda [13]. The basic idea is to order the destination processors into a sequence, then apply a binomial tree-based multicast [14] on these destinations. The chain concatenation ordering (CCO) algorithm first constructs as many partial order chains (POC) as possible from the network. A partial order chain is a sequence of destinations such that we can apply a binomial multicast on it without any contention. The CCO algorithm then concatenates these POCs into sequence where a binomial multicast is performed [13]. The sequence consists of fragments of processor sequences in which messages within the same fragment can be sent independently, therefore congestion is reduced. Based on the CCO algorithm, the source-partitioned CCO (called SPCCO) performs multiple multicasts simultaneously. Each multicast produces its own sequence (consisting of POCs), and each resulting sequence is shifted until the source appears at the beginning of the sequence. By shifting these sequence, the communication is "interleaved" according to the source, and communication hot-spots are avoided. However, both CCO and SPCCO use the idea of POC to reduce contention. Within a single POC different messages do not interfere with one another as long as they are from different sections within a POC. However, this POC structure may not always be preserved since the later binomial multicast is not aware of it.

To solve this problem, in [15] we proposed an agent-based multicast algorithm, which avoids network contention by localizing and interleaving message passings in multicast. Our agent-based approach starts with a recursive multicast algorithm. An agent for a multicast is chosen for each subtree of the routing tree. An agent is responsible for relaying (forwarding) the multicast messages to all the destinations in that subtree. This task is divided into subtasks for each subtree, where they are performed recursively. We generalize this algorithm to multiple multicast by choosing a *primary agent* for each multicast. The primary agent are chosen from the subtrees of the root of the routing tree, and are properly interleaved so that the tasks are distributed evenly. The primary agents for different multicasts exchange messages and then use the multicast algorithm to forward messages.

The key to the performance of the agent-based multicast strategy is the scheduling of message forwarding between agents as well as between an agent and the destination processors within each subtree. In our previous work we use a rudimentary scheduling for this purpose. The focus of this paper is an optimal scheduling algorithm, called *ForwardInSwitch*, for message forwarding. We provide theoretical analysis for the optimality and time complexity of *ForwardInSwitch*. Our experimental results also demonstrate significant performance improvement of our multicast algorithms in comparison with the CCO and SPCCO multicast algorithms.

The rest of the paper is organized as follows: Section 2 formally describes the communication model in this paper. Section 3 first describes our multicast algorithm, and then describes the generalization to multiple multicast. Section 4 presents the *ForwardInSwitch* optimal scheduling algorithm. Section 5 reports our experimental results, and finally we conclude with Section 6.

2   Model

We now describe the up-down routing [9] used in our multiple multicast algorithm. The up-down routing mechanism first uses a breadth-first search to build a spanning tree T for the switch connection graph $G = (V, E)$. Since T is a spanning tree of G, E is partitioned into two subsets – T and $E - T$. Those edges in T are referred to as *tree edges* and those in $E - T$ as *cross edges* [13]. Since the tree is built with a BFS, the cross edges can only connect switches whose levels in the T differ by at most 1. A tree edge going up the tree, or a cross edge going from a processor with a higher processor id to a processor with a lower one, are referred to as *up links*. The communication channels going the other direction are *down links*. In up-down routing a message must travel all the up links before it travels any down links.

We assume that a switch can deliver multiple messages simultaneously from ports to ports, as long as the messages are delivered from different source and destination ports. This assumption is consistent with current routing hardware technology. As a result, congestion on the communication links becomes the major bottleneck.

We consider three cases where link contention can be avoided. In the first case, as shown in Figure 1(a), all source/destination processors are connected to the same switch A. In this case, there will be no contention since the messages travel through different paths within the switch. In the second case, as shown in Figure 1(b), both source processors reside on A. In this case, both can send

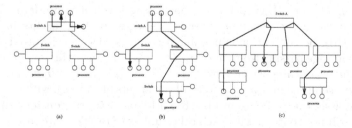

Fig. 1. Example cases that avoid contention on the inter-switch channels

messages to destinations in different subtrees of A simultaneously. Note that a destination node could be any processor in these two subtrees. In the third case two messages travel through four subtrees of switch A, as indicated in Figure 1 (c). If the two messages both go through switch A, there will be no link contention between them.

3   Agent-Based Algorithms

3.1   Single Multicast

For a given multicast message m and a switch v we will define two functions – an agent function $A(m, v)$ that returns a processor within the subtree rooted at v and will be responsible for relaying multicast message m, and a cost function $C(m, v)$ that estimates the total cost of sending m to all of its specified destinations within the subtree rooted at v.

We define these agent and cost functions recursively. Let $D(m, v)$ be the set of destination processors of message m that are connected to switch v. For a leaf v, $A(m, v)$ is defined to be an arbitrary destination processor in $D(m, v)$, and $C(m, v)$ is $\log |D(m, v)|$. For an internal node v, if $|D(m, v)| > 0$, we pick an arbitrary destination of m in $D(m, v)$ to be $A(m, v)$. Otherwise we consider all the children of v that m must be sent to, and set $A(m, v)$ to be the agent from these subtrees that has the highest cost. Formally, let $S(m, v)$ be the set of children of v that have destinations of m in their subtrees, then $A(m, v) = w$ such that $w \in S(v)$ and $C(m, w) \geq w'$ for all $w' \in S(v)$.   For the cost function part, if $|D(m, v)|$ is 0, the agents of tree nodes from $S(v)$ will first perform a multicast among themselves using a binomial multicast [14], then as soon as an agent a from $S(m, v)$ finishes receiving m, it recursively performs a multicast to all the destinations in the subtree where it is defined as the agent. The total communication cost is then defined as $C(m, v)$.

When $|D(m, v) > 0|$, the situation is more complicated since the agent of v can send m to other destinations in $D(m, v)$, or to the agents of $S(m, v)$. We apply a procedure *ForwardInSwitch* that determines the order for those in $D(m, v)$ and $S(m, v)$ to receive messages. The algorithm *ForwardInSwitch* takes $D(m, v)$ and $C(w, m)$ for all $w \in S(m, v)$ as inputs, then computes an optimal schedule and the total cost. The details of *ForwardInSwitch* will be given later.

When $|D(m, v)| > 0$, v does have some destination processors for message m and one of them is the agent of v. When the agent sends messages to those destinations in $D(m, v)$ (Figure 1 (a)), the messages will not interfere with each other. Also when the agent of v sends messages to those agents in $S(m, v)$ (Figure 1 (b)), no contention is possible if no cross edges are involved. In addition, the message passing from one category (Figure 1 (a)) will not contend with those in the other category (Figure 1 (b)). When $|D(m, v)| = 0$, we use a single multicast to send the messages among all the agents of $S(m, v)$, with one of them now being assigned as the agent of v. From Figure 1 (c) we conclude that these messages will not contend with each other unless cross edges are involved, since the agents of different subtrees in $S(m, v)$ will not be in the same subtree.

3.2   Multiple Multicast

Let r be the root of the up-down routing tree. The agent-based multiple multicast is carried out in three steps as described below. First for each message m we choose a *primary agent* among the agents of $S(m, r)$ - the set of subtrees of root r. Each source processor then sends its message to its primary agent. Second, the primary agent sends its message m to a destination d in $D(m, r)$ if any, and to the agents of $S(m, v)$. Finally, each agent a of $S(m, r)$ sends messages to its destinations by calling *RAM*, and a sends m to $D(m, r)$ with a binomial multicast.

4   ForwardInSwitch

We have two kinds of nodes in our *ForwardInSwitch* scheduling. The first is called *local nodes*, which are processors within a switch (or a local cluster). Local nodes can send and receive data among themselves. The second is *remote nodes*. Each remote node represents a remote agent that we need to send the message to. Once a remote agent receives the data from one of the local nodes, it will be responsible for distributing the data among the processors within that subtree.

Initially we have the agent local node as the source of the broadcast. The agent needs to send the data to all the other nodes (local and remote nodes) in the system. We define the *finishing time* as the time for all nodes in the system to receive the data, and, we would like to find a broadcast schedule with the minimum finishing time.

We assume that the local nodes are homogeneous, so that it takes one unit time for any local node to send a data to any other nodes. However, it takes very different amount of time for a remote node to receive a data, and this time is at least 1 time unit. To be more specific, when a local node sends data to another local node at time t, both local nodes can start sending data to another node at time $t + 1$. However, if a local node sends data to a remote node at time t, the local node can start sending data to another node at time $t + 1$, but the remote node will not complete its operation until $C(m, r)$, which will be determined recursively from bottom to the top of the routing tree. Recall that $C(m, r)$ is the cost for an agent r to send messages m to all the destination processors located in the subtree rooted at r. As a result we define the *finishing time* of a remote node r to be the $t + C(m, r)$, where t is the time the parent of r starts sending the data to r. The total time of *ForwardInSwitch* is then determined by the maximum of all nodes.

4.1   Scheduling Algorithm

Let n and m be the number of local and remote nodes. The remote nodes are $r_1, r_2, \ldots, r_m$ with costs $c_1, c_2, \ldots, c_m$. Without lose of generality we assume that $c_i \geq c_{i+1}$, for $1 \leq i \leq m - 1$. We use $l(n)$ to denote the level number of a node n. We first observe that the remote nodes should be scheduled according to non-decreasing order according to their costs. That is, there exists an optimal

ForwardInSwitch schedule in which $l(r_i) \leq l(r_{i+1})$, for $1 \leq i \leq m - 1$. If we assume that there exists an optimal *ForwardInSwitch* schedule in which $l(r_i) > l(r_{i+1})$ for some i, it is easy to see that by switching r_i and r_{i+1} the finishing time will not increase.

We use a binary search to determine the optimal *ForwardInSwitch* finishing time. If we could determine that, given a target finishing time T, whether all tree nodes can finish, we could use at most $O(\log C)$ round of testings to determine the optimal *ForwardInSwitch* finishing time, where C is maximum possible finish time. As a result, the key point of our algorithm is to determine, given a time constraint T, whether all nodes can finish in time.

We divide the remote nodes into two groups – *critical* and *non-critical*. A remote node r_i is critical at time t if $t + c_i$ is at least T, where T is the target finishing time constraint. If a remote node is critical, it should be scheduled immediately otherwise it will miss the deadline T. If the node is non-critical, then it can wait.

We now describe our testing algorithm which determines whether it is possible to obtain a *ForwardInSwitch* scheduling within time T. At every time step, all the local nodes that have already received the message, select the destinations according to the following priority. (1) critical remote nodes, (2) local nodes, (3) non-critical remote nodes.

Theorem 1. *There exists an optimal* ForwardInSwitch *schedule that obeys the priority.*

Proof. Since a critical node must be scheduled immediate to avoid missing its deadline, it has the highest priority. We only need to show that there exists an optimal *ForwardInSwitch* schedule that will schedule non-critical remote nodes only when there is *no* local node to send messages to.

We assume that there is an optimal schedule in which a non-critical remote node r is scheduled at time t and a local node b is scheduled at a later time $t' > t$. Let a be the local node that sends data to r in the optimal schedule. Now we will do the following changes. We will make a to send data to b instead of r at time t, and make b to send data to r at time $t+1$, then make b to send data to c at time $t+2$, where c is the node b sends data to at time $t' + 1$ in the optimal schedule. Since r is not critical at time t, delaying it to $t + 1$ will not miss the deadline T. The subtree rooted at c started at time $t' + 1$ in the original optimal schedule, and now starts at time $t + 2$. Since that $t' > t$, or $t' + 1 \geq t + 2$. The subtree of c will not be delayed either. ■

We use this checking algorithm to verify whether a finishing time T is feasible. From Theorem 1 we know that if there exists an optimal schedule for *ForwardInSwitch*, the checking algorithm will find it. Now with a binary search on T, we can easily determine the optimal T, hence the optimal *ForwardInSwitch* schedule. It is easy to see that the finish time will not be more than $n + \sum_{i=1}^{m} c_i$, so at most $O(\log(n + C))$ rounds of checking, where C is the summation of costs from remote nodes, suffice to find the optimal finish time.

5   Simulation Experiments and Results

In this section, we present results of simulation experiments to compare the algorithms proposed in Section 3 and the two order-chain-based algorithms proposed in prior works (CCO, SPCCO).

We developed a C++, discrete event-based simulator for our experiments. The simulator can model wormhole routing switches with arbitrary network topologies. We chose system parameters as follows. Communication start-up time was 5.0 microseconds, link transmission time was 10.5 nanoseconds, and routing delay at switch was 200 nanoseconds. The default buffer size at each port was assumed to be 1 flit. The default numbers of input ports and output ports were assumed to be 16. The network topologies were generated randomly. For each data point, the multicast performance was averaged over 100 different network topologies.

For all experiments, we assumed a default system configuration of a 512-processor system interconnected by 64 sixteen-port switches in an irregular topology. 50% of the ports on a switch are connected to processors, and the other 50% of the ports are connected to other switches. Links were not allowed between ports of the same switch. A random number generator was used to decide the port and switch or the processing node to which a given switch port should be connected to.

For our study, we varied each of the following parameters one at a time: the message length (NBM), the number of destinations in each multicast (ND), the number of simultaneous multicast operations (NM), the number of switches (NS), and the number of ports on a switch (HP). Since message length, number of multicast operations, and system size varied in our experiments, instead of using latency as the measurement of performance, we use *throughput*, which is defined by M/T, where M is the total length of the messages and T is the parallel completion time of the (multiple)multicast operation.

Effect of Number of Multicast Operations. First we examined the effect of variation in the number of multicast operations on the performance of the proposed algorithms. Other parameters were assumed to be as follows: number of switches $NS = 64$ (and thus 512 processors), number of ports connected to processors $HP = 8, 12$, and number of destinations in each multicast $ND = 153, 204, 537, 716$. The destinations were generated randomly. For each data point, the multicast performance was averaged over 50 different sets of destinations.

As shown in Figure 2, when there are few (less then eight) multicast operations, ordered-chain-based algorithms perform better than our agent-based algorithms. This is because when the number of multicast operations is small, message contention is not significant and thus the importance of reducing number of communication stages outweighs that of reducing message contention. However, when the number of multicast operations increases, the impact of message contention becomes more important and therefore the benefit of agent-based optimization becomes more significant.

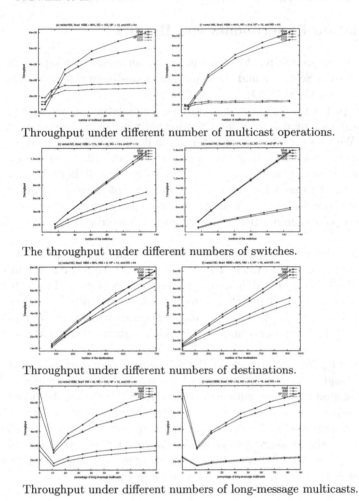

Throughput under different number of multicast operations.

The throughput under different numbers of switches.

Throughput under different numbers of destinations.

Throughput under different numbers of long-message multicasts.

Fig. 2. Simulation result comparison by varying different parameters

Effect of Number of Switches. We studied the scalability of the proposed algorithms on different systems sizes. We varied the number of switches from 16 to 128, with 50% of the ports connected to processors and the other 50% connected to switches. For each switch size, number of multicast operations NM=32. Number of multicast destinations ND=134, 179. For each data point, the multicast performance was averaged over 50 different sets of destinations.

As shown in Figure 2, the throughput of the agent-based algorithms, the throughput of the ordered-chain-based algorithms, and the improvement ratio of the agent-based algorithms over the ordered-chain-based algorithms all increase when the number of switches (and processors) increases. A possible reason is that when number of switches increases, the level of the up-down routing BFS tree also increase, hence the number of hops between the sender and the receiver of a cross-subtree message may increase. Longer path increases the potential of contention. Since our agent-based algorithms guarantee the path of each message be no more than 2 hops, they are scalable with respect to number of switches.

Effect of Number of Destinations. In this experiment, number of switches $NS = 64$ and number of ports connected to processors $HP = 8$. We chose two different numbers of multicast operations $NM = 4, 32$. We varied the number of destinations for each multicast from 100 to 900. Figure 2 shows the throughput of these algorithms. As we can see, the throughput of these algorithms increases when the number of destinations increases, and the improvement ratio of the agent-based algorithms over the ordered-chain-based algorithms also increases on size increase in destinations.

Effect of Message Length. We examined the effect of message length on the performance of proposed algorithms. We chose two message lengths, $128KB$ for short messages and $32MB$ for long messages, and varied the number of multicast operations with long messages (NBM). The source and destinations of a multicast were generated randomly. As shown in Figure 2, when the number of long-message multicast operations is small, the performance discrepancy between agent-based algorithms and the ordered-chain-based algorithms is small. The possible reason is that long messages are likely to increase the chance of contention, and when the number of long-message multicast operations is small, they may not be evenly distributed in the BFS tree and thus may cause hot-spots in communication.

6   Conclusion

This paper describes an agent-based approach for scheduling multiple multicast on switch-based networks. Our approach assigns an agent to each subtree of switches such that the agents can exchange information efficiently and independently. The entire multicast problem is recursively solved with each agent sending message to those switches that it is responsible for. Communication is localized by the assignment of agents to subtrees. In addition, the agent mechanism provides an easy mechanism in performing multiple multicasts simultaneously, with very low chances of network contention.

We compare the results with SPCCO [13] and found that SPCCO, a highly efficient multicast algorithm based on *Partial Ordered Chains*, incurs high contention in large cases. Our agent-based approach minimizes contention by properly interleaving multiple multicast and optimally scheduling message passings between agents and destination processors to avoid hot spots.

References

1. Dally, W.: Deadlock-free message routing in multiprocessor interconnection networks. IEEE Trans. Comput. **C-36**(5) (1987) 547–553
2. Duato, J.: On the design of deadlock-free adaptive routing algorithms for multicomputers. In: Proceedings of Parallel Architectures and Languages Europe 91. (1991)

3. Duato, J.: A necessary and sufficient condition for deadlock-free adaptive routing in wormhole networks. In: Proceedings of the 1994 International Conference on Parallel Proceeding. (1994)
4. Glass, C., Ni, L.: The turn model for adaptive routing. J. ACM **41** (1994) 847–902
5. Gaughan, P.T., Yalamanchili, S.: Adaptive routing protocols for hypercube interconnection networks. IEEE Computer **26**(5) (1993) 12–23
6. Gravano, G., Pifarre, G.D., Berman, P.E., Sanz, J.L.C.: Adaptive deadlock- and livelock-free routing with all minimal paths in torus networks. IEEE Trans. Parallel and Distributed Systems **5**(12) (1994) 1233–1251
7. P.K. McKinley, H. Xu, A.H.E., Ni, L.: Unicast-based multicast communication in wormhole-routed networks. IEEE Transactions on Parallel and Distributed Systems **5**(12) (1994) 1252–1265
8. Boden, N.J., Cohen, D., Felderman, R.F., Kulawik, A.E., Seitz, C.L., Seizovic, J., Su, W.: Myrinet - a gigabit per second local area network. IEEE Micro (1995) 29–36
9. et. al., M.D.S.: Autonet: A high-speed, self-configuring local area network using point-to-point links. Technical Report SRC research report 59, DEC (1990)
10. Horst, R.: Servernet deadlock avoidance and fractahedral topologies. In: Proceedings of the International Parallel Processing Symposium. (1996) 274–280
11. Qiao, W., Ni, L.: Adaptive routing in irregular networks using cut-through switches. In: Proceedings of the 1996 International Conference on Parallel Proceeding. (1996) I:52–60
12. Fan, K.P., King, C.T.: Efficient multicast on wormhole switch-based irregular networks of workstations and processor clusters. In: Proceedings of the Internationl Conference on High Performance Computing Systems. (1997)
13. Kesavan, R., Panda, D.K.: Efficient multicast on irregular switch-based cut-through networks with up-down routing. In: IEEE Trans. Parallel and Distributed Systems. Volume 12. (2001)
14. Leighton, F.T.: Introduction to Parallel Algorithms and Architectures: Arrays, Trees, hypercubes. (Morgan Kaufmann)
15. Lin, Y.F., Liu, P., Wu, J.J.: Efficient agent-based multicast on wormhole switch-based irregular networks. In: International Parallel and Distributed Processing Symposium. (2003)

Methods for Partitioning Data to Improve Parallel Execution Time for Sorting on Heterogeneous Clusters*

Christophe Cérin[1], Jean-Christophe Dubacq[1], and Jean-Louis Roch[2]

[1] Université de Paris Nord, LIPN, CNRS UMR 7030,
99 avenue J.B. Clément, 93430 Villetaneuse - France
{cerin, jcdubacq}@lipn.univ-paris13.fr
[2] ID-IMAG, CNRS - INRIA - INPG - UJF, Projet MOAIS,
51 Av. J. Kuntzmann, 38330 Montbonnot-Saint-Martin - France
Jean-Louis.Roch@imag.fr

Abstract. The aim of the paper is to introduce general techniques in order to optimize the parallel execution time of sorting on a distributed architectures with processors of various speeds. Such an application requires a partitioning step. For uniformly related processors (processors speeds are related by a constant factor), we develop a constant time technique for mastering processor load and execution time in an heterogeneous environment and also a technique to deal with unknown cost functions. For non uniformly related processors, we use a technique based on dynamic programming. Most of the time, the solutions are in $\mathcal{O}(p)$ (p is the number of processors), independent of the problem size n. Consequently, there is a small overhead regarding the problem we deal with but it is inherently limited by the knowing of time complexity of the portion of code following the partitioning.

Keywords: parallel in-core sorting, heterogeneous computing, complexity of parallel algorithms, data distribution.

The advent of parallel processing, in particular in the context of *cluster computing* is of particular interest with the available technology. A special class of *non homogeneous clusters* is under concern in the paper. We mean clusters whose global performances are correlated by a multiplicative factor. We depict a cluster by the mean of a vector set by the relative speeds of each processor.

In this paper we develop general techniques in order to control the execution time and the load balancing of each node for applications running in such environment. What is important over the application we consider here, is the meta-partitioning schema which is the key of success. All the approaches we develop can be considered as static methods: we predetermine the size of data that

---

* Work supported in part by France Agence Nationale de la Recherche under grants ANR-05-SSIA-0005-01 and ANR-05-SSIA-0005-05, programme ARA sécurité.

we have to exchange between processors in order to guarantee that all the processors end at the same time before we start the execution. So, this work can be considered in the domain of placement of tasks in an heterogeneous environment.

Many works have been done in data partitioning on heterogeneous platforms, among them Lastovetsky's and Reddy's work [1] that introduces a scheme for data partitioning when memory hierarchies from one CPU to another are different. There, the heterogeneity notion is related to the heterogeneity of the memory structure. Under the model, the speed of each processor is represented by a function of the size of the problem. The authors solve the problem of partitioning n elements over p heterogeneous processors in $\mathcal{O}(p^2 \times \log_2 n)$ time complexity.

Drozdowski and Lawenda in [2] propose two algorithms that gear the load chunk sizes to different communication and computation speeds of applications under the principle of divisible loads (computations which can be divided into parts of arbitrary sizes; for instance painting with black pixels a whole image). The problem is formalized as a linear problem solved either by branch and bound technique or a genetic algorithm. Despite the fact that the architecture is large enough (authors consider heterogeneous CPU and heterogeneous links), we can not apply it here because our problem cannot be expressed under the framework of 'divisible loads': in our case, we need to merge sorted chunks after the partitioning step and the cost is not a linear one... thus our new technique.

The organization of our paper is the following. In section 1 we introduce the problem of sorting in order to characterize the difficulties of partitioning data in an heterogeneous environment. The section motivates the work. In section 2 we recall our previous techniques and results. Section 3 is devoted to a new constant time solution and deals also with unknown cost functions. In section 4 we introduce a dynamic programming approach and we recall a technique that do not assume a model of processors related by constant integers but in this case the processor speed may be "unrelated". Section 5 is about experiments and section 6 concludes the paper.

1 Target Applications and Implementation on Heterogeneous Clusters

Assume that you have a set of p processors with different speeds, interconnected by a crossbar. Initially, the data is distributed across the p processors and according to the speeds: the slowest processor has less data than the quickest. This assumption describes the initial condition of the problem. In this section we detail our sorting application for which performance are directly related to this initial partitioning.

1.1 Parallel Sort

Efficient parallel sorting on clusters (see [3, 4, 5, 6, 7, 8] for the homogeneous case and [9, 10, 11, 12, 13] for the heterogeneous case) can be implemented in the following ways:

1. Each processor sorts locally its portion and picks up representative values in the sorted list. It sends the representative values to a dedicated node.
2. This node sorts what it receives from the processors and it keeps $p-1$ pivots; it distributes the pivots to all the processors.
3. Each processor partitions its sorted input according to the pivots and it sends $p-1$ portions to the others.
4. Each processor merges what it received from the others.

Note that the sorting in step 1 can be bypassed but in this case the last step is a sort not a merge. Moreover note that there is only one communication step: the representative values can be selected by sampling few candidates at a cost much lower than the exchange of values. In other words, when a value moves, it goes to the final destination node in one step.

2 Previous Results and Parallel Execution Time

Consider the simple problem of local sorting, such as presented in [10] (and our previous comments). The sizes n_i of data chunks on each node is assumed to be proportional to the speed of processors.

Let us now examine the impact on the parallel execution time of sorting of the initial distribution or, more precisely, the impact of the redistribution of data. We determine the impact in terms of the way of restructuring the code of the meta partitioning scheme that we have introduced above. In the previous section, when we had N data to sort on p processors depicted by their respective speeds $k1, \cdots , k_p$, we had needed to distribute to processor p_i an amount n_i of data such that:

$$n_1/k_1 = n_2/k_2 = ... = n_p/k_p \tag{1}$$

and

$$n_1 + n_2 + ... + n_p = N \tag{2}$$

The solution is:

$$\forall i, n_i = N \times k_i/(k_1 + k_2 + ... + k_p)$$

Now, since the sequential sorts are executed on n_i data at a cost proportional $n_i \ln n_i$ time cost (approximatively since there is a constant in front of this term), there is no reason that the nodes terminate at the same time since $n_1/k_1 \ln n_1 \neq n_2/k_2 \ln n_2 \neq \cdots \neq n_p/k_p \ln n_p$ in this case. The main idea that we have developed in [14] is to send to each processor an amount of data to be treated by the sequential sorts proportional to $n_i \ln n_i$. The goal is to minimize the global computation time $T = \min(\max_{i=1,...,p} n_i \ln n_i)$ under the constraints $\sum n_i = N$ and $n_i \geq 0$.

It is straightforward to see that an optimal solution is obtained if the computation time is the same for all processors (if a processor ends its computation before another one, it could have been assigned more work thus shortening the computation time of the busiest processor). The problem becomes to compute the data sizes $n'_1, \cdots , n'_p$ such that:

$$n_1' + n_2' + \cdots + n_p' = N \tag{3}$$

and such that

$$(n_1'/k_1) \ln n_1' = (n_2'/k_2) \ln n_2' = \cdots = (n_p'/k_p) \ln n_p' \tag{4}$$

We have shown that this new distribution converges to the initial distribution when N tends to infinity. We have also proved in [14] that a constant time solution based on Taylor developments leads to the following solution:

$$n_i = \frac{k_i}{K}N + \epsilon_i, \quad (1 \le i \le p) \text{ where } \epsilon_i = \frac{N}{\ln N}\left[\frac{k_i}{K^2}\sum_{j=1}^{p} k_j \ln\left(\frac{k_j}{k_i}\right)\right] \tag{5}$$

and where K is simply the sum of the k_i. These equations give the sizes that we must have to install initially on each processors to guaranty that the processors will terminate at the same time. The time cost of computing one k_i is $\mathcal{O}(p)$ and is independent of n which is an adequate property for the implementations since p is much lower and not of the same order than n.

One limitation of above the technique is that we assume that the cost time of the code following the partitioning step should admit a Taylor development. We introduce now a more general approach to solve the problem of partitioning data in an heterogeneous context. It is the central part of the work. We consider an analytic description of the partitioning when the processors are uniformly related: processor i has an intrinsic relative speed k_i.

3   General Exact Analytic Approach on Uniformly Related Processors

The problem we solved in past sections is to distribute batches of size N according to (4). We will first replace the execution time of the sorting function by a generic term $f(n)$ (which would be $f(n) = n \ln n$ for a sorting function, but could also be $f(n) = n^2$ for other sorting algorithms, or any function corresponding to different algorithms). We assume that f is a strictly increasing monotonous integer function. We can with this consider a more general approach to task distribution in parallel algorithms. Since our processors have an intrinsic relative speed k_i, the computation time of a task of size n_i will be $f(n_i)/k_i$. This (discrete) function can be extended to a (real) function $\tilde{f}$ by interpolation. We can try to solve this equation exactly through analytical computation. We define the common execution time T through the following equation:

$$T = \frac{\tilde{f}(n_1)}{k_1} = \frac{\tilde{f}(n_2)}{k_2} = \cdots = \frac{\tilde{f}(n_p)}{k_p} \tag{6}$$

and equation

$$n_1 + n_2 + \cdots + n_p = N \tag{7}$$

Let us recall that monotonous increasing functions can have an inverse function. Therefore, for all i, we have $\tilde{f}(n_i) = Tk_i$, and thus:

$$n_i = \tilde{f}^{-1}(Tk_i) \tag{8}$$

Therefore, we can rewrite (7) as:

$$\sum_{i=1}^{p} \tilde{f}^{-1}(Tk_i) = N \tag{9}$$

If we take our initial problem, we have only one unknown term in this equation which is T. The sum $\sum_{i=1}^{p} \tilde{f}^{-1}(Tk_i)$ is a strictly increasing function of T. If we suppose N large enough, there is a unique solution for T. The condition of N being large enough is not a rough constraint. $\tilde{f}^{-1}(T)$ is the number of data that can be treated in time T by a processor speed equals to 1. If we consider that $\tilde{f}^{-1}(0) = 0$ (which is reasonable enough), we obtain that $\sum_{i=1}^{p} \tilde{f}^{-1}(Tk_i) = 0$ for $T = 0$.

Having T, it is easy to compute all the values of $n_i = \tilde{f}^{-1}(Tk_i)$. We shall show later on how this can be used in several contexts. Note also that the computed values have to be rounded to fit in the integer numbers. If the numbers are rounded down, at most p elements will be left unassigned to a processor. The processors will therefore receive a batch of size $n_i = \left\lfloor \tilde{f}^{-1}(Tk_i) \right\rfloor + \delta_i$ to process. δ_i can be computed with the following (greedy) algorithm:

1. Compute initial affectations $\tilde{n}_i = \left\lfloor \tilde{f}^{-1}(Tk_i) \right\rfloor$ and set $\delta_i = 0$;
2. For each unassigned item of the batch of size N (at most p elements) do:
   (a) Choose i such that $(\tilde{n}_i + \delta_i + 1)/k_i$ is the smallest;
   (b) Set $\delta_i = \delta_i + 1$.

The running time of this algorithm is $O(p \log p)$ at most, so independant of the size of the data N.

3.1 Multiplicative Cost Functions

Let us consider now yet another cost function. f is a multiplicative function if it verifies $f(xy) = f(x)f(y)$. If f is multiplicative and admits an inverse function g, its inverse is also multiplicative:

$$g(ab) = g(f(g(a))f(g(b))) = g(f(g(a)g(b))) = g(a)g(b)$$

If $\tilde{f}$ is such a function (e.g. $f(n) = n^k$), we can solve equation (9) as follows:

$$N = \sum_{i=1}^{p} \tilde{f}^{-1}(Tk_i) = \sum_{i=1}^{p} \tilde{f}^{-1}(T)\tilde{f}^{-1}(k_i) = \tilde{f}^{-1}(T) \sum_{i=1}^{p} \tilde{f}^{-1}(k_i) \tag{10}$$

We can then extract the value of T:

$$\tilde{f}^{-1}(T) = \frac{N}{\sum_{i=1}^{p} \tilde{f}^{-1}(k_i)} \tag{11}$$

Combining it with (8) we obtain:

$$n_i = \tilde{f}^{-1}(Tk_i) = \tilde{f}^{-1}(T)\tilde{f}^{-1}(k_i) = \frac{\tilde{f}^{-1}(k_i)}{\sum_{i=1}^{p} \tilde{f}^{-1}(k_i)} N \tag{12}$$

Hence the following result:

Theorem 1. *If f is a cost function with the multiplicative property $f(ab) = f(a)f(b)$, then the size of the assigned sets is proportional to the size of the global batch with a coefficient that depends on the relative speed of the processor k_i:*

$$n_i = \frac{\tilde{f}^{-1}(k_i)}{\sum_{i=1}^{p} \tilde{f}^{-1}(k_i)} N$$

This results is compatible with the usual method for linear functions (split according to the relative speeds), and gives a nice generalization of the formula.

3.2   Sorting: The Polylogarithmic Function Case

Many algorithms have cost functions that are not multiplicative. This is the case for the cost $\Theta(n \log n)$ of the previous sequential part of our sorting algorithm, and more generally for polylogarithmic functions. However, in this case equation 9 can be solved numerically. Simple results show that polylogarithmic functions do not yield a proportionality constant independent of N.

Mathematical resolution for the case $n \ln n$. In the case $f(n) = n \ln n$, the inverse function can be computed. It makes use of the Lambert W function $W(x)$, defined as being the inverse function of xe^x. The inverse of $f : n \mapsto n \ln n$ is therefore $g : x \mapsto x/W(x)$.

The function $W(x)$ can be approached by well-known formulas, including the ones given in [15]. A development to the second order of the formula yields $W(x) = \ln x - \ln \ln(x) + o(1)$, and also:

$$\frac{x}{W(x)} = \frac{x}{\ln(x)} \frac{1}{1 - (\ln\ln(x)/\ln(x)) + o(1)} = \frac{x}{\ln(x)} \left(1 + \frac{\ln\ln(x)}{\ln(x)} + \mathcal{O}\left(\left(\frac{\ln\ln(x)}{\ln(x)}\right)^2\right)\right)$$

This approximation leads us to the following first-order approximation that can be used to numerically compute in $\mathcal{O}(p)$ the value of T:

Theorem 2. *Initial values of n_i can be asymptotically computed by*

$$\sum_{i=1}^{p} \frac{Tk_i + Tk_i \ln\ln(Tk_i)}{(\ln(Tk_i))^2} = N \text{ and } n_i = \frac{Tk_i + Tk_i \ln\ln(Tk_i)}{(\ln(Tk_i))^2}$$

3.3   Unknown Cost Functions

Our previous method also claims an approach to unknown cost functions. The general outline of the method is laid out, but needs refinement according to the specific needs of the software platform. When dealing with unknown cost functions, we assume no former knowledge of the local sorting algorithm, just linear speed adjustments (the collection of k_i). We assume however that the algorithm has a cost function, i.e. a monotonous increasing function of the size of the data C.[1] Several batch of data are submitted to our software. Our method builds an incremental model of the cost function. At first, data is given in chunks of size proportionnal to each node's k_i. The computation time on node i has a duration of T_{n_i} and thus a basic complexity of $C(n_i) = T_{n_i} k_i$. We can thus build a piecewise affine function (or more complex interpolated function, if heuristics require that) that represents the current knowledge of the system about the time cost $n \mapsto C(n)$. Other values will be computed by interpolation. The list of all *known points* can be sorted, to compute f efficiently.

The following algorithm is executed for each task:

1. For each node i, precompute the mapping $(T, i) \mapsto n_i$ as previously, using interpolated values for f if necessary (see below). Deduce a mapping $T \mapsto n$ by summing the mappings over all i.
2. Use a dichotomic search through $T \mapsto n$ mapping to find the ideal value of T (and thus of all the n_i) and assign chunks of data to node i;
3. When chunk i of size n_i is being treated:
    (a) Record the cost $C = T_{n_i} k_i$ of the computation for size n_i.
    (b) If n_i already had a non-interpolated value, choose a new value C' according to whatever strategy it fits for the precise platform and desired effect (e.g. mean value weighted by the occurrences of the various C found for n_i, mean value weighted by the complexity of the itemset, max value). Some strategies may require storing more informations than just the mapping $n \mapsto C(n)$.
    (c) If n_i was not a known point, set $C' = C$.
    (d) Ensure that the mapping as defined by $n \neq n_i \mapsto C(n)$ and the new value $n_i \mapsto C'$ is still monotonous increasing. If not, raise or lower values of neighboring known points (this is simple enough to do if the strategy is to represent the cost with a piecewise function). Various heuristics can be applied, such as using the weighted mean value of conflicting points for both points.
4. At this point, the precomputation of the mappings will yield consistent results for the dichotomic search. A new batch can begin.

The initial extrapolation needs care. An idea of the infinite behavior of the cost function toward infinity is a plus. In absence of any idea, the assumption that the cost is linear can be a starting point (a "linear guess"). All "linear guesses" will yield chunks of data of the same size (as in equation (4)). Once at least one point has been computed, the "linear guess" should use a ratio based on the complexity for the largest chunk size ever treated (e.g. if size $1,000$ yields a cost of $10,000$, the linear ratio should be at least 10).

---

[1] If some chunks are treated faster than smaller ones, their complexity will be falsely exaggerated by our approach and lead to discrepancies in the expected running time.

4 A Dynamic Programming Technique for Non-uniformly Related Processors

In the previous sections we have developed new constant time solution to estimate the amount of data that each processor should have in its local memory in order to ensure that the parallel sorts end at the same time. The complexity of the method is the same than the complexity of the method introduced in [14].

The class of functions that can be used according to the new method introduced in the paper is large enough to be useful in practical cases. In [14], the class of functions captured by the method is the class of functions that admit a Taylor development. It could be a limitation of the use of the two methods.

Moreover, the approach of [14] considers that the processor speeds are uniformly related, i.e. proportional to a given constant. This is a restriction in the framework of heterogeneous computers since the time to perform a computation on a given processor depends not only on the clock frequency but also on various complex factors (memory hierarchy, coprocessors for some operations).

In this section we provide a general method that provides an optimal partitioning n_i in the more general case. This method is based on dynamic programming strategy similar to the one used in FFTW to find the optimal split factor to compute the FFT of a vector [16].

Let us give some details of the dynamic approach. Let $f_i(m)$ be the computational cost of a problem of size m on machine i. Note that two distinct machines may implement different algorithms (e.g. quicksort or radix sort) or even the same generic algorithm but with specific threshold (e.g. Musser sort algorithm with processor specific algorithm to switch from quicksort to merge sort and insertion sort). Also, in the sequel the f_i are not assumed proportional.

Given N, an optimal partitioning $(n_1, \ldots, n_p)$ with $\sum_{i=1}^{p} n_i = N$ is defined as one that minimizes the parallel computation time $T(N, p)$;

$$T(N, p) = \max_{i=1,\ldots,p}\{f_i(n_i);\} = \min_{(x_1,\ldots,x_p)\in\mathbb{N}^p:\sum_{i=1}^{p} x_i=N} \max_{i=1,\ldots,p}\{f_i(x_i);\}$$

A dynamic programming approach leads to the following inductive characterization of the solution:$\forall (m, i)$ with $0 \leq m \leq N$ and $1 \leq i \leq p : T(m, i) = \min_{n_i=0..m} \max(f_i(n_i), C(m - n_i, i - 1))$.

Then, the computation of the optimal time $T(N, p)$ and of a related partition $(n_i)_{i=1,\ldots,p}$ is obtained iteratively in $\mathcal{O}(N^2.p)$ time and $\mathcal{O}(N.p)$ memory space.

The main advantage of the method is that it makes no assumption on the functions f_i that are non uniformly related in the general case. Yet, the potential drawback is the computational overhead for computing the n_i which may be larger than the cost of the parallel computation itself since $T(N, p) = o(N^2 p)$. However, it can be noticed, as in [16], that this overhead can be amortized if various input data are used with a same size N. Moreover, some values $T(m, p)$ for $m \leq K$ may be precomputed and stored. Than in this case, the overhead decreases to $O\left(p.\left(\frac{N}{K}\right)^2\right)$. Sampling few values for each n_i enables to reduce the overhead as desired, at the price of a loss of optimality.

5   Experiments

We have conducted experiments on the Grid-Explorer platform in order to compare our approach for partitioning with partitioning based only on the relative speeds. Grid-Explorer[2] is a project devoted to build a large scale experimental grid. The Grid-Explorer platform is connected also to the nation wide project Grid5000[3] which is the largest Grid project in France. We consider here only the Grid-Explorer platform which is built with bi-Opteron processors (2Ghz, model 246), 80GB of IDE disks (one per node). The interconnection network is made of Cisco switches allowing a bandwidth of 1Gb/s full-duplex between any two nodes. Currently, the Grid-Explorer platform has 216 computation nodes (432 CPU) and 32 network nodes (used for network emulation - not usefull in our case). So, the platform is an homogeneous platform.

For emulating heterogeneous CPU, two techniques can be used. One can use the CPUfreq driver available with Linux kernels (2.6 and above) and if the processor supports it; the other one is CPU burning. In this case, a thread with high priority is started on each node and consumes Mhz while another process is started for the main program. In our case, since we have bi-opteron processors we have chosen to run 2 processes per node and doing CPU burning, letting Linux to run them one per CPU. Feedback and experience running the CPUfreq driver on a bi-processor node, if it exists, is not frequent. This explain why we use the CPU burning technique.

Figure 1 shows the methodology of running experiments on the Grid-Explorer or Grid5000 platforms. Experimenters take care of deploying codes and reserve nodes. After that, they configure an environment (select specific packages and a Linux kernel, install them) and reboot the nodes according to the environment. The experiments take place only after installing this "software stack" and at a cost which is significant in term of time. We have implemented the sorting algorithm depicted in subsection 1.1 and according to Theorem 2 for the computation of the initial amount of data on each node for minimizing the total execution time. Note that each node generates its local portion on the local disk first, then we start to measure the time. It includes the time for reading from disk, the time to select and to exchange the pivots, the time for partitioning data according to the pivots, the time for redistributing (in memory) the partitions, the time for sorting and finally the time to write the result on the local disks.

We sort records and each record is 100 bytes long. The first 10 bytes is a random key of 10 printable characters. We are compliant with the requirements of Minute Sort[4] as much as possible in order to beat the record in a couple of weeks.

We proceed with 50 runs per experiment. We only consider here experiments with a ratio of 1.5 between processor speeds. This is a strong constraint: the more the ratio is high the more the difference in execution time is important and in favor of our algorithm. So we have two classes of processor but the choice

---

[2] See: http://www.lri.fr/~fci/GdX

[3] See: http://www.grid5000.fr

[4] See: http://research.microsoft.com/barc/SortBenchmark/

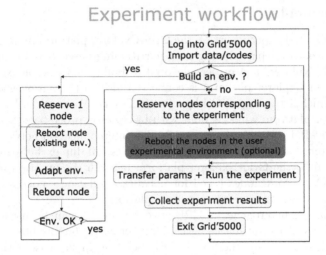

Fig. 1. Methodology of experiments on the Grid-Explorer platform

between the performance (1 or 1/1.5) is made at random. We set half of the processors with a performance of 1 and the remainder with a performance of 1/1.5. We recall that the emulation technique is 'CPU burning'.

Since we have observed that the communication time has a significant impact on the total execution time, we have developed two strategies and among them, one for using the second processor of the nodes. In the first implementation communication take place in a single thread that is to say in the thread also doing computation. In the second implementation we have created a thread for sending and a thread for receiving the partitions. We guess that the operating system allocates them on the 'second' processor of our bi-opteron cards equiped with a single Gigabit card for communication.

The input size is 541623000 records (54GB) because it provides about an execution time of one minute in the case of an homogeneous run using the entire 2Ghz. Note that it corresponds approximatively to 47% of the size of the 2005 Minute Sort record.

We run 3 experiments. Only experiments A.2 et A.3 use our technique to partition the data whereas experiment A.1 corresponds to a partitioning according to the relative speed only. In other words, experiment A.1 corresponds to the case where the CPU burns X.Mhz (where X is either 1Ghz or 1/1.5 GHz) but the performance vector is set according to an homogeneous cluster, we mean without using our method for re-balancing the work. Experiment A.2 also corresponds to the case where communication are not done in separate threads (and thus they are done on the same processor). Experiment A.3 corresponds to the case where the CPU burns X Mhz (also with X is either 1Ghz or 1/1.5 GHz) and communication are done in separate threads (and thus they are done on separate processors among the two available on a node). We use the pthread library and LAM-MPI 7.1.1 which is a safe-thread implementation of MPI. sorting 54GB on 96 nodes

A1 experiment	A2 experiment	A3 experiment
125.4s	112.7s	69.4s

Fig. 2. Summary of experiments

is depicted in Figure 2. We observe that the multithreaded code (A.3) for implementating the communication step is more efficient than the code using a single thread (A.2). This observation confirms that the utilization of the second processor is benefit for the execution time. Concerning the data partitioning strategy introduced in the paper, we observe a benefit of about 10% in using it (A.2) comparing to A.1. Moreover, A.3 and A.2 use the same partitioning step but they differ in the communication step. The typical cost of the communication step is about 33% of the execution time for A.3 and about 60% for A.2.

6 Conclusion

In this paper we address the problem of data partitioning in heterogeneous environments when relative speeds of processors are related by constant integers. We have introduced the sorting problem in order to exhibit inherent difficulties of the general problem.

We have proposed new $\mathcal{O}(p)$ solutions for a large class of time complexity functions. We have also mentioned how dynamic programming can find solutions in the case where cost functions are "unrelated" (we cannot depict the cpu performance by the mean of integers) and we have reminded a recent and promising result of Lastovetsky and Reddy related to a geometrical interpretation of the solution. We have also described methods to deal with unknown cost functions. Experiments based on heteroneous processors correlated by a factor of 1.5 and on a cluster of 96 nodes (192 AMD Opteron 246) show better performance with our technique compared to the case where processors are supposed to be homogeneous. The performance of our algorithm is even better if we consider higher factor for the heterogeneity notion, demonstrating the validity of our approach.

In any case, communication costs are not yet taken into account. It is an important challenge but the effort in modeling seems important. In fact you cannot mix, for instance, information before the partitioning with information after the partitioning in the same equation. Moreover, communications are difficult to precisely modelize in a complex grid archtitecture, where various network layers are involved (Internet/ADSL, high speed networks,...). In this context, a perspective is to adapt the static partitioning, such as proposed in this paper, by a dynamic on-line redistribution of some parts of the pre-allocated chunks in reaction to network overloads and resources idleness (e.g. distributed work stealing).

References

1. Lastovetsky, A., Reddy, R.: Data partitioning with a realistic performance model of networks of heterogenenous computers. In: Proc. 18th International Parallel and Distributed Processing Symposium (IPDPS'04), Santa-Fe, New-Mexico. (2004) CD–ROM publication
2. Drozdowski, M., Lawenda, M.: On optimun multi-installment divisible load processing in heterogeneous distributed systems. In 3648, L., ed.: Proc. 11th International Euro-Par Conference, Lisbon, Portugal. (2005) 231–240
3. Li, H., Sevcik, K.C.: Parallel sorting by overpartitioning. In: Proceedings of the 6th Annual Symposium on Parallel Algorithms and Architectures, New York, NY, USA, ACM Press (1994) 46–56
4. Reif, J.H., Valiant, L.G.: A Logarithmic time Sort for Linear Size Networks. Journal of the ACM **34**(1) (1987) 60–76
5. Reif, J.H., Valiant, L.G.: A logarithmic time sort for linear size networks. In: Proceedings of the Fifteenth Annual ACM Symposium on Theory of Computing, Boston, Massachusetts (1983) 10–16
6. Shi, H., Schaeffer, J.: Parallel sorting by regular sampling. Journal of Parallel and Distributed Computing **14**(4) (1992) 361–372
7. Li, X., Lu, P., Schaeffer, J., Shillington, J., Wong, P.S., Shi, H.: On the versatility of parallel sorting by regular sampling. Parallel Computing **19** (1993) 1079–1103
8. Helman, D.R., JáJá, J., Bader, D.A.: A new deterministic parallel sorting algorithm with an experimental evaluation. Tech. Rep. CS-TR-3670 and UMIACS-TR-96-54, Institute for Advanced Computer Studies, Univ. of Maryland (1996)
9. Cérin, C., Gaudiot, J.L.: Evaluation of two BSP libraries through parallel sorting on clusters. In: Proceedings of WCBC'00 (Workshop on Cluster-Based Computing) in conjunction with ICS'00 (International Conference on Supercomputing), Santa Fe, New Mexico (2000) pp 21–26
10. Cérin, C., Gaudiot, J.L.: An over-partitioning scheme for parallel sorting on clusters running at different speeds. In: Cluster 2000. IEEE International Conference on Cluster Computing. T.U. Chemnitz, Saxony, Germany. (Poster). (2000)
11. Cérin, C., Gaudiot, J.L.: Parallel sorting algorithms with sampling techniques on clusters with processors running at different speeds. In: HiPC'2000. 7th International Conference on High Performance Computing. Bangalore, India. Lecture Notes in Computer Science, Springer-Verlag (2000)
12. Cérin, C., Gaudiot, J.L.: On a scheme for parallel sorting on heterogeneous clusters. FGCS (Future Generation Computer Systems **18**(issue 4) (2002) The special issue is preliminary scheduled for publication in future vol.
13. Cérin, C.: An out-of-core sorting algorithm for clusters with processors at different speed. In: 16th International Parallel and Distributed Processing Symposium (IPDPS), Ft Lauderdale, Florida, USA. (2002) Available on CDROM from IEEE Computer Society
14. Cérin, C., Koskas, M., Jemni, M., Fkaier, H.: Improving parallel execution time of sorting on heterogeneous clusters. In: Proc. 16th Int. Symp. on Comp. Architecture and High Performance Computing (SBAC'04), Foz-do-Iguazu, Brazil. (2004)
15. Corless, R., Jeffrey, D., Knuth, D.: A sequence of series for the lambert w function. In: Proc. of ISSAC'97, Maui, Hawaii. W.W. Kuechlin (ed.). New York, ACM. (1997) 197–204
16. Frigo, M., Johnson, S.G.: The design and implementation of fftw3. In: Proceedings of the IEEE, Special issue on Program Generation, Optimization, and Platform Adaptation. (2005) 216–231

Detecting Unaffected Message Races in Parallel Programs*

Mi-Young Park and Yong-Kee Jun**

Computer Science, Gyeongsang National University,
Jinju, 660-701, South Korea
{park, jun}@race.gnu.ac.kr

Abstract. Detecting unaffected race conditions is important to debugging message-passing programs effectively, because such a message race can affect other races to occur or not. Unfortunately, the previous technique to efficiently detect unaffected races does not guarantee that all of the detected races are unaffected. This paper presents a novel technique that manages the states of the detected races by examining if every received message is affected until the execution terminates. Our technique guarantees to efficiently detect unaffected races, because it maintains affects-relations of the races all along the execution of program.

1 Introduction

In message-passing programs, a *message race* [4, 11, 17] occurs in a receive event, if two or more messages are sent over communication channels on which the receive listens and they are simultaneously in transit without guaranteeing the order of arrival of them. Message races should be detected for effectively debugging a large class of parallel or grid programs [7, 10, 23], because nondeterministic order of arrival of the racing messages causes unintended nondeterminism of programs. Especially, it is important to efficiently detect *unaffected races* before which no other races happened, because such races may make other affected races appeared or make them hidden.

Previous methods to detect races dynamically can be classified with the point of detection time into two classes: *on-the-fly detection* [1, 2, 3, 4, 11, 17, 18, 12, 21] and *post-mortem analysis* [14, 19, 22, 24]. On-the-fly detection detects partial information or only a subset of races appeared in an execution of program without requiring as much space as post-mortem analysis does for a trace file. Some on-the-fly techniques [1, 2, 12, 18] just verifies the existence of race, but the other set [3, 4, 11, 17, 21] can detect unaffected races. The most efficient technique [17] to detect unaffected races detects racing messages by halting at the located receive

---

* This work was supported in part by Grant No. R05-2003-000-12345-0 from the Basic Research Program of the Korea Science and Engineering Foundation.
** Corresponding author. Also involved in Research Institute of Computer and Information Communication (RICIC) as a research professor in Gyeongsang National University.

Y.-C. Chung and J.E. Moreira (Eds.): GPC 2006, LNCS 3947, pp. 187–196, 2006.
© Springer-Verlag Berlin Heidelberg 2006

event of the first race to occur in each process. However, this technique does not guarantee that all of the detected races are unaffected.

This paper presents a novel technique which guarantees to detect efficiently all unaffected races, because it maintains affects-relations of the races all along the execution of program. We tested our technique in MPI [23] using MPICH implementation [8] on a Linux cluster system which consists of four Compaq-Alpha processor nodes. We implemented our technique as a C-library using MPI Profiling Interface to make it transparent to user programs, and justified its efficiency and accuracy using a set of published benchmark programs [15, 9, 20].

The experimentation results show that the technique incurs overhead only about 1% more in its slowdown than the previous technique, but detects all of unaffected races which is a subset of races reported by the previous technique. This small overhead of detecting unaffected races is still important for debugging large-scale scientific programs which run on computational grids [6], because debugging such grid applications [10] is often a much more exhausting task than sequential or even parallel programs [25].

The following section explains the significance of detecting unaffected races and the serious problems of previous techniques in detecting such a kind of races. We present a novel solution in section 3 which captures affects-relations among processes and efficiently maintains the state transitions of the detected race to determine if it is an unaffected race. Section 4 shows the results of experimentation justifying that our technique is reasonable in its efficiency and is accurate enough using a set of published benchmarks. The final section summarizes our technique, and argues its significance with some future work.

2   Background

Message-passing programs [7, 10, 23] consists of a set of parallel processes that communicate with each other. We model a message-passing between processes as occurring over *logical channels* [17], and assume that each send or receive specifies a set of logical channels over which it operates to send copies of one message or to receive one message from the channels. If more than one channel has a message available, the receive nondeterministically chooses a channel among them to receive one message. We assume that any message sent over a channel is received by exactly one receive event, and all messages sent are eventually received at the corresponding receive. This model with logical channel is general, because most message-passing schemes can be represented.

A *message race* [4, 11, 18] occurs toward a receive event, if two or more messages are sent over communication channels on which the receive listens and that they are simultaneously in transit without guaranteeing the order of arrival of them. A message race is represented as $\langle r, M \rangle$, where r is a receive event and M is a set of racing messages toward r. Thus, r receives the message delivered first in M, and the send event s which sent a message in M does not satisfy $r \rightarrow s$. Here, $r \rightarrow s$ denotes a *happened-before* relation [13] which means r always occurs before s in all executions of the program. We denote a message

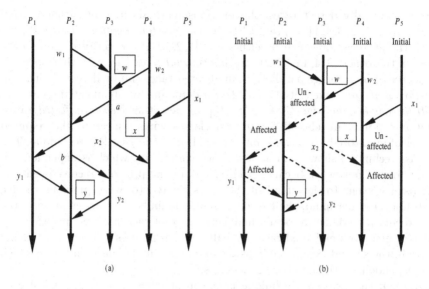

Fig. 1. Message Races

sent by a send event s as $msg(s)$. Figure 1(a) shows a partial order of events that occurred during an execution of message-passing program. A vertical arc in the figure represents an event stream executed by each process along with time; and a slanting arc between any two vertexes optionally labelled with their identifiers represents a delivery of message between a pair of send and receive operations.

Suppose that there exist any two message races $\{\langle m, M \rangle, \langle n, N \rangle\}$ in an execution of a program, and they satisfy $(m \to s \vee m \to n)$ where the message $msg(s) \in N$. Then the message $msg(s)$ is an *affected* message by $\langle m, M \rangle$ because $m \to s$; and the race $\langle n, N \rangle$ is an *affected* race by $\langle m, M \rangle$ because $m \to n$. And we say that $\langle m, M \rangle$ is an *unaffected* race, if there does not exist any message such that $msg(t) \in M$ satisfying $(n \to t)$ and there exists no such event that satisfies $(n \to m)$. For example, figure 1.b shows one unaffected race $\langle w, W \rangle$ where $W = \{msg(w_1), msg(w_2)\}$ and two affected races $\{\langle x, X \rangle, \langle y, Y \rangle\}$ where $X = \{msg(x_1), msg(x_2)\}$ and $Y = \{msg(y_1), msg(y_2)\}$; six affected messages by the unaffected race are represented with dotted arcs. $\{\langle x, X \rangle, \langle y, Y \rangle\}$ are affected by $\langle w, W \rangle$, because $msg(x_2) \in X$ satisfies $w \to x_2$ and $\langle y, Y \rangle$ satisfies $w \to y$. Unaffected races such like $\langle w, W \rangle$ is important to debugging message passing programs effectively, because those races occurs always in all execution instances with the same input and may make other affected races appeared or make them hidden. A *locally-unaffected race* is the first race to occur in a process. Although the locally-unaffected race of a process is unaffected by any other race occurred in the local process, it is not guaranteed to be unaffected from another race occurred in the other processes. For example, figure 1 shows that all of the races appeared in the figure are locally-unaffected races, two of which $\{\langle x, X \rangle, \langle y, Y \rangle\}$ are affected by another locally-unaffected race $\langle w, W \rangle$.

To dynamically detect races, the previous methods may be either *on-the-fly detection* [1, 2, 3, 4, 11, 17, 18, 12, 21] or *post-mortem analysis* [14, 19, 22, 24]. An on-the-fly techniques can be either one [1, 2, 12, 18] to verify the race *existence* or the other [3, 4, 11, 17, 21] to detect *unaffected races*. With respect to the degree of monitoring parallelism, unaffected races can be detected either in *One-thread-at-One-time* (OtOt) [3, 4, 21] for detecting locally-affected races or in *Multi-threads-at-One-time* (MtOt) [11, 17] for detecting *globally-affected* races. MtOt techniques are classified into two classes with respect to the required number of monitored executions: *one-pass* [11] and *two-pass* [17] technique. The one-pass technique shows impractical space complexity which is dependent on the number of messages, because it checks all of the previous receive events at each receive event to detect all of the races related to every previous receive event. On the other hand, the two-pass technique finds some information in the first execution to detect a locally-unaffected race of each process, and then try to detect globally-unaffected races by halting each process at every first racing receive in the second execution. This technique consumes space and time which are independent of the number of messages.

Although the two-pass technique is the most efficient to detect unaffected races, it can not guarantee that all of the detected races are globally-unaffected. It is because a process which is halted at its first racing receive cannot send messages to notify other processes of their being affected, and then such processes which can not receive such messages will report their affected races as unaffected erroneously. For example, consider the two-pass technique for an execution instance shown in figure 1. In the first execution, each process writes some information into a trace file to locate its locally-unaffected races $\{w \in P_3, x \in P_4, y \in P_2\}$. In the second execution, it halts the three processes at the location $\{w, x, y\}$, and then receives the racing messages into their receive buffers. This results in the three receive buffers of (P_2, P_3, P_4) to contain three sets of messages $(\emptyset, W, \alpha)$ respectively, where $W = \{msg(w_1), msg(w_2)\}$ and $\alpha = \{msg(x_1)\} \subseteq X$. Consequently, this two-pass technique reports two races $\{\langle w, W \rangle, \langle x, X \rangle\}$ as unaffected, but actually $\langle x, X \rangle$ is affected by $\langle w, W \rangle$ as shown in figure 1.b. This kind of erroneous reports is resulted from halting at w of P_3, and then not delivering $msg(x_2) \in X$ at P_4 to capture affects-relation.

3   Detecting Unaffected Races

Figure 2 shows our pass-1 algorithm. To decide if the current receive event is involved in the locally-unaffected race, it is necessary to determine if the receive event is involved in a race and if the race occurs first in the current process. The first line of pass-1 stores into *preRecv* the location of the previous receive event which received a message over the current channel. This is because that location makes it determine if the current receive is involved in a race in line 2 by examining the mutual concurrency between the previous receive and the send event which sent the current message. A vector timestamp [5, 16] is used for the concurrency information to check the happened-before [13] relation between

```
0  CheckReceivePass1(Send)
1  prevRecv := PrevBuf[thisChan];
2  if (prevRecv ↛ Send) ∧ (Send[me] → cutoff) then
3       cutoff := Send[me];
4       firstChan := thisChan;
5  endif
6  for all i in Channels do
7       PrevBuf[i] := Recv[me]
8  endfor
```

Fig. 2. Pass-1 Algorithm

every two events. Secondly, it determines if the detected race is the first to occur in the current process by comparing *cutoff*, which represents the location of the current locally-unaffected race, with $Send[me]$ which is the current process information in the received vector timestamp. If $Send[me]$ happened before *cutoff*, the currently detected race is the first race to occur until now in the process. For example, when $msg(y_2)$ is received in figure 1, *cutoff* of $\langle y, Y \rangle$ is b, because it is the most recent send event which happened before y_2 in P_2. Lastly, the current receive event $Recv[me]$ is stored into *PrevBuf* which has entries as many as the number of channels associated with the current receive event. This is because the current receive event will be the previous receive event *prevRecv* at the next receive event to detect races.

Figure 3 shows the pass-2 algorithm which uses *cutoff* and *firstChan* generated by the pass-1. This algorithm run at every receive event detects the first racing receive and the messages involved in the locally-unaffected race, and then calls an algorithm to manage the state of the detected race. The line 1 and 2 check the happened-before relation between *cutoff* and the current receive event, examine if *firstChan* is included in *Channels* which is a set of logical channels associated with the current receive event, and check if the receive is affected. This is because the current receive event is involved in the locally-unaffected race occurred in the process, if the receive is an unaffected event occurred first after *cutoff* and associated with *firstChan*. To produce affects-relation information that will be attached to messages to notify other processes of their being affected, the line 7 evaluates a disjunction of *affecting* and *Msg(affecting)*. It is because messages sent by the current process can affect other processes, if either a race occurred or affected messages were received from other process. The line 8 checks if the received message is racing toward the first racing receive denoted *firstRecv* in the process. The *firstRecv* that is not null means that there exists the first racing receive in the process, and the *firstRecv* that does not happen before *send* means that the received message is racing toward the first racing receive.

The line 12 passes three values to the state transition algorithm: *Msg(affecting)* indicating affects-relation information included in the received message, *state* indicating the current state of the race, and *racing* indicating if the received message races. First, the affects-relation information included in a received message is important to capture if a locally-unaffected race is affected via an affected message

```
 0  CheckReceivePass2(Send, recv, Msg, cutoff, firstChan)
 1  for all i in Channels do
 2      if (cutoff → recv) ∧ (firstChan = i) ∧ ¬ affecting) then
 3          firstRecv := recv;
 4          affecting := true;
 5      endif
 6  endfor
 7  affecting := affecting ∨ Msg[affecting];
 8  if (firstRecv = ¬ null ∧ firstRecv ↛ send) then
 9      racingMsg := racingMsg ∪ Msg;
10      racing := true
11  endif
12  state := CheckRace(state, Msg[affecting], racing);

13  CheckRace(state, affected, racing)
14  if (state = Initial ∧ ¬ affected ∧ racing) then
15      return Unaffected;
16  endif
17  if (state = Initial ∧ affected) then
18      return Affected;
19  endif
20  if (state = Unaffected ∧ affected ∧ racing) then
21      return Affected;
22  endif
```

Fig. 3. Pass-2 Algorithm

sent by other processes. In its initial state, for example, if a process receives an affected message before its locally-unaffected race occurs, then the race becomes affected then; if a process receives an affected message after its unaffected locally-unaffected race occurred, then the unaffected race becomes affected. Second, the existence of the first receive event toward which the currently received message races is important, because a race $\langle r, M \rangle$ is affected if there exists an affected message in M. For example, although a received message is affected, the state of $\langle r, M \rangle$ should not be changed if the message is not included in M. It is because the message can not affect the occurrence of $\langle r, M \rangle$.

There are three states of the detected race in each process: *Initial, Unaffected,* and *Affected.* Figure 3 shows our algorithm to manage race state transition. Figure 1(b) illustrates the states of the locally-unaffected races and the affected messages, when we apply this algorithm to figure 1(a). In the figure, a dotted line represents affected messages.

Given c is the number of logical channels and p is the number of processes, this technique requires $O(c)$-space for keeping information to locate the first race to occur in all the channels associated with every current receive, and $O(p)$-space for maintaining a vector timestamp used to check concurrency between any pair of send and receive events. Therefore the space complexity of this technique is $O(c + p)$ in both of the Pass-1 and Pass-2. In the time complexity, it requires $O(c)$-time to compare the location information in every channel at a receive, and $O(p)$-time to update the vector timestamp at each send or receive event. Therefore the time complexity of this technique is $O(c+p)$ in both of the Pass-1 and Pass-2.

4 Experimentation

Our cluster system consists of four Compaq-Alpha processor nodes, each of which is equipped with a mother-board specifically designed for the Alpha-21264 processor with 600 MHz clocks speed. Each main memory is 256MB ECC RAM with the capability of 1-bit error compensation, and the capacity of each cache memory is 2MB. Each hard disk stores up to 40GB via IDE interface. These nodes are connected via 100Mbps Fast Ethernet; a switching hub connected to each node through a 3Com Ethernet Network Interface Card. We installed Linux under kernel version 2.2.14-6 on the cluster system, and tested our technique in the *non-overtaking* MPI programs [23] for which we installed MPICH [8].

In addition to the algorithms introduced in the section 3, we implemented three additional functions to produce a vector timestamp [5] in each send or receive, to determine and write down { *cutoff*, *firstChan* } to a trace file in Pass-1, and to read *cutoff* and *firstChan* from the trace file for our Pass-2 algorithm. We implemented these functions using MPI Profiling Interface to make it transparent to user programs, so that users apply the library to their programs without modifying them. MPI Profiling Interface included in MPI specification allows anyone to intercept calls to the MPI library and perform arbitrary actions.

Actually, the number of the wrapped MPI functions are five synchronous functions but can be extended to asynchronous functions with ease: MPI_Comm-_size(), MPI_Comm_rank(), MPI_Send(), MPI_Recv(), and MPI_Finalize(). We implemented two different wrapped functions for each of Pass-1 and Pass-2, because our technique requires the different wrapped functions to be performed in the two passes of monitored executions. Consider the functions for Pass-1. MPI_Comm_size() and MPI_Comm_rank() initialize all data structures for detecting races. MPI_Send() produces a vector timestamp and attach it to messages to be sent to other processes. MPI_Recv() produces a vector timestamp using the sender's timestamp received, and determine { *cutoff*, *firstChan* } to find the first racing receive. MPI_Finalize() stores to a trace file { *cutoff*, *firstChan* } which are detected for a racing receive of locally-unaffected race. Consider the functions for Pass-2. MPI_Comm_size() and MPI_Comm_rank() initialize all data structures and read { *cutoff*, *firstChan* } from the trace file. MPI_Send produces a vector timestamp and attach it to messages with the boolean value of *affecting* to be sent to other processes. MPI_Finalize() reports the state of the detected locally-unaffected race in each process.

The benchmark programs are three MPI applications written in C language: *Broadcast* in MPBench [15], *Stress* in mpptest [9], and *Exchange* in PMB [20]. We measured the time overhead using MPI_Wtime() at each process invoked by each technique in the three benchmark programs. We measured three kinds of time: the time to run the original benchmark programs, the time to monitor

Table 1. Race Detected in the Modified *Stress*

pid	loc. of first racing receive	Netzer's Report		Our Report	
		locally-unaffected races	♯ of racing messages	locally-unaffected races	♯ of racing messages
0	4	Affected	1	Affected	3
1	5	Affected	0	Affected	3
2	1	Unaffected	2	Unaffected	2
3	1	Unaffected	2	Affected	3

the programs with the previous technique, and the time with our technique. We measured each kind of time in 10 times, and acquired the average time. For *Stress* and *Exchange* that shows no races, the two techniques showed very similar slowdowns; the worst case of our technique incurs overhead at most 1% more than the previous technique. Especially, the slowdowns of *Exchange* is smaller than those of *Stress*, although *Exchange* generates more messages than *Stress*. This shows that the overhead of message-passing is larger than the overhead of monitoring a program to detect races.

To evaluate accuracies of the two techniques, we modified *Stress* and compared those results of race detection with the analysis of trace files generated just for this job. We modified one static receive call in *Stress* source code to receive tagged messages with MPI_ANY_TAG to intentionally make races as bugs. Table 1 shows the results of the two techniques applied to the modified *Stress*. The two techniques are same in the reported location of the first racing receives, but are different in the views of the numbers of unaffected races and racing messages. The previous technique reported two unaffected races, and the other two races occurred in P_0 and P_1 are reported as races affected. On the other hand, our technique reported only one unaffected race occurred in P_2 in the modified program. The number of racing messages detected in the previous technique is less than ours. This is because the message to be sent after the point that a race occurs can not be sent to other processes by halting an execution of the process. Therefore, the previous technique is less accurate than our technique.

5 Conclusion

We presented a novel technique to efficiently maintain the state transition of the detected races, and to report all unaffected races. We justified our technique in the aspects of efficiency and accuracy using a set of published benchmark programs. From the results of the experimentation, we found that the two techniques have very similar slowdowns in the aspect of efficiency, and only our technique reports all unaffected races in the aspect of accuracy. This small overhead of detecting unaffected races is still important for debugging large-scale scientific programs which run on computational grids, because debugging such grid applications is often a much more exhausting task than sequential or even parallel programs.

When a programmer can set the value of $\{cutoff, firstChan\}$, our technique can be used in a stand-alone mode without running Pass-1. This technique therefore helps programmers avoid detecting intended races, and discriminate unaffected or affected races from unintended races. And, if programmers repetitively debug the detected races by applying the gradually increased value of $cutoff$, all of the races existed in each process can be detected. Future work includes the development of effective techniques to visualize the states of the detected races in various levels of visual abstractions.

References

1. Claudio, A. P., and J. D. Cunha, "A Race Detection Mechanism Embedded in a Conceptual Model for the Debugging of Message-Passing Distributed Programs," *Int'l Conf. on Parallel and Distributed Computing* (Euro-Par), Klagenfurt, Austria, LNCS, 2790: 57-65, Springer-Verlag, August 2003.
2. Cypher, R., and E. Leu, "Efficient Race Detection for Message-Passing Programs with Nonblocking Sends and Receives," *7th Symp. on Parallel and Distributed Processing*, pp. 534-541, IEEE, Oct. 1995.
3. Damodaran-Kamal, S. K., and J. M. Francioni, "Nondeterminacy: Testing and Debugging in Message Passing Parallel Programs," *ACM/ONR Workshop on Parallel and Distributed Debugging, Sigplan Notices*, 28(12): 118-128, ACM, Dec. 1993.
4. Damodaran-Kamal, S. K., and J. M. Francioni, "Testing Races in Parallel Programs with an OtOt Strategy," *Int'l Symp. on Software Testing and Analysis*, pp. 216-227, ACM, August 1994.
5. Fidge, C. J., "Partial Orders for Parallel Debugging," *SIGPLAN/SIGOPS Workshop on Parallel and Distributed Debugging*, pp. 183-194, ACM, May 1988.
6. Foster,I., and C. Kesselman, *The Grid: Blueprint for a New Computing Infrastructure*, Morgan-Kaufmann, 1999.
7. Geist, A., A. Beguelin, J. Dongarra, W. Jiang, R. Manchek, and V. Sunderam, "PVM: Parallel Virtual Machine," *A Users Guide and Tutorial for Networked Parallel Computing*, Cambridge, MIT Press, 1994.
8. Gropp, W., and E. Lusk, *User's Guide for Mpich, A Portable Implementation of MPI*, TR-ANL-96/6, Argonne National Laboratory, 1996.
9. Gropp, W., and E. Lusk, "Reproducible Measurements of MPI Performance Characteristics," *6th European PVM/MPI Users' Group Conf.*, LNCS, 1697:11-18, Springer-Verlag, Sept. 1999.
10. Karonis, N., B. Toonen, and I. Foster, "MPICH-G2: A Grid-Enabled Implementation of the Message Passing Interface," *J. of Parallel and Distributed Computing*, 63(5): 551-563, Academic Press, May 2003.
11. Kilgore, R., and C. Chase, "Re-execution of Distributed Programs to Detect Bugs Hidden by Racing Messages," *30th Annual Hawaii Int'l. Conf. on System Sciences*, Vol. 1, pp. 423-432, Jan. 1997.
12. Krammer, M. S. Müller, and M. M. Resch, "MPI Application Development Using the Analysis Tool MARMOT," *4th Int'l Conf. on Computational Science* (ICCS), LNCS, 3038: 464-471, Springer-Verlag, June 2004.
13. Lamport, L., "Time, Clocks, and the Ordering of Events in a Distributed System," *Communications of the ACM*, 21(7): 558-565, ACM, July 1978.

14. Lei, Y., and K. Tai, "Efficient Reachability Testing of Asynchronous Message-Passing Programs," *8th Int'l Conf. on Engineering of Complex Computer Systems* pp. 35-44, IEEE, Dec. 2002.
15. Mucci, P. J., and K. London, *The MPBench Report*, CEWES MSRC/PET TR-98-26, Nichols Research, Programming Environment Training (PET), Major Shred Res. Center (MSRC), DoD HPC Modernization Program CEWES, March 1998.
16. Mattern, F., "Virtual Time and Global States of Distributed Systems," *Parallel and Distributed Algorithms*, pp. 215-226, Elsevier Science, North holland, 1989.
17. Netzer, R. H. B., T. W. Brennan, and S. K. Damodaran-Kamal, "Debugging Race Conditions in Message-Passing Programs," *ACM Sigmetrics Symp. on Parallel and Distributed Tools* (SPDT), pp. 31-40, ACM, May 1996.
18. Netzer, R. H. B., and B. P. Miller, "Optimal Tracing and Replay for Debugging Message-Passing Parallel Programs," *Int'l Conf. on High Perf. Networking and Computing*, pp. 502-511, ACM/IEEE, Minneapolis, Minn., Nov. 1992.
19. Park, M., and Y. Jun, "Detecting Unaffected Race Conditions in Message-Passing Programs," *11th European PVM/MPI User's Group Meeting* (EuroPVM/MPI), Budapest, Hungary, LNCS, 3241: 268-276, Springer-Verlag, Sept. 2004.
20. Pallas GmbH, *Pallas MPI Benchmarks - PMB*, Pallas GmbH, Hermuelheimer Street 10, 50321 Bruehl, Germany, March 2000.
21. Park, M., Y. Kim, M. Kang, and Y. Jun, "Improving On-the-fly Race Detection for Message-Passing Programs," *Int'l Conf. of Computational Methods in Sciences and Engineering* (ICCMSE), Korinthos, Greece, *Lecture Series on Computer and Computational Science*, 4: 449-454, Brill Academic, Oct. 2005.
22. Park, M., S. Park, S. Bae, and Y. Jun, "Scalable Race Visualization for Debugging Message-Passing Programs," *Workshop on State-of-the-Art in Scientific Computing* (PARA), pp. 179-188, Copenhagen, Denmark, June 2004.
23. Snir, M., S. Otto, S. Huss-Lederman, D. Walker, and J. Dongarra, *MPI: The Complete Reference*, MIT Press, 1996.
24. Tai, K. C., "Race Analysis of Traces of Asynchronous Message-Passing Programs," *Int'l. Conf. on Dist. Computing Systems* (ICDCS), pp. 261-268, IEEE, May 1997.
25. Wang, W., B. Fang, H. Zhang, and Y. Yao, "Ad Hoc Debugging Environment for Grid Applications," *3rd Int'l Conf. on Grid and Cooperative Computing* (GCC), Wuhan, China, Oct. 2004. LNCS, 3251: 113-120, Springer-Verlag, Sept. 2004.

A Combined Technique of Non-uniform Loops

Sam Jin Jeong, Kun Hee Han, and Young Chul Park

Division of Information and Communication Engineering, Cheonan University,
Anseo-dong 115, Cheonan City, Korea 330-704
{sjjeong, hankh, ycpark}@cheonan.ac.kr

Abstract. This paper proposes efficient methods such as Improved Tiling Method for non-uniform dependence loops with only flow dependences and Improved Region Partitioning Method for loops with both flow and anti dependences. In the Improved Tiling Method, we propose our incrementing minimum dependence distance technique and loop interchanging technique. In Improved Region Partitioning Method, we eliminate anti dependences from the nested loop by variable renaming. After variable renaming, this method can divide the iteration space into two parallel regions as large as possible and one or less serial region as small as possible. By combination of existing methods and our proposed methods, it exposes more parallelism.

1 Introduction

The execution of DO loops spends most of time in computationally expensive programs. Therefore, an efficient approach for exploiting potential parallelism is to concentrate on the parallelism available in loops in ordinary programs [1].

Some parallelization techniques, based on Convex Hull theory [2] which has been proved to have enough information to handle non-uniform dependences, are minimum dependence distance tiling method [3], the unique set oriented partitioning method [4] and three region partitioning method [5], [6].

This paper will focus on parallelization of flow and anti dependence loops with non-uniform dependences.

Example 1.	Example 2.	Example 3.
do i = 1, 10	do i = 1, 10	do i = 1, 50
do j = 1, 10	do j = 1, 10	do j = 1, 50
A(2*i+3, j+1) = ...	A(2*j+3, i+j+5) = ...	A(3*i+1, 4*i+2*j+1) = ...
...=A(i+j+3, i+2*j+1)	... = A(2*i+j-1, 3*i-1)	...= A(2*i-4, i+j-4)
enddo	enddo	enddo
enddo	enddo	enddo

Example 1 illustrates a non-uniform dependence loop. Fig. 1(a) shows the dependence patterns of Example 1 in the iteration space.

Y.-C. Chung and J.E. Moreira (Eds.): GPC 2006, LNCS 3947, pp. 197–206, 2006.

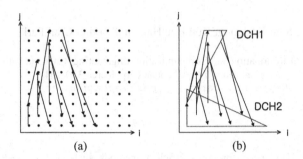

(a)   (b)

Fig. 1. (a) Iteration spaces with Non-uniform dependencies (b) CDCH of Example 1

2 Program Model and Dependence Analysis

The loop model has the form in Fig. 2, where $f_1(I, J)$, $f_2(I, J)$, $f_3(I, J)$, and $f_4(I, J)$ are linear functions of loop variables. The loop in Fig. 2 carries cross iteration dependences if and only if there exist four integers (i_1, j_1, i_2, j_2) satisfying the system of linear diophantine equations given by (1) and the system of inequalities given by (2). The general solution to these equations can be computed by the extended GCD and forms a **DCH** (Dependence Convex Hull).

do $I = l_1, u_1$
  do $J = l_2, u_2$
    $A(f_1(I, J), f_2(I, J)) =$ . . .
    . . . $= A(f_3(I, J), f_4(I, J))$
  enddo
enddo

Fig. 2. A doubly nested loop model

$$f_1(i_1, j_1) = f_3(i_2, j_2) \text{ and } f_2(i_1, j_1) = f_4(i_2, j_2) \tag{1}$$

$$l_1 \leq i_1, i_2 \leq u_1 \text{ and } l_2 \leq j_1, j_2 \leq u_2 \tag{2}$$

From (1), (i_1, j_1, i_2, j_2) can be represented as

$(i_1, j_1, i_2, j_2) = (g_1(i_2, j_2), g_2(i_2, j_2), g_3(i_1, j_1), g_4(i_1, j_1))$

where g_i are linear functions.

From (2), two sets of inequalities can be written as

$$l_1 \leq i_1 \leq u_1 \text{ and } l_2 \leq j_1 \leq u_2 \text{ and} \tag{3}$$

$l_1 \leq g_3(i_1, j_1) \leq u_1 \text{ and } l_2 \leq g_4(i_1, j_1) \leq u_2$

$$l_1 \leq i_2 \leq u_1 \text{ and } l_2 \leq j_2 \leq u_2 \text{ and} \tag{4}$$

$l_1 \leq g_1(i_2, j_2) \leq u_1 \text{ and } l_2 \leq g_2(i_2, j_2) \leq u_2$

And, (3) and (4) form DCHs denoted by DCH1 and DCH2, respectively [4]. The union of DCH1 and DCH2 is called Complete DCH (**CDCH**), and all dependences lie within the CDCH. Fig. 1(b) shows the CDCH of Example 1, which is given in [6].

If iteration (i_2, j_2) is dependent on iteration (i_1, j_1), then we have a dependence vector $d(i_1, j_1) = (d_i(i_1, j_1), d_j(i_1, j_1)) = (i_2\text{-}i_1, j_2\text{-}j_1)$

So, for DCH1, we have

$$d_i(i_1, j_1) = g_3(i_1, j_1) - i_1 = (\alpha_{11} - 1)i_1 + \beta_{11}j_1 + \gamma_{11} \text{ and} \tag{5}$$

$$d_j(i_1, j_1) = g_4(i_1, j_1) - j_1 = \alpha_{12}i_1 + (\beta_{12} - 1)j_1 + \gamma_{12}$$

For DCH2, we have

$$d_i(i_2, j_2) = i_2 - g_1(i_2, j_2) = (1 - \alpha_{21})i_2 - \beta_{21}j_2 - \gamma_{21} \text{ and} \tag{6}$$

$$d_j(i_2, j_2) = j_2 - g_2(i_2, j_2) = -\alpha_{22}i_2 + (1 - \beta_{22})j_2 - \gamma_{22}$$

The properties of DCH1 and DCH2 can be found in [4].

The dependence distance function $d(i_1, j_1)$ in flow dependence loops gives the dependence distances $d_i(i_1, j_1)$ and $d_j(i_1, j_1)$ in dimensions i and j, respectively. We can write these dependence distance functions in a general form as

$$d_i(i_1, j_1) = p_1 * i_1 + q_1 * j_1 + r_1 \tag{7}$$

$$d_i(i_2, j_2) = p_3 * i_2 + q_3 * j_2 + r_3$$

where p_i, q_i, and r_i are real values and i_1 and j_1 are integer variables of the iteration space.

3   Improved Tiling Method for Flow Dependence Loops

The minimum dependence distance tiling method [3] presents an algorithm to convert the extreme points with real coordinates to the extreme points with integer coordinates. The method obtains an IDCH from a DCH. It can compute d_{imin} and d_{jmin}, the minimum value of the dependence distance function $d_i(i_1, j_1)$ and $d_j(i_1, j_1)$ from the extreme points of the IDCH, respectively.

The properties for tiling of nested loops with flow dependence can be described as follows.

Property 1. *If there is only flow dependence in the loop, DCH1 contains flow dependence tails and DCH2 contains flow dependence heads.*

Property 2. *If there is only flow dependence in the loop, then $d_i(x, y) = 0$ or $d_j(x, y) = 0$ does not pass through any DCH.*

Property 3. *If there is only flow dependence in the loop, the minimum and maximum values of the dependence distance function $d(x_1, y_1)$ appear on the extreme points.*

Property 4. *If there is only flow dependence in the loop, the minimum dependence distance value d_{imin} is equal or greater than zero.*

Property 5. *If there is only flow dependence in the loop, the difference between the distance of a dependence and that of the next dependence, d_{inc}, is equal to or greater than zero.*

From property 5, when $p_1 > 0$ and $q_1 \geq 0$, we know that d_{inc} is equal to or greater than zero. For each i_1, d_{imin} is incremented as the value of i_1 is incremented. So, the second d_{imin} is equal to or greater than the first one, and the third one is greater than the second one, and so on.

The improved tiling method for doubly nested loops with non-uniform and flow dependence is described as Algorithm Tiling_Method, which is the algorithm of tiling loop by the incrementing minimum dependence distance as shown in Fig. 3.

This algorithm computes the incrementing minimum dependence distance, tiles the iteration space efficiently according to the incrementing minimum dependence distance, and transforms it into parallel loops.

```
Algorithm Tiling_Method(i₁, j₁, l₁, l₂, u₁, u₂, d_i(i₁, j₁))
    i₁, j₁: i and j value for the source of the first minimum
        dependence in the loop computed by the extreme points of the
        IDCH
    l₁, l₂, u₁, u₂: the lower and upper bounds of outer loop and inner
        loop, respectively
    d_i(i₁, j₁): the dependence distance function of the IDCH
    begin
        Step 1: when the first source point, (i₁, j₁), is given, the
            first minimum dependence distance d_imin and first tile size
            are computed.
        Step 2: Next d_imin is computed.
            If (next sink point is greater than bound), Goto Step 4.
        Step 3: Next tile size is computed, and Goto Step 2.
        Step 4: the original loop is transformed into n parallel tiles.
    end Tiling_Method.
```

Fig. 3. Algorithm of tiling loop by the incrementing minimum dependence distance

An example given in Example 3 illustrates the case that there is non-uniform and flow dependence. Fig. 4(a) shows CDCH(Complete Dependence Convex Hull) of Example 3. As the example, we can obtain the following results using the improved tiling method proposed in this section.

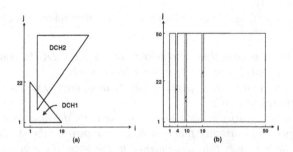

(a)   (b)

Fig. 4. (a) CDCH, (b) Tiling by minimum dependence distance in Example 3

The i value for the source of the first dependence in the second tile is 4. The i value in the third tile is 10, and next values are 19, 31, and 49. Then, we can divide the iteration space by four tiles as shown in Fig. 4(b).

4   Region Partitioning Method

In this section, we present an improved method to partition doubly nested loops with flow and anti dependence sets.

If the line $d_i(i, j) = 0$ passes through the CDCH, then it divides a DCH into DCH1 and DCH2 as shown in Fig. 5(a).

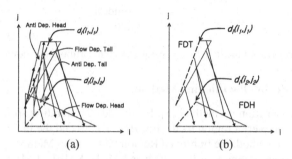

(a)   (b)

Fig. 5. (a) Dependence and Anti Dependence unique set, (b) FDT and FDH of Example 1

We define **FDT** and **FDH,** and four lines such as LMLH, RMLH, LMLT and RMLT as follows.

Definition 1. *If line $d_i(i_1, j_1) = 0$ intersects DCH1, the flow dependence tail set of the DCH1 is called as **FDT**.*

Definition 2. *If line $d_i(i_2, j_2) = 0$ intersects DCH2, the flow dependence head set of the DCH2 is called as **FDH**.*

Definition 3. *The line that can be formed by the two left most extreme points in FDT is called the **LMLT** $(dl_i(i_1, j_1) = 0)$. And the line by the two left most extreme points in FDT is called **RMLT** $(dr_i(i_1, j_1) = 0)$.*

Definition 4. *The line that can be formed by the two left most extreme points in FDH is called the **LMLH** $(dl_i(i_2, j_2) = 0)$. And the line by the two left most extreme points in FDH is called **RMLH** $(dr_i(i_2, j_2) = 0)$.*

Property 6. *Suppose line $d_i(i, j) = p*i+q*j+r$ passes through CDCH. If $q > 0$, FDT(FDH) is on the side of $d_i(i_1, j_1) \geq 0$ $(d_i(i_2, j_2) \geq 0)$, otherwise, FDT(FDH) is on the side of $d_i(i_1, j_1) \leq 0$ $(d_i(i_2, j_2) \leq 0)$.*

Fig. 5(b) shows FDH and FDT of the loop in Example 1 after variable renaming.

4.1   Two Parallel Region Partitioning Method

If intersection of FDT and FDH is empty, FDT does not overlap FDH and the iteration space is divided into two parallel regions, AREA1 and AREA2, by the line $d_i(i_2, j_2) = 0$ as shown in Fig. 5(b). From (6), we can get $d_i(i_2, j_2) = i_2/2 - j_2/2$, and the equation is $j = i$. So, the iteration space is divided into two parallel regions, AREA1 and AREA2, by the line $j = i$.

The execution order is AREA1 $\rightarrow$ AREA2. Transformed loops are given as follows.

```
/* AREA1 */                          /* AREA2 */
do i = l₁, u₁                        do i = l₁, u₁
    do j = max(l₂,⌈i⌉), u₂               do j = l₂, min(u₂,⌈i⌉)
        A(2*i+3, j+1) = ...                  A(2*i+3, j+1) = ...
        ... =A(2*j+i+1, i+j+3)               ... =A(2*j+i+1, i+j+3)
    enddo                                enddo
enddo                                enddo
```

Fig. 6. Transformation of the loop by two parallel region partitioning method in Example 1

4.2 Improved Region Partitioning Method

The three region partitioning method [5], [6] divides the iteration space into two parallel regions and one serial region by the line $d_i(i_1, j_1) = 0$ and the line $d_i(i_2, j_2) = 0$.

In our proposed method, the Improved Region Partitioning Method, we select one or two appropriate lines among four lines such as LMLH, RMLH, LMLT and RMLT, as given in Definition 3 and 4. One or two selected lines divide the iteration space into two parallel regions and/or less than one serial region.

To partition the iteration space, we use the Algorithm Region_Partition, which is the algorithm of selecting the bounds in the transformed loop in two-dimensional solution space as shown in Fig. 7. The main functionality of this algorithm is to select one or two appropriate lines among four lines by position of two given lines $d_i(i_1, j_1) = 0$ and $d_i(i_2, j_2) = 0$, and two real values q_1 and q_3 given in (7). From property 6, we know that the real value $q_1(q_3)$ determines whether the position of FDT(FDH) is on side of $d_i(i_1, j_1) \geq 0(d_i(i_2, j_2) \geq 0)$ or not. These two (or one) selected lines are the bounds of three (or two) loops.

```
Algorithm Region_Partition
INPUT: four lines (LMLT, RMLT, LMLH, RMLH)
OUTPUT: two parallel regions and/or less than one serial region
BEGIN
IF (line d_i(i₁, j₁)= 0 is on the left side of line d_i(i₂, j₂) = 0)
    Switch (q₁, q₃) BEGIN
        CASE 1: q₁ > 0 and q₃ > 0
            Select dl_i(i₂, j₂) = 0 (= LMLH) and d_i(i₁, j₁) = 0 (= RMLT);
            Call Transformation11(dl_i(i₂, j₂), d_i(i₁, j₁));
        CASE 2: q₁ > 0 and q₃ < 0
            /* FDH does not overlap FDT */
            Call Transformation12(d_i(i₁, j₁));
        CASE 3: q₁ < 0 and q₃ > 0
            Select d_i(i₁, j₁) = 0 (= LMLT) and d_i(i₂, j₂) = 0 (= RMLH);
            Call Transformation13(d_i(i₁, j₁), d_i(i₂, j₂));
        CASE 4: q₁ < 0 and q₃ < 0
            Select d_i(i₂, j₂) = 0 (= LMLH) and dr_i(i₁, j₁) = 0 (= RMLT);
            Call Transformation14(d_i(i₂, j₂), dr_i(i₁, j₁));
    End Switch
ELSE IF (d_i(i₁, j₁) = 0 is on the right side of d_i(i₂, j₂) = 0)
    Switch (q₁, q₃) BEGIN
        CASE 1: q₁ > 0 and q₃ > 0
```

```
          Select dl_i(i_1, j_1) = 0 (=LMLT) and d_i(i_2, j_2) = 0 (=RMLH);
          Call Transformation21(dl_i(i_1, j_1), d_i(i_2, j_2));
        CASE 2: q_1 > 0 and q_3 < 0
          Select d_i(i_2, j_2) = 0 (=LMLH) and d_i(i_1, j_1) = 0 (= RMLT)
          Call Transformation22(d_i(i_2, j_2), d_i(i_1, j_1));
        CASE 3: q_1 < 0 and q_3 > 0
          /* FDH does not overlap FDT */
          Call Transformation23(d_i(i_1, j_1));
        CASE 4: q_1 < 0 and q_3 < 0
          Select d_i(i_1, j_1) = 0 (=LMLT) and dr_i(i_2, j_2) = 0 (=RMLH);
          Call Transformation24(d_i(i_1, j_1), dr_i(i_2, j_2));
    End Switch
  ELSE /* the line d_i(i_1, j_1) intersects the line d_i(i_2, j_2) */
      Select d_i(i_1, j_1) = 0 and d_i(i_2, j_2) = 0;
      Call Transformation13(d_i(i_1, j_1), d_i(i_2, j_2));
  END Region_Partition
```

Fig. 7. Algorithm of selecting the bounds of the transformed loop

After selecting one or two appropriate lines, Algorithm Region_Partition executes one among eight procedures, *i.e.*, Transformation11 ~ Transformation24, which are algorithms of transforming the original loop as shown in [7]. In this algorithm, the expressions $j = A_1i+B_1$ and $j = A_2i+B_2$ used in the index bounds correspond to the first and the second input parameter in each procedure, respectively. We know that two input parameters can be the upper or lower bound in the transformed loops based on the corresponding region of the loop.

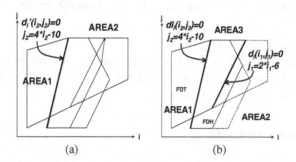

(a)   (b)

Fig. 8. Regions of the loop partitioned by (a) the improved region partitioning, (b) the unique set oriented partitioning in Example 2

Fig. 8(a) shows regions of the loop partitioned by our proposed technique in Example 2. In this case, the iteration space is divided into two parallel regions, AREA1 and AREA2, and one serial region, AREA3, by the two selected lines $j = 4i_2 - 10$ and $j = 2i_1 - 6$ as shown in Fig 6(a). The execution order is AREA1 $\rightarrow$ AREA3 $\rightarrow$ AREA2.

5   Combining Technique for Loop Parallelization

We consider these cases separately and propose suitable loop tiling and partitioning method as follows.

Case 1. DCH1 does not overlap DCH2.
In this case, we can find two parallel regions, DCH1 and DCH2, by the algorithm of finding DCH1 or DCH2 in two-dimensional solution space [2].

Case 2. There is only flow dependence and DCH1 overlaps DCH2.
When there is only flow dependence in the loop, we proposed the Improved Tiling Method in section 3. Our proposed method tiles the iteration space by the incrementing minimum dependence distance.

Case 3. FDT does not overlap with FDH.
When there are both flow and anti dependence sets, we eliminate anti dependence from the doubly nested loop by variable renaming. After variable renaming, if there remains only flow dependence in the nested loop and FDT does not overlap with FDH, the iterations within each area can be fully executed in parallel by the Two Parallel Region Partitioning Method in section 4.1.

And in our another proposed method - the Improved Region Partitioning Method in section 4.2, we can determine whether the intersection of FDT and FDH is empty by position of two given lines $d_i(i_1, j_1) = 0$ and $d_i(i_2, j_2) = 0$, and two real values. If the intersection of FDT and FDH is empty, we divide the iteration space into two parallel regions by the line $d_i(i_1, j_1) = 0$ or $d_i(i_2, j_2) = 0$.

Case 4. FDT overlaps with FDH and $d_i(i_1, j_1)=0$ does not intersect $d_i(i_2, j_2)=0$.
In this case, we proposed the Improved Region Partitioning Method in section 4.2. When FDT overlaps FDH, two selected lines among our defined four lines divide the iteration space into two parallel regions as large as possible and one serial region as small as possible.

Case 5. $d_i(i_1, j_1)=0$ intersects $d_i(i_2, j_2)=0$.
In this complicated case, Pean and Chen [8] presented the Optimized Dependence Convex Hull Partitioning Method (ODCHP), which divides the iteration space into many and variable sized parallel region.

6 Performance Analysis

Theoretical speedup for performance analysis can be computed as follows. The total time of execution is equal to the number of parallel regions, N_p, plus the number of sequential iterations, N_s. Generally, speedup is represented by the ratio of total sequential execution time to the execution time on parallel computer system as follows:

$$Speedup = (N_i * N_j)/(N_p + N_s)$$

where N_i, N_j are the size of loop i, j, respectively.

In Example 1, the three region partitioning method [5], [6] and the unique set oriented partitioning method [4] divide the iteration space into one parallel region, AREA2, and one serial region, AREA1, as shown in Fig. 9(a). So, the speedup that can be achieved by this method is $(10*10)/(1+45) = 2.2$.

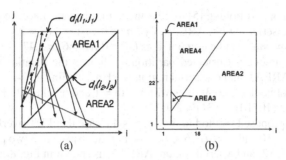

Fig. 9. Regions of the loop partitioned by (a) the three region partitioning in Example 1, (b) the unique sets oriented partitioning in Example 3

By the minimum dependence distance tiling method [3], the minimum value of $d_j(i, j)$, d_{jmin}, occurs at the extreme point $(1, 1)$ and $d_{jmin} = 2$. The space can be tiled with width = 1 and height = 2, thus 50 tiles are obtained. The speedup for this method is $(10*10)/(50) = 2$.

Applying our proposed method to this loop is the case which FDT does not overlap the FDH as shown in Fig. 5(b). The speedup for this method is $(10*10)/2 = 50$.

Fig. 4(a) shows original partitioning of Example 3. Applying the unique set oriented partitioning to this loop illustrates case 2 of [4]. This method can divides the iteration space into three parallel regions, and one serial region, AREA 3, as shown in Fig. 9(b). The speedup for this method is $(50*50)/(3+44) = 53.2$.

By the minimum dependence distance tiling method, d_{imin} occurs at the extreme point $(1, 1)$ and $d_{imin} = 3$. The space can be tiled with width = 3, thus 17 tiles are obtained. The speedup for this method is $(50*50)/17 = 147$.

By our proposed method, the Improved Tiling Method, this loop is tiled by four parallel areas as shown in Fig. 4(b). The speedup for this method is $(50*50)/4 = 625$.

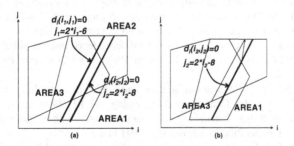

Fig. 10. Regions of the loop partitioned by (a) the improved region partitioning method, (b) the three region partitioning method in Example 2

In Example 2, the improved three region partitioning [6] can divide the iteration space into two parallel regions, AREA1 and AREA2, and one serial region, AREA3, by line $d_i(i_2, j_2) = 0$ and line $d_i(i_1, j_1) = 0$ as shown in Fig. 10(a). The speedup can be computed as $(10*10)/(2+55) = 1.75$.

The three region partitioning [5] divides the iteration space into one parallel region, AREA1, and one serial region, AREA3, by line $d_i(i_2, j_2) = 0$ $(j_2 = 2i_2 - 8)$ as shown in Fig. 10(b). The speedup can be computed as $(10*10)/(2+66) = 1.47$.

Applying the unique set oriented partitioning divides the iteration space into one parallel region, AREA1, and one serial region, AREA2, by line $j_2 = 4i_2 - 10$ as shown in Fig. 8(b). AREA2 is tiled into 34 tiles with width = 1 and height = 2, thus the speedup for this method is $(10*10)/(1+34) = 2.9$.

Applying the proposed method to this loop is the case that FDT overlaps with FDH. Two lines $j_2 = 4i_2 - 10$ and $j_1 = 2i_1 - 6$ divide the iteration space into two parallel regions, AREA1 and AREA2, and a serial region, AREA3, as shown in Fig. 8(a). The speedup for this method is $(10*10)/(2+18) = 5$.

In the above comparisons, our proposed partitioning method exploits more parallelism than the other related methods.

7 Conclusions

In this paper, we studied the problem of transforming nested loops with non-uniform dependences, and proposed efficient methods such as improved loop tiling method and region partitioning method to maximize parallelism.

In comparison with some previous partitioning methods, such as minimum dependence distance tiling, unique sets oriented partitioning and three region partitioning, our combination technique gives much better speedup and extracts more parallelism than other existing methods.

Our future research work is to improve parallelization for non-perfectly nested loop.

References

1. D. J. Lilja, "Exploiting the parallelism available in loop," *IEEE Computer*, (1994). 13-26
2. T. Tzen and L. Ni, "Dependence uniformization: A loop parallelization technique," IEEE Trans. Parallel and Distributed Systems, vol. 4, no. 5, (1993) 547-558
3. S. Punyamurtula and V. Chaudhary, "Minimum dependence distance tiling of nested loops with non-uniform dependences," in Proc. Symp. Parallel and Distributed Processing, (1994) 74-81
4. J. Ju and V. Chaudhary, "Unique sets oriented Partitioning of nested loops with non-uniform dependences," in Proc. Int. Conf. Parallel Processing, vol. III, (1996) 45-52
5. A. Zaafrani and M. R. Ito, "Parallel region execution of loops with irregular dependencies," in Proc. Int. Conf. Parallel Processing, vol. II, (1994) 11-19
6. C. K. Cho and M. H. Lee, "A Loop Parallization Method for Nested Loops with Non-uniform Dependences", in Proceedings of the International Conference on Parallel and Distributed Systems, (1997) 314-321
7. S. J. Jeong, "Maximizing Parallelism for Nested Loops with Non-uniform Dependences", in Lecture Notes in Computer Science 3046, Part IV, Springer-Verlag, (2004) 213-222
8. D. -L. Pean and C. Chen, "CDCHP: a new effective mechanism to maximize parallelism of nested loops with non-uniform dependences", The Journal of Systems and Software, vol. 56, (2001) 279-297

Neighbor-Aided Multicast Protocol
for Streaming Transmission on MANETs*

Min-Ping Lin, Chung-Ta King, and Ming-Tsung Sun

Department of Computer Science, National Tsing Hua University, Hsinchu, Taiwan
g924309@oz.nthu.edu.tw, king@cs.nthu.edu.tw,
g934344@oz.nthu.edu.tw

Abstract. Streaming transmission on MANETs requires a high data delivery rate, few jitters and short delay, while consuming little network bandwidth. This paper presents the Neighbor-Aided Multicast Protocol for Streaming transmission on MANET (NAMPS). NAMPS is an on-demand, mesh-based protocol which provides multiple paths for data transmission. The key issue in mesh-based streaming transmission is the maintenance of the mesh structure. This involves the detection of the change to the mesh and restructuring of the mesh. In this paper, we take advantage of the continuous streaming packets and broadcast signals in wireless radio to detect the changes in link states. For the restructuring problem, we propose to use mesh neighbor to maintain group information, which facilitates route recovery and optimization. The simulation results show that NAMPS has both high effectiveness and efficiency.

1 Introduction

Mobile ad-hoc networks (MANETs) are a kind of wireless networks that have no fixed infrastructure. The nodes in the network may move around and thus the network topology is dynamic. MANETs typically have high packet loss rate, low bandwidth, limited power, and high node failure rate. These characteristics make it challenging to design applications on MANETs.

There are many applications on MANETs that require communication between members of a group, i.e. *group communication*. Consider a group of tourists visiting a historical site. The guide can use a microphone attached to a mobile device, such as a PDA, to inform the members of the historical significances of that site. The messages of the voice stream are broadcasted to the group and the members can listen using the earphone of their mobile device. Since the group members may move around, we thus have a MANET.

Multimedia streaming applications require real-time transmission. They typically induce heavier traffic than normal data transmission. They are sensitive to delay,

---

* This work was supported in part by the National Science Council, R.O.C., under Grant NSC 93-2752-E-007-004-PAE, by the Advanced Mobile Context Aware Application & Service Technology Development Project of the Institute for Information Industry, and by the MOEA, R.O.C.

Y.-C. Chung and J.E. Moreira (Eds.): GPC 2006, LNCS 3947, pp. 207–216, 2006.

particularly delay variance (jitter). Excessive delay impairs human interaction. On the other hand, multimedia streaming can tolerate some amount of data losses. Packet losses may cause minor glitches, but they can be concealed if only a few. Finally, multimedia streaming transmits data continuously. Packets should be received in time and in order for "smooth" playback. Late arriving data is useless and may generate playback delay.

Many multicast protocols on MANETs have been proposed [5], but they do not address media streaming. The goal of this paper is to design a multicast protocol, called _Neighbor-Aided Multicast Protocol for Streaming_ (NAMPS), to support streaming transmissions on MANETs. NAMPS is mesh-based and does not require periodic transmission of control packets, which results in low communication overhead. It supports multiple multicast operations simultaneously, with sources creating the mesh structure "on-demand" when they have streaming data to send. NAMPS uses _mesh neighbors_ to facilitate route recovery and optimization on node mobility and topology change. Disconnected nodes could quickly find a new route to the group mesh using few control packets with the assistance of the closest mesh neighbors. In this way, NAMPS tries to minimize network cost while reducing network delay in streaming multicast.

The rest of this paper is organized as follows. Section 2 reviews existing multicast protocols on MANETs. Section 3 describes our NAMPS multicast protocol for data streaming. Section 4 evaluates the performance of NAMPS in simulation. Finally, conclusion of this work is presented in Section 5.

2   Related Works

A straightforward way to perform multicast on MANETs is flooding [7]. It works well for highly mobile ad hoc networks. However, blind flooding causes serious redundancy, contention, and collision. Multicast protocols to alleviate the problem on MANETs have been proposed, including: _tree-based approaches_ ([13], [16]), _mesh-based approaches_ ([4], [6], [9]), _stateless approaches_ ([3], [8]), and _hybrid approaches_ ([1], [14]).

It has been shown that ODMRP outperforms some of the other protocols [1] [6] [16] in presence of high mobility [10]. Its simplicity and exploitation of the broadcast nature of the wireless radio contribute to high data delivery rate for highly mobile ad hoc networks. Its use of up-to-date shortest routes may reduce the delay for packet delivery. However, each source in ODMRP has to flood control packets to the entire network periodically. Thus, as the number of multicast groups (sources) increases in the network, the control overhead also increases, causing congestion and reducing the data delivery ratio. There are many proposals [11] [12] to reduce the control overhead of ODMRP.

We can say that a protocol is _effective_ if it has high data delivery ratio, low latency, and few playback delays. On the other hand, we can say that a protocol is _efficient_ if it requires low control and data packet overhead. Most of the protocols mentioned above do not address both issues at the same time. In this paper, we try to address both issues and design a protocol having high effectiveness and high efficiency.

3 Protocol Description

Unlike other multicast protocols [9] that require periodic flooding of control packets to maintain the group membership and the mesh topology, NAMPS performs on-demand mesh creation and route recovery. Under the assumptions that all links in the wireless networks are symmetric and streaming packets are continuous during the transmission period, NAMPS takes the advantage of the continuous streaming data and the broadcast natural of wireless radio to detect link breakage. Forwarding nodes maintain the mesh by overhearing continuous streaming data packets sent by other downstream forwarding nodes. A forwarding node stops forwarding data packets when it does not hear data packets from its downstream nodes. In other words, useless routes will be "self-pruned" gradually without any control packet. Route recovery is initiated when a downstream node detects that its upstream node stops forwarding data packets. Note that we do not consider network partition in this work.

Some terminologies and notations used in this paper are listed below. Figure 1 illustrates an example. Let the total number of nodes in the network be **N**.

- *Group Members* (**G**): the nodes that are willing to receive the multicast data
- *Forwarding Nodes* (**F**): the nodes, perhaps non-members, that relay data packets for the members
- *Group Mesh* (**M**): consisting of forwarding nodes and group members, where the leaf nodes are group members, where $M = G \cup F$
- *Mesh Neighbors* (**B**): the nodes that are one-hop away from the group mesh except those already belonging to the group mesh, where $B \subset (N - M)$

Nodes near the group mesh are called *mesh neighbors*. Since most link failure recoveries can be localized to a small region [11], charging mesh neighbors to keep the group information facilitates route recovery and route optimization. The route recovery process initiated by a forwarding node requires less overhead, because it can find the mesh neighbors in fewer hops with a high probability. It follows that disconnected nodes can quickly find a new route to the group mesh with the assistance of the closest mesh neighbors. In addition, mesh neighbors can help route optimization when there is a better route via a mesh neighbor.

3.1 Packet Formats and Data Structures

There are seven types of packets in NAMPS, classified as control and data packets. The control packets have the same header format and the data packet header has one extra field "UpstreamNode". We use the IP option field to attach all the above headers.

Control Packets	
JoinQuery	a flooding packet sent by a source to create a mesh
JoinReply	a reply packet to a *JoinQuery* packet
RecoveryQuery	a route recovery packet broadcasted by a disconnected node
RecoveryReply	a reply packet to a *RecoveryQuery* packet
Optimization	a packet sent when a node detects a shorter route via itself
Ack	a packet sent after receiving a *RecoveryReply* or *Optimizaiton* packet for acknowledgement
Data Packets	
Data	a streaming data packet

In NAMPS, each node maintains the following data structures.

- **Routing Table:** A Routing Table is created on demand for each multicast group. When a new *JoinQuery* or *RecoveryQuery* packet is received, an entry is inserted in the Routing Table containing information as follows: The "UpstreamNode" column shows the next node when transmitting *JoinReply* or *RecoveryReply*. The "HopCount" value records the number of hops to the multicast source. The "Timestamp" value indicates the time when the upstream nodes were refreshed.
- **Member Table and Mesh Neighbor Table:** When a node joins a group, it inserts an entry to Member Table. Likewise, while a node becomes a neighbor of the group mesh, it inserts an entry to Mesh Neighbor Table.
- **Forwarding Node Table:** While a node becomes a forwarding node, it inserts an entry to its Forwarding Node Table for that group. Note that each forwarding node has only one upstream node but can have several downstream nodes.
- **Message Cache:** The message cache is used to detect duplicate *Data* packets, *JoinQuery* packets, or *RecoveryQuery* packets.

3.2 Multicast Mesh Creation

In NAMPS, group membership and multicast mesh are established by the source "on-demand". The mesh creation process is similar to ODMRP [9]. When a multicast source wants to start a session, it floods a *JoinQuery* packet to the entire network with a unique GroupID. On receiving a *JoinQuery* message, nodes willing to participate in the multicast group respond by broadcasting a *JoinReply* packet and fill the "NextHop" field of the packet with its upstream node. On receipt of a *JoinReply* message, each node checks whether the next hop address matches its own node ID. If it does, this node becomes a forwarding node. It then broadcasts its own *JoinReply* based on the match in its Routing Table. The *JoinReply* message gets propagated to the multicast source via the shortest path. These forwarding nodes are connected as a mesh joining all the group members. Each forwarding node and group member knows its corresponding upstream node and downstream node.

After establishing the multicast mesh, the source can multicast streaming data packets to the receivers. A multicast data packet contains a sequence number and a hop count value in addition to data payload. The sequence number is used for duplicate detection. When a forwarding node receives a new data packet, it rebroadcasts the packet. Since data packets are broadcasted by forwarding nodes to all their one-hop neighbors, a forwarding node or group member may receive redundant data packets which improve robustness.

3.3 Multicast Mesh Maintenance

Link breakage detection and self-pruning
NAMPS is a "soft-state" protocol which takes the advantage of broadcast natural of ad hoc networks. After the multicast mesh is created, non-forwarding-node group member periodically broadcasts the *JoinReply* packet containing its upstream node ID. Since streaming data packet is continuous, data packets and periodically broadcasted *JoinReply* packets can be used by the forwarding nodes to detect link breakage. This is done by "overhearing" the continuous data packets re-broadcasted by the downstream node. If the downstream forwarding node has not broadcasted data packets for a while or the "UpstreamNode" field of the data packets does not match its own node ID, the upstream node assumes that the link is broken.

Similarly, the upstream node of a non-forwarding-node group member insures the link connectivity according to the periodically broadcasted *JoinReply* packet sent by the group member. If an upstream node detects the link breakage and this node has no other downstream nodes, it changes itself to a non-forwarding node. Therefore, group members can leave the multicast group at any time without informing other nodes. Furthermore, while a downstream node detects that its upstream node stops forwarding data packets, it starts to recover the path.

Mesh neighbors
In general, most link failure recoveries can be localized to a small region along a previous route [11]. Mesh neighbors are used in NAMPS to assist route recovery and optimization. Since a packet is broadcasted to all neighboring nodes in a radio-based wireless network, a node can determine whether it is a mesh neighbor of the group by eavesdropping. Nodes which do not belong to the group mesh but detect the *Data* or *JoinReply* packet become a mesh neighbor. Because the header of data packets and *JoinReply* packets contain "HopCount", each mesh neighbor can calculate its own hop count in the Mesh Neighbor Table. These mesh neighbors keep additional information and behave as good neighbors to help its neighbor mesh. The neighborhood relationship is removed as the mesh neighbor no longer hears the data packet or *JoinReply* packet from the group mesh nodes of that group.

Route recovery
A route recovery process is invoked when a downstream node is disconnected from its upstream node because of node mobility. If a forwarding node **A** is disconnected from its upstream node **B** but can still receive data packets from another upstream node **C** due to the mesh topology, node **A** will then view node **C** as its new upstream node. Node **C** detects the new downstream node **A** by overhearing the data packet and then adds **A** to its Forwarding Node Table.

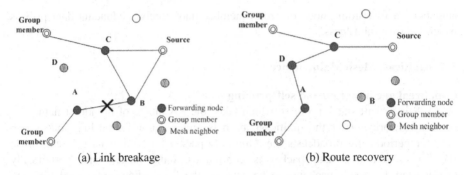

(a) Link breakage   (b) Route recovery

Fig. 1. Route recovery with the help of a mesh neighbor

If a node does not receive any data packet from its upstream node for a time interval, it assumes that the link between itself and its upstream node is broken. The timer interval of each node is related to its hop count. The larger the hop count, the longer the time interval. In Figure 1(a), if a node **A** is disconnected from its upstream node **B**, and if it has no other forwarding node in its one-hop range, it starts the route recovery process by broadcasting a *RecoveryQuery* with TTL=1. When a mesh neighbor **D** receives the *RecoveryQuery* packet, it broadcasts a *RecoveryReply* packet with node **A** in the "NextHop" field. After node **A** receives the *RecoveryReply* packet, it adds node **D** into the "UpstreamNode" column of its Forwarding Node Table and sends an *Ack* packet to Node **D**. Node **D** becomes a forwarding node after receiving the *Ack* packet. Node **C** detects the new downstream node **D** by overhearing the data packet sent by node **D** and then puts node **D** into its Forwarding Node Table. In this way, a new route is constructed. Node **B** will be pruned away from the group mesh. If more than one route is recovered, the node can choose one of them as its new route. The resulting graph is shown in Figure 1(b).

If the time of a route recovery process expires, the node will increase the TTL value of the *RecoveryQuery* packet and broadcast it again. In Figure 2(a), node **A** moves outside the range of its upstream node **B** and there is no mesh neighbor node

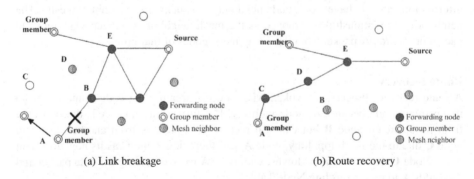

(a) Link breakage   (b) Route recovery

Fig. 2. Route recovery with the help of non-neighbor and neighbor nodes

beside it. Node **A** broadcasts a *RecoveryQuery* packet with TTL = 2 after its previous route process (with TTL = 1) expires. The intermediate node **C** records the group information in its Routing Table and rebroadcasts the packet. When the *RecoveryQuery* packet reaches the mesh neighbor node **D**, node **D** then sends *RecoveryReply* packet along the reverse path back to the disconnected node **A**. Upon receiving the *RecoveryReply* packet, node **A** sends an *Ack* packet along the new route to inform node **C** and node **D**. Node **C** and **D** then become forwarding nodes. A new route is thus re-built. Node **E** adds node **D** into its Forwarding Node Table after hearing the data packet from node **D**. Node **B** and its upstream node will be pruned away from the forwarding mesh, since it has no other downstream node. The resulting graph is shown in Figure 2(b).

4 Performance Evaluation

The simulation is based on the GloMoSim simulator [15]. In our experiments, the radio propagation range for each node was set to 250 meters and channel capacity to 2 Mbits/sec. IEEE 802.11 was used as the MAC protocol. We considered 100 wireless mobile nodes in the simulation. At the beginning of the simulation, nodes were uniformly placed in a 1200m × 1200m area. Node movements used the *random way-point* model [2] with no pausing. Each simulation was executed for 300 seconds of the simulation time.

There is one source for each multicast group. The group source and group members were randomly selected. All members joined the multicast group at the beginning of the simulation and remained members till the end of the simulation. The source node sent data in constant bit rate into the network. The data payload was set to 512 bytes. Data packets were generated at each source at a rate of 16 packets per second.

We compared NAMPS with Flooding [7] and ODMRP [9]. We assumed that no node was equipped with GPS, so a multicast source in ODMRP should periodically broadcast the "*JoinQuery*" packet. Parameters used for ODMRP are as follows: *JoinQuery* refresh interval is 3 seconds, *JoinReply* acknowledgment timeout is 75 ms, maximum *JoinReply* retransmissions is 3 times, and Fg_FLAG timeout is 6 seconds. Parameters for NAMPS are as follows: *JoinReply* broadcast interval is 3 seconds, route broken timeout is 1 second, recovery retransmission is 3 times, and self-prune timeout is 6 seconds.

To evaluate the performance of the proposed protocol, we use two metrics in this paper. The *average data delivery ratio* is defined as

$$((\sum_{i=1}^{K} n_i) / N * K),$$

where n_i is the number of packets received by each group member, and N and K are the total number of packets sent from the source and the number of group members, respectively. The second metric is the *average end-to-end delay*, which is defined as

$$(\sum_{i=1}^{K} (\sum_{j=1}^{n_i} t_{2j} - t_{1j}) / n_i * K),$$

where t_{1j} is the time a packet is sent from the source and t_{2j} is the time the packet is received by a particular group member. The parameters, n_i and K, are the same as the previous metric.

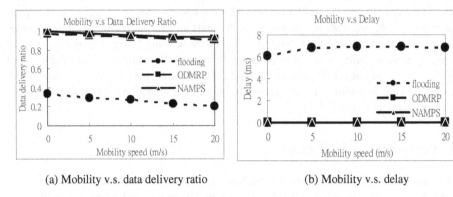

(a) Mobility v.s. data delivery ratio   (b) Mobility v.s. delay

Fig. 3. Effects of node mobility on system performance

We first examine the effects of node mobility on the system performance. From Figure 3, we see that both ODMRP and NAMPS can tolerate mobility change well. As the mobility increases, NAMPS slightly outperforms ODMRP. This is because ODMRP floods *JoinQuery* by piggybacking data packet requests, which results in more contention of the radio channel. In NAMPS, only leaf member nodes periodically broadcast control packets and nodes invoke the route recovery process on-demand. The mesh neighbors reduce the *ReocveryQeury* packets used in the route recovery process. Flooding shows a low data delivery ratio and long delays even with slow mobility. The results above show that NAMPS is more robust than ODMRP and Flooding in high mobility situations.

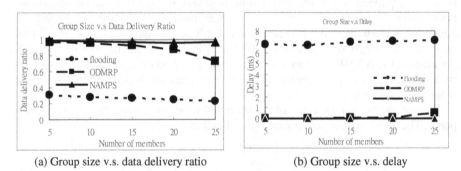

(a) Group size v.s. data delivery ratio   (b) Group size v.s. delay

Fig. 4. Effects of group size on system performance

We next examine the effects of group size. In Figure 4(a), we can see that, as the group size increases, NAMPS shows a high data delivery ratio compared to that of ODMRP. In ODMRP, when group members increase, the periodically flooded *JoinQuery* packets build more redundant routes to each group member. In NAMPS, useless routes are soon self-pruned. Flooding shows poor performance in this kind of traffic load. Figure 4(b) shows the average delay each data packet takes to reach the group members. ODMRP has too many forwarding nodes to relay the data packets in a large group size. This incurs more contention and collision, which in turn increases the delay time. NAMPS usually takes a shorter delay time to transmit data packets owing to the route optimization process and the assistance of mesh neighbors. The simulation result shows that NAMPS outperforms ODMRP since it uses an on-demand route recovery process and also takes the advantage of the mesh neighbors to reduce the control packet transmissions. These results also show that NAMPS is less affected by the group size than ODMRP.

5 Conclusion

In this paper, we propose NAMPS -- a robust, scalable, efficient, on-demand protocol for streaming data multicast in mobile ad hoc networks. It takes advantage of the broadcast natural of radio-based ad hoc networks and collects information from the packets that its one-hop neighbors broadcast to reduce the control packet overhead. We use the mesh neighbors to maintain group information to facilitate route recovery and optimization. Our simulation results show that NAMPS has better performance than Flooding and ODMRP under different mobility condition and group size. NAMPS achieves a higher data delivery ratio with a shorter end-to-end delay. For future works, we want to evaluate the performance of the protocol under multiple sources for a multicast group. We also want to modify and evaluate the performance of our protocol for other applications as well.

References

1. E. Bommaiah, M. Liu, A. McAuley, and R. Talpade, "AMRoute: Adhoc Multicast Routing Protocol," *Internet-Draft*, draft-talpade-manetamroute-00.txt, Aug. 1998, Work in progress.
2. J. Broch, D. Maltz, D. Johnson, Y. Hu, and J. Jetcheva, "A Performance Comparison of Multi-hop Wireless Ad Hoc Network Routing Protocols," *Proc. of ACM/IEEE MOBICOM* , pp. 85–97, October 1998.
3. K. Chen and K. Nahrstedt, "Effective Location-Guided Tree Construction Algorithms for Small Group Multicast in MANET," *Proc. INFOCOM*, 2002, pp. 1180–89.
4. C.-C. Chiang, M. Gerla, and L. Zhang, "Forwarding Group Multicast Protocol (FGMP) for Multihop, Mobile Wireless Networks," *Journal of Cluster Computing*, Special Issue on Mobile Computing, vol. 1, no. 2, 1998, pp. 187–96.
5. C. Cordeiro, H. Gossain, and D. Agrawal, "Multicast over Wireless Mobile Ad Hoc Networks: Present and Future Directions," *IEEE Network Magazine*, vol. 17, no. 1, pp. 52-59, January/February 2003.
6. J.J. Garcia-Luna-Aceves and E.L. Madruga, "The Core-Assisted Mesh Protocol," *IEEE Journal on Selected Areas in Communications*, vol. 17, no. 8, Aug. 1999, pp. 1380-1394.
7. C. Ho, K. Obraczka, G.. Tsudik, K. Viswanath, "Flooding for Reliable Multicast in Multi-hop Ad Hoc Networks," *Proc. of the 3rd International Workshop on Discrete Algorithms and Methods for Mobile Computing and Communications*, p.64-71, August 20-20, 1999, Seattle, Washington, United States.

8. L. Ji, and M. S. Corson, "Differential Destination Multicast — A MANET Multicast Routing Protocol for Small Groups," *Proc. INFOCOM*, pp. 1192–02.

9. S.-J. Lee, M. Gerla, and C.-C. Chiang, "On-Demand Multicast Routing Protocol," *Proc. of IEEE WCNC*, New Orleans, LA, Sep. 1999, pp. 1298-1304.

10. S.-J. Lee et al., "A Performance Comparison Study of Ad Hoc Wireless Multicast Protocols," *Proc. INFOCOM*, Mar. 2000, pp. 565–74.

11. S. Lee and C. Kim, "Neighbor Supporting Ad Hoc Multicast Routing Protocol," *Proc. ACM MobiHOC*, Aug 2000.

12. S. Park, D. Park, "Adaptive Core Multicast Routing Protocol," *Wireless Networks*, vol. 10(1), 2004, pp. 53-60.

13. E. M. Royer and C. E. Perkins, "Multicast Operation of the Ad Hoc On-Demand Distance Vector Routing Protocol," *Proc. ACM MOBICOM*, Aug. 1999, pp. 207–18.

14. P. Sinha, R. Sivakumar, V. Bharghavan, "MCEDAR: Multicast Core-Extraction Distributed Ad hoc Routing," *Proc. IEEE Wireless Communication and Network Conf.*, 1999.

15. *GloMoSim: A Scalable Simulation Environment for Wireless and Wired Network Systems*, Computer Science Dept, UCLA, http://pcl.cs.ucla.edu/projects/domains/glomosim.html

16. C.W. Wu, Y.C. Tay, and C.-K. Toh, "Ad hoc Multicast Routing Protocol Utilizing Increasing id-Numbers (AMRIS) Functional Specification," Internet-D*raft*, draft-ietf-manet-amris-spec-00.txt, Nov. 1998, Work in progress.

An Entropy-Based Stability QoS Multicast Routing Protocol in Ad Hoc Network

Baolin Sun[1,3], Layuan Li[1], Qiu Yang[2], and Yang Xiang[1]

[1] School of Computer Science and Technology,
Wuhan University of Technology, Wuhan, 430063, P.R. China
blsun@163.com
[2] School of Mathematics and Physics,
China University of Geosciences, Wuhan, 430074, P.R. China
[3] Department of Mathematics and Physics,
Wuhan University of Science and Engineering,
Wuhan, 430073, P.R. China

Abstract. Due to the dynamic nature of the network topology and restricted resources, quality of service (QoS) and multicast routing in MANET is a challenging task. This paper discusses the multicast routing problem with multiple QoS constraints, which may deal with the delay, bandwidth and cost metrics, and describes a network model for researching the Ad Hoc network QoS multicast routing problem. It presents an Entropy-based stability QoS Multicast Routing protocol in ad hoc network (EQMR). The key idea of EQMR algorithm is to construct the new metric-entropy and select the stability path with the help of entropy metric to reduce the number of route reconstruction so as to provide QoS guarantee in the ad hoc network. In this paper, the proof of correctness and complexity analysis of the EQMR are also given. The simulation results show that the proposed approach and parameters provide an accurate and efficient method of estimating and evaluating the route stability in dynamic mobile networks.

1 Introduction

Mobile ad hoc network (MANET) is a multi-hop wireless network formed by a collection of mobile nodes without the intervention of fixed infrastructure. They are autonomously formed without any pre-configured infrastructure or centralized control. Since nodes are mobile, the network topology changes at any time whenever a wireless link is broken or reestablished due to a pair of nodes moving toward or away from each other[1-7]. Moreover, they are usually deployed in an unattended environment, such as battlefields or disaster areas, and have to rely on battery power. These characteristics demand a new way of designing and operating this type of networks. For such networks, an effective routing protocol is critical for adapting to node mobility as well as possible channel error to provide a feasible path for data transmission.

The use of multicasting with the network has many benefits. Multicasting reduces the communication cost for applications that send the same data to

Y.-C. Chung and J.E. Moreira (Eds.): GPC 2006, LNCS 3947, pp. 217–226, 2006.

many recipients. Instead of sending via multiple unicast, multicast reduces the channel bandwidth, sender and router processing and delivery delay. In addition, multicast gives robust communication whereby the receiver address is unknown or modifiable without the knowledge of the source within the wireless environment[1-6,10]. Due to the wireless ad hoc networks' features and the enlarging of it's application area, the research on the designing theory and method of wireless ad hoc networks QoS multicast routing protocol has become an important research topic in network area. Recently, quite a few scholars proposed some impacting QoS algorithms of ad hoc networks[7-11].

Entropy[12,13,14] presents the uncertainty and a measure of the disorder in a system. There are some common characteristics among self-organization, entropy, and the location uncertainty in mobile ad hoc wireless networks. The corresponding methodology, results and observations can be used by the routing protocols to select the most stable route between a source and a destination, in an environment where multiple paths are available, as well as to create a convenient performance measure to be used for the evaluation of the stability and connectivity in mobile ad hoc networks.

In this paper, we designed an Entropy-based stability QoS Multicast Routing protocol in ad hoc network (EQMR). The key idea of EQMR protocol is to construct the new metric-entropy and select the stability path with the help of entropy metric to reduce the number of route reconstruction so as to provide QoS guarantee in the ad hoc network. The goal of this paper is to develop a protocol to find out QoS-based multicast routing provisioning for guaranteed QoS, and to reduce the protocol's complexity through the local broadcasting feature in the ad hoc networks.

The rest of the paper is organized as follows: In section 2, we present entropy metric in ad hoc network. Section 3 introduces the ad hoc network model and routing issues. Section 4 describes the EQMR protocol. Section 5 deals with proofs of correctness and complexity analysis of the EQMR. Some simulating results are provided in section 6. Finally, the paper concludes in section 7.

2   Entropy Metric

We also associate each node m with a set of variable features denoted by $a_{m,n}$ where node n is a neighbour of node m. In this paper, two nodes are considered neighbours if they can reach each other in one hop (e.g. direct communication). These variable features $a_{m,n}$ represent a measure of the relative speed among two nodes and are defined rigorously later in this section[12,13,14]. Any change of the system can be described as a change of variable values $a_{m,n}$ in the course of time t such as $a_{m,n}(t) \to a_{m,n}(t+\Delta_t)$. Let us also denote by $v(m,t)$ the velocity vector of node m and by $v(n,t)$ the velocity vector of node n at time t. Please note that velocity vectors $v(m,t)$ and $v(n,t)$ have two parameters, namely speed and direction. The relative velocity $v(m,n,t)$ between nodes m and n at time t is defined as:

$$v(m,n,t) = v(m,t) - v(n,t)$$

Let us also denote by $p(m,t)$ the position vector of node m and by $p(n,t)$ the position vector of node n at time t. Please note that position vectors $p(m,t)$ and $p(n,t)$ have two parameters, namely position. The relative position $p(m,n,t)$ between nodes m and n at time t is defined as:

$$p(m,n,t) = p(m,t) - p(n,t)$$

Then, the relative mobility between any pair (m, n) of nodes during some time interval is defined as their absolute relative speed and position averaged over time. Therefore, we have:

$$a_{m,n} = \frac{1}{N} \sum_{i=1}^{N} \frac{|p(m, n, t_i) + v(m, n, t_i) \times \Delta_{t_i}| - |p(m, n, t_{i+1})|}{R}$$

where N is the number of discrete times t_i that velocity information can be calculated and disseminated to other neighbouring nodes within time interval Δ_t. R is radio range of nodes. Based on this, we can define the entropy $H_m(t, \Delta_t)$ at mobile during time interval Δ_t. The entropy can be defined either within the whole neighbouring range of node (e.g., within set S_m), or for any subset of neighbouring nodes of interest. In general the entropy $H_m(t, \Delta_t)$ at mobile is calculated as follows:

$$H_m(t, \Delta_t) = \frac{-\sum_{k \in F_m} P_k(t, \Delta_t) \log P_k(t, \Delta_t)}{\log C(F_m)}$$

where $P_k(t, \Delta_t) = (a_{m,k} / \sum_{i \in F_m} a_{m,i})$.

In this relation by F_m we denote the set of the neighbouring nodes of node m, and by $C(F_m)$ the degree of set F_m. If we want to calculate the local network stability (with reference to node m), then F_m refers to the set that includes all the neighbouring nodes of mobile node m (e.g., $F_m = S_m$), while if we are interested in the stability of a part of a specific route then F_m represents the two neighbouring nodes of mobile node m over that route. As can be observed from the previous relation the entropy $H_m(t,\Delta_t)$ is normalized so that $0 \le H_m(t, \Delta_t) \le 1$. It should be noted that the entropy, as defined here, is small when the change of the variable values in the given region is severe and large when the change of the values is small [12,13,14]. Let us present the route stability (RS) between two nodes s and $u \in U$ during some interval Δ_t as RS. We also define and evaluate two different measures to estimate and quantify end to end route stability, denoted by $F'(s, u)$ and $F(s, u)$ and defined as follows respectively:

$$F(s, u) = \prod_{i=1}^{N_r} H_i(t, \Delta_t)$$

where N_r denotes the number of intermediate mobile nodes over a route between the two end nodes (s, u).

$$F(s, u) = -\ln F'(s, u) = -\sum_{i=1}^{N_r} \ln H_i(t, \Delta_t)$$

3   Network Model and Routing Issues

A network is usually represented as a weighted digraph $G = (N, E)$, where N denotes the set of nodes and E denotes the set of communication links connecting the nodes. $|N|$ and $|E|$ denote the number of nodes and links in the network respectively[2-6,9-11]. In $G(N, E)$, considering a QoS constrained multicast routing problem from a source node to multi-destination nodes, namely given a nonempty set $M = \{s, u_1, u_2, \ldots, u_m\}$, $M \subseteq N$, s is source node, $U = \{u_1, u_2, \ldots, u_m\}$ be a set of destination nodes. In multicast tree $T = (N_T, E_T)$, where $N_T \subseteq N$, $E_T \subseteq E$. If $C(T)$ is the cost of T, $P_T(s, u)$ is the path from source node s to destination $u \in U$ in T, $B_T(s, u)$ is the usable bandwidth of $P_T(s, u)$.

Definition 1: The cost of multicast tree T is:

$$C(T_e) = \sum_{e \in E_T} C(e), \quad e \in E_T.$$

Definition 2: The bandwidth, delay and stability route of multicast tree T is the value of link bandwidth, delay, and entropy metric in the path from source node s to each destination node $u \in U$. i.e.

$$B_T(s, u) = \min(B(e), e \in E_T).$$
$$D_T(s, d) = \max(\sum_{e \in P_T(n_0, d)} D(e), d \in U).$$
$$F_T(s, d) = \min(F'(e), e \in E_T).$$

Definition 3: Assume the minimum bandwidth constraint of multicast tree is B, the maximum delay constraint is D, the minimum entropy metric constraint of multicast tree is F, given a multicast demand R, then, the problem of bandwidth, delay, and entropy metric constrained multicast routing is to find a multicast tree T, satisfying:

(1) Bandwidth constraint: $B_T(s, d) \geq B$, $d \in U$.
(2) Delay constraint: $D_T(s, d) \leq D$, $d \in U$.
(3) Entropy metric constraint: $F_T(s, d) \leq F$, $d \in U$.

Suppose $S(R)$ is the set, $S(R)$ satisfies the conditions above, then, the multicast tree T which we find is:

$$C(T) = \min (C(T_s), T_s \in S(R))$$

Definition 4: In $G(N, E)$, for any $\forall (i, j) \in E$, $P(i, j)$ is the link from node i to node j, if $P(i, j)$ satisfying:

$$P(i, j) = (B(i, j) \geq B) \wedge (D(i, j) \leq D) \wedge (F'(i, j) \leq F)$$

Then we call $P(i, j)$ a feasible path.

Definition 5: In $G(N, E)$, for a source node s, destination node $j \in U$, the feasible path with minimum cost from s to j is called the optimal path, respresented as P_j.

4   EQMR Protocol

We are considering a full-connected, single source, flat network. The cost is different for different links between the nodes in the network. As mobile multimedia applications and group communication become more and more popular for wireless users, ad hoc networks have to support QoS for multicasting. In EQMR, the multicast tree is formed incrementally, and source node s is an initiate's multicast tree, namely:

Multicast route discovery begins either when a node wishes to join a multicast group or when it has data to send to a multicast group and does not have a current route to it.

(1) Source node s constructs a explorer frame p and diffuses it to node s' neighboring node with limitation, in other words, node s sends a explorer frame to every neighboring node i with feasible path from node s, frame p records every intermediate nodes it passes, including source s. Table 1 shows the structure of a explorer frame packet.

Table 1. Explorer frame packet format

Multicast source address	Multicast group ID	QoS parameters
Hop-count	List of forwarding nodes	

(2) If neighboring node i receives the explorer frame from s with constrained time window, then it transfers this frame to all its neighboring nodes with feasible path except source node, discarding any frame it receives over the time limit, and at the same time, node j will remember the originating node of frame p. we called the originating node the previous node of node j.

(3) Because every explorer frame p moves only along feasible path, and every intermediate node points to its previously node, any destination node $u(u \in U)$ receives an explorer frame p, and $P(s,u)$ is feasible path (if there are more than one feasible paths from s to u, then choosing the path with minimum cost), and the optimal path is found, the node u will discard all frames received over limited time. At the same time, node u reverse-sends a resource reserves information and acknowledge reply to source node s, add u into the multicast tree, then u keeps all other feasible paths recorded by other explorer frame as backup paths.

(4) For any node g receiving resource reserves request, if g not in $P(s,u)$, then g discards the information, otherwise it reserves the resource and then executes one or two of the following:

a. If g already is a node of T, then it discards the resource reserves information, continuously transfers acknowledgement reply.

b. If g is not a node of T, then g transfers the resource reserves information.

(5) Acknowledge reply finds the path to the source node s through the previous node's information kept among the intermediate nods, meanwhile, the

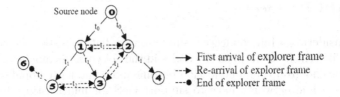

Fig. 1. The QoS multicast explorer frame initiation process

intermediate nodes update their previously node's information through the source of the acknowledge reply information.

(6) When resource reserves information or acknowledge reply information finally reaches source node, the destination nodes are added into the multicast tree successfully.

Fig. 1 shows the QoS multicast explorer frame initiation process.

In our protocol, the multicast tree's development process is the asymptotic process in which all destination nodes are added into the multicast tree. For any multicast task in networks, every time in the process to construct the multicast tree, any node in the network originates and sends one explorer frame at most. Because only optimal paths are recorded in the explorer frame, any explorer frame which reachs destination node and not be discarded records a feasible path from source node to destination node. When node s receives resource reservation request or acknowledge reply information, the node is added into the multicast tree successfully. Additionally, in protocol, the node s will set a time limit to deal with the problems, such as discarding information or finding no feasible path.

5   Proofs of Correctness and Complexity Analysis of the EQMR

5.1   Proof of Correctness

Theorem 1: The feasible path searched by EQMR is loop-free.

Proof: For $\forall u \in U$, if p is a explorer frame with destination node u, $P(s,j)$ is a path recorded by the frame, then u will choose $P(s,j)$ plus link (j,u) as path $P(s,u)$. If there is a loop in $P(s,u)$, then there must be a node a ($a \neq u$) choosing two optimal explorer frames or sending out two explorer frames along path $P(s,j)$. This contradicts with our assumed that each node can only send out an explorer frame at most. So $P(s,u)$ is loop-free.

Theorem 2: Whenever during EQMR's routing searching process, all paths searched construct a multicast tree T.

Proof: Every searched path will be identified by the explorer frames. In EQMR, any nodes can only send out one explorer frame, and receive one or multi-frames. So all these nodes will construct a searching tree structure, namely multicast tree T.

Theorem 3: If a feasible path exists, it must be searched by EQMR.

Proof: We can prove with counterevidence method. If a feasible path exists, but EQMR fails to find it, then assign $P(i,j)$ be the first link along the path, but EQMR fails to find it. Because $P(i,j)$ is a link unfound along the path, and u_j must be one destination node, u_j is not in initial state. According to theorem 2, u_j is in state of failure state, then u_i must search all out links including $P(i,j)$, which is contradiction with our assumption. Thus, the theorem holds.

5.2 The Complexity Analysis

We can analyze the complex feature of QoS multicast routing protocol through the calculation complex of derived multicast tree and needed message. The former mainly concerns the cost required for the derived multicast tree's message exchange. In EQMR, we can calculate path through nodes. For any node in the networks, if there are k nodes within its transmission range, namely k neighbors, then the node can receive k explorer frames at most. If it needs a unit time to deal a frame for a node, then the node will take up k time units at most. So at the worst case, the complex is $O(k)$ for node's calculation time, in EQMR, every node sends out an explorer frame at most, so when EQMR searches a multicast tree, the message complex is $O(|N|)$ at most worst case.

6 Simulation Experiments

6.1 Simulation Model

To effectively evaluate EQMR's performance, we compare it with other famous multicast routing protocols MAODV[10] for cost to control information, average link-connect time, the success rate to find the path and the feature of data transmission. Our simulation modeled a network of mobile nodes placed randomly within 1000m × 1000m area[15]. There were no network partitions throughout the simulation. Each simulation is executed for 600 seconds of simulation time. Multiple runs with different seed values were conducted for each scenario and collected data was averaged over those runs. Table 2 lists the simulation parameters which are used as default values unless otherwise specified.

6.2 Simulation Results

The results of the simulation are positive with respect to performance. We use the NS-2 simulator[16] to evaluate the EQMR protocol.

Fig.2 depicts a comparison of cost to control information two protocols. We can see that EQMR's cost is smaller than that of MAODV with the increase of the scale of the network, the extend QoS constraints into MAODV, the cost to control information also increases; but for EQMR, with its feasible path and QoS restrictive diffuse scheme, the growth of cost to control information is lower, so EQMR will not incur the flooding storm. Due to the scarcity of wireless Ad

Table 2. Simulation parameters

Number of nodes	100
Terrain range	1000m × 1000m
Transmission range	250 m
seconds Node's mobility speed	0-10 m/s
Mobility model	Random way point
Channel bandwidth	3 Mbps
Links delay	20-200 ms
Traffic type	CBR
Data payload	512 bytes/packet
Node pause time	0-10 seconds
Examined routing protocol	MAODV

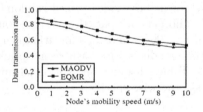

Fig. 2. Cost-Comparison with control information

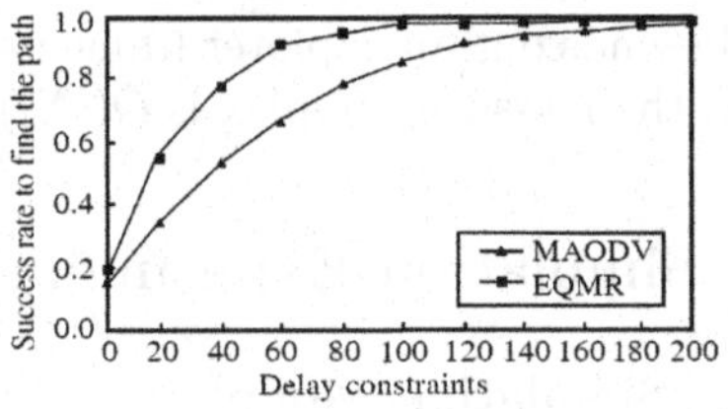

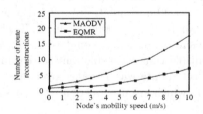

Fig. 3. Comparison of success rate to find the path

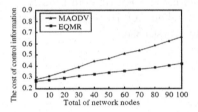

Fig. 4. Comparison of data transmission rate

Fig. 5. Number of route reconstructions against mobility

Hoc network resource, to ad hoc network multicast routing problems, EQMR has apparent advantages.

Fig.3 depicts a comparison among success rate to find the path through MAODV, EQMR protocols. With the relaxation of delay constraints, the success rate becomes larger for MAODV, EQMR protocols, and EQMR success rate is still higher than that of MAODV, which mean EQMR is more suitable for the routing choosing under timely data transmission application and dynamic network structure.

Fig. 4 depicts the comparison of data transmission rate under nodes' changing movement speed for these three protocols: the faster the node's movement speed, the smaller the protocol's data transmission rate, due to the fact that when the movement speed increase for the nodes, the network's topology structure changes faster. From the Fig. 4 we can see that when the node's movement speed increases, EQMR data transmission rate is higher than that of MAODV. When the node movement speed is control with a range, the network's topology structure will not change fast, the link's break rate of the multicast tree is low, make EQMR QoS constraints assured within most of user's movement speed range, so EQMR has a good performance within the network node's constrained movement speed scope.

Fig. 5 depicts a comparison of number of route reconstructions against mobility through MAODV, EQMR protocols. Whenever path error occurs, it needs to reconstruct, and route number of reconstructions characterize the route's stability to some extent. From Fig. 5 we can see that the times of route reconstructions for EQMR is superior and more stable.

7   Conclusion

This paper discusses the multicast routing problem with multiple QoS constraints, which may deal with the delay, bandwidth and cost metrics, and describes a network model for researching the Ad Hoc network QoS multicast routing problem. It presents an Entropy-based stability QoS Multicast Routing protocol in ad hoc network (EQMR). The key idea of EQMR protocol is to construct the new metric-entropy and select the stability path with the help of entropy metric to reduce the number of route reconstruction so as to provide QoS guarantee in the ad hoc network. In this paper, the proof of correctness and complexity analysis of the EQMR are also given. The simulation results show that the proposed approach and parameters provide an accurate and efficient method of estimating and evaluating the route stability in dynamic mobile networks.

Acknowledgement

This work is supported by National Natural Science Foundation of China (No. 60172035, 90304018), NSF of Hubei Province of China (No. 2005ABA231).

References

1. Li, L. Y., Li, C. L.: A QoS-guaranteed multicast routing protocol. Computer Communications, Vol. 27, No. 1, (2004) 59-69
2. Li, L. Y., Li, C. L.: A distributed QoS-aware multicast routing protocol. ACTA INFORMATICA, Vol. 40, No. 3, (2003) 211-233

3. Li, L. Y., Li, C. L.: A QoS multicast routing protocol for dynamic group topology. EOROPAR 2003 Parallel Processing, LNCS 2790, Springer Verlag, (2003) 980-988

4. Li, C. L., Lu, Z. D., Li, L. Y.: Design and implementation of a distributed computing environment model for object-oriented networks programming. Computer Communications, Vol. 25, No. 5, (2002) 516-521

5. Sun, B.L., Li, L.Y.: A QoS Based Multicast Routing Protocol in Ad Hoc Networks. Chinese Journal of Computers, Vol. 27, No.10, (2004) 1402-1407 (in Chinese)

6. Sun, B.L., Yang, Q., et al.: Fuzzy QoS Controllers in Diff-Serv Scheduler using Genetic Algorithms. Computational Intelligence and Security (CIS 2005), LNAI 3801, Springer-Verlag, (2005) 101-106

7. Wang, H.T., Zheng, S.R., Song, L.H.: The Researches on Guarantee Mechanisms of QoS in Ad Hoc network. Journal of China Institute of Communications, Vol. 23, No. 10, (2002) 114-120 (in Chinese)

8. Shen, H., Shi, B.X., Zou, L., et al.: The Location-Based QoS Routing Algorithm in Ad Hoc Network. Journal of China Institute of Communications, Vol. 24, No. 9, (2003) 27-34 (in Chinese)

9. Chen, S., Nahrstedt, K.: Distributed Quality-of-Service Routing in Ad Hoc Networks. IEEE Journal on Selected Areas in Communications, Vol. 17, No. 8, (1999) 1488-1505

10. Royer, E.M., Perkins, C.E.: Multicast Operation of the Ad Hoc On-Demand Distance Vector Routing Protocol. ACM MOBICOM, August, (1999) 207-218

11. Lin, C.-R.: On-demand QoS Routing in Multihop Mobile Networks. In Proc. of IEEE INFOCOM 2001, (2001) 1735-1744

12. An,B., Papavassiliou, S.: An Entropy-Based Model for Supporting and Evaluating Route Stability in Mobile Ad hoc Wireless Networks, IEEE Communications Letters, Vol. 6, No. 8, (2002) 328-330

13. Shiozaki, A.: Edge extraction using entropy operator, Comp. Vis., Graphics, Image Processing, Vol. 36, (1986) 1-9

14. Bush, S.F., Smith, N.: The Limits of Motion Prediction Support for Ad Hoc Wireless Network Performance. The International Conference on Wireless Networks, Vegas, Nevada, June 27-30, (2005)

15. Waxman, B.: Routing of Multipoint Connections. IEEE Journal on Selected Areas in Communications, No. 6, (1988) 1617-1622

16. The Network Simulator - ns-2,: http://www.isi.edu/nsnam/ns/.

On the Performance of a Hybrid Routing Protocol for Blueweb: A Bluetooth-Based Multihop Ad Hoc Network

Chih-Min Yu and Chia-Chi Huang

Dept. of Communication Engineering, National Chiao Tung University,
Hsinchu, Taiwan 300, Republic of China
hankycm@ms47.hinet.net, huangcc@cc.nctu.edu.tw

Abstract. Blueweb is a self-organizing Bluetooth-based multihop network with an efficient scatternet formation algorithm. Blueweb's scatternet formation uses two mechanisms. One is the role exchange mechanism in which only slave nodes serve as relays throughout the whole scatternet. The other one is the return connection mechanism in which we convert the scatternet from a tree-shaped to a web-shaped topology. In this paper, a modified source routing protocol is proposed for Blueweb in which we combine the proactive method locally with the reactive method globally to discover the optimal path for packet transmission. In addition, we use computer simulations to evaluate the routing performance of Blueweb with a uniform end-to-end traffic model. Our simulation results show that Blueweb can achieve good system performance with the modified source routing protocol.

1 Introduction

Bluetooth is emerging as a potential technology for short-range wireless ad hoc network [1]. This technology enables the design of low power, low cost, and short-range radio [2] that can be embedded in existing portable devices. Initially, Bluetooth technology is designed as a cable replacement solution among portable and fixed electronic devices. Today, people tend to use a number of mobile devices such as cellular phones, PDA's, digital cameras, laptop computers, and so on. Consequently, there exists a strong demand for connecting these devices into networks. As a result, Bluetooth becomes an ideal candidate for the construction of ad hoc personal area networks.

A Bluetooth-based multihop ad hoc network brings some challenges. Besides the methods of device discovery for a node to participate in multiple piconets, the scatternet formation algorithm and the routing protocol are two major technical issues. The scatternet formation algorithm [3]-[6] deals with the problem of how to construct individual piconets and connect them together into a scatternet. On the other hand, the routing protocol deals with the problem of delivering messages efficiently in such a scatternet.

Until now, a number of routing protocols have been proposed for Bluetooth multihop networks [6]-[9]. In the proactive approach, such as in the Bluetree [6], each master node maintains a routing table. The main problem here is the overhead in routing information exchanges, although little delay is involved in determining a route. In

Y.-C. Chung and J.E. Moreira (Eds.): GPC 2006, LNCS 3947, pp. 227–236, 2006.
© Springer-Verlag Berlin Heidelberg 2006

the reactive approach [7][8], a flooding method is usually used to search for the optimal path from a source node to a destination node and this will incur a certain amount of delay. However, the reactive approach provides better network scalability. In [9], the performance of a hybrid routing protocol is presented for Bluetooth scatternets and it consumes small amount of storage, low routing overhead, and low route discovery latency. Nevertheless, the paper did not try to combine this hybrid routing protocol with a scatternet formation algorithm for Bluetooth scatternet to achieve its excellent routing performance.

In this paper, a modified source routing protocol for Blueweb [10] is proposed to provide the shortest path routing among nodes. The routing information is collected at each master node during the scatternet formation. This is a hybrid routing protocol in which we use the proactive approach locally and the reactive approach globally to discover the optimal path for source routing. In addition, a uniform end-to-end traffic model [11] is used to simulate and demonstrate the routing performance of Blueweb.

The rest of this paper is organized as follows: In Section 2, we describe the scatternet formation algorithm of Blueweb. In Section 3, a modified source routing protocol for the Blueweb architecture is proposed. In Section 4, computer simulations are used to evaluate the system performance of Blueweb. Finally, a conclusion is stated in Section 5.

2 Blueweb Scatternet Formation Algorithm

The scatternet formation of Blueweb is executed in two phases. In the first phase, a coordinator called the route master initiates the scatternet formation procedure by paging up to 7 neighboring slave nodes, and forms the first piconet. The slave nodes then switch their roles to masters (called S/M nodes). Each S/M node only pages one additional neighboring slave node. After each S/M node connects to its slave, a role exchange mechanism is executed to make the S/M node function as a relay and make the slave node function as a master. Then the new master node begins to page up to 7 neighboring slave nodes. This procedure is iterated until the leaf nodes of the tree are reached and a tree-shaped topology is created.

In the second phase, a return connection mechanism is used to generate more connection paths among nodes and the tree-shaped topology is converted into a web-shaped topology. Fig. 1 illustrates a simple Blueweb topology example.

3 Blueweb Routing Protocol

In the Blueweb scatternet formation period, some routing information can be exchanged among masters. In the first phase of scatternet formation, each master keeps a record of its directly connected upstream master. As a result, a query path can be easily formed by connecting all the masters in the upstream direction to the route master.

In the second phase of scatternet formation, each returning master will pass its own piconet information together with a list of its directly connected masters to the route master via its upstream masters. At the same time, each returning master including the route master will pass its own piconet information to its directly connected masters.

Here, we define the directly connected neighboring piconets within its neighboring N tiers of a master as the N-tier piconets of the master. The associated N-tier piconet information will be stored in the master's *N-tier piconet table*. In addition, those masters affected by the return connection mechanism will update their N-tier piconet table via relays. As a result, each master will keep its own piconet information and its N-tier piconet information. This information is used locally when a node inquires the master for a path to deliver packets.

After finishing the second phase of scatternet formation, the route master will have the routing information of all nodes and store it in a *piconet list table*. This table contains a list of all the masters and their associated slaves. Meanwhile, the route master will compute the shortest path for any two-piconet pair using the all-pairs shortest path algorithm [12]. This shortest path information is stored in a *scatternet routing table* and is used when any node inquires the route master for routing information to deliver packets.

In order to implement this routing protocol, a piconet-layer addressing scheme can be used. This scheme combines the Bluetooth active member address (AM_ADDR) with piconet identification (PID) to address each Bluetooth device throughout the whole scatternet. In a piconet, each slave is assigned a 3-bit AM_ADDR by its master. In addition, the PID is used to distinguish different piconets in the scatternet.

The PID's are assigned on a layer-by-layer basis in the downstream direction during the first phase of scatternet formation. For example, the route master is the only layer 1 node and uses 1 as its PID. Its first attached master is assigned 1.1 as its PID, the second attached master is assigned 1.2 as its PID, and so on. In this way, a layer 3 master will be assigned a PID of $1.a_2.a_3$. We refer this addressing method as a piconet-layer addressing scheme. This addressing scheme can be applied to Blueweb architecture directly. An example of this scatternet addressing scheme for Blueweb is shown in Fig. 1.

Based on the routing information collected by all the masters including the route master, a modified source routing protocol is developed. This is a hybrid routing protocol and operates in two phases. In the first phase, an optimal path from source to destination is searched. In the second phase, the optimal path is used to transmit the packets.

Besides, a packet format is also designed for implementing our routing protocol. This packet format is similar to RVM (Routing Vector Method) [7] and is shown in Fig. 2. The SRC field contains the address of the source node according to the piconet-layer addressing scheme. The DST field contains either the 48-bit Bluetooth address for a query packet or the address of the destination node for a reply packet or a data packet. The PATH field contains either the address of the route master for a query packet or a sequence of PID's according to the piconet-layer addressing scheme for a reply packet or a data packet.

For example in Fig. 1, when the node S with address 1.1.1.1 sends a packet to the destination node D, the node S will query its affiliated master with a query packet for routing information. If the master node has the node D information in its N-tier piconet table, the master will reply the routing path to the slave node directly. Then, the source node will embed the routing path in the PATH field and transmit the packet. Otherwise, the queried master 1.1.1 will forward this query message directly to the

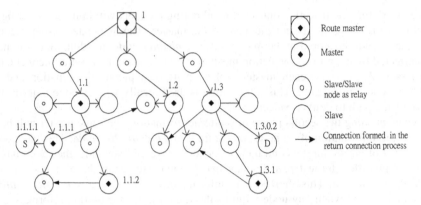

Fig. 1. An example of a connected Blueweb topology

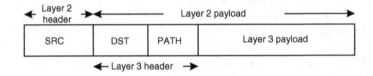

Fig. 2. Blueweb packet format

route master 1 via its upstream master 1.1. In this scenario, the header fields for a sequence of query packets are shown in Table 1.

When the route master receives the query packet, it will first look up in its piconet list table for the associated piconet addresses and then look up in the scatternet routing table for the optimal path. The route master then sends back the optimal routing path to the source node via the downstream master nodes according to the piconet address of SRC field. The optimal path contains a sequence of PID's in the PATH field. The header fields for a sequence of reply packets are shown in Table 2.

In the packet transmission phase, when a master receives a packet from another node, it strips off its PID in the PATH field and forwards this packet to the next piconet according to the next PID in the PATH field. In this way, the packet will finally reach the destination node D. The header fields for a sequence of data packets are listed in Table 3. Overall, the detailed Blueweb routing algorithm is described by the pseudo code listed in Fig. 3.

Table 1. Header fields for a sequence of query packets

Query packet sequence	SRC	DST	PATH
Node S queries its master	1.1.1.1	D's Bluetooth address	1
Queried master forwards to its upstream master	1.1.1.1	D's Bluetooth address	1
Upstream master forwards to the route master	1.1.1.1	D's Bluetooth address	1

Table 2. Header fields for a sequence of reply packets

Reply packet sequence	SRC	DST	PATH
Route master sends routing path to downstream master	1.1.1.1	1.3.0.2	1.1.1;1.2;1.3
Downstream master passes this information to the queried master	1.1.1.1	1.3.0.2	1.1.1;1.2;1.3
The queried master passes this information to the query node S	1.1.1.1	1.3.0.2	1.1.1;1.2;1.3

Table 3. Header fields for a sequence of data packets

Reply transmission sequence	SRC	DST	PATH
Node S sends packet to destination node D	1.1.1.1	1.3.0.2	1.1.1;1.2;1.3
The master of node S forwards to the next piconet	1.1.1.1	1.3.0.2	1.2;1.3
The immediate master forwards this data packet to the master node of destination	1.1.1.1	1.3.0.2	1.3
The packet reaches the destination node D	1.1.1.1	1.3.0.2	0

```
Routing algorithm () {
    If the source node is a master
        It checks whether it has its destination's routing information
        If this master has destination's routing information
            The source node transmits its packets directly
        Else it forwards the query message to the route master
            The route master replies the routing path to the source node
            The source node transmits its packets by source routing
        End
    Elseif this node is a relay or slave
        The source node queries its immediate upstream master
        If this master has its destination's routing information
            It replies the routing path to the source node
            The source node transmits its packets using the routing path
        Else it forwards the query message to the route master and
            The route master replies the routing path to the source node
            The source node transmits its packets using the routing path
        End
    End
}
```

Fig. 3. Blueweb routing algorithm

4 System Performance Simulation

In our simulation scenario, the scatternet topologies simulated were constructed by using the scatternet formation algorithms as described in Section 2. Overall, we simulated ten topologies each with 20, 30, and 40 nodes randomly distributed in the same geographical area.

For data transmission, packets were generated in each node according to a Poisson arrival pattern. Here, we assumed only a single packet was sent in each routing session. Each data packet was assumed to last five time slots. Each route query packet and each route reply packet were assumed to last one time slot. Each node was provided a FIFO queue with a length of 80 packets. The source-destination pair in each routing session was selected randomly and packets were forwarded by using the Blueweb routing protocol. To evaluate the system performance, we calculated some selected performance metrics over twenty seconds of simulation time for each topology. Table 4 summarized the simulation parameters.

Table 4. The simulation parameters

Simulation time (seconds)	20
Number of nodes	20, 30, 40
Traffic pattern	Poisson arrival
Scheduling scheme	Round robin
Routing protocols	Modified source routing
FIFO buffer size	80 packets
Source-destination pair	Randomly selected
Query or reply packet	1 time slot
Data packet (for each routing session)	5 time slots

4.1 System Performance

In this section, several performance metrics are evaluated by computer simulation to demonstrate the system performance of the Blueweb scatternet. These performance metrics include average packet throughput, average packet delay, packet dropping probability, and so on.

4.1.1 Average Packet Throughput

The average packet throughput is defined as the ratio of the total number of successfully finished routing packets over the total simulation time in second. This parameter reflects the system capacity of a scatternet.

The simulation results for average packet throughput of Blueweb are presented in Fig. 4. The average packet throughput increases continuously as the routing packet generation rate increases. This is because the modified source routing protocol together with the web-shaped architecture greatly enhances the system performance. Nevertheless, the throughput performance will finally become saturated. Fig. 4 also shows the performance of all the two-tier cases achieve better throughput performance than the corresponding one-tier simulated cases of Blueweb.

4.1.2 Average Packet Delay

The average packet delay metric is defined as the average packet transmission time from the first transmitted bit at the source node to the last received bit at the destination node for every routing packet. In addition, our simulation adopts the Poisson arrival traffic pattern, the round robin scheduling algorithm, and the modified source routing protocol to evaluate this performance metric in a uniform traffic model.

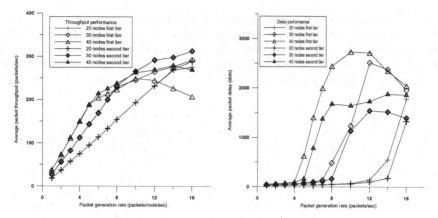

Fig. 4. Average packet throughput   **Fig. 5.** Average packet delay

Fig. 5 shows the average packet delay performance of Blueweb. The average packet delay increases as the packet generation rate increases. In addition, the 20-node cases generate the smallest average delay since it produces the smallest average path length out of all simulated cases. Clearly, the two-tier cases achieve better delay performance than the one-tier cases of Blueweb. We observed that the delay perform-ance deteriorated very quickly when the traffic load begins to saturate the network. This happens when the route master and other masters eventually become bottlenecks and cause network saturation.

Due to the fact that a smaller packet incurs larger system overhead, the average packet delay in Fig. 5 can be reduced further when more than one packet are transmit-ted in each packet.

4.1.3 Packet Dropping Probability

A packet dropping probability metric is used to evaluate the effect of scatternet con-gestion caused by the buffer overflow phenomenon in some nodes. When the FIFO buffer in a node overflows, the affected routing packets including both the newly generated and currently active routing packets were dropped. The packet dropping probability is defined as the ratio of the total number of dropped packets over the total number of generated packets in all nodes.

Fig. 6 shows the packet dropping probability of Blueweb. Clearly, the 20-node cases achieve the best performance on the packet dropping probability. In addition, the two-tier cases also have better dropping probability performance than the one-tier cases. As observed from our simulation, the route master and all other masters will start to drop packets when network saturation happened.

4.1.4 Average Packet Query Time

The average route query time is defined as the average transmission time of query packet to discover a path from either the piconet master or the route master. The query time to the piconet master is defined as the local query time, and the query time to the route master is defined as the global query time.

Fig. 7 shows the average route query time performance (including both the local and global query time) represents about two third of the overall average packet delay time. In addition, the query performance of the two-tier cases is reduced significantly from the one-tier cases. Because the local query with a larger local routing table effectively shares the working load of global query.

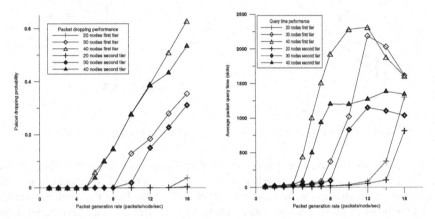

Fig. 6. Packet dropping probability   **Fig. 7.** Average packet query time

4.1.5 Probability of Querying the Route Master

The probability of querying the route master is defined as the ratio of the total number of queries to the route master over the total number of queries (including both the local and global queries). Fig. 8 shows the two-tier approach can reduce 20% in the probability of querying the route master as compared with one-tier approach. We also observed that most of the path queries are done at the route master instead of local masters in the one-tier cases. This phenomenon may cause the route master to saturate easily and become the bottleneck of packet transmission in Blueweb. Nevertheless,

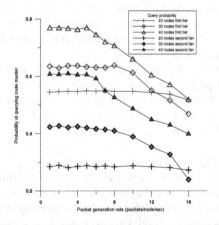

Fig. 8. Probability of querying the route master

Fig. 7 and Fig. 8 show that the two-tier approach of the modified source routing protocol can improve the routing performance significantly.

5 Conclusions

In this paper, a modified source routing protocol is proposed for Blueweb. During the scatternet formation process, the routing information is exchanged among masters and the routing tables needed for the modified source routing protocol is established at the same time. Using computer simulations, we simulate and demonstrate the system performance of Blueweb with a uniform end-to-end traffic model. Our simulation results show that Blueweb can achieve good system performance with this modified source routing protocol.

In addition, our modified source routing protocol provides the following features. First, this is a hybrid routing protocol that takes the advantages of both proactive and reactive routing protocols. Second, the query-based source routing protocol generates low overhead and small route query latency that is especially useful in the transmission of large batch of data packets. Third, the size of the piconet routing table of each master can be increased to include its N-tier ($N \geq 2$) piconet information when the size of scatternet grows up. This property makes the scatternet easily expandable into a large network.

References

1. http://www.bluetooth.com. *Specification of the Bluetooth System*, Volume 1, Core. Version 1.1, February 22 2001.
2. Johansson, P., Johansson, N., Korner, U.; Elg, J.and Svennarp, G, "Short range radio based ad hoc networking: performance and properties," *IEEE International Conference on Communications*, vol.3, pp. 1414-1420, 1999.
3. Zhifang Wang, Thomas, R.J., and Haas, Z., "Bluenet – A New Scatternet Formation Scheme," *Proceedings of the 35th Annual Hawaii International Conference on System Sciences*, pp. 779-787, 2001.
4. Chiara Petrioli, Stefano Basagni, and Imrich Chlamtac, "Configuring BlueStars: Multihop Scatternet Formation for Bluetooth Networks", *IEEE Transaction on Computers*, vol. 52, no.6, pp.779-790, June 2003.
5. Yong Liu, Myung J. Lee, and Tarek N. Saadawi, "A Bluetooth Scatternet-Route Structure for Multihop Ad Hoc Networks", *IEEE Journal on Selected Areas in Communications*, vol. 21, no. 2, pp. 229-239, Feb. 2003.
6. Zaruba, G.V., Basagni, S.and Chlamtac, I. "Bluetrees-scatternet formation to enable Bluetooth-based ad hoc networks," *IEEE International Conference on Communications*, vol.1, pp. 273 –277, June 2001.
7. P. Bhagwat and A. Segall, "A Routing Vector Method (RVM) for Routing in Bluetooth Scatternets," *IEEE International Workshop on Mobile Multimedia Communications*, pp. 375-379, 1999.
8. *Prabhu, B.J.and Chockalingam, A.* "A Routing Protocol and Energy Efficient Techniques in Bluetooth Scatternets," *IEEE International Conference on Communications*, 2002. ICC 2002. pp. 3336 –3340.

9. R. Kapoor and M. Gerla, "A zone routing protocol for Bluetooth scatternets", *IEEE Wireless Communications and Networking*, vol.3, pp. 1459-1464, March 2003.
10. C. M. Yu and C. C. Huang, "Introduction to Blueweb: A New Bluetooth-based Multihop Ad Hoc Network," *International Conference on Wireless Network*, June 2004.
11. D. Miorandi, A. Trainito, and A. Zanella, "On efficient topologies for Bluetooth scatternets," in *Lecture Notes in Computer Science*, vol. 2775, Proc. 8th IFIP TC6 Int. Conf. (PWC 2003), Sept. 2003, pp. 726–740.
12. E. Horowitz, S. Sahni, and D. Mehta, *Fundamentals of Data Structures in C++*, Computer Science Press, New York, 1995.

An Adaptive and Scalable Resource Advertisement and Discovery Strategy for Mobile Ad Hoc Networks

Donggeon Noh[1] and Heonshik Shin[2]

[1] Seoul National Univ., School of Computer Science and Engineering, 301-551,
151-742 Kwanak-gu, Sillim-dong, Seoul, Korea
dgnoh@mobisys.snu.ac.kr
[2] Seoul National Univ., School of Computer Science and Engineering, 301-502,
151-742 Kwanak-gu, Sillim-dong, Seoul, Korea
shinhs@snu.ac.kr

Abstract. Effective resource advertisement and discovery (*Ad/D*) are particularly important in mobile ad hoc networks (*MANETs*), due to network dynamics and resource constraints of wireless nodes. In this paper, we propose an adaptive and scalable resource *Ad/D* technique for *MANETs*. Based on a variable zone size, it combines push-based *Ad/D* with a pull-based *Ad/D* that uses a modified bordercasting resolution protocol. The scheme avoids redundant flooding and reduces system overhead by piggybacking resource information on the routing-layer packet, and adapts locally to changing conditions, such as mobility and popularity levels, in a *MANET*. Simulation results verify that our scheme can track a changing network environment while reducing the resource *Ad/D* network overheads, thereby saving resources, decreasing latency and being scalable to large *MANETs*.

1 Introduction

Rapid advances in network application technology and its pervasive influence over our society demand an efficient way to locate resources[1] over the network. Particularly, in self-configurable networks which are to be easily deployed and reconfigured automatically when extended with new hardware and/or software capabilities, it is necessary to efficiently execute the advertisement and discovery (*Ad/D*) of the network resources. Mobile ad hoc networks (*MANETs*) are a special form of such self-configurable networks with their own peculiarities, such as network dynamics, resource constraints at the constituent nodes, and no centralized mechanisms for managing the network. Because of these characteristics, the development of resource discovery strategies for *MANETs* poses interesting challenges:

1. Enabling resource-constrained, wireless devices to discover resources dynamically, while minimizing both the control traffic and latency.
2. Enabling resource discovery in large-scale *MANETs*.
3. Enabling lightweight resource discovery for resource-poor constituent nodes.

---

[1] The resources of a network are made up of many kinds of service and information, including peripherals, computation, storage, and the network itself.

Y.-C. Chung and J.E. Moreira (Eds.): GPC 2006, LNCS 3947, pp. 237–249, 2006.
© Springer-Verlag Berlin Heidelberg 2006

To meet these requirements, we present *RADIZ* (resource *Ad/D* protocol with independent zone), which is a directory-less hybrid adaptive resource *Ad/D* strategy integrated with a network-layer protocol. *RADIZ* provides a zone size determination algorithm for hybrid *Ad/D*, which considers the network characteristic (i.e. mobility and call rate) and the popularity of the resource. In addition, it offers a lightweight implementation of resource *Ad/D* by using existing routing control packets. Moreover, it provides an efficient resource discovery mechanism for on-demand (i.e. pull-based) resource finding. These characteristics allow *RADIZ* to support *Ad/D* with a relatively low overhead and latency, making it applicable to large-scale *MANETs* (i.e. those with at least 100 nodes), unlike other directory-less *Ad/D* schemes.

The rest of this paper is organized as follows. The next section contains an analysis of existing resource *Ad/D* strategies for *MANET*. Section 3 describes the characteristics of our adaptive and scalable resource *Ad/D* strategy. We then give an overview of the simulation environment and present an evaluation of our strategy in Section 4. Finally, conclusions are drawn and future works are discussed in Section 5.

2   Resource *Ad/D* for *MANETs*

In a *MANET* scenario, it can be argued that the directory-less resource *Ad/D* model is more suitable than the directory model, because it can be performed in a completely distributed fashion and there is no need for any infrastructure. In the directory-less model for *MANETs*, users actively send out resource request messages and servers listen for these messages at a well-determined network interface and port. Users can also learn about the available resources in a passive way by listening for resource advertisements that are generated by the servers.[2]

In several existing directory-less resource *Ad/D* implementations, resource *Ad/D* models are applied at the middleware layer [6], [7]. These models have to be supported by underlying ad hoc routing protocols. Both the *Ad/D* protocol and the routing protocol can invoke redundant flooding of the network, and this inevitably incurs a large overhead. Additionally, these are rather heavyweight solutions, because they must be implemented as an independent layer. Both of these problems can be a serious drawback in *MANETs*, in which there is often a shortage of network and computing power.

A consideration of these problems motivates the integration of resource *Ad/D* protocols with routing protocols. A resource *Ad/D* protocol has already been integrated with a proactive routing protocol [8] and also with a reactive routing protocol [1], [2], [3]. More recently, two strategies, *RUBI* [5] and *HAID* [4], have been designed by integrating a hybrid resource *Ad/D* protocol with a simple routing protocol, and this approach shows improved performance. However, the size of the push-based resource zone is simply determined by the transmission range of the node in *RUBI*, or by the popularity of the resource provider node in *HAID*. Furthermore, neither Oh *et al* [4] nor Harbird *et al* [5] simulate their schemes in large-scale *MANETs*.

---

[2] We refer to these methods of resource *Ad/D* as the pull-based *Ad/D* model and the push-based *Ad/D* model respectively. The hybrid resource *Ad/D* model is a hybrid of these two models.

We conclude that existing directory-less resource *Ad/D* protocols have shortcomings: in particular, a poor ability to adapt to dynamic network changes (e.g. mobility and call rate level in the network, popularity level of the resource), low efficiency of resource discovery algorithms, and dubious scalability.

3 RADIZ

RADIZ is an adaptive hybrid resource *Ad/D* protocol integrated with the *IZR* routing protocol, as summarized in Figure 1. Integration with the routing protocol is intended to result in a lightweight scheme and to reduce the amount of unnecessary network flooding. The hybrid resource model is used to provide efficient advertisement and discovery. But, *RADIZ* also allows nodes to adapt their own zone radii dynamically and automatically as the network environment changes. And these changing zone radii are used to provide an efficient resource query mechanism.

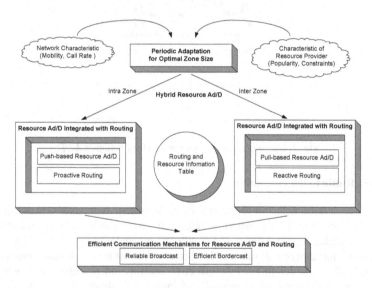

Fig. 1. Overview of the *RAIDZ* strategy

3.1 Hybrid Resource *Ad/D* Strategy Integrated with a Routing Protocol

Redundant flooding operations by middleware-oriented resource *Ad/D* strategies can expose serious deficiencies in *MANET* environments, which are by nature poor in resources. By piggybacking the resource information on the routing control packet, we can implement a lightweight *Ad/D* scheme which can obtain the resource and routing information for an expected resource provider simultaneously.

Our *RADIZ* scheme also uses a hybrid resource model, which allows each node to perform push-based *Ad/D* in its zone, and pull-based *Ad/D* elsewhere. This is made possible by integrating the resource *Ad/D* process with a hybrid routing protocol. Previous studies of routing [10], [11] have shown that a hybrid routing protocol is more efficient than simple proactive or reactive protocols, in the context of a *MANET*. Therefore, by integrating the resource *Ad/D* protocol with an effective hybrid routing protocol (i.e. *IZR*), we expect to achieve a more efficient resource *Ad/D* model. We will introduce an extended version of the *IARP* (intra routing protocol) packet, which carries resource information piggyback, and call it the *IAIP* (intra integrated protocol) packet. And the *IERP* (inter routing protocol) packet is likewise expanded to become the *IEIP* (inter integrated protocol) packet. The architecture of the framework for integrating hybrid *Ad/D* and routing is provided in Figure 2.

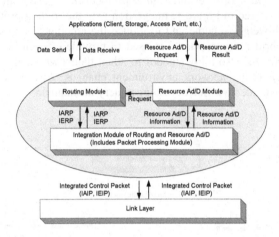

Fig. 2. Integrated framework for a hybrid resource *Ad/D*

3.2 Zone Radius Determination

In *RADIZ*, each node determines the size of its own zone independently, while taking into account the state of the network (e.g. call rate, mobility). Resource providers must also consider popularity (e.g. the number of resource invocations). For example, if the network has a high call rate and low mobility, most nodes should have relatively large zone radii, in order to perform effective routing and resource *Ad/D* with minimum impact on the network overhead and latency. Additionally, the provider of a more popular resource operates more efficiently with a larger zone.

Since *RADIZ* integrates the resource *Ad/D* protocol with the routing protocol, the zone of a resource provider node is now the push-based *Ad/D* zone as well as the proactive routing zone. But the zone of a resource user node is only the proactive routing zone, and does not include push-based *Ad/D* since a user has nothing to advertise. Nevertheless, the zone of a user node is still significant in the resource *Ad/D* process, because it determines the base from which we can perform effective on-demand resource discovery, as explained in Section 3.4.

We determine zone sizes using a modified version of the *IZR* algorithm, which is a hybrid of the *Min_Searching* and *Adaptive_Traffic_Estimation (ATE)* algorithms [12], tailored to integrated *Ad/D*. The proactive traffic of a node is a nondecreasing function of the zone radius, and the reactive traffic is a nonincreasing function of the radius [12].

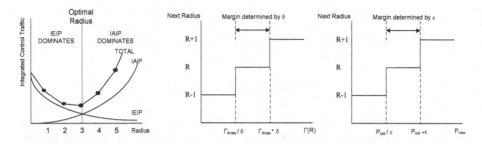

Fig. 3. A hybrid zone determination algorithm of *RADIZ*: (a) *Min_Searching*, (b) *Adaptive_Traffic_Estimation (ATE)*, and (c) Additional part of *ATE* for resource provider

Hence, the total control traffic, which is a sum of these two components, is a convex function. Figure 3(a) shows how the *IAIP*, *IEIP* and total control traffic vary with zone radius. In this figure, the total control traffic is a minimum when the zone radius is 3. At each node, the *Min_Searching* algorithm can find the minimum point on the integrated control traffic curve by repeated refinement of the zone size in increments and decrements of one hop. More specifically, each node estimates the integrated control packet traffic at each time step. If the amount of traffic has fallen, the next change to the radius is in the same sense; if the traffic has increased, the radius is changed in the opposite directions.

Once the lowest point on the control traffic curve has been found, the ratio of the *IEIP* component to the *IAIP* component at the optimal zone radius is set to Γ_{thres}, which is periodically used by the *ATE* algorithm to tune the zone radius. Let $\Gamma(R)$ be the ratio of the *IEIP* traffic to the *IAIP* traffic, measured at a network node during an estimation interval during which the zone radius is R. Simplistically, we can now compare $\Gamma(R)$ with Γ_{thres} to determine whether the zone radius should shrink or grow. However, since frequent changes of zone size can make the network unstable, a delayed triggering mechanism is introduced by the use of a multiplicative hysteresis term, δ. As illustrated in Figure 3(b), if $\Gamma(R) > \Gamma_{thres} \cdot \delta$, then the radius is increased by one hop; if $\Gamma(R) < \Gamma_{thres} / \delta$, the radius is decreased by one hop.

In the case of a resource provider, the popularity of the resource as well as the network state must be considered by the *ATE* algorithm. For this reason, a resource provider periodically monitors the frequency of invocation of its resource. As shown in Figure 3(c) if P_{new} (the invocation frequency during the current period) is higher than P_{old} (the invocation frequency during the last period), then the radius is increased by one hop, and vice versa. A delayed triggering mechanism is also used here to prevent frequent changes of zone size. The multiplicative hysteresis term is ε.

With this hybrid algorithm, each node adapts to dynamic changes in the network environment with little computational overhead.

3.3 Push-Based Resource Ad/D

In *RADIZ*, each resource provider performs push-based resource advertisement in its dynamic zone. The provider periodically broadcasts an advertisement message to all nodes within its zone, and resource users within that zone learn passively about the resource by receiving these advertisements.

Fig. 4. *RPM* (resource publicity message) format

In order to implement integrated push-based resource advertisement, we designed the *IAIP* packet format. We will refer to an *IAIP* packet used in the *Ad/D* mechanism as an *RPM* (resource publicity message). Figure 4 shows that an *RPM* is composed of two parts. One is the routing control part used by the *IARP*. The other is the resource information part which includes the resource type, the resource lifetime and additional information about the resource, such as its functional interface and *QoS* (quality of service) level. This resource information part can be modified as required. If the target service architecture is service-oriented and based on web services, then *WSDL* (web services description language) can be used for resource description. In this paper, we focus on the *Ad/D* architecture, and not on the device-level or service-level interoperability. Therefore, we use a simple resource information description.

The resource type is predefined across all the nodes and the resource lifetime field is used to support the renewal cycle of the resource provider. If a node which receives an *RPM* does not receive it again during the lifetime of that resource, the node invalidates that resource information. This allows the network to accommodate quickly to the disappearance of a resource provider. The additional information field includes the functional interface and dynamic *QoS* attributes of the resource. The *QoS* specification includes: (i) scalability information, which specifies the capacity of the resource to service additional requests over a specified period of time; (ii) the performance and capacity of the host, including its available energy, computation power, and network bandwidth. This specification of *QoS* parameters is optional but, for each parameter, the following attributes must be specified: name, value and expiration. The *TTL* (time to live) field is initially set to its own zone radius.

3.4 On-Demand Pull-Based Resource Discovery

RADIZ uses the *BRP* (bordercast resolution protocol) [9] as a pull-based resource discovery method. It provides efficient mechanisms for sending a query to peripheral nodes[3], and for routing the query outward from the source beyond its own zone. Additionally, it provides a query detection mechanism to prevent query overlap.

With independent zone radii, the zone of one node may be completely included in the zone of another. In this case, the first node cannot explore any new zone when it receives a query from the second node. Processing such a query wastes the resources of the first node. *BRP* avoids this situation by assigning query processing to nodes which are able to explore new zones. Figure 5 illustrates the example of bordercasting by a node with a zone radius of 3. To start bordercasting, the *BRP* constructs a

---

[3] A peripheral node is a node whose minimum distance to the source node is exactly equal to the zone radius.

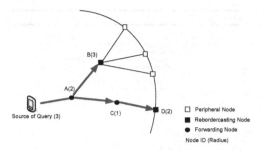

Fig. 5. Example of bordercasting using *BRP*

bor-dercast tree that connects the source node to all peripheral nodes. Then it chooses rebordercasting nodes on the basis of the zone radius of each node and the query detection mechanism. In Figure 5, Nodes *B* and *D* are chosen as rebordercasting nodes, since they are the closest to the source node of all the nodes which are able to access the outside of the zone and which have not previously received the current query. The resource user unicasts a resource query message to these rebordercasting nodes. Lastly, the rebordercasting node executes query processing, and if it still has no information about the target resource, it performs bordercasting again.

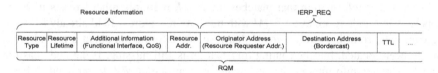

Fig. 6. Pull-based *RQM* (resource query message) format

In order to achieve pull-based resource discovery using bordercasting, we need an *RQM* (resource query message) and an *RRM* (resource reply message), which add resource information to the general *IERP* request packet (*IERP_REQ*) and to the *IERP* reply packet (*IERP_REP*) respectively. The format of pull-based *RQM* message is shown in Figure 6. The lifetime and resource address fields of the *RQM* are initially empty and are used temporarily before an *RRM* is generated. The resource type and additional information fields should initially be filled with identification of the resource information that the user wants to find. The destination address field of the *RQM* contains the address of a rebordercast node supplied by the source node.

The *RRM* has similar format to the *RQM*. It contains the resource information which the *RQM* has found. After an *RRM* has been created by a node which has the necessary information, it is sent to the node from which the *RQM* was received, as part of a backtracking process that leads back to the node that initiated bordercasting.

The query processing algorithm is shown in Figure 7. When a rebordercasting node receives a resource query, it performs the query processing algorithm. If a node has the information about the resource provider which matches the *RQM*, and the routing information for that resource provider node, that node creates an *RRM* that contains

```
Query-Processing (RQM)

 1   If Check_RA (RQM) == NULL  then              //RA (Resource Address)
 2           If Have_Resource_Info (RT(RQM)) then  //RT (Resource Type)
 3                   If Have_Route_Info (RA(RQM)) then
 4                           Make_RRM (Resource_Info, Route_Info)
 5                           Reply (RRM)
 6                   else
 7                           Fill_RQM (Resource_Info) // RA is filled
 8                           Bordercasting (RQM)
 9                   end If
10           else
11                   Bordercasting (RQM)
12           end if
13   else
14           If Have_Route_Info (RA(RQM)) then
15                   Make_RRM (Resource_Info, Route_Info)
16                   Reply (RRM)
17           else
18                   If Have_Alter_Resource_Info_With_Routing_Info (RT(RQM)) then
19                           Make_RRM (Resource_Info, Route_Info)
20                           Reply (RRM)
21                   else
22                           Bordercasting (RQM)
23                   end if
24           end if
25   end if
```

Fig. 7. Pseudo-code for the query processing and bordercasting algorithm

this resource and routing information and sends it back by the reverse path. But if the node only has resource information, and no routing information for the provider, it only fills the resource information fields of the *RQM* and rebordercasts it. If a node has no resource information that matches the *RQM*, it simply rebordercasts it. Now, suppose that a node receives an *RQM* with the resource address field already filled in. We can infer from this kind of *RQM* that resource information about a provider has already been located, but the routing information is still missing. If the node has the required routing information, it can create an appropriate *RRM* and send it back. However, if it has no routing information about that resource provider, but it does have resource and routing information about an alternative resource provider, it creates an *RRM* with information about that alternative provider and sends it back.

4   Performance Evaluation

We designed a simulation to evaluate the performance of *RADIZ*. Extended *NS2* from Cornell University [4] was used to implement *RADIZ*. On top of the *IEEE 802.11 MAC* protocol, *OLSR* [14] was used as the proactive routing protocol integrated with a push-based resource *Ad/D* protocol, and *AODV* [13] was used as the reactive routing protocol integrated with a pull-based resource *Ad/D* protocol.

4.1   Simulation Model

We created network containing different numbers of nodes (50, 100, 150, 200), spread randomly over an area of 1000×1000 m^2. Five nodes are resource providers. All nodes in the network have advance knowledge of the resource types. Each simulation ran for 500 seconds and there were 30 runs in total.

---

[4] http://wnl.ece.cornell.edu/Software/zrp/ns2

There are several parameters that we can use to characterize a network. The first is the mean speed of the nodes. The faster their relative speed, the more dynamic the network is. The second parameter is the mean pause time, which controls how long a node can remain in one place before moving. The longer the pause time, the more stable the network is. The third parameter is the *MSID* (mean session interarrival delay) which corresponds to the call rate of the nodes. The smaller the *MSID*, the more frequent calls are. From the resource provider's point of view, there is one further parameter which is the *MTNR* (mean time to next request). It represents the popularity of the resource.

In order to simulate the resource *Ad/D* traffic, a randomly chosen node sends a resource query message to one resource provider. The interarrival times between queries to each provider are exponentially distributed with a given *MTNR* (1s, 10s). Since *RADIZ* is integrated with the *IZR* routing protocol, we need to simulate routing traffic as well as resource *Ad/D* traffic. We therefore make each node send a certain number of data packets to a randomly chosen destination. The number of data packets per session follows a Poisson distribution with an average of 10 packets. The interarrival time between sessions at each node is exponentially distributed with a given *MSID* (3s, 150s). The source of a particular session generates 1Kbit data packets at the constant rate of 16 packets per second.

4.2 Simulation Results

To evaluate the performance of *RADIZ*, we implemented five different resource *Ad/D* strategies and conducted a simulation of each strategy. *ZRP-RDP* is the resource *Ad/D* protocol integrated with *ZRP*, and *AODV-RDP* is the *Ad/D* protocol integrated with *AODV*. We will also refer to pull-based *RDP* and push-based *RDP*, which are the resource *Ad/D* protocols separated from the routing protocol.

Figure 8 shows comparative results for average traffic and latency for different resource *Ad/D* strategies. In this experiment, we only simulated the resource *Ad/D* traffic and not the routing traffic. The mean speed of the nodes is 0.5 m/s, the pause time is 100s and the *MTNR* of each resource node is 1s. The value of δ, ε for delayed triggering is 10 and 1.5 respectively. As Figure 8 (a) indicates, *RADIZ* saves between 20% and 65% of the control traffic related to resource *Ad/D* when the number of nodes is 50. The average control traffic mentioned in this figure refers to the control packets passing through each node during the simulation. Therefore, the total number of control packets in the network can be reduced substantially by using *RADIZ*. Moreover, the larger the number of nodes, the more definite the difference in traffic overhead is between *RADIZ* and the other strategies. Among other strategies, *ZRP-RDP* shows the best performance when the zone radius is 1 hop, but this pre-defined uniform radius may not be suited to other environments. The traffic overhead of *RADIZ* does not increase exponentially as the number of nodes increases, which shows that *RADIZ* is suitable for large-scale ad-hoc networks. We can also infer that the nodes have found an approximately optimal radius from the fact that, using *RADIZ*, the traffic is less than it is for *ZRP-RDP*, whether the zone radius is 1 or 2. The average zone radius during this experiment was about 1.45. Figure 8(b) shows that *RADIZ* also shows the best performance in term of latency.

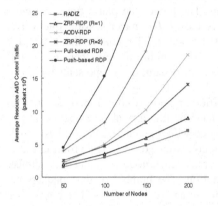

Fig. 8. Performance of *RADIZ* with only resource *Ad/D* traffic: (a) Average resource *Ad/D* control traffic and (b) Average *Ad/D* query latency

To observe the performance of *RADIZ* in a more realistic environment, in which resource *Ad/D* and routing traffic coexist, we simulated resource *Ad/D* traffic and routing traffic simultaneously. We also changed the network environment 250 seconds after the start of the simulation in order to assess the adaptability of *RADIZ*. The network characteristics and traffic model that we simulated are set out in Table 1. Figure 9 shows the effect on the average control traffic of varying the resource *Ad/D* strategy and the number of nodes. Again, *RADIZ* gives the best performance among the six strategies, and the differential performance grows with the number of nodes. Moreover, *RADIZ* saves much more traffic overhead in this realistic scenario than in a static environment in which there is only resource *Ad/D* traffic.

In order to study the performance of *RADIZ* in more detail, we analyzed the traffic for each strategy at each period, in a 100-node network. Figure 10(a) shows the results. In Period 1, *RADIZ*, *ZRP-RDP* with a zone radius of 1, and *AODV-RDP*

Table 1. Simulation environment with realistic traffic

		Period 1 (0s~250s)	Period 2 (250s~500s)
Network Environment	Average Speed	15 m/s	0.5 m/s
	Pause Time	10 s	100 s
Service Ad/D Traffic	MTNR	10 s	1 s
Routing Traffic	MSID	150 s	3 s

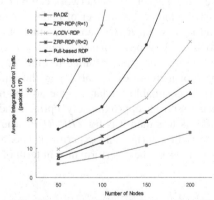

Fig. 9. Average integrated control traffic with both resource *Ad/D* and routing traffic

produce relatively little traffic, while *ZRP-RDP* with a zone radius of 2, and push-based *RDP* generate much more. We suggest that this occurs because a high level of *IAIP* traffic is incurred by zone maintenance, when there is a rapidly changing network topology and a high probability of link failure. In Period 2, however, *RADIZ* and *ZRP-RDP* with a zone radius of 2 show relatively little traffic, while *AODV-RDP* and pull-based *RDP* are now much busier. This result indicates that it is more efficient to maintain larger zones when there is a relatively stable network environment and a Figure 10(a), high call rate, which are the characteristics of Period 2. As we can see from *RADIZ* has better performance than all the other schemes, in terms of the total number of control packets, over both periods.

We also plotted the average zone radius of the nodes over time while varying the δ, ε., As we can see from Figure 10(b), the average zone radius of a node is about 1 in Period 1, and grows to 2.4 in Period 2. The high value of δ, ε can mean that adaptation to changing network characteristics is slow. The average zone radii of the five resource providers are 3.3 in Period 2, which shows that the zone determination algorithm used by *RADIZ* can track a changing network environment while maintaining approximately optimal zone radii. Our confidence in the validity of this assertion is strengthened by the strong performance of *ZRP-RDP* with a zone radius of 1 during Period 1, and with a zone radius of 2 during Period 2, as shown in Figure 10 (a).

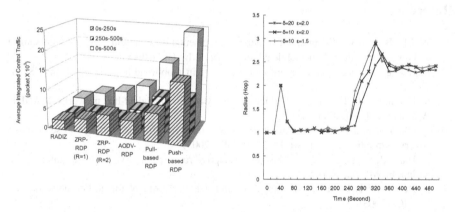

Fig. 10. Adaptability of RADIZ with both resource Ad/D and routing traffic (100-node network): (a) Average integrated control traffic and (b) Average zone radius

5 Conclusions and Future Work

The characteristics of *MANETs*, such as the potentially highly dynamic topology and the inclusion of heterogeneous wireless nodes whose energy needs to be saved for enhanced autonomy, require special care in the handling of distributed resource provisioning. In particular, the discovery of resources must allow access to the whole *MANET*, to ensure availability, while limiting resource consumption. However, existing directory-less discovery protocols designed for *MANETs* are short of adaptability and scalability.

RADIZ is a new lightweight adaptive resource *Ad/D* strategy integrated with the *IZR* routing protocol. It avoids the use of redundant flooding mechanisms by integrating the *Ad/D* and routing protocols, and can perform more effective resource *Ad/D* by applying a hybrid resource *Ad/D* model which combines the pull-based and push-based approaches. The system overhead is substantially reduced because *RADIZ* extends the existing routing packet, rather then requiring separate resource *Ad/D* packets. In addition, each node can have its own zone size to facilitate local adaptation to dynamic changes in the network environment. Maintaining an optimal zone around each node allows *RADIZ* to provide an efficient query routing and processing mechanism. The reduced overheads incurred in using *RADIZ* can translate to lower power consumption, less congestion, and reduced memory and processing requirements. Due to these advantages of *RADIZ*, it has the scalability necessary for large-scale *MANETs* containing several hundreds nodes unlike previous directory-less resource *Ad/D* strategies.

In future, we plan to improve the zone size determination algorithm, which may involve considering the resource status or the number of providers supplying the same type of resource. We also intend to refine the bordercasting mechanism and to undertake a more mathematical analysis of the integrated traffic model used by *RADIZ*.

References

1. W. Ma, B. Wu, W. Zhang, and L. Cheng.: Implementation of a light service advertisement and discovery protocol for mobile ad hoc network. In: GLOBECOM. (2003)
2. L. Cheng.: Service advertisement and discovery in mobile ad-hoc networks. In: CSCW. (2002)
3. R. Koodli and C. E. Perkins.: Service discovery in on-demand ad-hoc networks. MANET-WG Internet Draft, IETF. (2002)
4. C. Oh, Y. Ko, and Y. Roh.: An integrated approach for efficient routing and service discovery in mobile ad hoc networks. In: CCNC. (2005)
5. R. Harbird, S. Halies, and C. Mascolo.: Adaptive resource discovery for ubiquitous computing. In: MPAC. (2004)
6. S. Helal.: Konark – a service discovery and delivery protocol for ad-hoc networks. In: WCNC. (2003)
7. R. Hermann, D. Husemann, M. Moser, M. Nidd, C. Rohner, and A. Schade.: DEAPspace: transient ad-hoc networking of pervasive devices. The International Journal of Computer and Telecommunications Networking, Vol. 35 (2001) 411-428
8. U. C. Kozat and L. Tassiulas.: Network layer support for service discovery in mobile ad hoc networks. In: INFOCOM. (2003)
9. Z. J. Haas, M. R. Pearlman, and P. Samar.: The bordercast resolution protocol (BRP) for ad hoc networks. MANET-WG Internet Draft, IETF. (2002)
10. Z. J. Haas, M. R. Pearlman, and P. Samar.: The zone routing protocol (ZRP) for ad hoc networks. MANET-WG Internet Draft, IETF. (2002)
11. P. Samar, M. R. Pearlman, and Z. J. Hass.: Independent zone routing: an adaptive hybrid routing framework for ad hoc wireless networks. IEEE/ACM Transactions on Networking, Vol. 12 (2004) 595-608
12. M. R. Pearlman and Z. J. Haas.: Determination of the optimal configuration for the zone routing protocol. IEEE Communications, Vol. 17 (1999) 1395-1414

13. C. E. Perkins, E. M. Belding-Royer, and S. Das.: Ad hoc on-demand distance vector (AODV) routing. RFC 3561, IETF. (2003)
14. T. Clausen and P. Jacquet.: Optimized link state routing protocol (OLSR). RFC 3626, IETF. (2003)
15. U. Kozar and L. Tassiulas.: Service discovery in mobile ad hoc networks: An overall perspective on architectural choices and network layer support issues. Ad Hoc Networks, Vol. 2 (2004) 23-44
16. F. Sailhan and V. Issarny.: Scalable service discovery for MANET. In: PerCom. (2005)

Binding Multiple Applications on Wireless Sensor Networks

Ali Hammad Akbar, Ahmad Ali Iqbal, and Ki-Hyung Kim[1]

Graduate School of Information and Communication,
Ajou University, Suwon, 443-749, Korea
{hammad, ahmad, kkim86}@ajou.ac.kr

Abstract. Multiple applications can be invoked simultaneously on single sensor network through pre-emptive or late binding. Triggering multiple applications on sensor networks at a post-deployment stage results into complex interactions between them. In this paper, we discuss considerations for multiservice sensor networks such as resource allocation and energy conservation. First, we identify the uniqueness of node selection strategies for such multi-service sensor networks. Second, we discuss their effects on network usability and longevity. We present a holistic nodes election protocol for such networks. Simulation results show increased longevity of networks when our protocol is implemented on the network.

1 Introduction

Wireless sensor networks (WSNs) are a new breed of networks that are application centric and mission oriented. Distributed in nature, these networks comprise miniaturized hardware platforms and software environments adapted to a wide variety of applications. So far, most of the application frameworks suggested for wireless sensor networks have assumed a single service supported by sensor nodes deployed in the region of interest (ROI). Such single service architectures are relatively simpler in implementation and management. Management architectures of some existing applications, however, support change of mission in due course of sensor lifetime.

The problem of sensor nodes management and their network-wide coordination takes altogether a different outlook once multiple applications are considered from the service perspective of sensor networks. For example, a sensor network that renders multiple services simultaneously in the form of application overlays risks of computation and communication contradictions. Consider Fig.1 for the sake of illustration where four applications running on the same sensor network share both the nodes' as well as the network's resources. A resource heavy application's requirements might compromise another or all the other applications' quality of service (QoS). Similarly, due to bidding against only the best resources by applications, part of the sensor network might be under-utilized [1]. The problems highlighted above can be mitigated by pre-emptive application binding on the sensor nodes. However, it is not a valid assumption in most of today's applications scenarios of sensor networks. There is a

---

[1] Corresponding author.

Y.-C. Chung and J.E. Moreira (Eds.): GPC 2006, LNCS 3947, pp. 250–258, 2006.

need for orchestrating nodes' and network resources in run time. Therefore late binding of applications on sensor networks will be a plausible proposition in futuristic applications. Our contribution here is to propose a protocol that helps applications to commit resources on the sensor nodes in a fair manner. This load balancing protocol ensures that all the nodes are effectively utilized to serve multiple applications. The performance of our protocol shows an increase system longevity by allowing nodes closer to the application sinks to conserve energy.

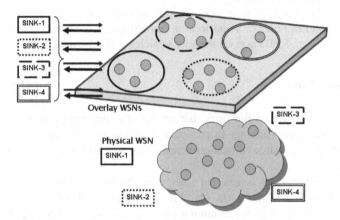

Fig. 1. Multiple applications support by a single wireless sensor network

The paper is organized as follows. In section 2, we present scenarios that entail multiple services provisioning on single sensor network. In section 3, we present the work reported so far that studies various aspects of multiservice provisioning networks. In section 4 we present specific questions that pose challenge to the design of such a multiservice WSN. Assumptions necessary to propose our scheme are outlined in section 5. Section 6 thoroughly presents the nodes' resource bidding and reservation protocol. Simulation results and performance analysis are discussed in section 7. Section 8 concludes the paper.

2   Scenario Illustrating Multiple Services Provisioning on a Singular Wireless Sensor Networks

In this section, we present a scenario to provide motivation for our research. The scenario will be elaborated for requirements in the next section.

2.1   Scenario: Military Applications

For military applications, primary considerations remain robustness, accuracy, and timeliness. State-of-the-art vibration, acoustic and magnetic sensors for object diversity are employed and onboard algorithms are used to optimize their performance. E.g., sensor-cued images of detected threats may be rapidly relayed to chief command for real-time threat identification and prosecution. Following applications may be rendered by sensor nodes:

Target tracking: Sensor nodes are randomly deployed through unarmed air vehicle (UAV) in the battle zone to track enemy vehicles, measure the location of the vehicle and send this information to the central command for decision making.

Mine detection: Nodes performing tracking may be assigned another task of mine detection simultaneously to facilitate infantry and armoured personnel carriers to penetrate into the enemy territory.

Friend or foe: Finally, these sensor nodes may also signal friend or foe (FoF) to central command in order to avoid loss or casualty through friendly fire by detecting the presence of e.g., RFID tags on friendly vehicles and personnel.

3 Related Work

In this section, we discuss the work that relates to issues regarding sensor networks with multiservice provisioning. In particular, we review schemes and protocols that support node and resource allocation schemes for binding applications onto sensor networks.

Yang Yu et al presents issues that emerge in allocating resources for a single service under various constraints in [2]. They formulate task allocation on a sensor network as Integer Linear Programming problem and as a 3-phase heuristic. Using simulations, they analyze energy-latency tradeoffs for the two schemes.

A more recent work by the same author in [3] has pinpointed the exact issue of multiservice provisioning by adopting a middleware approach. They also identify the need for resource management in cluster-based sensor networks.

A management approach is presented by Linnyer et al in [4]. They give MANNA architecture for specifying functional, information, and physical management of sensor networks. The authors itemizes the management functions such as topology discovery function, node operating state control function, and network connectivity discovery function etc. However, this paper does not propose a new resource allocation and optimization protocol.

Well known routing schemes such as [5]-[8] address optimizations over energy efficiency, reducing communication overhead, scalability and reliability. However, there is no explicit mention to support multiple services in either of the schemes.

In summary, no work reported so far proposes nodes' resource allocation protocol that considers network lifetime and network utilization simultaneously.

4 Purported Challenges

Consider Fig. 2 where sensor nodes are part of various applications simultaneously being executed on a WSN. There are specific sinks associated with every application, though shown for just three for visual clarity. Applications solicit for resources on individual sensor nodes through gateways to carrying out sensing for them. Another important concern is that all the sensor nodes in the ROI must be used as fairly as possible, else the network is underutilized. With usual greedy approach of choosing the closest nodes with appropriate resources, it is quite likely that multiple applications will acquire sensing nodes in the fringes of the network. The nodes in the centre of the network may go unused.

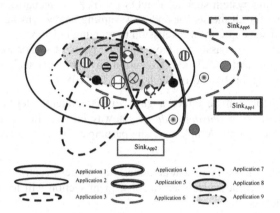

Fig. 2. Applications sharing sensor nodes and application specific sinks

These observations and requirements pose the following questions that we sought answers for in the next section.

Question#1: How can gateways acquire nodes for their applications such that nodes closer to gateways are highly available for routing data?

Question#2: How can load be balanced amongst the sensor nodes in the ROI?

Question#3: How can a system be made dynamic such that it optimizes energy-latency-load for applications with differing QoS requirements?

These questions when seen in the context of network and node resources intrigue our minds to put forth resource allocation protocol. In the following sections, we define nodes' resource bidding and allocation protocol and its variants in detail.

5 Model and Assumptions

In this section, we formulate the role of entities and other key assumptions that interplay in the proposed protocol.

Communication: Sensor nodes transmit data that can be received by one hop neighbours. All the non-destined nodes can overhear the transmission. This phenomenon is useful in establishing the behaviour of the surrounding nodes in dense deployments.

Caching: The sensor nodes have the capability to cache the data or control messages. This assumption allows a node to hold data or control information until some specific timers expire.

Deployment: Sensor nodes are randomly deployed in the region of interest. This will result into non-uniform accessibility of nodes' resources to application gateways.

Node architecture and constraints: Every sensor node in the network has resources that enable it to execute certain tasks. Intelligence in a sensor node is provided through an operating system such as TinyOS [9]. For our scenario, we assume a homogeneous model for all the sensor nodes. Assuming heavy sensing applications, we model the ratio of sensing-cum-transmission to relaying is 1:0.3.

A single sensor node chassis can have multiple types of sensors, e.g., thermal sensor, a photodetector, and a CCD etc. Execution environments such as TinyOS® provide concurrency support by add-ins such as MATE [10].

Node types: A node can be either a *gateway* (equivalently termed as *sink* when deemed appropriate) or a *sensing node*. A gateway initiates the resource solicitation on behalf of an application. A sink node can participate in sensing and/or routing data for a specific gateway.

Routing protocol: It is assumed that an underlying address-centric routing protocol is in-place. The protocol messages used in subsequent section will form the payload of the usual data packets.

6 Nodes' Resource Bidding and Reservation Protocol

The protocol answers the challenge questions raised in section 4 by providing the following features:

- The selection of nodes and their resources is based on their current load and remaining battery energy.
- Nodes that are closer to gateways are involved in sensing activities to a lesser extent. This ensures network longevity.
- Nodes that are farther from the application gateways, which otherwise were ignored, also participate in sensing activities. This yields a higher degree of network utilization.

In remainder of the section, we present the details of our proposed protocol. The operation of the protocol is performed using following algorithms and packet formats.

A. Application Advertisement Message

An application advertises its bid to solicit sensor nodes and their resources for its application tasks through *Application_Join_Req* message. This advertisement is received by all one-hop neighbours. The packet format for Application_Join message is shown in Fig. 3 and explained below.

Flag	App_ID	TTL	Threshold

Fig. 3. Packet format for application advertisement message

Flag: *Application_Join_Req* message; 00
Application_ID: Identifies a unique application. It is used to match a request to a reply

TTL: Time to live; A hop count field that decrements on every hop.

Threshold: A field specified by the application. The node at which TTL equals threshold, it may join an application as a sensing node. This field prevents nodes closer to the sink from becoming part of a specific application. Thus nodes deep inside the network are chosen for sensing tasks and nodes closer to the gateway forward the sensed data.

B. Node Reply Message

A node or set of nodes within one-hop neighbourhood of a gateway receive *Application_Join_Req* message. From here on, we may refer to the sensor node under consideration as *this* node. Each of *these* nodes starts a timer called *Join_TimeOut*. The duration of timer will depend upon the following factors:

Current_Application_Load: A number that shows the number of applications *this* node is already part of. Thus greater load on the sensor node will result into longer timer duration.

Remaining_Battery: It represents the remaining units of energy affordable by *this* sensor node. Incase there is enough battery power, timer duration will be shortened.

A node can reply back to the gateway in either of the messages given below. Fig. 4 shows a general format of sensor node reply message.

Flag	App_ID

Fig. 4. Packet format for sensor node reply message

Application_Join_Rep message: 01
The timer of *this* node has expired. The *TTL* field does not equal the *Threshold* field now. The node has not overheard any neighboring node replying back to the gateway. It implies that this node is the only node in one hop vicinity to the gateway. Or there may be some nodes that are beyond the reception range of *this* node. The node expresses its willingness to act as a router, and rebroadcasts the *Application_Join_Req* message.

Application_Join_Rep message: 10
The timer of *this* node has expired. The *TTL* field equals the *Threshold* field now. The node has not overheard any neighboring node replying back to the gateway. The node may expresses its willingness to act as a sensor node and a router. It rebroadcasts the *Application_Join_Req* message.

Application_Join_Rep message: 11
The timer of *this* node has expired. The *TTL* field equals the *Threshold* field now. The node has not overheard any neighboring node replying back to the gateway. The node only agrees to be a router for the application. It rebroadcasts the *Application_Join_Req* message.

Incase a node overhears a neighboring node replying back to the gateway, it gives up any activity pertaining to this application and clears the timer. This is an indication that there are ample number of nodes available in this area offering spatial redundancy.

By analyzing the working of the proposed protocol, we realize that the *Application_Join_Req* message diverges inside the topology as it traverses through multiple hops. Hence, we refer to this phenomenon as divergecast. This protocol is greedy in approach. Using this scheme, an application can acquire sensing nodes for as long as the *TTL* does not expire.

In the following subsection, we present and discuss a variant of divergecast that yields a different set of advantages.

6.1 Acknowledgment-Based Variant to the Proposed Protocol

In this version of the proposed protocol we introduce the notion of one-hop acknowledgement. It means that in reply to *Application_Join_Req* message from the gateway, receiving nodes generate an *Acknowledgement*. The format of *Acknowledgment* may include node parameters such as current load and remaining battery. Now the gateway decides which next hop node to select. The operation is performed recursively till all the gateways commit nodes' resources on the network. Here, the *Application_Join_Req* message follows a unicast transmission model. This approach cautiously reserves resources, making it more apt for energy starved sensor nodes.

Both the original protocol and its variant have their advantages. However, to make the best out of the two, a policy can be spelled out at the application gateway that allows a switch over to either of the protocols in the real time environments.

The following might form the guidelines for making a policy for soliciting and committing resources in a sensor network.

Traffic type: If the traffic load is high, the variant protocol might be considered. It is due to the fact that higher traffic load means more contention at the link layer. In order to undermine the effect of contention, lesser nodes should be involved in forwarding of data packets.

Application type: If the application defines a minimal coverage in the ROI, it is necessary to use the original proposal. Otherwise, adopting the variant will be a communication-savvy approach.

7 Performance Evaluation

A simulator based on the system in section 6 was developed in c++ to evaluate our approach. The simulations were obtained for a topology of 400 nodes that were randomly distributed across an area of 60*60 units as shown in Fig. 5. A total 25 sinks contested against resources by sending out their *Application_Join_Req* requests. The number of nodes that successfully joined the applications during the simulation time were recorded. By introducing the role of threshold field and associating it with TTL resulted into performance gains. The number of nodes that die during the simulation time were also recorded to see the effect of multiple applications running simultaneously.

Fig 6 shows the performance of the proposed protocol, i.e., divergecast, under two conditions. Compare Fig. 6(a) and Fig. 6(b); when the difference between Threshold and TTL is large, the Application_Join_Req message goes inside the sensor network.

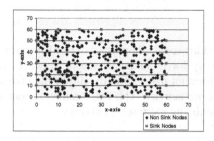

Fig. 5. Simulation topology used for proposed protocol

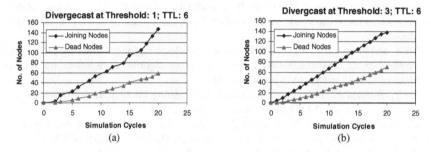

Fig. 6. Performance of proposed protocol

This allows an increased number of nodes to join the contending applications. Similarly, the number of nodes that die because of drained energy is also reduced considerably.

Fig. 7(a) shows similar scenario when the difference between threshold and TTL is three hop. It means that nodes at three hops distance from the sink can join as sensing nodes. The results of Fig. 7(b) show an increase in number of nodes that join the network by a margin of 10. The compromise, however is the longer time for nodes joining. The nodes that die during the simulation shown both in Fig 7(a) and (b) show that using the propsed scheme network longevity can be achieved.

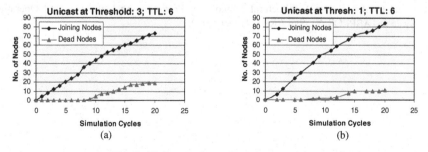

Fig. 7. Unicast variant of proposed protocol

8 Conclusion

In this paper, we have addressed the important issue of interplay between load balancing and network longevity for multiservice sensor networks. We have presented an overlay for resource allocation that implicitly allows the nodes to balance their routing load with local sensing activity. Through simulation, our proposal demonstrates its efficacy in terms of utilizing more sensor nodes.

References

1. Jonathan L., Jeff S., Matt W., Mema R., and Margo S.: Open Problems in Data Collection Networks. Proceeding of 11th ACM SIGOPS European Workshop 2004, Leuven Belgium, (2004)
2. Yu Y. and Prasanna V. K.: Energy-balanced task allocation for collaborative processing in wireless sensor networks. MONET special issue on Algorithmic Solutions for Wireless, Mobile, Ad Hoc and Sensor Networks, (2003)
3. Yu Y., Bhaskar K., Prasanna, V.K.: Issues in Designing Middleware for Wireless Sensor Networks. Network, IEEE Vol. 18, Issue 1, (2004), 15-24
4. Linnyer B. R., Jose M. N., Antonio A. F.: MANNA: A Management Architecture for Wireless Sensor Networks. In IEEE Communication Magazine, vol. 41, (2003)
5. W. Heinzelman, J. Kulik, and H. Balakrishnan, "Negotiation Based Protocols for Disseminating Information in Wireless Sensor Networks," *Wireless Networks*, Vol. 8, pp. 169-185, 2002.
6. Chalermek I., Ramesh G., Deborah E. Directed Diffusion: A Scalable and Robust Communication Paradigm for Sensor Networks. Proceedings of the Sixth Annual ACM/IEEE International Conference on Mobile Computing and Networks (MobiCOM 2000), Boston MA, Aug. 2000.
7. Kemal A., Mohamed Y.A survey on routing protocols for wireless sensor networks. Ad hoc Networks, pp. 325-349, Mar. 2005.
8. Tatiana B., Nirupama B., Sanjay J. A Performance Comparison of Data Dissemination Protocols for Sensor Networks. In Proceedings of IEEE Globecom Wireless Ad Hoc and Sensor Networks Workshop (Globecom 2004), Dallas Texas, Nov. 2004.
9. TinyOS Community Forum (www.tinyos.net)
10. Phil L., David C. Maté: A Virtual Machine for Tiny Networked Sensors," 10th International Conference on Architectural Support for Programming Languages and Operating Systems (ASPLOS-X), San Jose, CA, Oct. 2002.

Model-Aided Metadata Management for Wireless Sensor Networks*

Chongqing Zhang, Haibing Guan, Minglu Li, Min-You Wu,
Wenzhe Zhang, and Feilong Tang

Department of Computer Science and Engineering,
Shanghai Jiaotong University, Shanghai, China
zhangchongqing@sjtu.edu.cn

Abstract. Metadata are abstraction and knowledge of wireless sensor networks
and are used to provide adequate information for query processing. The purpose
of metadata management is to provide adequate information for query processing, while at the same time to make the cost of maintaining the metadata as low
as possible. In this paper, we discuss new issues about metadata management in
wireless sensor networks; and propose a metadata management solution which
includes an architecture and a model-aided approach for the base station to collect meta-data from sensor nodes. Experimental results show the effectiveness
of our solution.

1 Introduction

With the rapid advancement in wireless communications technology and micro-
electro-mechanical systems (MEMS) technology, the wide deployment of large-scale
wireless sensor networks (WSNs) has been made possible. Due to their features of
reliability, accuracy, flexibility, cost-effectiveness and ease of deployment, WSNs are
promising to be used in a wide range of applications, such as environmental monitoring, target tracking, etc [1].

A WSN is a data-centric network [2] and can be viewed as a distributed database [3].
In order to reply a query submitted by a user effectively, a WSN needs to parse and
optimize the query so as to work out an efficient query plan. The query parsing and
optimization work are generally done on the base station with more powerful computation ability and rich resources. After the query plan is worked out, it will be disseminated into the WSN. The decomposed query is executed on sensor nodes and may bring
forth sensing tasks and in-network processing tasks that can save energy significantly by
reducing the bandwidth usage [4].

Then there are several questions. Without knowing the knowledge of the WSN in
priori, how does the base station parse and optimize the queries to work out query
plans of high efficiency? How does an in-network processing function know the
meaning of the data it processes? How does a node adjust itself to satisfy several
queries? The answer to above questions is metadata. In a traditional DB system,
metadata are defined as the descriptive data used by the DBMS to describe the data

---

* This paper is supported by Natural Science Foundation of Shanghai (No.05ZR14081).

Y.-C. Chung and J.E. Moreira (Eds.): GPC 2006, LNCS 3947, pp. 259–268, 2006.

that it manages. But in fact the scope of metadata is beyond this definition. Metadata include data schema, definition of tables and views, statistics of data, storage paths, data distribution information, and so on. Metadata are stored in special tables called the system catalogs. Metadata are frequently accessed and have great influence on the performance of the DBMS so that metadata deserve being carefully designed and managed [5].

There has been substantial work [6, 7, 8, 9, 10, 11, 12] on adopting database techniques to solve the problem of collecting data in wireless sensor network. Several works [6, 9, 10] have mentioned metadata more or less. The special nature of a WSN makes it differ significantly from a traditional database system in many aspects. These differences mean new challenges of metadata management in WSNs. Yet there is not a work dedicated to the research of this issue.

In this paper, we define metadata in a WSN as the descriptive data used to describe the WSN system, including the environment, the nodes and their states, measurement data, and the WSN as a whole entity; metadata are knowledge of the WSN system and can be used for the purpose of querying processing. We try to answer following questions: What metadata are needed for query processing in a WSN? How to formalize these metadata? How do the nodes and the base station manage the metadata in a WSN? How does the base station efficiently collect metadata from nodes in a WSN?

The remainder of this paper is organized as follows. In section II, by discussing query and metadata, challenges of metadata management and definition of metadata are introduced. We introduce the solution in next two sections, that is, the management architecture in section III and the metadata collecting approach in section IV. Experimental results are presented in section V to show the effectiveness of our solution. In section VI, related work is reviewed. We conclude and describe the future work in section VII.

2   Query Processing and Metadata in WSNs

In this section, we first give the WSN model on which we base our research work. Then we discuss query processing in WSNs. Based on the discussion, new challenges of metadata management are introduced.

2.1   Wireless Sensor Network Model

Without loss of generality, the WSN model in this paper is based on following assumptions: 1) A WSN is composed of a base station and large number of nodes scattered on a plane. Each node has a unique identifier. 2) Each node is aware of its location by some localizing techniques, such as GPS or other ranging localization techniques [13]. 3) Base station and nodes can move at a relatively low speed. Nodes don't have to be homogeneous.

2.2   Query Processing in WSNs

Although a WSN can be viewed as a distributed database, its special nature makes it differ significantly from a traditional database system in many aspects. A WSN is composed of a base station and large number of sensor nodes. Base station and nodes play different part in query processing. Query parsing and query optimization are mainly carried out on base station and sensing and in-network processing are carried out on nodes. As a result, new solutions for querying WSNs are needed. Figure 1 illustrates what operations happen in the course of query processing in WSNs.

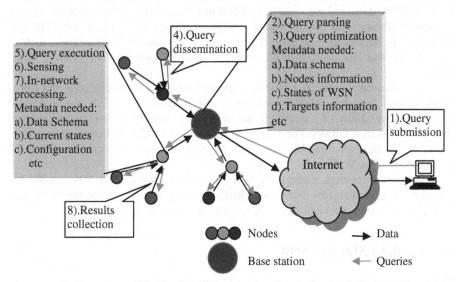

Fig. 1. Operations of Query Processing

Just as Figure 1 reveals, the process of query processing in a WSN has following operations: query parsing, query optimization, query dissemination, query execution, sensing, in-network processing, aggregation, and result collecting, etc. All these operations need the help of metadata. For example, the query parsing and optimization work is generally done on the base station, so the base station needs to maintain metadata, such as nodes distribution and topology of the WSN, for the use of query parsing and optimization.

Note different metadata are needed by different kinds of queries. There is a diversity of applications for WSNs, and accordingly there are different kinds of queries for WSNs. And there are different ways to categorize the types of queries [14], such as long-running continuous queries and one-shot queries, aggregate queries and non-aggregate queries, complex queries and simple queries, etc. It seems there is not a one-fit-all solution to handle all types of queries. Every type of queries has its own nature, which means that it should be treated specially. As a result, the metadata to support those types of queries are different.

2.3 Challenges of Metadata Management

To cater for the new characteristics of WSNs so as to help a WSN process queries effectively, new metadata management solution is demanded. In the following, we summarize new challenges of metadata management in WSNs:

1) Distribution of metadata. In a DBMS, metadata are generally stored concentratedly. While in a WSN, metadata are totally stored distributedly. Both base station and nodes need to maintain corresponding metadata for their use.

2) Formalization of metadata. In a DBMS, most metadata are rather stable, only some statistical metadata are dynamic. While in a WSN, there are errors and uncertainty in WSN data; and the metadata related to the residual energy, topology, etc are of high variability. This not only means metadata already used in traditional DB systems need to be modified to meet the need of WSNs, but new techniques, such as probabilistic and stochastic methods, may be taken to formalize and manage metadata.

3) Metadata collection. In a DBMS, metadata are generally predefined and stored concentratedly, and this makes it relatively easy to maintain. In a WSN, the distributed storage and variability of metadata make metadata management work more complex than what it is in a DBMS. For example, base station need to collect metadata from sensor nodes and calculate those metadata to work out new metadata describing the global states of the WSN.

4) Cost consideration. Energy efficiency is always an important issue in WSNs. Metadata management also consumes energy, computing and storage resources. For example, collecting metadata from nodes consumes the energy of nodes.

3 Metadata Management

The purpose of metadata management is to provide adequate information for query processing, while at the same time to make the cost of maintaining the metadata as low as possible. To do this, we need to face the challenges discussed in last section. As a reply to those challenges, we propose a solution in this section and next section to solve the problems. The solution includes two parts: an architecture and a model-aided metadata collecting approach. The architecture is addressed in this section.

3.1 Metadata Management Architecture

From discussed above, we know metadata can be classified according to two criteria: distribution and variability. Further, metadata can be classified into four types: static metadata on base station, dynamic metadata on base station, static metadata on nodes and dynamic metadata on nodes. Different management solutions are adopted for these different types of metadata.

As for a sensor node, static metadata can be prestored in the flash of the node in advance. When the node boots up, the static metadata are read into memory. Dynamic metadata change with the states of the node and cannot be prestored. There should be a process that monitors the states changes of the node and update the metadata accordingly. As for base station, similar strategy can be adopted for the static metadata. However, things for dynamic metadata are quite different from what they are on sensor nodes. The base station needs to collect metadata from sensor nodes dynamically and calculate those metadata to generate new metadata that reflect the states of the WSN.

In order to manage the metadata effectively we propose an architecture to help the WSN to manage metadata. The architecture is shown in Figure2, and the primary work that the metadata manager needs to do is also given.

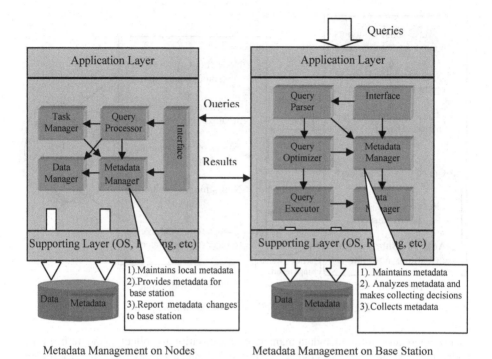

Metadata Management on Nodes   Metadata Management on Base Station

Fig. 2. Metadata Management Architecture

4 Collecting Metadata from Nodes

Designing an effective approach for collecting metadata from node is a challenging work and deserves being studied carefully. We need to take energy efficiency, fidelity of the data, network scale, collecting methods and the regularity of metadata into consideration. To meet these challenges, models are created on base station and are used to guide the collecting of metadata.

4.1 Metadata Collecting Approach

Based on above discussion, we propose an approach for collecting metadata from nodes. Following are the strategies adopted by the approach to lower the cost:

1) Models reflecting how the state of the WSN changes is created on base station to help managing metadata.

2) Push and pull are all used and play different roles respectively.

3) Flexible strategies can be adopted to compose queries for querying metadata.

4) Nodes are grouped into different groups according to their positions, types and other attributes.

5) In-network processing, such as aggregation and compression, can be used to reduce the traffic caused by metadata.

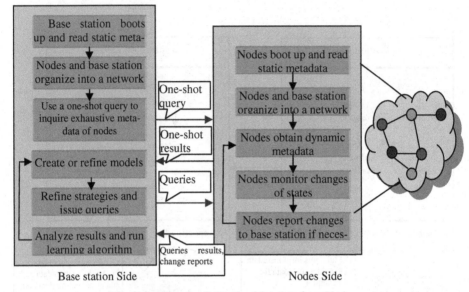

Fig. 3. Solution for Collecting Metadata from Nodes

The approach for the metadata manager of base station to collect metadata from the nodes is based on above strategies. As figure 3 depicts, the approach has following functional steps among which steps 3, 4, 5, 6 run on base station, steps 2, 7 run on nodes, and step 1 runs on both base station and nodes.

1) After being deployed, base station and nodes boot up and read static metadata into memory; then they organize into an integral WSN.

2) Nodes get dynamic metadata such as locations, neighbors, residual energy, etc.

3) At the base station side, the metadata manager issues a one-shot query to inquire exhaustive metadata of nodes, including ID, location, hardware and software configuration, resources, and functions, etc.

4) Using the retrieved metadata, models, such as nodes distribution, coverage map, topology map, etc are created. Corresponding structures for managing metadata, e.g. different kinds of groups, are created according to the actual condition of the WSN. Then the metadata manager can provide basic help for query processing.

5) Based on the models and the measurement data returned by nodes, the metadata manager can use more elaborate queries to inquire metadata of the nodes.

6) With more metadata are collected, the accuracy of models can be refined gradually by the learning algorithm.

7) On a node, metadata manager monitors the states changes and updates metadata accordingly. It replies to the metadata queries by sending back metadata and it also reports unlooked-for metadata to base station.

5   Experimental Results

As Figure 4, one of the simulation scenes, shows, the WSN model consists of 200 sensor nodes that are uniformly placed in a 300m×300m square area. The base station is located at the center of the simulation area. All nodes have same transmission ranges of 40 meters. The initial energy of a sensor node is 5 joules, and the energy of the base station is infinite. We assume the WSN is deployed to monitor fires; and nodes are equipped with sensors to measure temperature. A node is in sleep mode in most of time and wakes up every 30 seconds to check if there is a fire. If there is a fire, then the node sends a data packet to one of its parents chosen randomly every 5 seconds. If there is not a fire, then the node sleeps and will wake up in 30 seconds again. Nodes within the circle of 40 meters of a fire can monitor the fire. Two fires happen somewhere in the field randomly every 1 minute; and the lifetime of a fire is 1 minutes. The energy needed for a sensor nodes to sense, receive and transmit a packet on average are 2×10^{-6} joule, 2×10^{-6} joule, and 1×10^{-5} joule respectively. The power for a mobile node to move is 5×10^{-5} w. For simplicity, a query command or a reply is also regarded as a packet and consume as much communication energy as a measurement data packet.

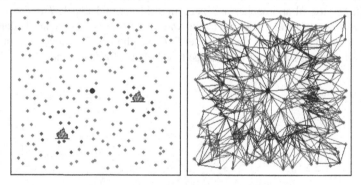

Fig. 4. A Scene of Simulation WSNs

We use two metrics, energy cost and fidelity to evaluate different approaches in our simulation. Energy cost is the energy consumption of disseminating queries from base station to nodes and transmitting metadata from nodes to base station. We simply calculate the energy cost by take count of the data packets used for collecting metadata, including the queries for metadata. The higher the value is; the worse is the performance. Fidelity can be evaluated by the errors between the metadata given by base station and the metadata on sensor nodes. We use two errors: average error and max error to evaluate the fidelity of all approaches.

We compare five metadata management approaches: 1) approach denoted as NMLQ is not model-aided, and metadata are reported to the base station periodically; 2) approach denoted as NMR is not model-aided, and nodes only report metadata as significant changes happen; 3) approach denoted as MLQ is model-aided, and metadata are reported to the base station periodically; 4) approach denoted as MOQ is model-aided, metadata are collected with one-shot queries which means a node sends metadata to the base station only when it receives a query command; 5) approach denoted as MR is model-aided, and nodes report metadata as significant changes happen.

Table 1. Settings of Experiments

	Immobile Nodes	Mobile Nodes
NMLQ	$T > 1$ minutes	$T > 30$ seconds
MLQ	$T > 1$ minutes	$T > 30$ seconds
NMR	DataSend(T) > 12	DataSend(T) > 12 or C(Neighbors, T) > 2
MR	DataSend(T) > 12	DataSend(T) > 12 or C(Neighbors, T) > 2
MOQ	$(T_{dt} < 0.6)$ and $(T_{route} > 0.8)$	$(T_n < 0.6)$ or $((T_{dt} < 0.4)$ and $(T_{route} > 0.8))$

20 simulation scenes are used to evaluate the metadata management approaches. Energy cost, average error, and maximum error are calculated by averaging the simulation results of all scenes. We use DataSend to calculate average error and maximum error. Settings for all approaches are listed in Table 1. In Table 1, T denotes the time interval from the last time when metadata was sent till now; DataSend(T) denotes the number of data packets sent during time T; C(Neighbors, T) denotes the number of neighbors that changed during T; T_{dt} is the threshold set for DataSend.

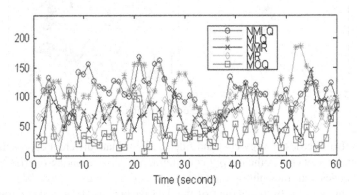

Fig. 5. Energy Cost of All Approaches

Figure 5 and Figure 6 show the energy cost of five metadata collecting approaches. Figure 5 compares the absolute energy cost of all approaches in one minute in detail; while Figure 6 shows total energy cost in 10 minutes of all approaches. It can be seen that NMLQ consumes as much energy as MLQ; NMR also consumes as much energy as MR; and the energy cost by MOQ is less than other four approaches. It will be seen later that the error of MOQ is also less than other four approaches.

Figure 7 and Figure 8 respectively compare average errors and maximum errors of five approaches in 3 minutes. Horizontal axes in both figures are time; and vertical axes are average error and maximum error that have the unit of packet. As for NMLQ and MLQ, because immobile nodes send metadata packets every 1 minutes and mobile

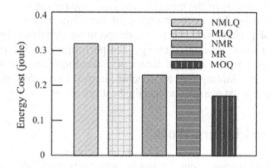

Fig. 6. Energy Consumption of All Approaches

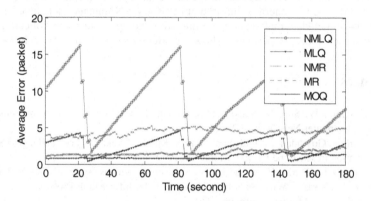

Fig. 7. Average Error of All Approaches

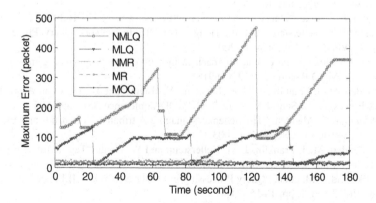

Fig. 8. Maximum Error of All Approaches

nodes send metadata packets every 30 seconds and arrivals of the packets at the base station are distributed in an extremely short time, so the average errors and maximum errors of NMLQ and MLQ appear to be periodic. When the base station receives the metadata, the errors reach their minimum points. After then, the errors gradually increase till the next arrivals of the metadata packets. The reason of the maximum error of NMR is a fixed value lies in the nodes send metadata packet to the base station when the number of packets sent reaches corresponding threshold. From the figures, although consuming same amount of energy, the performances of model-aided MLQ and MR outscore the performances of their corresponding non-model-aided counterpart: NMLQ and NMR. Among five approaches, helped by models, one-shot queries-based MOQ consumes least energy and has the best precision.

6 Conclusion and Future Work

The issue of metadata management for query processing in WSNs was addressed in this paper. We discussed the new characteristics of query processing in WSNs and new demands for metadata. As an answer to the new challenges of metadata management in WSNs, we proposed a general solution that helps a WSN manage metadata. The solution includes a metadata management architecture and approaches for collecting metadata from sensor nodes. Experiments show the effectiveness of our approaches.

References

1. I.F. Akyildiz, W. Su*, Y. Sankarasubramaniam, E. Cayirci. "A survey on sensor networks". Computer Networks, 2002.
2. D. Estrin, R. Govindan, J. Heidemann, and S. Kumar, "Next century challenges: Scalable coordination in sensor networks". MobiCom 1999.
3. P. Bonnet, J. E. Gehrke, P. Seshadri. "Towards sensor database systems". MDM 2001.
4. F. Zhao, L. Guibas. "Wireless Sensor Networks : An Information Processing Approach". Boston: Elsevier-Morgan Kaufmann; 2004.
5. R. Ramakrishnan, J. Gehrke. "Database Management Systems" (Third Edition), The McGraw-Hill Companies, Inc, 2003
6. Y. Yao, J. E. Gehrke. "Query Processing for Sensor Networks". CIDR 2003.
7. S. Madden, J. Hellerstein, and W. Hong. "TinyDB: In-Network Query Processing in TinyOS". Version 0.4, September 2003.
8. Y. Yao, J. Gehrke. "The cougar approach to in-network query processing in sensor networks". SIGMOD Record, 2002,31(3):918.
9. S. Madden, M. J. Franklin, J. M. Hellerstein, W. Hong: "The Design of an Acquisitional Query Processor For Sensor Networks". SIGMOD Conference 2003: 491-502
10. W. Wong and S. Madden. "TinySchema: Managing Attributes, Commands and Events in TinyOS". Version 1.1, September 2003.
11. S. R. Madden, M. J. Franklin, J. M. Hellerstein, and W. Hong. "Tag: A tiny aggregation service for ad-hoc sensor networks". In OSDI 2002.
12. J. Gehrke and S. Madden. "Query Processing in Sensor Networks", IEEE Pervasive Computing, Vol. 3, No. 1, pp. 46-55, 2004.
13. C. Savarese, J. M. Rabaey, and J. Beutel. "Locationing in distributed ad-hoc wireless sensor networks". ICASSP 2001.
14. N. Sadagopan, B. Krishnamachari, and A. Helmy, "Active Query Forwarding in Sensor Networks (ACQUIRE)", SNPA 2003.

Availability Considerations for Wireless Sensor Grids

Ali Hammad Akbar[1], Ki-Hyung Kim[1,*], Seung-Jin Bang[2],
Waleed Mansoor[1], and Won-Sik Yoon[3]

[1] Graduate School of Information and Communication,
Ajou University, Suwon, Korea, 443-749
[2] Dept. of Mathematics,
Ajou University, Suwon, Korea, 443-749
[3] School of Electrical Engineering,
Ajou University, Suwon, Korea, 443-749
{hammad, kkim86, math, waleed, wsyoon}@ajou.ac.kr

Abstract. In this paper, we derive and analyze network availability for sensor grids by considering an elaborate energy consumption model. Sensor grids that form chain topologies are compared for two widely known grid traversal models, namely staircase and Delannoy number. Based upon the mathematical model, we analyze two sleep modes, viz, synchronous and asynchronous for their effects on the network availability of sensor grids with regard to energy conservation and packet loss. We also propose a non-uniform, asynchronous sleep scheme in sensor grids which allows nodes to sleep in a manner such that nodes closer to the gateway sleep less than the nodes in the fringes. The performance results show that the proposed scheme prolongs network availability effectively in sensor grids.

1 Introduction

Wireless sensor networks are autonomous networks that are expected to render a broad range of services in the emerging ubiquitous era. Once, deployed, either in an ad hoc manner or in a preconceived arrangement into the environments, they are expected to continue to function unattended. Optimization schemes concerning their functional behaviour are widely studied to extend their lifetime, while meeting performance objectives amicably [1]. Serviceability of sensor nodes is gauged by their continued operation in the sensor network; an issue of network availability. Various interpretations of network availability as identified in [2] have emerged into parallel research directions. For example, in [3], the authors propose a scheme to adjust the sleep-awake periods of sensor nodes for energy optimization, consequently extending operational lifetime. In [4], the authors ascertain relationship between node transmission power control and lifetime by suggesting topology control algorithms.

Assuming mostly ad hoc deployments, studies of sensor nodes and networks have seldom exploited prior knowledge of sensor networks, e.g., location information of sensor nodes. Exceedingly complex and computationally expensive schemes for

---

* Corresponding author.

Y.-C. Chung and J.E. Moreira (Eds.): GPC 2006, LNCS 3947, pp. 269–278, 2006.
© Springer-Verlag Berlin Heidelberg 2006

sensor networks can therefore be tailored into light-weight equivalents by utilizing such knowledge base.

In this paper, we target sensor grids, considering them to be candidates for future applications in target tracking and surveillance [5]. In [6], we derived network availability expression for sensor grids and analyzed the network availability for two widely known lattice path traversal models, namely Delannoy number and staircase-based traversals.

In this paper, we revisit the derivation and analysis of network availability of sensor grids for the two lattice path traversal models under a thorough range of assumptions. We then analyze two widely known sleep modes, viz, synchronous and asynchronous for their effects on the network availability of sensor grids with regards to energy conservation and packet loss. Finally, we propose a non-uniform, asynchronous sleep scheme in sensor grids which allows nodes to sleep in a manner such that nodes closer to the gateway sleep less than those in the fringes. The performance results show that the proposed scheme prolongs network availability effectively in sensor grids.

The organization of the paper is as the following. In section II, we present sensor grid model and formulate assumptions necessary to make it practicable. In section III, we derive an expression for network availability by considering a range of node and network parameters. Section IV presents our proposed scheme that makes nodes sleep in a non-uniform manner. We present simulation-based performance evaluation for the proposed scheme in Section V. Section VI summarizes the contributions and concludes the paper.

2 Model and Assumptions

As given in Fig. 1, we consider a reference grid of $n \times k$ equidistant sensor nodes. Each node has an index as $(1,1),\ldots,(i,j),\ldots,(n,k)$, where i and j refer to rows and columns of the grid, respectively. Following assumptions are made to formulate the model;

- Every sensor node maintains energy availability tables of neighbouring nodes.
- Whenever a sensing node transmits data, it is overheard by all its neighboring nodes that are one hop away. A neighboring node only relays the data in a unicast manner towards the collector if i) it has the highest energy level amongst the candidate relay nodes and ii) it is closer to the collector as compared to the sending node, i.e., it is a downstream neighbor.
- Every node in the sensor grid senses an event and sends it towards the gateway. Intermediate nodes relay it downstream towards the gateway through the last node.
- h_{ij} is the initial energy of the sensor node (i,j) at the reference time t_0, distributed across the network as $\eta_{ij} e^{-\eta_{ij} t}$ with mean $1/\eta_{ij}$.

- The sensing process is a random memoryless process that takes place whenever an event occurs. It is assumed that the occurrence of an event is Poisson distributed with mean λ_{ij} [7].

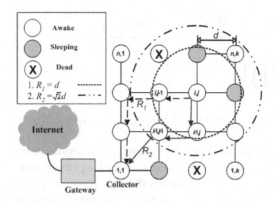

Fig. 1. Reference topology of sensor networks

- Since the inter-arrival time of Poisson distribution is exponential, the energy consumptions due to these activities are exponentially distributed with mean $1/\beta_{ij}$ and $1/\gamma_{ij}$ respectively.
- Sensor node (i,j) consumes energy at a rate of a_{ij} per second to remain awake. It means that even if there is no sensing and relaying activity, sensor node energy will be drained at a constant rate in idle time.
- Sensor node (i,j) consumes energy at a rate of a'_{ij} per second during the time they sleep. Different schemes suggest different levels of energy consumption while sleeping. For example, [8] suggests that the energy consumption ratio during the awake state and sleep is 1:0.05. While a node is sleeping, it does not perform relaying for other nodes' data. From the routing perspective, it is equivalent to a soft failure.
- When a node dies, either due to battery drainage or component failure, it ceases to perform any sensing operation. Due to the dead node, a hole is created in the network that undermines relaying activity of other nodes.

In the following section, we derive the network availability of a two-dimensional topology in the form of Chapman-Kolmogorov equations [7] for two special cases of data relaying models, namely Staircase and Delannoy number-based lattice path traversals.

3 Mathematical Analysis

We denote y_{ij} as the total energy consumed by sensor node (i,j) in sensing, relaying, during sleep, and in idle mode. Furthermore, x_{ij} denotes energy consumption just being sensing and relaying data only. $F_t(x_{ij})$, $\forall ij=\{11, \ldots,1k,21,\ldots,2k,\ldots n1,\ldots,nk\}$ is the joint probability density function (pdf) of all nodes at time t. Since Poisson processes are pure birth processes, the joint pdf of all the sensor nodes can be given by the differential-difference equation as

$$\frac{dF_t}{dt}(x_{ij}) = -\sum_{i=1}^{n}\sum_{j=1}^{k}\lambda_{ij}F_t(x_{ij}) + \sum_{i=1}^{n}\sum_{j=1}^{k}\lambda_{ij}\beta_{ij}$$

$$\times \prod_{l=1}^{i-1}\prod_{m=1}^{j-1}\gamma_{lm}\int_{y_{11}=0}^{x_{11}}\cdots\int_{y_{ij}=0}^{x_{ij}}F_t\left(y_{11},...,y_{ij},...,x_{nk}\right)\times$$

$$\exp\left[-\beta_{ij}\left(x_{ij}-y_{ij}\right)-\sum_{l=1}^{i-1}\sum_{m=1}^{j-1}\gamma_{lm}\left(x_{lm}-y_{lm}\right)\right]dy_{11}...\,dy_{ij}. \tag{1}$$

Equation (1) reflects overall energy consumption in awake state and in active state, i.e., during sensing and relaying data. An interesting observation is that the second term on the right hand side of (1) implies that due to sensing and relaying activity, the energy consumption reaches from y_{ij} to x_{ij}. Considering (1) to be an initial value problem, we obtain $R_t(s_{ij})$ as Laplace transform of $F_t(x_{ij})$:

$$R_t(s_{ij}) = \exp\left[-\left(\sum_{i=1}^{n}\sum_{j=1}^{k}\lambda_{ij} - \sum_{i=1}^{n}\sum_{j=1}^{k}\lambda_{ij}\frac{\beta_{ij}}{s_{ij}+\beta_{ij}}\prod_{l=1}^{(i-1)}\prod_{m=1}^{(j-1)}\frac{\gamma_{lm}}{s_{lm}+\gamma_{lm}}\right)\times t\right]. \tag{2}$$

Now if we include the notion that all the sensor nodes synchronously adopt sleep mode on detecting no activity, the total energy consumption of entire sensor network is now characterized by an individual node's energy consumption. The energy consumption is now given by $y_{ij}=x_{ij}+a_{ij}t_1+a'_{ij}t_2$; t_1 is the time for which sensor nodes are awake and t_2 is the time for which sensor nodes sleep, i.e., $t=t_1+t_2$. Since it is assumed that all the nodes of a sensor grid in the region of interest sleep and wake-up at the same time, i.e., nodes follow synchronous sleeping schedules, a synchronization mechanism needs to be incorporated amongst the sensor nodes [8]. According to the expression for y_{ij}, introduction of sleep mode into sensor nodes suggests reduction in the overall energy consumption of the sensor networks proportionate to the sleep duration of sensor nodes. Let $Z_t(s_{ij})$ be the Laplace transform of $F_t(y_{ij})$.

$$Z_t(s_{ij}) = R_t(s_{ij})\times\exp\left[\sum_{i=1}^{n}\sum_{j=1}^{k}a_{ij}s_{ij}t_1 + \sum_{i=1}^{n}\sum_{j=1}^{k}a'_{ij}s_{ij}t_2\right]. \tag{3}$$

In this paper, availability A_t is adopted to be a measure of network lifetime and is defined as the probability that all the nodes along all the paths are alive. Inserting (2) into (3) and manipulating the variables, the network availability is given by

$$A_t = \exp\left[\begin{array}{c}(-\sum_{i=1}^{n}\sum_{j=1}^{k}\eta_j a_{ij} - \sum_{i=1}^{n}\sum_{j=1}^{k}\lambda_{ij} + \\ \sum_{i=1}^{n}\sum_{j=1}^{k}\frac{\lambda_{ij}\beta_{ij}}{\eta_{ij}+\beta_{ij}}\prod_{l=1}^{(i-1)}\prod_{m=1}^{(j-1)}\frac{\gamma_{lm}}{\eta_{lm}+\gamma_{lm}})\times t_1 - (\sum_{i=1}^{n}\sum_{j=1}^{k}\eta_j a'_{ij})\times t_2\end{array}\right]. \tag{4}$$

At this stage, we investigate the effect of regulating the transmission power on network availability of spatial distributions of sensor nodes by considering two unicast data relaying models, i.e., Delannoy number-based and staircase lattice path traversals. If the transmission range is adjusted to R_1 as shown in Fig. 1, staircase lattice paths are used, i.e., only leftwards or downwards (←↓) links are formed en-route to relay data from the sensing node to the gateway, and assuming a square topology, (4) can be transformed as

$$
A_{t_1} = \exp\left[\left\{ -n^2\eta a + n^2\lambda - \frac{\lambda\beta}{(\eta+\beta)} \frac{\sum_{i=0}^{n-1}(1+i)(\frac{\gamma}{\gamma+\eta})^i +}{\sum_{j=1}^{n-1}(n-j)(\frac{\gamma}{\gamma+\eta})^{(n-1)+j}} \right\} \times t_1 \\ -(n^2\eta a') \times t_2 \right].
$$

(5)

Similarly, adjusting the power level such that the transmission range changes to R_2, the data relaying activity turns out to be a different lattice path traversal, i.e., paths from sensing node to the gateway are formed by leftwards, downwards or diagonal-downwards (←↓↘) links as given by Delannoy numbers [8]. The network availability of (4) is now given as

$$
A_{t_2} = \exp\left[\begin{array}{l} \left\{ n^2\eta a + n^2\lambda - \\ -\left\{ \frac{\lambda\beta}{(\eta+\beta)} \left(\sum_{i=0}^{n-1} (2i+1)(\frac{\gamma}{\gamma+\eta})^i \right) \right\} \times t_1 \\ -(n^2\eta a') \times t_2 \end{array} \right].
$$

(6)

The parameters in (5) and (6) are all assumed to be independent of $i, j, l,$ and m i.e., $a_{ij}=a, a'_{ij}=a', \lambda_{ij}=\lambda, \beta_{ij}=\beta, \eta_{ij}=\eta, \eta_{lm}=\eta,$ and $\gamma_{lm}=\gamma$. The numeric values are adopted from [9] as: $a = 15$ μJ/s, $a' = 1.5$ μJ/s, $\lambda = 0.083$ packets per second, $1/\eta = 12960$ J, $1/\beta = 42.61$ J, $1/\gamma_S = 140.87$ J for staircase and $1/\gamma_D = 280$ J for Delannoy. The number of nodes varies from 4 (or $n = 2$) to 1600 (or $n = 40$).

Fig. 2 plots the network availabilities of (5) and (6) for various node and network parameters. According to Fig. 2, when $d = 1000$ m, $1/\eta_{ij} = 12960$ J, detection

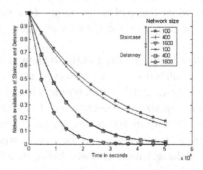

Fig. 2. Network availabilities for two grid traversal schemes

rate = 0.000005, and the numerical plots are obtained for $t = 0$ seconds to $t = 15552000$ seconds (six months), staircase lattice path traversal shows intuitive advantage over Delannoy number's traversal due to half power consumption for small to medium sized networks. For large to extremely large networks, however, Delannoy number-based lattice path traversal offers up to 1% increase in the network availability as compared to staircase's. It is due to the fact that increased transmission range results into an effective decrease in the number of hops traversed from sensing nodes to the gateway as compared to staircase's, saving the relaying energy for an increasing number of nodes that use diagonal paths.

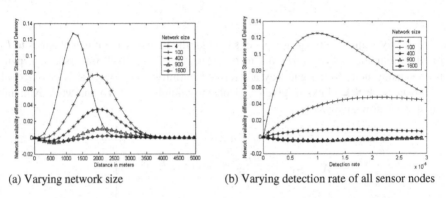

(a) Varying network size   (b) Varying detection rate of all sensor nodes

Fig. 3. Difference between network availabilities under design considerations

Fig. 3 (a) is the difference between (5) and (6) to show the effect of distance varia-tion onto network availability. It was observed at $t=1000000$ seconds (11.57 days) for the two data relay models under consideration. The grid size was varied from 100 m to 5000 m with a step size of 150 m. For very large networks, i.e., for a network size of 1600 nodes or more, when the inter-node distance is increased for a fixed number of sensor nodes, staircase is a better choice for relaying until the network size be-comes exceedingly large. As can be seen, Delannoy number-based lattice path tra-versal starts to outperform staircase-based data relay because of 40 percent more transmission range only when the grid is too large. This suggests an advantage of increasing the transmission power on the network availability for wide spatial distri-butions of sensor nodes.

Fig. 3 (b) is the difference between (5) and (6) to show the effect of detection rate variation onto network availability. It was observed at $t=1000000$ seconds (11.57 days) for the two data relay models under consideration. The detection rate varies from 0 to 0.00003 with a step size of 9.09091×10^{-7}. For small to medium sized net-works, e.g., for network sizes up to 100 nodes, staircase traversal shows better per-formance, however when the network sizes are large, e.g., when the number of sensor nodes is more than 400, Delannoy number-based lattice path traversal offers up to 0.5 percent more network availability as compared to staircase-based data relay.

4 Proposed Non-uniform Asynchronous Sleep Scheme

As defined in (3) and throughout our analytical modelling, we adopted synchronous sleep mode for the sensor grid. The choice of synchronous sleep mode owes to simpler treatment of network availability. In this energy conservation scheme, since all the nodes sleep and wake up at the same time, there is no data relaying loss. However, this choice is a compromise between energy conservation and sensing fidelity. Once all the nodes sleep simultaneously, the probability of an event not being sensed increases in proportion to the sleep duration.

In contrast to synchronous sleep mode, a sensor network may implement asynchronous sleep mode. For such sensor networks, sensing fidelity is relatively higher. The nodes that are awake sense an event and send this information towards the gateway. The sleeping nodes, however, do not participate in their relaying activity [8]. As more nodes sleep, more relaying paths become unavailable, thus affecting the overall relaying activity. Sensor networks that incorporate sleep mode conserve energy at one hand but waste the relaying energy on the other. This implicit phenomenon occurs simultaneously to energy conservation. Thus the overall data relay activity is compromised for individual nodes' energy conservation. Coming back to the comparison of two data relay models, Delannoy number-based traversal is a better candidate for asynchronous sleep-schedule implementing sensor grids because it offers an additional number of increasing paths of the order of $\sum_{k=0}^{n} \frac{(n)!}{(n-k)!(k)!} \frac{(n+k)!}{(n)!(k)!} - \frac{(2n-2)!}{(n-1)!(n-1)!}$ as compared to Staircase, avoiding sleeping nodes effectively. Delannoy number-based traversal can reduce such an adverse effect of sleeping nodes.

We suggest that the sleep schedules for sensor nodes deployed as a grid can be governed by an interesting observation and an intuitive scheme that follows. Owing to the lattice mathematics, when a node ij sleeps, it cannot participate in relaying the data of up to $(n-i+1)(n-j+1)-1$ nodes. This data loss is unrecoverable for real time applications. For non-real time applications, the data loss is compensated through retransmissions. Not all types of sensor networks, however encourage retransmissions. This relay loss is therefore critical in determining the sleeping behaviour of sensor bodes. For sensor grids supporting retransmissions, such loss will generate retransmissions; energy wastage.

In this paper, we propose that nodes closest to the gateway, say e.g., node $(1,1)$ should adopt sleep schedules with the smallest durations, commensurate to the relaying load. This sleep schedule may be communicated to one hop neighbours to adjust their sleep schedules, in a similar manner as proposed in [10]. Consequently, nodes located on the outskirts may opt to adjust their sleep schedules according to the occurrence of events that they sense and the sleep schedules of downstream neighbours.

The proposed scheme can be generalized for sensor fields which form chain topologies of sensor nodes. More appropriately, for scenarios where multiple sources sense data and relay to a single sink through multiple hops. This idea is envisaged to complement proposed routing protocols such as two-tier data dissemination model that forms a grid from the sensing node towards the sink [11].

5 Performance Analysis

A simulator based on the system in section IV was developed in C++ to evaluate our scheme. The simulation results were obtained for a topology of 10×10 nodes that were placed in the form of a two-dimensional grid. We assumed the free space radio propagation model. The gateway or sink node is located at the bottom-left corner of the grid. All the nodes in the grid generate packets towards the gateway in a uniform distribution. The routing of packets towards the gateway follows the model described in section II. In case of data loss due to sleeping or dead node(s) along the routing path, a source node retransmits end-to-end. Detailed network parameters are summarized in Table 1.

Table 1. Simulation parameters

Simulation Parameters		Value
Node energy consumption (J)	Tx (←↓)	3
	Tx (↙)	5
	Rx	3
	Constant drain	1
	Sleep	0
	Sense	2
Initial energy of nodes (J)		2000
Sleep duty cycle of nodes		0.3
Max. Retransmissions		1

Network availability was obtained as a performance index which is defined as the ratio of nodes that are alive to the total number of nodes at the initialization time of simulation.

Fig. 4 (a) illustrates simulation results obtained for staircase lattice path traversal under the three scenarios as shown in the legend. The advantage using our scheme is

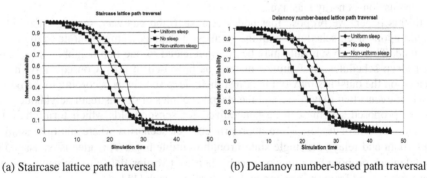

(a) Staircase lattice path traversal   (b) Delannoy number-based path traversal

Fig. 4. Network availability comparison for sleep schemes

clear. Nodes closer to the gateway either do not sleep or sleep less. Thus they do not loose any routing data. It results into network wide energy saving when compared with uniform sleeping scheme. Obviously, the scenario that does not implement any sleeping strategy has the lowest availability.

Fig. 4 (b) shows the comparison and simulation results asserting the usability of non-uniform sleep scheme in Delannoy number-based traversal. A fractional gain in network availability is observed in this traversal when compared to staircase traversal for all the three scenarios. This agrees with our earlier mathematical results that Delannoy number-based lattice path traversal performs better than staircase extending network longevity.

6 Conclusion

In this paper, we study the spatio-temporal effects of transmission power adjustment onto network availability of sensor nodes deployed across a two-dimensional space that implement sleep mode under a variety of constraints. We observe that doubling the transmission power of sensor nodes in sensor grids can help incorporate diagonal neighbours into the data relay path from sensing nodes to the gateway, especially in dense and large deployments of sensor nodes. This results into better network availability due to a decrease in effective number of hops for very large deployment of sensor nodes. It is clearly against the apparent notion that lifetime reduces by increasing the transmission power. This observation should be considered valid only for sensor grids that form chain topologies. It might be deemed appropriate as a future work to deliberate on other topologies of sensor nodes.

It is also noticeable that increasing the transmission power also increases the probability of finding alternate paths for two cases; first, when the sensor nodes are distributed in a wide area; second, when sensor nodes sleep to conserve energy and make the intermediate paths unavailable. We propose a non-uniform, asynchronous sleep scheme in sensor grids which allows nodes to sleep in a manner such that nodes closer to the gateway sleep less than those in the fringes. The performance results show that the proposed scheme prolongs network availability effectively in sensor grids.

References

1. Tilak, S., Ghazaleh, N. B. A., and W. Heinzelman.: A Taxonomy of Wireless Micro-Sensor Network Models. ACM SIGMOBILE Mobile Computer and Communications Review, vol. 6, issue. 2 (2002)
2. Sauve, J. P., Coelho, F.E.S.: Availability Considerations in Network Design. Proceedings of International Symposium on Dependable Computing, Pacific Rim, (2001), 119-126
3. Schurgers, C., Tsiatsis, V., Ganeriwal S., and Mani, S.: Optimizing Sensor Networks in the Energy-Latency-Density Design Space. IEEE Transactions on Mobile Computing, vol. 1, no. 1, (2002), 70-80
4. Liu, J., Li, B. Distributed Topology Control in Wireless Sensor Networks with Asymmetric Links.: IEEE GlobeComm, vol. 3, (2003), 1257-1262

5. Chakrabarty, K.: Grid Coverage for Surveillance and Target Location in Distributed Sensor Networks. IEEE Transactions on Computers, vol. 51, no.12, (2002), 1448-53
6. Akbar, A. H., Yoon, W. S., and Kim, J. H.: Effect of Transmission Power Adjustments on Network Availability. Information Technology Journal, 4(3), 2005 271-273
7. Kleinrock, L.: Queuing Systems Volume I: Theory. Cambridge University Press (1997)
8. Gao, Q.: Analysis of energy conservation in sensor networks. Wireless Networks, Kluwer Press
9. Bhardwaj, M., Garnett, T., and Chandrakasan, A. P.: Upper Bounds on the Lifetime of Sensor Networks. in Proceedings of ICC, (2001), 785-790
10. Ye, W., Heidemann, J., and Estrin, D.: An Energy-Efficient MAC Protocol for Wireless Sensor Networks. IEEE INFOCOM, vol. 3, (2002), 1567– 1576
11. Ye, F., Luo, H., Cheng, J., Lu, S., and Zhang, L.: A Two-Tier Data Dissemination Model for Large-Scale Wireless Sensor Networks. 8th ACM/IEEE MobiCOMM, (2002), 148-149

An Energy-Aware Position-Based Routing Strategy

Linfeng Yuan[*,**], Zongkai Yang, Liang Ou,
Wenqing Cheng, and Xu Du

Department of Electronics and Information Engineering,
Huazhong University of Science and Technology,
Wuhan, Hubei Province, 430074, P.R. China
yuanlf@163.com

Abstract. In sensor networks, the nodes are always equipped with limited power source, energy-awareness must be carefully considered in the design of sensor networks. According to the analysis of the classical positioned-based routing protocols, this paper introduces a novel concept of Effective Transmission (ET) which ensures each forwarding node is not only farther from the source node, but also nearer to the destination node with respect to its sender. An energy-aware routing protocol based on ET is proposed. It decreases the energy consumption for each hop in the transmission. The simulation results show the routing protocol is effective on the performance of energy consumption while comparing with some other routing protocols.

1 Introduction

Wireless Sensor Network (WSN) technology is declared as one of the most important technologies for the 21st century and it will play an important role in our future lives [1]. It recently received tremendous attention from both academia and industry because of its promise of a wide range of potential applications in both civil and military areas. A WSN consists of a large number of small sensor nodes with sensing, data processing, and communication capabilities, which are deployed in a region of interest and collaborate to accomplish a common task, such as environmental monitoring, military surveillance, and industry process control. Distinguished from traditional wireless networks, WSNs are characterized of dense node deployment, unreliable sensor node, frequent topology change, and severe power, computation, and memory constraints. These unique characteristics and constraints present many new challenges to the design and implementation of WSNs. Energy efficiency is the key to prolonging the network lifetime and is thus of primary importance in WSNs [2].

---

[*] This work is supported by the National Natural Science Foundation of China (No. 60572049) and the Natural Science Foundation of Hubei Province, China (No. 2005ABA264).
[**] Corresponding author.

Y.-C. Chung and J.E. Moreira (Eds.): GPC 2006, LNCS 3947, pp. 279–288, 2006.

Although many networking protocols and algorithms have been developed for traditional wireless ad hoc networks, they cannot effectively address the unique characteristics and constraints and application requirements of sensor networks. To meet the new challenges, innovative protocols and algorithms are needed to achieve energy efficiency. It is highly desirable to develop new energy-efficient protocols for topology discovery, self-organization, route discovery, and data dissemination.

At the same time, position is another important issue in wireless network. It is natural to utilize location-aware routing [3]. But most of these routing protocols (GRS [4], MFR [5], COMPASS [6]) do not consider energy consumption carefully. The position-based protocols [3, 7] only ensure that the forwarding candidate is nearer to the destination node and don't care whether the forwarding candidate is farther from the source node when comparing with the preceding node. So they have not maximized each hop's transmission area and thus bring less efficiency.

This paper proposes an energy-aware routing protocol in sensor networks. We put forward a novel concept of Effective Transmission (ET) that ensures the forwarding candidate is not only nearer to the sink, but also farther from the source node with respect to its preceding node. So it can limit the area of the candidate nodes and efficiently decrease the transmission energy to the least on each hop. Each intermediate node can decide its next forwarding node according to the value of decisive energy factor. The energy efficiency will be achieved in this transmission mode.

2   Effective Transmission Model

The main idea in this paper is to propose an effective way to reduce the energy consumption from the source node to the destination node during the transmission. The optimum forwarding candidate is chosen according to the computation results of each link's energy consumption. And this choice is based on a position-based transmission model. So we will first discuss this model in this section.

Suppose each node's transmission radius is R, we give the following definitions.

Definition 1. *The* distance *of node A and node B is given by $d(A, B) = \sqrt{(A_x - B_x)^2 + (A_y - B_y)^2}$.* $\square$

The distance between node A and B can also simply be denoted as AB. That is $AB = d(A, B)$.

Definition 2. Neighbors *of node V_i are defined as* $\{N(V_i) = V_j | d(V_i, V_j) \leq R, j \neq i\}$. $\square$

Definition 3. Effective Transmission (ET) *ensures each forwarding node is farther from the source node and nearer to the destination node with respect to its preceding node.* $\square$

Definition 4. *The* Forwarding Candidate Set (FCS) *of node V_i is formed by the nodes in V_i's neighbors that comply with the criteria of ET.* $\square$

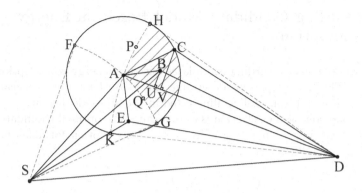

Fig. 1. ET and FCS model

Given the source node S and the destination node D, the node V_i's FCS is

$$FCS(V_i) = \{V_j | d(V_j, S) > d(V_i, S), d(V_j, D) < d(V_i, D), V_j \in N(V_i)\}. \quad (1)$$

In Figure 1, S is the center of arc $FAQG$ and D is the center of arc $HPAK$. Nodes H, C, G are on the circle with the center point of A and its transmission radius is R. Three arcs of APH, HCG and GQA, as illustrated in the shadow part, surround the FCS area of sender A.

Some position-based routing algorithms only require the forwarding candidate is nearer to the destination. For example, in Figure 1, node B and node E are the forwarding candidates of node A because $BD < AD$ and $ED < AD$. But candidate E is less efficient since $ES < AS$, while B can bring effective transmission since $BS > AS$.

Theorem 1. *The overall path is guaranteed to be loop free when the routing scheme selects next hop nodes if they have ET.* □

Proof: Denote PS as the routing path set,
$m = |PS|, V_i \in PS, V_j \in PS, 1 \le i < j \le m - 1, V_1 = S, V_m = D$.
If the routing path is not loop free, it means there must be a node V_j whose forwarding node is its ancestor V_i. According to the condition of ET, there is

$$SV_i < SV_{i+1} < \cdots < SV_{j-1} < SV_j. \quad (2)$$

If V_i is V_j's forwarding node, there is

$$SV_j < SV_i. \quad (3)$$

Equation (3) is contrary to equation (2). So there does not exist a node whose forwarding node is its ancestor. The theorem holds. □

3 Forwarding Candidate Model Based on Energy Consumption

The selection of the forwarding candidates based on energy consumption needs two steps. The first step is to determine the FCS. That is to determine the candidates who can bring ET as illustrated in the above definitions.

The second step of the selection is to determine the optimal candidate within the FCS. According to paper [8], the energy consumption formulas in sensor networks are as follows,

$$E_{Rx}(l) = E_{Rx-elec}(l) = lE_{elec} \tag{4}$$

$$E_{T_x}(l, d) = E_{Tx-elec}(l) + E_{Tx-amp}(l, d)$$
$$= \begin{cases} lE_{elec} + l\varepsilon_{fs}d^2, & d < d_0 \\ lE_{elec} + l\varepsilon_{mp}d^4, & d \geq d_0 \end{cases} \tag{5}$$

where E_{elec} is the electronics energy, $\varepsilon_{fs}d^2$ is the amplifier energy in the free space and $\varepsilon_{mp}d^4$ is the amplifier energy in the multipath fading channel models, l is data size (bit), d is transmission distance, d_0 is a distance threshold. In a densely deployed sensor network (it means $d < d_0$), the first transmission energy formula is used here. For an intermediate node in the routing path, the energy consumption is

$$E(l) = E_{Rx}(l) + E_{Tx}(l, d) = 2lE_{elec} + l\varepsilon_{fs}d^2 \tag{6}$$

Whatever angle-based or distance-based is used in position-based routing protocol, the only one goal is energy efficiency. Given a sender node A, there are two candidate nodes B and C. We compare the energy consumption relaying by each node.

If the packets are propagated via node B, the energy consumption for the transmitting from A to B is

$$E_{B1}(l) = E_{Tx}(l, d(A, B)) = lE_{elec} + l\varepsilon_{fs}d^2(A, B) \tag{7}$$

The energy consumption for receiving of node B is

$$E_{B2}(l) = E_{Rx}(l) = lE_{elec} \tag{8}$$

The energy consumption for the transmitting from B to the destination node D is

$$E_{B3}(l) = E_{Tx}(l, d(B, D)) = lE_{elec} + l\varepsilon_{fs}d^2(B, D) \tag{9}$$

So the total energy consumption relaying by node B is

$$E_B(l) = E_{B1}(l) + E_{B2}(l) + E_{B3}(l)$$
$$= 3lE_{elec} + l\varepsilon_{fs}(d^2(A, B) + d^2(B, D)) \tag{10}$$

Similarly, the total energy consumption relaying by C is

$$E_C(l) = E_{C1}(l) + E_{C2}(l) + E_{C3}(l)$$
$$= 3lE_{elec} + l\varepsilon_{fs}(d^2(A,C) + d^2(C,D)) \tag{11}$$

So the differences between the transmission via the two nodes lie in $(d^2(A,B) + d^2(B,D))$ and $(d^2(A,C) + d^2(C,D))$. We denote the decisive energy factor (DEF) as

$$DE_A(B) = d^2(A,B) + d^2(B,D) \tag{12}$$
$$DE_A(C) = d^2(A,C) + d^2(C,D) \tag{13}$$

If the energy consumption through node B is less than that through node C, node B is more appropriate to be chosen as the forwarding node. It means that

$$E_B(l) < E_C(l) \tag{14}$$

From equations (10), (11) and (12), (13), equation (14) means

$$DE_A(B) < DE_A(C) \tag{15}$$

So for a specific data size, the energy consumption is decided by the Decisive Energy Factor (DEF). The sender node can compare each node in the FCS by computing each DEF. And from the opinion of the energy consumption, the sender will select the node with the least DEF as the optimal candidate.

Many other position-based routing protocols cannot ensure the least energy consumption. In SPEED [3] and GRS [4], the sender selects its neighbors the closest one to its destination. MFR [5] demands the packet is forwarded to the neighbor whose progress is the maximum. In Figure 1, there are two candidate nodes B and C of sender node A, suppose $CD = 7, BD = 8, AC = 5, AB = 3, BU \perp AD$, $CV \perp AD$. From the opinion of SPEED and GRS, since $CD < BD$, node C is a better candidate node than node B. And from the opinion of MFR, since $AV > AU$, node C is also better than node B as a candidate node. But from the energy consumption formulas,

$$DE_A(C) = AC^2 + CD^2 > AB^2 + BD^2 = DE_A(B) \tag{16}$$

Equation (16) shows that the energy consumption via node B is less than that via node C, so node B is a better candidate node than node C. In the COMPASS [6] routing method, it selects the neighbor that its direction to the sender is the closest to the direction from the sender to the destination. It often brings more hops to the destination node than the other protocols, so it also cannot ensure the efficient energy consumption.

4   Energy-Aware Routing Protocol Based on Effective Transmission

4.1   Candidate Selection

The sender node compares each element in the $FCS(V_i)$ by the Decisive Energy Factor (DEF) and chooses the node with the least value as the optimal forwarding node.

If the sender node has sent its query and receives no reply after a certain period, it means that no candidate is available according to the constraint of ET. Our protocol will automatically adopt an adaptive selection adjustment method. The sender node initiates another query for the forwarding candidates with a looser constraint that only requires the candidates are closer to the destination node. After receiving the replies from the candidates, the sender node compares each candidate's selection function and indicates the node with the least value as the forwarding node.

4.2   Protocol Description

The sender node V_i (beginning from the source node S) broadcasts its own coordinates together with the coordinates of the source node and the sink node. Each receiver candidate V_j determines whether to join the routing path selection based on its residual energy and the comparison results of SV_j vs SV_i, V_jD vs V_iD. Only if the residual energy is above the threshold and $SV_j > SV_i, V_jD < V_iD$, will V_j compute the Decisive Energy Factor (DEF) and send it back to its sender node V_i.

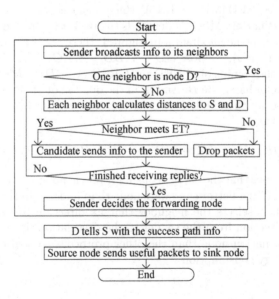

Fig. 2. Protocol implementation flow chart

After receiving the replies from the candidates, the sender node V_i compares each DEF and selects the candidate with the least value as its forwarding node. Then the sender node V_i sends the decision to that node. If the sender node has not received any reply for a certain period, it will initiate another query with the constraint that the candidate nodes are closer to the sink compared with the sender node.

The process lasts until the forwarding candidate is the sink node. Then the sink node sends the information of the path establishment to the source node along the routing path adversely. After receiving this success information, the source node S can now send useful packets to the sink node. Figure 2 is the implementation flow chart.

5   Simulation Results

In this section, we evaluate the performance of our proposed routing protocol in the ns-2 simulator. The sensing area is 200m x 200m and the radio range is 30m for each node. The initial energy of each node is 2J. The simulation will start from 1s and stop at 30s. Each packet size is 36 bytes. The interval time among each packet is 1s. We evaluate the following performance metrics:

- Energy consumption during the transmission.
- Success link ratio.

We denote our proposed solution as ET protocol, and we will evaluate the performance by comparing ET with SPEED, GRS, MFR, COMPASS.

5.1   Energy Consumption

In the simulation, we calculate the energy consumption of all the nodes in the routing path during the transmission per 4 seconds and get the results shown in Figure 3. In the figure, we can find that the energy consumption in ET protocol is least and COMPASS costs most energy. Because COMPASS selects the neighbor that its direction to the sender is the closest to the direction from the sender to the destination, it needs more hops to the destination node and need more energy consumption for the propagation. In our simulation, there are only 9 hops from the source node to the destination node in ET protocol, but 11 hops are existed in COMPASS protocol. The figure also shows SPEED protocol consumes more energy than ET protocol. This can explain that SPEED protocol can get higher transmission rate at the cost of energy consumption at some time comparing with ET protocol.

In order to illustrate the energy consumption statistically, we randomly generate 30 network topologies based on the above environmental settings and calculate the whole energy consumption in the routing path at the time of 30 seconds for every topology with each protocol. Then we compute the mean energy consumption for all the topologies for each protocol. Figure 4 shows the simulation result. The figure shows that the mean energy of ET protocol is the least one

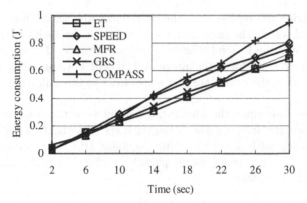

Fig. 3. Energy consumption during the transmission

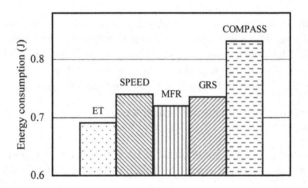

Fig. 4. Mean energy consumption with different topologies

and COMPASS costs most mean energy consumption. The energy consumption in SPEED protocol is a little higher than that in GRS protocol and MFR protocol. It is ET protocol has considered energy metric and other protocols have not carefully considered energy metric that ET protocol becomes a more efficient transmission scheme for the energy consumption.

5.2   Success Link Ratio

We change the number of nodes and evaluate the probability that the source node can successfully find a route to the destination node in each routing protocol. When selecting a certain number of nodes, we test each routing protocol in 50 different topologies and calculate how many times the source node can find a route to the destination node. Figure 5 shows the simulation results.

The figure indicates that the success link ratio for each protocol has small differences with the others. When the number is under 150, ET's link ratio is a few lower than the others. This is because the selection area in the ET protocol is smaller than those in the other protocols. But in the densely distributed network, ET can get almost the same success link ratio with the others, as illustrated in

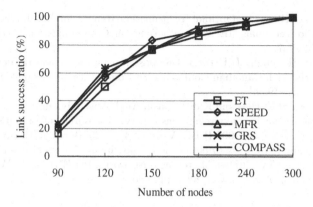

Fig. 5. Success link ratio at different number of nodes

the figure when the number of nodes is above 150. And it is the smaller selection area that makes ET protocol more accurate and more efficient to find a routing path.

6 Conclusions

Many excellent protocols have been developed for ad hoc networks. However, sensor networks have additional requirements that were not specifically addressed. Energy efficiency is one of those important issues. The most existing position-based routing protocols have not considered energy consumption carefully. This paper proposed an effective energy-aware position-based routing protocol in sensor networks. The novel concept of ET is introduced for the forwarding candidate selection. The simulation results indicate that the proposed routing protocol can get low energy consumption when comparing with some other routing protocols. Moreover, it can also achieve about the same success link ratio after providing effective transmission.

References

1. John A. Stankovic, Tarek F. Abdelzaher, Chenyang Lu, Lui Sha, and Jennifer C. Hou, Real-Time Communication and Coordination in Embedded Sensor Networks, Proceedings of the IEEE, Vol.91, No.7, July 2003, pp: 1002-1022.
2. Jamal N. Al-karaki, Ahmed E. Kamal, Routing techniques in wireless sensor networks: a survey, Wireless Communications, IEEE [see also IEEE Personal Communications], Volume: 11, Issue: 6, Dec. 2004, pp. 6-28.
3. Tian He, J.A. Stankovic, Chenyang Lu, T. Abdelzaher, SPEED: a stateless protocol for real-time communication in sensor networks, Proceedings of the 23rd International Conference on Distributed Computing Systems, 19-22 May 2003, pp. 46-55.
4. G.G. Finn, Routing and Addressing Problem in Large Metropolitan-Scale Internetworks, ISI res. Rep ISU/RF-87-180, Mar 1987.

5. H. Takagi. L. Kleinrock, Optimal Transmission Ranges for Randomly Distributed Packet Radio Terminals, IEEE Transactions on Communications, Vol. 32, no. 3, 1984, pp. 246-257.
6. E. Kranakis, H. Singh, J. Urrutia, Compass routing on geometric networks, Proceedings of the 11th Canadian Conference on Computational Geometry. Vancouver, Canada, August 1999.
7. Wook Choi, Sajal K. Das, and Kalyan Basu, Angle-based dynamic path construction for route load balancing in wireless sensor networks, Wireless Communications and Networking Conference, 2004 IEEE, Volume: 4, 21-25 March 2004, pp. 2474-2479.
8. W.B.Heinzelman, A.P.Chandrakasan, H.Balakrishnan, An application-specific protocol architecture for Wireless Microsensor Networks, IEEE Tran. On Wireless Communications, Vol. 1, No. 4, Oct 2002, pp. 660-670.

Introduction of Grid Computing Application Projects at the NASA Earth Science Technology Office[*]

Kai-Dee Chu[1], Liping Di[2], and Peter Thornton[3]

[1] Global Science & Technology, Inc.,
NASA ESTO Technology Integration Manager
[2] Laboratory for Advanced Information Technology and Standards (LAITS),
George Mason University
[3] National Center for Atmospheric Research (NCAR)

Abstract. In 2003, NASA Earth Science Technology Office (ESTO) awarded funding for 20 new investigations in information systems technology development under the Advanced Information Systems Technology (AIST) Program. Two of the selected proposals specifically used Grid computing technology in their Earth science applications:

(1) Integration of OGC and Grid Technologies for Earth science modeling and applications
The Open Geospatial Consortium (OGC) web service technologies are developed to provide interoperable access and services of geospatial data while the Grid technology is developed for sharing data, storage, and computational powers of high-end computing facilities within a virtual organization. The built-in OGC geospatial services include subsetting, resampling, georectification, reprojection, reformatting, and visualization. The technology integration will make Grid technology geospatially enabled and compatible with OGC standards and, at the same time, make OGC technology Grid enabled.

(2) Grid-BGC: A Grid-computing architecture for terrestrial biogeochemical modeling
The objective of the Grid-BGC project creates an end-to-end technological solution for high-end Earth system modeling that will reduce the costs and risks associated with research on the global carbon cycle and its coupling to climate. The system can provide a robust end-to-end processing environment that permits computation at the supercomputer level and addresses the associated demands for massive on-line and near-line input and output data streams.

1 Integration of OGC and Grid Technologies for Earth Science Modeling and Applications

1.1 Project Description

Open Geospatial Consortium (OGC) is an international organization promoting the interoperability and sharing of geospatial resources and services in the distributed

---

[*] These projects are currently funded by NASA Earth Science Technology Office (ESTO), Advanced Information Systems Technology (AIST) Program.

Y.-C. Chung and J.E. Moreira (Eds.): GPC 2006, LNCS 3947, pp. 289–298, 2006.

environment through the development of volunteer-based implementation specifications. OGC specifications are widely used by geospatial communities for sharing data and resources and are becoming ISO standards. The recently developed OGC web-services specifications allow seamless access to geospatial data in a distributed environment, regardless of the format, projection, resolution, and the archive location. The fundamental ones include Web Coverage Services (WCS), Web Feature Services (WFS), Web Map Services (WMS), and Web Registries Services (WRS). They form the foundation for OGC web-based interoperable data access.

The OGC technology allows users to specify the requirements for the data they want. An OGC compliant server has to preprocess the data on-demand based on users' requirements and then returns the data back to users in the form specified by users. At the end, users get the data that exactly match their requirements in both the contents and the structure (e.g., format, projection, spatial and temporal coverage, etc). This will significantly reduce the time needed for users to acquire and preprocess the data before they can be used in models or analysis packages.

The Laboratory for Advanced Information Technology and Standards (LAITS) of George Mason University has developed NASA Hierarchical Data Format for Earth Observing System (HDF-EOS) Web Geographic Information System Software Suite (NWGISS) to test OGC interfaces in NASA's data environment. It is the only OGC compliant servers and client system in the world that works with all generic HDF-EOS files. Funded by ESTO, OGC, and the Earth Science Data and Information System Project (ESDISP), NWGISS provides interoperable, personalized, on-demand data access and services (IPODAS) to Earth Observing Systems Data and Information System (EOSDIS) data with built-in georectification, reprojection, subsetting, resampling, reformatting, and visualization functions. Currently, NWGISS consists of five components: a Map Server, a Coverage Server, a Catalog Server, a multi-protocol geoinformation client (MPGC), and a Toolbox. The map server serves HDF-EOS data as maps to any OGC-compliant map clients. The coverage server allows clients to access multi-dimensional data at user specified geographic location, parameters, projection, and formats. The catalog server provides the catalog search capabilities to catalog clients. MPGC enables users to search WRS server and to access data served by OGC web coverage, map, and feature servers. It also provides a set of data manipulation, processing, and analysis functions at user's desktop.

The main work of this project is to integrate Grid and OGC technologies. Based on the preliminary analysis of the two technologies and the EOSDIS data environment, the integration took place between the backend of the NWGISS OGC servers and front-end of data Grid services. The key is to make Grid-managed data accessible through NWGISS OGC servers.

Figure 1 shows the architecture of the integrated system. The first phase is the initial integration, which includes the setup of the development environment, preliminary design of the integration, and implementation of WCS access to Grid-managed data. The second phase is the data naming and location transparency, which includes investigating the use of Data Grid and Replica Services (metadata catalogues, replication location management, reliable file transfer services, and

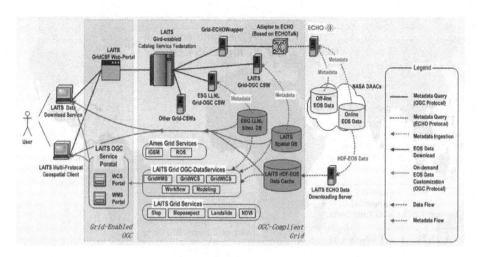

Fig. 1. Integrated Architecture of Geospatially-Enabled OGC-Compatible Data Grid

network caches) to provide naming and location independence for data used by NWGISS and revising NWGISS to invoke such Grid services. The approach to investigating the Data Grid and Replica Services will be to configure a Data Grid testbed. This will be followed by the integration of NWGISS data catalogs into a data Grid catalog and the investigation of naming approaches, followed by interfacing NWGISS with data generators and Data Grid Replica Location service.

The third phase is the virtual dataset research and development. Virtual datasets are those the Grid knows how to produce on-demand, but not produced (materialized) yet. The concept of virtual datasets is being implemented in the high-energy physics Grid project, but is not tested anywhere in Earth science. This project has implemented the Virtual Data services (materialized data catalog, virtual data catalog, abstract planner, concrete planner) to provide the on-the-fly data transformation services needed by NWGISS.

1.2 Project Accomplishments

In order to show the real power of Grid technology for use in Earth science modeling and application, the project has successfully built a creditable, realistic Grid virtual organization as the project testbed among members of the project team and Committee on Earth Observation Satellites (CEOS). The virtual organization (VO) testbed includes 7 machines with realistic NASA data environment and large amount of data. Figure 2 shows the structure of virtual organization at the end of May 2005.

The flagship computer in the VO is LAITS' Apple Cluster server. The machine is hosted at the network laboratory of NASA Earth Science Data and Information System Project (ESDISP) in NASA Goddard Space Flight Center (GSFC). The server at Lawrence Livermore National Laboratory (LLNL) is used as the gateway between the Earth System Grid (ESG) project and this project.

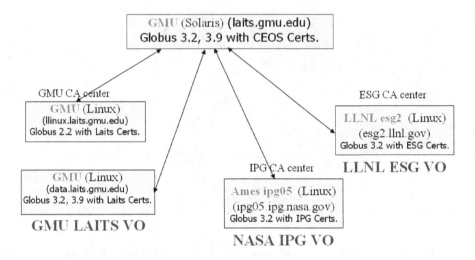

Fig. 2. Structure of Virtual Organization

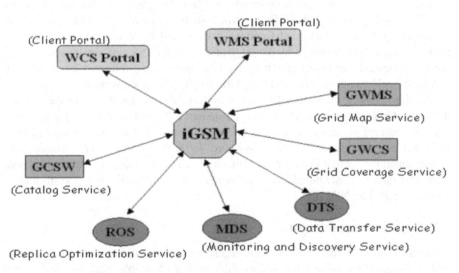

Fig. 3. Portal and Service Interface to intelligent Grid Service Mediator (iGSM)

An intelligent Grid Service Mediator (iGSM) was implemented to mediate the resources in a Grid to fulfill the geodata request from WCS and WMS portals. The iGSM was enhanced to work with Globus Replica Optimization Service (ROS),Monitoring and Discovery Service (MDS), and Data Transfer Services (DTS) for best utilization of the Grid resources. Figure 3 shows the services that iGSM works with. In the figure, the ROS, MDS and DTS are Globus services. The GWMS, GWCS and GCSW are the Grid-enabled geospatial services developed by this project. And the WCS and WMS are the portals developed by this project.

1.3 Integrated Grid-Enabled OGC Applications

With the development of Grid-enabled geospatial services components, we are ready
to establish a geospatial data grid at our testbed that can provide on-demand
geospatial data services through OGC interfaces. Figure 4 shows how the geospatial
grid fulfills a data request from OGC client. The scenario is based on the access pattern
that an OGC client first searches the data in Grid and then retrieves the data. The
following paragraphs explain the request and response sequences labeled in the figure.

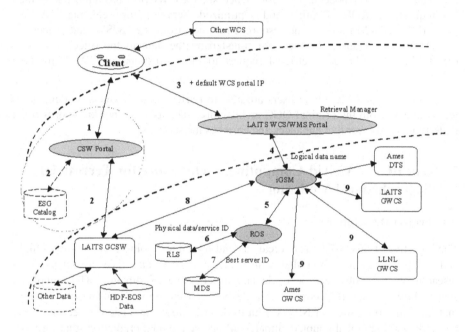

Fig. 4. A Data Request Scenario with the Geospatial Grid

(1) The OGC client issues a search request to CSW portal to find if the data the client
    wants exist in the Grid.
(2) The CSW portal propagates the request to GCWS at LAITS and ESG data
    catalog. Those catalogs will return with the logical names of the matched datasets
    as well as proper metadata to the portal. The portal then integrates the results
    from individual catalog services and returns the result to OGC client.
(3) Based on the search result, the OGC client formulates a WCS data retrieval
    request for retrieving a dataset from the Grid. The request is then sent to the
    default WCS portal, in our case, the LAITS WCS portal.
(4) The portal then sends the whole request to iGSM to mange the retrieval.
(5) iGSM sends the logical name to ROS for resolving the physical name and
    location of the requested dataset.
(6) ROS sent the logical name to RLS to find a list of physical file name and service
    ID for the datasets.

(7) With the physical name and service ID, ROS then query MDS to find the best available server. Then ROS returns an optimized Physical File Name Information (PFNInfo) object to iGSM. Each PFNInfo contains a physical file name, a GridWCS service ID, and the host where the data file located. The service ID could be either a valid or NULL ID.

(8) If the ID is a valid ID, iGSM sends a request to the GCSW for corresponding GridWCS/WMS URL to the service ID. If the ID is NULL, iGSM sends a request to GCSW for finding an available GWCS(s) /GWMS(s) which accepts data from other node in the Grid. Once such a GWCS(s) is found, iGSM then requests a ROS (Replica and Optimized Service) for selecting the best GridWCS/WMS among the resources returned from the GCSW and requests a DTS (Data Transfer Service) for transferring the data to the selected system.

(9) iGSM sends the data retrieval request to the corresponding GWCS for data retrieval.

As a result, the OGC client users are able to retrieve data products on demand as was available from the original OGC architecture. The users do not know or feel the underlying Grid layer that enhances and enriches the services.

2 Grid-BGC: A Grid-Computing Architecture for Terrestrial Biogeochemical Modeling

2.1 Project Description

The objective of this project is to create an end-to-end technological solution for high-end Earth system modeling that will reduce the costs and risks associated with research on the global carbon cycle and its coupling to climate. The completed system bridges gaps in process and scale between the remote sensing observations that form the foundation of NASA's Earth Science Strategic Vision for carbon cycle research, and the global coupled climate-carbon cycle model predictions that form the culmination of that Strategic Vision. This project takes advantage of recent developments in Grid technologies to reduce the costs of this research by providing an integrated software system that links remote computational, storage, analysis, and visualization hardware components, reducing the need for on-site access to expensive hardware.

The completed system also helps achieve NASA Earth Science strategic goals in global carbon cycle research by making it practical to link remote sensing observations to global coupled climate-carbon cycle simulations through a hierarchical interaction with a high-resolution regional model of terrestrial biogeo-chemical cycles. The high-resolution model predicts many of the same quantities as the coarse-resolution global coupled models, so acts as a useful conduit for passing process-level understanding to the global scale through focused model-model evaluations.

The Grid-BGC system consists of a single user-oriented software framework that integrates the following five technology components:

(1) A data ingest and interpolation engine that acquires ground-based observations of surface weather as its lowest-level input data and produces high-resolution gridded outputs of surface weather fields.

(2) A state-of-the-art model of terrestrial carbon, water, and nitrogen cycles that acquires gridded surface weather fields from the interpolation engine, performs a configurable sequence of simulations, and produces a high-volume multi-dimensional gridded output dataset. Model code and documentation is on-line at http://www.cgd.ucar.edu/tss/staff/thornton/rnd.html

(3) A post-processing engine that acquires and summarizes the high-resolution biogeochemical model output, evaluates the model results against operational in-situ and remote-sensing observations, and performs spatial scaling analyses against global coupled climate system model outputs.

(4) A visualization engine that acquires analyzed or summarized output from the post-processing engine and produces static and dynamic visualizations to assist the user in assessing experimental results, developing new experiments, and effectively conveying high-volume high-resolution model output and model evaluation information to a broad scientific audience.

(5) A mass storage system with high-speed connection to the computational engines. See description of the National Center for Atmospheric Research (NCAR) Mass Storage System (MSS) on-line at http://www.scd.ucar.edu/main/mss.html

Over the past several years, since the development of the interpolation and carbon cycle components of the proposed system, the development team has received a growing number of requests for assistance in implementing large gridded simulations employing these components. Because of the lack of a software framework that integrates these components and addresses the parallel computational requirements for these large simulations, it was impossible to respond positively to more than one or two such requests per year. NCAR undertook the development of the prototype system to demonstrate that there was a viable technological solution that would permit the efficient implementation of large simulations with a low start-up cost in terms of time and hardware expense. In the course of this exercise a more comprehensive vision was formed for an end-to-end software framework to facilitate the development, implementation, and evaluation of high-resolution carbon cycle simulations requiring supercomputer levels of parallel computation, which is the system we have developed under the current NASA project. The architectural design block diagram can be seen at Figure 5.

2.2 Project Accomplishments

The list below expands on the project overview, providing a description of the project accomplishments including reference to particular technology components that will be deployed:

(1) Use emerging Grid-Compute technologies to provide a research-quality platform for terrestrial carbon cycle modeling.

(2) Provide a Web Portal user interface to organize the complicated workflow and data object dependencies that are typical of very large gridded ecosystem model implementations.

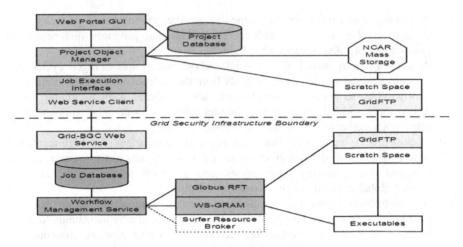

Fig. 5. Grid-BGC Current Architecture Design Diagram

(3) Connect Portal-based simulation definition and control with automated job execution on remote supercomputer platforms, eliminating direct user interaction with the remote computational resources.

(4) Provide automated data streaming for very large model input and output datasets between the Portal, remote computational resources, and a remote mass storage facility.

(5) Provide robust analysis and visualization tools through the Portal.

(6) Demonstrate end-to-end functionality with a research-quality application (U.S. 1 km gridded simulations, targeting application to the North American Carbon Program).

(7) Focus on the needs of real researchers, through multiple iterations of platform development and beta-testing.

Most of the developed services are applicable to other application domains and can be reused in future systems that address those domains. We have demonstrated this capability by re-tasking the current back-end grid service components to run the Parallel Ocean Program (POP), developed by DOE at the Los Alamos National Laboratory and a component of NCAR's Community Climate System Model (CCSM). An example of the application of Grid-BGC is shown in Figure 6. This project satisfies the pressing need for a research-quality software infrastructure to support simulations of terrestrial biogeochemistry over large domains at high spatial resolution.

2.3 Science Relevance of Grid-BGC

Our system will help to answer two of the fundamental questions defining the NASA Earth Science Mission: "How well can we predict future changes in the Earth system?" and "How do ecosystems respond to and affect global environmental change and the global carbon cycle?". The Earth Science Strategic Vision for 2003 to 2025

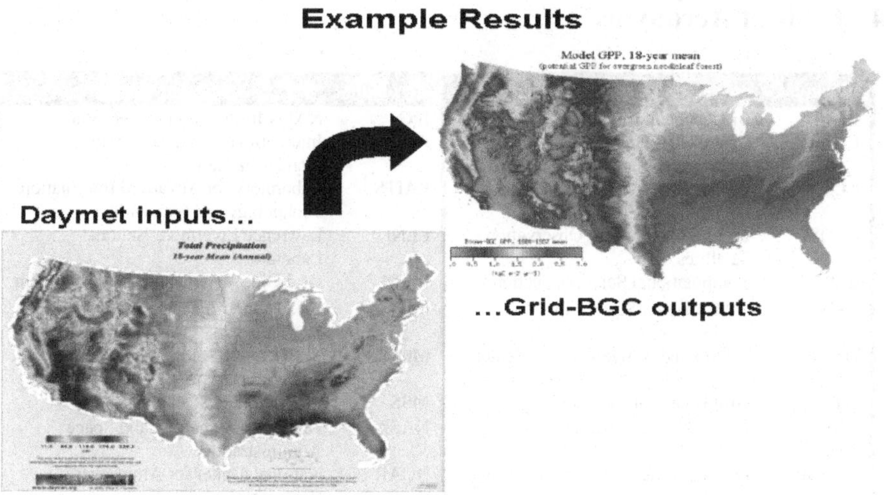

Example Results

Daymet Inputs...

...Grid-BGC outputs

Fig. 6. An example of the typical simulation domain targeted by the project, showing schematically the information flow from the Daymet model processing that produces gridded surface weather fields, to the Biome-BGC model processing that ingests these fields and produces estimates of the state and flux variables for carbon, nitrogen, and water cycles.

calls for the research community to "develop and test models to bring diverse observations to bear on the fundamental Earth Science questions", and later to "develop a collaborative synthetic environment to facilitate understanding and enable remote use of models and results." If our project is a success, we will have made substantial progress toward both of these goals. Our vision for this technology is to bring the modeling capabilities for regional terrestrial carbon cycle science up to the level of technical readiness that already exists for large remote-sensing data distribution systems and global coupled climate-carbon simulation systems. This addresses a critical gap in scales between the observations available for evaluation of carbon cycle simulations and the current simulation platforms. The technology developed under this project will significantly provide an evaluation framework for the terrestrial component of carbon cycle research at the scales appropriate to the remote sensing technology planned through 2010.

3 Lessons Learned

A surprising amount of our time has been spent on basic network administration and security due to network performance and firewall restrictions. A dedicated domain expert and the point of contact for each virtual organization is essential to the success of the project. Maintaining configuration management across independent agencies and centers is difficult but extremely important. Each tool/software upgrade should be carefully planned and executed in order to minimize service disruptions. Listen carefully to the concerns of the end users, and communicate frequently among the collaborators so that a healthy feedback loop can be formed to ensure the success of the project.

4 Table of Acronyms

Acronym	Elaboration	Acronym	Elaboration
BGC	Biogeochemical	IPG	NASA Information Power Grid
CA	Grid Certificates and Authentications	ISO	International Organization for Standardization
CCSM	Community Climate System Model	LAITS	Laboratory for Advanced Information Technology and Standards
CEOS	Committee on Earth Observation Satellites	LLNL	Lawrence Livermore National Laboratory
CSS	Computational Sciences Section	MCS	Grid Globus Metadata Catalog System
CSW	OGC Catalog Service for Web	MDS	Grid Monitoring and Discovery Service
DAAC	Distributed Active Archive Center	MODIS	MODerate-resolution Image Spectrometer
DTS	Grid Data Transfer Service	MSS	Mass Storage System
EOS	Earth Observing System	NASA	National Aeronautics and Space Administration
EOSDIS	EOS data and information system	NCAR	National Center for Atmospheric Research
ESDISP	NASA Earth Science Data and Information System Project	POP	Parallel Ocean Program
ESG	Earth System Grid of Department of Energy	PFNInfo	Physical File Name Information
ESTO	Earth Science Technology Office	RLS	Grid Replica Location Service
GRAM	Grid Resources Allocation and Management	ROS	Grid Replica Optimization Service
GSFC	NASA Goddard Space Flight Center	SAN	Storage Area Network
GCSW	Grid-enabled OGC Catalog Service for Web	SCD	Scientific Computing Division
GWCS	Grid-enabled OGC Web Coverage Service	OGC	Open Geospatial Consortium
GWMS	Grid-enabled OGC Web Map Service	UCAR	University Corporation for Atmospheric Research
HDF	Hierarchical Data Format	VO	Grid Virtual Organization
HDF-EOS	EOS profile of HDF	WCS	OGC Web Coverage Service
iGSM	Intelligent Grid Service Mediator	WMS	OGC Web Map Service

Modeling Message-Passing Overhead on NCHC Formosa PC Cluster

Chau-Yi Chou, Hsi-Ya Chang, Shuen-Tai Wang, and Shou-Cheng Tcheng

National Center For High-Performance Computing

Abstract. The communication plays a role in the overall system performance. The characterization of the communication overhead is very important to estimate the global performance of parallel applications and to detect possible bottlenecks. In this work, we evaluate and model the performance of the message-passing libraries on NCHC Formosa PC Cluster, a large cluster system with dual processor nodes and connected by Gigabits Ethernet networks. Our aim is to fairly characterize the communication primitives using general models and performance metrics. We use the formulae to estimate the communication time of a real application program for molecular dynamics simulation. We hope that it is able to provide some useful information for performance prediction and scientific computing.

1 Introduction

The improvement of the microprocessor and network has been so rapid for the last many years that has enabled PC clusters to compete with conventional supercomputers. In fact many powerful supercomputers currently in use are made of microprocessors and which usually are even a generation behind the fastest processors used in PCs. Furthermore, the availability of low-cost and fast interconnection network allows many research groups to put together commodity off-the-shelf PCs to build parallel high-performance computers. Having the advantage of delivering high-performance at low-cost, PC clusters are becoming one of the most important platforms for HPC [1-5].

Message passing plays a crucial role in distributed computation. The overheads incurred with message passing can severely limit the performance on these applications. Without knowing these overheads, users cannot make informed code-optimizing decisions, such as the tradeoffs between higher parallelism and increased communication overheads [6].

Xu and Hwang [6] have already proposed communication overhead models for machines like IBM SP2, Cray T3D, and Intel Paragon. Likewise, Prieto et al. [7] proposed models for Cray T3E and SGI Origin 2000, Touriño and Doallo [8] for Fujitsu AP3000 platform, and Gunawan and Cai [9] for Myrinet-based cluster system. Yet, there has been no formulation for clusters with Gigabit Ethernet so far.

NCHC Formosa PC Cluster [10] is a high-performance, cost-effective parallel computing system dedicated to serve a diverse group of researchers for computational

Y.-C. Chung and J.E. Moreira (Eds.): GPC 2006, LNCS 3947, pp. 299–307, 2006.

science applications. The system consists of 150 dual-Xeon PCs (i.e., 300 Intel Xeon processors) connected by a private subnet with 1000 Mbits/s Gigabits Ethernet. It has a theoretical peak speed of 1680 Gflops/s with the Linpack performance score being 997 Gflops/s, the best score of Taiwan on the 22nd Top500 List [11].

We will establish the formulae of point-to-point, broadcast, and reduce message passing on Formosa PC Cluster, and estimate the communication time of a real application program for molecular dynamics simulation by using the formulae.

Our aim is to estimate communication overheads with simple expressions, which can help application developers to design or migrate parallel programs more efficiently.

The rest of the paper is organized as follows. The communication model and measurement methodology is in section 2. In section 3 we present the results of some commonly used MPI functions. A case study is evaluated in section 4. Some concluding remarks are made in section 5.

2 Communication Model and Measurement Methodology

Table 1 lists the variables used in the communication models in this Section.

Table 1. Definition of the variables

Variable	Definition or Meaning
t	the communication time in microseconds
m	Message size in bytes
t_0	the latency (or startup time) in microseconds
r_∞	the asymptotic bandwidth in MB/s
n	the number of processors

2.1 Hockney's Model

Hockney [9, 12] has proposed a model to characterize the communication time (in microseconds) for a point-to-point communication [13]. The model is described as:

$t(m) = t_0 + \dfrac{m}{r_\infty}$, where m is the transferred message size in bytes, r_∞ is the asymptotic bandwidth in MB/s, which is defined as the maximal bandwidth achievable when the message length approaches infinity, and t_0 is the latency (or startup time).

2.2 Xu and Hwang's Model

The Hockney's model in the prior section is only for point-to-point communication. The communication time is only dependent on message size. For collective communication, Xu and Hwang [6] developed a generalized communication model based on Hockney's model: $t(m,n) = t_0(n) + \dfrac{m}{r_\infty(n)}$, where n is the number of processors, the communication time is a function of n and m now, and both the latency and the asymptotic bandwidth are also functions of n.

2.3 Gunawan and Cai's Model

Gunawan and Cai [9] divides the transferred messages into two groups, then fit the model of communication overhead in Myrinet environment, respectively. The above models in Sections 2.1 and 2.2, respectively, are rewritten as follows.

$$t(m) = \begin{cases} t_0 + \dfrac{m}{r_p}, m \leq m_p \\ t_0 + \dfrac{m}{r_\infty}, m > m_p \end{cases} \quad \text{and} \quad t(m,n) = \begin{cases} t_0(n) + \dfrac{m}{r_p(n)}, m \leq m_p \\ t_0(n) + \dfrac{m}{r_\infty(n)}, m > m_p \end{cases},$$

where r_p is the peak bandwidth achieved at the message size $m = m_p$. The model suggests that there should be two ranges for the performance metrics. One for the message size $m \leq m_p$ where the message still fits the cache size and another for the message size $m > m_p$ where the cache no longer can hold the message in one operation.

2.4 Measurement Methodology

In our experiment, we measured the MPI communication overhead likely as follows.

```
While (Static Check is O.K) {
    Barrier synchronization;
    for (i=0; i < ITERS+5; i++) {
        if (i==5) get start_time;
    MPI_communication;
    }
    get end_time;
    local_time=(end_time- start_time)/ ITERS;
    communication_time = maximum reduce(local_times);
    compute statics;
}
```

Our test bed is composed of eight dedicated nodes (16 processors). Because our system consists of dual processor nodes only, we use 2, 4, 6, 8, 10, 12, 14, and 16 processors for measuring sample data. The only exception is the pingpong case where we use one processor of each two dedicated nodes to pass message.

After five iterations for startup, we repeat one thousand times of the tested MPI functions, and then calculate the mean of these iterations. The data is called a "sample". In the paper, we have taken one thousand samples. Harmonic mean [14] was used since it gets rid of outliers better than the arithmetic mean [5,9]. Moreover, we repeated the measurement until the standard error of the mean was within 10% of the mean with 95% confidence level [14].

In our work, we used the Intel compiler 8.0 with option "-O3". And the LAM 7.0.6 [15] is adopted as the MPI library.

3   Results

3.1   Point to Point (Hockney's Model)

The results of the well-known ping-pong method [6] are clearly shown in Table 2. The detail description of the standard error is in [14]. From the table, we show that the throughput of the system is about 90.14 MB/sec, near the peak performance of 1000Mbits Ethernet. The projection function of the Hockney's model is

$$t(m) = 51.8 + 0.011\ m. \tag{1}$$

Table 2. Pingpong results on NCHC Formosa PC Cluster

Message length (bytes)	Bandwidth (MB/s)
1	0.020±0.0000
2	0.038±0.0013
4	0.070±0.0000
8	0.141±0.0010
16	0.285±0.0017
32	0.560±0.0052
64	1.106±0.0067
128	2.132±0.0291
256	4.043±0.0151
512	7.145±0.0201
1024	11.580±0.0319
2048	18.970±0.0158
4096	30.554±0.0317
8192	48.859±0.0422
16384	65.020±0.0767
32768	75.108±0.0413
65536	84.145±0.0696
131072	78.655±0.0811
262144	83.702±0.0286
524288	87.104±0.0190
1048576	88.516±0.1199
2097152	87.644±1.7322
4194304	89.642±0.1073
8388608	89.678±0.2283
16777216	89.974±0.0986
33554432	90.001±0.0134
67108864	88.685±1.2288
134217728	90.045±0.0226
268435456	90.141±0.0966

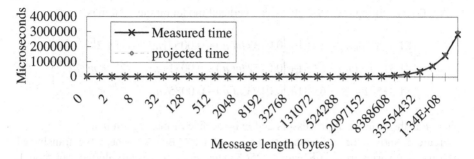

Fig. 1. Measured versus projected times for point-to-point communication

Figure 1 is the comparative analysis of projection function and measured data. The projected and measured values nearly coincide with each other.

3.2 MPI_BCAST

Figure 2 is the throughput of the MPI_BCAST on 16 processors. We observe that the maximum occurred at message length=32KB, and the highest value for the second curve at message length=16MB.

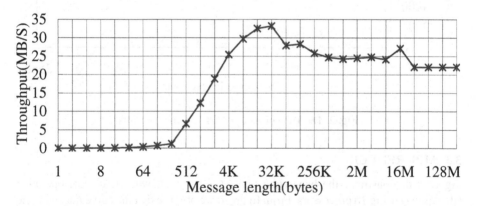

Fig. 2. The throughput of MPI_BCAST on 16 processors

Therefore, we extend the Gunawan & Cai's model as

$$t(n,m) = \begin{cases} t_0(n) + \dfrac{m}{r_p(n)}, & m \le m_p \\[2mm] t_0(n) + \dfrac{m}{r_q(n)}, & m_p < m \le m_q \\[2mm] t_0(n) + \dfrac{m}{r_\infty(n)}, & m_q < m \end{cases}.$$

After curve fitting, the MPI_BCAST overhead model on the system is

$$
t(n,m) = \begin{cases}
81.3154\,ln(\,n\,) - 63.81 + [0.0137\,ln(\,n\,) - 0.0057]m, & m \leq 2^{15} \\
81.3154\,ln(\,n\,) - 63.81 + [0.0152\,ln(\,n\,) - 0.0031]m, & 2^{15} < m \leq 2^{24} \\
81.3154\,ln(\,n\,) - 63.81 + [0.0193\,ln(\,n\,) - 0.0085]m, & 2^{24} < m
\end{cases} \qquad (2)
$$

where n is the number of processors and m is the size of message in byte.

Figure 3 shows the communication time of MPI_BCAST where the transferred message size varies from 16Kbytes to 256Kbytes. Four curves are plotted: our model, Xu & Hwang's model, Gunawan & Cai's model and by measurement. Our model appears to be closer to the measurement than the other models .

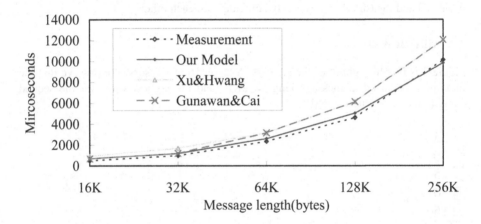

Fig. 3. The Time of MPI_BCAST on 16 processors

3.3 MPI_REDUCE

Figure 4 demonstrates the bandwidth of MPI_ REDUCE with MPI_SUM operation (float point) using 16 processors. From figure 4, we observe that the curve may be fitted by using Gunawan & Cai's model accurately. Then we obtain the projection function of MPI_REDUCE in the following formulae.

$$
t(2,m) = \begin{cases}
0.119 + 0.0025m, & m \leq 2^{6} \\
0.119 + 0.0042m, & 2^{6} < m
\end{cases},
$$

$$
t(n,m) = \begin{cases}
0.0014\,ln(\,n\,) + 0.123 + [0.0141\,ln(\,n\,) - 0.0109]m, & m \leq 2^{13} \\
0.0014\,ln(\,n\,) + 0.123 + [0.0143\,ln(\,n\,) - 0.0046]m, & 2^{13} < m
\end{cases} \quad for\ n > 2 \qquad (3)
$$

where n is the number of processors and m is the size of message in byte.

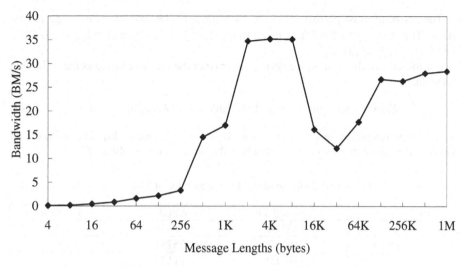

Fig. 4. The throughput of `MPI_REDUCE` on 16 processors

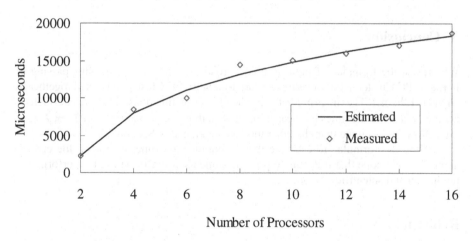

Fig. 5. The Time of transferring 512 KB Message by `MPI_REDUCE`

Figure 5 shows the communication time of `MPI_REDUCE` while transferring 512 KB message in various numbers of processors by projection function and by measurement. The two curves nearly coincide.

4   Case Study: Molecular Dynamics Simulation

The program *Modyn* is a representative benchmark in computational chemistry domain, which simulates molecular dynamics. It can efficiently simulates the molecular dynamics of Lennard-Jones atoms [16].

The program must perform MPI_ALLREDUCE of 750,008 bytes message in one stage. The MPI_ALLREDUCE is equal to one MPI_BCAST plus one MPI_REDUCE, i.e., Eq.(2) and Eq.(3).

For the sake of discussion, we define the error of the estimated time as the following formula.

$$Error = (\text{Measured Time - Estimated Time}) / \text{Measured Time} \qquad (4)$$

The experimentally measured time and the estimated time by Eq.(2) and Eq.(3) on various number of processors are listed in Table 4. The error is about 7%.

Table 4. The Measured and Estimated Time of Modyn (in sec.)

Number of Procs	Measured Time	Estimated Time	Error(%)
8	43560	40338	7
16	59837	55731	7
32	76780	71123	7
64	93437	86516	7

5 Conclusion

We present the formulae of point-to-point, broadcast, and reduce message passing on Formosa PC Cluster, a dual-processor shared-memory PC Cluster connected together by Gigabits Ethernet. The times predicted by the projection functions of Eqs. (1) through (3) are pretty close to the times by measurement. The three stages model of MPI_BCAST in Eq. (2) is more accurate than the other models mentioned in Section 3.2.

Appling the formulae to estimate the communication time of *Modyn*, the error is about 7%. We hope that it is able to provide some useful information for performance prediction and scientific computing.

References

1. Sterling, T., Becker, D., Savarese, D., et al.: BEOWULF: A Parallel Workstation for Scientific Computation. Proc. Of the 1995 International Conf. On Parallel Processing (1995)
2. Sterling, T., Savarese,D., Becker, D., et al.: Communication Overhead for Space Science Applications on the Beowulf Parallel Workstation. Proc. of 4th IEEE Symposium on High Performance Distributed Computing (1995)
3. Reschke, C., Sterling T. and Ridge, D.: A Design Study of Alternative Network Topologies for the Beowulf Parallel Workstation. Proceedings of the 5th IEEE Symposium on High Performance and Distributed Computing (1996)
4. Ridge, D., Becker, D. and Merkey, P.: Beowulf: Harnessing the Power of Parallelism in a Pile-of-PCs. Proceedings of IEEE Aerospace (1997)
5. Pfister G. F.: In Search of Clusters. Prentice-Hall, Inc. (1998)

6. Xu, Z. and Hwang, K.: Modeling Communication Overhead: MPI and MPL Performance on the IBM SP2. IEEE Parallel & Distributed Technology **4**(1) (1996) 9-23

7. Prieto, M., Espadas, D., Llorente, I. M. and Tirado, F.: Message Passing Evaluation and Analysis on Cray T3E and SGI Origin 2000 Systems. In 5th Int'l Euro-Par Conference **1685** (1999) 173-182

8. Touriño, J. and Doallo, R.: Characterization of Message-Passing Overhead on the AP3000 Multicomputer. International Conference on Parallel Processing (2001)

9. Gunawan, T. and Cai, W.: Performance Analysis of a Myrinet-Based Cluster. Cluster Computing **6** (2003) 229-313

10. NCHC Formosa PC Cluster Home Page, **http://formosa.nchc.org.tw**

11. Top 500 List, **http://www.top500.org**

12. Hockney, R. W.: Performance Parameters and benchmarking of supercomputers, Parallel Computing **17** (1991) 1111-1130

13. Hockney, R. W.: The Communication Challenge for MPP: Intel Paragon and Meiko CS-2. Parallel Computing **20** (1994) 389-398

14. Burns, G.., Daoud, R. and Vaigl, J.: LAM:An Open Cluster Environment for MPI. Proceedings of Supercomputing Symposium'94 (1994) 379-386

15. Lichten, W.: Data and Error Analysis. Prentice Hall (1998)

16. Huang, Kuo-Chan, Chang, His-Ya, Shen, Cherng-Yeu, Chou, Chau-Yi, Tcheng, Shou-Cheng. :Benchmarking and Performance Evaluation of NCHC PC Cluster. High Performance Computing in the Asia-Pacific Region (200)

Evaluation of the Device Driver Availability in Dawning4000A

Yuanxia You [1,2], Dan Meng [1], Gang Xue [3], and Jie Ma [1]

[1] National Research Center for Intelligent Computer Systems,
Institute of Computing Technology, Chinese Academy of Sciences,
Beijing 100080, P.R. China
[2] Graduate University of the Chinese Academy of Sciences, Beijing 100039, P.R. China
[3] Shanghai Supercomputer Center, Shanghai 201203, P.R. China
yyx@ncic.ac.cn

Abstract. Device drivers were claimed to be the most error prone in kernel source. A lot of error tolerance or error prevention approaches have been developed or suggested after this claim. But after analyzing the event log and maintenance record of Dawning4000A for three month, we find that device driver errors are not the most crucial crash causes in this previous TOP10 supercomputer. We believe device driver errors need developing and debugging efforts, rather than tolerance. We also suggest drivers to achieve better tolerance to device errors, especially on storage device.

1 Introduction

Large-scale Linux clusters are widely deployed in recent years. As node quantity becomes larger, components becomes more complex, node error and failure turns out to be more and more crucial to the availability and serviceability of the entire cluster. On the other hand, node MTBF of Dawning4000A (D4KA) has reached 200,000 hours, and the inherent redundant node of cluster provide the best fault tolerant infrastructure. For years people believe that the node failures are easier to be caused by software than hardware. Among all the software components in a commercial cluster, system software is the most likely to cause node failure, especially for the OS [1][2][3].

Static scan and analyse on OpenBSD and Linux kernel source codes show that the device drivers have the highest error rates than all other kernel modules [4]. Some people studied how these source code errors impact the kernel [5] [8], and others tried to reduce or tolerate their impacts [6]. Therefore, device driver errors and their behaviors are one of the emphases during our research on the node error and failure of D4KA.

This research used the event log and maintenance records of D4KA from Jul. 6, 2005 to Oct. 6 2005. The device drivers in D4KA can be classified into three catalogues: i) storage related, including HBA card and SCSI disk drivers, ii) network related, including Myrinet card driver and firmware, Gigabits Ethernet and Megabits Ethernet card drivers, iii) management and control related, such as KVM card driver.

Y.-C. Chung and J.E. Moreira (Eds.): GPC 2006, LNCS 3947, pp. 308–313, 2006.

After carefully inspection and classification, we find that Myrinet card driver and firmware are the only drivers that have ever fallen into error context on D4KA. Only Myrinet related utilities have happened oopses among all drivers, but these oopses are not regular and routinely.

Why device drivers' errors are noisy in source code, but quiet in production runtime? We believe the reasons are as following:

- D4KA's light weighted kernel eliminated useless but possibly faulty drivers
- Matured runtime eliminated high error rate drivers
- Developers paid more attention on important and widely used devices, such as SCSI HBA.

Section 4 describes the detail of reboot analyses of D4KA, and demonstrates those reboots that were caused by driver errors; section 5 compares static kernel error rate with the reboot causes of D4KA, and shows the gap between them; section 6 evaluate the efficiency of fault isolation on driver errors based on both static results and productive reboot analyses.

2 Related Works

[4] is a milestone research on kernel error analyse. Their authors implemented uniformed trace on the entire kernel sources upon different versions based on identified kernel error patterns. They concluded that device drivers have the highest error rate among the whole kernel. After that, several further researches evaluated the possibility to isolate and tolerate a faulty driver in a running kernel [6]. Others examined the behavior of the kernel when driver or similar error happens [5]. Some people even proposed user space drivers to provide a less sensitive kernel infrastructure [9]. All these works imply that the quality of driver in open source operating systems is difficult to improve as quickly and well as core functions and modules of kernel.

On the contrary, OSDL supplies driver-hardening guidance to decrease bug quantity and improve fault tolerance in drivers [7]. But this guidance is too rigid and complicated for developers to follow.

3 Approach

D4KA has 512 computing nodes, 16 storage nodes, and 4 management nodes. There are mainly four connections in D4KA: Myrinet, Gigabits Ethernet, SAN, and Megabits Ethernet. Megabyte Ethernet is a management connection, which we used to collecting event log from every computing nodes and storage nodes to management nodes.

The event logs used in the research are collected through UDP based network syslog on dedicated connections to dedicated log collecting nodes, together with maintenance and analysis records. Linux kernel has limited network event messages. Besides, SCSI errors are only transferred over this network connection; no SCSI command errors will be recorded on node's local disk. These measures can prevent domino effect when error happens on either NIC or SCSI device and (or) driver.

4 Node Crash Analyse in D4KA

Node crash is the extreme result of kernel error. As is pointed out by [5], Linux kernel is most sensitive to four major errors: NULL pointer, illegal kernel paging request, invalid operation code, and general protection failure. These crashes are always followed by node reboots before the node can be used again. We examined reboot in D4KA to get ideas on how node crashes.

The methods to catalog these reboots include:

- Collecting every possible reboot causes from the log.
- Evaluating the gravity priority of each cause. Among the causes discovered, network core lockup has the highest priority, and Myrinet firmware failure the lowest.
- Classifying each reboot to each cause according to the highest priority messages before reboot.

Figure 1 shows the reboot statistics in D4KA.

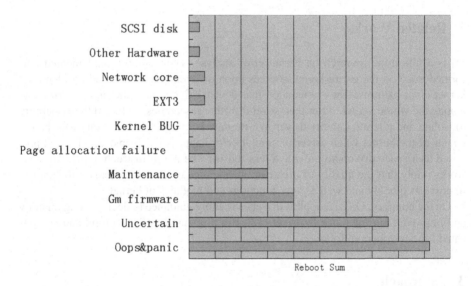

Fig. 1. Reboot statistics in D4KA

From Figure 1 we confirmed that hardware is really an unimportant cause for node reboot. Only SCSI disks and some other minor hardware have ever crashed the node. Maintenance reboot are different. Most of maintenance reboots are not after crash.

Next we analyzed software caused node crash, resulting in Figure 2:

Memory error, like NULL pointer, is only considered when it is the first error after node startup. Thus memory based error propagation will not disturb to find the original cause. From Figure 2, we can conclude that:

- The software caused node crash in D4KA is limited to several causes.
- A single driver conflict between Myrinet and nVidia leads to the largest portion of software caused node crash, almost 56%.
- Myrinet driver and firmware errors contribute to more than 70% of node crash.
- All the other node crashes have no relationship with any device driver error.
- Transient hardware errors can propagate to IO system and then lead to permanent data error and file system crash (see the last line in Figure 2).

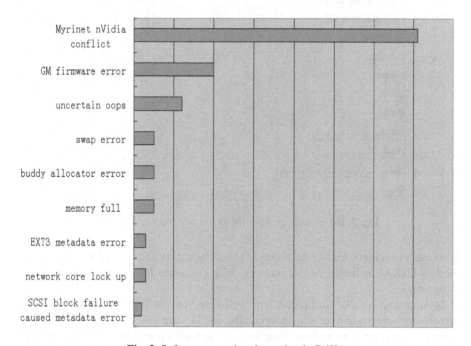

Fig. 2. Software caused node crashes in D4KA

5 Comparison with Static Research

Static analyses show that device driver has significant errors or bugs. *More than 90% of Block, Free and Intr errors and more than 70% of Lock Null and Var errors are from device drivers* [4]. This is a milestone research on open source OS kernel errors. Although this is totally true for source code, no one has validated it in productive environment.

Even in source code, driver error distribution is still different from the coarse grain data in [4]. Following Figure 3 is a simple driver quantity and error rate statistics based on Linux kernel bugzilla for version 2.4:

Figure 3 implies an important fact: error rate is unbalanced inside device drivers. Mature or widely used device, like SCSI disk & HBA card, and network interface card, usually got more effort from their developers and testers. They also got more assistance

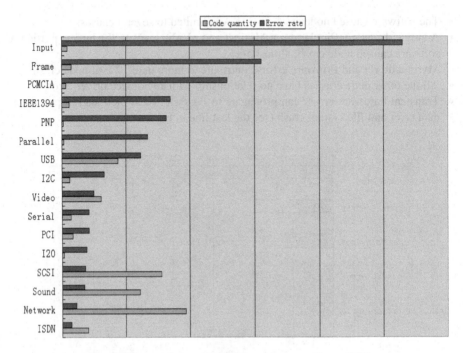

Fig. 3. Driver code quantity (MB) and error rate (errors/MB)

from users to achieve high code quality. From Figure 3 we can see that the main device used in D4KA, including SCSI, network, PCI, etc. often has relatively lower driver error rate.

Myrinet and nVidia confliction is a well-know caveat in GM driver. These two drivers are correct when running individually, and this can also be easily avoided by not running *gm_board_info* in some situation. This runtime error cannot be scanned by the compiler in [4]. Except the confliction mentioned above is excluded, GM firmware error is the only case of device driver error in D4KA, and it leads to 20 OS crash.

From this comparison, we can claim that in large scale Linux cluster as Dawning4000A, device driver error rate is not higher than other part of the kernel, except specific drivers for custom device.

6   Evaluation the Efficiency of Error Isolation

Some researches tend to tolerate driver errors during runtime, that is, isolating the kernel from faulty drivers. These driver can be isolated in either kernel [6] or user space [9]. The isolation can catch error modification and access of fragile shared memory. When errors are activated and propagated to the isolation border, isolation can help to kill the drivers and prevent the kernel from crash.

This passive protection results in unavoidable slow down. Furthermore, it protects only the kernel, neither driver nor application. For large-scale cluster systems for advanced scientific applications, slow down and kernel oriented (not node oriented) protection are all unacceptable. However, these are what must to be paid for tolerating a driver which has a much higher error rate than other parts of the kernel. The worst thing happens when several kinds of OS crashes, such as hardware address conflicts, memory full error, allocation error, ext3 error propagation, and SCSI disk error propagation, which happened in D4KA, are very difficult to be tolerated only by current isolation and stop methods.

On the contrary, from section 4 and 5, we know that after eliminating buggy drivers from kernel, testing in production environment, and updating to newer versions, driver's error rate can be reduced to a comparable low level as other parts of the kernel.

The trick here is to balance the cost between development and production [10]. For private OS like Windows, driver vendors usually have no chance to trace into kernel code to improve driver quality. Desktop user would rather fail one or more applications than crash the Windows OS and restart. For mature clusters as D4KA, more efforts should be paid not on tolerate a faulty driver, but on tolerating a reliable SCSI disk to prevent error data propagation from memory onto disk.

7 Conclusions

This paper analyzed the reboot and crash cases in one of the largest commercial Linux cluster, Dawning4000A, and tried to evaluate the device driver errors and their impact on node failure. Compared with previous researches on OS errors, we concluded that device driver error is not the largest node crash cause of D4KA, compared with static scan result. In D4KA, high error rate drivers have been eliminated in construction and test period. We suggested improving the error propagation prevention mechanism in device drivers as SCSI.

References

1. J.Gray, High-Availability Computer Systems, IEEE Computer, Sep. 1991
2. J.Gray, A Census of Tandem System Availability Between 1985 and 1990, Technical Report, 1990
3. J.Xu, Z.Kalbarczyk, etc, Networked Windows NT System Field Failure Data Analysis, Proceedings of the 1999 Pacific Rim International Symposium on Dependable Computing.
4. A.Chou, J.Yang, etc, An Empirical Study of Operating Systems Errors, SOSP 2001
5. W.Gu, Z.Kalbarczyk, Characterization of Linux Kernel Behavior under Errors, DSN 2003
6. M.M. Swift, B.N. Bershad, Improving the Reliability of Commodity Operating Systems.
7. Device Driver Hardening Design Specification, Intel Corp. IBM Corp 2002
8. A.Albinet, J.Arlat, etc, Characterization of the Impact of Faulty Drivers on the Robustness of the Linux Kernel, DSN 2004
9. Peter Chubb, Get More Device Drivers out of the Kernel, OLS 2004
10. D.S.Bai, W.Y. Yun, Optimum Number of Errors Corrected before Releasing a Software System, IEEE Trans. On Reliability, Vol 37, Issue 1, 1988

HyMPI – A MPI Implementation for Heterogeneous High Performance Systems

Franciso Isidro Massetto[*], Augusto Mendes Gomes Junior[**],
and Liria Matsumoto Sato

Politechnic School – University of São Paulo – São Paulo, Brazil
{francisco.massetto, augusto.gomes, liria.sato}@poli.usp.br

Abstract. This paper presents the HyMPI, a runtime system to integrate several MPI implementations, used to develop Heterogeneous High Performance Applications. This means that a single image system can be composed by mono and multiprocessor nodes running several Operating Systems and MPI implementations, as well as, heterogeneous clusters as nodes of the system. HyMPI supports blocking and non-blocking point-to-point communication and collective communication primitive in order to increase the range of High Performance Applications that can use it and to keep compatibility with MPI Standard.

1 Introduction

Since MPI[1] became thoroughly used in the development of applications of high performance, among them, clusters and computational grids, several researches involving these subjects began to appear.

MPI is considered an interface standard. This way, there are several implementations, each one with your own characteristic, portability and platform. However, one of the largest limitations of the MPI is the integration of different implementations. This challenge has motivated the development of researches, some of them with real results that allow executing applications that can make use of several MPI implementations in a clear way.

This work presents the HyMPI – Hybrid MPI [2], a set of MPI primitives that allow the integration of heterogeneous environment. It means that, through the HyMPI is possible to integrate, in a single system, monoprocessors and multiprocessors machines, besides computers clusters. This integration allows that different machines that execute different Operating Systems and have different MPI implementations installed can communicate to each other and to heterogeneous clusters in a transparent way.

Thus, with the use of HyMPI, it is possible to create a high performance system formed by monoprocessor nodes, SMP machines, homogeneous and heterogeneous clusters.

This article is structured as follows: in section 2 we present the works related to HyMPI, it means, implementations that support integration of several implementations.

---

[*] Professor at Centro Universitário UNIFIEO and Anhembi Morumbi University.
[**] Professor at Anhembi Morumbi University.

Y.-C. Chung and J.E. Moreira (Eds.): GPC 2006, LNCS 3947, pp. 314–323, 2006.
© Springer-Verlag Berlin Heidelberg 2006

In section 3, it is presented the structure and architecture of HyMPI, as well as the communication primitives supported and the communication protocol. Section 4 illustrates some tests and results reached with HyMPI. Finally in section 5, we show the conclusions and present some future works.

2 Related Work

The researches effort to integrate several MPI implementations, as to execute in clusters environment as in grids, has produced results, among them are IMPI [3], PVMPI [4], MPICH-G2 [5], PACX-MPI [6], STAMPI [7] and MetaMPI [8].

IMPI is a standard that defines rules and aspects of interoperability among different MPI implementations. LAM-MPI [9] implements this pattern, including the daemon impid, responsible for the communication among the nodes of different implementations.

In IMPI, there is a global nomination among the processes, that is, if there is a set of n processes executing with implementation A (ranks from 0 to $n-1$) and m processes executing with implementation B (ranks from 0 to $m-1$), we will have processes with rank between 0 and $m+n-1$. The IMPI architecture can be seen through Figure 1.

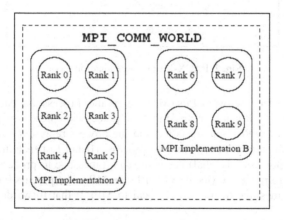

Fig. 1. IMPI Architecture

In this figure, we can notice two clients. Client 0 has 2 hosts executing a MPI implementation and Client 1 has 1 host executing another MPI implementation. The communication among the hosts of Client 1 is accomplished through MPI messages. For a process of Client 0 to communicate with a process of Client 1, an intermediate process is made necessary. This process, called server is responsible for interoperability among the clients. A message of a process in Client 0 is sent to the server process that forwards it to the process of Client 1.

The messages among clients of different MPI implementations pass, obligatorily, through the server. Besides the message forwarding, authentication protocols, service negotiation and data security among the clients.

PACX-MPI also has a global numbering schema accessible for all the process, however, PACX-MPI implements interoperability among "pseudo-mpi" processes. It means, for each different MPI implementation, the process of rank 0 and 1 are responsible, respectively, for sending and receiving messages of process of other implementations. This communication is made via TCP, where the process 0 from implementation A connects itself to process 1 from implementation B and vice-versa. As well as in IMPI, there is a local numbering (for each implementation) and a global numbering (including all implementations), as can be seen in Figure 2.

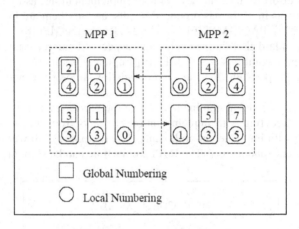

Fig. 2. PACX-MPI Communication model

In this figure, there are two MPPs (Massive Parallel Processors), each one running a MPI implementation. It can be noticed that the processes represent by circles are local numbering of each MPI implementation and the process represent by squares are the ones of global numbering, unassuming the processes 0 and 1 of each implementation.

This way, if process 3 (global) needs to send a message to process 5 (global), the message is sent to process 0 (local to MPP1) via MPI. The process 0 of MPP1 sends, via TCP/IP the message to process 1 (local to MPP2) that forwards it to process 5 (global).

MPICH-G2 is a MPI implementation, based on MPICH implementation of Argone Lab, for Grids environments, which uses services from Globus Toolkit 3 [10]. MPICH-G2 can be used in two distinct scenarios: in the first scenario there is a cluster of workstations with nodes executing different operating systems and/or MPI implementations. The second scenario illustrates a set of MPPs (Massive Parallel Processors) dispersed through a WAN that can be integrated to increase performance.

This way, MPICH-G2 creates a mesh of connections among the several processes to make possible the communication, as shows Figure 3. For a MPI application uses the MPICH-G2 resources, it is necessary that some services of Globus Toolkit's infrastructure are installed and available, in the workstations and in MPP.

Finally, PVMPI has a hybrid communication model, where MPI is used for intra-cluster communication and PVM [11] for inter-cluster communication. This way, PVM processes work as a "bridge" among several MPI implementations.

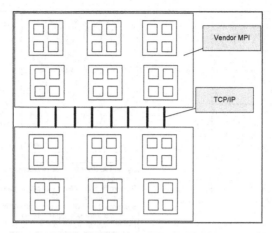

Fig. 3. MPICH-G2 Architecture

3 HyMPI – Hybrid MPI

Hybrid MPI [2] is an execution time system that aims to integrate nodes that execute different operating systems and MPI implementations. Besides, it possible to integrate computer clusters as nodes of this system.

The term "hybrid" was used to describe HyMPI, because HyMPI can be used in an environment with mono and multiprocessor nodes. In case of monoprocessor nodes, it can integrate nodes executing different operating systems and MPI implementations. Among the multiprocessor nodes, HyMPI allows using a computer cluster, where the nodes of this cluster also can execute different operating systems and different MPI implementations.

The communication strategy in HyMPI is defined taking into account the existent types of nodes. It means that are created mesh of connections among the nodes that have different MPI implementations and/or Operating Systems. In case of a node be a cluster, there is a process in the front-end machine, that we will call GATEWAY, responsible for the forwarding of messages for the others nodes that compose the cluster.

This way, all the nodes will create connections amongst them and with the GATEWAY process to communicate with the nodes belonging to the cluster.

3.1 System Architecture

To exemplify the HyMPI architecture, let us take as example a system formed by: a SMP machine with 4 processors, a Linux operating system and LAM-MPI (A). A machine SMP with 4 processors also, Windows Operating System and MPI-Pro (B) and, finally, a heterogeneous cluster with 16 nodes, 8 of them with Windows and MPICH library and the other 8 nodes with Linux and MPICH library (C).

Each MPI implementation has a MPI_COMM_WORLD communicator that identifies its processes from 0 to n-1. Supposing that there is, in this case, a process for each processor, we would have 4 distinct process numbering: from 0 to 3 in systems A and B and twice from 0 to 7 in system C, due to different implementations, as illustrates Figure 4.

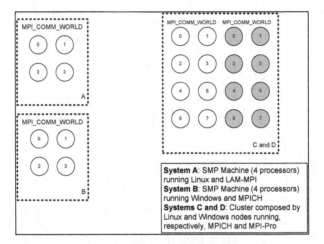

Fig. 4. Different Systems running combinations of Operating Systems and MPI implementations

Considering the heterogeneity of the environment, we would have 4 different processes numberings, taking into account the MPI implementation in each one of the environments. HyMPI uses the models adopted in IMPI and PACXMPI creating a global numbering for all processes. In this scenario and, considering a process for each processor, we would have a process numbering from 0 to 23.

The communication among several processes in HyMPI is accomplished creating a communication mesh among all the processes. However, for the nodes inside of a cluster, there is the need of a message to be forwarded through the cluster front-end machine. It means that there is a process in the cluster front-end machine, called GATEWAY, responsible for forwarding the messages inside and out of the cluster.

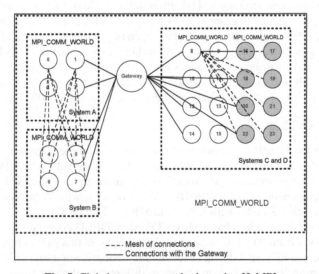

Fig. 5. Global processes numbering using HyMPI

This way, all the nodes that are not part of the cluster should maintain connections with the GATEWAY process, as well as the nodes that are part of the cluster, as shows Figure 5.

In this figure, we can notice that the nodes that are not part of the cluster, but execute different Operating Systems and MPI implementations create a mesh of connections, amongst themselves and also with the GATEWAY process, located in the cluster font-end machine. As the cluster of Figure 5 is also composed of heterogeneous nodes, communication meshes are created among these nodes and also with the GATEWAY process. In that way, every message that enters or leaves the cluster, obligatorily pass through the GATEWAY process.

3.2 Architecture of An Application That Uses HyMPI

As said previously, HyMPI is a set of libraries of execution time that must be connected to the MPI application. An advantage of this model is that HyMPI maintain the compatibility with the MPI interface, avoiding rewriting the code. On the other hand, the application should be recompiled and re-linked with the libraries. Figure 6 shows the architecture of a HyMPI application.

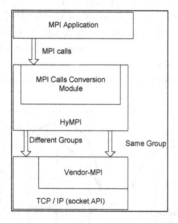

Fig. 6. Architecture of an Application that uses HyMPI

As it can be noticed in the figure, the communication among the processes of same implementation is done through a MPI native interface (vendor MPI) and the whole communication among the nodes of different Operating Systems and/or MPI implementations is accomplished through the Sockets TCP/IP API.

HyMPI offers a set of primitives in ANSI C that includes:

− Initialization and finalization of the environment
− Blocking and Non-Blocking Point-to-Point Communication
− Collective Communication

Besides, some utility and environment control functions were developed, aiming to offer larger resources in the development of MPI applications.

3.3 Communication Strategy

The communication among the processes using HyMPI uses distinct approaches, considering the king of node that composes the system. The communication among the nodes that are not part of the clusters is accomplished directly by a TCP/IP channel, while a communication among nodes that are inside of a cluster and outside of a cluster is accomplished using a intermediate process, called GATEWAY. In that way, we can detail the communication strategy as it follows:

3.3.1 Blocking Point-to-Point Communication

The blocking point-to-point communication can be done directly, in case the processes that will communicate are in the same sub-network. Alternatively, the communication can be made through the gateway process, where the sender sends a control header, containing, among other information, the global number of the target process. The message is, then buffered and forwarded in a blocking way to the receiver.

3.3.2 Non-blocking Point-to-Point Communication

According to the MPI specification [2], what differentiates the non-blocking communication of the blocking communication is the possibility of the sender process to manipulate the message buffer while it is being sent.

This way the non-blocking communication in HyMPI, when done directly, uses operating system primitives for non-blocking sending. When there is the need of the process to send a message via gateway, the message is sent from the transmitter to the gateway in a non-blocking way. The gateway buffers the whole message and forwards it normally (it means, in a blocking way) to the target process.

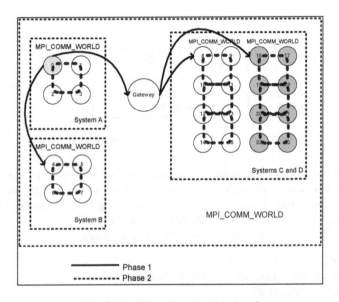

Fig. 7. Two-Phase Broadcast protocol

3.3.3 Collective Communication

HyMPI follows the same collective sending specification defined in IMPI. A two phase's protocol is used, where there are a global and a local phase. Figure 7 shows the operation of the MPI_Bcast primitive.

Supposing that the process of rank "0" (global) wants to broadcast a message. In the first phase of the protocol (global phase), it sends a message to all the processes of rank 0 of each implementation (called local root).

This sending can be made directly (through the point-to-point channel for processes in a same sub-network) or through the gateway (for processes in different sub-networks).

After all the local root nodes receive their respective copies of the message, they are responsible for doing the Broadcast among their pairs of same implementation. This second phase is called local phase.

4 Development and Tests

In the test phase, some parallel algorithms were implemented to test the communication viability in HyMPI. The environment of tests included systems composed of homogeneous and heterogeneous workstations and systems composed of workstations and a heterogeneous cluster. In this developing stage, versions of Windows-compatible and Linux-compatible libraries were implemented, intending to extend for a larger variety of operating systems. The tested system is composed by two SMP machines, each one running a different operating System (Windows and Linux) and different MPI implementations (MPIPro and MPICH, respectively) and a heterogeneous cluster, composed by eight nodes, where four of them are running Windows and MPICH and the other four nodes running Linux and LAM-MPI. The gateway machine is running Windows.

Among the developed algorithms, stands out the HEAT2D [12], based on a simplified two-dimensional heat equation domain decomposition. An array contains cells that indicate heat in a metal foil. The boundaries are held at zero throughout the simulation. During the time-stepping, an array containing two domains is used; these domains alternate between old data and new data.

This parallel version uses a master-slave approach, where the grid is decomposed by the master process and then it is distributed in lines for the slaves. To each instant of time the slave processes should change the data of their borders with their neighbors, because the effective temperature of each point of the grid depends on the values of the instant of previous time, added of their neighbors' values. When the task is completed by the slave, it returns its results to the master process.

In this algorithm, point-to-point primitives (MPI_Send e MPI_Recv) are used to communicate the slaves with their neighbors and the MPI_Barrier primitive is used to synchronize all the slaves with the master process.

Another algorithm is a parallel version of MergeSort [13], that also uses a master-slave approach for distribution and accomplishment of tasks and makes use of point-to-point and collective primitives for tasks distribution from the master. Finally, a Matrix Multiplication algorithm with point-to-point primitives was also used.

Table 1 shows some execution times obtained with both algorithms.

Table 1. Execution times (in seconds)

Algorithm	Test A	Test B	Test C	Test D
Heat2D	70.187	66.231	72.514	80.749
MergeSort	15.880	13.983	16.003	20.830
Matrix Multiplication (1000x1000)	11.008	8.503	11.632	13.065
Matrix Multiplication (2000x2000)	66.019	57.688	62.850	72.140

The Test A is a homogeneous system, composed by nodes with Linux and LAM-MPI. Test B is another homogeneous system composed by nodes with Windows and MPI-PRO. Test C is a heterogeneous cluster only with nodes monoprocessor running Linux with LAM and Windows with MPICH. Finally Test D is a heterogeneous system, composed by workstations running Windows with MPICH, workstations running Linux and LAM and a heterogeneous cluster, with nodes running Windows and MPI-Pro and Linux with MPICH.

As seen in Table 1, Test D has greater execution times because most of messages between slaves must go through Gateway process, and it becomes a bottleneck.

5   Conclusions and Future Work

This paper presented HyMPI, a MPI-compatible message-passing interface that allows integration, in a single system, several SMP nodes, each one running a different Operating System and/or MPI implementation. Besides that, it's possible to have, as a node, homogeneous and heterogeneous clusters (i.e., clusters with nodes running different OS and MPI implementations).

Comparing qualitatively HyMPI with other implementations, can be noticed some differences and similarities. Similarities are related to the process numbering, as seeing in MPICH-G2, PACX-MPI and IMPI Standard. The more significant difference among HyMPI and the other implementations is the capability to integrate SMP machines, homogeneous and heterogeneous clusters as nodes of the system. To accomplish this feature, HyMPI combines different strategies, which are present in MPICH-G2, PACX-MPI and IMPI, i.e., creating meshes of connections among process running different OS and MPI implementations, and having a process to forward messages between nodes inside and outside clusters. The gateway process, considering clusters features, is a bottleneck for the communication.

The quantitative analysis of the obtained results shows that HyMPI is viable, because communication among different nodes was possible, considering point-to-point and collective communication. However more detailed comparative analysis between HyMPI and the other implementations will be performed. Besides that, other MPI primitives will be implemented in order to increase the compatibility between HyMPI and the MPI standard.

References

1. SNIR M., GROPP W., "MPI the Complete Reference". The MIT Press (1998).
2. MASSETTO, F. I., SATO, L. M., GOMES, A. M., "HMPI – Hybrid MPI". 14th IEEE International Symposium on High Performance Distributed Computing, 2005.
3. GEORGE, W., HAGEDORN, J., DEVANEY, J.: "IMPI: Making MPI Interoperable". Journal of Research of the National Institute of Standards and Technology. Vol 105. (2000).
4. FAGG, G., DONGARRA, J., GEIST, A., "Heterogeneous MPI Application Interoperation and Process management under PVMPI", Recent Advances in Parallel Virtual Machine and Message Passing Interface', (1997).
5. KARONIS, N., TOONEN, B., FOSTER, I.: "MPICH-G2: A Grid-Enabled Implementation of the Message Passing Interface". Journal of Parallel and Distributed Computing (JPDC), Vol. 63, No. 5, pp. 551-563 (2003).
6. GABRIEL E., RESCH M., RUHLE R.. "Implementing MPI with optimized algorithms for metacomputing". In Message Passing Interface Developer's and Users Conference (1999).
7. IMAMURA, T., et al. "An architecture of Stampi: MPI library on a cluster of parallel computers". In Recent Advances in Parallel Virutal Machine and Message Passing Interface, vol 1908 of Lecture Notes In Computer Science, (2000)
8. POEPPE, M, SCHUCH, S., BEMMERL, T.: "A Message Passing Interface Library for Inhomogeneous Coupled Clusters". Proceedings of ACM/IEEE International Parallel and Distributed Processing Symposium (IPDPS 2003), Workshop for Communication Architecture in Clusters (2003)
9. LAM Team. LAM/MPI Parallel Computing, MPI General Information. Avaliable at http://www.lam-mpi.org/mpi/
10. The Globus Project. Available at http://www.globus.org
11. GEIST A., BEGUELIN, A., "PVM Parallel Virtual Machine – A Users' guide and tutorial for networked parallel computing". The MIT Press (1994).
12. BARNEY, B. Lecture notes. Available at http://carbon.cudenver.edu/csprojects/ csc5809F99/ mpi_examples/ 2d_heat_equation.html
13. JACKSON, B. Lecture Notes. Available at http://carbon.cudenver.edu/csprojects/ csc5809F99/mpi_examples/merge_sort.html

Performance Improvement by Data Management Layer in a Grid RPC System

Yoshiaki Aida, Yoshihiro Nakajima, Mitsuhisa Sato,
Tetsuya Sakurai, Daisuke Takahashi, and Taisuke Boku

Department of System and Information Engineering, University of Tsukuba,
Tennodai 1-1-1, Tsukuba-shi, Ibaraki 305-8577, Japan
{aida, ynaka}@hpcs.cs.tsukuba.ac.jp,
{msato, sakurai, daisuke, taisuke}@cs.tsukuba.ac.jp

Abstract. A grid RPC system provides a useful and intuitive programming interface for master-worker type applications in a grid environment. In many grid applications, such as parameter search programs, both master and workers are often required to have a large amount of common data. Since in the RPC model the data must be transferred from the master directly to each worker, the master is sometimes a bottleneck, resulting in poor performance. In order to improve the performance in such cases, we propose a model to decouple the data transfer by a data management layer from the RPC programming. We have designed and implemented a prototype data transfer layer called OmniStorage to OmniRPC, which is a grid RPC system for parallel programming in a grid environment. This allows efficient data transmission of a large amount of data by placing intermediate relay servers, taking the network topology into account, to route the communication and cache the common data in the server. We have evaluated the performance of the proposed system by using synthetic workloads and a real grid application. The results show that OmniStorage can improve the performance of OmniRPC applications compared to the case of using only OmniRPC.

1 Introduction

Recent advances in wide-area networking technology and infrastructure have made it possible to construct large-scale, high-performance distributed computing environments, or computational grids, that provide dependable, consistent and pervasive access to enormous computational resources. Grid technology enables integration of the computing resources in the wide-area network and the sharing of huge amounts of data distributed in several places. In order to make use of computing resources in a grid environment, the RPC-style system is particularly useful in that it provides an easy-to-use, intuitive programming interface that allows users of the grid system to easily make grid-enabled applications. Several systems adopt Grid RPC as a basic model of computation, including Ninf[9], NetSolve[2] and CORBA[5]. We are currently developing a grid RPC system called OmniRPC[6][7] for parallel programming in cluster and grid environments.

Y.-C. Chung and J.E. Moreira (Eds.): GPC 2006, LNCS 3947, pp. 324–335, 2006.

Grid RPC provides an effective programming model for typical grid applications, such as parametric search programs and task parallel programs. In these programs, a grid RPC program is composed of a master that performs remote procedure calls in parallel and several workers that execute the procedures called by the master in remote nodes. In many cases, programs are required to share a large amount of data among the workers. For instance, in some parametric search applications, the workers often have the same common data, and then receive different parameters from the master to execute different computations at remote nodes in parallel. In the RPC model, communication occurs only between the master and a worker when the master issues the remote procedure call and receives the results from the invoked remote procedure. Since the master sends data to every worker as arguments of remote procedure calls, the master may become a bottleneck when the the data size is large. Furthermore, if an RPC system does not support data persistence in workers, which cannot hold any data between calls, the master must send the same data at every call.

In this paper, we propose a programming model to decouple the data transmission from the RPC model to allow the data to be transferred efficiently according to the usage of data and the network topology. In particular, we focus on efficient data transfer from the master to the workers, which often is required in many typical grid applications. We have designed and implemented a prototype data transfer layer for the OmniRPC grid RPC system called OmniStorage. OmniStorage can improve the data transfer by arranging intermediate servers that relay data at appropriate nodes between the master and worker in a network. This allows data transfer routing that takes the network topology into account. The data can be cached in an intermediate relay server located between the master and worker where the master calls a number of procedures with the same data. For example, a typical computing resource in a grid environment is a cluster of PCs. By setting a relay server at the master node of the cluster, a data may be cached in the master node so that the data can be shared by a fast network inside the cluster.

The OmniRPC provides a partial data persistence facility called "automatic-initializable remote module" to hold only data given by an initialize function of the remote executable module. This allows multiple transmission of the same initial data to be avoided. However, the data must be sent directly from the master to each worker when the remote module is invoked. If the initial data is large, the master may be a bottleneck. Furthermore, since the remote modules are invoked on demand, the invocation of workers is sometimes delayed, resulting in poor scalability. Decoupling data transmission by OmniStorage from RPC calls can make the invocations of remote modules faster.

Beck, et al.[1] proposed a general framework to combine NetSolve and IBP for the use of storage in grid RPC programming. Del-Fabbro, et al.[4] presented a data management scheme in their grid RPC system, DIET. While the DIET data management is designed on top of the DIET infrastructure, we have designed the data transfer layer as a different layer from OmniRPC, focusing on the data transfer from the master to the workers. Our contributions are as follows:

- We propose a model to decouple the data transmission from the RPC for typical grid applications, which are required to have a large amount of common data.
- We have designed OmniStorage as a prototype data transfer layer for OmniRPC and have evaluated the performance by synthetic workloads and a real grid application in our grid testbed. Our application is a master-worker parallel eigenvalue computation, which requires only one minute per job with 50 MB of initial data.
- The performance improvement by using OmniStorage is shown by comparing the results of tests conducted with and without OmniStorage.

The next section presents an overview of OmniRPC. Section 3 presents the proposed model that decouples the RPC layer into RPC invocation and data transfer. Section 4 describes the implementation of the newly developed OmniStorage. The performance of OmniStorage is evaluated in Section 5. Section 6 describes previous works related to the present study. Finally, Section 7 presents our conclusions and future works.

2   Background: A Grid RPC System OmniRPC

OmniRPC is Grid RPC programming middleware that exploits computing resources that are geographically distributed with an intuitive programming interface. The OmniRPC system inherits Ninf's APIs[8]. One of the target execution platforms of OmniRPC is a cluster-of-clusters, in other words, OmniRPC handles multiple clusters as a virtualized cluster. OmniRPC supports the parallel master/worker programming model, so the user can use asynchronous call APIs in order to create a parallel program. OmniRPC also provides both simple procedure call APIs and APIs with data persistence. Simple procedure call APIs do not specify any hosts, and the system automatically allocates idle nodes for the procedure call. APIs with data persistence allows the worker to hold the state between different calls so that multiple data transmissions of the same data are avoided. Although data persistence allows efficient execution, the master has to manage the location of the remote node.

OmniRPC provides data persistence through the "automatic-initializable remote module" facility to hold only data given by an initialize function of the remote executable module. Any remote procedure in the module can use the initial data by a simple procedure call API once the module is invoked with the initialize function. This allows both flexible allocation of remote nodes and efficient execution by data persistence.

OmniRPC can multiplex the communication between the client process and remote worker processes in order to enable the users to exploit clusters composed by private address and to use thousands of remote hosts because the number of connections in the client program is reduced.

Figure 1 shows an overview of OmniRPC. In this figure, the master is calling the calculation node of the cluster by multiplexed connection. When the client program is started, OmniRPC's agent is invoked on the host specified in the host

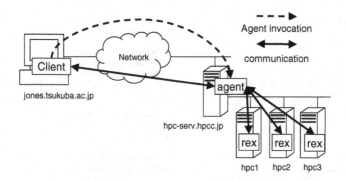

Fig. 1. OmniRPC Overview

configuration file of OmniRPC. Next, when the client program calls a remote procedure, the agent runs the remote execution program at calculation nodes. In the execution of an OmniRPC application, the executable module containing the remote procedures are invoked on demand when the procedure is first called.

3   Decoupling Data Transfer from the RPC Model

In this section, we present a programming model to decouple the data transmission from the RPC model.

We have designed a prototype data transfer layer called OmniStorage to allow the data to be transferred efficiently according to the usage of data and the network topology.

3.1   RPC Parallel Programming with Data Transfer Layer: OmniStorage

In the simple RPC model, communication occurs only between the master and a worker when the master issues the remote procedure call and receives the results from the invoked remote procedure. Even if the data sent to each worker is the same, the master sends the data to the worker through one-to-one communications.

Figure 2 shows a simple parallel program using OmniRPC asynchronous calls for a master-worker parallel program.

When the size of the data is large, the master may become a bottleneck. To solve the problem, we decouple the transmission of data from the RPC model, and make use of the layer to transfer the common data. OmniStorage is a data transfer layer for OmniRPC. Using OmniStorage, the master registers common data on this layer beforehand, after the workers receive the data from this layer. Figure 3 shows an example using OmniStorage's API. The master calls "OmstPutData()" before asynchronous calls to the remote procedures to

```
/* master program */              /* master program */
int main(){                       int main(){
  ...                               ...
                                    OmstPutData("MyData",
                                     data, OMST_INTEGER * DATALEN);
  for(i = 0; i < n; i++){           for(i = 0; i < n; i++){
   req[i]=OmniRpcCallAsync("MyProcedure", i,   req[i]=OmniRpcCallAsync("MyProcedure", i);
     data, results);
  }                                 }
  OmniRpcWaitAll(n, req);           OmniRpcWaitAll(n, req);
  ...                               ...
}                                 }

/* worker's IDL */                /* worker's IDL */
Define MyProcedure(int IN parameter,   Define MyProcedure(int IN parameter){
           IN data[], OUT results[]){
                                    OmstGetData("MyData",
                                     data, OMST_INTEGER * DATALEN);
  /* Program in C */                 /* Program in C */
  ...                                ...
}                                 }
```

Fig. 2. A sample program using only Om-   **Fig. 3.** A sample program using the API
niRPC asynchronous calls   of OmniStorage

register the data, and then the workers can call "OmstGetData()" to retrieve
the data before calculation. To identify data, the master and worker access data
by a unique name "MyData" along with its size. OmniStorage also provides APIs
that transfer a file by its directory path.

Compared to the case of using only the RPC shown in Figure 2, OmniStorage
can improve the data transfer by arranging intermediate servers that relay data
at appropriate nodes. For example, if the workers are nodes in a PC cluster,
OmniStorage can optimize communication by setting the relay server at the
master node of the cluster. Once the data is transferred and cached in the server
through a wide area network, the data is then transferred to the worker nodes
using the fast network of the PC cluster. Since the master may send the data
only once, the master will no longer be a bottleneck.

The APIs of OmniStorage are summarized as follows:

- int OmstPutData(const char *dataname, const void *data, int datasize);
  OmstPutData() puts the data indicated by "data" into the cache at the host
  wh
- int OmstPutFile(const char *dataname, const char *path);
  OmstPutFile() puts the data into the cache. The source of the data is not
  the m
- int OmstGetData(const char *dataname, void *data, int datasize);
  OmstGetData() retrieves the data from OmniStorage system and writes data
  into t
- int OmstGetFile(const char *dataname, const char *path);
  OmstPutFile() retrieves the data from the OmniStorage system and writes
  the dat

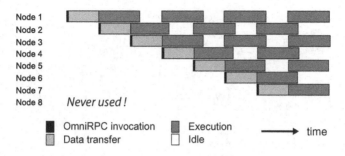

Fig. 4. Problem with a large amount of initial data in OmniRPC. This figure shows a timing chart for the case of a parallel program executed by OmniRPC on eight calculation nodes. This application has 16 jobs. As shown, if the initialization takes a long time, the chart will become sparse.

3.2 Problem of Applications Requiring a Large Amount of Initial Data

In parallel applications such as parametric search, the input data needed by a remote program can be separated into two parts: the initial data and parameters. While the initial data is the same for every worker and is often large, the parameters are small.

To support such a application, the OmniRPC has a facility for transferring initial data when invoking a remote program. This facility enables the reuse of the initial data at other RPCs, removing multiple transmission of the same data. In the current implementation of OmniRPC, the workers are invoked on demand when the actual calls are performed so that its invocation process is serialized. When the amount of initial data is large, it takes longer to invoke all of the remote programs as the number of workers increases. This sometimes limits the scalability of OmniRPC programs. Figure 4 shows a typical situation that occurs in sucases. By decoupling the data transfer for a large amount of initial data by using OmniStorage, we can reduce the time to invoke all workers.

4   Implementation of OmniStorage

In this section, we describe the implementation of OmniStorage.

Figure 5 shows that dataflow in OmniStorage. There are tree kinds of components, as follows:

- The node denoted "C" is an OmniRPC client host that submits jobs to workers.
- The node denoted "W" is a worker host that executes a job for a called procedure. The node denoted "R" is a relay host that relays data transfer between client host and worker host.

When a PC cluster is used for a pool of workers, it is useful for the relay host to be set up at the master node of a PC cluster. In OmniStorage, the connection

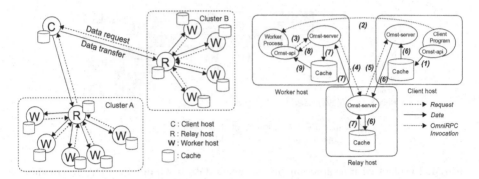

Fig. 5. Dataflow in OmniStorage   **Fig. 6.** Behavior of OmniStorage

to each host forms a tree topology without any cycle. Data is transferred from the root, and all hosts can cache received data.

Figure 6 illustrates the behavior of OmniStorage system. Hereinafter, the number enclosed with parentheses corresponds to the number in this figure. In addition, "Omst-server" and "Omst-api" indicate OmniStorage's server process and its API, respectively.

(1) The client program registers data to the cache in master hosts by Omst-api. (`OmstPutData`)
(2) The remote program is invoked by OmniRPC. (`OmniRpcCallAsync`)
(3) The invoked remote program checks whether the requested data is in the local cache. If the data is not found, Omst-api sends a request for the data to the local Omst-server.
(4) The Omst-server receives the request from Omst-api, and requests the data from the Omst-server at an upstream relay host.
(5) The Omst-server in the upstream relay host checks if the requested data is in the local cache. If the data is not found, the Omst-server again requests the data from the Omst-server at its upstream client host.
(6) The Omst-server at the client host retrieves the data from the local cache and sends it to the relay host. The data is stored in the cache of the relay host.
(7) The Omst-server at the relay host retrieves the data from the local cache, and sends it back to the worker host. The data is stored in the cache of worker host.
(8) The Omst-server sends a response to the Omst-api.
(9) The Omst-api reads the data from local cache and stores it in memory.

A series of operations from (1) to (9) are executed when no data is found in either the worker host or the relay host. If the data already exists in the cache of worker host, it executes from (3) to (9). On the other hand, if the data exists in the cache of the relay host, it executes from (5) to (7). As a result, a job executed first in a worker executes all steps from (1) to (9) because none of the remote hosts have data at the beginning, except the client host. However, the job that uses the same existing data uses the cache on the way to the client host. In particular, when the same worker executes the second job, Omst-api can read the local cache directly. In this case, the OmniStorage system is not accessed.

5   Performance Evaluation

5.1   Experimental Setting

For the experiment, we used two PC clusters connected by different networks. In addition, we used two hosts as clients: cTsukuba and cTitech. Those host nodes are located at the University of Tsukuba and at the Tokyo Institute of Technology, respectively. Table 1 shows the experimental setup. Figure 7 shows the network bandwidth between hosts and clusters.

Table 1. Machine configurations in the grid testbed

Site	Cluster Name	Machine	Memory	Network	Nodes
HPCC.JP	Dennis	Dual Xeon 2.4 GHz	1 GB	1 Gb Ethernet	16
Univ. of Tsukuba	Kaede	Dual Xeon 3.2 GHz	2 GB	1 Gb Ethernet	64

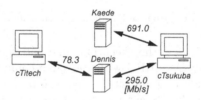

Fig. 7. Network bandwidth

5.2   Basic Performance

We measured the basic performance and characteristics of OmniStorage using a synthetic program that models an RPC application with OmniRPC's data transmission mechanism. This program sends a certain amount of initial data from master to worker processes. We changed initial data size and the execution time per RPC, which are simulated by sleep system call.

We compared the performance of two versions of model program: "OmniRPC + OmniStorage" and "OmniRPC only". "OmniRPC + OmniStorage" used OmniStorage to transfer initial data, and "OmniRPC only" transferred initial data by using `OmniRpcModuleInit`.

We varied the size of transferred data as 1, 16, 128, 512 and 1,024 MB and the execution time of one RPC as 5, 60 and 300 seconds, respectively. A total of 32 RPCs were to be performed, and 16 calculation nodes were used with an OmniRPC agent process at each cluster. We used "cTitech" and "Dennis" for the client host and the cluster, respectively.

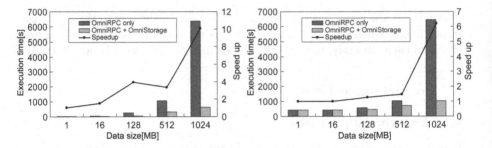

Fig. 8. Performance for an execution time of 5 seconds

Fig. 9. Performance for an execution time of 60 seconds

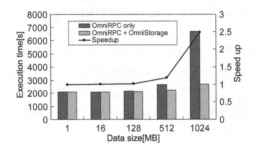

Fig. 10. Performance for an execution time of 300 seconds

Figures 8, 9 and 10 show the execution time and speed up ratio based on the time for using only OmniRPC with the same configuration. OmniStorage can reduce the execution time for all data sizes, especially in the case of 1,024 MB data transmission. The larger the data transmission, the greater the improvement by OmniStorage. The execution time increases rapidly by using only OmniRPC when the data size exceeds 512 MB.

5.3   Master-Worker Parallel Eigenvalue Solver

We examined the scalability of OmniStorage with respect to the number of calculation nodes using master-worker parallel eigenvalue solver program[11]. This program is used to solve large-scale eigenvalue problems in parallel by solving the equation that corresponds to a point on the circumference in the complex space. In this experiment, we compared the performance of multiple clusters and a single cluster. We used the data set in which the degree of parallelism is 80 for both cases. The number of the eigenvalue computation worker to 80.

First, we evaluated the scalability in only the Kaede cluster acceding to the number of nodes used. Figure 11 shows the execution time and speed up ratio based on the execution time in one node on the Kaede cluster. We found that OmniStorage improved the performance up to 32 nodes. On the other hand, there were limited improvements in the performance of the application beyond 16 nodes when only OmniRPC is used without OmniStorage. This is because the

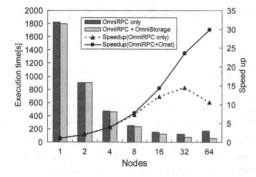

Fig. 11. Execution time and speed up of parallel eigenvalue calculation program

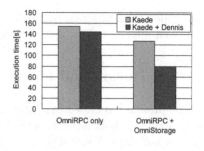

Fig. 12. Comparison of execution time of parallel eigenvalue calculation program by number of clusters

execution time of the eigenvalue calculation job changes widely and the degree of parallelism of the data-set that was used is limited to 80.

Next, we examined the performance of OmniStorage at two clusters. We used both cTsukuba and Kaede. Figure 12 shows the execution time of the program using two clusters. The speed-up when using only OmniRPC remains approximately 1.06 times when only the Kaede cluster is used. However, the speed-up when OmniStorage is used is 1.58 times that when only the Kaede cluster is used. We found that OmniStorage improves the performance when using multiple clusters.

6 Related Works

NetSolve[2] can treat persistent data by using two components of Distributed Storage Infrastructure (DSI) and RequestSequencing in the process in which RPC is called. DSI manages the arrangement of the data that the program on the callee side uses and makes the data transfer from the client program to the worker program efficient by using the cache.

IBP[1] is middleware for large-scale data transfer in grid applications that provides users with sharing of storage resources and allows client processes to manipulate the state of data by using several APIs, such as IBP_allocate, IBP_store and IBP_load. The greatest difference between IBP and OmniStorage is the degree of allowance for data management by client process. In IBP, users should consider the data location during programming. In contrast, transferring and managing data is done automatically by OmniStorage.

DIET[4] manages the persistent data by using the data identifier. If data is sent from the client once, then the Agent can manage thereafter and the data is used on the callee side. The management of data has been achieved by using two components: a Logical Data Manager and a Physical Data Manager. The Logical Data Manager manages data identifier information on an Agent mounted with CORBA. The Physical Data Manager manages actual data. This system is developed for a program constructed with a directed acyclic graph and has not yet been applied to real applications.

7   Conclusion and Future Work

In the present paper, we have proposed a model to decouple the data transfer by a data management layer from the RPC programming for sharing larges amounts of common data. We designed and implemented a prototype data management layer, OmniStorage, that transfers common initial data according to the network configuration. We found that OmniStorage achieved efficient initial data transfer to workers and that using OmniStorage together OmniRPC can improve the performance of applications with large-scale initial data transfer. Moreover, we showed that several computer resources on the wide-area network can be used as scalable when OmniStorage accompanies the transmission of large-scale data in the programming model of master/worker type applications.

The current design of OmniStorage focuses on only the distribution of data from master to worker. We will extend this to include a function to collect the data of the calculation results. For example, an application such as Phylogenetic Analysis by Maximum Likelihood (PAML) programs needs to collect very large result data. At the same time, we will employ an efficient lookup mechanism such as a distributed hash table (DHT) for the data storage in large scale environment.

Since the data management layer can be replaced with the same OmniStorage APIs, we will exploit the possibility of using Bittorrent[3] or Gfarm[10] as the data transfer layer.

References

1. Alessandro Bassi, Micah Beck, Terry Moore, James S. Plank, Martin Swany, Rich Wolski, and Graham Fagg. The internet backplane protocol: a study in resource sharing. *Future Gener. Comput. Syst.*, 19(4):551–562, 2003.
2. H. Casanova and J. Dongarra. Netsolve: A network server for solving computational science problems, 1996.
3. B. Cohen. Incentives build robustness in bittorrent, 2003.
4. Bruno Del-Fabbro, David Laiymani, Jean-Marc Nicod, and Laurent Philippe. Data management in grid applications providers. In *DFMA '05: Proceedings of the First International Conference on Distributed Frameworks for Multimedia Applications (DFMA'05)*, pages 315–322, 2005.
5. Object Management group. http;//www.omg.org.
6. Mitsuhisa Sato, Taisuke Boku, and Daisuke Takahashi. OmniRPC:grid RPC system for parallel programming in grid environment. *IPSJ Transactions on Computing System*, Vol. 44(No. SIG11 (ACS 3)):34–45, 2003.
7. Yoshihiro Nakajima, Mitsuhisa Sato, Taisuke Boku, Daisuke Takahashi, and Hitoshi Gotoh. Performance evaluation of omnirpc in a grid environment. In *SAINT-W '04: Proceedings of the 2004 Symposium on Applications and the Internet-Workshops (SAINT 2004 Workshops)*, page 658, 2004.
8. Ninf Project. http://ninf.apgrid.org/.

9. M. Sato, H. Nakada, S. Sekiguchi, S. Matsuoka, U. Nagashima, and H. Takagi. Ninf: A network based information library for global world-wide computing infrastructure, 1997.

10. Osamu Tatebe, Youhei Morita, Satoshi Matsuoka, Noriyuki Soda, and Satoshi Sekiguchi. Grid datafarm architecture for petascale data intensive computing. In *CCGRID '02: Proceedings of the 2nd IEEE/ACM International Symposium on Cluster Computing and the Grid*, page 102, Washington, DC, USA, 2002. IEEE Computer Society.

11. Tetsuya Sakurai, Hiroto Tadano, Kentaro Hayakawa, Mitsuhisa Sato, Daisuke Takahashi, Umpei Nagashima, Yuichi Inatomi, Hiroaki Umeda, and Toshio Watanabe. A master-worker type parallel method for large-scale eigenvalue problems. *IPSJ Transactions on Computing System*, Vol. 46(No. SIG7):1–8, 2005.

Effective Dynamic Replica Maintenance Algorithm for the Grid Environment

Rashedur M. Rahman[1], Ken Barker[1], and Reda Alhajj[1,2]

[1] Department of Computer Science, University of Calgary, Calgary, AB, Canada
[2] Department of Computer Science, Global University, Beirut, Lebanon
{rahmanm, barker, alhajj}@cpsc.ucalgary.ca

Abstract. Replication in Data Grid reduces access latency and bandwidth consumption by creating multiple data copies. One of the challenges in data replication is to select the candidate sites where replicas should be placed, which is known as the allocation problem. One performance metric to determine the best place to host replicas is select for optimum average response time. We use the p-median model for the replica placement problem. The p-median model has been exploited in urban planning to find locations where new facilities should be built. In our problem, the p-median model finds the locations of p candidate sites to place a replica that optimize the aggregated response time. Motivated by the fact that the Grid environment is highly dynamic, we propose a dynamic replica maintenance algorithm that re-allocates replicas to new candidate sites when a performance metric degrades significantly. Simulation results demonstrate that the dynamic maintenance algorithm with static placement decisions performs best in dynamic environments like Data Grids.

1 Introduction

The term "Grid" is derived from an analogy to the electrical power supplier in the sense that it has pervasive access to power and can draw any resources from the distributed resource pool. Thus, a household draws electricity from power sockets irrespective of their physical location and the location of access points [9]. Foster *et al.* [8] define the Grid concept as "coordinated resource sharing and problem solving in dynamic, multi-institutional virtual organizations". Grid computing accommodates very diverse resource types including storage devices, CPU power, files, special cases of devices such as sensors, radio telescopes, satellite receivers, and others. These resources may be distributed across many organizations among different geographical locations. Large scientific initiatives such as global climate change, high energy physics, and computational genomics require large data collections which are now being crated in various locations. Data replication is critical as Data Grids are developed to permit data sharing across many organizations in geographically disperse locations [13]. The general idea of replication is to store copies of data in different locations so that data can be easily recovered if one copy at one location is lost or unavailable. Moreover, if data can be kept close to users via replication, data access performance can be improved dramatically. Replication facilitates load balancing and improves

Y.-C. Chung and J.E. Moreira (Eds.): GPC 2006, LNCS 3947, pp. 336–345, 2006.
© Springer-Verlag Berlin Heidelberg 2006

reliability by creating multiple data copies. However, the files in the Grid are large (*i.e.*, 500MB-1GB) so replication to every site is infeasible. One of the challenges is to locate the candidate sites for replica placement. One approach is to place replica at sites that optimize aggregated response time. Response time is calculated by multiplying the number of requests at site i with the distance between the nearest replication site to the requester. The sum of the response times for all sites constitute the aggregated response time. We will use the terms *total response time* and *aggregated response time* interchangeably throughout this research. We propose a p-median model [10] that finds the locations of p candidate sites to place a replica that will minimize the aggregated response time. However, the optimization problem is NP-hard so a large network requires an unacceptable computation time without directing to the optimal solution [5]. Therefore, heuristics are needed that can generate optimal/near-optimal solutions for the p-median model. The Lagrangean Relaxation technique is one popular heuristic technique because it provides bounds on the objective function. Lagrangean technique solves the p-median model by locating p candidate sites to place replicas optimally. The Grid environment is highly dynamic where user requests and network latency vary constantly. Candidate sites that hold replicas currently may not be the best sites to fetch replicas subsequently. Thus, we propose a dynamic replica maintenance algorithm that first finds the optimal/near-optimal cumulative aggregated response time for certain K periods by allowing relocation with a positive transportation cost, and then compare it with current cumulative aggregated response time. The current response time is calculated by adding aggregated response time for K periods assuming that replicas are placed at sites that provide the optimal value using p-median at period $K=1$. The relocation decision is then made based on the comparison, *i.e.,* if the difference is greater than an allowable threshold.

The rest of the paper is organized as follows. Section 2 presents related work. Optimal static replica placement strategy is discussed in Section 3. Dynamic replica maintenance strategy is presented in Section 4. The simulation model is described in Section 5. Section 6 evaluates and compares the replication strategies. Section 7 concludes and indicates possible future research directions.

2   Related Work

Kavitha et al. [11] propose a strategy for creating replicas automatically in a generic decentralized peer-to-peer network. The goal of their model is to maintain replica availability with some probabilistic measure. Ranganathan and Foster [13] discuss various replication strategies for a hierarchical DataGrid architecture. They test six different replication strategies. Kavitha et al. [12] develop a family of job scheduling and replication algorithms and use simulation studies to evaluate them. Three different replica placement algorithms are considered and combined with four scheduling strategies. They show that when there is no replication, simple local scheduling performs best. However, when a replication is used scheduling jobs to sites containing the required data is better. The key lesson for our study is that dynamic replication reduces hotspots created by popular data and enables load sharing. OptorSim [1] is a simulator developed as a part of European DataGrid project to carry out different replication and scheduling algorithms. The simulator uses an economic model in which sites buy and sell files using an auction mechanism.

Several research efforts [1, 12, 13] only consider user requests for replica placement and ignore network latencies. However, network bandwidth plays a vital role in large file transfers. Substantial transfer time is saved if we place file replicas at neighboring sites with limited bandwidth but high request rates. Earlier work [14] shows that considering both the current network state and file requests produce better results than file requests times alone. The replication algorithm selects one site per iteration to host replica by optimizing risk or utility indexes. In this research we extend our earlier work to account for spiky request patterns by locating p candidate sites simultaneously rather than one site per iteration. Besides, we propose a dynamic replica maintenance algorithm to relocate replicas to new sites if performance metric degrades significantly.

3   Static Replica Placement Algorithm

Our objective is to find the p best candidate (replication) sites such that the total response time for all of the requesting sites is minimized. The identified problem is closely analogous to the *p-median* model [10] used extensively for facility location problems in urban planning. In the following sections we formally restate the model and provide a heuristic based approach that leads to optimal/near-optimal solution for our replica placement problem.

3.1   P-Median Model

The p-median model is formulated with the following equations:

$$\text{Minimize} \sum_{i=1}^{n} \sum_{j=1}^{n} h_i d_{ij} y_{ij} \tag{1}$$

$$\text{Subject to} \sum_{j=1}^{n} x_j = p \tag{2}$$

$$\sum_{j=1}^{n} y_{ij} = 1, \ i = 1,\ldots,n \tag{3}$$

$$y_{ij} - x_j \le 0, \ i = 1,\ldots,n \quad j = 1,\ldots,n \tag{4}$$

$$x_j \in (0,1), \quad j = 1,\ldots,n \tag{5}$$

$$y_{ij} \in (0,1), \ j = 1,\ldots,n \ ; \ i = 1,\ldots,n \tag{6}$$

$$y_{ij} = \begin{cases} 1 \text{ if requesting site } i \text{ is allocated to replication site } j \\ 0 \text{ otherwise} \end{cases} \tag{7}$$

The objective function (1) minimizes the request-weighted distance between each requesting site and the nearest replication site. Constraint (2) states that exactly p sites are to be located to place the replica. Constraint (3) states that each requesting site should be allocated exactly one replication site from which it can fetch the replica. Constraint (4) states that requests at site i can only be assigned at replication site j if a replica is placed at site j. Constraints (5-6) are general integrity constraints. Here, h_i represents requests at site i. For a small network and small value of p, any of the well-known algorithms such as branch and bound [5] can be used to solve the p-median problem optimally. For a large number of constraints and variables, the problem is classified as NP-Hard [5]; hence, should be solved heuristically.

3.2 Lagrangean Relaxation: A Heuristic Approach

A major benefit of the Lagrangean heuristic [6] over other heuristic approaches is that it gives both upper and lower bounds for the objective function. Thus, it provides a range in which the optimal value of the solution lies. The basic idea is to relax some constraints of the original model and add those constraints, multiplied by Lagrange multiplier to the objective function. We then try to solve the relaxed problem optimally. The model uses a search technique to find a set of values for Lagrange multipliers that lead to a solution of the problem that satisfies the relaxed constraints. If the lower and upper bound of the solution coincide, we have found the optimal solution; otherwise, we can iterate or search for the best Lagrange multipliers until the gap between the upper and lower bound is acceptably narrow.

3.2.1 Lower Bound Calculation

If we relax constraint (3) and add this one into objective function, the relaxed problem can be stated as Equations (8-9).

$$\text{Minimize} \sum_{i=1}^{n}\sum_{j=1}^{n} h_i d_{ij} y_{ij} + \sum_{i=1}^{n} \lambda_i \left(1 - \sum_{i=1}^{n} y_{ij}\right) \tag{8}$$

$$= \sum_{i=1}^{n}\sum_{j=1}^{n} \left(h_i d_{ij} - \lambda_i\right) y_{ij} + \sum_{i=1}^{n} \lambda_i \tag{9}$$

The other constraints (2, 4-7) remain the same as in the p-median problem. To minimize the objective function in (9), we would like to set $y_{ij}=1$ if its coefficient $\left(h_i d_{ij} - \lambda_i\right) < 0$, and $y_{ij}=0$ otherwise. To set the value of y_{ij}, i.e., $y_{ij}=1$, the corresponding x_j's value should be 1 (by Constraint 4). However, Constraint (2) states that we can choose at most p replica sites for which $x_j=1$. Therefore, we have to rank the values of V_j, where V_j is defined by $v_j = \sum_{i=1}^{n} \min\left(0, h_i d_{ij} - \lambda_i\right)$. Find the p smallest values of V_j that have the largest impact on the objective function. Set the corresponding $x_j=1$. Then set $y_{ij}=1$, if $x_j=1$ and $\left(h_i d_{ij} - \lambda_i\right) < 0$, otherwise set $y_{ij}=0$. Calculate the lower bound of the solution (Z_{LB}) by finding the objective function from Constraint (9), which includes y_{ij} which is set to 1.

3.2.2 Upper Bound Calculation

Recall that in the relaxed problem we relax Constraint (2) which states that each requesting site must be assigned to a replication site is eased. The objective function value found by the lower bound program ignores this constraint. Therefore, this constraint may remain unsatisfied, which leads to an infeasible solution to the original problem. We must find an upper bound (Z_{UB}) of the objective function by assigning each requesting site to the nearest replication site. The replication sites are found from the lower bound calculation, i.e., the sites for which the corresponding $x_j=1$.

3.2.3 Multiplier Adjustment

The Lagrange Multipliers are updated by the following steps:

1. Define subgradients G_i^t for the relaxed constraint in the current iteration by:

$$G_i^t = \sum_{j=1}^{n} \left(1 - y_{ij}^{\ t}\right) i = 1,..., n \cdot$$

2. Define a step size $\quad T^t = \dfrac{\pi \left(z_{UB}^t - z_{LB}^t\right)}{\sum\limits_{i=1}^{n} \left(G_i^t\right)^2}\quad$ where π is initially set to 2. If there is

not much improvement after a certain number of iterations, π is replaced by $\dfrac{\pi}{2}$.

3. With this step size, the values of λ_i are updated by the following relationship:

$$\lambda_i^{t+1} = \max\left(0, \lambda_i^n + T^n G_i^t\right) i = 1,..., n$$

The algorithm terminates either after a specified number of iterations or if the value of π becomes sufficiently small. More discussion about this Lagrangean relaxation technique and its application to p-median problem can be found elsewhere [4, 5].

4   Dynamic Maintainability of Static Placement

The Lagrangean relaxation technique assures the optimal or near-optimal solution based on the user requests and network characteristics for the current period. However, the candidate sites that hold replicas currently may not be the best sites to fetch replica if the user requests and network latency changes. Therefore, relocation should to be considered if the performance is to be maintained. But, it is costly. To determine the performance degradation occurring in last K time periods, we must determine the optimal cumulative average response time for K time periods if reallocation is permitted while accounting for transfer costs. Fortunately, the solution of this aspect of the problem also finds the replica placement needed to achieve an optimal/near optimal cumulative average response time. Wesolowsky and Truscott [16] analyze a multi-period facility location-allocation problem that allows facilities to move. They propose a dynamic model that minimizes three factors, (1) distributing cost, (2) construction and removal cost for a given time period, and (3) determining possible facility allocation to achieve the optimal/near-optimal cumulative cost.

$$\text{Minimize} \sum_{k=1}^{K}\sum_{i=1}^{n}\sum_{j=1}^{n} h_i^k d_{ij}^{\ k} y_{ij}^{\ k} + \sum_{k=2}^{K}\sum_{j=1}^{N} c_j^{\ k} a_j^{\ k} \tag{10}$$

$$\text{Subject to} \sum_{j=1}^{n} x_j^{\ k} = p \quad \text{for } k=1.,2...,K \tag{11}$$

$$\sum_{j=1}^{n} y_{ij}^{\ k} = 1, \ i = 1,.....,n \ ; \ k=1,2,...,K \tag{12}$$

$$y_{ij}^{\ k} - x_j^{\ k} \leq 0, \ i = 1,.....,n \ ; \ j = 1,....., \ n \ ; k=1,2,...,K \tag{13}$$

$$x_j^k \in (0,1), \quad j = 1,....., \; n \; ; k=1,2,...,K \tag{14}$$

$$y_{ij}^k \in (0,1), \quad j = 1,....., \; n \; ; i = 1,.....,n \; ; k=1,2,...,K \tag{15}$$

$$y_{ij}^k = \begin{cases} 1 \text{ if requesting site } i \text{ is allocated to replication site } j \text{ at period } k \\ 0 \text{ otherwise} \end{cases} \tag{16}$$

$$a_j^k = \begin{cases} 1 \text{ if a replica is relocated at site } j \text{ in period k} \\ 0 \text{ otherwise} \end{cases} \tag{17}$$

$$c_j^k = \text{the t ansportation cost of the} \tag{18}$$
file from nearest replication site to node j at period k

Performance monitoring in Data Grid is often done by a meta-scheduler or re-source broker. To remove a file from a site's local storage, the resource broker must send a message; a small overhead message to initiate the much larger file transfer. We will also ignore the cost of removing a file from local storage. We use their dynamic model [16] to find the optimal cumulative total response time for K periods.

Equations (10-16) are the multi-period versions of (1-7), respectively. Constraint (17) ensures that we can consider the reallocation cost if a replica is relocated on that site. Wesolowsky *et al.* [16] use dynamic programming to solve the mathematical model optimally for a small network size and limited number of periods. For a large network and large value of K, the dynamic programming generates huge state spaces and stages. Therefore, the authors suggest heuristics to generate good solutions.

We can use the Lagrangean relaxation technique to generate the optimal or near-optimal solutions to the dynamic model. Once achieved, we compare this result with the current one. The current result is calculated by adding total response time for K periods assuming that replicas are placed to the sites that gave the optimal value for the p-median problem at period $K=1$. We must then decide if relocation is appropriate. Table 1 presents 4 cases to consider when to determine if relocation should occur, and it also identifies a candidate target. For simplicity, we consider 2-median problem and 3 time periods for the dynamic model. We compare the current result (CR) with optimal result (OR) and check whether the difference is more than the allowable threshold (T). For example, the solution found by the p-median problem at period $K=1$ suggests that the replica should be placed at Site A and Site B. We must analyze the performance of this placement decision based on three consecutive periods: the first period when the static optimal decision was made and the next two periods.

Table 1. Replica Reallocation Decision

Case	(CR–OR)>T	Period 1	Period 2	Period 3	Decision
1	No	A, B	A, B	A, B	No Relocation
2	No	A, B	A, B	C, D	Relocate at C, D
3	Yes	X, Y	X, Y	X,Y	Relocate at X, Y
4	Yes	P, Q	R, S	M, N	Re-optimize by p- median with aver-age requests and average bandwidth for last 3 periods

In Case 1, we find that the optimal solution complies with our early decision so replicas are placed correctly. In Case 2, we find an optimal solution which suggests that replica should be placed at Site A and Site B for time period 1 and 2. But to get the optimal value, we should consider relocation to Sites C and D for time period 3. So, we can relocate at C and D at the end of time period 3. In Case 3, we found that site (X, Y) is giving the optimal cumulative response time suggesting that Site (X,Y) shows consistent performance since the last three periods; even we consider the relocation cost, *i.e.*, transportation time of a file to sites X, Y from the best candidates (which are currently A and B). Moreover, the difference between current and optimal solutions is above the prescribed threshold. Case 4 addresses a random situation where we are not able to find a set of sites that perform satisfactory throughout the last three time periods. Moreover, the tolerance level is above the threshold, so we must consider relocation. Unfortunately, the sites must now be found by solving the *p*-median problem that takes average request and average network latency as parameters. The averages are calculated by averaging the request and latency for the last three time periods.

5 Simulation

Replica placement algorithms must be tested thoroughly before deploying them in real Data Grid environments. One way to achieve a realistic evaluation of the various strategies is through simulation that carefully reflects real Data Grids. On a Data Grid, different jobs are submitted from various sites. Mean job execution time is a good measure of effectiveness of the replication strategies. Jobs in the Data Grid request a number of files. If the file is at a local site, response time is assumed to be zero; otherwise the file must be transferred from the nearest replication site. Thus, job execution time incorporates the response time required to transport a file. The best replication strategy minimizes the mean job execution time and minimizes the average response time. Our replica placement algorithms are evaluated with a simulator written in Java. The simulation generates random background traffic and grid data requests.

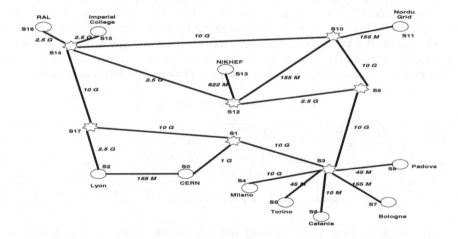

Fig. 1. The EU Data Grid and their associated network geometry

The study of our replica placement algorithms is carried out using a model of the *EU Data Grid Testbed* 1 [1] sites and their associated network geometry. Site 0 is the CERN (European Organization for Nuclear Research) location. Initially all master files are distributed to CERN. A master file contains the original copy of some data samples and cannot be deleted. Each circle in Figure 1 represents a testbed site and a star represents a router. Each link between two sites shows the available network bandwidth. The network bandwidth is expressed in Mbits/sec (M) or Gbits/sec (G). We include the storage capacity at each router, *i.e.*, intermediate nodes. The intermediate nodes have higher storage capacity than the testbed sites, but smaller capacity than CERN. Placing data at intermediate nodes moves it closer, and hence more accessible to testbed sites. File requests are generated from the testbed sites.

Our program's input is from two configuration files. One file describes the network topology, *i.e.,* links between different sites, available network bandwidth between sites, and the size of disk storage of each site. The second configuration file contains information about the number of requests generated by each testbed site and the current network load. Network load is varied to test the impact on our replication algorithm. We consider low, medium and heavy traffic. File requests may either follow uniform distribution or normal distribution. We set three maximum values for uniform file requests where each testbed site can generate requests that are uniformly distributed with a maximum of 10, 30, or 50. We also consider ten random normal requests with different mean and variance. The testbed site that generates each of those random requests is chosen arbitrarily. We consider uniform and normal requests with diverse variances to analyze how well the replication algorithms perform when there is no correlation among previous requests, *i.e.*, they are totally random.

6 Simulation Results

Each site records the time taken for each file requested to be transferred to it. This time record forms the basis to compare various replication strategies. We compare our replication algorithm with respect to average response time. Response time is the time that elapses from a request for a file until it receives the complete file. The average of all response times for the length of the simulation is calculated. The best replication strategy will have lowest response time. Each file is 100 MB in size. After some initial runs, we place a replica at sites that will optimize either one of the objectives, *i.e.*, the request objective, static p-median, and dynamic p-median. Best_Client strategy considers the request objective. After six (K=6) time periods, we consider relocation. For simplicity, we set the Threshold to zero (T=0), *i.e.*, we consider relocation when we can find an optimum aggregated response for the last six periods better than the current accumulated response time. We test our algorithm for p=5. We calculate the average response time for future requests in different network load by assuming the replicas are now at the candidate sites.

We accumulate the average response time for the next sixty runs to analyze the performance of the replica placement algorithms. We also vary the network load with other background traffic to see its impact on the replication algorithm. The results of accumulated average response time (in seconds) are shown in Table 2; they show that

Table 2. Average response time for different models, network loads, user requests (p=5)

Traffic	Request	Best_Client	Static P-Median	Dynamic P-Median
Low	Uniform (10)	2883	896	714
Medium	Uniform (10)	8765	1669	1368
High	Uniform (10)	9906	2975	1737
Low	Uniform (30)	8216	2734	1753
Medium	Uniform (30)	17140	4205	3310
High	Uniform (30)	25189	7862	5320
Low	Uniform (50)	15483	3434	3184
Medium	Uniform (50)	25115	7243	6054
High	Uniform (50)	28649	12585	6798
Low	Normal	40970	7925	7076
Medium	Normal	86454	16381	11714
High	Normal	57585	16547	12232

the response time increases with increasing requests. There is a strong correlation between response time and user requests as one would expect. We have highest average response time in peak period. We include the dynamic traffic condition and random requests to see the impact on the dynamic model. The dynamic model that considers the relocation shows significant performance improvement compared to static and best-client model in different background traffic conditions as well when user requests vary randomly (uniform random), or the future requests are normally distributed and centered on previous requests. We can get a significant performance improvement with dynamic model if the previous best paths become congested because of high background traffic or if current user requests vary significantly.

The simulation was carried out on a Pentium 4 processor 2GHz with 512 MB RAM. With current network size, the computational time is only 10 seconds on average to reach a solution using static or dynamic p-median model.

7   Conclusions

We consider a p-median model for the replica placement problem. The model finds the locations of p candidate sites to place replica that will minimize the aggregated response time. Due to the dynamic nature of the Grid, the placement decision may not be optimal for subsequent periods. Therefore, we need to decide about relocation. However, relocation needs transportation cost for transferring the file to the relocated sites. We propose a dynamic replica maintenance algorithm that suggest for a relocation of candidate sites by considering the relocation cost. The decision of relocation is made when the performance metric degrades significantly in last K time periods. We validate our model by using a model of the EU Data Grid testbed 1 sites and their associated network geometry. However, we need to decide on the value of p for our p-median problem that gives a satisfactory response time to the requesting sites. Moreover, the term Threshold (T) needs to be calculated before using the dynamic maintenance algorithm. Its value should not be too small or too large. One choice is to use a value that changes proportionally based on average response time of each time period.

References

1. Bell W., et al., OptorSim- A Grid Simulator for Studying Dynamic Data Replication Strategies. *Journal of High Performance Computing Applications*, 17(4), 2003.
2. Buyya R., Abramson D., and Giddy J., Nimrod/G: An Architecture of a Resource Management and Scheduling System in a Global Computational Grid, *Proc. of HPC Asia*, pp.283-289, Beijing, China, 2000.
3. Chervenak A., et al., The Data Grid: To wards and Architecture for the Distributed Management and Analysis of Large Scientific Data Sets. *Journal of Network and Computer Applications*, 23(3), pp.187-200, 2000.
4. Daskin M.S., Network and Discrete Location Models: Algorithms and Applications, John Wiley & Sons, 1995.
5. Drezner Z., and Hamacher H. W., Facility Location Applications and Theory, Springer Verlag, Berlin, Germany, 2002.
6. Fisher M.L., The Lagrangian relaxation method for solving integer programming problems, *Management Science*, 27, 1-18.
7. Foster I., Internet Computing and the Emerging Grid, Nature Web Matters, 2000.
8. Foster, I., Kesselman C., Tuecke S., The Anatomy of the Grid: Enabling Scalable Virtual Organizations. *J. Supercomputer Applications*, 5(3), 2001.
9. Foster I. and Kesselman C., The Grid: Blueprint for a New Computing Infrastructure.
10. Hakami S., Optimum location of switching centers and the absolute centers and medians of a graph, *Operations Research*, 12, 450-459.
11. Kavitha R., Iamnitchi A. and Foster I., Improving Data   Availability through Dynamic Model Driven Replication in Large Peer-to-Peer Communities. *Proc. of Global and Peer-to-Peer Computing on Large Scale Distributed Systems Workshop*, Berlin, 2002.
12. Kavitha R., and Foster I., Decoupling Computation and Data Scheduling in Distributed Data-Intensive Applications. Proceedings of IEEE International Symposium on High Performance Distributed Computing Edinburgh, Scotland, July 2002
13. Kavitha R., and Foster I., Design and Evaluation of Replication Strategies for a High Performance Data Grid, in Computing and High Energy and Nuclear Physics 2001.
14. Rahman R. M., Barker K. and Alhajj R., Replica Placement on Data Grid: Considering Utility and Risk. *Proc. of IEEE Intrn'l Conf. on Coding and Computing*, 2005.
15. Toregas C., et al., The location of emergency service facilities, *Operations Research*, 19, 1363-1373.
16. Wesolowsky G.O. and Truscott W.G., The multiperiod location-allocation problem with relocation of facilities. *Management Science*, 22, Sept., 1975.

A Lightweight Cyclic Reference Counting Algorithm*

Chin-Yang Lin and Ting-Wei Hou

Department of Engineering Science, National Cheng Kung University,
No. 1, Ta-Hsueh Rd., Tainan 701, Taiwan
{chinyang, hou}@nc.es.ncku.edu.tw

Abstract. This paper focuses on a major weakness of reference counting technique - the lack of collecting cyclic garbage. Most reference counted systems handle this problem by either invoking a global mark-sweep collector occasionally, or incorporating a local ("partial") tracing collector that considers only the cycle candidates (objects) but needs several traces on them. This paper proposes a "lightweight" cycle detector, which is based on the partial tracing approach but collects garbage cycles in a simpler and more efficient way. Key to the algorithm is the removal of multiple traces on the cycle candidates - It effectively reclaims garbage cycles in only one trace. We have evaluated the algorithm in the Jikes Research Virtual Machine, where a set of benchmark programs from SPECjvm98 were applied. The experiments demonstrate the efficiency and practicability of the lightweight cycle detector, compared to a modern cycle detector that requires multiple traces on objects.

1 Introduction

Reference counting [7] is intuitive for garbage collection. It has several advantages [11], such as simplicity in implementation, allowing immediate reuse of objects, and good locality of reference. Particularly, the work of reference counting is interleaved with the running program's execution (mutations). Such an incremental property makes it easy to maintain the responsiveness (i.e. shorter pauses) and thus suitable for highly interactive systems. Unlike tracing-based method [19], the overhead of reference counting is proportional to the work on object mutations, and it works well regardless of heap size as it need not traverse all of the objects in the heap.

Reference counting has two main problems: (1) Run-time overhead of tracking pointers and (2) memory leaks. First, reference counting tracks pointers by continuously monitoring mutations (e.g. increment, decrement and zero-check). Deleting a pointer to an object may introduce numerous updates on reference counts (i.e. recursive freeing), which depends on the size of the sub-graph below the deleted pointer. The cost can thus be expensive and unbounded. A widely used solution to this problem is the deferred reference counting [9]. Its main idea is to avoid examining heavily mutated references immediately, such as stack variables and registers. Instead, they are only examined periodically. Only references from heap objects are counted immediately, and references from local variables are ignored. Since most of the

---

* This research was supported by the National Science Council of R.O.C. under contract NSC 92-2213-E-006-045.

Y.-C. Chung and J.E. Moreira (Eds.): GPC 2006, LNCS 3947, pp. 346–359, 2006.

references are likely to be from local variables, the cost of maintaining reference counts is greatly reduced. Such a deferral (or lazy) concept are also adopted in several modern RC algorithms [3, 2, 13, 5] which have different buffering strategies and all reduce the overhead of tracking pointers significantly.

The second problem (memory leaks) often refers to the inability to reclaim cyclic structures (i.e. reference counts never become zero in a garbage cycle). Since memory leaks may occur when the mutator generates large garbage cycles, it is generally considered the greatest drawback of reference counting and a major reason why many prior systems give up reference counting.

Since McBeth [18] noticed the inability of reference counting to collect garbage cycles, two main techniques for cycle collection have been proposed. One approach [8] is to invoke a "global" mark-sweep collector infrequently, in which, the garbage cycles are reclaimed in the sweep phase since they will not be visited in the mark phase. This may have tough time with large heap as it needs to trace the entire heap. The alternative is to incorporate a local ("partial") tracing collector that considers only the cycle candidates (i.e. the local sub-graphs suspected to contain cyclic garbage) [6, 17] and thus has a major benefit in that it often takes a smaller sub-graph as input. However, it traces objects multiple times (normally three times per object) for finding dead cycles. This can also introduce a significant delay because objects may be traced again and again. Even so, we would remind that the increasing memory trend will make the "partial" tracing approach more attractive. Since Christopher [6] introduced the original partial tracing scheme, several works related to it, either for uni-processor or for multiprocessor, have been proposed in the literature [17, 15, 10, 16, 14, 3, 2, 20].

On the other hand, reference counting may also become the preferred method for garbage collection as soon as the heap grows larger. Such a perception has been noticed in recent state-of-the-art works [3, 2, 20], and actually it is a major motivation for this paper. We believe that reference counting will become more attractive in the future, which would hinge on how the garbage cycles can be handled efficiently.

This paper proposes a "lightweight" cycle detector, which is based on the partial tracing approach but detects cycles in a simpler and more efficient way. Specially, we present a novel and practical idea that a garbage cycle can be reclaimed as soon as the sub-graph containing the cycle is detected as garbage, where the sub-graph is an object graph rooted at a candidate cycle root (i.e. an object whose count is decremented to a nonzero value). That is, we can consider the entire sub-graph, instead of individual cycles, as the basic unit of cycle collection. According to this idea, we propose a new algorithm to handle the cycle problem, which is lightweight since it takes only one traversal of the sub-graphs. Compared to those algorithms based on [17, 15] that walks sub-graphs in multiple rounds, we reduce the complexity from $3O(n)$ to $O(n)$, where n is the size of the considered object graph. Additionally, the quadratic complexity of those algorithms (noticed in [3, 2]) will not appear in our algorithm. In practice, we have evaluated the algorithm in the Jikes Research Virtual Machine [1], where a set of benchmark programs from SPECjvm98 [21] were applied. The experiments show that the lightweight cycle collector is practical in use and able to reclaim garbage cycles of large programs efficiently.

The rest of the paper is organized as follows. Section 2 describes the background, basic terminology and definitions. Section 3 presents the algorithm in detail. Section 4 contains a proof of correctness. Section 5 is our experiments and is followed by our conclusions.

2 Background

This section presents the basic terminology and definitions used in this paper and reviewing the cyclic reference counting algorithms to which this paper is relevant.

A directed graph is used to model the reachability, where the objects and references involved are considered to form a graph, with the objects being the nodes and the references being the edges. The terms "edge", "pointer" and "reference" are interchangeable, and the same goes for "object" and "node". In this paper, a strongly connected component (*SCC*) in the graph is used to represent a cyclic structure. A strongly connected component is a maximal set of objects in the graph such that every pair of objects are mutually reachable (i.e. there is a path from each object to the other). A *SCC* is *trivial* if it contains a single object without self loops. Any directed graph can be decomposed into a number of individual *SCCs*.

Garbage is objects that are unreachable from any of the system roots. For a *SCC*, we call the edges in the sub-graph induced by the *SCC* internal pointers and the edges from outside *external pointers*. A *SCC* is called a *garbage cycle* if there are no external pointers to it, since any external pointer may make the *SCC* reachable from some objects in use (or system roots).

Since any garbage cycle can only be generated on deleting a pointer, a typical algorithm [17] performs the local search starting from any object whose reference count is just decremented to a nonzero value. Since a starting object may be the first encountered member of a garbage cycle, it is called a *candidate root* (of a garbage cycle), written *CR*. The local search for cycle detection involves several *depth-first searches* (DFS) over the sub-graph below a *CR*. First, the sub-graph is traversed, in which each visited object is marked as potential garbage, and the reference counts due to internal pointers are subtracted. Second, each marked object with nonzero count is unmarked, and the reference counts of the object and its transitive closure are restored. Finally, the objects still marked are deemed garbage and are then reclaimed.

Lins [15] improved it by performing the local search lazily, in which a special buffer called Roots is used for queuing each *CR* and then *CRs* in Roots are batch processed for cycle collection when the buffer overflows, CPU is idle or memory is exhausted, etc. Many unimportant *CRs* are filtered out and thus the redundant local searches are largely reduced.

More recently, Bacon et al. [3, 2] improved Lins' algorithm [15] by performing the tracing of all candidates simultaneously, in which, the entire transitive closure of Roots is considered as a whole and the number of traced objects is thus bounded. This algorithm was also extended to a concurrent cycle collection algorithm. In [20], the sliding views technique [13] was incorporated into Bacon and Rajan's previous work [3], which decreases the redundant cost of tracing again by reducing the number of *CRs* significantly. All these cycle collection algorithms are called partial tracing algorithms since they only consider the cycle candidates instead of the entire heap. Such a local tracing scheme is also known as trial deletion.

3 The Algorithm

This section describes the proposed algorithm, which is based on the partial tracing scheme and takes the same computation graph as the trial deletion algorithms. The main difference with trial deletion is that the new algorithm has a new scheme for collecting cycles, which is based on a novel hypothesis that a garbage cycle can be reclaimed as soon as the sub-graph containing the cycle is detected as garbage, where the sub-graph is an object graph rooted at a candidate root (*CR*). We call it a light-weight cycle detector because of two key benefits: (1) it takes only one traversal over the computation graph, which results in better efficiency; and (2) it is linear in the size of the sub-graphs traced, avoiding the worst case of Lins' algorithm [15] (i.e. the quadratic complexity noticed in [3, 2]).

3.1 The Computation Graph

To manage the sub-graphs that may include garbage cycles, the new algorithm uses a similar strategy to [15, 3] - all the *CR*s are placed into a buffer, denoted `Roots`; periodically, *CR*s in `Roots` are batch processed for cycle collection.

A *collection cycle* is defined as a single complete execution of the lightweight cycle collector (starting at a specific trigger point for processing *CR*s in `Roots`). The entire work of a collection cycle is divided into n work units, where n is the number of (live) *CR*s in `Roots` and each work unit is a single execution of a cycle detection procedure starting from a *CR* in `Roots`. The *ith* work unit is written W_i, and the sub-graph traced (considered) during W_i is denoted G_i. It is assumed that each *CR* can only be queued once per collection cycle (i.e. no duplicate *CR*s in `Roots`).

According to these definitions, the lightweight cycle collector performs each work unit, say W_i, in a collection cycle in two steps. First, the collector performs a local search on G_i, in which, each object traced (entered) is marked and the number of external pointers to G_i is computed. In the second step, the collector reclaims G_i if the number of external pointers is zero (i.e. G_i is unreachable). We next present how a local search is performed on G_i, followed by a pseudocode explanation.

3.2 The Traversal Procedure

A main idea of the lightweight cycle collector is to consider a single sub-graph, instead of individual cycles, as the basic unit of cycle collection. Let G be the sub-graph considered for cycle collection in a work unit, and SCC_1, ..., SCC_n be the SCCs contained in G. During the collection, the lightweight collector reclaims G only if SCC_1, ..., SCC_n are all detected to be unreachable (dead). That is, the reclamation of a dead SCC in G could be delayed until every SCC in G is dead. Under this concept, G is considered for collection as a whole, and thus it will no longer matter how many cycles are contained in G and which of these cycles are dead.

In our work, G contains garbage cycles and is eligible for collection only if G has no incoming edges from outside (i.e. there exists no external pointer coming from objects outside of G). Let `Pi` and `Pe` be, respectively, the number of internal pointers and external pointers for G. Then we have R = Pi + Pe, where

$$R = \sum_{S \, in \, G} RC(S).$$

This equation is trivial since each object's reference count is only contributed by pointers that are either internal or external. Based on this, we examine whether G is referenced by external pointers (i.e. compute Pe) according to the following two facts: (1) the collector can gather the reference count of each object in G through a single traversal over G, which helps to compute R; (2) each (internal) pointer coming from any of the objects in G must be traced during a traversal over G, which helps to count Pi. That is, after a single traversal over G, R and Pi would be computed, and so Pe is available. Then, G is considered garbage and eligible for reclamation if Pe = 0.

3.3 Pseudocode and Explanation

The pseudocode of the lightweight algorithm is shown in Fig. 1, where we only present the key procedures of the lightweight cycle collector. Assume that the input is the computation graph defined in section 3.1 and a global buffer for queuing candidate roots called Roots. For each object S, apart from the reference count, denoted $RC(S)$, S also contains an *ID* field, written $ID(S)$, which is used for labeling objects in the same sub-graph considered in a work unit. For a given work unit W_i that is just been finished, each object in G_i must be labeled by the same *ID*, where the *ID* is maintained in an increasing number. Additionally, the collector keeps the last used *ID* that has been applied in the previous collection cycle for the current collection cycle, which is for distinguishing objects that are not labeled in the current collection cycle. The algorithm makes use of two global variables, CurID and PreMaxID, for managing this information. More precisely, for a given object S at any time (See Lemma 1):

- $ID(S) = 0$ => S has never been labeled in any collection cycle.
- $0 < ID(S) \leq$ PreMaxID => S has been labeled in a previous collection cycle.
- $ID(S) >$ PreMaxID   => S has been labeled in the current collection cycle.

In addition to assisting the graph traversal, the labeling mechanism also helps in efficiency, in which, it prevents the same object from being considered (traced) more than once per collection cycle, and therefore the problem of repeated traversals over objects mentioned in [3] is avoided. Actually, the complexity of the lightweight algorithm is linear in the size of the computation graph. It requires $O(N + E)$ worst-case time for collection, where N is the number of nodes (objects) and E is the number of edges (pointers) in the graph. Furthermore, compared to those algorithms based on [17, 15] that walks sub-graphs in multiple rounds, the lightweight algorithm only walks sub-graphs in one round and thus results in much better efficiency. In [22], it takes one round to walk sub-graphs, gathering some dependency information. A filtering procedure is then performed for discovering garbage cycles. However, the filtering procedure may result in a performance bottleneck ($O(n^3)$ in the worst case).

We now describe the details of the pseudocode. Triggering a collection cycle is to invoke the procedure CollectCycles, which tries to process *CR*s in Roots. For

```
CollectCycles()
1. for each live object S in Roots
2.    remove S from Roots;
3.    if(ID(S) ≤ PreMaxID)
4.       DoTraversal(S);
5.       CollectGarbage();
6.       CurID := CurID + 1;
7. PreMaxID := CurID - 1;

DoTraversal(S: Object)
1. empty CycleCandidates;
2. ID(S) := CurID;
3. Pe := RC(S);
4. append S to CycleCandidates;
5. Traverse(S);

Traverse(S: Object)
1. for T in children(S)
2.    if(ID(T) ≤ PreMaxID)
3.       ID(T) := CurID;
4.       Pe := Pe + RC(T);
5.       Pe := Pe - 1;      /* finding an internal edge */
6.       append T to CycleCandidates;
7.       Traverse(T);
8.    else
9.       if(ID(T) = CurID)
10.         Pe := Pe - 1;   /* finding an internal edge */

CollectGarbage()
1. if(Pe = 0)
2.    for S in CycleCandidates
3.       ReclaimObject(S);

ReclaimObject(S: Object)
1. for T in children(S) such that S is alive
2.    if(ID(T) ≠ CurID)
3.       Decrement(T);
4. Free(S);
```

Fig. 1. The Lightweight Cycle Collection Algorithm

every *CR* that will be considered for processing, it must be alive and have never been labeled in the current collection cycle (avoiding revisiting objects per collection cycle). That is, *ID(CR)* must fall in the range from 0 to PreMaxID (i.e. the last-used *ID* in the previous collection cycle). Each *CR* processed means that a work unit has been finished, which consumes an *ID* number and involves two procedures: DoTraversal, which performs a local search for detecting garbage cycles; and CollectGarbage, which actually reclaims garbage objects (if available). Finally, PreMaxID is updated for the next collection cycle.

The procedures DoTraversal and Traverse collaborate to do a local search for a given work unit, aimed at traversing the sub-graph below a *CR* with a DFS, where only the objects that have "not" been labeled in the current collection cycle will be labeled (or relabeled if it has already been labeled in a previous collection cycle) by a new *ID* (i.e. `CurID`). During the traversal, the number of external pointers to the sub-graph (i.e. Pe) is computed as follows. The variable `Pe` (initially 0) is increased by the reference count of an object that is labeled in the current work unit and is decreased by one upon finding an internal pointer. The former is trivial. The latter must be done by exactly counting the number of edges (pointers) to those objects associated with the same *ID* (i.e. `CurID`), which can be seen from `Traverse`.

In addition, all the objects labeled in the same work unit are regarded as cycle candidates and will be put into a buffer called `CycleCandidates`. This buffer is used for queuing the references of "potential" garbage objects considered in a work unit and is emptied per work unit. Once the sub-graph considered in the work unit is detected to be garbage (i.e. Pe = 0), all the objects in `CycleCandidates` can be collected directly (i.e. the work done in the procedure `CollectGarbage`). Finally, the procedure `ReclaimObject` is responsible for reclaiming each dead object in `CycleCandidates`. Normally, before a dead object *S* can be actually freed, the reference counts due to the pointers out of *S* should be decremented. Specially, since all the dead objects are in `CycleCandidates` and the decrements of reference counts due to the internal pointers are redundant, `ReclaimObject` only consider the decrements of reference counts due to the external pointers. It can be seen from `ReclaimObject` that a pointer is considered for decrement only when it points to an object whose *ID* is "not" `CurID`.

4   Proof of Correctness

A cycle collector is *safe* if every object collected is indeed garbage; *complete* if it eventually collects all garbage cycles. We first prove the *safety* of the proposed algorithm. Then, we describe the case that a garbage cycle may not be reclaimed immediately by the algorithm, which would affect the *completeness* of the algorithm in theory. We next introduce a method for improving the *completeness*, which makes the lightweight algorithm fully *complete*. Finally, we present the proof of *completeness*.

4.1   Safety: Correctness Proof

Lemma 1. *Let S be an object considered in a given collection cycle. If ID(S) ≤* Pre-MaxID, *S must have never been labeled in the current collection cycle.*

Proof. The hypothesis implies either that *S* has not been labeled (i.e. *ID(S)* = 0) or that *S* has been labeled with an *ID* smaller than `PreMaxID`. The former case is trivial. In the latter case, whether *S* was labeled in the current collection cycle depends on how `PreMaxID` is managed in the algorithm. Also, the only place to update `PreMaxID` is at the end of a collection cycle (at line 7 of `CollectCycles`), which indicates, for any collection cycle, `PreMaxID` represents the last *ID* used in the previous collection cycle. Suppose *S* was labeled in the current collection cycle. *ID(S)* must be greater than `PreMaxID`, contradicting the hypothesis. Thus, the lemma is proved.

Lemma 2. *Let R be a live candidate root. When* `DoTraversal(R)` *finishes, R and the objects that are reachable from R but have never been labeled in the current collection cycle must be labeled with the same ID number.*

Proof. During the execution of `DoTraversal(R)`, R is first labeled with a new *ID* number (i.e. `CurID`) at line 2 of `DoTraversal`. Then, for each object *T* reachable from *R*, it may be labeled with the same *ID* through `Traverse`. Also, *T* is labeled with `CurID` only if $ID(T) \leq$ `PreMaxID`, at line(2-3) of `Traverse`. By Lemma 1, *T* must have never been labeled in the current collection cycle. The lemma is proved.

Lemma 3. *Let R be a live candidate root and G be the sub-graph induced by the objects labeled during the execution of* `DoTraversal(R)`. *If* `Pe` = 0, *G must be garbage.*

Proof. By Lemma 2, all the objects in *G* must be labeled with the same *ID*. During the execution of `DoTraversal(R)`, `Pe` is initially 0 and is computed in two aspects. First, for every object *S* in *G*, *RC(S)* is accumulated to `Pe`, at line 3 of `DoTraversal` and line 4 of `Traverse`. Second, when visiting an edge in *G* (i.e. an internal pointer), `Pe` is decreased by one. At line 5 of `Traverse`, an internal pointer is found since the object the pointer points to is labeled with `CurID` (i.e. the object must be contained in *G*). At line (8-10) of `Traverse`, an internal pointer is counted only when the pointer points to an object whose *ID* is `CurID`. That is because, by Lemma 2, such a pointer must be contained in *G*. In this case (line (8-10) of `Traverse`), if the object pointed to has an *ID* larger than `PreMaxID` and smaller than `CurID`, the object must have already been considered in the current collection cycle (before *R* is taken). That is, the object has been labeled in a previous work unit of the current collection cycle. By Lemma 2, such an object is not contained in *G* and so the pointer is also not covered in *G*. Consequently, when `DoTraversal(R)` finishes, `Pe` means the difference between the sum of the in-degree of the objects in *G* and the total number of edges in *G*. The hypothesis (`Pe` = 0) implies there exists no (external) pointer coming from objects outside of *G*. Clearly, *G* is fully unreachable and must be garbage.

Theorem 1 (Safety). *Only garbage objects are collected by the algorithm.*

Proof. For each collection cycle (i.e. `CollectCycles`), `CollectGarbage` is the only place to reclaim objects, which is always performed after an invocation of `DoTraversal`. By Lemma 2, the objects labeled during the execution of `DoTraversal` are assigned the same *ID*, in which, those objects are also added to `CycleCandidates`, at line 4 of `DoTraversal` and line 6 of `Traverse`. Moreover, Lemma 3 indicates that `Pe` is available when `DoTraversal` finishes, and those objects in `CycleCandidates` must be garbage if `Pe` = 0. At line (1-3) of `CollectGarbage`, every object in `CycleCandidates` will be reclaimed (by `ReclaimObject`) only if `Pe` = 0. Thus, the theorem is proved.

4.2 Completeness: Correctness Proof

In theory, there exists a case that a garbage cycle may not be reclaimed immediately. Let G be a sub-graph rooted at a candidate root R that is considered for cycle collection. Suppose G is composed of two $SCCs$ (cycles), SCC_i and SCC_j, where SCC_i is dead and is rooted at R (i.e. there must be a directed path from SCC_i to SCC_j.). In this case, SCC_i is collected only if SCC_j is dead. If SCC_j is alive, SCC_i will not be collected in the current work unit, since the algorithm only computes Pe for G and so SCC_j results in Pe > 0. That is, the reclamation of a dead SCC (garbage cycle) may be postponed to a subsequent collection cycle if there is a live SCC reachable from the dead SCC. In theory, such a case may cause some garbage cycles to remain in heap for a long time and even not reclaimed eventually. The *completeness* is thus affected. In section 5, our experiments show that the lightweight algorithm does not suffer from this problem and is practical in use.

Actually, this problem has been improved by our design of making the algorithm linear, in which, sub-graphs considered in different work units are processed independently and so a dead sub-graph can be reclaimed immediately without being interfered with by other sub-graphs. To further complement the lack of the *completeness*, we present an intuitive way to incorporate a backup cycle collector, defined as follows.

Definition 1. *A backup cycle collector incorporated into the lightweight cycle collector is a cycle collector such that*

(1) It is based on the partial tracing scheme.
(2) It can collect garbage cycles existing in a sub-graph considered for collection.
(3) It only considers the candidate roots not collected by the lightweight collector.
(4) It is triggered on demand.

The first statement indicates the backup cycle collector performs search locally. The second one implies that it must be *complete*, which aims at handling the case that some garbage cycles may not be reclaimed by the lightweight cycle collector immediately. In the third statement, the backup cycle collector is confined to the cases that the lightweight cycle collector fails. In the implementation, another buffer would be used for storing the candidate roots that are not timely collected by the lightweight cycle collector (i.e. the case of Pe $\neq$ 0). Finally, the backup cycle collector should be timely triggered when the lightweight cycle collector can not reclaim garbage cycles effectively. In the implementation, the backup cycle collector can be simply triggered as the memory is still low after a limited number of collection cycles, in which, CollectCycles will determine whether to switch to the backup cycle collector.

Theorem 2(Completeness). *All garbage cycles are eventually collected by the lightweight cycle collector that is complemented by a backup cycle collector defined in Definition 1.*

Proof. The lightweight algorithm uses the same computation graph as other trial deletion algorithms. All potential garbage cycles are thus considered for collection. Let G be a sub-graph rooted at a candidate root R that is considered for cycle collection, and

$SCC_1, \ldots, SCC_n$ be the *SCCs* (or cycles) contained in G such that there is a path from SCC_i to SCC_j, if $i < j$. The base case is $n = 1$, where G forms a single *SCC* (cycle). If the *SCC* is dead (a garbage cycle), there must be no pointers from outside of G. Thus, when DoTraversal(R) finishes, Pe must be zero and so the *SCC* is immediately reclaimed by CollectGarbage. Actually, this is the case that the lightweight cycle collector is *complete* itself in theory (i.e. without any backup cycle collector).

In case of $n \geq 1$, suppose SCC_k is garbage. It is easy to see that for every $1 \leq i < k$, SCC_i must also be garbage (since SCC_k is reachable from SCC_i). In this case, SCC_k can be reclaimed only if, for every $k < j \leq n$, SCC_j is unreachable from outside of G. That is because a reachable SCC_j can introduce an external pointer, which leads to Pe $\neq 0$. Hence, if there exists a live SCC_j, SCC_k can not be reclaimed immediately, and R will be added to a buffer, by Definition 1. Let BackupRoots be the buffer. SCC_k may be reclaimed in a subsequent collection cycle; otherwise, it will be reclaimed by the timely triggered backup cycle collector, where the candidate roots in BackupRoots will be considered for cycle collection. Consequently, all garbage cycles are eventually collected by the algorithm. The theorem is proved.

5 Experiments

We have performed experiments to evaluate the effectiveness of our cycle collection algorithm in comparison with the "synchronous" trial deletion algorithm from Bacon and Rajan [3]. The compared algorithm is a recent state-of-the-art cycle collector and has already been implemented in the Jikes Research Virtual Machine (Jikes RVM), an open-source Java virtual machine developed by IBM Watson Research Center [1]. The lightweight cycle collector was implemented in the Jikes RVM without using any backup cycle collector defined in Definition 1. (In the rest of this section, the term "trial deletion" refers to the compared algorithm unless otherwise indicated.)

5.1 Experimental Platform and Benchmarks

Our experiments used the version 2.3.1 of Jikes RVM along with the memory management toolkit JMTk (now MMTk [4]), which were executed on the platform: 2.0 GHz AMD Athlon, and 1GB of physical memory running Linux 2.4.20.

To better concentrate on the comparison of the cycle collection, we implemented the lightweight cycle collector in Jikes RVM by simply replacing the cycle detection code of the trial deletion implementation [3] with all the relevant strategies unmodified, such as how Roots are maintained and when to trigger a garbage collection or a cycle detection. We added a single word to the object header for the *ID* field per object and built RVM using the baseline compiler and a reference counting implementation based on the work from Yossi Levanoni and Erez Petrank [12].

We used eight benchmarks from SPECjvm98 [21], which were run at the default size of 100. We ran each of the benchmarks in RVM without specifying further command-line arguments, except for the options of defining available heap sizes. Additionally, each of the experiments was run 5 times and the average is reported.

5.2 Results and Discussion

We compare the cycle collection time between the lightweight (LW) algorithm and the synchronous trial deletion (TD) algorithm [3]. To better show the practicality of LW, the benchmarks were run on varying heap size, from tight to relaxed condition. Most of the benchmarks can be run in a reasonable range between 30MB and 120MB.The only exception is the benchmark _213_javac, which is unable to run to completion until the maximum heap size of 84MB as LW is used; and the same goes for TD, where the required heap size is 78MB. Such a situation has already been reported in [5]. Bacon et al. [2] have also noticed the performance problem with _213_javac - it produces lots of garbage cycles and so requires a large amount of cycle collection work. That is why we measured it in another range from 90MB to 180MB.

Fig. 2 presents the results, in which, the time reflects only the work for triggered cycle detection, and the cycle collection time ratio of LW to TD is reported (The lower the ratio, the better LW performs compared to TD). Table 1 further shows the number of triggered cycle detection for each running of the benchmarks, including the maximum and average number of triggered cycle detection. It can be seen that no cycle detection is triggered for the benchmarks _222_mpegaudio and _228_jack. They are thus are not presented in Fig. 2. In fact, our execution of _228_jack shows that the average number of triggered garbage collection is 17 and 16, respectively for LW and TD. However, there is no cycle detection triggered within the execution of those garbage collections. As for _222_mpegaudio, it has a relatively small allocation [2], and thus the garbage collection is almost not necessary with the current heap settings.

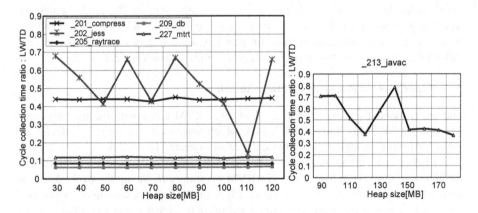

Fig. 2. Cycle collection time ratio: LW/TD

Except for _222_mpegaudio and _228_jack, Fig. 2 exhibits the effectiveness of our cycle collection algorithm in several aspects. The first exciting result is that, like TD, LW can execute each of the benchmarks to completion at the acceptable memory settings. This is especially meaningful for _201_compress and _213_javac [2, 5]. Unlike _213_javac that creates lots of garbage cycles, _201_compress only creates a

Table 1. The number of triggered cycle detection

	201		202		205		209		213		222		227		228	
	max	avg.	max	avg.	max	avg.	max	avg.	max	avg.	max	avg.	max	avg.	max	avg.
LW	8	8	8	3.4	1	1	1	1	10	4.4	-	-	1	1	-	-
TD	8	8	7	2.7	1	1	1	1	8	4.1	-	-	1	1	-	-

number of garbage cycles. However, those cycles lead to many huge objects and so it runs out of memory if the garbage cycles can not be timely collected. Our experiments show that LW can improve the cost of the cycle collection about 56% and 47% on average, respectively, for 201_compress and _213_javac.

Recall that LW, in theory, may cause some garbage cycles to remain in heap for a long time, and this implementation of LW has not really incorporated any backup cycle collector defined in Definition 1 (since this lets us have more attention on the effectiveness of our new idea). Once the difficult case happens frequently, LW would require more space due to the garbage cycles that can not be reclaimed immediately, which may thus introduce more cycle detection triggers. The experiments show that the theoretical problem does not really affect the practicality of LW, even if no backup cycle collector is used. In Table 1, the number of triggered cycle detection between LW and TD is very close, also implicitly demonstrating the effectiveness of LW.

In Fig. 2, LW indeed outperforms TD in each of the six cases. However, the surprising results for _205_raytrace, _209_db and _227_mtrt do not exactly expose the efficiency, since the cycle detection is triggered only once. To get better understanding of this, we did the experiments again for these three benchmarks as well as _222_mpegaudio and _228_jack, in which, the cycle detection is permanently turned on (i.e., let each triggered garbage collection always perform the cycle detection).

The results are respectively presented in Fig. 3 and Table 2. The number of triggers increases for most of the benchmarks, except for _222_mpegaudio. On average, LW is up to 63% faster (_209_db) and at least 12% faster (_227_mtrt) than TD. Though LW still outperforms in this experiment, in practice, permanently turning on the cycle

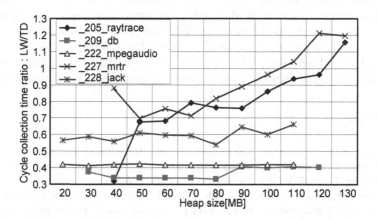

Fig. 3. Cycle collection time ratio: LW/TD (with enforced cycle detection)

Table 2. The number of triggered cycle detection (with enforced cycle detection)

	205		209		222		227		228	
	max	avg.	max	avg.	max	avg.	max	avg.	max	avg.
LW	13	10.7	13	9.6	2	2	17	11.4	62	20.2
TD	15	11.2	12	8.9	2	2	18	12	35	16.3

detection would not be a good idea for LW, since LW may cause more overhead if the difficult case occurs frequently. The garbage cycles not reclaimed immediately may thus be considered repeatedly. In Fig. 3, the results for _227_mtrt and _205_raytrace show that the benefit of LW degrades gradually as the heap size increases. In fact, the cycle collection cost of these two benchmarks tends to be down for both LW and TD as the heap size increases, while the trend for LW is relatively low (not presented here). A potential reason is that some garbage cycles may not be collected for a long time and be reconsidered repeatedly. Though this is not a frequent case in our experiments, it also gives us a motivation to consider using a backup cycle collector.

Over all, the experiments demonstrate that the lightweight cycle collector is practical and able to reclaim garbage cycles of real programs efficiently, which also confirms our new hypothesis - a garbage cycle can be reclaimed as soon as the sub-graph containing the cycle is detected as garbage.

6 Conclusions

Key to this work is a novel hypothesis that a garbage cycle can be reclaimed as soon as the sub-graph containing the cycle is detected as garbage, where the sub-graph is an object graph considered for cycle collection. We developed a lightweight synchronous cycle collector, which performs search locally and handles the cycle problem by walking graph only once, thus reducing the complexity from $3O(n)$ to $O(n)$.

We have implemented the lightweight cycle collector in the Jikes RVM for effectiveness evaluation, where eight SPECjvm98 benchmarks were used. The experiments show the effectiveness of the new algorithm, compared to a modern trial deletion algorithm. Particularly, the theoretical problem that a garbage cycle may not be reclaimed immediately does not really affect the practicality. In addition, we have presented the detailed pseudocode and a proof of correctness of the new algorithm.

References

1. Alpern, B., et al.: Implementing Jalape˜no in Java. In OOPSLA'99 Conference Proceedings:Object-Oriented Programming Systems, Languages, and Applications (Denver, Colorado, Oct. 1999). SIGPLAN Notices, 34, 10, (1999) 314–324.
2. Bacon, D.F., Attanasio, C.R., Lee, H.B., Rajan, V.T., and Smith, S.: Java without the coffee breaks: A nonintrusive multiprocessor garbage collector. In Proceedings of SIGPLAN 2001 Conference on Programming Languages Design and Implementation, ACM SIGPLAN Notices, Snowbird, Utah, June 2001.

3. Bacon, D.F., and Rajan, V.T.: Concurrent cycle collection in reference counted systems. In Proceedings of 15th European Conference on Object-Oriented Programming, ECOOP 2001, Budapest, Hungary, June 18-22, vol. 2072 of Lecture Notes in Computer Science, Springer-Verlag, (2001) 207-235.
4. Blackburn, S.M., Cheng, P., and McKinley, K.S.: Oil and water? High performance garbage collection in Java with MMTk. In International Conference on Software Engineering, 2004.
5. Blackburn, S.M., and McKinley, K.S.: Ulterior reference counting: Fast garbage collection without a long wait. In ACM Conference on Object-Oriented Programming Systems, Languages, and Applications, Anaheim, CA, (2003) 244-358.
6. Christopher, T.W.: Reference count garbage collection. Software Practice and Experience, 14 (6) (1984) 503-507.
7. Collins, G.E.: A method for overlapping and erasure of lists. Commun. ACM 3, 12 (1960) 655-657.
8. Detreville, J.: Experience with concurrent garbage collectors for Modula-2+. Tech. Rep. 64, DEC Systems Research Center, Palo Alto, California, 1990.
9. Deutsch, L.P., and Bobrow, D.G.: An efficient incremental automatic garbage collector. Commun. ACM, 19, 9 (1976) 522-526.
10. Jones, R.E., and Lins, R.D.: Cyclic weighted reference counting without delay. In PARLE'93 Parallel Architectures and Languages Europe, A. Bode, M. Reeve, and G. Wolf, Eds., vol. 694 of Lecture Notes in Computer Science, Springer-Verlag, (1993) 712–715.
11. Jones, R.E., and Lins, R.D.: Garbage Collection. John Wiley and Sons, 1996.
12. Levanoni, Y., and Petrank, E.: A scalable reference counting garbage collector. Technical Report CS-0967, Technion - Israel Institute of Technology, Haifa, Israel, Nov. 1999.
13. Levanoni, Y., and Petrank, E.: An on-the-fly reference counting garbage collector for Java. In ACM Conference Proceedings on Object-Oriented Programming Systems, Languages, and Applications, Tampa, FL, (2001) 367-380.
14. Lins, R.D.: An efficient algorithm for cyclic reference counting. Inf. Process. Lett. 83, (2002) 145-150.
15. Lins, R.D.: Cyclic reference counting with lazy mark-scan. Inf. Process. Lett. 44, 4 (1992) 215-220.
16. Lins, R.D.: Generational cyclic reference counting. Inf. Process. Lett. 46, 1 (1993) 19-20.
17. Martinez, A.D., Wachenchauzer, R., and Lins, R.D.: Cyclic reference counting with local mark-scan. Inf. Process. Lett. 34, 1 (1990) 31-35.
18. McBeth, J.H.: On the reference counter method. Commun. ACM 6, 9 (1963) 575.
19. McCarthy, J.: Recursive functions of symbolic expressions and their computation by machine. Commun. ACM 3, (1960) 184-195.
20. Paz, H., Petrank, E., Bacon, D.F., Rajan, V.T., and Kolodner, E.K.: An efficient on-the-fly cycle collection. In Proceedings of the 14th International Conference on Compiler Construction, Edinburgh. Springer-Verlag, April 2005.
21. S. P. E. Corporation: Specjvm98 documentation. March 1999.
22. Ye, X., and Keane, J.: Collecting cyclic garbage in distributed systems. In International Symposium on Parallel Architectures, Algorithms and Networks, Taipei, Taiwan, 1997.

Distributed Garbage Collection for Mobile Actor Systems: The Pseudo Root Approach

Wei-Jen Wang and Carlos A. Varela

Department of Computer Science,
Rensselaer Polytechnic Institute,
Troy, NY 12180, USA
{wangw5, cvarela}@cs.rpi.edu
http://www.cs.rpi.edu/wwc/

Abstract. Automatic distributed garbage collection (GC) gives abstraction to grid application development, promoting code quality and improving resource management. Unreachability of *active objects* or *actors* from the root set is not a sufficient condition to collect actor garbage, making passive object GC algorithms unsafe when directly used on actor systems. In practical actor languages, all actors have references to the root set since they can interact with users, *e.g.*, through standard input or output streams. Based on this observation, we introduce *pseudo roots*: a dynamic set of actors that can be viewed as the root set. Pseudo roots use protected (undeletable) references to ensure that no actors are erroneously collected even with messages in transit. Following this idea, we introduce a new direction of actor GC, and demonstrate it by developing a distributed GC framework. The framework can thus be used for automatic life time management of mobile reactive processes with unordered asynchronous communication.

1 Introduction

Large applications running on the grid, or on the internet, require runtime reconfigurability for better performance, *e.g.*, relocating application sub-components to improve locality without affecting the semantics of the distributed system. A runtime reconfigurable distributed system can be easily defined by the actor model of computation [2, 8]. The actor model provides a unit of encapsulation for a thread of control along with internal state. An actor is either *unblocked* or *blocked*. It is unblocked if it is processing a message or has messages in its message box, and it is blocked otherwise. Communication between actors is purely asynchronous: non-blocking and non-First-In-First-Out (non-FIFO). However, communication is guaranteed: all messages are eventually and fairly delivered. In response to an incoming message, an actor can use its thread of control to modify its encapsulated internal state, send messages to other actors, create actors, or migrate to another host.

Many programming languages have partial or total support for actor semantics, such as SALSA, ABCL, THAL, Erlang, E, and Nomadic Pict. Some libraries also support actor creation and use in object-oriented languages, such as

Y.-C. Chung and J.E. Moreira (Eds.): GPC 2006, LNCS 3947, pp. 360–372, 2006.

the Actor Foundry for Java, Broadway for C++, and Actalk for Smalltalk. In designing these languages or systems, memory reuse becomes an important issue to support dynamic data structures — such as linked lists. Automatic garbage collection is the key to enable memory reuse and to reduce programmers' efforts on their error-prone manual memory management.

The problem of distributed garbage collection (GC) is difficult because of: 1) information distribution, 2) lack of a global clock, 3) concurrent activities, and 4) possible failures of the network or computing nodes. These factors complicate detection of a consistent global state of a distributed system. Comparing to object-oriented systems, a pure actor system demands automatic GC as well, even more, because of its distributed, mobile, and resource-consuming nature. Actor GC is traditionally considered as a harder problem than passive object GC because of two additional difficulties to overcome:

1. Simply following the references from the root set of actors does not work in the actor GC model. Figure 1 explains the difference between the actor garbage collection model and the passive object GC model.
2. Unordered asynchronous message delivery complicates the actor garbage collection problem. Most existing algorithms cannot tolerate out-of-order messages.

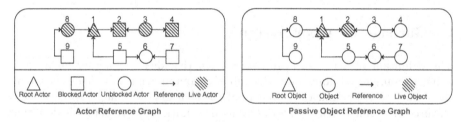

Fig. 1. Actor 3, 4, and 8 are live because they can potentially send messages to the root. Object 3, 4, and 8 are garbage because they are not reachable from the root.

Previous distributed GC algorithms (including actor GC algorithms) rely on First-In-First-Out (FIFO) communication which simplifies detection of a consistent global state. A distributed object GC algorithm either adopts: 1) a lightweight reference counting/listing approach which cannot collect distributed mutually referenced data structures (*cycles*), 2) a trace-based approach which requires a consistent state of a distributed system, or 3) a hybrid approach [1].

In actor-oriented programming languages, an actor must be able to access resources which are encapsulated in service actors. To access a resource, an actor requires a reference to it. This implies that actors keep persistent references to some special service actors — such as the file system service and the standard output service. Furthermore, an actor can explicitly create references to public services. For instance, an actor can dynamically convert a string into a reference to communicate with a service actor, analogous to accessing a web service by a web browser using a URL.

Actor mobility is another new challenge to overcome. The concept of *in-transit* actors complicates the design of actor communication — locality of actors can change, which means even simulated FIFO communication with message redelivery is impractical, or at least limits concurrency by unnecessarily waiting for message redelivery. FIFO communication is an assumption of existing distributed GC algorithms. For instance, distributed reference counting algorithms demand FIFO communication to ensure that a reference-deletion system message does not precede any application messages.

This research differs from previous actor GC models by introducing: 1) asynchronous, unordered message delivery of both application messages and system messages, 2) resource access rights, and 3) actor mobility.

The remainder of the paper is organized as follows: In Section 2 we give the definition of garbage in actor systems. In Section 3 we propose the pseudo root approach — a mobile actor garbage collection model for distributed actor-oriented programming languages. In Section 4 we present an implementation of the proposed actor GC model. In Section 5 we briefly describe a concurrent, snapshot-based global actor garbage collector to collect distributed cyclic garbage. In Section 6 we show experimental results. In Section 7 we discuss related work. Section 8 contains concluding remarks and future work.

2   Garbage in Actor Systems

The definition of actor garbage comes from the idea of whether an actor is doing meaningful computation. Meaningful computation is defined as having the ability to communicate with any of the *root actors*, that is, to access any resource or public service. The widely used definition of live actors is described in [12]. Conceptually, an actor is live if it is a root or it can either potentially: 1) receive messages from the root actors or 2) send messages to the root actors. The set of actor garbage is then defined as the complement of the set of live actors. To formally describe our new actor GC model, we introduce the following definitions:

- **Blocked actor:** An actor is blocked if it has no pending messages in its message box, nor any message being processed. Otherwise it is unblocked.
- **Reference:** A reference indicates an address of an actor. Actor A can only send messages to Actor B if A has a reference pointing to B.
- **Inverse reference:** An inverse reference is a conceptual reference in the counter-direction of an existing reference.
- **Acquaintance:** Let Actor A have a reference pointing to Actor B. B is an acquaintance of A, and A is an inverse acquaintance of B.
- **Root actor:** An actor is a root actor if it encapsulates a resource, or if it is a public service — such as I/O devices, web services, and databases.

The original definition of live actors is denotational because it uses the concept of "potential" message delivery and reception. To make it more operational, we use the term *"potentially live"* [7] to define live actors.

- **Potentially live actors:**
  - Every unblocked actor and root actor is potentially live.
  - Every acquaintance of a potentially live actor is potentially live.
- **Live actors:**
  - A root actor is live.
  - Every acquaintance of a live actor is live.
  - Every potentially live, inverse acquaintance of a live actor is live.

3   The Pseudo Root Approach

The pseudo root approach is based on the *live unblocked actor principle* — a principle which says every unblocked actor should be treated as a live actor. Every practical actor programming language design abides by this principle. With the principle, we integrate message delivery and reference passing into reference graph representation — *sender pseudo roots* and *protected references*. The pseudo root approach together with *imprecise inverse reference listing* enables the use of unordered, asynchronous communication.

The Live Unblocked Actor Principle. Without program analysis techniques, the ability of an actor to access resources provided by an actor-oriented programming language implies explicit reference creation to access service actors. The ability to access local service actors (e.g. the standard output) and explicit reference creation to public service actors make the following statement true: *"every actor has persistent references to root actors"*. This statement is important because it changes the meaning of actor GC, making actor GC similar to passive object GC. It leads to the *live unblocked actor principle*, which says every unblocked actor is live. The live unblocked actor principle is easy to prove. Since each unblocked actor is: 1) an inverse acquaintance of the root actors and 2) defined as potentially live, it is live according to the definition of actor GC.

With the live unblocked actor principle, every unblocked actor can be viewed as a root. Liveness of blocked actors depends on the transitive reachability from unblocked actors and root actors. If a blocked actor is transitively reachable from an unblocked actor or a root actor, it is defined as potentially live. With persistent root references, such potentially live, blocked actors are live because they are inverse acquaintances of some root actors. This idea leads to the core concept of *pseudo root* actor GC.

Pseudo Root Actor Garbage Collection. The pseudo root actor GC starts actor garbage collection by identifying some live (not necessarily root) or even garbage actors as pseudo roots. There are three kinds of pseudo root actors: 1) root actors, 2) unblocked actors, and 3) *sender pseudo root actors*. The sender pseudo root actor refers to an actor which has sent a message and the message has not yet been received. The goal of sender pseudo roots is to prevent

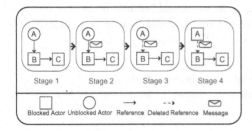 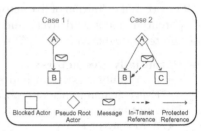

Fig. 2. The left side of the figure shows a possible race condition of mutation and message passing. The right side of the figure illustrates both kinds of sender pseudo root actors.

erroneous garbage collection of actors, either targets of in-transit messages or whose references are part of in-transit messages. A sender pseudo root always contains at least one protected reference — a reference that has been used to deliver messages which are currently in transit, or a reference to represent an actor referenced by an in-transit message — which we call an *in-transit refer-ence*. A protected reference cannot be deleted until the message sender knows the in-transit messages have been received correctly.

Asynchronous communication introduces the following problem (see the left side of Figure 2): application messages from Actor A to Actor B can be in transit, but the reference held by Actor A can be removed. Stage 3 shows that Actor B and C are likely to be erroneously reclaimed, while Stage 4 shows that all of the actors are possibly erroneously reclaimed. Our solution is to temporarily keep the reference to Actor B undeleted and identify Actor A as live (Case 1 of the right side of Figure 2). This approach guarantees liveness of Actor B by tracing from Actor A. Actor A is named the *sender pseudo root* because it has an in-transit message to Actor B and it is not a real root. Furthermore, it can be garbage but cannot be collected. The reference from A to B is protected and A is considered live until A knows that the in-transit message is delivered.

To prevent erroneous GC, actors pointed by in-transit references must uncon-ditionally remain live until the receiver receives the message. A similar solution can be re-used to guarantee the liveness of the referenced actor: the sender becomes a sender pseudo root and keeps the reference to the referenced actor undeleted (Case 2).

Using pseudo roots, *the persistent references to roots can be ignored*. Figure 3 illustrates an example of the mapping of pseudo root actor GC. We can now safely ignore: 1) dynamic creation of references to public services and 2) persis-tent references to local services.

Imprecise Inverse Reference Listing. In a distributed environment, an inter-node referenced actor must be considered live from the perspective of lo-cal GC. To know whether an actor is inter-node referenced, each actor should maintain inverse references to indicate if it is inter-node referenced. This ap-proach usually refers to *reference listing*. Maintaining precise inverse references

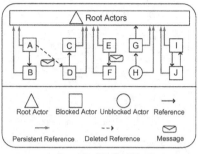
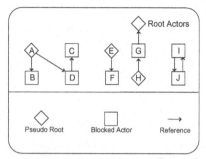

An Example of the Real World   The Corresponding Pseudo Root Actor Reference Graph

Fig. 3. An example of pseudo root actor garbage collection which maps the real state of the given system to a pseudo root actor reference graph

in an asynchronous way is performance-expensive. Fortunately, imprecise inverse references are acceptable if all inter-node referenced actors can be identified as live — inter-node referenced actors can be pseudo root actors (we call them the *global pseudo roots*), or reachable from another local pseudo root to guarantee their liveness.

4   Implementation of the Pseudo Root Approach

To implement the proposed pseudo root approach, we propose the *actor garbage detection protocol.* The actor garbage detection protocol, implemented as part of the SALSA programming language [28, 34], consists of four sub-protocols — the *asynchronous ACK protocol*, the *reference passing protocol*, the *migration protocol*, and the *reference deletion protocol*. Messages are divided into two categories — the *application messages* which require asynchronous acknowledgements, and the *system messages* that will not trigger any asynchronous acknowledgement.

The Asynchronous ACK Protocol. The asynchronous ACK protocol is designed to help identifying sender pseudo roots. Each reference maintains a counter, count, for expected acknowledgements. A reference can be deleted only if its expected acknowledgement count is zero. An actor is a sender pseudo root if the total expected acknowledgements of its references are greater than zero. The protocol is shown in the left upper part of Figure 4, in which actor sender sends a message to actor receiver. The event handler OnSend is triggered when an application message is sent; the event handler OnReceive is invoked when a message is received. If a message to receive requires an acknowledgement, the event handler OnReceive will generate an acknowledgement to the message sender. The message handler ACK is asynchronously executed by an actor to decrease the expected acknowledgement count of the reference to actor receiver held by actor sender. With the asynchronous ACK protocol, the garbage collector can identify sender pseudo roots and protected references from the perspective of implementation:

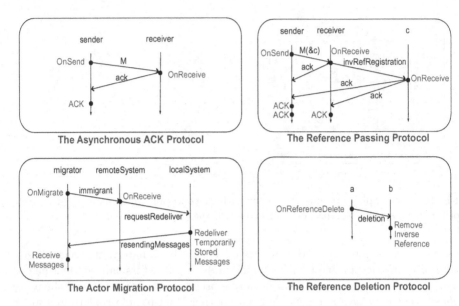

Fig. 4. The actor garbage detection sub-protocols

- A *sender pseudo root* is one whose total expected acknowledgement count of its references is greater than zero.
- A *protected reference* is one whose expected acknowledgement count is greater than zero. A protected reference cannot be deleted.

The Reference Passing Protocol. The reference passing protocol specifies how to build inverse references in an asynchronous manner. A typical scenario of reference passing is to send a message M containing a reference to c, from **sender** to **receiver**. The reference (**sender,receiver**) and the reference (**sender,c**) are protected at the beginning by increasing their expected acknowledgement counts. Then **sender** sends the application message M to **receiver**. Right after **receiver** has received the message, it generates an application message **invRefRegistration** to c to register the inverse reference of (**receiver,c**) in c. A special acknowledgement from c to **sender** is then sent to decrease the count of the protected reference (**sender,c**). Making **invRefRegistration** an application message is to ensure that reference deletion of reference (**receiver,c**) always happens after c has built the corresponding inverse reference. The protocol is shown in the right upper side of Figure 4.

The Migration Protocol. Implementation of the migration protocol requires assistance from two special actors, **remoteSystem** at a remote computing node, and **localSystem** at the local computing node. An actor migrates by encoding itself into a message, and then delivers the message to **remoteSystem**. During this period, messages to the migrating actor are stored at **localSystem**. After migration, **localSystem** delivers the temporarily stored messages to the migrated actor asynchronously. Every migrating actor becomes a pseudo root by increasing the expected acknowledgement count of its self reference. The migrating actor decreases the expected acknowledgement count of its self reference when it receives the temporarily stored messages. The protocol is shown in the left lower side of Figure 4.

The Reference Deletion Protocol. A reference can be deleted if it is not protected — its expected acknowledgement count must be zero. The deletion automatically creates a system message to the acquaintance of the actor deleting the reference to remove the inverse reference held by the acquaintance. The protocol is shown in the right lower side of Figure 4.

Safety of Actor Garbage Detection Protocol. The safety of local actor GC in a distributed environment is guaranteed by the following invariants:

1. Let $x \neq y$. If Actor y is referenced by a non-pseudo-root actor x, actor y must have an inverse reference to Actor x.
2. If an actor is referenced by several pseudo roots, either it has at least one inverse reference to one of the pseudo roots, or it is a pseudo root.

The above two invariants together guarantee *the property of one-step back tracing safety*. The property says that if an actor is inter-node referenced, the actor either can be identified as a remotely dependent pseudo root by one-step back tracing through its registered inverse references, or is reachable from some local pseudo roots.

5   Collecting Distributed Cyclic Actor Garbage

In order to collect distributed cyclic garbage, we need to obtain a consistent global view of the system. With the help of the pseudo root approach, we have devised a logically centralized global garbage collector, which is concurrent (does not stop applications), asynchronous, and non-FIFO. The global collector triggers distributed GC periodically, decides which computing nodes to include, asks each computing node to return a local snapshot, merges the snapshots, identifies garbage, and then notifies each computing node of the garbage list. Before snapshots are returned, deleted references or inverse references are preserved for consistency. Migrating or migrated actors are removed from the group of GC, and actors referenced by them are identified as pseudo roots directly. Actors that have been unblocked or are currently unblocked during garbage collection are also pseudo roots. Details of the global collector can be found in [32].

6   Experimental Results

Major concerns on the performance of distributed applications are mostly the degree of parallelism and the application execution time. In this section, we use several types of applications to measure the impact of the proposed actor GC mechanism in terms of real execution time and overhead percentage. The results are shown in Table 1, and each result of a benchmark application is the average of ten execution times. To show the impact of GC, the measurement for actor GC uses two different mechanisms: *No GC* and *DGC*. "No GC" means nothing is used; "DGC" means local garbage collectors are activated every two seconds or in case of insufficient memory, and distributed GC starts every 20 seconds. The results of local GC experiments can be found in [32].

Distributed Benchmark Application

Each distributed benchmark application is executed at four dual-processor Solaris machines. These machines are connected by Ethernet. The benchmark applications are described as follows:

- Distributed Fibonacci number with locality (Dfibl): *Dfibl* optimizes the number of inter-node messages by locating four sub-computing trees at each computing node.
- Distributed Fibonacci number without locality (Dfibn): *Dfibn* distributes the actors in a breadth-first-search manner.
- Distributed N queens number (DNQ): *DNQ* equally distributes the actors at four computing nodes.
- Distributed Matrix multiplication (DMX): *DMX* divides the first input matrix into four sub-matrices, sends the sub-matrices and the second matrix to four computing nodes, performs one matrix multiplication operation, and then merges the data at the computing node that initializes the computation.

Table 1. The distributed garbage collection experimental results (measured in seconds)

Mechanism	Application(Argument)/Number of Actors							
	Dfibl(39) /177	Dfibl(42) /753	Dfibn(39) /177	Dfibn(42) /753	DNQ(16) /211	DNQ(18) /273	DMX(100²) /5	DMX(150²) /5
No GC (Real)	1.722	3.974	3.216	8.527	13.120	426.151	6.165	39.011
DGC (Real)	2.091	4.957	3.761	9.940	17.531	461.757	6.715	38.955
DGC Overhead (Real)	21%	25%	17%	17%	34%	8%	9%	0%

7 Related Work

Distributed garbage collection has been studied for decades. The area of distributed passive object collection algorithms can be roughly divided into two categories — the reference counting (or listing) based algorithms and the indirect distributed garbage collection algorithms. The reference counting (or listing) based algorithms cannot collect distributed cyclic garbage — such as [16, 4, 20, 21, 3, 33, 25]. They are similar to the proposed actor garbage detection protocol but they tend to be more synchronous — all of them rely on First-In-

First-Out (FIFO) communication or timestamp based FIFO (simulated FIFO) communication, and some of them are even totally synchronous by using remote-procedure-call [4]. Since actor communication is asynchronous and unordered, these algorithms cannot be reused directly by actor systems.

There are various indirect distributed garbage collection algorithms for passive object systems. The most important feature of these algorithms is that they collect at least some distributed cyclic garbage. Hughes' algorithm [10] uses global timestamp propagation from roots which is very sensitive to failures. Liskov et al. [13] present a client-server based algorithm which requires every local collector to report inter-node references to a server. Vestal's algorithm [31] tries to virtually delete a reference to see whether or not an object is garbage. Maheshwari et al. [17, 18] and Le Fessant [15] propose heuristics based algorithms to suspect some objects as garbage and then to verify the suspects. Lang et al. [14] propose a group-based tracing algorithm to collect garbage hierarchically. Rodrigues et al. [23] present a dynamically partitioning approach to form a group of objects for global garbage collection. Veiga et al. [29] propose a heuristics and snapshot based algorithm, in which any change to the snapshots may force current global garbage collection to quit. Hudson et al. [9] propose a generational collector where the address space of each computing node is divided into several disjoint blocks (cars), and cars are grouped together into several distributed trains. A car/train can be disposed of if there are no incoming inter-car/inter-train references to it. Blackburn et al. [5] suggest a methodology to derive a distributed garbage collection algorithm from an existing distributed termination detection algorithm [19], in which the distributed garbage collection algorithm developers must design another algorithm to guarantee a consistent global state. All of the above algorithms cannot be reused directly in actor systems because actors and passive objects are different in nature.

Marking algorithms for actor garbage collection are relatively various, including Push-Pull, Is-Black by Kafura et al. [12], Dickman's algorithm [7], and the actor transformation algorithm by Vardhan and Agha [26, 27]. Most distributed actor garbage collection algorithms are snapshot based. The algorithm proposed by Kafura et al. [11] uses the Chandy-Lamport snapshot algorithm [6] to determine a precise global state, which is expensive and requires FIFO communication to flush communication channels. Venkatasubramanian et al. [30] assume a two-dimensional grid network topology, and the algorithm also requires FIFO communication to flush communication channels. Puaut's algorithm [22] is client-server based, and requires each computing node to maintain a timestamp vector to simulate a global clock. Vardhan's algorithm [26] transforms each local actor reference graph into a passive object reference graph, and uses Schelvis' algorithm [24] for global garbage collection. It assumes: FIFO communication, and periodically performs stop-the-world garbage collection. All existing actor garbage collection algorithms violate the asynchronous, unordered assumption of actor communication, and all of them do not support the concept of actor migration.

8   Conclusion and Future Work

In this paper, we have redefined garbage actors to make the definition more operational. We also introduced the concept of pseudo roots, making actor GC easier to understand and to implement. The most important contribution of this paper is *the actor garbage collection framework for actor-oriented programming languages*. Implementation of actor GC is available since version 1.0 of the SALSA programming language [34, 28]. Unlike existing actor GC algorithms, the proposed framework does not require FIFO communication or stop-the-world synchronization. Furthermore, it supports actor migration and it works concurrently with mutation operations. This feature reduces interruption of users' applications. The proposed logically centralized global garbage collector is safe in the case of failures since it does not collect actors which are referenced by unknown actors.

Future research focuses on the idea of resource access restrictions, which is part of distributed resource management. By applying the resource access restrictions to actors, the live unblocked actor principle is no longer true — not every actor has references to the root actors. Another direction of this research is to modify the partitioning based passive object GC algorithms to increase scalability. Last but not least, testing the GC algorithms on real-world applications running on large-scale distributed environments is necessary to further evaluate their scalability and performance.

Acknowledgements

We would like to acknowledge the National Science Foundation (NSF CAREER Award No. CNS-0448407) for partial support for this research.

References

1. S. E. Abdullahi and A. Ringwood. Garbage collecting the internet: A survey of distributed garbage collection. *ACM Computing Surveys*, 30(3):330–373, 1998.
2. G. Agha. *Actors: A Model of Concurrent Computation in Distributed Systems*. MIT Press, 1986.
3. D. I. Bevan. Distributed garbage collection using reference counting. In *PARLE'87*, volume 258/259 of *Lecture Notes in Computer Science*, pages 176–187, Eindhoven, The Netherlands, June 1987. Springer-Verlag.
4. A. Birrell, D. Evers, G. Nelson, S. Owicki, and E. Wobber. Distributed garbage collection for network objects. Technical Report 116, DEC Systems Research Center, 130 Lytton Avenue, Palo Alto, CA 94301, Dec. 1993.
5. S. M. Blackburn, R. L. Hudson, R. Morrison, J. E. B. Moss, D. S. Munro, and J. Zigman. Starting with termination: a methodology for building distributed garbage collection algorithms. *Aust. Comput. Sci. Commun.*, 23(1):20–28, 2001.
6. K. M. Chandy and L. Lamport. Distributed snapshots: Determining global states of distributed systems. *ACM Transactions on Computer Systems*, 3(1):63–75, 1985.

7. P. Dickman. Incremental, distributed orphan detection and actor garbage collection using graph partitioning and Euler cycles. In *WDAG'96*, volume 1151 of *Lecture Notes in Computer Science*, Bologna, Oct. 1996. Springer-Verlag.

8. Hewitt, C. Viewing control structures as patterns of passing messages. *Journal of Artificial Intelligence*, 8(3):323–364, June 1977.

9. R. L. Hudson, R. Morrison, J. E. B. Moss, and D. S. Munro. Garbage collecting the world: One car at a time. *SIGPLAN Not.*, 32(10):162–175, 1997.

10. J. Hughes. A distributed garbage collection algorithm. In *Record of the 1985 Conference on Functional Programming and Computer Architecture*, volume 201 of *LNCS*, pages 256–272, Nancy, France, Sept. 1985. Springer-Verlag.

11. D. Kafura, M. Mukherji, and D. Washabaugh. Concurrent and distributed garbage collection of active objects. *IEEE TPDS*, 6(4), April 1995.

12. D. Kafura, D. Washabaugh, and J. Nelson. Garbage collection of actors. In *OOP-SLA'90*, pages 126–134. ACM Press, October 1990.

13. R. Ladin and B. Liskov. Garbage collection of a distributed heap. In *International Conference on Distributed Computing Systems*, Yokohama, June 1992.

14. B. Lang, C. Queinnec, and J. Piquer. Garbage collecting the world. In *POPL'92*, pages 39–50. ACM Press, 1992.

15. F. Le Fessant. Detecting distributed cycles of garbage in large-scale systems. In *Principles of Distributed Computing (PODC)*, Rhodes Island, Aug. 2001.

16. C. Lermen and D. Maurer. A protocol for distributed reference counting. In *ACM Symposium on Lisp and Functional Programming*, ACM SIGPLAN Notices, pages 343–350, Cambridge, MA, Aug. 1986. ACM Press.

17. U. Maheshwari and B. Liskov. Collecting cyclic distributed garbage by controlled migration. In *PODC'95*, 1995.

18. U. Maheshwari and B. Liskov. Collecting cyclic distributed garbage by back tracing. In *PODC'97*, pages 239–248, Santa Barbara, CA, 1997. ACM Press.

19. J. Matocha and T. Camp. A taxonomy of distributed termination detection algorithms. *J. Syst. Softw.*, 43(3):207–221, 1998.

20. L. Moreau. Tree rerooting in distributed garbage collection: Implementation and performance evaluation. *Higher-Order and Symbolic Computation*, 14(4):357–386, 2001.

21. J. M. Piquer. Indirect reference counting: A distributed garbage collection algorithm. In *PARLE'91*, volume 505 of *Lecture Notes in Computer Science*, Eindhoven, The Netherlands, June 1991. Springer-Verlag.

22. I. Puaut. A distributed garbage collector for active objects. In *OOPSLA'94*, pages 113–128. ACM Press, 1994.

23. H. Rodrigues and R. Jones. A cyclic distributed garbage collector for Network Objects. In *WDAG'96*, volume 1151 of *Lecture Notes in Computer Science*, pages 123–140, Bologna, Oct. 1996. Springer-Verlag.

24. M. Schelvis. Incremental distribution of timestamp packets — a new approach to distributed garbage collection. *ACM SIGPLAN Notices*, 24(10):37–48, 1989.

25. M. Shapiro, P. Dickman, and D. Plainfossé. SSP chains: Robust, distributed references supporting acyclic garbage collection. Rapports de Recherche 1799, INRIA, Nov. 1992.

26. A. Vardhan. Distributed garbage collection of active objects: A transformation and its applications to java programming. Master's thesis, UIUC, Urbana Champaig, Illinois, 1998.

27. A. Vardhan and G. Agha. Using passive object garbage collection algorithms. In *ISMM'02*, ACM SIGPLAN Notices, pages 106–113, Berlin, June 2002. ACM Press.

28. C. A. Varela and G. Agha. Programming dynamically reconfigurable open systems with SALSA. *ACM SIGPLAN Notices. OOPSLA'2001 Intriguing Technology Track Proceedings*, 36(12):20–34, Dec. 2001.
29. L. Veiga and P. Ferreira. Asynchronous complete distributed garbage collection. In O. Babaoglu and K. Marzullo, editors, *IPDPS 2005*, Denver, Colorado, USA, Apr. 2005.
30. N. Venkatasubramanian, G. Agha, and C. Talcott. Scalable distributed garbage collection for systems of active objects. In *IWMM'92*, volume 637 of *Lecture Notes in Computer Science*. Springer-Verlag, 1992.
31. S. C. Vestal. *Garbage collection: An exercise in distributed, fault-tolerant programming*. PhD thesis, University of Washington, Seattle, WA, 1987.
32. W. Wang and C. A. Varela. Distributed garbage collection for mobile actor systems: The pseudo root approach. Technical Report 06-04, Dept. of Computer Science, R.P.I., Feb. 2006. Extended Version of the GPC'06 Paper.
33. P. Watson and I. Watson. An efficient garbage collection scheme for parallel computer architectures. In *PARLE'87*, volume 258/259 of *Lecture Notes in Computer Science*, pages 432–443, Eindhoven, The Netherlands, June 1987. Springer-Verlag.
34. Worldwide Computing Laboratory. The SALSA Programming Language, 2002. Work in Progress. http://www.cs.rpi.edu/wwc/salsa/.

A Grid-Based Node Split Algorithm for Managing Current Location Data

Jae-Kwan Yun, Seung-Won Lee, Dong-Suk Hong, Dong-Oh Kim, and Ki-Joon Han

School of Computer Science & Engineering, Konkuk University,
1, Hwayang-Dong, Gwangjin-Gu, Seoul 143-701, Korea
{jkyun, swlee, dshong, dokim, kjhan}@db.konkuk.ac.kr

Abstract. There is rapidly increasing interest in Location Based Service(LBS) which utilizes location data of moving objects. To efficiently manage the huge amounts of location data in LBS, the GALIS (Gracefully Aging Location Information System) architecture, a cluster-based distributed computing architecture, is proposed. The GALIS using the non-uniform 2-level grid algorithm performs load balancing and indexing for nodes. However, the non-uniform 2-level grid algorithm has a problem creating unnecessary nodes when moving objects are crowded in a certain area. Therefore, a new node split algorithm, which is more efficient for various distribution of moving objects, is proposed in this paper. Because the algorithm proposed in this paper considers spatial distribution for the current location of moving objects, it can perform efficient load balancing without creating unnecessary nodes even when moving objects are congested in a certain area. Besides, the various data distribution configuration for moving objects has been experimented by implementing node split simulators and it's been verified that the proposed algorithm splits nodes more efficiently than the existing algorithm.

1 Introduction

According to the development of wireless mobile communication technology, mobile devices such as mobile phone and PDA(Personal Digital Assistants) have been prevailed, and as location measurement technology like GPS is developed, LBS which utilizes location data of moving objects becomes attractive. In order to provide this service, the location data management system is required to manage the location data of moving objects efficiently [1,2,3,4].

The GALIS architecture proposed for LBS is designed for a cluster-based distributed computing architecture to handle the large amount of moving objects [5,6]. The GALIS is composed of the SLDS(Short-term Location Data Subsystem) for management of the current location data and the LLDS(Long-term Location Data Subsystem) for management of the past location data. The SLDS divides the entire service area into smaller ones based upon the non-uniform 2-level grid algorithm, and each node processes the movement of moving objects in different area. The non-uniform 2-level grid algorithm implemented in the GALIS is a method proposed for load balancing and indexing of moving objects, and to provide load balancing, it divides one node into two nodes when the number of moving objects which processed in a certain node exceeds the specific limit.

Y.-C. Chung and J.E. Moreira (Eds.): GPC 2006, LNCS 3947, pp. 373–384, 2006.
© Springer-Verlag Berlin Heidelberg 2006

The non-uniform 2-level grid algorithm basically has a 2-split structure and performs node split based on the central position of the splitting area as a basis [7]. Because this algorithm doesn't consider the current location data distribution of moving objects, unnecessary nodes would be created, and it has a problem of load unbalancing between nodes.

Therefore, in this paper, we proposed an efficient node split algorithm that is appropriate to the SLDS of the GALIS architecture. Since the proposed algorithm considers the size of area and the number of moving objects for the two nodes after split, it doesn't create unnecessary nodes and can solve the problem of load unbalancing between nodes.

This paper is organized as follows. The GALIS architecture, the non-uniform 2-level grid algorithm, and the problems of the non-uniform 2-level grid algorithm are described with examples in chapter 2. A new node split algorithm is proposed in chapter 3 and the results from the experiment and performance evaluation are analyzed in chapter 4. Finally, the conclusion and future work are described in chapter 5.

2 Related Works

In this chapter, the GALIS architecture, the non-uniform 2-level grid algorithm for the management of location data of moving objects, and problems of the non-uniform 2-level grid algorithm are described.

2.1 GALIS Architecture

The GALIS, which is for LBS, has a cluster-based distributed computing architecture with multiple nodes, and each node is able to process the movement of moving objects in different area.

Figure 1 shows the GALIS architecture. The GALIS consists of the SLDS for current location data management and the LLDS for past location data management. The SLDS uses a main memory DBMS(Database Management System) in order to efficiently process the periodic update of current location data and the LLDS uses a disk-based DBMS for managing past location data[8]. Each node in the SLDS is named the SDP(Short-term Data Processor) and it manages current location information of moving objects in a Macro-cell area. One node of the SDP is called the SDP Master and the rest of them are called the SDP Worker.

The LLDS also has a similar form of the SLDS, and each node in the LLDS consists of the LDP (Long-term Data Processor) Master and the LDP Worker. The SLDS and the LLDS also have Coordinators for load balancing. The SDP Master receives current location information of moving objects in real time and has a role of transmitting it to the other SDP and the LDP master. Each Coordinator node observes the number of moving objects that are processed in the SDP or the LDP and performs dynamic load balancing using the non-uniform 2-level grid algorithm [9].

2.2 Non-uniform 2-Level Grid Algorithm

When the whole area that needs to be processed for LBS is considered as a two-dimensional plane, this two-dimensional plane is divided into n areas and each

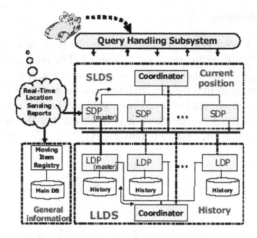

Fig. 1. The GALIS architecture

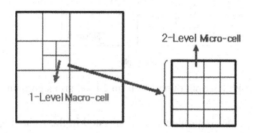

Fig. 2. Structure of non-uniform 2-level grid algorithm

divided area is called Macro-cell in the GALIS. Macro-cell can be composed of different sized rectangle areas. Split of Macro-cell occurs when the number of moving objects included in a Macro-cell exceeds the pre-defined maximum number, and the split method takes the central position of axis x and of axis y alternately and makes split. Merge with adjacent Macro-cell occurs, on the other hand, when the number of moving objects included in a Macro-cell less than the pre-defined minimum number.

Location information regarding moving objects included in each Macro-cell boundary is processed by a single node and a Macro-cell, in turn, is divided into an area called Micro-cell that has a regular real-world size of $100m$ by $100m$. Micro-cell is organized to index current location information of moving objects in a node and it especially uses the z-ordering technique for indexing [9]. When moving object data is inserted using the z-ordering technique, the system can recognize the number of moving objects which are included in a specific Micro-cell.

The left side in Figure 2 shows the whole service area that has been divided into 10 Macro-cells and the right side shows a single Macro-cell that has been divided into 16 regular sized Micro-cells.

2.3 Problem Definitions

The non-uniform 2-level grid algorithm has a problem of load unbalancing between nodes and a problem of unnecessary node creation. The creation of unnecessary node can make split impossible when a certain node needs to be split. Also, the problem of load unbalancing implies that the system resources are not optimally utilized.

Figure 3 shows a node state that has been split by the non-uniform 2-level grid algorithm. Before Figure 3 is explained, it is assumed that the system serving whole area in Figure 3 can use three nodes at maximum.

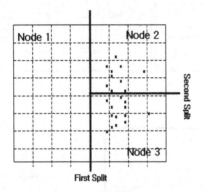

Fig. 3. Split of non-uniform 2-level grid algorithm

In Figure 3, when moving objects are congested in the right side area, the first split can not distribute them into two nodes because it occurs at the middle point of axis x. Therefore, through the second split, the moving objects can be distributed into node 2 and node 3. Even in this state, the number of moving objects in node 1, 2, and 3 are still in unbalance. Node 1, in this case, still processes a certain area even though there is no real load at all(i.e., the number of moving objects = 0) and thus, shortage of nodes can cause split impossible when split is needed in case some moving objects move from node 2 to node 3.

3   Node Split Algorithm

A new node split algorithm is suggested and explained in this chapter. This node split algorithm is divided into two parts; selection of the candidate split positions and selection of the final split position.

3.1   Selection of Candidate Split Positions

The number of moving objects after split is one thing that needs to be considered in the node split algorithm. Because the node split algorithm decides the split position by consideration of the number of moving objects in the node after split, the optimal number of moving objects limited by a single node after split during the process of the

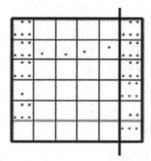

Fig. 4. Example of split without consideration of area size

algorithm must be known. The optimal number is the same as the half of the number of moving objects in the current node. This number is called the optimal number of moving objects after split.

When only the number of moving objects is considered to decide the split position, unbalance of area processed by the node can be made. Figure 4 shows an example of split that can occur when the size of area is not considered.

In Figure 4, the size of one node can be very small because the size of area is not considered although the number of moving objects is appropriately divided. In this case, another split may become necessary when moving objects in the smaller area move a little to another node. To solve the problem, the optimal number of moving objects after split is recalculated and expressed by a *scope value* having the maximum and minimum values. This scope value is defined as a loosely optimal value and the candidate split positions are selected by using this loosely optimal value.

An algorithm for selecting the candidate split positions uses a two-dimensional integer array that has the number of moving objects included in the cell, and $cell_{ij}$ means the number of moving objects in the cell located at i-th cell of axis x across with j-th cell of axis y. The number of moving objects in a specific Macro-cell that can be known due to the characteristic of the SLDS is used in the algorithm. The algorithm also takes the coefficient variable (CV) of the optimal value and the number of moving objects (MONum) being processed by the current node as its input.

A split position selection method begins with finding the optimal value (MinLOPT) and the loosely optimal value (MaxLOPT) after split. The algorithm for finding these values is described in Figure 5. Next, based upon split axis information accepted, the number of moving objects in the first column are summed and stored in a one-dimensional array in case of axis x, the next column stores the accumulated value by adding the values stored in the previous column to the number of moving objects in the current column. In case of axis y, the same process as axis x is performed for the row. Thus the obtained one-dimensional array is defined as the *cumulative array* (CA) and is marked as CA^x for the axis x and as CA^y for the axis y. In addition, CA^x_i (CA^y_i) indicates the i-th element of CA^x (CA^y). CA is automatically sorted because it contains accumulated values.

CA and the loosely optimal value are used to select the candidate split positions. From each sorted CA, an appropriate position into which the loosely optimal value

```
Algorithm: Candidate Split Positions Selection (cells, CV, MONum)
OPT ← MONum / 2                          // Optimal Split Position is set by the half of MONum after split
MinLOPT ← OPT – (OPT * (CV/100))         // Optimal value
MaxLOPT ← OPT + (OPT * (CV/100))         // Loosly optimal value
for i from 1 to the number of x axis cell do    // Compute Cumulative Array(CA) for x axis
        for j from 1 to the number of y axis cell do
                CAˣᵢ ← CAˣᵢ + cellsⱼ
        end for
end for
for i from 1 to the number of y axis cell do    // Compute Cumulative Array(CA) for y axis
        for j from 1 to the number of x axis cell do
                CAʸᵢ ← CAʸᵢ + cellsⱼ
        end for
end for
// Select CSP(Candidate Split Position)
//CSPˣ is computed by the CSP that has value between MinLOPT and MaxLOPT over x axis
i ← 1
while CAˣᵢ < MaxLOPT
    if CAˣᵢ > MinLOPT
        CSPˣ ← CSPˣ ∪ i
    end if
    i ← i + 1
end while
//CSPʸ is computed by the CSP that has value between MinLOPT and MaxLOPT over y axis
i ← 1
while CAʸᵢ < MaxLOPT
    if CAʸᵢ > MinLOPT
        CSPʸ ← CSPʸ ∪ i
    end if
    i ← i + 1
end while
return CSP
```

Fig. 5. Selection algorithm for candidate split positions

can be inserted is found and stored in CSP which contains a set of candidate split positions. The candidate split positions based on axis x are marked as CSP^x and those based on axis y is marked as CSP^y. The values stored in CSP are integer values that indicate the position to be split in the Micro-cell.

3.2 Selection of Final Split Position

After the candidate split positions are stored in CSP, we have to select a final split position. DF, an important element in the selection of the final split position, shows the difference in the number of moving objects in two nodes and in ratio of area, and the candidate split position having the smallest difference is selected as the final split position. The formula for finding DF is as follow.

$$DF = |\ MONum_1/MicroNum_1 - MONum_2/MicroNum_2\ |$$

When split is made on the basis of the candidate split positions, two nodes after split are called node 1 and node 2, and $MONum_1$ ($MONum_2$) and $MicroNum_1$ ($MicroNum_2$) represent the number of moving objects and the number of Micro-cells processed by node 1 (node 2), respectively.

Figure 6 shows the algorithm that computes DF for each candidate split position and selects the final split position which has the minimum DF value.

```
Algorithm: Final Split Position Selection (CSP, MONum)
xSize ← the number of x axis cell
ySize ← the number of y axis cell
MinDF ← MONum              // Minimum value of DF
for each i ∈ CSPˣ do
// DF, which uses each element of CSPˣ on calculation, is computed by the difference of number of moving
// objects divided by the number of micro-cells of two regions after split
   DF ← |CAˣᵢ /(ySize*i)-(MONum-xCAˣᵢ)/(ySize*(xSize-i)|
   if DF < MinDF then        // Select the position having the minimum number of moving objects
      T ← ∅
      T ← T ∪ i
      MinDF ← DF
   else if DF = MinDF then    // if DF is MinDF then store i
      T ← T ∪ i
   end if
end for
// DF, which uses each element of CSPʸ on calculation, is computed by the difference of number of moving
// objects divided by the number of micro-cells of two regions after split
for each i ∈ CSPʸ do
   DF ← |CAʸᵢ /(xSize*i) - (MONum-yCAʸᵢ)/(xSize*(ySize-i)|
   if DF < MinDF then        // Select the position having the minimum number of moving objects
      T ← ∅
      T ← T ∪ i
      MinDF ← DF
   else if DF = MinDF then    // if DF is MinDF then store i
      T ← T ∪ i
   end if
end for
return T   //T has the minimal DF value
```

Fig. 6. Selection algorithm for final split position

If more than one final split position is selected, the algorithm selects the position having the minimum number of moving objects among the cells adjacent to the split position. In this case, more than one position could be selected. If that's the case, the split position nearest to the central position of the selected positions is finally selected.

4 Experiment and Performance Evaluation

This chapter describes moving object data used in the experiment and explains node split simulators implemented for performance evaluation of two algorithms, that is, our advanced node split algorithm and the non-uniform 2-level grid algorithm. Last, the two algorithms are compared each other with respect to the following three points; the number of nodes used for node split, the number of splits and merges, and the degree of load balance.

4.1 Moving Object Data

We have utilized GSTD[10] to create moving object data used in the experiment, and 1,000 moving objects and 10 timestamps were taken. In addition, six different distribution types of data were created to experiment various type of moving objects for different cases. The shape of six types of moving object data is shown in Figure 7.

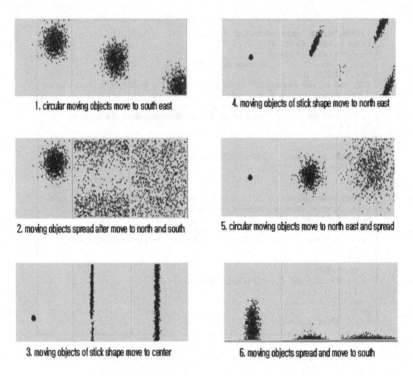

1. circular moving objects move to south east

4. moving objects of stick shape move to north east

2. moving objects spread after move to north and south

5. circular moving objects move to north east and spread

3. moving objects of stick shape move to center

6. moving objects spread and move to south

Fig. 7. Six types of moving object data

4.2 Node Split Simulators

In order to evaluate the proposed algorithm, node split simulators were implemented in this paper. There are two types of node split simulators; one is executed by the non-uniform 2-level grid algorithm and the other is executed by the advanced node split algorithm proposed in this paper. Set-up variables for the two simulators are shown in Table 1.

Values set up for the experiment are shown in Table 2. The same values are used for the two algorithms. CV in Table 2 is an additional set-up variable for the optimal value and is only used in the simulator utilizing the advance node split algorithm and it is not used in the simulator utilizing the non-uniform 2-level grid algorithm.

Table 1. Common variables for simulators

Variable Name	Description
MAXMONUM	Maximum number of moving objects that can be processed in a single node
MINMONUM	Minimum number of moving objects for node merge
NODENUM	Total number of nodes
TSNUM	Number of timestamps in input data
MONUM	Number of moving objects in input data
CV	Variable coefficient for optimal value

Table 2. Set-up values for simulators

Algorithm Set-up Variables	Non-uniform 2- level grid algorithm	Advanced node split algorithm
MAXMONUM	100	100
MINMONUM	50	50
NODENUM	30	30
TSNUM	10	10
MONUM	1000	1000
CV	N/A	10

4.3 Evaluation and Analysis of Performance

Evaluation of performance has been done by comparing the average number of nodes used for load balancing, the number of splits and merges, and the degree of load balance for six different types of moving object data.

Split shape from the execution result of simulators can be observed by timestamps. Figure 8 shows split shape of the first moving object data type, among six experimental data types, where moving objects move toward to the south.

Above part in Figure 8 shows split shape at the third timestamp and lower part shows another split shape at the last timestamp. By looking at Figure 8, it is clear that the non-uniform 2-level algorithm can create unnecessary nodes that have no load at all for split and in the advanced node split algorithm, the load of every node is distributed evenly.

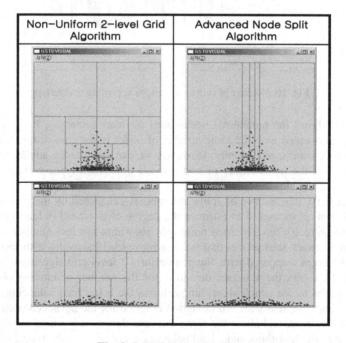

Fig. 8. Split shape by simulators

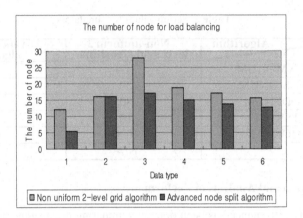

Fig. 9. Number of nodes used for load balancing

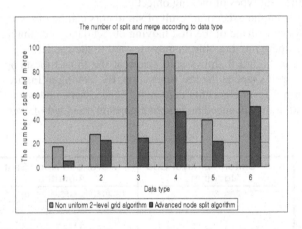

Fig. 10. Number of splits and merges according to data types

Figure 9 shows the number of nodes used for load balancing. It shows that load balance is performed with the same number of nodes in the case of type 2 data where moving objects are spread evenly. However, we can see that the advanced node split algorithm uses the less number of nodes in all other data types compared with the non-uniform 2-level grid algorithm.

In Figure 10, the number of splits and merges calculated by the simulators using two algorithms is measured to estimate the degree of overhead in load balancing. As shown in Figure 10, the advanced node split algorithm has less number of splits and merges in all cases, thus proves that it can achieve load balancing with less amount of splits and merges compared with the non uniform 2-level grid algorithm.

Figure 11 shows the standard deviation for the number of moving objects processed by nodes to see which algorithm performs the better load balancing. Except for the type 2 data, the less standard deviation is found for the advanced node split algorithm in every case, and about the same standard deviation is found in type 2 data. It means that both algorithms make load balance evenly only for the type 2 data, but the

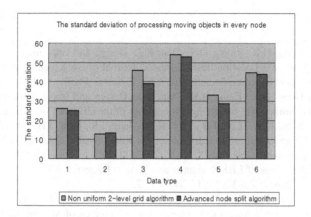

Fig. 11. Standard deviation of moving objects in each node

advanced node split algorithm always performs the better load balance in all other data types compared with the non uniform 2-level grid algorithm.

5   Conclusion and Future Work

In this paper, we proposed an advanced node split algorithm for the SLDS of the GALIS architecture proposed for LBS. The role of the SLDS is to manage current location data of moving objects. The proposed algorithm is able to solve the problems caused by the existing non-uniform 2-level grid algorithm since it considers the distribution of moving object data and performs the node split based upon the state of the node that has already split.

To evaluate and compare the proposed algorithm with the non-uniform 2-level grid algorithm, two node split simulators have been implemented and six types of moving object data are created by using the GSTD in this paper. The paper has proved, by performance evaluation experimented against six different types of moving object data, that the proposed algorithm always performs the better load balance using less number of nodes than the non-uniform 2-level grid algorithm without creating unnecessary nodes. It also has confirmed that the advanced node split algorithm can reduce the amount of communication cost between nodes with creating the less number of splits and merges.

The load balance has been made based upon the maximum and minimum number of moving objects that has pre-set for now, but further study on how to adapt the maximum and minimum number of moving objects in accordance with different system capacity will be needed in the near future.

Acknowledgements

This research was supported by the MIC(Ministry of Information and Communication), Korea, under the ITRC(Information Technology Research Center) support program supervised by the IITA(Institute of Information Technology Assessment).

References

1. Lee, S.W., Kang, H.K., Hong, D.S., Han, K.J.: Design and Implementation of Extended SLDS for Real-time Location-based Services. Journal of the Korea Open Geographic Information System Research Society. Vol.7, No.2. (2005) 47-56.
2. Lee, S.W., Hong, D.S., Kang, H.K., Han, K.J.: Design and Implementation of Extended SLDS for Dynamic Load Balancing. Proceedings of the GIS/RS Conference (2005) 37-44.
3. Cho, D.S., Nam, K.W., Lee, J.H., Min, K.W., Jang, I.S., Park, J.H.: Information System with Very Large Location Data. Journal of the Korea System Science Society Special Interest Group on Databases. Vol.18, No.4. (2002) 11-22.
4. Han, K.J.: A Review of LBS Standards and Trends. Information Policy on National Computerization Agency. Vol.10, No.4. (2003) 3-17.
5. Kim, M.H., Kim, K.H., Nah, Y.M., Lee, J.W., Wang, T.H., Lee, J.H., Yang, Y.K.: Distributed Adaptive Architecture for Managing Large Volumes of Moving Items. Society for Design and Process Science, IDPT-Vol.2. (2003) 737-744.
6. Nah, Y.M., Kim, K.H., Wang, T.H., Kim, M.H., Lee, J.H., Yang, Y.K.: A Cluster-based TMO-structured Scalable Approach for Location Information Systems. Proceedings of the 9th IEEE International Workshop on Object-oriented Real-time Dependable Systems (2003) 225-233.
7. Theodoridis, Y., Silva, J. R. O., Nascimento, M. A.: On the Generation of Spatiotemporal Datasets. Proceedings of the 6th International Symposium on Large Spatial Databases (1999) 147-164.
8. Nah, Y.M., Wang, T.H., Kim, K.H.(Kane), Kim, M.H., Yang, Y.K.: TMO-structured Cluster-based Real-time Management of Location Data on Massive Volume of Moving Items. Proceedings of STFES (2003) 89-92.
9. Nah, Y.M., Kim, K.H., Wang, T.H., Kim, M.H., Lee, J.H., Yang, Y.K.: GALIS: Cluster-based Scalable Architecture for LBS systems. Proceedings of the Korea Information Science Society Conference. Vol.18, No.4. (2002) 66-80.
10. Pfoser, D., Theodoridis, Y.: Generating Semantics-Based Trajectories of Moving Objects. Journal of Computers, Environment and Urban Systems (2003) 243-263.

Cicada: A Highly-Precise Easy-Embedded and Omni-Directional Indoor Location Sensing System

Hongliang Gu, Yuanchun Shi, Yu Chen, Bibo Wang, and Wenfeng Jiang

Computer Science and Technology Department, Tsinghua University,
Beijing 100084, P.R. China
ghl02@mails.tsinghua.edu.cn,
{shiyc, yuchen}@tsinghua.edu.cn,
wangbibo@tsinghua.org.cn, jiangwf04@mails.tsinghua.edu.cn

Abstract. For supporting location-aware computing in indoor environments, the location sensing/positioning system not only need to provide objects' precise location, but also should own such characteristics as: isotropy and convenience for portability. In this paper, we present an indoor location sensing system, Cicada. This System is based on the TDOA (time difference of arrival) between Radiofrequency and ultrasound to estimate distance, and adopts a technology integrating Slide Window Filter (SWF) and Extended Kalman Filter (EKF) to calculate location. Consequently, it not only can determine the coordinate location within 5cm average deviation either for static objects or for mobile objects, but also owns a nearly omni-directional working area. Moreover, it is able to run independently, mini and light so that it is very easy to be portable and even embedded into people's paraphernalia.

1 Introduction

Location-awareness is a paramount characteristic of many computing fields, such as pervasive/ubiquitous computing, mobile computing, and many applications, such as location-dependent information services [1] and location-aware instruction [2]. The location sensing/positioning system, which provides objects' location, is a most underlying component of location-aware computing. Although Global Positioning System (GPS) [3] is renowned for its outstanding performance outdoors, it does not work well in indoor and urban environments. Thus, design and implementation of indoor location sensing system is urgent for location-aware computing in an indoor environment, e.g. in Smart Space [4]. Besides provision of location, location-aware computing in indoor environments gives the location sensing system other requirements:

- Precision. In Smart Space, persons, the important located objects, are always fairly close. To distinguish person-sized objects, location precision is expected to be less than 1 dm. Moreover, because persons keep moving, the system should be able to determine almost as precise location for mobile objects as for static objects.
- Isotropy. In a building the located unit carried by a person keeps changing its direction along with his/her activities. The system should be immune to the varying of direction, that is, its working area should be omni-directional.

Y.-C. Chung and J.E. Moreira (Eds.): GPC 2006, LNCS 3947, pp. 385–394, 2006.

- Convenience for portability. It means the located unit (the portable part of system) is mini and light enough to be portable. Moreover, it had better run independently, namely it can work without help of other portable devices, e.g. a computer or PDA.

Compared with the guidelines of indoor location sensing system, several popular systems can not meet the all-around requirements more or less. Aiming at this, we present our indoor location sensing system, Cicada.

2 Working Principle and Framework

Being somewhat similar to the physical principle of Cricket [5], Cicada is also based on the TDOA between RF (radiofrequency) and ultrasound. Being different from Cricket, Cicada is of active mode. The framework of Cicada is shown in Fig. 1.

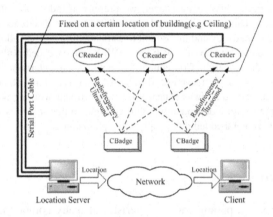

Fig. 1. Working principle and framework of Cicada

As Fig. 1 shows, Cicada consists of three main parts: CBadge, CReader and Location Server. CBadges are carried by users or attached to those objects located, which emit RF and Ultrasound at the same time periodically. And each RF corresponding to each CBadge modulates the CBadge's ID. CReaders are deployed on the fixed location of a building, e.g. ceilings, whose coordinate location are known by beforehand measurement. Because the propaganda speeds of RF and Ultrasound are different, the TDOA between them from a CBadge to a CReader is direct proportional to the distance between them, where the coefficient is the velocity of sound in air (neglecting the propaganda time of RF). According to the theory, a CReader can infer the distance from a CBadge, and then report it to a dedicated computer, Location Server, through a serial port cable. The Location Server collects all distance and calculates out location. Applications can acquire location from the Location Server as its clients.

The close-up of CBadge and CReader is shown in Fig. 2. A RMB coin and a ruler (the unit is cm) are nearby. The CBadge has a rechargeable 3V lithium battery attached on its back. The omni-directional ultrasound transmitter of CBadge is composed of 5 ultrasound sensors being mutually orthogonal. The CReader has two ports:

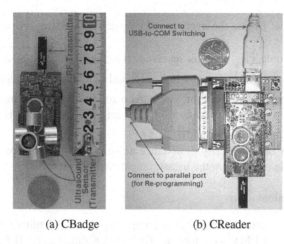

(a) CBadge   (b) CReader

Fig. 2. The CBadge and CReader in Cicada

one is USB, which connects to the serial port of a computer by a USB-to-COM Switching; and another is parallel port, which connects to a computer's parallel port. The parallel port is unplugged unless CReader is re-programmed. And when Cicada runs, the USB port must connect to the Location Server (being plugged) all the time.

3 Positioning Algorithm

After acquiring the distance set from CReaders, how to infer objects' coordinate location is concerned with the positioning algorithm. In Cicada, the positioning computation includes two phases: distance filter and location calculation.

3.1 Distance Filter

Due to ultrasound's reflection, obstruction and diffraction from wall, furniture and instruments etc, the indoor multi-path effect occurs very often. That is, quite a few of distances is invalid because they do not traverse along a LOS (line-of-sight). Before the distances go into location calculation, the invalid value of them must be filtered out carefully. Here Cicada adopts a method called Slide Window Filter (SWF).

The data received from CReaders includes CReader's ID, CBadge's ID, distance between the CReader and the CBadge, and the timestamp when the CBadge emits its signal, which is quaternion $[r,b,d,t]$. If the CReader and CBadge are given, the data from CReaders is a set of pairs $[t_i, d_i], i = 1, 2, \cdots$ according to time's ascendant order. Define a distance tuple D as the triple $D_i = [t_i, d_i, v_i]$, where $v_i = (d_i - d_{i-1})/(t_i - t_{i-1})$. A slide widow is a cyclic queuing to stores recent distance tuple for each pair of CReader and CBadge.

In slide widow, what the rear points at is the distance tuple received most recently, and what the front points at is the distance tuple received earliest, which was dequeued just now. Define the average velocity of slide widow as $\overline{V} = \frac{1}{n}\sum_{i=1}^{n} v_i$. When

a new distance tuple $N = [t,d,v]$ is received, if $v \le \min\{\alpha\overline{V}, V_{max}\}$, it will be added into the slide window; otherwise it will be rejected as an invalid distance. Here V_{max} is the maximal velocity of objects' moving, and α represents the maximal acceleration. For example, in our actual applications, V_{max} is set to 1.5m/s, which is a typical moving velocity for human indoors, and $\alpha = 1.5$.

SWF can filter out a majority of distance noise caused by multi-path effect. However it is incapable of handling the measurement error (noise) itself.

3.2   Location Calculation

On location's calculation method, after comparing with an intuitive method, Linear Equations Method (LEM), we adopt the Extended Kalman Filter (EKF) as Cicada's location calculation algorithm at last.

3.2.1 Naïve Method

The distances from all CReaders with the same timestamp and CBadge's ID are guaranteed to come from a CBadge at a time. Because the positions of the CReaders reporting the distances are known, the distances with the CReaders' position can be notated as pairs $[p_i, d_i]$ $i = 0, \cdots, n-1$, where p_i is a 3-D coordinate value being also notated as (x_i, y_i, z_i) , and n is the pairs' total number. If the unknown CBadge's position is $\phi = (x, y, z)$, the Linear Equations Method (LEM) is to solve the quadratic system of equations below:

$$\begin{cases} (x-x_0)^2 + (y-y_0)^2 + (z-z_0)^2 = d_0^2 \\ \cdots \quad \cdots \\ (x-x_{n-1})^2 + (y-y_{n-1})^2 + (z-z_{n-1})^2 = d_{n-1}^2 \end{cases} \quad (1)$$

Let each equation above minus each other, we get a non-homogeneous linear system of n-1 equations, which can be notated as a form of matrix:

$$AX = b \qquad (2)$$

Apparently when $n > 4$, we get an over-constrained system. In the presence of measurement errors, there may not be a unique solution to the equation above. For avoiding this, we take a transformation on it:

$$A^T AX = A^T b \Rightarrow KX = B \qquad (3)$$

Where $K_{3\times3} = A^T A$, and $B_{3\times1} = A^T b$. The equation above is the main algorithm of Linear Equations Method (LEM). When $n > 4$, LEM can guarantee that $\sum_{i=1}^{n} (\|\phi - p_i\| - d_i)^2$ is minimal [6]. Nevertheless, LEM has several drawbacks:

1. Be disabled when the number of distance at a time is less than 4.

In those cases, we have to take the most recent distance stored in the slide windows as the received distances which are not actually received to make up 4 equations. Actually, those distances from the slide windows are not received simultaneously, which violate the simultaneity condition of distance, especially for mobile objects.

2. Take no account of the measurement noise on distance.

Due to environmental causes, the measured distances often deviate from the actual value more or less. The deviation is called measurement noise, which is inevitable.

3. Always generate large error, due to ill-conditioned coefficient matrix.

By experiments we find that the coefficient matrix K of (3) often becomes ill-conditioned. That is, any little change of the elements in K which is generated by measurement noise will result in a great change of X value by tens of times.

Because LEM considers naively that the location calculation is to directly solve the quadratic equations, we also call it naïve method or intuitive method. Though having quite a few drawbacks, LEM is regarded as a basic contrastive method with others.

Because LEM considers naively that the location calculation is to directly solve the quadratic equations, we also call it naïve method or intuitive method. Though having quite a few drawbacks, LEM is regarded as a basic contrastive method with others.

3.2.2 EKF Method

Aiming at the drawbacks of Naïve Method, we adopt another method, Extended Kalman Filter (EKF), to calculate location. Kalman Filter [7] is an optimal estimation method for a linear dynamic system perturbed by Gaussian white noise, while Extended Kalman Filter [8] is the Kalman Filter extended for non-linear system. EKF is composed of circular iterations, and each of iterations is called a time-step, which consists of two phases: prediction and correction, and each time-step can guarantee that the error covariance between the estimated value and actual value is minimal. Moreover, since EKF works on time domain, it owns low computation complexity, against those working on frequency domain, such as Wiener filter. On location calculation, Cicada adopts the EKF based on position-velocity model (PV model), which is described as follows:

In PV model, we set the state vector of EKF to a vector with 6 components, notated as $X = [x, y, z, vx, vy, vz]^T$, where (x, y, z) is object's 3-D coordinate position, and (vx, vy, vz) is object's velocity on 3 axes respectively. Because in Cicada the measurement value is only the distance, we let measurement vector m be the measured distance, which is a scalar value. So we get the system's equations of PV model:

$$\begin{cases} x_k = x_{k-1} + vx_{k-1}\Delta T + \frac{1}{2}ax_{k-1}\Delta T^2 \\ y_k = y_{k-1} + vy_{k-1}\Delta T + \frac{1}{2}ay_{k-1}\Delta T^2 \\ z_k = z_{k-1} + vz_{k-1}\Delta T + \frac{1}{2}az_{k-1}\Delta T^2 \\ vx_k = vx_{k-1} + ax_{k-1}\Delta T \\ vy_k = vy_{k-1} + ay_{k-1}\Delta T \\ vz_k = vz_{k-1} + az_{k-1}\Delta T \end{cases} \qquad (4)$$

Here, ΔT is the time difference between adjacent time-steps, and (ax, ay, az) is the acceleration on 3 axes respectively, which are regarded as zero-mean Gaussian white noises, namely $ax, ay, az \sim N(0, q)$. The system's equations in the matrix form is :

$$\begin{cases} X_k = \Phi X_{k-1} + \Gamma W_{k-1} \\ m_k = h(X_k) + \gamma_k \end{cases} \tag{5}$$

Here $\Phi = \begin{pmatrix} I_3 & \Delta T * I_3 \\ 0 & I_3 \end{pmatrix}$, $\Gamma = \begin{pmatrix} \dfrac{\Delta T^2}{2} * I_3 \\ \Delta T * I_3 \end{pmatrix}$, $W_k = \begin{pmatrix} ax \\ ay \\ az \end{pmatrix}$, I_3 is an 3×3 identity matrix,

and. γ_k is the measurement error, and it is also a zero-mean Gaussian white noise, namely $\gamma \sim N(0, r)$ where r is called *measurement noise covariance matrix*. $h(X_k) = \sqrt{(x_k - x_R)^2 + (y_k - y_R)^2 + (z_k - z_R)^2}$, where (x_R, y_R, z_R) is the known CReader's position. We define H as the Jacobian of h:

$$H(X) = \frac{1}{h(X)} [(x - x_R) \quad (y - y_R) \quad (z - z_R) \quad 0 \quad 0 \quad 0] \tag{6}$$

In the system's equations, the white noises ax, ay, az and γ are mutually independent. So we define the process noise covariance matrix Q_k as:

$$Q_k = E[W_k W_k^T] = q * I_3 \tag{7}$$

According to the theory of EKF, we can acquire the all computing equations (namely the iterator) of PV model as follows:

1. Prediction phase

$$X_k^{(-)} = \Phi X_{k-1}^{(+)} \tag{8}$$

$$P_k^{(-)} = \Phi P_{k-1}^{(+)} \Phi^T + \Gamma Q_{k-1} \Gamma^T \tag{9}$$

Here $X_k^{(-)}$ is the predicted state, and $P_k^{(-)}$ is the predicted error covariance.

2. Correction phase

$$K_k = P_k^{(-)} H_k^T (H_k P_k^{(-)} H_k^T + r)^{-1} \tag{10}$$

$$X_k^{(+)} = X_k^{(-)} + K_k [m_k - h(X_k^{(-)})] \tag{11}$$

$$P_k^{(+)} = P_k^{(-)} - K_k H_k P_k^{(-)} \tag{12}$$

Here K_k is Kalman gain, H_k is an abbreviation of $H(X_k)$, $P_k^{(+)}$ is the corrected error covariance, and $X_k^{(+)}$ is the corrected state as well as the output of EKF.

3.2.3 The Parameters of EKF

As a parameter of EKF, the measurement noise variance represents the average error during measuring distance. We put a pair of CReader and CBadge face-to-face on a line at various distances from 0.2m to 4m, and record about 300 samples reported by the CReader. By comparing the samples with actual distance, we know that the average measure error is 4.3cm, so $r = 4.3^2 \approx 18$. The process noise variance is more difficult to determine. For static objects, we set $q = 0$. For mobile objects, in our experiment, the device carrying a CBadge moves around a ring track, providing the perimeter C and cycle time T are measured, so the process noise variance is near to:

$$\sqrt{q} = \bar{a} = \frac{v}{T/4} = \frac{C/T}{T/4} = \frac{4C}{T^2} \tag{13}$$

4 Performance Evaluation

We conducted an experiment to evaluate the positioning performance of Cicada. In the experiment, we deploy 6 CReaders in a room, and divide the experiment into 3 groups: mobile-LEM experiment, mobile-EKF experiment, and static experiment. In mobile-LEM experiment we mount a CBadge on the top of a small trolley with a height of 83.5cm, and let the trolley move along a rectangle track at an average velocity of 11cm/s. The location calculation of mobile-LEM experiment adopts LEM. The scenario of the mobile-EKF experiment is the same as that of the mobile-LEM, and the unique difference from mobile-LEM experiment is that its location calculation adopts EKF. In the static experiment the CBadge is put on the 9 locations, and location calculation also adopts EKF. The whole scenario's plan-form is shown in Fig. 3.

Before the experiment, we still test out some approximate blind areas, which are also labeled in Fig. 3. A blind area is the area where less than 4 CReaders can hear the CBadge's whistle along LOS. As a result, we record the about 2780 position data in the mobile-EKF experiment, 400 position data in the mobile-LEM experiment, and 90

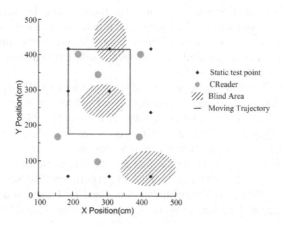

Fig. 3. The experiment scenario

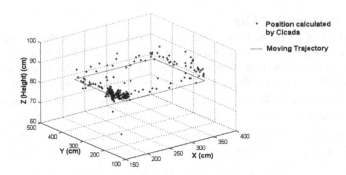

Fig. 4. The position data in mobile-EKF experiment

position data in the static experiment. As an example, the data in mobile-EKF experiment is shown in Fig. 4.

By our survey means available now, it is different to know the exact actual location of mobile objects at a certain time, while it is easy to get that of the static objects. Fortunately, because in the 3 groups of experiments the objects' heights are invariable, both for the mobile objects and for the static objects, it is easy to survey the z-axis error. In view of this cause, we first compare the z-axis error of the three experiment groups, and then infer the distance error according to the ratio of z-axis error to distance error in the static experiment. The z-axis error CDF (cumulative distribution function) of 3 groups of experiments is shown in Fig. 5.

As Fig. 5 shows, a half (the occurrence = 48%) error of the static experiment renders is no more than 2.2cm), that (the occurrence = 53%) of the mobile-EKF experiment is no more than 2.3cm too, but that (the occurrence = 47%) of the mobile-LEM reaches 18cm. The cause why the performance of the previous two are much higher than that of the last one is that the previous two adopt position-velocity model EKF while the last one adopts the LEM. This phenomenon illustrates EKF can not only minimize the effect of Gaussian white noise that LEM can not do, but also it is more immune to blind areas than LEM. Even if only a distance is received, EKF can still realize the state's prediction and correction. On the contrary, because in those cases LEM resorts to the distances in slide windows which violate the simultaneity condition, it generates a larger error for mobile objects. This result also proves the importance of location calculation method, and meanwhile explains why Cicada adopts EKF as its location calculation at last.

As is seen from Fig. 5 too, the error distribution of mobile-EKF experiment is quite almost near to that of the static experiment. And a little of difference is that, the maximal error of static experiment is no more than 6cm, the 99.8% error of mobile-EKF is no more than 12cm, and its maximal error reaches 21cm. This result proves that Cicada can guarantee the average height deviation (error) at a sub-decimeter level, either for static objects or for mobile objects. The cause of difference between both experiments is likely to be that, in the static experiment, the Slide Window Filter has enough time to filter out the invalid distance and EKF has enough time-steps to converge to the actual location, while those conditions can hardly be met in the mobile experiment.

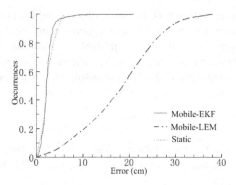

Fig. 5. The z-axis error CDF of three groups of experiments

Table 1. The error of the static experiment

	Each Dimension			3-D
	x	y	z	(distance)
Average error (cm)	2. 346	2. 450	2. 220	4. 359
Dimension error/Distance error	0. 538	0. 562	0. 510	

Although those discussed above focus on only one-dimension (height) error, we can also know the distance error (3 dimensions error). The each dimension error and distance error in the static experiment are shown in Table 1.

As Table 1 shows, the ratios of each dimension average error to the distance average error are approximately equal, and all near to $\sqrt{3}\big/3 \approx 0.578$. By utilizing this conclusion, we can infer the distance error in the mobile experiment according to the height error:

$$E_d = \sqrt{3} \times E_h \qquad (14)$$

Where E_d is the distance average error, and E_h is the height average error. By the equation, we can conclude that Cicada can provide the average location precision of about 5cm both for static objects and for mobile objects, a sub-decimeter precision.

Another experiment is designed to test the direction sensitivity of Cicada. In the experiment, a pair of CReader and CBadge is put apart at a distance of 2m. We adjust their orienting angle from -90° to +90°, and record the distance date they report. The result shows, no matter what the orienting angle is, the CReader can report the distance all the time, and meanwhile all error is below 15cm, an acceptable range.

The physical characteristics of Cicada are also listed as follows. Size: 8.8*3.0*4.3cm; weight: 50g (with batteries). Besides, the CBadge can work without connection to any PDA or computer. That is, Cicada can run independently.

5 Conclusion

In this paper, we have presented Cicada, an active system for locating indoor objects. The experiments illuminate that Cicada can not only provide a high location precision of about 5cm median resolution both for static objects and for mobile objects, but also its working area is omni-directional. Moreover, being mini, light and able to run independently, it is convenient enough to be portable or embedded into people's paraphernalia. Those advantages illuminate that, Cicada meets the various requirements of location-aware computing well, and it is a promising indoor location sensing system.

References

1. Dik Lun Lee, Jianliang Xu, Baihua Zheng, Wang-Chien Lee: Data Management in Location-Dependent Information Services. Pervasive computing, IEEE Press, Vol 1, No 3, pp. 65-72, 2002.
2. Hongliang Gu, Yuanchun Shi, Guangyou Xu, et al: A Core Model Supporting Location-Aware Computing in Smart Classroom. Proc 4th International Conference on Web-based Learning, pp.1-13, 2005.
3. McNeff, J.G.: The global positioning system. IEEE Transactions on Microwave Theory and Techniques, Vol 50, No 3, pp.645-652, 2002.
4. The introduction to smart space: http://www.nist.gov/smartspace/.
5. Allen Ka Lun Miu: Design and Implementation of an Indoor Mobile Navigation System. Master thesis, Massachusetts Institute of Technology, 2002.
6. S. Van Huffel, J.Vanderwalle: The Total Least Square Problem: Computational Aspects and Analysis. Society for Industrial and Applied Mathematics, Philadelphia, 1991.
7. Greg Welch, Gary Bishop: An Introduction to the Kalman Filter. Tutorial of SIGGRAPH 2001, pp.1-81, 2001.
8. Mohinder S. Grewal, Angus P. Andrews: Kalman filtering: theory and practice. Prentice-Hall Inc, New Jersey, USA, 1993.

Searchable Virtual File System: Toward an Intelligent Ubiquitous Storage

YongJoo Song, YongJin Choi, HyunBin Lee,
Donggook Kim, and Daeyeon Park

Korea Advanced Institute of Science and Technology,
Yuseong-gu, Daejeon 305-701, Republic of Korea
{yjsong, yjchoi, hblee, dgkim}@sslab.kaist.ac.kr,
daeyeon@ee.kaist.ac.kr

Abstract. As moving toward ubiquitous environment, demand for a easy data-lookup is growing rapidly. In an ocean of the exploding data, users should use some tools to find an right data. Intelligent ubiquitous applications also make the data-lookup service essential to the ubiquitous computing framework. This paper proposes a new, searchable, backward-compatible, virtual file system (S-VFS) for a easy file-lookup. We add the lookup functionality to VFS, the *de facto* standard layer in the file system. Users don't need to remember a full path to find a file any longer. Instead, each file has the attributes to use at lookup. S-VFS maintains the attributes in a normal file per partition. The indexing structures for the attributes are placed on a separated partition. Using the attribute files and the indexing structures, S-VFS processes queries provided by users and returns the result as a form of directory. In spite of this modification in VFS, S-VFS uses the legacy file systems without any modification. Since S-VFS supports the full backward compatibility, users can even browse hierarchically with the legacy path name.

1   Introduction

People say the ubiquitous computing world, in which the ubiquitous devices surrounds users with a lot of convenient services. To develop and support the services easily, ubiquitous frameworks are proposed [1] [2]. Modahl at el [3] surveyed and summarized the frameworks. They classified the components of the subsystems, including the Data Storage component. The Data Storage handles significant structured data movement between distributed nodes [4] , and so it requires the functionality of *Searching* and *Sharing*.

In addition, searching (or lookup) is becoming essential in the data management. As the Internet is widely used, people access the more information and the more files. Now, the local disk is too large and the files are too many to know where the desired file is. Marsden [5] proposed a file browser searches using the attributes of files. The searchable file systems are also proposed. Semantic File System [6] is the first attempt to find a file without the directory browsing, and inherited by BeFS [7] and LogicFS [8]. Commercially, Spotlight by Apple is a file management technique with a lookup functionality. Microsoft also attempts

Y.-C. Chung and J.E. Moreira (Eds.): GPC 2006, LNCS 3947, pp. 395–404, 2006.
© Springer-Verlag Berlin Heidelberg 2006

to add some searchable structures in WinFS - the next generation file system in Windows Longhorn. These file systems commonly modify a actual file system. They add the attribute fields in the metadata of each files and some indexing structure for querying.

We are motivated by the insight that *file system* in kernel is originally in charge of the data management. But the current file systems do not have enough functionality for searching, since previous research into file systems has mainly focused on the performance and the reliability. So, the Data Storage component is playing the role of searching in the middleware over file system layer. Note that the middleware approach means a redundant data management layer over file system, the original management layer in kernel. Previous file system approaches can't be a complete solution since they gave up the backward compatibility. Users should move the whole files to the new file system and not able to share with the others. Also they should give up the novel mechanisms for the performance like clustering, grouping, journalingand defragmentation [9], since the new searchable file system doesn't implement those mechanisms. We note that it is because of the integrating the lookup into the actual file system. *Virtual file system* layer would be the right place to have the functionality of searching and sharing without giving up the legacy file systems.

Searchable Virtual File System (S-VFS) makes the whole data space searchable. Like BeFS [7] and LogicFS [8], S-VFS also uses the attribute to look up a file. Users or applications give some attributes and values to the files, and retrieve using a query. However, VFS approach and the requirement of the backward compatibility need more mechanisms. First, a new query syntax is addressed to use S-VFS. S-VFS doesn't make the separated interface for the query. We integrate the query into the legacy interface of the *path*. The single query interface of S-VFS supports both the query and the browsing via path, even including the mixture form of those. Second, we propose a separated and dedicated partition for indexing of the attributes. S-VFS searches the whole mounted file systems, not only a partition. So indexing structure should be independent to a partition. We place the indexes at the separated partition and it is updated every mount operation. Finally, we also design a new mechanism for the attribute management. S-VFS is a modified VFS, but doesn't modify an actual file system. That means i-node can't be modified to insert the attributes like BeFS [7]. S-VFS manages the attributes as a normal file per partition. The attribute file has all information to retrieve a file, and is accessed only by S-VFS. Also, it accelerates the query processing by the parent caching.

The rest of this paper is organized as follows. Section 2 proposes the new design of Searchable VFS. The detailed internal structures are described in Section 3. Section 4 presents the steps of query processing. Section 5 provides the performance results. Finally, Section 6 concludes this paper.

2   Design

Virtual File System(VFS) is the root of naming and the adequate layer to implement a searching function. A design philosophy of Searchable-VFS is to support the *generalized query* with *backward compatibility*. S-VFS uses only the legacy file lookup interface *open()* and *opendir()*. Via the same interface, users can browse the single name space hierarchically, as well as search with some condition. S-VFS processes the generalized - even including the mixture of hierarchical path and searching condition - query. The following section describes the syntax of attribute and query supported by S-VFS. An Architectural overview is also presented. Again, note that there is no change in the implementation of actual file systems.

2.1 Attribute and Query

The attribute is mainly used to characterize a file [6] [8], and allows users to search a desired file without memorizing the whole path. Any name-value pair, $(name, value)$, can be an attribute. For example, a music file, *yesterday.mp3*, has three attributes in Fig 1; $(time, 3 : 40)$, $(singer, beatles)$ and $(genre, pop)$. The type of the attribute is pre-defined but can be any type, for example, int, float, string, enum and so on. S-VFS allows even the directory to have attributes. The directory attributes enable to describe a group attribute. In Fig 1, the attributes of the directory *favorite* say "it has music files selected at 2005." By the directory attribute, users can find the pre-grouped files. S-VFS supports the directory search.

Query generally consists of the required attributes. Users make a query with the desired attributes set and searching engine processes it and returns the result set. In S-VFS, the query is not only the set of attributes. A query Q can have directory path d and query fragment q. d means the required path which the target files should have. q represents the legacy query consists of required attributes. S-VFS processes q and d and even the repeated mixture of them.

Fig 2 presents the generalized query using the mixture of q and d. The query $Q1$ can be divided into $d1$, $q1$ and $d2$. The user is requiring the files with the following conditions; in the directory *proceeding* ($d2$) made in May 1 or 2 ($q1$), which is the one of the children of */home/yjsong* ($d1$). No previous work supports the mixed query like this. Using the single generalized query interface, S-VFS support both the hierarchical browsing and queryable interface including the mixture of them. So there is no need to modify the legacy applications.

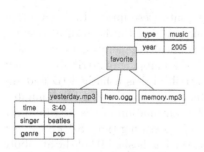

Fig. 1. An example of attributes

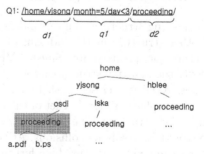

Fig. 2. Query in S-VFS

2.2   S-VFS Architecture

For the search functionality, S-VFS maintains two data structures, indexing partition and attribute table. S-VFS mimics the indexing of DBMS using the indexing partition. At OS installation time, the indexing partition has to be created like the swap partition. the partition is accessed only by S-VFS for indexing and searching. It consists of attribute hash table and indexing structures. The detailed structures will be described in the next section.

Attributes per file is managed as an attribute table in a normal file per partition. The table file contains all attributes of all files in its own partition. During the query processing, S-VFS first selects a distinct attribute in the query and searches the indexing structure for the attribute. And the remaining exact conditions are matched using the attribute table file. Heuristic for choosing a distinct attribute has been a hot issue in the research area of DBMS [10] , and it's out of the scope of this paper.

3   Data Structures

3.1   Indexing

S-VFS maintains a partition dedicated for the indexing structures. The indexing partition has the number of indexing structures equal to the number of the attributes. It means that all the files are sorted by each attributes.

During the query processing, S-VFS selects a distinct attribute. Index partition returns the indexing structure sorted by the distinct attribute. An indexing structure can be any form, B$^+$tree, hash table, Bloom filter [11] and even simple linked list(Fig 3). The only guideline is that they should get the minimum and maximum value of the query and result the sorted file list. B$^+$tree would be efficient for the attribute *create_time*. For attribute *keyword*, hash table may be better. User or system selects a proper indexing structure at adding an attribute.

Implementation of indexing structure should use the disk by block unit. Page cache is also used for the caching effect during the query processing.

3.2   Attribute Description Table

The indexing structure contains indexes. Attribute Description Table (ADT) is the other structure in the indexing partition, pointing the head of a indexing structure for an attribute. Since S-VFS dynamically generates, modifies and removes the indexing structures, there should be a mapping of attributes to their indexes. ADT is a closed hash table. Each attribute has a hashed ID and the mapping is placed at the bucket of the ID. The bucket has the first block number of indexing structure. The hashed ID and the information of the attribute are also stored for resolving collisions. At the query processing time, S-VFS can get the exact indexing structure by referring to ADT. The hashed ID of the attribute is used to the direct referencing, not a iterative lookup.

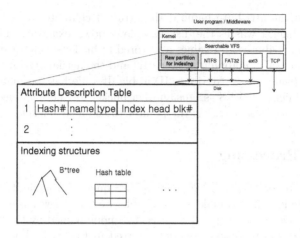

Fig. 3. Raw partition for indexing

3.3 Attribute Table

S-VFS creates the files named "attributes.svfs" at the root of each disk partition. The files have the attribute table that maintains all attribute information in each partition. The attribute table is a closed hash table that uses the hashed i-node number as a key(Fig 4). Each file of a partition has its bucket in the *attributes.svfs* at the root of the partition.

The bucket consists of the i-node number of the file, the reserved space for parent cache and the attributes information the file has. The parent cache is for accelerating the processing of the mixed query. Each bucket maintains the bucket number of the parent and the tree depth from the root directory. The detailed usage of the parent cache will be described in the next section.

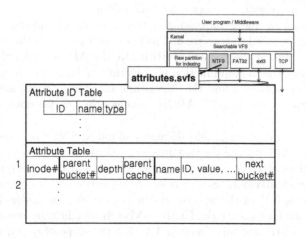

Fig. 4. Attribute Table as a normal file

The type of the attribute name is the array of character. The string of the name in each bucket wastes the disk and slows down exact-matching in query processing. So attributes and values are stored in buckets as a form of ID-value pair, $(ID, value)$. The mapping between ID and the actual attribute name is in the head of *attributes.svfs*, Attribute ID Table. If a file has too many attributes to store in its bucket, S-VFS assigns another bucket for the remained attributes. The last element of the bucket is the pointer to the next bucket.

4   Query Processing

S-VFS is an extended VFS. S-VFS makes VFS queryable while it still supports hierarchical file lookup. To make it searchable, we use a new *namei* function. In VFS, *namei* traverses a path and returns the i-node named by the path. S-VFS uses *modified-namei* to process queries inserted in the path. The procedure of query processing is shown in pseudo code form in Algorithm 4.1.

Algorithm 4.1. HIERARCHICAL_LOOKUP(parent, path)

(d, q, r) = **parse_path**(path);
inode = **namei_from**(parent, d);   //4.1.1 hierarchical traverse
if $(q \neq null)$
   inode = SEARCH(inode, q);   //4.1.2 query processing
  else
  return inode;
HIERARCHICAL_LOOKUP(inode, r);   //4.1.3 repeat from 1

To separate the query fragment q from the path, S-VFS call **parse_path**, which returns the first directory path d and the first query fragment q. r means the remained path except q and d. In the example of Fig 2, (d, q, r) is $(/home/yjsong/, month = 5/day < 3/, proceeding/)$.

The first step of query processing is the hierarchical traverse. The legacy namei function is called to traverse d. The parameter *parent* is the start point of traversing. It is *null* at the first call of HIERARCHICAL_LOOKUP. If there is no query to process, the lookup function returns the results of directory traversing. q, if exists, is processed using the Algorithm 4.2. The first parameter *parent* means the scope of searching. SEARCH processes the query among the children files of *parent*.

S-VFS doesn't maintain a multi-dimensional index. S-VFS first uses the index of the distinct attribute and the remained conditions are iteratively matched. To select the distinct attribute from *query*, **parse_query** divides the query into the fragment for each attribute. S-VFS refers ADT(section 3.2) to get the indexing structure(section 3.1) of the selected distinct query dq. The indexing structure can pick out the files satisfy dq. Lastly, **isMatch** matches the remained conditions using the attribute table(section 3.3). For the scope of query, **isParent** is another condition of the exact matching. S-VFS makes a virtual directory that has the final list of the files. HIERARCHICAL_LOOKUP recursively repeats to traverse the remained path r. The traverse would be ended when there is no query to process.

Algorithm 4.2. SEARCH(parent, query)

---

qlist = **parse_query**(query);
select a distinct query dq from qlist   //4.2.1 select a distinct condition
indexing_structure = **ADT**(dq.attribute_name);
flist = **indexing_structure(dq)**;   //4.2.2 lookup by the distinct condition
create a virtual directory vd
for each (file in flist){
  attributes = **AttributeTable**(file);
  if (**isMatch**(qlist, attributes) && **isParent**(parent, file)) //4.2.3 exact matching
    insert file into vd;
}
return vd.inode;

Limiting the scope of query is very expensive. There are only two ways to get the limited result. The one is to use a candidate file set first. If a query q should be processed within the scope of *parent*, the candidate set is the list of all files in the subdirectories of *parent*. The condition of q should be matched iteratively, and any indexing structure can't be used since indexing structures are not available for all scopes.

S-VFS takes the other approach, checking *parent* later. S-VFS checks whether a file is a child of *parent* during the last iterative matching. It's also an expensive task. S-VFS has *parent cache* in the attribute table to accelerate the checking. S-VFS checks the parents of a file following *parent bucket pointer* and *depth* in the attribute table. Parent cache stores the result of the checking and eliminates the repeated checking.

Let's back to the example of Fig 2, Fig 5 presents the processing steps of the example. At first, the query $Q1$ is divided into $(d1, q1, d2)$. By Algorithm 4.1, S-VFS traverses $d1$, $/home/yjsong/$, and gets i-node number and the bucket number 5 in the attribute table. S-VFS performs Algorithm 4.2 with the parameters $(5, month = 5/day < 3)$. Let's assume that the distinct attribute is *day* in this case.[1] The distinct query dq is $day < 3$. S-VFS gets the head block number 50 from the ADT in the raw partition for indexing. Using the indexing structure, S-VFS gets the bucket list of files which satisfy $day < 3$. The last conditions are $month = 5$ and $parent = yjsong$(that is, $parentbucket = 5$). By Algorithm 4.2.3, S-VFS iteratively matches the last conditions using the attribute table. In Fig 5, the directory *proceeding* in the bucket 9 matches $month = 5$. To check the parent, S-VFS follows the parent bucket field. S-VFS meets *osdi* and it has the number of the target parent bucket 5. Or, S-VFS climbs until the depth is

---

[1] To choose a distinct attribute, we made a simple heuristic using the query cost mechanism like [10] . S-VFS maintains the cost information in ADT.

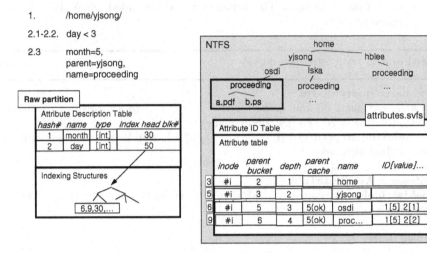

Fig. 5. An example of query processing

smaller than that of the target parent, 2. Since the parent checking is successful, S-VFS puts OK at the parent cache field on the path. At the next checking for another file, S-VFS can refer OK or NOK sign in the cache.

After the last matching, we get the virtual directory which means $/home/yjsong/month = 5/day < 3/$. S-VFS repeats Algorithm 4.1 with the directory. It will only traverse a directory *proceeding*. Here is the optional technique to enhance the processing. In Algorithm 4.1, the first path in r can be moved to the last condition in q. In case of Fig 5, $(/home/yjsong/, month = 5/day < 3/, proceeding/)$ can be transformed to $(/home/yjsong/, month = 5/day < 3/name = proceeding, null)$. This query transformation may reduce the number of the iteration of Algorithm 4.1.

5   Evaluation

We assess the performance of our S-VFS on improving the speed of looking up files. Experiments were conducted on the linux server with Intel Pentium-III 800MHz processor, 256MB memory, a 61.4GB Maxtor 5400RPM E-IDE drive. S-VFS mechanisms are implemented in the application layer and the actual disk partitions. We uses a simple open hash table for the indexing structures in the raw partition.

We evaluated S-VFS with the lookup performance. The test program searches the target files selected randomly among a working set. We used a linux kernel source tree as a working set. The linux kernel 2.6.7-21 source tree has 34,007 files and we selects a subset of the tree as a working set. We varies the number of files in the working set from 10 to 34,007. The lookup test is iterated to get the meaningful average elapsed time.

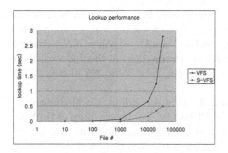

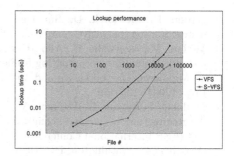

Fig. 6. Lookup performance   **Fig. 7.** Lookup performance - log scale

Fig 6 presents the average lookup time. X-axis is the log-scaled number of files in the working set. Y-axis is the elapsed time per lookup. When the test program uses the legacy VFS, it should traverse the whole working set to lookup the target file. So the lookup time is in direct proportion to the number of files in the working set. Using S-VFS, the lookup times are ignorable by the order of hundreds of files in the working set. When the working set size is over the 10,000, S-VFS shows the lookup performance logarithmically proportional to the working set size.

Fig 7 is a log-scaled Y-axis version of Fig 6. VFS test shows the straight proportional line in Fig 7, too. S-VFS shows the minimum lookup time about a number of milliseconds. It means the fixed overhead of S-VFS for accessing the ADT, the indexing structure, and the attribute table. Because of the overhead, the legacy VFS shows the better performance at the small working set. As growing the size of the working set, the indexing structure lookup time becomes dominant. The results over 10,000 files presents the strongest point of S-VFS lookup, logarithmical proportion to the working set size.

6   Conclusions

In this paper, we have presented the searchable virtual file system, S-VFS. S-VFS makes the name space of file systems searchable. S-VFS doesn't need any changes in the actual file systems and the legacy applications. So S-VFS can support the ubiquitous middleware and storage with the minimum effort. Currently, S-VFS is in an initial prototype state. However, our new concepts for the VFS layer introduces a number of challenges for the ubiquitous middleware and storage system.

It is another challenge to consider the concurrency and the consistency in the access of S-VFS data structures. While the data structures of S-VFS already are free to access concurrently, it can be a performance bottleneck.

References

1. Romn, M., Hess, C., Cerqueira, R., Ranganathan, A., Campbell, R.H., Nahrstedt, K.: Gaia: a middleware platform for active spaces. SIGMOBILE Mob. Comput. Commun. Rev. **6**(4) (2002) 65–67

2. Garlan, D., Siewiorek, D., Smailagic, A., Steenkiste, P.: Project aura: Toward distraction-free pervasive computing (2002)
3. Modahl, M., Agarwalla, B., Abowd, G., Ramachandran, U., Saponas, T.S.: Toward a standard ubiquitous computing framework. In: Proceedings of the 2nd workshop on Middleware for pervasive and ad-hoc computing, New York, NY, USA, ACM Press (2004) 135–139
4. Modahl, M., Bagrak, I., Wolenetz, M., Hutto, P., Ramachandran, U.: Mediabroker: An architecture for pervasive computing. In: PERCOM '04: Proceedings of the Second IEEE International Conference on Pervasive Computing and Communications (PerCom'04), Washington, DC, USA, IEEE Computer Society (2004) 253
5. Marsden, G., Cairns, D.E.: Improving the usability of the hierarchical file system. In: SAICSIT '03: Proceedings of the 2003 annual research conference of the South African institute of computer scientists and information technologists on Enablement through technology, , Republic of South Africa, South African Institute for Computer Scientists and Information Technologists (2003) 122–129
6. Gifford, D.K., Jouvelot, P., Sheldon, M.A., James W. O'Toole, J.: Semantic file systems. In: SOSP '91: Proceedings of the thirteenth ACM symposium on Operating systems principles, New York, NY, USA, ACM Press (1991) 16–25
7. Giampaolo, D.: Practical File System Design with the Be File System. Morgan Kaufmann Publishers Inc., San Francisco, CA, USA (1998)
8. Padioleau, Y., Ridoux, O.: A logic file system. In: USENIX '03: Proceedings of USENIX 2003 Annual Technical Conference. (2003) 99–112
9. Ahn, W.H., Park, D.: Mitigating data fragmentation for small file access. IEICE Trans. Information and Systems $E86-D(6)$ (2003) 1126–1133
10. Reiss, F.R., Kanungo, T.: A characterization of the sensitivity of query optimization to storage access cost parameters. In: SIGMOD '03: Proceedings of the 2003 ACM SIGMOD international conference on Management of data, New York, NY, USA, ACM Press (2003) 385–396
11. Koloniari, G., Pitoura, E.: Bloom-based filters for hierarchical data. In: the 5th Workshop on Distributed Data and Structures (WDAS). (2003)

A Collaborative Privacy-Enhanced Alibi Phone

Hsien-Ting Cheng[1], Ching-Lun Lin[2], and Hao-hua Chuinst[1]

[1] Department of Computer Science and Information Engineering,
Graduate Institute of Networking and Multimedia,
National Taiwan University, Taipei, Taiwan
{r92006, hchu}@csie.ntu.edu.tw
[2] Department of Computer Science,
Columbia University,
New York, NY 10027, USA
cl2399@columbia.edu

Abstract. This paper presents a collaborative privacy protection approach that not only filters context information and reduces its granularity, but also intelligently replaces the filtered-out context with an artificial context considered appropriate by its user. The benefit of this approach is that individuals accessing the filtered context cannot detect the presence of filtering, namely, filtering becomes imperceptible. This new approach is used as a basis for designing, implementing and evaluating a collaborative privacy-enhanced alibi phone, allowing user to imperceptibly conceal surrounding ambient sound from callers, while leaving callers unaware of this filtering.

1 Introduction

Many individuals feel that they reveal more (context) information to others regarding their daily life than is necessary. For example, when receiving a voice call or participating in a video conferencing session, individuals not only disclose to callers our voice and facial expression, which is the only information they actually want them to hear/see. Microphones and cameras also capture and transmit ambient sound and background scenery to callers, reveal additional context information regarding our current location and activities. In some situations, such additional information can cause unnecessary embarrassment and misunderstanding to the callees. To avoid these situations, many callees often refuse to communicate with callers when they consider it inconvenient. This work uses the following two scenarios to illustrate situations like those described above:

1. Joe has told his girlfriend Jane that he was going to play basketball with his male friends. Unfortunately, some of his male friends did not show up, leading to cancellation of the basketball game. Instead, Joe decided to meet some female friends in a coffee shop for a friendly chat. At the coffee shop, Joe then receives a phone call from Jane. Joe was hesitant to answer this call,

Y.-C. Chung and J.E. Moreira (Eds.): GPC 2006, LNCS 3947, pp. 405–414, 2006.

because he was concerned that Jane would hear that he was with female friends, possibly causing an unnecessary misunderstanding.

2. Joe noticed a video phone call from his supervisor while he was entertaining an unexpected client at a local jazz bar. Since this was an unexpected visit, Joe had not informed his supervisor Jill about it. Again, Joe was hesitant to pick up the video phone call because he did not want Jill to see or hear the bar environment and loud Jazz music and thus conclude that Joe was slacking off from work.

A simple solution to the above dilemmas would be to filter out the ambient sound and background scene [1]. However, this simple solution is insufficient in situations in which the callers are expecting certain types of ambient sound or background scenes from the callees. In the 1st scenario, Jane would expect Joe to be in the basketball court and expect to hear the sound of basketball being played. In the 2nd scenario, Jill would expect Joe to be working in a busy office and expect see sights and hear sounds confirming this. The ideal solution should produce the expected ambient noise and background scene V the basketball court or the busy office. Notably, filtering alone can lead to a noticeable absence of ambient sound and background scenes, particularly when callers are expecting callees to be in certain places with distinctive ambient sounds and scenes. Filtering may create the undesirable impression that callees are intentionally and explicitly hiding certain information from callers. Therefore, a new approach to privacy protection is required that does not simply protect the context information of callees, but simultaneously can make such filtering imperceptible to callers.

This paper proposes a new privacy protection approach that not only filters out context information, but also intelligently substitutes the filtered-out context information with artificial context information considered appropriate by its user, thus creating the appearance of imperceptible filtering to callers. This approach is collaborative in the sense that other peers on the network who may have access to such artificial context information can help by contributing them. Based on this new approach, this work has designed an audio-based privacy protection system for use with a mobile phone. To achieve imperceptible filtering, it is designed to do the following: (1) filter out background ambient sound from the voice of the callee, (2) find an appropriate ambient sound source expected by the caller over a peer network, and (3) mix the selected ambient sound source with the voice of the callee. Consider the 1st scenario described previously. When his privacy-enhanced cell phone detects that Joe is not currently at the expected location on the basketball court, it can filter out the background chatter of Joes female friends, find an ambient sound source on a basketball court and mix this ambient sound with Joes voice. Consequently, Jane will hear ambient sound resembling the location where she expects Joe to be, namely a basketball court. Joe thus can feel comfortable picking up phone calls anytime anywhere regardless of his current ambient environments.

2   Related Work

Previous works on protecting context information were focused primarily on information filtering and granularities. Project Aura [2] proposed an access control mechanism for filtering out fine-grained information from raw context data, so that the provided context information would match the access privileges given to the request. For example, location information can be determined based on an image captured by a camera. If a user is only granted access to the location information, Aura will filter out and remove the image, and return only a text-based location description. In comparison, the proposed system not only filters information granularity, but also intelligently substitutes the filtered-out context information with the artificial context information. As a result, the proposed system can create the appearance of imperceptible filtering to people accessing the context information of call recipients.

Several commercial products are available that can eliminate ambient noises. The Boom Noise Canceling Headset [2] enables users to communicate clearly in loud noisy environments. This headset can be plugged into most cellular phones. The headset is fitted with two microphones. The mouthpiece microphone collects the voice of the user together with some of the ambient noises surrounding the user. Meanwhile, the noise microphone picks up all the ambient noise but little of the users voice. The handset subtracts the ambient noise gathered by the noise microphone from the audio signals gathered by the mouthpiece microphone. The net result of the subtraction is a pure recording of the speakers voice.

Some cellular phone service providers, such as TransAsia Telecom in Taiwan [3], are currently offering services that enable users to mix background music into their phone calls locally and centrally, respectively. To use these services, users must establish a schedule for mixing the music or sound effect, such as noise of traffic jam, a circus parade, a thunderstorm, a ringing phone, into the phone call. Additionally, users can decide what and how to mix the music or sound effect based on the identity of the callee/caller. Nevertheless, the proposed system differs from these services in several respects. First, both of the previous system lack the ambient noise filtering feature, which will be crucial in a location with extremely noise background, simply mixing is unable to replace the original ambient noise. Second, the previous service provided by TransAsia Telecom [3] is designed to make phone calls more entertaining rather than being designed to provide privacy protection. Moreover, the selection of background music for mixing with voice in previous systems is static and limited, only some prerecorded sound effect are available. Our proposed system can search through a peer network of collaborative users and the available background sound at their current locations, to find the desired ambient and mix it in real time, which actually meets the requirements of users.

A group of cell phone users have formed an alibi and excuse club [4], to provide more substantial excuses, club member has to pick up a phone to let the boss know of a buddys tardiness and make his wife believe her husband has an important meeting when he is really at bar. Such club uses a real manual conversation to hide context information, however, even the founder of the club admits there existing moral problems from an integrity standpoint.

3   Challenges and Approach

This study identifies the following technical challenges in realizing this privacy-enhanced phone.

- Detecting whether the user is at the expected location. Detecting this requires the user to maintain a schedule of whether he/she is expected to be at different times. By consulting the schedule of a user and comparing his/her expected location with his/her current location, the system can determine whether the user is at the expected location. Currently, the most popular locating system is GPS. However, GPS does not work indoors. To overcome this problem, the proposed system pre-defines some location profiles, such as office, transportation, countryside, and so on. User can then manually change current location profile. Additionally, audio recognition techniques can be applied to ambient environment sound to automatically infer the current location profile of the user.
- Quickly locate an appropriate ambient sound source at the expected location. The amount of time required to locate an appropriate ambient sound source must not exceed a few phone rings, which is the amount of time the caller is willing to wait for the callee to answer the call. If no appropriate ambient sound can be identified sufficiently quickly, the caller might abandon the call, as well as the callee may miss the phone call.
- Filter out background ambient sound and mix the selected ambient sound in real time. Audio filtering and mixing have been active areas of research on speech processing. When selecting speech processing techniques for the proposed system, the limited processing power on mobile devices must be considered, and the real time constraints of voice calls.
- Security attacks: numerous attacks can be made on the proposed system to check if a user is using an alibi background sound. Consider the following attack. To find out whether Joe is at his expected location, an attacker (or his/her friend) can make a phone call to Joe from Joes expected location. If Joe is currently not at the expected location, his cell phone will geocast a message over the peer network that requests the ambient sound source at the expected location. The attacker (or his/her friend) will then receive this request message from Joe immediately after calling Joe. This means that the attacker can tell whether Joe is at the expected place or not, depending on whether the attacker receives an ambient sound request at the expected place or not. In the 2nd attack, the attacker can monitor the data packet containing requests for ambient sound sources. The attacker can then extract the IP address in the data packet and map it to the likely physical location.
- Reliability: an active ambient sound source can sometimes fail during a call. Failures can result from wireless network disconnection, the source device running out of battery, and so on. Since failure of ambient sound source can make filtering visible to the callers, the proposed system has to be reliable under all these unexpected conditions.
- Peer-to-peer architecture vs. centralized architecture: two possible methods exist for building a peer network of collaborative users: peer-to-peer vs.

centralized. In section 5, advantages and disadvantages of these two approaches are compared, and the peer-to-peer method is chosen for implementation.

4   Design

Figure 1 shows the design of our privacy-enhanced Phone. The design comprises four components: Context Agent, Location Scheduler, Ambient Sound Locator, and Voice Processor. The executing flow is described through the following five steps:

1. Receive a ring-tone on a mobile.
2. Context Agent determines the current location of the callee via GPS or by checking the pre-defined location of the user.
3. Location Scheduler compares the current location of the callee with his/her expected location schedule. If the callee is not at the expected location, they are prompted to see if they need ambient sound at the expected location.
4. Ambient Sound Locator identifies several ambient sound sources and selects one as the active sound source.
5. Voice Processor filters out the original ambient sound and mixes in the ambient sound source.

This work has implemented the phone on HP iPAQ running the Microsoft Windows CE Operating System. This study has developed and deployed a voice processor capable of filtering and mixing ambient sounds. The ambient sound mixer is implemented by adding two waveforms and then adjusting the coefficients a and b to yield the optimum performance.

$$S(t_k) = aS_1(t_k) + bS_2(t_k) \tag{1}$$

S_1, S_2: voice signal; t_k: time index

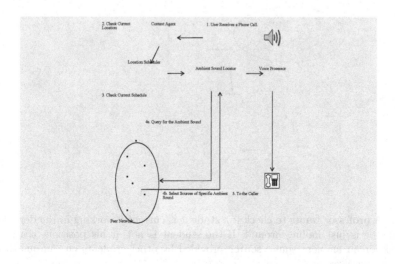

Fig. 1. The executing flow of the privacy-enhanced phone

However, designing a smooth and effective ambient sound filter is more complex than mixing. Developing such a filter is equivalent to the problem of noise reduction in the field of speech processing. This study examines two general approaches for noise reduction. The 1st approach employs the whole voice sequence as an input, and then calculates a global optimal noise signal. This approach requires advance knowledge of the entire voice sequence. The 2nd approach is a frame-by-frame method based on the Wiener Filter [5] that takes two frames at a time, and then calculates noise signals locally. This approach has the advantage property of online frame-by-frame processing, which is applicable to the targeted voice conferencing application. In addition, the 2nd approach is fast enough to run in real time. Therefore, it is used.

5   Centralized vs. P2P Architecture

Two possible approaches exist for realizing the peer network of collaborative users who can help others by acting as ambient sound sources: centralized vs. peer-to-peer (P2P). In a centralized architecture, the system maintains a directory server of client locations, which can be accomplished by server periodically polling the locations of clients or alternatively client pushing the location information to the server. The location directory server responds to a client request for the ambient sound sources at a specified location or a location profile. The centralized architecture can also deploy powerful, stationary voice processing servers for running audio filtering and mixing software, and thus can alleviate the problem of limited processing and power for mobile devices. In the

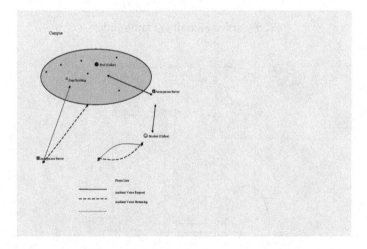

Fig. 2. A professor wants to check if a student is currently working in the department building or is just fooling around. If the student is not at his position, the student can ask for an ambient sound source provided by other students on campus through anonymous server.

centralized architecture, all voice and data communications must go through some centralized servers that are responsible for the privacy and security protection of users making requests or providing ambient sound sources.

However, the centralized architecture requires infrastructure support for deployment. Therefore, this work favors the P2P architecture; namely, direct peer node communications between the requestors and providers of ambient sound sources [6]. This work favors the P2P architecture because the application presented in this work fundamentally has a P2P flavor V in which the participating users act as service providers sharing their ambient sounds, and also act as service consumers when they require ambient sounds.

To address the security attacks described in section 2, this work proposes using anonymous redirection servers. The security attacks involve an attacker who can monitor the data packet containing requests for ambient sound sources, and then infer physical location using the IP address in the data packet. Using anonymous servers stops this attack because the requests are redirected through anonymous servers, and these anonymous servers can then remove the IP address from the request. This is shown in Fig 2.

6   Evalution

This work evaluated the performance of the privacy enhanced phone both objectively and subjectively. In objective part, the evaluation metrics include ambient sound filtering quality and communication delay; user study was conducted subjectively to evaluate the audible sound quality and the psychological state of user.

6.1   Objective Evaluation

- Ambient sound filtering: To measure the noise reduction performance of the Weiner Filter, this work employs segmental SNR (signal-to-noise ratio) improvement which is calculated by:

$$SNR_{improve} = segSNR_{out} - segSNR_{in} \tag{2}$$

  Three types of background noise (speech, jazz, rock music) are artificially added to a sample of clean speech. Each noise has different SNR: -5dB and 5dB. Table 1 lists the noise reduction results.
- Communication delay: the communication delay time was measured, including the processing times for audio filtering and mixing, and network delay. The results listed in Table 2 exhibited good performance in terms of voice processing time and network delay time. Experiments were performed under three different conditions: without filtering and mixing, with filtering only, and with both filtering and mixing.

6.2   Subjective Evaluation: User Study

The system design should consider actual audible sound quality and user psychological state. Current systems are all unable to transmit and mix ambient

Table 1. The improvement of the noise reduction using Weiner Filter for three different noise types: speech, jazz, and rock music. And each type with two inputs SNR (measured in dB).

Noise type	Speech		Jazz		Rock Music	
Input SNR	5	−5	5	−5	5	−5
Improvement	7.3	11.6	8.9	13.3	8.2	12.7

Table 2. Delay time (process + transmit): evaluated with none of filter and mixer, filter only, and both filter and mix respectively

	None	Filter Only	Both Filter and Mix
Delay time (sec)	0.64	1.53	1.71

sound in real time. Thus, current systems cannot provide users with full privacy protection. This study describes the actual experiences of 32 participants who evaluated the system from different perspectives.

This User Study aims to understand the services offered by the proposed system and whether its performance can meet expectations. A comparison is made with overall system efficiency to see whether the proposed system achieves better efficiency. Additionally, this study surveys user satisfaction with the proposed system. The following outlines complete process and results.

Independent Variables: The calling procedure of individual users.

Dependent Variables: Actual subjective sound heard, call quality transmission, privacy protection, subjective satisfaction ranked based on overall calling experience, user perception of call quality, and system user friendliness.

Participants: Thirty-two participants aged 20-40 years old were selected for the survey. The subjects were frequent PDA and web phone users who possessed their own PDAs. Few of the participants had any experience with ambient sound filtering or mixing.

Procedures: Participants were briefed on the goals and procedures of the user study. The participants were provided a demonstration of the procedures for dialing using the PDA. The entire evaluation comprised two stages. In stage one, each participant was asked to answer three phone calls made to them. The first call involved asking the participants to answer an unfiltered call. The second call involved filtering of ambient sound. The third call used the proposed system for filtering and mixing various ambient sounds as required. In stage two, each participant was asked to rate the overall quality of the proposed system. The score is ranging from 1 to 5 where higher value indicates better performance. In addition, each participant completed the survey form with their background details and personal experience.

Results: The result shows 62.5

- The subject is the boss: Employees feel uncomfortable about the boss being aware of their location.

- The subject is the boyfriend or girlfriend: Relationships with the opposite sex are sometimes complicated, and sometimes when a person in a relationship ends up unexpectedly in a place not previously reported to their partner, even when there is nothing wrong, they may feel concerned about potential misunderstandings should their partner discover their true whereabouts.
- The subjects are parents: Students/adolescents sometimes frequent places that parents disapprove of, for example pubs, KTVs, billiard halls, and video game parlors. When the parents call and find that the children are in such places, the children are likely to feel that their privacy has been invaded. Additionally, children can also feel apologetic at causing their parents unnecessary worry by letting them know they are frequenting such places.

Almost all collected feedbacks are positive. The average score rated by all participants is 4.37. There are 93.75% of participants willing to use the proposed system to protect their privacy. Most users have a high regard for the privacy protection offered by the proposed system. These users consider that the system provides better protection than the previous ambient sound filter telephone system. Furthermore, the proposed system locates and mixes in the desired ambient sounds nearly in real-time, fully satisfying user privacy considerations. However, some users feel that the system efficiency and voice quality can still be improved.

7 Future Work

As shown in Table 1, ambient sound filtering quality for speech is lower than when the filtering is applied to other noise. We believe that this is due to the fact that there is a small difference between the voice of the user and background speech; therefore they are more difficult to distinguish. Future studies can attempt to enhance the filter to enable it to fully detect and remove background speech.

The current system is designed and implemented using the P2P architecture. Future studies should seek to improve this P2P application in the areas of scalability, security and privacy, quality of services, performance, fault tolerance, and so on. We believe that this new system for privacy protection is easily applicable to video and can help users avoid sharing sensitive background scenes withy callers. Future studies can develop video filtering and mixing methods that can substitute existing backgrounds with other scene without making callers aware of the deception.

References

1. The Boom Noise Canceling Headset.
   http://www.thetravelinsider.info/roadwarriorcontent/boomheadset.htm (2003)
2. U. Hengartner, P. Steenkiste: Access Control to Information in Pervasive Computing Environments. HotOS. (2003)

3. TransAsis Telecommunicatios, Taiwan.
   http://www.hank.net.tw/channel/TL/BGM/service.htm (2002)
4. Elisa Batista: Phone become alibi for liars.
   http://www.wired.com/news/wireless/0,1382,63439,00.html (2004)
5. Speech Processing, Transmission and Quality Aspects (STQ); Distributed speech
   recognition; Advanced front-end feature extraction algorithm; Compression algorithms. ETSI ES 202 050 v.1.1.3 5.1 Noise Reduction. (2003)
6. Q. Lv, P. Cao, E. Cohen, K. Li, and S. Shenker: Search and replication in unstructured peer-to-peer networks. Proc. of the 16th ACM Intl Conf. on Supercomputing.
   (2002)

The Semantic Grid: Requirements, Infrastructure and Methodology

Kashif Iqbal[1], Stefan Decker[1], and Mark Baker[2]

[1] Digital Enterprise Research Institute,
National University of Ireland, Galway
{kashif.iqbal, Stefan.decker}@deri.org
[2] Advanced Computing and Emerging Technologies (ACET) Centre,
The University of Reading
mark.baker@computer.org

Abstract. The Grid offers a number of advantages for undertaking computation, information processing, and collaboration, which can be applied to both science and industry. In this paper, we will discuss where Semantic Web technology can augment grid technology to help bring it to its full potential; especially with applications in e-Science, e-Research, and e-Business. The proposed marriage between Semantic Web and the Grid is known as Semantic Grid. The Semantic Grid is an extension of the current grid in which information and services are given well-defined meaning, enabling computers and people to work together for efficiently and effectively. The Semantic Grid vision is not new, but what we focus on in this paper are the areas where Semantic Web technologies can supplement grid technologies. In particular the key components for a Semantic Grid infrastructure and a methodology to realize this infrastructure by describing the state of the art of the most relevant technologies.

1 Introduction

Web Services provide a standard means of interoperability among different software applications, running on heterogeneous platforms for seamless application integration. Programs providing simple services can interact with each other to compose sophisticated value-added services (Orchestration). Web Services are built around ubiquitous, open Web and Internet standards such as TCP/IP, HTTP/S, Java, HTML, and XML, as well as other standard technologies such as SOAP, WSDL, and UDDI [1]. Web Services standards define the format of the message, specify the interface to which a message is sent, describe conventions for mapping the contents of the message into and out of the programs implementing the service, and define mechanisms to publish and discover service interfaces.

The Semantic Web [12] is an extension of the current Web in which information is given well defined meaning, allowing more efficient and effective cooperation among computers and people . It encompasses the idea that data can be defined and linked in a way so that it can be effectively discovered, automated, integrated, and reused across a variety of applications. The Web can reach its full potential, if its data can be shared and processed by automated tools as well as by people. On the other hand

Y.-C. Chung and J.E. Moreira (Eds.): GPC 2006, LNCS 3947, pp. 415–426, 2006.
© Springer-Verlag Berlin Heidelberg 2006

Semantic Web services based on existing Semantic Web and Web Services standards focuses on describing Web Services interfaces in a machine processable way, so that that these service descriptions can be processed by software agents in order to automate the tasks of service discovery, composition and invocation with minimal or no human intervention.

Grid technologies that are build on top of the Web facilitating global sharing of not just information, but also of resources ranging from computational and data storage devices to scientific instruments. Resource sharing among physically distributed organizations governed by their own administrative policies remains a challenge. Grid technologies attempt to overcome these problems by providing the protocols, services and software components needed to allow flexible and controlled resource sharing on a large scale. One concept at the heart of grid is the Virtual Organization (VO) [2]. It is a dynamic collection of individuals, institutions and resources that can be grouped together in order to share resources as they tackle common tasks. Emerging applications require that grid middleware should allow new capabilities to be constructed dynamically and transparently from a range of distributed services. In order to engineer new grid applications it is desirable to reuse existing components and information resources and to assemble and co-ordinate these in a flexible manner. Partially, for this reason, the Grid has moved away from a collection of protocols to a service-oriented approach. The Open Grid services Architecture (OGSA) [3] unifies Web Services with grid requirements and techniques. This paper highlights how and where the Semantic Web technology can augment various parts of the Grid.

The rest of the paper is organized as follows: Section 2 describes the vision of Semantic Grid community. Section 3 highlights the requirements for the Semantic Grid. Section 4 continues the discussion on the Semantic Grid Infrastructure and architecture and Section 5 discusses the methodology and state of the art of the technologies. Finally Section 6 discusses issues and future directions for Semantic Grid efforts.

2 The Semantic Grid Vision

Both the Grid and the Semantic Web communities started separately as two distinct research efforts in computer science. Until recently the Grid and the Semantic Web communities were working individually, despite the convergence of their respective visions and commonalities in their interests and challenges. Both have a need for computationally accessible and sharable metadata to support automated information discovery, integration and aggregation. Both operate in a large-scale, distributed, dynamic, and error-prone environments. The Semantic Grid is an initiative to develop effective methods for enabling such complex infrastructures.

According to the Semantic Grid community, the vision (see Figure 1) reflects that both the Grid and Semantic Web efforts are not orthogonal to each other. Fundamentally, they are both about joining resources together in order to achieve new things. For instance, to build new grid applications, we can reuse and reprocess the available services, data, workflows and indeed knowledge, from existing sources. We need the Grid to virtualize the heterogeneity of the underlying resources, the latest

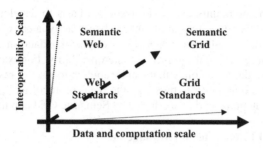

Fig. 1. Semantic Grid Vision [4]

grid problem is to assemble new services, or even new grids, quickly, easily and as automatically as possible from diverse resources. By analogy with the Semantic Web, the Semantic Grid is an extension of the current grid in which information and services are given well-defined meaning, better enabling computers and people to work in cooperation [4]. We believe the most logical way of realizing the Semantic Grid vision is to apply Semantic Web technologies into grid developments, from the machinery of the Grid infrastructure (such as Grid services) up to the Grid applications. It is important to note that the 'semantics' permeate the full vertical extent of the Grid and is not just a semantic (or knowledge) layer on top: it is semantics in, on and for the Grid. As the Semantic Web is to the Web, so is the Semantic Grid to the Grid.

3 Semantic Grid Requirements

In this section, we will identify the key application areas where Semantic Web technology can be applied to bring the grid to its full potential. The discussion will lead towards a Semantic Grid roadmap.

3.1 Security, Trust and Provenance

Security is one of the key building blocks for VOs. There are requirements for trust, authentication, encryption, privacy, non-repudiation and digital rights management when multiple stakeholders with their local administrative domains and usage policies are involved. Policies need to be expressed and applied to multiple resources with a consistent interpretation, so that automated reasoning can be undertaken to identify the correct role that should be assigned to members, based on their credentials and local and VO-wide policies. The expression and propagation of trust based on delegation of credentials, so that automated reasoning can be undertaken, has a key role during collaborations within a VO or between multiple VOs. Provenance and the context of information have to be identified in order to judge the quality of the content and the associated services. These are necessary when integrating data from different sources in a grid environment.

We believe that Semantic Web has much to offer for grid security, trust and provenance requirements identified in the previous paragraph. Ontology and rule-based languages with context support (e.g. OWL [8], Triple [6]) as well as tools from the Semantic Web community can be utilized as a basis to develop policy and trust ontologies and to facilitate reasoning mechanisms associated with them. Service mediation is another challenge whenever we discuss data integration between heterogeneous sources and sinks to provide interoperability. For example, while using a single ontology to describe policy that can be applied to a set of resources. Currently the Semantic Web community is pursuing the data, protocol and process mediation challenges, their outcomes will be exploited by Semantic Grid community.

3.2 Dynamic VO Life Cycle and Management

As described in section 1, a VO may consist of individuals, institutions and resources that may be grouped together, so that common tasks can be undertaken. A VO is a dynamic environment as resources, services and users may join and leave at anytime. For many grid applications these requirements vary over time so it is hard to tell exactly in advance, what services it will need in a given system. Thus, new services composed of different individuals, institutions and resources are needed to handle dynamic workloads and varying needs of volatile properties of Grid applications including scale, timeliness and quality of service. Beside the dynamic characteristics of VOs, still the process of building, managing and destroying a VO requires a lot of human intervention in terms of efforts and is very time consuming and tedious. For instance, it took more than a year to form a virtual organization for ESG (Earth System Grid) [11] after the exchange of several emails, face-to-face meetings and phone calls.

We believe Semantic Web tools and technologies can be used to, for example,

- Help in selecting the best resources to deliver the desired service,
- Divide work in the most effective way between the resources,
- Monitor an ongoing operation of the VO and to alter it when appropriate,
- Dissolve collaboration when they are no longer sustainable within a VO lifecycle.

Semantic Web models and languages, including RDF [7], OWL and WSMO [10], can be used to realize these requirements by providing declarative models for describing the workflow for a VO's life cycle, via an expressive policy language, which can facilitate sophisticated reasoning over policies in order to identify the role for an individual, institution or resource based on their credentials and the usage policies of VO.

3.3 Workflow Model and Enactment

In this section, we will identify some of the issues related to the workflows description, discovery and enactment at the resource or service level. To support the creation of a VO's services, a system needs descriptions (such as workflows) to facilitate the composition of multiple resources, and mechanisms for creating and enacting these in a distributed manner. Whenever we talk about composition, we think in terms of discovery and integration of possibly heterogeneous distributed data and components, and in terms of their control and data flow. An aim of the Semantic Web community is, but not limited, to provide solutions for such information and data integration challenges for complex resource sharing in scientific workflows. Resource description and discovery for workflows is described separately in section 3.5.

Declarative models are required to support the design of complex workflows encompassing heterogeneous data sets, components and other workflows. Existing Semantic Web languages like OWL-S [9] define a process (workflow) using the OWL-S process model ontology. On the other hand, WSMO is aiming to use abstract state machines language to define the process model and execution semantics for workflows description and execution.

Another challenge during the process of service composition where semantics can be of help is where services are semantically equivalent but structurally incompatible, i.e. their semantic descriptions match the request, but data and control flow differs. To handle such situations it becomes necessary to annotate data sets, workflows and other components to facilitate efficient matching. Execution semantics are required to formally describe the operational behavior of a given system. On the other hand, information captured in the form of execution semantics can be used for automating control and data flows and to define alternative control and data flows (dynamic workflows) for exception handling in case of partial failures. Ontologies can be used with monitoring data also. Here the ontology can be used for defining relationships and capacity planning during workflow execution. There is currently little that exists to handle partial failures and capacity planning in grid workflows systems.

3.4 Annotations and Metadata

From the classification of a model to publish the scientific analysis, it is necessary to have annotations and metadata that enrich the description of any digital content. This meta-content may apply to data, information, or knowledge and depends on agreed interpretations. While the basic metadata infrastructure already exists in the shape of RDF and Dublin Core [14], metadata issues have not been fully addressed in current grid deployments. It is relatively straightforward to deploy some of the technologies in this area, and this should be promoted [5]. RDF and RDFS [13], for example, are already used for encoding metadata and annotations as shared vocabularies. However, there is still a need for work in the area of tools and methods to support the design and deployment of ontologies. Annotation tools and methods need to be developed so that emerging metadata and ontologies can be applied to the large amount of content that will be generated and consumed by grid applications.

To further clarify, we look at one application area for annotations and meta-data (semantics) in the Web Services Resource Framework (WSRF) [15]. In WSRF, every WS-Resource has zero or more properties expressed as XML elements, representing a view of the resources state. The element schema is then referenced from a WSDL description of the interface, advertising that Web Services with this interface have this known set of properties. As both XML and WSDL are solely based on their syntax, the semantics of the data are required for information discovery and integration tasks. Both the WSDL description of the interface and the resource properties document can be annotated using explicit semantics provided by existing ontology languages, i.e. OWL-S and WSMO, and metadata standards, i.e. RDF, RDFS and Dublin Core. These annotations can then be utilized for automated discovery and inference support.

3.5 Resource Description, Discovery, and Use

In grid systems, the resources may range from digital content to services provided by various computational and data resources, to particular instruments. For creating VOs dynamically, appropriate grid resources should be discovered and selected after negotiation on the fly. The phases for efficient and dynamic resource discovery and selection, through coordination and negotiation among various entities, mandates the generation and processing of job, resource, choreography and SLA descriptions. They further require on-demand and dynamically planned use of resources in order to meet the requirements of an existing virtual organization or forming a new one. On the other hand, a system should be able to store and retrieve these descriptions in a timely and efficient manner, which may require the federation of resources.

We strongly believe that the Semantic Web tools and languages can augment grid technologies in creating, storing and processing these machine processable descriptions of resources, jobs and SLAs. OWL-S and WSMO are ongoing research efforts for describing requests and Web Services functionality in a way that can help in the automation of service discovery and composition. WS-Choreography and WS-Agreement are the recommended specifications for coordination and negotiation tasks. WS-Choreography will use RDF and OWL to define the semantics of the choreography language. A registry for semantic data should provide a more sophisticated data model for storage and processing of semantic content.

4   Semantic Grid Infrastructure and Architecture

In section 3, we have identified a number of requirements for semantics in grid environments. This section will identify the key building blocks for semantic infrastructure in order to satisfy the Semantic Grid requirements.

4.1 Information Models and Ontologies

Heterogeneous and distributed systems, such as the Grid, are dependent upon information acquired from unrelated applications, resources, instruments, components and sub-systems. To be effectively managed, such information will need to conform to a common information model. An information model describes the salient entity attributes, relationships and characteristics needed to complete the process in question [16], thus, it is the modelling of information requirements for a particular domain.

The information model provides an abstraction of the real world into constructs that can be represented in computer systems, e.g., objects, properties, behavior, and relationships. It is not tied to any particular implementation and can be used to exchange information among different domains. We need an information model for the Grid because it allows multiple domain experts contribute to a problem's description. Ontologies [28] are a key technology for information and domain modelling. They interweave human understanding of symbols with their machine-processability. More recently, the concept of ontology is also becoming widespread in fields, such as intelligent information integration, cooperative information systems, information retrieval, electronic commerce, Semantic Web Services and knowledge management. The reason ontologies are becoming so popular is largely due to what they promise of a shared and common understanding of a domain that can be communicated between people and application systems. Concisely, ontologies are a formal and consensual specification of conceptualizations that provide a shared and common understanding of a domain, an understanding that can be communicated across people and application systems.

In the Semantic Grid framework, ontologies will be used to define the terminology that will be used by other elements of WSRF and OGSA specifications.

4.2 A Metadata Framework

There is a need to improve access to large source of information about grid resources and for the development of better search, retrieval, and organizational tools.

Metadata is a fundamental part of the solution to these challenges. The effective use of metadata among applications, however, requires common conventions about semantics, syntax, and structure. Communities define the semantics, or meaning of metadata that address their particular needs. Syntax is the systematic arrangement of data elements for machine-processing, it facilitates the exchange and use of metadata among multiple applications. Structure can be thought of as a formal constraint on the syntax for the consistent representation of semantics. These three elements standardized semantics, a definitive syntax, and a framework for exchange, provide an architecture for resource description that can work across all subject areas on the Grid. Although, developing a single and complete vocabulary for resource description is a difficult problem. However, tackling this effort in a modular fashion, allows for an incremental solution with manageable constituent parts.

4.3 An Architecture for the Semantic Grid

The Open Grid Services Architecture (OGSA) [3] provides a conceptual framework for grid systems based on Web Services concepts and technologies. Figure 2-(a) shows the overall OGSA architecture. OGSA being an architecture for the Grid naturally fulfills the requirements as a Semantic Grid architecture too, but additional services are required for handling semantic data. We will identify these services, while also describing OGSA services.

OGSA shown in Figure 2-(a) defines several services that are required in a Grid environment. These include:

1. Infrastructure services, which leverage Web services technologies to structure OGSA-based, systems according to the design principle of Service-Oriented Architecture.
2. Execution Management Services deal with the problems of task initiation and management.
3. Data Services, which are responsible for efficient data access, consistency, persistency, integration and location management.
4. Resource Management Services, which allow the management of an individual resource, management of resources in a grid, i.e. resource reservation, monitoring and control, and monitoring of grid infrastructure.
5. Security Services, which provide controlled access to resources, which can be in various administrative domains with different access and security policies.

6. Self-Management Services, which includes SLA, policies and service level manager models.
7. Information Services provide access and can manipulate information about applications, resources and services in a Grid environment. For the Semantic Grid, we need knowledge bases in order to effectively and efficiently store and retrieve semantic information.
8. Semantic Services should be introduced into OGSA to provide the modelling, creation, attachment, management, and visualization of semantic data (ontologies and metadata). It may also include a rule based approach for data integration and mediation.

As explain in section 2, the Semantic Grid implies semantics into grid and onto Grid. Figure 2-(b) explains this implication by placing Semantic Services vertically along the layers of the OGSA model. Ontologies developed using Semantic Services can be used to enrich services ranging from infrastructure services in OGSA to Grid applications built on top of OGSA. According to OGSA, Infrastructure Services are based on Web Services specified by OGSI or WSRF.

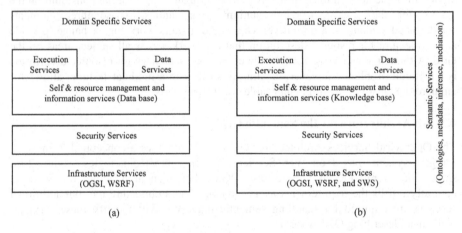

(a)   (b)

Fig. 2. OGSA for Grids (a) and OGSA for Semantic Grid (b)

5 Methodology and State of the Art

We believe that in order to build the Semantic Grid infrastructure, we need to cross discipline boundaries, which means: The Semantic Grid should inherit current technologies by building bridges in order to fill the technology gaps. Moreover, existing grid and web applications should be able to seamlessly migrate into the Semantic Grid environment. The Semantic Grid community should exploit the advances in the areas of the Grid, the Semantic Web and Web Services, in order to gather use cases and model elaborated sets of requirements from distinct for the Semantic Grid infrastructure. We also think that there is a need for a Semantic Grid roadmap in order to guide the Semantic Grid efforts in future.

In rest of the section, we will explain the state of the art of various technologies, most relevant to the Semantic Grid infrastructure and can serve as building blocks.

5.1 The Semantic Web – Metadata and Ontologies

The Dublin Core Metadata Element Set (DCMES) [14] can be viewed as the common semantic building block of Web metadata. It consists of 15 broad categories (elements) that are useful for creating simple, easy-to-understand descriptions for most information resources. Most communities, like the Grid, need additional semantics to describe their resources. DCMES facilitates the combination of various modules of metadata to form descriptions that are more complex. The DCMES is the basic block, but other chunks of metadata can be combined with it to form richer descriptions.

The Resource Description Framework (RDF) [7] is an infrastructure that enables the encoding, exchange and reuse of structured metadata. RDF is an application of XML that imposes needed structural constraints to provide unambiguous methods for expressing semantics. RDF additionally provides a means for publishing both human-readable and machine-processable vocabularies designed to encourage the reuse and extension of metadata semantics between communities. The structural constraints of RDF impose the consistent encoding and exchange of standardized metadata that allow interoperability of separate packages of metadata defined by different resource description communities. RDF Schema [13] is an RDF's vocabulary description language that is a semantic extension, as defined in RDF. RDFS provides mechanisms for describing groups of related resources and the relationships between these resources. OWL, the Web Ontology Language [8], is designed and developed for use by applications that need to process the content of information, rather than just presenting information to humans. OWL facilitates greater machine interpretability of Web content than that supported by XML, RDF, and RDFS by providing additional vocabulary along with a formal semantics. There have been some efforts [17] in modelling various aspects of the Grid using OWL.

5.2 Information and Process Modelling

Some of the efforts in information modelling for describing IT resources in general and Grid resources in particular include CIM and the GLUE schema. Graphical languages, like UML [20], are equally effective for representing information and process models. However, several other formalisms exist for modelling Grid processes (workflows) like Petri nets, and DAG.

The CIM (Common Information Model) [18] from the DMTF (Distributed Management Task Force) is the standard that provides a common model for describing computer and network information. CIM infrastructure is an approach to the management of systems and networks that applies the basic structuring and conceptualization techniques of the object-oriented paradigm. The approach uses a uniform modeling formalism that together with the basic repertoire of object-oriented constructs supports the cooperative development of object-oriented schemas across multiple organizations. A management schema is provided to establish a common conceptual framework at the level of a fundamental typology, both with respect to classification, to association, and to a basic set of classes intended to establish a common framework for a description of the managed environment.

GLUE (Grid Laboratory Uniform Environment) schema [19] collaborative effort focusing on interoperability between US and EU HEP Grid related projects, which started in April 2002. In particular, the focus was on modelling all those resources that participate in a Grid system and that are requested to be discoverable and monitored. The effort targeted at core grid services, i.e. resource discovery and monitoring, authorization and authentication, data movement infrastructure, common software deployment procedures, and preserving coexistence for collective services. The ultimate objective was to produce a schema available for a Grid Information Services (GIS) as if concepts and relationships are properly modelled, the same information can be retrieved from different GISs relying on different technologies.

The Directed Acyclic Graph Manager (DAGMan) [21] is a meta-scheduler for Condor jobs. A directed acyclic graph (DAG) is used to represent a set of programs (workflow) where the input, output, or execution of one or more programs is dependent on one or more other programs. The programs are nodes (vertices) in the graph, and the edges (arcs) identify the dependencies. DAGMan submits jobs to Condor in an order represented by a DAG and processes the results.

Petri nets are formalism for modelling dynamic systems. They are graphical, mathematically normalized, and well analysable. Petri nets have been applied to a large number of areas, including communication protocols, performance evaluation, and distributed systems [22], because they are very general and were the first to model concurrency [23].

5.3 Semantic Web Services

Semantic Web Services (SWS) facilitate and semi-automate the consumption of resource functionality, through rich service or resource descriptions based on formal semantics. We believe that these formal descriptions provided by SWS can be extended to describe grid services and resources by using a formal ontology for WSRF and can form the basis for Semantic Grid Infrastructure. However, seamless integration and ad-hoc cooperation between various business parties or dynamic collaborations on the Web and Grid can be achieved only, if tools for handling semantically enhanced services are provided.

OWL-S [9] provisions Web Service providers with a core set of markup language constructs for describing the properties and capabilities of their services in unambiguous, computer-interpretable form. OWL-S markup of Web Services facilitates the automation of tasks including automated discovery, execution, interoperation, composition and execution monitoring. OWL-S also provides a workflow-oriented orchestration language to describe a workflow model, for the composition of Semantic Web Services.

The Web Services Modelling Ontology (WSMO) [10] initiative is one of the several research efforts currently underway working to develop a conceptual model, language and execution environment for SWS. WSMO aims to provide both workflow and conversational model (WSMO Orchestration and Choreography [24] based on Abstract State Machines (ASMs) [25]. Enhancing existing Web Services standards with semantics markup standardized through the WSMO initiative will promotes existing Web Services standards for semantic-enabled integration. The Web Services Execution Environment (WSMX) [26] is one of the WSMO initiatives aiming to provide an execution environment for discovery, selection, mediation, invocation and interoperation of the SWS.

5.4 The Globus Toolkit

The Globus Toolkit [27] provides an open source software infrastructure for resource and data management of autonomous distributed systems with provisions for policy extensibility and co-allocation. The Globus project is an American multi-institutional research effort that seeks to enable the construction of grids. The Globus Toolkit provides the basic services and capabilities required to construct Computational, Data or Service Grids. The toolkit consists of a set of components that implement basic services, such as security, resource location, resource management, and communications. The basic services implemented by key components within GT4 (latest release of Globus Toolkit) include grid security (GSI, WS-Security, CAS etc.), grid resource management (GRAM), data management (GridFTP, RLS, OGSA-DAI, RFT and XIO), information services (MDS2 and WS-Index) and WS Core.

6   Issues and Future Directions

In this paper we have identified the requirements for the Semantic Grid and discussed its infrastructure by identifying the relevant technologies and building blocks, especially how the Semantic Web can augment existing Grid technologies and by explaining state of the art of various other relevant technologies. However, we foresee that this integration of the Semantic Web and Grid technologies under the Semantic Grid effort will not lead to just a one-way migration path, i.e. the Semantic Web supplementing the Grid. Rather we strongly believe that Grid technologies have much to offer as well, in terms of computational and storage resources to store and process ontologies, a secure, robust, scalable resource and data management infrastructure to share resources.

References

1. Web Services: The Next Big Thing By: Jack Martin
2. Foster, I., Kesselman, C. and Tuecke, S. The Anatomy of the Grid: Enabling Scalable Virtual Organizations. International Journal of Supercomputer Applications, 15 (3). 200-222. 2001.
3. Foster, I., Kesselman, C., Nick, J. and Tueske, S., "The Physiology of the Grid: An Open Grid services Architecture for Distributed Systems Integration", Globus, Project.
4. http://www.semanticgrid.org/vision.html
5. David de Roure, Nicholas R. Jennings, senior member, IEEE, and Nigel R. Shadbolt. The Semantic Grid: Past, Present, and Future, Invited Paper, IEEE proceedings, March 2005.
6. TRIPLE, http://triple.semanticweb.org/
7. W3C Resource Description Framework, http://www.w3.org/RDF/
8. W3C Ontology Web Language, http://www.w3.org/2004/OWL/

9. OWL for Services, http://www.daml.org/services/owl-s/
10. Web Service Modeling Ontology, http://www.wsmo.org
11. Earth System Grid (ESG), https://www.earthsystemgrid.org/
12. W3C Semantic Web, http://www.w3.org/2001/sw/
13. W3C RDF Schema, http://www.w3.org/TR/rdf-schema/
14. Dublin Core meta data initiative, http://dublincore.org/
15. Web Service Resource Framework (WSRF) http://www.oasis-pen.org/committees/tc_home. php? wg_abbrev=wsrf
16. Information Model, http://mayoresearch.mayo.edu/mayo/research/bmi/grant_dev_eval_term_full.cfm
17. http://www.csm.ornl.gov/~7lp/ontos.html
18. http://www.dmtf.org/standards/cim/
19. http://infnforge.cnaf.infn.it/glueinfomodel/
20. http://www.uml.org/
21. http://www.cs.wisc.edu/condor/dagman/
22. T. Murata. Petri nets: properties, analysis, and applications. Proceedings of the IEEE, 77(4):541–580, 1989.
23. J. C. M. Baeten. A brief history of process algebra. Rapport CSR 04-02, TU Eindhoven, 2004.
24. WSMO Choreography and Orchestration Working Draft, http://www.wsmo.org/TR/d14/v0.1/
25. Abstract State Machines, http://www.eecs.umich.edu/gasm/
26. Web Service Execution Environment, http://www.wsmx.org/
27. Globus Toolkit, http://www.globus.org/
28. D. Fensel and M. Musen: Special Issue on Semantic Web Technology, IEEE Intelligent Systems, 16(2), 2001.

MPLS Inter Domain Services Routing Architecture and Model Based on P2P Semantic Grid

Chongying Cao[1,2], Jing Yang[3], and Guoqing Zhang[1]

[1] Institute of Computing Technology, Chinese Academy of Sciences,
P.O. Box 2704, Beijing 100080, China
[2] Graduate School of the Chinese Academy of Sciences, Beijing, China
[3] UTStarCom Company, China
caocy@ict.ac.cn, Jamesy@utstarcom.com, gqzhang@ict.ac.cn

Abstract. Service routing across different MPLS and access networks domain is the critical problem in next generation networks. BGP is a de facto inter domain routing standard, but it can not satisfy the inter domain traffic engineering. It doesn't take into account service metrics. These cause routing efficiency of BGP very low. To solve the problem, we propose a new architecture to setup service semantic P2P grid. Based on the architecture, we define the formal model of service semantic network, including how to map network service to service ontology and construct a service semantic network. We use a common network measurement platform to get information which is imported to set up time and space relationships among their service ontology. According to these relationships, we setup index structure of a service routing. Using the index structure, we can easily setup service routing across different MPLS and access network domains.

1 Introduction

With the development of society, the requirements to communicate across all kinds of networks become more and more important. Next generation services are very different from the services provided today. It brings great challenges to the MPLS networks, which will be the core networks in the next generation network (NGN). Service routing is an overlay network routing, which provides related service capability. For example, we often need to setup VPN services across different MPLS network domains.

The Border Gateway Protocol (BGP) [1] is a de facto standard for inter domain routing. It is also used between MPLS domains to setup routing. As a path vector routing protocol, BGP is similar to any other distance vector routing protocol that doesn't take into account service metrics. Its criteria for selecting the best path are based on the length of AS path. In the next generation network, service will become richer, which need to support multimedia, openness and virtualization. In BGP, bearer and control is not completely decomposed. These causes BGP hardly support different service routing according to the open service requirement of NGN. It makes service routing across different MPLS domains become a NP-hard problem. This brings great complexity to the network interconnection. If we use underlying network protocols to connect different domain for NGN services, it will become N^2 problem. At the same

Y.-C. Chung and J.E. Moreira (Eds.): GPC 2006, LNCS 3947, pp. 427–436, 2006.
© Springer-Verlag Berlin Heidelberg 2006

time, different MPLS and access network domains are owned by different network providers, they have different service providing methods and policies, which make them lacking common languages to understand each other. Such kind of problems can not be solved by reinforcing the underlay network algorithms [2].

Due to these reasons, service routings across different network domains are difficult to be setup. To solve the problem, we must open MPLS network capability. OGSA [16] is a good platform to converge different MPLS service. At the same time, the semantic provide the common language among different MPLS service domains. Then we introduce an innovative idea —— service semantic P2P grid architecture and model to organize the resources of service routing across different network domain based on ontology.

The rest of the paper is organized as follows. In section 2, we introduce the related research works. According to the comparison, we set up architecture for the service semantic P2P network in section 3. In the section 4, we setup the model. After set upping the architecture, we give the formal definition of the service semantic P2P networks and solve how to map service ontology. After setting up a service network graph, we use index structure to improve the routing efficiency. Network measurement will reduce the complexity of service routing and improve its efficiency. Based on network measurement, we provide the P2P routing constructing methods. In the section 5, we make a conclusion.

2   Related Works

There are many researches to improve BGP protocol [12]. Many heuristics also have been proposed due to its NP-completeness [14]. Due to complexity imposed on router, their improving arranges are limited. High complexity prevents their practical applications. Some algorithms only suit for a specific network, which can't support different service routing.

To solve the online computing overhead, overlay network is proposed to decompose the functions from routers [13] recently. However, they do not possess details of the underlying network, and control over routing on the underlay. In telecommunication domain, Parlay Gateway [3] has been proposed to open the network capabilities. Its connectivity manager API [4] and policy manager API [5] can be used to abstract the MPLS network capabilities and policy management capability to setup the MPLS inter domain routing. However, Parlay is based on CORBA, one fine-grain management architecture, which is close-coupled. Web Services [6] is used to provide loose-couple in Parlay Gateway, but it run short of the dynamic resource management. To setup routing across heterogeneous MPLS domains, service convergence and virtualization is the key. Parlay can't provide such kind of capability. OGSA (Open Grid Services Architecture) [16] is such service convergence and virtualization platform. Due to its new mechanism, such as soft state management, grid services [16] can be used.

Parlay doesn't concern routing between different domains in MPLS network. P2P routing can provide such scalability. Many research efforts have been focused on improving searching efficiency by designing good P2P routing and discovery protocols, and so on. Xiaohui Gu of University of Illinois gave a framework to composite the QoS-aware service for large-scale peer-to-peer systems [7]. To get the network status between peer nodes, measure must be considered. To minimize the number of nodes that a query probes, heuristic-based approaches was employed to direct a search to only a fraction of the node population. These approaches can be further divided into three categories: random walk [8], employing summarization [9], and organizing nodes with similar contents or sharing interests into groups [10].

However, current peer-to-peer routing algorithms are based on key words, which can hardly solve those problems whose key words are more than one. Different service relationships are very complex for those only can be solved through key words. Different network providers have their own service definitions and policies, which are understood by each others hardly. Semantic Network was proposed, which can make the network resources become a large database. In particular, the notion of Semantic Overlay Networks (SONs) [11] is a way to group together peers sharing the same schema information. Thus, peers employing one or more concepts of the same thematic hierarchy are semantically related and belong to the same SON. This approach facilitates routing, since a peer can easily identify relevant peers instead of broadcasting query requests on the networks.

3 Architecture

To setup service routing across different MPLS networks and access networks domains, we design semantic P2P grid Architecture as figure 1. At first, we need use Parlay API to open the MPLS network capability, which includes connectivity management and policy management. For each MPLS border node, relative service node is setup. These service nodes decompose the functions from MPLS border nodes and Parlay Gateway, and provide a distributed computation. These capabilities opened are wrapped as Grid Services, which can effectively manage MPLS network resources and their states. We use the OGSA platform —— Globus to converge service. On the foundation, we set up a single semantic image —— ontology. Ontology [8] is a formal, explicit specification of a shared conceptualization. The Ontology is gotten through a knowledge platform —— Semantic Grid. Through ontology, we can get, describe, express and compose services to set up service routing across different MPLS domains

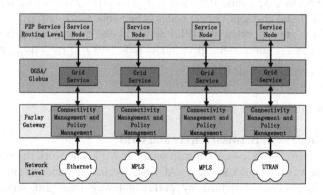

Fig. 1. System Architecture

and other networks. At the same time, different service relationships can be set up through semantic. In semantic grid level, different MPLS domains and other access networks can understand each other through ontology, and become a transparent homogeneity network. In such a homogeneity network, we can use semantic to set up P2P service routing.

4   System Model

4.1   Service Semantic Network Model

We give a formal definition for service semantic network model based on semantic p2p gird, which will be used to setup service routing across different MPLS network and access network domains. Our P2P service routing system P is constituted by a set of peers, each of which includes a set of mapping function that specify the semantic relationships with network services delegated by other peers. In the model, service paths in MPLS domains are mapped by Parlay Gateway. Every MPLS Parlay service will be mapped to a peer based on service ontology. The Services Semantic P2P Overlay Network forward according to the service ontology.

Definition 1: Formally each service peer node $p \in P$ is defined as a service tuple $p = (O, S, L, M)$, where

- O is the basic bearer service of node p, which is ontology of service.
- S is the source service of node p, which is defined by different network providers in different MPLS and access networks domains and mapped by Parlay Gateway.
- L is a set of local mapping assertions between O and S. Each local mapping assertion is an expression of the form $L(S){\to}O$.
- M is a set of P2P mapping assertions between two peer nodes of the same service ontology in different MPLS domains.

According to Definition 1, we can define a service semantic P2P grid model for service routing between different MPLS domains which are composed of these peer nodes.

Definition 2: Service Semantic P2P Grid $SSPG(O) = (P(O),E)$ is a network which is composed of all basic grid service peer nodes in Semantic Grid platform over the Parlay Gateways which are supported by MPLS networks and their access networks, where $P(o)=\{p_i \in P | o \in O(p_i)\}$ are service peer node sets, and $E=\{e(p_i, p_j) | \forall p_i \in P(o), \exists p_j \in P(o) \cap (p_i, p_j)\}$ are service semantic link sets.

4.2   Vertical Integration

4.2.1   Mapping Model Between Parlay and Grid

According to above model, we must map underlay MPLS network resource provided by parlay gateway into grid services. At first, we use a standardization center to translate MPLS service provided by parlay gateway into grid services. In the standardization center, we translate Parlay Service according to the Parlay API, which will expose the connectivity capability and policy Management capability of MPLS networks, into Grid service. Then we register such kinds of service into the grid domain which will manage the MPLS domain.

Parlay consists of two kinds of interfaces: Framework interface and Service interfaces —— Service Capability Features (SCF). We can reconstruct these interfaces into Grid Service. Grid Services provide several function interfaces. The GridServiceBase object is the base of all Grid services and implements the standard OGSI GridService PortType. It also provides APIs to modify instance specific properties, as well as APIs for querying and modifying service data. The ServiceDataSet interface provides the management for the service data. A service can be created by simply extending from GridServiceImpl, but it is not recommended because of its limited flexibility. One of solution adopted in GT3 Core is called Operation Provider model or the dynamic delegation model. Instead of extending from the base implementation classes, you only provide an implementation of the operations (as defined in WSDL) that you would like to expose to remote clients.

Here we use the parlay interface IpVPrN as an example (figure 2). The enterprise operator can create a new virtual provisioned pipe (VPrP) in an existing private network (VPN) with this VPN interface. Such a pipe is extended between specific SAPs/sites. Each pipe is associated with QoS parameters identified with a specific Diffserv Codepoint. The interface IpVPrN aggregate the MPLS traffic trunk MIB —— mplsTunnelTable to manage through the interface ImplsTunnelTable. At the same time, we translate the data definition in Parlay specification into the ServiceData, which will be managed through ServiceDataSet. Last, we will implement the GridServiceBase. Then a Grid service VPrNGridServiceImpl to manage the VPN in the MPLS domain is created.

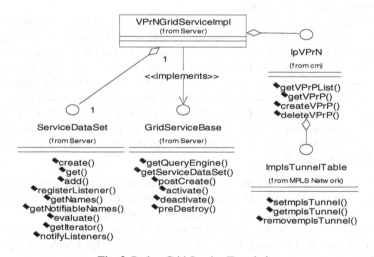

Fig. 2. Parlay-Grid Service Translation

4.2.2 Service Ontology Model

In the model, there are two levels —— concept level and service resource level. According to definition 1, we map the services provided by one Parlay Gateway in service resource level to one service ontology in concept level which is also the basic bearer service. The Semantic Web is a mesh of information linked up in such a way as to be easily processable by machines, on a global scale. You can think of it as being an efficient way of representing data on the World Wide Web, or as a globally linked database. So we describe the network resource as a database, which is mapped to an orthogonal resource space. The resource space of basic bearer service O can be decomposed into n dimensions, in which each node can dynamically manage a resource or a set of related resource.

Definition 3: In resource orthogonal space RS, each node can be represented as $O_{RS}(D_1, D_2, ..., D_n)$, where attribute $D = \{X_{i1}, X_{i2}, ..., X_{ik}\}$, where X_{ij} is a coordinate value for it.

Semantic Network separates concept and its property. Concept is static, but its property may change. We use grid service to map related resource to support service ontology. For service routing based on ontology, the service capability will be ensured; the service routing can ensure the users' requirements.

According to the definition 3, we can setup basic bearer grid services. In different MPLS domains and access networks, every service can be represented as a minimal logic unit, which is a feature description set S. Due to one feature information is related to a pair of <attribute class (c), attribute value (v)>, then a service can be represented as: $S = \{<c_1, v_1>, <c_2, v_2>, <c_3, v_3>, ..., <c_n, v_n>\}$. Using $L(S) \rightarrow O$, we can map the feature information into the orthogonal resource space of service ontology.

4.3 Horizontal Integration

4.3.1 Service Network Graph

In the model, the service network graph (SNG) (Figure 3) represents a "snap-shot" of the MPLS routing resource states. The inter domain service routing consists of a list of composable grid services, which is connected into a service path. S is the grid service vector of the service pipe which provided by parlay gateway. Formally, we define the vectors S as follows: $S = [s_1, s_2, ..., s_n]$. These vectors represent the service capability of the service ontology, including traffic attributes, resource attributes and other service management constraints. A, B, C, D are MPLS network domains, A^s, B^s, C^s, D^s are grid service domains translated from the MPLS services provided by parlay gateway. According to the above service ontology model, we can set up a service network graph.

A SNG is defined as follows:

(1) *SNG nodes:* The service node of SNG represents the border grid service node mapped from a MPLS node. In service network domain B^s, both a^s and b^s are the border service nodes, which is mapped from border node a and b.

(2) *SNG edges:* Edges from source border node to destination border grid node within a MPLS domain. In domain B^s, $<a^s, b^s>$ is the service edge which is mapped from underlay network edge.

(3) *SNG service instances:* In a SNG edge, a grid service instance represents a traffic trunk across an underlay physical path. Its resource requirement vector S^{req} (a, b) can be satisfied by the corresponding service pipe provided by the parlay gateway. In domain B, S_1 and S_2 are two grid service instances, which represent different service pipes. S_1 is across the physical path (a, b), S_2 is across the physical path (a, c) and (c, b).

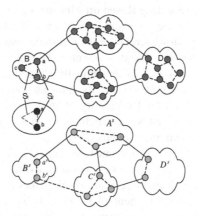

Fig. 3. Service Network Graph

4.3.2 Index Structure

Maintaining the global view of the service network graph is difficult. After constructing service network graph through mapping, we must organize the view of the service network. So we set up an index structure by employing three levels of summarization (Fig 4). The lowest level is *Parlay Gateway level*. The second level is named as *service ontology peer level*; all information owned by a peer is summarized according to service ontology. In the level, peers are the grid service instances which wrap service pipe provided by parlay gateway. Finally, in the third level, named as *semantic grid level*, all information contained by a peer group is registered in the semantic grid. Each semantic grid maintains two pieces of summaries: the super level summaries of its

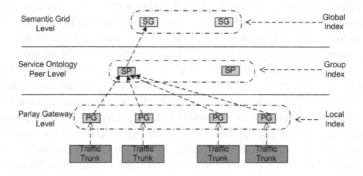

Fig. 4. Index Structure

group and its neighboring groups, and peer level summaries of its group. By examining super level summaries, a super peer can determine which peer group is relevant. Since the number of summaries may be large, to further improve the efficiency of the system, we maintain indexes on the summary information. We name the three indexes for parlay gateway, service ontology peer, and semantic grid level summaries as *local index*, *group index*, and *global index*, respectively.

4.3.3 Setup P2P Service Routing Based on Measurement

Due to the service ontology, we can setup a service routing through mapping between neighbor service ontology. However, Ontology is a static concept model which doesn't concern the dynamic behaviors, but its content and service object is being changed dynamically and network resource is dynamically changing. In order to support the service ontology, we must use grid services' dynamic mapping capability to support the service ontology. Using such kind capability of grid service, service ontology can ensure the network resource status on which they can setup service semantic links which satisfy the inter domain traffic engineering.

To get such kind of capability, we must get network status information through measurement. To solve the problem, we propose a hybrid approach that combines service ontology and network measurement, which makes routing limited to smallest range. Common network measurement platform is being researched, for example, routing underlay [17]. The common network measurement platform will use BGP, Traceroute and Ping to get the network information. Service measurement is also an import issue. In each MPLS domain, all opened service capability, are registered in grid register server based on semantic. According to the semantic, each MPLS domain can sent service measurement requirement to neighbor domains. When a neighbor MPLS domain receives such kind of requirements, it would response according to its policy. Such kind of common measurement platform is also based on grid service. This platform setups measurement for same kind of grid service for MPLS service routing.

4.3.4 Setup P2P Service Routing Methods

P2P semantic grid provides the access port to the grid service based on the service ontology. In the each semantic grid, there is a MPLS parlay service access engine. It helps us to match and search MPLS route service dynamically. The semantic access engine provides a bridge between the MPLS parlay service and semantic grid. Above service network graph provide the mapped grid service for MPLS domain. Using the index structure based on ontology, we can find the entry and match service to the service ontology peer group for G(S, a, d). Then we can get a reduced service network graph $G'(S, a, d)$ for G(S, a, d), where a is the source service node, d is destination service node, S is the service ontology. A common network measurement platform gets a set of network domains which can satisfy the service routing requirements. Through service ontology mapping and their neighbor list, we get a peer group. According to the index structure, we can get the entry to semantic grid. Then we can use some P2P routing algorithm to compute service routing. So we can setup an algorithm about how to match service based on ontology to setup P2P service routing in Service Routing Algorithm 1:

Service Routing Algorithm 1

| ServiceRouting(*a, d, S*)

Step 1: Get shared measurement result from service node according to the service request.
Step 2: According to the measurement result, we can sent a service request to the related semantic grid domains.
Step 3: Semantic grid match service request based on the ontology and find the service instance group. If it fails, return. Otherwise go to step 4.

Step 4: Return the service ontology metric of the service and service instance.
Step 5: Use P2P algorithm to find MPLS service routing across different MPLS domains on the service network graph. |

5 Conclusion and Future Works

In this paper, we analysis the problem in the MPLS inter domain service routing and related works. We propose a new architecture to setup MPLS inter domain routing based on semantic P2P grid. Through Parlay Gateway, we expose the resource of underlay network. OGSA platform provide good service convergence capability. Using grid service, we can manage the resource dynamically. Semantic network makes different network homogeneity, which make different network became same kind of service network. At the same time, P2P provide scalability. The new service convergence platform will be a trend to solve the service routing across different network domains. In the future, we still need to research the related routing algorithms and dynamic resource management algorithms in the new architecture and model.

Acknowledgement

We are grateful to the support of "Next generation Internet collaborative project between China and Japan (IPv6-CJ)".

References

1. Y. Rekhter, T. Li, "A Border Gateway Protocol 4 (BEP-4)" (RFC 1771), March, 1995
2. David D. Clark, Craig Partridge, J. Christopher Ramming and John T. Wroclawski, "A Knowledge Plane for the Internet", SIGCOMM 2003
3. Ard-Jan Moerdijk and Lucas Klostermann, "Opening the networks with Parlay/OSA: standards and aspects behind the APIs", IEEE Network, Volume 17, Issue 3, May-June 2003 Page(s):58 - 64
4. "Open Service Access (OSA); Application Programming Interface (API); Part 10: Connectivity Manager SCF (Parlay 3)", ETSI ES 201 915-10 v1.4.1 (2003-07)
5. "Open Service Access (OSA); Application Programming Interface (API); Part 13: Policy management SCF", ETSI ES 201 915-13 v1.4.1 (2003-01)
6. "Parlay Web Services Overview (version 1.0)"☐October 31, 2002, http://www.parlay.org.

 7. Xiaohui Gu, et al, "QoS-aware service composition for large-scale peer-to-peer systems"
 8. Q. Lv, P. Cao, E. Cohen, K. Li and S. Shenker, "Search and Replication in Unstructured Peer-to-Peer Networks", In ICS'02, June 2002
 9. S. Rhea and J. Kubiatowicz, "Probabilistic Location and Routing", In IEEE INFOCOM 2002, June 2002
10. M. Schwartz, "A Scalable, Non-Hierarchical Resource Discovery Mechanism Based on Probabilities Protocols", Technical Report CU-CS-474-90, University of Colorado, 1990
11. A Crespo, H Garcia-Molina, "Semantic Overlay Networks", 2003, http://www-db.standford.edu/ ~crespo/publication/op2p.pdf
12. Timothy G. Griffin, F. Bruce Shepherd, and Gordon Wilfong, "The Stable Paths Problem and Inter domain Routing", IEEE/ACM TRANSACTIONS ON NETWORKING, VOL.10, NO.2, APRIL 2002
13. Sharad Agarwal, Chen-Nee Chuah, Randy H. Katz, "OPCA: Robust Interdomain Policy Routing and Traffic Control", OPENARCH 2003
14. M.S. Garey, D.S. Johnson, "Computers and Intractability: A Guide to the Theory of NP-Completeness", W.H. Freeman, New York, 1979
15. Studer R, Benjamins V R, Fensel D, "Knowledge Engineering, Principles and Methods", Data and Knowledge Engineering, 1998, 25(1-2)
16. Ian Foster et al., "The Physiology of the Grid: An Open Grid Services Architecture for Distributed Systems Integration", June, 2002
17. Aki Nakao, Larry Peterson, Andy Bavier, "A Routing Underlay for Overlay Networks", in *Proceedings of the SIGCOMM 2003,* Karlsruhe, Germany, August 2003

Semantic Metadata Models in References Sharing and Retrieval System SemreX*

Hao Wu and Hai Jin

Cluster and Grid Computing Lab,
Huazhong University of Science and Technology, Wuhan, 430074, China
hjin@hust.edu.cn

Abstract. Peer-to-Peer (P2P) systems are a new paradigm for information sharing and some systems have successfully been deployed. It has been argued that current P2P systems suffer from the lack of semantics. Therefore combining P2P solutions with Semantic Web technologies for knowledge sharing become a new trend. SemreX is a P2P based semantic-enabled knowledge management system for sharing references metadata. In SemreX, we need to handle heterogeneous literature formats, and present a shared understanding about publications knowledge. Meanwhile, peers in SemreX require some compromises with respect to the use of semantic knowledge models for self-description. In this paper, we propose metadata models that combine features of ontology, for encoding and aligning semantic information from references, and for a flexible description of knowledge located in a peer. We describe these models and discuss the roles of the models in the SemreX environment as well as their creations and applications.

1 Introduction

Peer-to-Peer (P2P) systems are a new successful paradigm for information sharing. It has been argued that current P2P systems suffer from the lack of semantics; therefore combining P2P solutions with Semantic Web technologies for knowledge sharing become a new trend. Recently, there have been several research projects concerned with knowledge management in a P2P setting (called P2PKM[1]); examples include Edutella [2], SWAP [3], Edamok [4], and others [5][6]. In such P2PKM systems, resources usually are expressed or annotated with knowledge representation language such as RDF, OWL. For different knowledge applications, there need different domain metadata models (or domain ontologies). In addition, to retrieve relevant knowledge in a P2PKM system, one needs to find one or more peers to provide the knowledge. For this purpose, there need to be content-based routing indices. However, how to obtain the aggregated descriptions of peers to establish these routing indices remains questionable. Such a self-description would outline in a few relevant concepts what kind of knowledge the peer contains. In this paper, we present a similar P2PKM system SemreX, which is designed for references sharing and retrieval. Our

---

* This work is supported by National Basic 973 Research Program of China under grant No.2003CB317003.

Y.-C. Chung and J.E. Moreira (Eds.): GPC 2006, LNCS 3947, pp. 437–446, 2006.

approach to use metadata model to deal with the existing issues, including literature resource expression and self-description of peers, are focused.

The paper is structured as follows. In section 2 we briefly introduce the SemreX. Section 3 presents metadata models in SemreX. Metadata model for publications and metadata for peers, and their usage are discussed in detail. Finally, we conclude our works and discuss future work.

2 References Sharing and Retrieval System SemreX

Searching scientific references from the Internet is a frequent and important behavior for researchers. There is a common phenomenon that a paper in a remote server is downloaded many times by different researchers in a lab. If a paper is downloaded from WAN only once and shared in the LAN, it will reduce the unnecessary WAN traffic and searching time greatly. Furthermore, researchers in a lab usually have the same or similar research interests. If a member reads a good paper and broadcasts this message, the total group will benefit from it. To share and exchange references efficiently, SemreX is proposed and implemented. Bibster [7] is a similar semantics-based bibliographic P2P system, and is as an application of the SWAP project. Compared with Bibster, SemreX is more concise because the size of source files of SemreX is much less than that of Bibster. In addition, SemreX supports heterogeneous data and permits the sharing of researchers' private comments of papers.

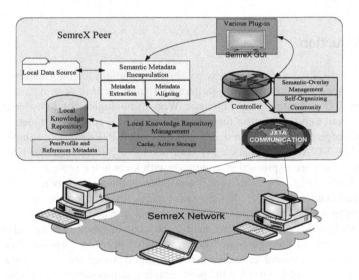

Fig. 1. Architecture of SemreX Peer

The software architecture of SemreX (shown in Fig.1) includes the human-machine interface, P2P communication layer, semantic information abstracting and classifying, semantic topology and routing, local knowledge repository management. The human-machine interface receives user's commands, shows query results, and calls services provided by other modules. At present, the automatic semantic information abstracting and classifying module mainly categorizes each paper into a sub-classification of ontology, according to the information from the references data in the original PDF files. In addition, SemreX provides a graphical interface, which lets user categorize papers into sub-classification by hand and add some private comments to each paper.

SemreX supports both automatic semantic information abstracting and manual re-marking. To describe the semantic information, a private ontology "SemreX: Reference" is created by our team, which gives some special information to bibliographies description. "SemreX: PeerProfile" is also utilized to self-describe a peer's knowledge resource. The users of SemreX can categorize papers into an accurate sub-classification according to literature taxonomy, such as ACM CCS (http://www.acm.org/class/1998/), and evaluate and grade papers. The manual evaluation information of references has higher priority than the automatic semantic information abstracting results in SemreX.

All the metadata in SemreX are stored in the RDF repository. When publication's metadata and the peer profile instances are encapsulated and aligned by RDF schemas, they are imported into *Local Knowledge Repository* (LKR), through LKR management infrastructure to query, delete and update.

3 Metadata Models in SemreX

3.1 Metadata Model for Publications

The same document can exist in different formats e.g. Postscript, PDF, BibTEX, or ASCII text. However with general metadata formats, different versions of the same document can be described in one record, whereas in the hard print version these would be regarded as different editions.

The most well-known metadata initiative is the *Dublin Core* (DC) which defines fifteen metadata elements for simple resource discovery. One of the specific purposes of DC is to support cross-domain resource discovery. DC has the metadata elements for publications, but for its initiative target, it does not focus on bibliographic domain.

The SWRC [8] is an ontology for modeling a research community, including persons, organizations, and bibliographic metadata. It is used in various projects and applications, such as Bibster, the AIFB portal, and the SemIPort projects. Closest to the SWRC are the *AKT reference ontology* (http://www.acm.org/class/1998/) developed by the AKT project and the *Knowledge Web portal ontology* (http://knowledgeweb.semantic-web.org/) developed by the Knowledge Web consortium. Both contain similar concepts and relationships as the SWRC ontology and serve a similar purpose. There are also other bibliographic ontology described in OWL (Web Ontology Language) on the web, such as *eBiquity Publication Ontology Resource* (http://ebiquity.umbc.edu/v2.1/ontology/ publication.owl) and *BibTEX Definition in Web Ontology Language* (http://visus.mit. edu/bibtex/ 0.1/).

We compare these similar metadata models for publications and find some characteristics listed as follows:

- Most ontology written in OWL. AKT reference ontology is expressed by OCML and Ontolinga; SWRC originally is written with DAML, whereas others are defined in OWL.
- More than 80% concepts and relationships among them are commonly defined and covered. For example, the concept about bibliographic format such as article, book, proceedings, master thesis, Ph.D. dissertation, and technical report.
- Most of them do not support ontology mapping mechanism. Only *AKT reference ontology* supports mapping mechanism for aligning other new defined concepts and relationships to original ontology.

Compared with these reference models, the publication metadata model in SemreX is specifically designed for wrapping the metadata extracted from scientific documents, and SemreX mainly aims at sharing key attributes of a scientific document. Therefore we select a minimized concept and relationships set which covers these key attributes such as document title, authors, abstract, key words, and most used publication information.

```
A: <ref:Publication rdf:about="urn://grid.hust.edu.cn/semrex#xxxxxx">
     <rdf:type rdf:resource="http://grid.hust.edu.cn/ontologies/
     refonto-yymmdd.owl #Proceedings" />
     <ref:title>Semantic Metadata Models in References Sharing and Retrieval System Sem-
     reX</ref:title> ... ...
     <ref:author>Hao Wu</ref:author> <ref:author>Hai Jin</ref:author>
     <ref:authors>Hao Wu, Hai Jin</ref:authors>
     <ref:publish>In Proceedings of GPC2006</ref:publish>
     <ref:year>2005</ref:year>
     <ref:abstract> Peer-to-Peer systems..., ..., We describe these models ...</ref:abstract>
     <ref:key>1</ref:key>
     <ref:url>http://grid.hust.edu.cn/papers/</ref:url>
     <ref:keywords>Metadata, Semantic Web, P2P </ref:keywords>
     <ref:classification> Semantic Web and P2P </ref:classification>
     <ref:comment>
        <ref:Person> Yijiao Yu </ref:Person>
        <ref:content> some remarks on this paper </ref:content>
        ... ...
     </ref:comment>   ... ...
   </ref:Publication>

B: <ref:Reference  rdf:about="urn://grid.hust.edu.cn/semrex#xxxxxx">
     <rdf:type  rdf:resource="http://grid.hust.edu.cn/ontologies/
     refonto-yymmdd.owl #Reference" />
     <ref:key>2</ref:key>
     <ref:title> The SWRC Ontology - Semantic Web for Research Communities </ref:title>
     <ref:authors>York Sure, Stephan Bloehdorn, Peter Haase, Jens Hartmann, Daniel Oberle
     </ref:authors>
     <ref: publish > In Proceedings of the 12th Portuguese Conference on Artificial Intelli-
     gence (EPIA 2005) </ref: publish >
     <ref:year>2005</ref:year>
   </ref:Reference>
```

Fig. 2. Example for Aligning Reference Item to Metadata Model

Another important characteristic is that our publication ontology model reflects the upper user's requirement. For a scientific researcher, when he/she gets a publication, firstly he/she wants to know whether the publication is valuable, or how valuable the publication is. These questions should be resolved when he/she finishes reviewing. However, if some researchers have already reviewed this publication, furthermore, they gave their comment on it. By the annotation tools, these comments and evaluations are combined with those metadata extracted from documents. Through SemreX communication network, these helpful and valuable information can be shared by others, especially play a key role for guiding the reader. This approach can seriously improve the effective of literature sharing.

One example using SemreX ontology to wrap metadata of this paper is shown as follows. Part A shows the metadata of this paper. Part B shows one reference cited by the paper. Class ref:comment is defined to encoding a reviewer's remarks, and more complex definition also can be introduced to replace it.

3.1.1 Generating Metadata from Literature

Extracting semantic metadata from the content of documents is a different task. Most existing file formats do not contain semantic markup, and it remains a difficult task to distinguish between sections of a text-based document.

BibTEX: BibTEX provides metadata attributes (entry types) for nearly every kind of bibliographic entry which has its own set of attributes describing a reference. The tag-based syntax of BibTEX is at the moment the most well-known (exchange-) format for bibliography metadata, especially on the World Wide Web.

Extracting metadata from BibTEX format is easier than PDF format and PS format. Through parsing the BibTEX format tags and extracting the corresponding metadata, we can easily align these metadata to RDF-based metadata model of publications. The bib2rdf (http://www.cs.vu.nl//~mcaklein/bib2rdf/) tool translates the structured data contained in BibTEX bibliographies into an RDF-compliant form, which makes a vast amount of bibliographical information available for semantic web applications.

PS and PDF: Postscript is a programming language that is designed to specify the layout of the printed page. Postscript printers and postscript display software use an interpreter, often GhostScript (http://www.cs.wisc.edu/~ghost/) to convert the page description into the displayed graphics. The *Portable Document Format* (PDF) is built upon the PostScript format and contains similar font and metrics information. Due to this, we can treat them with same approach.

Several methods have been proposed to extract metadata from a PS or a PDF document. One is to use the spatial knowledge [9] we have of documents to classify certain elements; for example, a title generally appears at the top of a page and is in a larger font size. The technique requires extraction of text from a document and associating information about the font, metrics, and axis location to each line. Moreover, a rule set can be applied to these strings to produce increasingly accurate candidates for a particular element.

For simple and open purpose, we adopt the popular method of classifying documents by employing statistical frequencies of words to categorize elements. This method is more appropriate for document summarization tasks. We refer to the open source tools and develop Java-based tools to parse metadata from text. Before actual parsing, we use open source converters such as Pstotext (PostScript to text converter), Pdf2txt (PDF to text converter) to redirect text from the printer to a text file. Then these texts are as data sources for *Metadata Generating Process* (MGP) to post-process.

3.1.2 Metadata Generating Process

Metadata Generating Process includes two phases, extracting and aligning, shown in Fig.3. Among extracting phase, documents with different formats are passed to the Document Parser to call corresponding parser, such as BIBTEX parser, PDF parser and PS parser, to process the document and extract prerequisite metadata into unattached fields. Experimental data play a key role to steering the statistical-based parser to analysis and extract documents. We use many statistical rules to fuzzy process in extracting metadata. One example is shown as following:

```
public int GetTitleProb(String Token, int Pos, int To-
tal)
  {
  int iWords = GetWordCount(Token);
  double Prob = 0.007*iWords*iWords*iWords*iWords -
0.254*iWords*iWords*iWords + 2.1452*iWords*iWords +
8.6235*iWords - 10.129;
  if(Prob < 0) Prob = 0;
  else if(Prob > 100) Prob = 100;
  return (int)Prob;
  }
```

Its function is to estimate the probability of current reference field (Token) being a reference title. The formula and coefficients are set according to statistical rule.

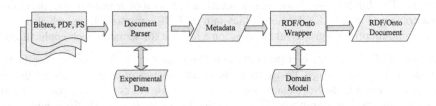

Fig. 3. Metadata Generating Process

Among aligning phase, these unattached metadata fields with corresponding semantic are sent to RDF/onto Wrapper to align these metadata to the domain model, in this paper are RDF Schema and Reference Ontology. Finally the .rdf file is created to store the literature's metadata. The RDF file provides a common style to represent and store metadata of literatures. These files can be imported to the RDF repository or be distributed directly through P2P network for sharing.

The literature document possesses various characteristics. At present, we focus on parsing PDF. Many literature organizations or digital libraries adopt or support PDF as their document format, especially in China where most digital libraries such as CNKI (http://www.edu.cnki.net/), CALIS (http://www.calis.edu.cn/calisnew/) have their private document formats. However, all of them also support PDF format, therefore PDF is regarded as the de facto standard format of digital library among Chinese research groups. In addition, XMP (*Extensible Metadata Platform*) can be utilized to annotate the PDF-based literatures with extracted metadata automatically.

3.2 Peer Metadata Model

The SemreX network utilizes the semantic topology [10] to optimize the query routing and message forwarding. Having rich metadata about others will enable peers to form communities and to have a notion of what a community is about. Having community descriptions provides an aggregated view of the network, allows users to choose which communities to join, detects new trends, or finds useful information.

Semantic-based peer description method has been applied in works, such as [4]-[6], [11], [12]. Most of them provide useful but simple information of peer descriptions, such as in [4]-[6]. [11] and [12] both provide relatively complete model, but they do not address the partition of information layer about a peer. Different from them, we elaborately design profile model for SemreX on the base of these former works. The metadata model supports flexible usage, where we divide the knowledge associated with a peer into three parts: network layer, focusing on network information; content layer, specialized in describing resources on a peer, and expertise layer, designing for a brief and effective style to create semantic overlay. Fig.4 shows the core parts of Peer Metadata Model, which are illustrated in detail as follows.

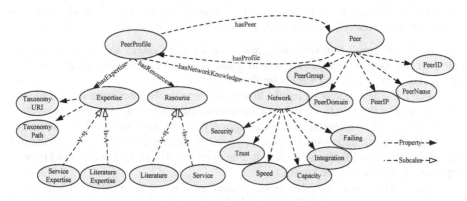

Fig. 4. The Core of Peer Metadata Model

For each peer, we have to know some basic information to identify it in a pure P2P network. The information is grouped in the *Peer* object, such as *Peer ID*, *Peer Name*, *Peer IP*, *Peer Domain* and *Peer Group*. Each peer links to a *PeerProfile* object. This object contains the meta-information of local knowledge base or links to it. The size of each profile is fairly small, and is unrelated to how much data is collected about the peer. Therefore a router can keep a few thousand active peer profiles without any significant overhead.

As far as *PeerProfile* concerned, it plays key roles in fields like:

(1) Building semantic overlay [10]. The semantic overlay relies on the knowledge of the peers about the expertise of other peers, and it can be described by the relation:

Knows $\subseteq P \times P$, where *Know (p1, p2)* means that peer *p1* knows about the expertise of peer *p2*. The semantic overlay in combination with the expertise-based peer similarity computation is the basis for semantic routing [10].

(2) Self-grouping for community. Community-based exchange is popular and effective. Different peers sharing the common resources and interests can group together to communicate each other. Under P2P environments, the community need be created dynamically, thus each peer need to know other peers' resources. *PeerProfile* just plays a bridge between peers and as a base for self-grouping policies.

(3) Creating global resource views for SemreX network. Resource view provides an intuitive style for people learning about the resources status on P2P network. When one peer collects enough well-defined peer profiles, a good and clear global resource view can be created to help retrieval and search manually.

Gathering this kind of profile information is a knowledge acquisition issue; one can get manually or automatically extracting profile information from the knowledge base or from the user's behavior.

3.2.1 Network Layer of PeerProfile

Each peer has a set of network information points collected, including statistics about how long it takes for them to reply to a network database query, how often their tunnels fail, and how many new peers they are able to introduce, as well as simple data points such as when we last heard from them or when the last communication error occurred. Collecting these data is in favor of analyzing the P2P network behaviors and designing more effective network architecture.

Speed: The speed estimates how many round trip messages we can send through the peer in a minute. For this estimation it just looks at previous performance, weighing recent data, and extrapolates it for the future.

Capacity: The capacity estimates how many tunnels the peer would agree to participate in over the next hour. Its computation is similar with speed estimation.

Integration: The integration is important only for the network database, as the detection code is not necessary for generally well connected networks. This calculation itself simply tracks the times the peer is able to tell us about a peer we do not know or updated data for a peer we know.

Failing: The failing calculation keeps track of a few data points and determines whether the peer is overloaded or is unable to continue its agreements.

Trust and *Security* are important when the P2P is for commercial purpose.

We drill through each peer's profile to come up with a few key calculations, and based upon those, we organize each peer into groups such as fast, capable, well integrated, trusted, not failing, and failing. Such network knowledge is easily acquired by underlying P2P platform (e.g. JXTA [14]), and be an assistant in peer selection with expertise for forwarding. When the router wants to build a tunnel, it looks for fast peers; when it wants to test peers it simply chooses capable ones; while for routing, the failings will not be taken into account. Of course, this relies on real-time information collection and precise calculation.

3.2.2 Content Layer of PeerProfile

The peer profile ontology has a major class *Resource* which is crucial for enabling profile-based peer management and resource discovery. *Resource* has several properties, such as: *Name, Category, Amount, URI*, and *Location*.

Resource is an abstract class with its subclasses, such as *Literature, Web Service*, which covers several possible types of resources hosted at a given peer. Each subclass has its own properties, synchronously inherits general information from class *Resource*. *Resource* also holds the capacity for timed content update, query and request language support definition. It also utilizes services registry, since SemreX also conceives of the services discovery on it [13].

3.2.3 Expertise Layer of PeerProfile

The class *Expertise* has two important attributes:

TaxonomyURI. This label contains the URL of any open or user-defined taxonomy, such as ACM CCS (http://www.acm.org/class/1998/) for digital library, the NAICS (http://www.census.gov/epcd/www/naics.html) and the UNSPSC (http://eccma.org/unspsc/browse/) for most web services registry.

TaxonomyTopic. This label represents topics path from a root to the most specific topic which an instance belongs to in a classification, e.g. *ACMCCS98 /Information Storage and Retrieval / Information Search and Retrieval/ Selection Process* (from ACM CCS) and */Travel and Food and Lodging and Entertainment Services /Travel facilitation /Travel agents /Tour arrangement services* (from UNISPC).

Expertise is designed for a brief style to build semantic overlay. Comparing the *TaxonomyTopic* of two *Expertise*s can easily decide the semantic neighborhood of two peers by taxonomy [10]. This is a key base for building semantic topology.

4 Conclusion and Future Works

We have built a prototype system of SemreX for sharing metadata of publications. For each processing, the bibliographic files are converted to text files, and metadata are extracted and wrapped into RDF file according to the reference ontology. The publications are also classified by literature's taxonomy. One RDF repository is created in memory to store these metadata. The user can search the publication in local peer, or from other peers through semantic overlay. We also prepare many data to test the model, the MGP works well in parsing PDF formats. At present, the whole system is under testing. More evaluations and practical usages must be done to improve the models in the future. Further development will make it more friendly and strong.

References

1. M. Ehrig, C. Schmitz, S. Staab, J. Tane, and C. Tempich, "Towards Evaluation of Peer-to-Peer-based Distributed Knowledge Management Systems", *Proceedings of the AAAI Spring Symposium on Agent-Mediated Knowledge Management (AMKM-2003)*, Springer LNAI, Vol.2926, 2004, pp.73-88.

2. W. Nejdl, B. Wolf, C. Qu, S. Decker, M. Sintek, A. Naeve, M. Nilsson, M. Palmer, and T. Risch, "EDUTELLA: A P2P Networking Infrastructure Based on RDF", *Proceedings of Eleventh International World Wide Web Conference*, 2002, pp.604-615.
3. M. Ehrig, C. Tempich, J. Broekstra, F. van Harmelen, M. Sabou, R. Siebes, S. Staab, and H. Stuckenschmidt, "SWAP: Ontology-based Knowledge Management with Peer-to-Peer", *Proceedings of the 1st National Workshop Ontologie-basiertes Wissensmanagement (WOW2003)*, Bonn, 2003, pp.17-20.
4. M. Bonifacio, R. Cuel, G. Mameli, and M. Nori, "A Peer-to-Peer Architecture for Distributed Knowledge Management", *Proceedings of 3rd International Symposium on Multi-Agent Systems, Large Complex Systems, and E-Businesses (MALCEB'02)*, 2002.
5. S. S. Raza Abidi and X. L. Pang, "Knowledge Sharing Over P2P Knowledge Networks: A Peer Ontology and Semantic Overlay Driven Approach", *Proceedings of International Conference on Knowledge Management*, 2004.
6. S. Castano, A. Ferrara, S. Montanelli, and D. Zucchelli, "HELIOS: A General Framework for Ontology-based Knowledge Sharing and Evolution in P2P Systems", *Proceedings of 2nd Web Semantics Workshop*, Prague, Czech Republic, 2003.
7. P. Haase, B. Schnizler, J. Broekstra, M. Ehrig, F. van Harmelen, M. Menken, P. Mika, M. Plechawski, P. Pyszlak, R. Siebes, S. Staab, and C. Tempich, "Bibster: A Semantics-Based Bibliographic Peer-to-Peer System", *Proceedings of the 3rd International Semantic Web Conference*, Hiroshima, Japan, 2004, pp.122-136.
8. Y. Sure, S. Bloehdorn, P. Haase, J. Hartmann, and D. Oberle, "The SWRC Ontology - Semantic Web for Research Communities", *Proceedings of the 12th Portuguese Conference on Artificial Intelligence (EPIA 2005)*, 2005.
9. G. Giuffrida, E. C. Shek, and J. Yang, "Knowledge-based Metadata Extraction from Post-Script Files", *Proceedings of the fifth ACM Conference on Digital Libraries*, San Antonio, Texas, United States, June 2000, pp.77-84.
10. H. Chen, H. Jin, and X. Ning, "Semantic Peer-to-Peer Overlay for Efficient Content Locating", *Proceedings of 2006 APWeb Workshops (MEGA'06)*, 2006, pp.545-554.
11. M. Ehrig, P. Haase, R. Siebes, S. Staab, H. Stuckenschmidt, R. Studer, and C. Tempich, "The SWAP Data and Metadata Model for Semantics-based Peer-to-Peer Systems", *Proceedings of First German Conference on Multiagent Technologies (MATES-2003)*, Springer LNAI, Vol.2831, Erfurt, Germany, 2003, pp.144-155.
12. O. Parkhomenko, Y. Y. Lee, and E. K. Park, "Ontology-driven Peer Profiling in Peer-to-Peer Enabled Semantic Web", *Proceedings of the Twelfth ACM International Conference on Information and Knowledge Management (CIKM 2003)*, 2003, pp.564-567.
13. H. Wu, H. Jin, and H. Chen, "Semantic-Overlay-Driven Web Services Discovery", *Proceedings of the First International Conference on Semantics, Knowledge and Grid (SKG2005)*, 2005.
14. Y. Yu and H. Jin, "Building a Semantic P2P Scientific References Sharing System with JXTA", *Proceedings of the Asia-Pacific Web Conference*, 2006, pp.937-942.

Clustering Large Scale of XML Documents

Tong Wang[1], Da-Xin Liu[1], Xuan-Zuo Lin[2], Wei Sun[1], and Gufran Ahmad[1]

[1] Department of Computer Science and Technology, Harbin Engineering University, China
Wangtong@hrbeu.edu.cn
[2] Northeast Agriculture University, Harbin, China
xuanzuolin@sina.com

Abstract. Clustering is able to facilitate Information Retrieval. This paper addresses the issue of clustering a large number of XML documents. We propose ICX algorithm with a novel similarity metric based on quantitative path. In our approach, each document is firstly represented by path sequences extracted from XML trees. Then these sequences are mapped into quantitative path, by which the distance between documents can be computed with low complexity. Finally, the desired clusters are constructed by utilizing ICX method with literal local search. Experimental results, based on XML documents obtained from DBLP, show the effectiveness and good performance of the proposed techniques.

1 Introduction

Since XML is becoming the pervasive web data exchange format, much research effort is currently devoted to support the storage and retrieval of large collections of such documents. Our research is driven by the hypothesis that closely associated documents tend to be relevant to the same requests, so that grouping similar documents accelerates the search [1]. However, traditional text clustering approaches [2] didn't take the structural information of XML into account. This paper considers the structure of XML and extracts paths from documents.

Many researchers [3][4][5] measure structural similarity using the "edit distance" between tree structures. However, the edit distance between two documents has time complexity at least $O(n^2)$ and the algorithm requires computing the distance for each document-pair. Thus, it is unsuitable for a collection of large documents.

In this paper, we introduce a novel indirect clustering method ICX for XML documents. The contributions are as follows: ① a novel distance metric is proposed based on quantitative path sequence, called QX_path. This metric calculation is simple with low computational complexity, which is fit for clustering high-volume XML documents. ② Based on the metric above, an improved C-means ICX method is proposed. This method solves local optima problem and the experiment compared with C-means shows its efficiency.

The remaining of the paper is organized as follows: section 2 is the feature extraction and similarity metric; section 3 introduced ICX clustering method; section 4 shows experiment evaluation. We conclude in section 5.

Y.-C. Chung and J.E. Moreira (Eds.): GPC 2006, LNCS 3947, pp. 447–455, 2006.
© Springer-Verlag Berlin Heidelberg 2006

2 Model Representation and Similarity Metric

Compared to traditional Vector Space Model (VSM), we use a different metric, called QX_path. In this model, each document is expressed by path sequences, and then is transformed to QX_path according to tag-mapping table. Finally, we define the similarity calculation, which has a lower time complexity.

2.1 Document Representation

XML document can be viewed as a labeled tree. In our case, we define here document model tree D_T.

Definition 1. XML document tree. Suppose a countable infinite set E of element labels (tags), a countable infinite set A of attribute names. An *XML document tree* is defined to be $d = (V, lab, ele, att, v_r)$ where V is a finite set of nodes in d; lab is a function from V to $E \cup A$; *ele* is a partial function from V to a sequence of V nodes such that for any $v \in V$, if *ele(v)* is defined then $lab(v) \in E$; *att* is a partial function from $V \times A$ to V such that for any $v \in V$ and $l \in A$, if $att(v,l) = v_1$, then $lab(v) \in E$ and $lab(v_1) = l$; v_r is a distinguished node in V called root of d, $lab(v_r) = root$.

Figure 1 shows an example of XML document tree. The model is a rooted, directed, and unordered tree. A path in D_T is sequence of nodes $v_1, v_2, v_3, ..., v_n$, through which we can traverse step by step in D_T. In addition, there exists one and only one path from node v_i to node v_j for each v_i and v_j, $v_i \neq v_j$. Before we formally define QX_path, we first give the definition of X_path.

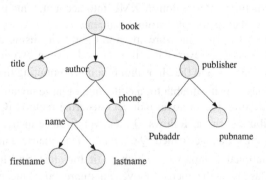

Fig. 1. XML document tree

Definition 2. Path Sequence. Given v_i and D_T, the path sequence of v_i is defined as an ordered sequence of tag names from *root* to v_i, denoted as

$$X\_path_{v_i}^{D_T} = \{v_0, v_1, ..., v_m\} \quad \text{where } v_k \in \sum_{D_T} , k \in [1...m]$$

Given node v_i and v_p, we define v_i is *nested* in v_p w.r.t. $i < p \wedge v_i, v_p \in X \_ path_{v_i}^{D_T}$.
Note that $X \_ path$ describes hierarchical and structural information of the XML document D_{Tk}, for it shows how v_i is nested in D_{Tk}. Furthermore, in XML document collection, an XML document D_{Tk} consists of many $X \_ path_{v_i}^{D_{Tk}}$ sequences, denoted as follows.

$$D_{Ti} = \{ X \_ path_{v1}^{D_{Tk}}, X \_ path_{v2}^{D_{Tk}}, ..., X \_ path_{vn}^{D_{Tk}} \} .\tag{1}$$

2.2 Similarity Metric

For clustering methods, similarity metric is foremost and related directly to the computing complexity. This paper proposes a novel distance metric based on quantitative $QX \_ path$ with low complexity. And our idea is inspired by numeric transformation of liner space [10]: Let the size of the alphabet be c, with an established order on the symbols in the alphabet. Choose an integer d>2c. Let a string of length n be $S_1, S_2, ..., S_n$, with each symbol S_i mapped to an integer t_i between 1 and c. t_i depicts the symbol position in the string, where $1 < t_i < c$. Thus, the string can be mapped to linear expression $t_1 / d + t_2 / d^2 + ... + t_n / d^n$.

In our approach, we map $X \_ path$ to numeric $QX \_ path$, by which we compute the similarity metric between each documents. Given document collection D_{Tall}, occurring tags collection T_{all} and size of tags collection $| T_{all} |$, $X \_ paths$ can be translated to $QX \_ paths$ according to the tag-mapping table. When the mapping table is constructed, WordNet Java API [7] is employed to consider semantics of tag (v_i) in each document and determine whether two tags are synonyms.

Table 1. Tag-mapping table of Fig.1

tag	position	tag	position
book	1	phone	6
title	2	pubaddr	7
author	3	pubname	8
pub-lisher	4	firstname	9
name	5	lastname	10

Definition 3. Quantitative XML path sequence ($QX \_ path$). Given $N_{D_{Tk}}(v_i)$, the mapping function from v_i of D_{Tk} to numeric representation, we define the quantitative path as follows:

$$QX \_ path_{v_i}^{D_{Tk}} = N_{D_{Tk}}(v_1) / d + N_{D_{Tk}}(v_2) / d^2 + ... + N_{D_{Tk}}(v_i) / d^i .\tag{2}$$

where d=2$| T_{all} |$+1.

The method has the ability to preserve "prefix " properties: the nearer the node to the root, the more discriminable contribution the node has to the structure. That is to say, we needn't represent all the paths from root. When the distance of paths is computed, the root-to-leaf paths can represent almost all the structural information extracted from the XML tree.

Note that equation 1 can be turned into equation 3. In this process, the structural information can be mapped into rational numbers, which can reduce the expense of similarity calculation subsequently.

$$D_{T_i} = \{QX\_path_{v1}^{D_{Tx}}, QX\_path_{v2}^{D_{Tx}}, ..., QX\_path_{vn}^{D_{Tx}}\} . \tag{3}$$

Example1. As is shown in table1, T_{all} ={book, title, author, publisher, name, phone, pubaddr, name, firstname, lastname}, $|T_{all}|$=10. Let's take some paths as an example:

$X\_path_{firstname}^{D_T} = \{book, author, name, firstname\}$,

$X\_path_{title}^{D_T} = \{book, title\}$.

The corresponding rational number will be:

$QX\_path_{firstname}^{D_T} = N_{D_T}(book)/|T_{all}| + N_{D_T}(author)/|T_{all}|^2 +$

$N_{D_T}(name)/|T_{all}|^3 + N_{D_T}(firstname)/|T_{all}|^4 = 1/21 + 3/21^2 + 4/21^4 + 5/21^5$

$QX\_path_{title}^{D_T} = N_{D_T}(book)/|T_{all}| + N_{D_T}(title)/|T_{all}|^2 = 1/21 + 2/21^2$

Based on the above feature extraction, we define the distance metric between D_{Tx} and D_{Ty} .

$$Dist(D_{Tx}, D_{Ty}) = \sqrt{\sum_{v_i \in D_{Tx}} \sum_{v_j \in D_{Ty}} |QX\_path_{v_i}^{D_{Tx}} - QX\_path_{v_j}^{D_{Ty}}|} . \tag{4}$$

The time complexity of the metric calculation is satisfactory. Traditional distance metrics often requires mapping features into vectors and dealing with them in the high-dimensional Vector Space Model (VSM) [11][12], in which time complexity is expensive. While the Quantitative path is an indirect distance method, for it only measures the documents through paths they contain.

Meanwhile, as mentioned above, tree edit distance [3] is unfit for large XML documents, because the computational expense of metric is $O(n^2)$. In our case, the distance between two documents has time complexity $O(p^2)$, where p denotes the scales of QX_path s and is far less than the scale of document collections.

3 ICX Cluster Technique

Document clustering is to categorize the documents based on similarity without the prior knowledge on the taxonomy. And it has two beneficial aspects: efforts in integrating XML documents with different structures and semantics can be alleviated because reconciling analogous and relatively small document collection is easier. Besides, ranges of queries can be dramatically decreased to applicable documents after relevant documents are aggregated together.

Section 2 introduces the distance metric of the clustering. In this chapter, we at first introduce the basic C-means clustering method briefly. Then, we present the Improved C-means methods for XML document, called ICX.

3.1 Standard C-Means Clustering

C-means is a partitional clustering algorithm based on the firm foundation of analysis of variances. It clusters a group of data objects into a predefined number of clusters. It starts with randomly initial cluster centroids and keeps reassigning the data objects in the dataset to centroids based on the similarity between the data object and the centroids. The reassignment procedure will not stop until a convergence criterion is met (e.g., the fixed iteration number, or the cluster result does not change after a certain number of iterations). The C-means algorithm can be summarized as:

1. Randomly select cluster centroids to set an initial dataset partition.
2. Assign each data object to the closest cluster centroids.
3. Recalculate the cluster centroid $c_j = \dfrac{1}{n_j} \sum_{\forall d_j \in S_j} d_j$

   where d_j denotes the data object that belong to cluster S_j; c_j stands for the centroid; n_j is the number of data object that belong to cluster S_j.
4. Repeat step 2 and 3 until the convergence is achieved.

3.2 ICX Method

C-means algorithm is efficient, with time complexity $O(ntk)$, where n is the size of dataset, k is the clusters and t is the circle time. Recent studies have shown that partitional clustering algorithms are more suitable for clustering large datasets [6].

However, It is well known that the main drawback of the C-means algorithm is that the result is sensitive to the selection of the initial cluster centroids and may converge to the local optima [14]. To solve the problem, ICX method is proposed. The main idea is that when a solution can be no more improved□the algorithm makes the next iteration after an appropriate disturbance on the local minimum solution. Thus the algorithm can skip out of the local minimum and in the meanwhile, reach the whole search space.

Algorithm ICX
Input: n: number of XML collection; k: number of clusters
Output: k cluster
1. Randomly select one initial partition $P_k = \{C_i\}, (i = 1,....,k)$
2. Initialize current best partition
3. Give terminate condition of algorithm; $\varepsilon > 0$; maximum iterant times n of object function;
4. do {
5.   Search locally in P_k to get a local minimum $f_{local-opt}$ and its corresponding partition P_k^*;

6.   do
7. $\{ P_k = P_k^*;\ f_{local-opt} = f_{opti} ;\}$
8.   until ($f_{local-opt} > f_{opt}$);
9.   Randomly select one object v_i
10.   If v_i is not chosen, Assign v_i to other clusters by computing:

$$\Delta f = \sum_{i=1}^{k} \sum_{v_i \in S_i^*} |v_i - c_i^{'}|^2 - \sum_{i=1}^{k} \sum_{v_i \in S_i} |v_i - c_i|^2$$

11.   t=t+1
12.   If $\Delta f < \varepsilon$
13. $f_{local-opt} = f_{local-opt} + \Delta f$
14.   If $f_{local-opt} < f_{opti}$
15. $f_{opti} = f_{local-opt};\ P_k^{'} = P_k;\ t = 0$
16.   } until (t<n)

At first, ICX algorithm randomly finds a local centroid vector by standard c-means clustering method. From the line 9 to line15 indicates the local search process. Firstly, we select a vector v_i of cluster S_i randomly and reassigned to cluster S_j, the centroid vectors will be updated according to equations $c_i^{'} = \dfrac{n_i \times c_i - v_i}{n_i - 1}$ and $c_j^{'} = \dfrac{n_j \times c_j + v_i}{n_j + 1}$, where n_i and n_j is the number of XML documents. Then, we measure the influence of this reassignment using the increment $\Delta f = \sum_{i=1}^{k} \sum_{v_i \in S_i^*} |v_i - c_i^{'}|^2 - \sum_{i=1}^{k} \sum_{v_i \in S_i} |v_i - c_i|^2$. If $\Delta f < \varepsilon$, the algorithm regards current partition as local minimum and starts the local search; otherwise, the algorithm assigns the vector v_i to other clusters. During the process, if v_i is assigned for k times, we have to try to choose another $v_j (v_i \neq v_j)$. The disturbance can help for skipping out of the local resolutions to improve the quality of cluster solutions.

4 Experiments and Analysis

Our experiments were conducted on a workstation of 1.5GHz Intel Pentium 4 machine with 512 MB main memory.

4.1 Dataset

We choose a variety of XML datasets including two widely used real datasets and one synthetic dataset, Xmark. One real dataset is obtained from DBLP [16], the bibliographical data of scientific conferences and journals; the other is Swiss Prot, a real-life data set with annotations on proteins; Xmark, a synthetic dataset that models transactions on an on-line auction site. Compared with DBLP, the data in Xmark is relatively tilted and sparse, with more complex structures.

The test subset of DBLP we used consists of 10 different ACM Journals. Each journal with 100 documents is grouped, denoted by $G_i, 1 \leq i \leq 10$. We mix these documents together and cluster them for our test. In the context of clustering, we can also produce 10 categories, denoted by $C_i, 1 \leq i \leq 10$. Similarly, the subset of Protein set contains 1324 document that have been classified into 54 categories.

For the synthetic dataset, Xmark, our experiment is based on the hypothesis that the documents with the same DTD will be clustered in the same class. When we generate files using Xmark, the scale parameter of Xmark is 0.2. That is, each generated document is 20M or so. We get 5 DTD (Data Type Definition) documents [18] and for each DTD generate 20, 40, 60, 80, 100 XML documents, respectively. The five generated datasets are denoted as Xmark1, Xmark2, Xmark3, Xmark4 and Xmark5, respectively.

4.2 Measurement

In order to measure the clustering accuracy, we take the DBLP as an example. As mentioned above, the groups we specify beforehand are denoted by G_i, and the final clustered groups in the experiments are denoted by C_i. The δ function is given by

$$\delta(d_1, d_2, C_i) = \begin{cases} 0, & if \ \exists j, d_1, d_2 \in G_j \\ 1, & if \ \neg \exists j, d_1, d_2 \in G_j \end{cases} . \tag{5}$$

where $d_1 \ d_2$ are documents from C_i category. To quantify the clustering accuracy of ICX technique, we define Classified Error Rate (CER) as follows.

$$CER = \frac{\sum_i \sum_{m,n \in C_i \wedge m \neq n} \delta(m,n,C_i)}{\sum_i [i \times (i-1)/2]} \tag{6}$$

If there is no pair of documents occurring in both C and G classes, the error rate will reach the maximum value, e.g., combination $C_i^2 = i \times (i-1)/2$. CER is a relative error rate value, $0 \leq CER \leq 1$.

4.3 Results Analysis

In order to compare to naïve method, which uses the standard C-means method, we also implement the naïve clustering method. Besides, the documents were parsed into labeled trees via the parser developed by Zhang et al [15] in pre-process.

In the stage of standard C-means procedure, the choice of k is often ad hoc, larger than the number of classes in general. In our case, we choose the class number. Since C-means is sensitive to the input order of vectors, we did each experiment several times and obtained the mean of CER. Fig.2 shows the results of the two methods.

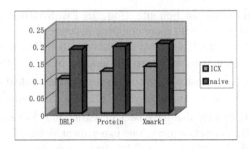

Fig. 2. Classified Error Rate of two methods: ICX and naïve method

The first case is to test the accuracy of ICX method. From figure2, for all the datasets, it is obvious that CER value of ICX outperformed that of naïve clustering. That's to say, the local search in ICX method significantly improves the clustering quality.

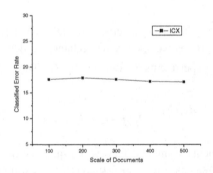

Fig. 3. The scalability of ICX method. The test dataset is Xmark datasets: Xmark1 (n=100), Xmark2(n=200), Xmark3(n=300), Xmark4(n=400) and Xmark5(n=500), respectively.

Then, we test the scalability of ICAXC. In this experiment, Xmark1, Xmark2, Xmark3, Xmark4 and Xmark5 are used as the test dataset, one by one. Figure 3 shows that the Classified Error Rate of these dataset varies very small when the number of the documents increases. It demonstrates that ICX algorithm is a robust and stable algorithm when the scale of dataset is large. Thus, the proposed method can be used for clustering a high-volume XML documents collection over the web.

5 Conclusion

In order to cluster high-volume XML documents efficiently, we have proposed a indirect distance metric based on quantitative path information. To improve the clustering quality, an improved C-means clustering is applied in our case. Experimental results show the proposed method is efficient for large scale of XML documents.

References

1. Faloutsos C. Oard D. A survey of information retrieval and filtering methods. Department of Computer Science. University of M aryland, Technical Report, CS-TR-3514, (1995)
2. O. Zamir, O. Etzioni, O. Madani, and R.M. Karp, "Fast and Intuitive Clustering of Web Documents," Proc. Second Int'l Conf.Knowledge Discovery and Data Mining,(1997) 287-290
3. A. Nierman and H.V. Jagadish, "Evaluating Structural Similarity in XML Documents," Proc. Fifth Int'l Workshop Web and Databases (2002)
4. Gianni Costa, Giuseppe Manco, Riccardo Ortale, Andrea Tagarelli: A Tree-Based Approach to Clustering XML Documents by Structure. PKDD 2004. (2004) 137-148
5. Theodore Dalamagas, Tao Cheng, Klaas-Jan Winkel, Timos K. Sellis: A Methodology for Clustering XML documents using Tree Summaries and Structural Distance Metrics. HDMS (2004)
6. Al-Sultan, K. S. and Khan, M. M..Computational experience on four algorithms forthe hard clustering problem. Pattern Recogn. Lett.17, 3, (1996) 295–308.
7. George A. Miller, Richard Beckwith, Introduction to WordNet: An On-line Lexical Database International journal of Lexicography, 3(4), (1990)235-312.
8. Mong-Li Lee, Liang Huai Yang, Wynne Hsu, Xia Yang: XClust: clustering XML schemas for effective integration. CIKM 2002, 292-299
9. Aoying Zhou, Weining Qian, Hailei Qian: Clustering DTDs: An Interactive Two-Level Ap-proach. J. Comput. Sci. Technol. 17(6) (2002) 807-819
10. H. V. Jagadish, Nick Koudas, Divesh Srivastava: On Effective Multi-Dimensional Indexing for Strings. Proceedings of the ACM SIGMOD Conference on Management of Data. (2000) 403-414
11. Antoine Doucet, Helena Ahonen-Myka: Naive Clustering of a large XML Document Collection. INEX Workshop 2002.(2002) 81-87
12. X. Cui, T. E. Potok, and P. Palathingal, Document Clustering using Particle Swarm Optimi-zation, In Proceedings of the 2005 IEEE Swarm Intelligence Symposium, June, 2005, Pasa-dena, California, USA,(2005)
13. Abiteboul, S., Buneman, P., Suciu, D.: Data On The Web: From relations to Semistructured Data and XML. Morgan Kaufmann Publishers, San Francisco, California,(2000)
14. Selim, S. Z. And Ismail, M. A.. K-means type algorithms: A generalized convergence theorem and characterization of local optimality. IEEE Trans. Pattern Anal. Mach. Intell. 6, (1984) 81–87
15. S. Zhang, J. T. L.Wang, and K. G. Herbert. Xml query by example. International Journal of Computational Intelligence and Applications, Vol. 2, No.3 (2002) 329–337
16. DBLP Computer Science Bibliography. 2004. http:// www.informatik.uni-trier.de/~ley/db/

QoS-Driven Grid Resource Selection Based on Novel Neural Networks

Xianwen Hao, Yu Dai, Bin Zhang, Tingwei Chen, and Lei Yang

College of Information Science and Engineering, Northeastern University,
Shenyang, 110004, China
haoxianwen@hotmail.com, zhangbin@mail.neu.edu.cn

Abstract. The dynamics nature of grid environment brings challenges for applications to offer nontrivial QoS on distributed, heterogeneous resources. It's a better way to select the suitable grid resources constrained by QoS. In this paper we propose the application QoS model and metrics as the standard of resource selection. We also give consideration of the existence of data dependence between the tasks composing an application and apply it to the QoS model. And we solve the resource selection problem efficiently using novel neural networks.

1 Introduction

Grid computing is evolving as the next major distributed enterprise application platform offering nontrivial QoS [1]. But the native dynamics, distributed, and heterogeneous characteristics make it challenging for applications to offer designed QoS in such a grid environment. To guarantee the application QoS is a hot point in the study of task scheduling and migration, and the primary problem is to select suitable resources.

Unlike science computing and freedom computing, enterprise computing need carefully consider the duration and price of an application, and also need to consider the availability, successful execution rate, reputation etc. In current research [7,8,9,10] on QoS model of Grid resources, few of them consider duration and price in a synthetic view, let alone considering other factors.

In this paper we consider all the factors mentioned above, and propose the application QoS model and metrics as the standard of resource selection. We also give consideration of the existence of data dependence between the tasks composing an application and apply it to the QoS model. And we turn the resource selection problem to be a multistage decision-making problem, and solve it in novel neural networks.

The rest of this paper is organized as follows. In section two, we firstly give the application's QoS model and metrics, and then propose a new QoS-driven resource selection mechanism. In section three, we propose a new neural network method to solve this multistage decision-making problem. In section four, experimentation

Y.-C. Chung and J.E. Moreira (Eds.): GPC 2006, LNCS 3947, pp. 456–465, 2006.
© Springer-Verlag Berlin Heidelberg 2006

indicates that the approach we proposed is more effective in satisfied results. In section five, we present related works. In section six, we summarize the contribution of this paper and our future work.

2 QoS-Driven Resource Selection

We can use a state chart to express a grid application and it contains two parts: tasks and the dependencies either dataflow or control-flow between tasks. A sample application expressed by state chart is shown in Fig.1.

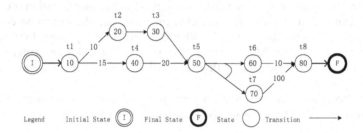

Fig. 1. A sample application expressed by state chart

In fig.1, states express the tasks t1 to t8 composing the application A. Task t2 and t3 can be done in parallel with t4. Either t6 or t7 can be done according to the result of t5. The numeric on the state expresses the workload of each task and the numeric on the arc is the data to be transferred.

All kinds of applications mentioned above need supporting from a subset of resources. Facing the plenty of all kinds of heterogeneous and distributed resources, how to allocate the most suitable resources becomes a key issue. Resource allocation includes 2 phases; the first is Resource Discovery, the process of locating a set of resources on which to schedule the task(s) of an application. And the second phase is Resource Selection, the process of selecting candidate resources from the set of resources that come out of the procedure of Resource Discovery. Then the problem of selection comes since there may be a large number of resources can fulfill the requirement. So there must be a criterion to evaluate resources based on which to do the selection.

2.1 QoS Evaluation Model

In papers [7,9,10], the concept of QoS in Grid is mentioned, but there is no broadly accepted QoS model proposed. Thus, we propose a task QoS evaluation model that takes consideration of a popular model of a single service [11] and an extended QoS evaluation model for application under specific resource allocation in the following. For each criterion, we provide a definition, and show how to compute its value for a given task (or application).

2.1.1 Task QoS Evaluation Model

Before mapping task to resource, the execution time and price are uncertain, and the QoS model cannot be given to a task without the mapping. So we give a definition task QoS as follows.

Definition 1 (Task QoS). A task QoS means the task's service quality running on given resource. It can be expressed as a vector:

$$Q(t,r)=<Du(t,r),Pr(t,r),Av(t,r),Su(t,r),Re(t,r)>$$

Du(t,r):Execution duration. Given a task t and a resource r, the execution duration Du(t,r) measures the expected delay in seconds between the moment when task t has sent to r and the moment when the task t finishes. The execution duration is computed using the expression Du(t,r)=L(r)+M(t)/Pe(r),meaning that the execution duration is the sum of the processing time M(t)/Pe(r)and the waiting time L(r) for local scheduling on resource r. M(t) expresses the workload of task t and Pe(r) expresses the performance of resource r. e.g., Pe(r) is speed ,in millions of cycles per second ,of computing resource r.

Pr(t,r):Execution price. Given a task t and resource r, the execution price Pr(t,r) is the fee that task t's execution on the resource r. The execution price is computed using the expression

Pr(t,r)=M(t)/Pe(r)*Pr(r), Pr(r) expresses the price of resource r.

Av(t,r): Availability. Given a task t and resource r, the availability Av(t,r) of a task t is the probability that the task is accessible on the resource r. The value of the availability of a task is computed using the following expression Av(t,r)=Ta(r)/ , where Ta(r) is the total amount of time (in seconds) in which resource r is available during the last   seconds. The value of may vary depending on a particular application. For example, in applications where tasks are more frequently accessed, a small value of   gives a more accurate approximation for the availability of resource. If the task is less frequently accessed, using a larger   value is more appropriate.

Su(t,r): Successful execution rate(SER). Given a task t and resource r, the successful execution rate Su(t,r) is the probability that request to task t on resource r is correctly responded. The value of the success rate is computed from data of past invocations using the expression Su(t,r)=Nc(r)/K, where Nc(r) is the number of times that all the tasks on resource r has been successfully completed within the maximum expected time frame, and K is the total number of invocations.

Re(t,r): Reputation. Given a task t and resource r, the reputation Re(t,r) of a task t is a measure of its trustworthiness on resource r. It mainly depends on end user's experiences of using the tasks on resource r. Different end users may have different opinions on the same task. The value of the reputation is defined as the average ranking given to the tasks on special resource r by end users, i.e., $Re(t, r) = \sum_{i=1}^{n} Ri / n\phi$, where Ri is the end user's ranking on a task's reputation on resource r, n is the number of times the tasks has been graded on resource r. Usually, end users are given a range to rank tasks. Φ is the upper limit of the reputation range [0, Φ].

2.1.2 Application QoS Evaluation Model

As for the application, in addition to consider the basic QoS of tasks, the dependence degree between tasks needs to be considered seriously. Especially for the application with heavy data dependence, large amount of time is consumed on the data transfer between tasks on different resource nodes .the transaction of data dependence effects the application's QoS. So we propose a different QoS vector for application as followings:

$$Q(A):<Du(A),Pr(A),Av(A),Su(A),Re(A),DD(A)>$$

Where Q(A) indicates the QoS of application A; the new-coming element DD (A) indicates the dependence degree of A, we give its definition as follows:

Definition 2 (Dependence Degree between Two Tasks). $\forall t_i, t_{i-1} \in T \wedge t_{i-1} \rightarrow t_i$, $DD(t_{i-1} \rightarrow t_i)$ indicates the dependence degree between task t_{i-1} and t_i and symbol "$\rightarrow$" presents that task t_{i-1} is invoked just before t_i, in other words, the output parameters of t_{i-1} will be given to task t_i as its input parameters. T expresses the set of tasks.

In the following, we give a formula of $DD(t_{i-1} \rightarrow t_i)$:

$$DD(t_{i-1} \rightarrow t_i) = L_n(r(t_{i-1}), r(t_i)) + D(t_{i-1}, t_i) / B(r(t_{i-1}), r(t_i))$$, where $r(t_i)$ is the resource where task i is allocated, $B(r(t_{i-1}), r(t_i))$ is the network bandwidth between the two resources where t_{i-1} and t_i allocated, and $L_n(r(t_{i-1}), r(t_i))$ the network latency of them.

Definition 3 (Dependence Degree of Application). DD(A) is the sum of dependence degrees of all the task pairs.

It is computed using the following expression $DD(A) = \sum_{i=1}^{N} DD(t_{i-1} \rightarrow t_i)$, where N is the amount of tasks in A.

Among the 6 quality factors, some could be negative, i.e., the higher the value, the lower the quality. Others are positive. From another aspect of the criteria, some of them are linear which can be added, others are non linear. In order to use a uniform computing model to express the element in the QoS vector, we use function Score, which turns each element to a form which follows the ascent property, has the addable property and makes the problem a linear one (see table 1 Function Score Column). After that we transform the scores to value between 0 and 1 so as to keep balance among 6 factors, using function f(x)=(x-Min(x))/(Max(x)-Min(x)). At last we add the scores. Table 1 illustrates the procedure simply.

Table 1. Aggregation Functions for Application QoS Model

	Function Score	Aggregation Function
Duration	Score(Du(r,t))= 1/Du(r,t)	Du(A)= ∑f(Score(Du(r,t)))
Price	Score(Pr(r,t))=1/Pr(r,t)	Pr(A)= ∑f(Score(Pr(r,t)))
Availability	Score(Av(r,t))=ln(Av(r,t))	Av(A)= ∑f(Score(Av(r,t)))
SER	Score (Su(r,t))=ln(Su(r,t))	Su(A)= ∑f(Score (Su(r,t)))
Reputation	Score (Re(r,t))=Re(r,t)	Re(A)= ∑f(Score (Re(r,t)))
Dependence Degree	Score(DD(r,t))=1/DD(r,t)	DD(A)=∑f(Score (DD(r,t)))

And then we can use a Multiple Criteria Decision Making (MCDM) [2] technique to give an overall evaluation for application A as follows:

$$Q(A) = \frac{Du(A)*w_{du} + Pr(A)*w_{pr} + Av(A)*w_{av} + Su(A)*w_{su} + Re(A)*w_{re} + DD(A)*w_{dd}}{w_{du} + w_{pr} + w_{av} + w_{su} + w_{re} + w_{dd}} \quad (1)$$

Where w_{du}, w_{pr}, w_{av}, w_{su}, w_{re} and w_{dd} are the *weights* assigned by the users.

From such formula, we know the purpose of selection is to find a set of resources for application A that makes the formula (1) get the max value.

Above all, we have established the evaluation model for both task and application, and we will discuss how such QoS evaluation models can do the selection in the following.

2.2 QoS-Driven Dynamic Selection Process

2.2.1 Dividing Phase
In order to do the selection easily, we will use the approaches that have been proposed in paper [3] to divide the complex structure into simple one that is just a sequent structure. A fraction of dividing example of Fig.1 is given in Fig.2.

And we must declare that after select the best satisfied concrete resources in the dividing graph, in order to achieve the original effect of the complex one, a work of combination of each divided graph into original one is needed. And for our aim is to select the best resources for application, we will pay little attention to the combination work.

Fig. 2. A fraction of dividing example of Fig.1

2.2.2 Substituting and Weighting Phase
As we have mentioned in section 2, in the state chart we just identify the tasks composing the application. For each task in a dividing graph, there are a large number of candidate resources on which the tasks can fulfill the function as user needed. So the first work needed to do is to enumerate the discovered resources for each task.

After the work above, then we will use the QoS evaluation proposed above to do the selection. Before doing this, we need a method to express the task-resource pair and QoS properties both the basic one and dependence degree.For such reason, we decide to use a weighted graph G= (V, E) to express such problem where $\forall a_{ij} \in V$, a_{ij} signifies task i on its candidate resource j and E signifies a set of arcs presenting the execution order between tasks. And based on expression (1), we can calculate the weight of arc $(t_{i-1} \rightarrow t_i)$ as expression (2),

$$weight(t_{i-1} \rightarrow t_i) = \frac{\left(\begin{array}{l} Score(Du(t_i,r_i))*W_{pr} + Score(\Pr(t_i,r_i))*W_{du} + Score(Av(t_i,r_i))*W_{av} \\ + Score(Su(t_i,r_i))*W_{su} + Score(\text{Re}(t_i,r_i))*W_{re} + DD(t_{i-1} \rightarrow t_i)*W_{dd} \end{array} \right)}{\left(W_{pr} + W_{du} + W_{av} + W_{su} + W_{re} + W_{dd} \right)} \quad (2)$$

and we can generate the Graph G as Fig.3 shows:

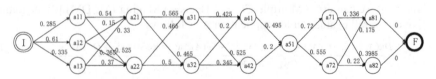

Fig. 3. Graph of task-resource assignment

Then, selection becomes a process in which single one resource of each task will be picked out based on the weight and then formed an executable application.

In essence, the process of resource selection is more or less a multistage decision making problem. We address the neural networks to be a solution since its high parallel computational power.

3 Neural Networks for QoS-Driven Resource Selection

Current approaches based on the Hopfield Neural networks, always are used to solve the problem of shortest path (SP) which apply the neuron matrix proposed by Rauch and Winarske [4] or the optimized one proposed by Thomopoulos [5] to identify the optimal path. However, such approaches are not suitable to solve the multistage decision-making problem for they normally makes all the decisions as neurons for every stage. To express the path in fig.3, 16×9 neurons are needed, in such method.

According to the unique feature of such multistage decision-making problem, we propose a structure which is a $s{\times}d$ matrix $V = (V_{ij})$ as follows:

$$ZYDNeuronMatrix = \begin{vmatrix} 1 & 0 & 1 & 1 & 0 & 1 & 0 & 0 & 1 \\ 0 & 1 & 0 & 0 & 1 & 0 & 0 & 1 & 0 \\ 0 & 0 & 0 & 0 & 0 & 0 & 1 & 0 & 0 \end{vmatrix}^{T}$$

Where i signifies the stage in the graph G and j signifies the node numbered j in stage i, $V_{ij}=0$ if node j of stage i is not selected while $V_{ij}=1$ the otherwise. From this, we know that the task needs 9×3 neurons. For Fig.3, ZYDNeuronMatrix expresses the application A, $I \rightarrow a_{12} \rightarrow a_{21} \rightarrow a_{31} \rightarrow a_{42} \rightarrow a_{51} \rightarrow a_{73} \rightarrow a_{82} \rightarrow F$. We can see that the overall neurons in this structure are less than the traditional one.

3.1 Algorithm Description

We adopt the ZYDNeuronMatrix to express the application A. Our aim is to find out the optimal selection through computing the QoS(A). We establish an energy function $E1$ signifying the QoS(A) and punishment function G which ensures that for each row there is only one and at most one nonzero entry.

$$E1 = \sum_{i=1}^{s}\sum_{j=1}^{d}\sum_{k=1}^{d}\left(V_{ij} * V_{i+1,k} * weight[i][j][i+1][k]\right), \text{ where } \forall j \leq d, \quad V_{s+1,j}=0 \tag{3}$$

$$G = -A * \sum_{i=1}^{s}\left(\sum_{j=1}^{d}V_{ij}-1\right)^{2}, \text{ where } A \text{ is a constant and } A{\geq}0 \tag{4}$$

Combining formula (3) and (4), the ultimate energy is established as follows:

$$E = \sum_{i=1}^{s}\sum_{j=1}^{d}\sum_{k=1}^{d}\left(V_{ij} * V_{i+1,k} * weight[i][j][i+1][k]\right) - A * \sum_{i=1}^{s}\left(\sum_{j=1}^{d}V_{ij}-1\right)^{2} \tag{5}$$

From paper [4], we have $\dfrac{\partial E}{\partial V_{ij}} = -\dfrac{\partial V_{ij}}{\partial t}$. Then we can delude that

$$\frac{\partial E}{\partial t} = -\frac{\partial E}{\partial V_{ij}}\frac{\partial V_{ij}}{\partial t} = -\left(\frac{\partial E}{\partial V_{ij}}\right)^2 \leq 0 \tag{6}$$

Formula (6) proves that the NN follows a gradient-descent of the energy, and ultimately it will keep the state unchangeable. Then, our aim is to change the state of NN, and find the state that can fulfill (6). That is to say, change the state as expression (7) used in paper [5] to fulfill expression (8).

$$V_{ij}(t+1) = \frac{1}{2}\left(1 + \tanh\left(\sum_{x \neq i}\sum_{y \neq j} weight \quad [x][y][i][j] * V_{xy}(t)\right)\right) \tag{7}$$

$$\frac{\partial E}{\partial V_{ij}} = \sum_k weight \ [i][j][i+1][k] * V_{i+1,k}(t) - 2 * A * \left(\sum_j V_{ij}(t) - 1\right) = 0 \tag{8}$$

In fig.4, we give an algorithm to describe the whole process of selection.

```
Procedure Selection_Algorithm
begin
   Set the MaxStep of iteration.
   Generate the first state.
   while the step less than MaxStep do
      For each step,
         Compute the in- and external state of neuron,
         And compute the function energy.
      if the state is the Ultimate_State then
         Output the result,
      else
         Generate the next state.
   endwhile
End Selection_Algorithm
```

Fig. 4. Selection process

Based on such algorithm, we can do the multistage decision-making problem and get the optimal Resource Selection in the term of better constraint evaluation value.

4 Experimentation

In order to verify the approach we proposed in this paper, we use the example application A as section 2 discussed, and we just discuss a fraction of it showed in fig.2. Table 2 lists the decomposed tasks in the first column "Task". The candidate resources are shown in the second column "Candidate resources". These candidates were discovered from resource registries. The scores of basic QoS factors and task dependence degree are shown in the third and the fourth column in the Table 2. QoS2 is the total value computed by the proposed QoS evaluation model while QoS1 is the value based on basic QoS standard. And two formulas are given in the following.

$$QoS2(S) = Score(Q_{pr}) * 0.2 + Score(Q_{du}) * 0.1 + Score(Q_{rat}) * 0.1 + Score(Q_{rep}) * 0.05 + Score(Q_{av}) * 0.05 + Q_{MD} * 0.5 \tag{9}$$

$$QoS1(S) = (Score(Q_{pr}) * 0.2 + Score(Q_{du}) * 0.1 + Score(Q_{rat}) * 0.1 + Score(Q_{rep}) * 0.05 + Score(Q_{av}) * 0.05)/0.5 \tag{10}$$

Table 2. QoS of Application "A" and Computing Process

Task	Candidate Resource	Score of Basic QoS Parameters						Score of Dependence Degree	QoS2
		Duration	Price	SER	Reputation	Availability	QoS1		
a1	a11	0.1	0.2	0.3	0	0.3	0.17	DD(I→a11)=0.4	0.285
	a12	0.1	0.3	0.2	0.5	0.3	0.22	DD(I→a12)=1	0.61
	a13	0	0.4	0	0.2	0.2	0.12	DD(I→a13)=0.55	0.335
a2	a21	0.2	0.1	0.5	0.4	0.4	0.28	DD(a11→a21)=0.8	0.54
								DD(a12→a21)=0.3	0.15
								DD(a13→a21)=0.66	0.33
	a22	0.5	0.4	0.6	0.7	0.8	0.55	DD(a11→a22)=0.5	0.525
								DD(a12→a22)=0.53	0.265
								DD(a13→a22)=0.74	0.37
a3	a31	0.5	0	0.1	0.1	1	0.33	DD (a21→a31)=0.8	0.565
								DD (a22→a31)=0.93	0.465
	a32	0.9	0.6	0.4	0.6	0.4	0.66	DD (a21→a32)=0.27	0.465
								DD (a22→a32)=1	0.5
a4	a41	0.6	0.3	0.7	0.5	0.6	0.55	DD (a31→a41)=0.3	0.425
								DD (a32→a41)=0.4	0.2
	a42	0.3	0.5	0.8	0.8	0.7	0.53	DD (a31→a42)=0.52	0.525
								DD (a32→a42)=0.69	0.345
a5	a51	0.4	0.9	0.9	0.9	0.8	0.69	DD (a41→a51)=0.3	0.495
								DD (a42→a51)=0.4	0.2
a7	a71	1	0.4	1	0.6	0	0.74	DD (a51→a61)=0.7	0.72
	a72	0.2	1	0.8	0.8	0.9	0.61	DD (a51→a62)=0.5	0.555
a8	a81	0.9	0.7	0.2	1	0.32	0.672	DD (a71→a81)=0	0.336
								DD (a71→a82)=0.35	0.175
	a82	0.34	0.5	0.3	0.5	0.41	0.387	DD (a72→a81)=0.41	0.3985
								DD (a72→a82)=0.44	0.22

In table 2, the task value is calculated and we will establish the Neural Network matrix for such problem. The matrix is shown as follows:

$$ZYDNeuronMatrix = \begin{vmatrix} 1 & 0 & 1 & 1 & 0 & 1 & 0 & 0 & 1 \\ 0 & 1 & 0 & 0 & 1 & 0 & 0 & 1 & 0 \\ 0 & 0 & 0 & 0 & 0 & 0 & 10 & 0 & 0 \end{vmatrix}^{T}$$

Finally, through using the Algorithm 1 presented in section 3 and only after 34 times iteration, we can get the ultimate application as follows:

Fig. 5. The ultimate application of Table 1 using proposed QoS evaluation model

Furthermore, while just considering the basic QoS parameters the ultimate application can be seen in Figure 6. From Figure 6, and according to Table 2, task a71 and task a81 have the most slow data transfer rate, and it's the worse situation for application A.

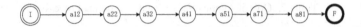

Fig. 6. The ultimate application of Table 1 using basic QoS evaluation model

From such experimentation, we can conclude that the QoS evaluation model is effective and the neural network model we proposed has power in dealing with such resource selection problem for applications with data dependence.

5 Related Works

In paper [6], Scheduling of workflows is supported by the Gridbus Workflow Engine which otherwise has similar properties with respect to the scheduling of data intensive applications.

In paper [7], the authors investigate some of the relevant issues that must be considered in designing grid applications that deliver appropriate QoS for commercial applications: definition of metrics, relationships between resource allocation and SLAs, and QoS-related mechanisms.

In paper [8], the authors consider a very general case in which applications are decomposed into tasks that exhibit precedence relationships, and provided a framework for building heuristic solutions for NP-hard problem.

In papers [9,10], the authors introduce a novel QoS guided task scheduling algorithm for Grid computing. The algorithm is based on a general adaptive scheduling heuristics that includes QoS guidance. And the authors propose the conception of QoS of resource. But In their study, only one dimension QoS is considered.

6 Conclusions and Future Work

In summary, we have presented a new application QoS evaluation model, composed by factors latency, price, availability, successful execution rate, reputation and dependence degree. Compared with current popular methods, we do better in resource selection with such model we proposed, especially for application with heavy data transfer due to the consideration of the factor dependence degree. When consider the selection process, we employ Neural Network to solve the multistage decision-making problem. We revolutionized the popular matrix and build a suitable energy function to solve such unique problem. And the experimentation shows that the mathematical model we proposed is more pragmatic than others in dealing with resource selection for a grid application and the neural network model we proposed is more effective.

Our future work will be focused on optimizing the QoS evaluation model. The dependence degree factor needs a better depiction, which is now only expressed by the data transfer time. Moreover, a better method of designating the suitable weight is worth considering. Lastly, adopting new algorithms to optimize the neural network we proposed will also be explored.

References

1. I. Foster, A. Roy, and V. Sander: A quality of service architecture that combines resource reservation and application adaptation. The 8th International Workshop on Quality of Service - IEEE (2000)
2. L.R. Ford Jr. and D.R. Fulkerson: Flows in Networks. Princeton University Press, Princeton, N.J. (1962)
3. Yu T. and Lin K.J.: Service Selection Algorithms for Web Services with End-to-end QoS Constraints. IEEE International Conference on E-Commerce Technology (CEC'04). California (2004)
4. L Zhang, S C A Thomopoulos: Neural network implementation of the shortest path algorithm for traffic routing in communication networks. The Int'l Joint Conf on Neural Networks, Washington DC (1989)
5. Herbert E Raugh, Theo Winarske: Neural Networks for Routing Communication Traffic. IEEE Control System Mag (1998)
6. J. Yu and R. Buyya: A novel architecture for realizing grid work_ow using tuple spaces. *Proceedings of the Fifth IEEE/ACM International Workshop on Grid Computing (GRID'04)*. Pittsburgh, PA,USA: IEEE Computer Society (2004)
7. Daniel A. Menascé, E. Casalicchio: Quality of Service Aspects and Metrics in Grid Computing. Proc. 2004 Computer Measurement Group Conference, Las Vegas, NV (2004).
8. Daniel A. Menascé, E. Casalicchio: A Framework for Resource Allocation in Grid Computing. Proc. 12th Annual Meeting of the IEEE/ACM International Symposium on Modeling, Analysis, and Simulation of Computer and Telecommunication Systems (MASCOTS), Volendam, The Netherlands (2004)
9. Xiaoshan He, Xian-He Sun, and Gregor von Laszewski: QoS Guided Min-Min Heuristic for Grid Task Scheduling. Journal of Computer Science and Technology, Special Issue on Grid Computing, 18(4) (2003)
10. X. He, X.-H. Sun, and G. Laszewski: A QoS Guided Scheduling Algorithm for the Computational Grid. The Proc. of the International Workshop on Grid and Cooperative Computing (GCC02), Hainan, Chian (2002)
11. Liangzhao Zeng, Boualem Benatallah, etc.: QoS-Aware Middleware for Web Services Composition. IEEE Transactions on Software Engineering, Vol. 30, No.5 (2004)

Towards Decentralized Load Balancing in a Computational Grid Environment

Kai Lu, Riky Subrata, and Albert Y. Zomaya

Networks & Systems Lab, School of Information Technologies,
University of Sydney, NSW 2006, Australia
{kailu, efax, zomaya}@it.usyd.edu.au

Abstract. Load balancing has been a key concern for locally distributed multi-processor systems. The emergence of computational grid extends this problem, such as scalability, heterogeneity of computing resources and considerable communication delay. In this paper, we study the problem of scheduling a large number of CPU-intensive jobs on such systems. The time spent by a job in the system is considered as the main issue that needs to be minimized. The proposed dynamic algorithm of scheduling jobs consists of two policies: Instantaneous Distribution Policy (IDP) and Load Adjustment Policy (LAP). Our algorithm does not address directly the load balancing problem since it is completely unrealistic in such large environments, but we will show that even a non-perfectly load balanced system can behave reasonably well by taking into account the jobs' time demands. The proposed algorithm is evaluated by a series of simulations.

1 Introduction

Computational grid is a promising platform that provides plenty of resources for high performance computing [1]. The grids comprise a variety of high-performance architectures – ranging from workstation networks to supercomputers. One of the biggest advantages of a grid environment over an isolated distributed system is that the participating computing resources can be utilized more efficiently. However, to fully exploit such grid systems, resource management and scheduling are key grid services, where issues of load balancing represent a common concern for most grid infrastructure developers.

Load balancer found in traditional computing system help harness the computational power provided by a pool of workstations within one domain [2]. With the growth in the scale of computational grid, a number of new challenges are presented, including heterogeneous computing resources, and considerable communication delay – the communication delay among computing resources is always one of the most costly and the least reliable factor in grid computing.

In this paper, we propose a load balancing algorithm especially designed to tackle the above new challenges of computing grid. Our algorithm is dynamic, sender-initiated and decentralized. Our algorithm comprises of two specific policies for load distribution that are driven by performance benefit jobs can gain, which are Instantaneous Distribution Policy (IDP) and Load Adjustment Policy respectively (LAP). In order to reduce/minimize the state-collection overhead in our proposed LB strategy, state information exchange is done via mutual information feedback.

Y.-C. Chung and J.E. Moreira (Eds.): GPC 2006, LNCS 3947, pp. 466–477, 2006.

The remainder of the paper is organized as follows. Section 2 presents related work. Section 3 presents the system model. Sections 4 describes in details the design of the proposed algorithm. In section 5, the performance of our algorithm is evaluated in a series of simulations. Finally, this paper is concluded in section 6.

2 Related Works

In this section, we will give an overview of related work. LB algorithms can be classified into static and dynamic approaches [3].

Static LB algorithms (e.g. [4]) assume that *a priori* information about all the characteristics of the jobs, the computing nodes and the communication network are known and provided. LB decisions are made deterministically or probabilistically at compile time and remain constant during runtime. The static approach is simple and has minimal runtime overhead. However, it has two major disadvantages. Firstly, the workload distribution of many applications cannot be predicted before program execution. Secondly, it assumes that the characteristics of the computing resources and communication network are all known in advance and remain constant. Such an assumption may not apply to a grid environment.

In contrast, dynamic LB algorithms attempt to use the runtime state information to make more informative decisions in sharing the system load. Dynamic LB algorithms can be further classified into a centralized approach and a decentralized approach. In the centralized approach (e.g. [5, 6]), one node in the distributed system acts as the central controller. It has a global view of the load information in the system, and decides how to allocate jobs to each of the nodes. Many authors argue that it is difficult for this approach to address communication overhead and administration of remote workstations. When the system size increases, the global knowledge of the system's attributes (like the total work load) is prohibitive due to the communication overhead produced, and the central controller may become a system bottleneck and the single point of failure.

In the decentralized approach (e.g. [7]), all nodes in the distributed system are involved in making the LB decision. Since the LB decisions are distributed, it is costly to let each node obtain the dynamic state information of the whole system. Hence, most algorithms [8-10] only use partial information stored in the local node to make a sub-optimal decision.

LB algorithms have been extensively studied in the literature, but most of the studies mentioned above only considered some over-simplified assumptions that are not applicable for the Grid Computing environment. For example, most of them assume that all the nodes have the same processing power, and that the inter-node communication delay is negligible (e.g. nearest-neighbor algorithm[9, 10]). Some studies (e.g. [11]) also assumed the existence of an efficient broadcasting service on the communication network.

3 System Model

It is assumed that the grid system consists of a collection of sites S connected by a communication network, as shown in Fig. 1. The set S contains n sites, labeled as

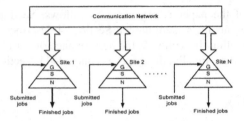

Fig. 1. Logical view of decentralized Load Balancing architecture

$s_1,...,s_n$. Each site may contain multiple computing nodes and each computing node may be equipped with multiple processors. The sites in the grid system may have different computing capability. The computing capability reflects relative capability compared with the computing capability of the slowest site in the system, denoted as APW_i.

3.1 Architecture Model

Logically, the site architecture is hierarchical and is divided into three levels: the Grid-Level, the Site-Level and the Node-Level. The Grid-Level scheduler is responsible for load control among grid sites. The Site-Level consists of a collection of computing nodes. The Site-Level scheduler can fully control the computing nodes within the site but cannot operate the computing nodes in other sites directly. The management of jobs at Site-Level is addressed by many research and commercial systems [2]: Condor, Load Sharing Facility, Portable Batch System, LoadLeveler, etc. The Node-Level is a computing node. To clarify the statement and emphasize our main idea, we simplify the model of grid site as one computing node with a single processor. Actually, our scheduling algorithm can be easily extended to accommodate aforementioned complicated cases.

3.2 Communication Model

The sites S is fully interconnected, meaning that there exists at least one communication path between any two sites in S. The only way for inter-site communication is through message passing. There is a non-trivial communication delay on the communication network between the sites. The communication delay is different between different pairs of sites. The underlying network protocol guarantees that messages sent across the network are received in the order sent. There is no efficient broadcasting service available.

Our communication model represents the network performance between any site pair (s_i, s_j) using two parameters: a transmission delay TD_{ij} and a data transmission rate BW_{ij}. The communication time for sending an m bytes message between these sites is then given by $TD_{ij}+m/BW_{ij}$. TD_{ij} includes a start-up cost and delays incurred by contention at intermediate links on the path between s_i and s_j. TD_{ij} and BW_{ij} can be dynamically forecasted by the Network Weather Service [12]. Some other research works [13-15] on estimating host distance between any two IP addresses are also proposed.

3.3 Job and Job Queue Model

For any site $s_i \in S$, there are jobs arriving at s_i. The jobs are assumed to be computationally intensive and mutually independent. As soon as a job arrives, it must be assigned to exactly one site for processing. When a job is completed, the executing site will return the results to the originating site of the job. We use J to denote the set of all jobs generated at S, $J = \{j_1, \ldots, j_k\}$. Although in most cases the execution time of a job can not be predicted accurately, it can be estimated by using some approaches. Several papers [12, 16-17] have attempted to address the problem. In this paper, the estimations are assumed to be perfectly accurate.

We assume that there exists a global job-waiting queue at each site. We use $GJQ(s_i)$ to denote the global job-waiting queue of the site s_i. The jobs in the global job–waiting queue are processed in "First-Come-First-Serve" order.

3.4 Job Migration

Some researchers have considered job migration (migration of partly executed jobs) in their LB algorithms (e.g. [18, 19]). However, job migration is far from trivial in practice. It involves collecting all system states (e.g. virtual memory image, process control blocks, unread I/O buffer, data pointers, timers etc.) of the job, which is large and complex. Many studies (e.g. [11, 20, 21]) have shown that: (1) job migration is often difficult in practice, (2) the operation is generally expensive in most systems, and (3) there are no significant benefits of such a mechanism over those offered by non-migratory counterparts. Hence, we do not consider the migration of partly-executed jobs in this paper.

A more conservative approach is used to reduce the rate at which jobs are moved form one site to another. This can be achieved by restricting the maximum number of jobs transmitted between sites (i.e. maximum one job) at any given time. This approach might be less responsive in some cases, but is more robust and requires minimal processing power and time at each site.

3.5 Objective

The objective of our LB algorithm is defined by:

$$\text{minimize} \left(\frac{\sum_{j_i \in J} \text{respTime}\,(j_i)}{m} \right)$$

where m represents the total number of jobs in J, and $\text{respTime}(j_i)$ denotes the completion time of j_i. In other words, our goal is to minimize the average job response time, denoted as ART in the paper.

4 Proposed Dynamic Load Balancing Algorithm

Dynamic LB algorithms can be classified into sender-initiated algorithms, receiver-initiated algorithms and symmetrically-initiated algorithms according to their location policies [22, 23]. Sender-initiated algorithms let the heavily loaded sites take the initiative to request the lightly loaded sites to receive the jobs; while receiver initiated algorithms let the lightly loaded sites invite heavily loaded sites to send their jobs. Symmetrically-initiated algorithms combine the advantages of these two by requiring both senders and receivers to look for appropriate sites. In this study, we only consider sender-initiated algorithms.

Our objective is achieved by considering proximity information among neighbor sites to guide load assignments. Our algorithm has two advantages: First, the load information from neighboring sites tends to be more accurate than from non-neighboring sites because of shorter communication delay, so the policy allows load balancing to perform efficiently. Second, the load migration cost is minimized while load balancing happens among a site and its neighboring sites.

In the following sections we discuss in details the proposed decentralized dynamic LB algorithm.

4.1 Neighbors

Each scheduler automatically maintains k number of neighboring sites $NSet_i$, which the scheduler will use to select a neighboring site for offloading jobs. Neighbors for each site are formed in terms of transmission delay. For a site s_i, a site s_j is considered as its neighboring site as long as the transmission delay between the site s_j and s_i is within ε times of the transmission delay between the site s_i and the nearest site. For our experiments, we have found $\varepsilon=1.5$ to yield very good results and this value is used throughout the experiments.

4.2 Load Index

Most algorithms in the literature solely use the instantaneous run-queue length (i.e. the number of jobs being served or waiting) as the load index of a computing node [11, 24]. This approach is based on the 'join the shortest queue' intuition. The run-queue length may be a good load index if we assume that all the nodes of the system are homogeneous and the inter-node communication delay is negligible or constant. However, it is not a reliable load indicator in a heterogeneous environment. It ignores the variations in computing power. Owing to the above reasons, we do not use the run-queue length as the load indicator. Instead, an accumulative job execution time is utilized. $\forall s_i \in S$, the load index of s_i at a particular instant of time t is defined as $LD_{i,t}$ = $TET_{i,t} + RET_{i,t}$, where $TET_{i,t}$ is the total estimated job execution time of all jobs currently waiting in job queue on s_i at time instant t, $RET_{i,t}$ is the estimated remaining time of the job currently being processed by site s_i at time instant t.

4.3 Execution Cost

Unlike conventional approaches that only consider the load index in calculating the cost of executing a job on a computing node, we include the dynamic communication cost in the cost calculation. It is because the dynamic and considerable communication cost may have a great influence on the performance of a LB algorithm in the grid environment. It may be more efficient to send a job to a node with heavier load but small communication cost.

$\forall\ s_i, s_j \in S$, the execution cost of sending a job $j_x \in J$ from s_i to s_j at time instant t is estimated by s_i as

If $\text{TRAN\_IN}(j_x, s_i, s_j, t) \geq \text{LD}_{j,t}$ Then
$\quad\quad EC(j_x, s_i, s_j, t) = \text{TRAN\_IN}(j_x, s_i, s_j, t) + ETC(j_x, s_j) + \text{TRAN\_OUT}(j_x, s_j, s_i, t)$
Else
$\quad\quad EC(j_x, s_i, s_j, t) = \text{LD}_{j,t} + ETC(j_x, s_j) + \text{TRAN\_OUT}(j_x, s_j, s_i, t)$

where $\text{TRAN\_IN}(j_x, s_i, s_j, t)$ measures how long it takes to transfer a job from site s_i to site s_j. $\text{TRAN\_OUT}(j_x, s_j, s_i, t)$ measures how long it takes to transfer a job result from site s_j to site s_i. $\text{LD}_{j,t}$ is the recent load index of site s_j at the time instant t that are recorded in the site s_i. $ETC(j_x, s_j)$ denotes the expected execution time of job j_x at site s_j.

4.4 Performance Benefit

The performance benefit associated to a job j_x is based on the idea that better migration can be done by assigning a job to a grid site that would "benefit" most in terms of expected response time if that grid site is assigned to it. Let the value of performance benefit of a job j_x be the difference between its estimated response time at local site and its estimated response time at a remote site, labeled as B_x.

4.5 Information Policy

Each site s_i maintains the state information of other sites by using a state object O_i. The state object helps a site to estimate the load of other sites at any time without message transfer. Each item $O_i[j]$ is a state object and has a property list (LD, LT): $O_i[j].LD$ denotes the load information of site s_j, and $O_i[j].LT$ denotes the site s_j's local time when the load status information is reported.

Each site collects and maintains the state information of only its neighbors. $O_i[j].LD$ and $O_i[j].LT$ is maintained through message exchanges with neighbors. We could not use state-broadcast because the broadcast services are not available in grid. We also could not use state-polling approach because it has a few problems in practice; Firstly, if the polling interval is small, it will generate a large amount of network traffic. Secondly, as the job needs to wait for the polling result, polling will increase the response time of the waiting job.

Thus, in order to minimize the overhead of information collection, state information exchange is done by mutual information feedback. Specifically, when s_i transfers a job j_x to a neighbor s_j for processing. s_i appends the load information of itself and its neighbors to the job transfer request sent to s_j by piggybacking. s_j then updates the corresponding load information in its state object by comparing the timestamps if the sites contained in the transfer request belong to its neighbors. Similarly, s_j inserts the current load information of itself and its neighbors in the job acknowledge or completions reply to s_i, so s_i can update its state objects. Further, for any site $s_i \in S$, if the state object element $O_i[j]$ ($\forall s_j \in NSet_i, i \neq j$) has not been updated for a predefined period T_P, then the LB scheduler will send an information exchange message to s_j.

4.6 Transfer Policy and Location Policy

Our transfer and location policies are a combination of two policies – *instantaneous distribution policy* (ID) and *load adjustment policy* (LAP). These are described below.

4.6.1 Instantaneous Distribution Policy (IDP)

When a new job arrives at site s_i, the LB algorithm decides whether it is to be sent to the site s_i or other neighboring sites $NSet_i$. The decision depends on the fact whether it can get performance benefit if it is distributed to one of its neighboring sites. The policy also tries to control the job processing rate on each site in the system. The following algorithm describes the instantaneous distribution policy:

Algorithm 1. (Instantaneous Distribution Policy):

$\forall j_x \in J$ with bornSite$(j_x) = s_i \in S$: /* bornSite(j_x) denotes the originating site of j_x */

For each s_j in $NSet_i$

    Calculate EC(j_x, s_i, s_j, t)

    Calculate related benefit value B_x

Find the neighboring site s_j that gives the maximum B_x

If $B_x > \theta$ then /* θ is a positive real constant close to zero */

    Transfer the job j_x to the neighboring site s_j

    Update load index of site s_j recorded at the site s_i

Else

    GJQ$(s_i) \leftarrow$ enqueue(j_x) /* put the job j_x in the job queue GJQ(s_i) */

4.6.2 Load Adjustment Policy (LAP)

The load adjustment policy for a site s_i tries to continuously reduce load difference among the site s_i and its neighbors $NSet_i$ by migrating jobs from heavily loaded sites to lightly loaded neighboring sites. The load adjustment policy is triggered whenever a site s_i receives updated load information of its neighbors. The LB algorithm will use the most recent load status information to decide whether a migration is initiated. The job benefits most in the global job queue GJQ(s_i) considered first for migration. The load adjustment policy algorithm for a site s_i is described below.

Algorithm 2. (Load Adjustment Policy):

For each s_x in $NSet_i$

    For each Job j_x in GJQ(s_i)

        Calculate EC(j_x, s_i, s_x, t)

For each Job j_x in GJQ(s_i)

    Find the site s_y that gives the minimum execution cost

    Calculate related benefit value B_x

Sort the jobs in GJQ(s_i) in ascending order by their benefit value

Pick the Job j_y with the biggest benefit value B_y

Find the neighboring site s_j that gives the maximum B_y to j_y

If $B_y > \theta$ then /* θ is a positive real constant close to zero */

    Remove the job j_y from GJQ(s_i)

    Transfer the job j_y to the neighboring site s_j

    Update load index of site s_j recorded at the site s_i

---

5 Experiments

We only consider sender-initiated algorithms. In the simulation, our algorithm (labeled as DLB) is compared with the following algorithms:

- Local. All jobs are locally processed by their originating sites.
- Random. A site is selected at random to process the arriving job.

5.1 Simulation Model

In this section, we study the performance of the algorithms under different system parameters via simulations. Several assumptions were devised for the simulation model. These are:

- The grid system consists of $n = 32$ sites.
- Jobs arrive at each site s_i, $i=1, 2,\ldots, n$ according to a Poisson process with rate λ_i $= \lambda \times P_i$, where $P_i = 1/n$. The actual inter arrival time of jobs is adjusted to give the required overall average system loading (see below).
- The service times of jobs are assumed to follow a two-phase hyperexponential distribution [25] with mean $X = 1.0$ time unit and coefficient of variation $CV = 4$.
- The transmission delay between any site pairs is chosen from a lognormal distribution with a mean of $\tau = 0.05$ time unit and a standard deviation $\sigma_c = 0.5$.
- To simplify the model and simulation, the transmission time for a job or job result is assumed to be subject to the same delays as the transmission delay.
- Let ρ be the required average system utilization for our simulation, which is the average job arrival rate divided by the average job processing rate. Using this definition, we adjust the job mean inter-arrival time $1/\lambda$ needed to get the desired $\rho = 0.8$.

Further to the above, we have period for periodic information exchange, $T_p = 10$ time unit, and Number of random partners/neighbors for information update, $\omega_p = 2$. For each simulation run, the simulation time is set to 1,300 time units, during which, the first 300 time units are considered as "warm-up time". After the warm-up time, we trace the jobs' born time, processing time and death time. We carry out each measurement three times with different random seeds. Except for experiment S2, all the other experiments are highly heterogeneous, and use the system configuration shown in Table 1.

Table 1. Heterogeneous system configuration

Relative processing power	1	2	5	10
Number of sites	12	8	8	4

5.2 Effect of System Utilization

In experiment S1, we carry out a series of simulations for a system that has a relatively high heterogeneity, under different system utilization parameter ρ. We vary the

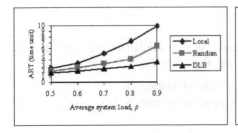   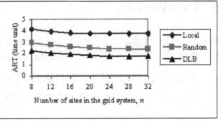

Fig. 2. (a) Average response time in S1 (b) Average response time in S2

system load by varying the mean inter-arrival time (initiation time) of the jobs, $1/\lambda$. Results are shown in Fig. 2(a); The higher the load, the higher the mean response time the algorithms. We can conclude from observing Fig. 2(a) that the DLB algorithm performs significantly better than the other two algorithms. When the system loading becomes high, the difference between the average response time of algorithm DLB and other two algorithms increases. DLB yields an average response time which is 56% less than Local and 32% less than Random.

5.3 Effect of System Size

In experiment S2, we focus our analysis on the case where the number of sites in the grid system is varied. We consider a low heterogeneous system consisting of two site classes with class 1 *APW* of 1 and class 2 *APW* of 10. We divided the sites equally between the two site classes. By observing the average response time of the three algorithms when the number of sites increases from 8 to 32, as shown in Fig. 2(b), we conclude that the response time of the system that results from applying the DLB is lower than the response time of the other algorithms under all *n*. DA has an average improvement factor of 51% and 26% over Local and Random, respectively.

5.4 Effect of Communication Delay

In experiment S3, we vary the mean network trasmission delay, τ, from 0.05 to 0.3 time units. The results shown in Fig. 3(a) shows that the DLB consistently gives the best performance across all the values of τ. DLB gives an average improvement of 32% over Random. The performance is especially apparent when the mean transmission delay is

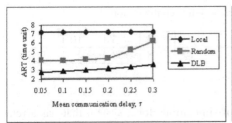   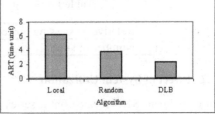

Fig. 3. (a) Average response time in S3 (b) Average response time in S4

high; The increasing rate of DLB is much smaller than that of Random.We suggest that this is because DLB takes the communication delay into account and use the Mutual Information Feedback policy for information collection between a site and its neighbors.

5.5 Effect with Different Job Arrival Pattern

All the experiment results discussed in the previous experiments are generated under the assumption that all sites have the same job arrival rate. In reality, job arrival rates usually differ from one site to another. To evaluate the effect of different job arrival rate on the average response time, we have conducted another experiemnt S4, in which we randomly choose ten of the sites as lightly-loaded site (ρ=0.3), eleven of the sites as moderately-loaded sites (ρ=0.6) and eleven of the sites as highly-loaded sites (ρ=0.9). It can be observed from the Fig. 3(b) that the average response time with DLB algorithm has an average improvement of 55% and 33% over Local and Random, respectively.

6 Conclusion and Future Work

The computing grid is a new type of distributed computing that involves heterogeneous grid sites from different organizations. Due to the concerns of scalability, site heterogeneity and significant communication overheads, these characteristics make grid systems different from the traditional distributed systems and have a significant impact on the performance of load balancing. In this paper, we have proposed a decentralized dynamic LB algorithm to cater for these characteristics.

Due to heterogeneity in computing capability, we did not use the run-queue length as load index. Instead, our algorithm defines the load index as accumulated job execution time at grid sites. Our algorithm operates on two job scheduling and load balancing policies. The first is *Instantaneous Distribution Policy*, which tries to control the job processing rate on each site in the system. The second is *Load Adjustment Policy*, which tries to continuously reduce load difference among a site and its neighbor sites. From the system perspective, our LB scheme, taking into account the different network communication delay between sites can reduce the cost of load movement, and enable quick response to load imbalances. In other word, our strategy is "greedy" in the sense that it tries, at each step, to make jobs assignments at lightly loaded site. Rather than using the conventional state-broadcast or state-polling approaches, state information exchange in our algorithm is done via mutual information feedback to reduce communication overheads. Through simulation experiments, it is found that our algorithm can give a shorter average job response time than the Local and Random Load Balancing algorithm over a wide range of system parameters.

Our research in this area is still in its beginning stage and there is much work worthy of further study. Here we list some for consideration. First, we have not modeled the impact of accuracy of job execution time estimation on the effectiveness of our proposed LB algorithm. Second, we can modify our algorithm to account for the resource requirements of jobs, i.e. jobs which need a set of CPUs. Third, in practical grid systems, the related files for a job need to be transferred through much slower

Internet links if the job is scheduled to run on a remote site. Thus, corresponding execution scheme for data distribution need to be studied. Finally, we do not take network and hardware failure into account in this study. A failure model may be employed to study the influence. Owing to the dynamic nature of the practical grid environment, designing an ideal load balancing algorithm still remains a challenge. We hope our algorithm can serve as examples for the continuing work in searching for a general and practical solution.

References

1. Foster, I. and Kesselman, C. (eds.). The Grid: Blueprint for a New Computing Infrastructure. Morgan Kaufmann, 1999.
2. El-Ghazawi, T., K. Gaj, N. Alexandridis, F. Vroman, N. Nguyen, J. Radzikowski, P. Samipagdi and S. Suboh, "A Performance Study of Job Management Systems," Concurrency and Computation: Practice and Experience 16(13): 1229–1246 (2004)
3. Casavant TL, Kuhl JG. A taxonomy of scheduling in general-purpose distributed computing systems. IEEE Transactions on Software Engineering 1988; 14(2):141–154.
4. C. Kim and H. Kameda. An algorithm for optimal static load balancing in distributed computer systems. *IEEE Trans Comput.*, 41(3):381–384, March 1992.
5. Lin H-C, Raghavendra CS. A dynamic load-balancing policy with a central job dispatcher (LBC). IEEE Transactions on Software Engineering 1992; 18(2): 145–158.
6. Mitzenmacher M., "The power of Two Choices in Randomized Load Balancing," IEEE Trans. Parallel and Distributed Systems, vol. 12, no. 10, pp. 1094–1104, October 2001.
7. Shivaratri NG, Krueger P, singhal M. Load distributing for locally distributed systems. Computer 1992; 33–44.
8. Barak A. and La'adan O., The MOSIX Multicomputer Operating System for High Performance Cluster Computing. Journal of Future Generation Computer Systems, Vol. 13, No. 4–5, pp. 361–372, March 1998.
9. P. Sanders. Analysis of nearest neighbor load balancing algorithms for random loads. Parallel Computing, 25(80), 1999
10. C. Xu, F. Lau, B. Monien, and R. Luling. Nearest neighbor algorithms for load balancing in parallel computers. Concurrency, Practice and Experience, 7:736, 1995.
11. S. Zhou. A trace-driven simulation study of dynamic load balancing. IEEE Transactions on Software Engineering, 14(9): 1327–1341, Sept. 1988.
12. R. Wolski, N. Spring, and J. Hayes, "The network weather service: A distributed resource performance forecasting service for metacomputing," Journal of Future Generation Computing Systems, vol. 15, pp. 757–768, 1999.
13. P.Francis, S. Jamin, C. Jin, Y. Jin, D. Raz, Y. Shavitt, and L. Zhang. IDMaps: a global internet host distance estimation service. IEEE/ACM Transactions on Networking (TON), 9(5): 525–540, 2001
14. A. Agrawal, H. Casanova. Clustering hosts in P2P and global computing platforms. CCGrid 2003. 3rd IEEE/ACM International Symposium on 12-15 May 2003 Page(s): 367 – 373
15. W. Theilmann, K. Rothermel. Dynamic distance maps of the Internet. INFOCOM 2000. Nineteenth Annual Joint Conference of the IEEE Computer and Communications Societies. Proceedings. IEEE Volume 1, 26-30 March 2000 Page(s):275–284 vol.1

16. S. Xian-He and W. Ming, "GHS: A performance prediction and task scheduling system for Grid computing," IEEE International Parallel and Distributed Processing Symposium (IPDPS 2003), 2003.
17. G. R. Nudd, D. J. Kerbyson, E. Papaefstathiou, S. C. Perry, J. S. Harper, and D. V. Wilcox. PACE – a toolset for the performance predictionof parallel and distributed systems. Int. J. High Performance Computing Applications 3(2000), 228–251
18. Amir Y, Awerbuch B, Barak A, Borgstrom S, Keren A. An opportunity cost approach for job assignment in a scalable computing cluster. IEEE Transactions on Parallel and Distributed Systems 2000; 11(7): 760–768.
19. Mor Harchol-Balter and Allen Downey. "Exploiting Process Lifetime Distributions for Dynamic Load Balancing," Proceedings of ACM sigmetrics '98 Conference on Measurement and Modeling of Computer Systems, May 1997, pp. 115–126
20. Eager DL, Lazowska ED, Zahorjan J. The limited performance benefits of migrating active processes for load sharing. Proceedings of the 12th ACM Symposium on Operating Systems Principles, 1988; 63–72.
21. Zhu W, Socko P, Kiepuszewski B. Migration impact on load balancing—an experience on amoeba. Operating Systems Review 1997; 31(1): 43–53.
22. P. Krueger and N. G. Shivaratri. Adaptive location policies for global scheduling. IEEE Transactions on Software Engineering, 20(6): 432–444, June 1994.
23. Eager DL, Lazowska ED, Zahorjan J. A comparison of receiver initiated and sender initiated adaptive load sharing. Performance Evaluation 1986; 6:53–68.
24. Kunz T. The influence of different workload descriptions on a heuristic load balancing scheme. IEEE Transactions on Software Engineering 1991; 17(7): 725–730.
25. T. Thanalapati and S. Dandamudi. An efficient adaptive scheduling scheme for distributed memory multicomputers. IEEE Transactions on Parallel and Distributed Systems, 12(7):758–768, July 2001.

A Resource-Autonomy Based Monitoring Architecture for Grids*

Meizhi Hu[1], Guangwen Yang[2], and Weimin Zheng[2]

Department of Computer Science and Technology,
Tsinghua University, Beijing, 100084, China
[1]hmq02@mails.tsinghua.edu.cn
[2]{ygw,zwm-dcs}@tsinghua.edu.cn

Abstract. Grid computing becomes more and more popular in integrating distributed heterogeneous resources. Despite all that, efficient monitoring to resources of different ownership in Grids remains a challenge. In this paper a novel resource-autonomy based grid monitoring architecture named PIMISA (Plug-In Monitoring and Information Service Architecture) is proposed to address this problem. GMA and SOA are subtly explored in the "Two-Level-Logic" philosophy of PIMISA: only measurement and control metadata of resources are globally published, while monitoring data communication between elements of different ownerships are handled by means of service invocation. The monitoring within the scope of an ownership follows a close-loop structure: a dynamic configurable set of management logic is kept, and resource states are analyzed at real time so that corresponding control indications could be made by decision-making. Moreover, above procedure can be achieved by a "Third-Party Mount" mode to leverage caused load on resources proportion to their capabilities. A prototype is currently under development, and therefore, the implementation scheme of PIMISA is presented in mathematical format.

1 Introduction

Grids aim to integrate miscellaneous distributed heterogeneous resources seamlessly to provide nontrivial computational services. In recent years it becomes more and more mature [1]. Much work has been focused on resource collaboration problems like service discovery, negotiation, service composition, scheduling, etc. In contrast, the issues of resource monitoring are seldom addressed in current studies. Our experience on grid computing convinces that an efficient grid monitoring solution is necessary to promote the prosperity of Grids in practice.

Compared to traditional resource monitoring, grid monitoring must handle complicate issues such as heterogeneity and various ownership. Generally, resource providers always put distinct restrictions on their own shared resources. And sometimes, they do not like to expose sensitive performance data but still

---

* This Work is supported by Natural Science Foundation of China under Grant 60573110, 60373005, 90412011, and 973 Project under Grant 2003CB3169007.

Y.-C. Chung and J.E. Moreira (Eds.): GPC 2006, LNCS 3947, pp. 478–487, 2006.

do use them for inner management. Due to heterogeneity, different components or parts of Grids may require quite diverse monitoring specifications. Thus, global identical monitoring implementations as traditional monitoring solutions do seem unreasonable and far from satisfaction in Grid context.

In this paper we present a novel resource-autonomy based grid monitoring architecture named PIMISA (Plug-In Monitoring and Information Service Architecture). The primary grid monitoring idea in PIMISA is a "Two-Level-Logic": autonomy is guaranteed at resource local level, and atop of that, monitoring-related components of system global level are built. The "Two-Level-Logic" philosophy separates resource local management from system global management, which brings great flexibility and scalability. Resource autonomy shields underlying heterogeneity and various ownerships for components of system global level, facilitating them to wholly focus on their own business logic. And based on the autonomy feature of underlying shared resources, global unified access manner and data structure at high logic level are more acceptable in practice. We mainly address the resource autonomy issues in this paper.

PIMISA follows both GMA and SOA, exploring subtly their elite in proper place. Only necessary measurement and control metadata of resource are globally published. This reduces the volume of global-maintained data. Data communication between elements of different ownership is handled by means of service invocation, by translating diverse data syntax and semantic to a global common scheme. Pay attention that, interaction within the scope of same ownership might utilize any other technologies.

A close-loop structure is employed to achieve resource autonomy in PIMISA. Resource providers predefine some local resource management logic that could be modified dynamically. And real-time states are continuously collected and analyzed so that corresponding control indications could be extracted from management logic and sent to execute accordingly. Above procedure is referred as decision-making. Taking into account that such decision-making might cause substantial cost, it is suggested that a "Third-Party Mount" mode can attain good effects in making the caused load on resources proportional to their capabilities by shifting all or part of management cost from busy/low-performance resources to free/high-performance resources. This can also be considered as a kind of load balance.

The remainder of this paper is organized as follows. Related work is briefly examined in Sect. 2, and then we introduce PIMISA elaborately in Sect. 3. Section 4 gives the implementation scheme. Finally, conclusion and future work are given in Section 5.

2   Related Work

Over the last several years, there have been numerous distributed monitoring solutions or toolkits, such as SNMP, Ganglia [2], MonALISA [3], etc. However, many of them have such assumptions as homogeneous resources, identical resource monitoring specifications. And poor interoperability has been achieved between them so far. Different ownership of resources in Grids means resource providers are permitted to choose any monitoring tools as they like. That is, there may be multiple kinds of monitoring tools working at the same time in a grid system. Additional effort should be made to achieve an acceptable level of interoperability. From the architecture viewpoint, they are orthogonal to our work.

Such monitoring solutions as Autopilot/Virtue, CODE [4] presented a close-loop structure featuring the synchronization feedback mechanism to enable dynamic control based on real-time measurements. Upon this structure, no standards have been widely agreed to follow, which also means poor interoperability between different implementations. In addition, because resource states always have short validity, high synchronization ability to events is implied to gain full control on resources. In wide-area network environment, this requirement is not so reasonable.

MDS [14] from Globus project and GMA [5] proposed by GGF presented other two monitoring structures: hierarchy model and Producer/Consumer model. Above two models share some common ideas that elements are required to register with somewhere global known for information publishing. Latest version of MDS obeys WSRF [9] in implementation, and is generally used in scenarios where values of objects change not so fast (e.g. OS_TYPE). GMA logically separates the discovery of events from the event transmission, making asynchronism of above two procedures a reality. Therefore it is widely followed in many projects, such as R-GMA [15] and GridMon [6]. However, GMA gives no clear implemental specification, which may result in great difference between different implementations.

Absorbing advantages of above models, PIMISA presents a "Two-Level-Logic" monitoring philosophy to cope with complex issues of monitoring heterogeneous resources of different ownership in Grids: at the system global level, only measurement and control metadata required for object location/discovery are exported to public know, and data communication between elements of different ownership are handled by means of service invocation, which means access interfaces to the external are wrapped to services; At resource local level, a close-loop structured decision-making procedure is made use of to monitor resource activities at real-time, realizing autonomy within an ownership efficiently. Moreover, a "Third-Party Mount" decision-making mode is utilized to make caused load proportion to resource capabilities.

3   Design

3.1   Resource Autonomy and "Third-Party Mount" Mode

Shared resources in Grids firstly belong to their owners (also known as "domain" in the remainder). Therefore, besides to obey global management rules of the grid system they should also behave as their owners want at the same time. For example, a resource should react to probe from upper system components as grid systems require, and stop to receive computational tasks from grid users as its owner prescribe when its CPU_LOAD exceeds 80%. Above two aspects are referred as "Grid Activities" (GA) and "Local Activities" (LA) of resources respectively. As previously discussed, management logic sets of different domains might enormously vary. Our idea to guarantee both GA and LA of resources is to realize "Resource Autonomy" at resource local level: each domain independently keeps a dynamically configurable set of management logic to its own shared resources, making no influence to other domains, and it is the duty of local deployed monitoring components to ensure resource GA and LA compliant to requirements from all sides by employing a close-loop structure. To monitoring non-local resources, a domain must get the authorization in advance from other domains. Here, we only involve management logic that can be translated to quantity-comparable expressions.

Although resources in Grids are argued to have good network connectivity and computational capacity [7], the case can not be ignored that resources with low configuration are allowed to be shared in Grids. The decision-making procedure of close-loop structure might cause substantial cost on resources, which probably is unacceptable to some resources, especially to those with low-hardware-configuration or busy in task execution. To overcome this potential irrationality, a "Third-Party Mount" mode is suggested: the decision-making of one domain can be handled in other domains as long as good agreement could be negotiated between these domains. The negotiation can be achieved by out-of-band means and is beyond our discussion, but it is assumed in this paper that all domains are honest and well behaved.

3.2 Architecture

Both SOA and GMA are subtly explored in PIMISA. The architecture is shown in Fig. 1. Domains are all registered to Directory Service (DS) to publish necessary discovery and location information, including monitoring related metadata. At the edge of domains, only Measurement Services (MS) and Control Services (CS) are exposed to shield heterogeneous monitoring issues within domains from upper global system components, enabling them focus on business requirements. DS, MS, and CS are expected to be WSRF/WSN compliant in implementation to follow the latest outcome from SOA community.

Inside a domain, Management Logic Set (MLS) is used to store management logic of local resources. Sensor Manager (SM) and Actuator Manager (AM) are responsible for management of sensors collecting real-time resource performance data and actuators executing control indications (For brevity sensors and actuators are omitted in Fig. 1). Decision-Making takes resource performance data from SM or MS as input, decides resource real-time states, and send predefined control indications to AM or CS to execute if the conditions of some management logic are satisfied.

Mounter is used to mount resources of other domains into local site so that local domain can handle decision-making procedure for those domains. In "Third-Party Mount" scenario, not only related sensors and actuators deployed on

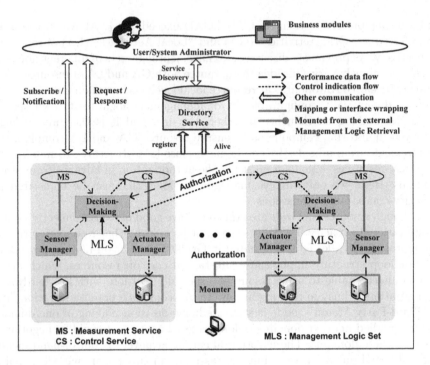

Fig. 1. PIMISA Architecture

mounted resources are registered to local SM and AM, but also the management logic of mounted resources is injected into local MLS.

In PIMISA, a domain could authorizes management capability of its resources to other domains, making them could define and store management logic to local resources in their MLS. Pay attention that a domain has no management capability of mounted resources until it is authorized by the master domain of mounted resources. Independently running domains must interact by means of service invocation if they are of different ownership, while it may not be the case for communication within a same ownership or decision-making relevant communication between mounted resources and mounting domains.

4   Implementation

The prototype is under development at present. Some snapshots are shown in Fig. 2. As a compromise, a few mathematical expressions and pseudocodes to current prototype implementation are given in this section.

4.1   Prerequisite

A hierarchical naming style is adopted in PIMISA. Domains, resources, metrics, and actuations are globally identified as *"DomainID"*, *"DomainID:ResourceID"*,

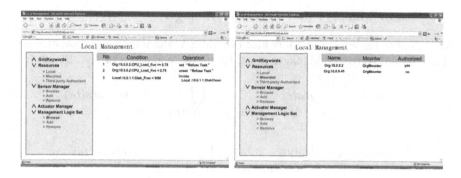

Fig. 2. Prototype Snapshot

"*DomainID:ResourceID:MetricID*" and "*DomainID:ResourceID:ActuationID*".
Define following sets and functions for notation simplification:

- resources(*object*): resources contained by *object*
- thirdParty(*dID*): domains whose resources are mounted to domain *dID*
- targetDomains(*dID*): domains authorizing the management capability of their resources to domain *dID*. Obviously, $dID \in targetDomains(dID)$
- domains(*dID*) = thirdParty(*dID*) ∪ targetDomains(*dID*)
- mLogics(*object*): management logic related to *object*. For domain *dID*,
$$mLogics(dID) = \bigcup_{rID \in resources(dID)} mLogics(dID : rID)$$
- sensors(*object*): sensors deployed in the scope of *object*. For domain *dID*,
$$sensors(dID) = \bigcup_{rID \in resources(dID)} sensors(dID : rID)$$
- actuators(*object*): actuators deployed in the scope of *object*. For domain *dID*,
$$actuators(dID) = \bigcup_{rID \in resources(dID)} actuators(dID : rID)$$
- metrics(*object*): metrics exposed by *object*. For domain *dID*,
$$metrics(dID) = \bigcup_{rID \in resources(dID)} metrics(dID : rID)$$
$$= \bigcup_{rID \in resources(dID)} metrics(sensors(dID : rID))$$
- actuations(*object*): control indications (a.k.a *actuations*) exposed by *object*. For domain *dID*,
$$actuations(dID) = \bigcup_{rID \in resources(dID)} actuations(dID : rID)$$
$$= \bigcup_{rID \in resources(dID)} actuations(actuators(dID : rID))$$
- duty(*module*, *fun*): objects targeted by element *module* on function *fun*. In the next discussion we would assign *fun* to following values of "integrate", "collect", "actuate", "contain" to respectively denote "integration", "data collection", "indication execution", and "contain" functions of components.

In addition, it is also assumed that there are some keywords with special meanings in Grids. For example, "Refuse Task" may used to denote computational tasks from grid system would be rejected by a domain. Use "*GridKeyWords*" to represent these keywords.

4.2   Sensor Manager and Actuator Manager

According to resource autonomy idea of PIMISA, the implementation of Sensor Manager and Actuator Manager must satisfy the equations of 1, 2, 3 and 4.

$$duty(SM, integrate) \subseteq \bigcup_{td \in thirdParty(dID) \cup \{dID\}} sensors(td) \qquad (1)$$

$$duty(SM, collect) \subseteq \bigcup_{td \in thirdParty(dID) \cup \{dID\}} metrics(td) \qquad (2)$$

$$duty(AM, integrate) \subseteq \bigcup_{td \in thirdParty(dID) \cup \{dID\}} actuators(td) \qquad (3)$$

$$duty(AM, actuate) \subseteq \bigcup_{td \in thirdParty(dID) \cup \{dID\}} actuations(td) \qquad (4)$$

4.3   Management Logic and MLS

Management logic has such expressions as "$Condition \rightarrow Operation$". $Condition$ is a quantity expression about metrics, and $Operation$ is a set of control indications that need to be executed when $Condition$ is satisfied. Refer the $Condition/Operation$ only covering one metric/control indication as $AtomCon/AtomOp$. Logical functor "$\vee$" and "$\wedge$" can be used to orchestrate complex $Conditions$ from $AtomCons$. Only "$\wedge$" is allowed in $Operation$ composition, and the order of $AtomOps$ is immutable. For example, "$CPU\_LOAD\_FIVE > 0.70$" (AC1) and "$Memory\_Free > 50M$ (AC2) are two $AtomCons$, "set the keywords of Refuse Task to true" (AO1) and "reduce collection frequency of CPU_LOAD_FIVE to half" (AO2) are two $AtomOps$, "AC1 $\wedge$ AC2", "AC1 $\vee$ AC2", and "AO1 $\wedge$ AO2" are legal, while "AO1 $\vee$ AO2" is not permitted, and "AO1 $\wedge$ AO2" is not equivalent to "AO2 $\wedge$ AO1".

The management logic $mLogic$ must satisfy the equations of 5 and 6. And MLS deployed in domain dID should satify the equation of 7.

$$metrics(mLogic) \subseteq \bigcup_{rID \in resources(mLogic)} metrics(rID) \qquad (5)$$

$$actuations(mLogic) \subseteq \bigcup_{rID \in resources(mLogic)} actuations(rID) \qquad (6)$$

$$duty(MLS, contain) \subseteq \bigcup_{rID \in resources(tID), tID \in domains(dID)} mLogics(rID) \qquad (7)$$

4.4 Decision-Making

The decision-making component actually acts as a domain administrator. It continuously retrieves performance data of cared resources either from target Measurement Services or Sensor Managers, evaluates the conditions of kept management logics in local MLS using resource real-time states. If the conditions of some management logic are satisfied, every control indication in their operations would be sent to corresponding Control Service or Actuator Manager to execute. We do recommend that performance data retrieval and control indication transmission between domains are handled by means of service invocation, so that current standards like WSRF and WSN can be followed. And the "subscribe/notification" mechanism us envisioned to work well, under which the program of this component is pictured in Fig. 3.

```
while (ture) {
    if (notification event arrives) {
        (1) parse the event, extract all pairs of < domainID:resourceID:MetricID, value > to the set of State;
        (2) for each management logic mLogic in local MLS {
            if (State satisfy the condition of mLogic)
                send out every control indication in Operation of mLogic in proper order
        } //for
    } //if-notification
} //while
```

Fig. 3. Decision-making Program under Subscribe/Notification Mechanism

4.5 Security Consideration

In our current plan, security in PIMISA mainly covers followings: (1) authentication of users or components; (2) Access control for users to elements in Grids; (3) read restrictions of a user to certain metric of a resource; (4) authorization to a control indication of an element in Grids; (5) the permission to mount third-party resources. Extant tools like GSI [8] are good groundwork to achieve them. Above security issues have not been involved in our prototype.

5 Conclusion and Future Work

In this paper a novel resource-autonomy based grid monitoring architecture named PIMISA is proposed. To cope with the highly complicated issues of monitoring distributed heterogeneous resources of different ownership in Grids, PIMISA adopts a "Two-Level-Logic" philosophy: resource activities are guaranteed at local level to strictly obey what their owners want, so that components at system global level can wholly focus on business requirements. GMA and SOA are subtly explored in that, only measurement and control metadata of resources are globally published, and monitoring data communication between elements of different ownerships are handled by means of service invocation. At resource local scope a close-loop structure is used to realize real-time management: not only to decide resource states of that time, but also to run decision-making procedure to send predefined control indications. Since the decision-making might raise substantial cost on resources, a "Third-Party Mount" mode is used to leverage the cost proportional to resource capabilities.

In current development of PIMISA prototype, only monitoring of hardware resources are considered, and at system global level only Directory Service is under construction. At next step we intend to study a general mechanism for certain kinds of application software monitoring, and build some modules with good interoperability with some popular log toolkits like Log4J [10]. Service Monitoring in Grids is also our working object in the future encouraged by several outcomes from industrial community, such as MUWS [11, 12] and MOWS [13]. Security especially precise access control to metrics and control indications of resources is another important future task we plan to go in for.

References

1. Ian Foster, Carl Kesselman, *The Grid2: Blueprint for a New Computing Infrastructure*, San Francisco: Margan Kaufmann Publishers Inc., (2003)
2. Matthew L. Massie, Brent N. Chun, and David E. Culler, *The Ganglia Distributed Monitoring System: Design, Implementation, and Experience*, Parallel Computing, Vol. 30, Issue 7, July (2004)
3. H.B.Newman, I.C.Legrand, P.Voicu, C.Cirstoiu, *MonALISA: A Distributed Monitoring Service Architecture*, In the proceedings of Computing in High Energy and Nuclear Physics, March (2003)
4. W.Smith, *A Framework for control and observation in distributed environments*, NASA Advanced Supercomputing Division, NASA Ames Research Center, (2001), Available at http://www.nas.nasa.gov/*sim*wwsmith/papers.html
5. B.Tierney, R. Aydt, D. Gunter, W.Smith, V. Taylor, R. Wolski, and M. Swany, *A Grid Monitoring Architecuture*, Global Grid Forum Performance Working Group (2002)
6. Zha Li, Xu Zhiwei, Lin Guozhang et al., *A LDAP Based Monitoring System for Grid*, Journal of Computer Research and Development, (2002), Vol 39(8), 930 936
7. I. Foster, A. Iamnitchi, *On Death, Taxes, and the Convergence of Peer-to-Peer and Grid Computing*, In 2nd International Workshop on Peer-to-Peer Systems (IPTPS'03), (2003)
8. GSI (Grid Security Infrastructure) overview, http://www.globus.org/security/overview.html
9. WSRF website, http://www.oasis-open.org/committees/tc_home.php?wg_abbrev =wsrf
10. Log4J website, http://logging.apache.org/log4j/docs/index.html
11. William Vambenepe (Ed.), *Web Services Distributed Management: Management Using Web Services (MUWS 1.0) Part 1*, Committee Draft, OASIS, (2004), http://www.oasis-open.org/apps/org/workgroup/wsdm/download.php/10558/cd-wsdmmuws- part1-1.0.pdf
12. William Vambenepe (Ed.), *Web Services Distributed Management: Management Using Web Services (MUWS 1.0) Part 2*, Committee Draft," OASIS, (2004), http://www.oasis-open.org/apps/org/workgroup/wsdm/download.php/10557/cd-wsdmmuws- part2-1.0.pdf

13. Igor Sedukhin (Ed.), *Web Services Distributed Management: Management of Web Services (WSDM-MOWS) 1.0*, Committee Draft, OASIS, (2004), http://www.oasis-open.org/apps/org/workgroup/wsdm/download.php/10567/cd-wsdm-mows-1.0.pdf
14. MDS website, http://www.globus.org/mds/
15. R-GMA website, http://www.r-gma.org/

Machine Learning-Based Adaptive Load Balancing Framework for Distributed Object Computing

Tarek Helmy and S.A. Shahab

College of Computer Science and Engineering,
King Fahd University of Petroleum and Mineral,
Dhahran 31261, Kingdom of Saudi Arabia
{helmy, sadnans}@ccse.kfupm.edu.sa

Abstract. Distributed object computing is widely envisioned to be the desired distributed software development paradigm due to the higher modularity and the capability of handling machine and operating system heterogeneity. In this paper, we address the issue of judicious load balancing in distributed object computing systems. In order to decrease response time and to utilize services effectively, we have proposed and implemented a new technique based on machine learning for adaptive and flexible load balancing mechanism within the framework of distributed middleware. We have chosen Jini 2.0 to build our experimental middleware platform, on which our proposed approach as well as other related techniques are implemented and compared. Extensive experiments are conducted to investigate the effectiveness of the proposed technique, which is found to be consistently better in comparison with existing techniques.

Keywords: Distributed object computing, Jini, Load balancing, Middleware layer, Reinforcement Learning, Q-Learning.

1 Introduction

The constantly increasing performance of personal computers accompanied by rapidly growing network bandwidth has equipped the Internet with a large pool of abundant and inexpensive computational resources. A wide range of large scale, distributed and parallel scientific problems that require massive computation could benefit tremendously from this huge pool of inexpensive resources if we have the ability to find and utilize them efficiently and securely. Devising a scalable architecture to find these resources and distributing the computation efficiently among them is necessary to achieve worldwide execution of programs. Therefore, an adaptive and flexible high-performance distributed middleware services need to be developed to address the challenges of dynamicity, heterogeneity, load balancing, fault tolerance, and security over highly dynamic large scale computer networks.

In Jini terminology [9], a directory service is a lookup (or registry). References stored in the directory are service items registered with the lookup which generally include proxy for services. Service providers store proxies with lookup service during bootstrap and are required to refresh or renew their leases. Clients are computer-based entities who wish to access the services listed in the Jini lookup service. They must

Y.-C. Chung and J.E. Moreira (Eds.): GPC 2006, LNCS 3947, pp. 488–497, 2006.
© Springer-Verlag Berlin Heidelberg 2006

search the Jini registry (lookup) for services they want to utilize. Clients specify a service template which may include service attributes such as provider name, model, specific properties etc. It is quite possible that search templates provided by clients are general enough to fetch more than one service proxies or it may also possible to have more than one service providers offering services with similar attributes, like in case of printing service. It is the responsibility of clients to decide which service proxy to utilize in order to get the desired Quality of Service (QoS).

In this paper we have addressed the issue of load balancing at middleware layer. The paper is organized in this fashion. Section 2 deals with survey of proposed techniques and related work concerning load balancing at middleware layer. Section 3 deals with some introduction to reinforcement learning and its application in proposed strategy. Section 4 demonstrates our proposed architecture for service provider and client hosts to facilitate Q-Learning process. Section 5 shows simulation and experimental results and finally section 6 concludes the paper.

2 Related Works

There have been some approaches proposed in the literature for load balancing. In this paper, we are concerned with those load balancing approaches that are implemented at middleware layer. Round-robin scheme was proposed in [6]. It simply causes a request to be forwarded to the next member and does not take load into account. Random scheme was also proposed in [6], which is non-adaptive strategy and also does not take load into account. It simply forwards clients requests to an object group member residing at a random location. Least loaded scheme was utilized by [4]. The goal of this strategy is to ensure load differences fall within a certain tolerance, i.e., it attempts to ensure that the average difference in load between each location/member is minimized. Another approach proposed in [5], was to incorporate a load monitor module within middleware layer. Various metrics such as CPU, memory, network usage were supplied to load prediction module. Based on the predictions, the system was able to dynamically adjust its configuration by transferring load to other services so as to minimize the response time. Under the threshold-based approach [7], server can trigger load-balancing actions if its load level exceeds a certain threshold. The bidding approach proposed in [3], views the computers as resources and the jobs as consumers. Clients bid for CPU time; only the winners can execute jobs on server. However, because the bidding process takes non-negligible time, it is not suitable for LAN environment. Fuzzy logic based load balancing scheme was also proposed in [10]. This scheme incorporates a separate service for load balancing. Service providers are required to send server load information to the load balancing service. In addition to this, the load balancing service measures remote method invocation time by invoking a bench mark remote method on each service provider. These metrics are then fuzzified using pre-defined membership functions. After fuzzification, inference rules are employed to infer the fuzzy value of output which is defuzzified using output graph.

While round robin and random assignment of load to the servers are not adaptive in nature, fuzzy logic based load balancing suffers from these deficiencies:

- Requirement of a separate service proxy for load balancing will increase the lease management overhead and it will create unnecessary traffic between lookup services and load balancing service. The leasing model [9] enables distributed components to explicitly limit the duration of their agreed cooperation. This removes any possible ambiguity about when such agreements are terminated and thereby allows components to safely reclaim resources that had been associated with them.
- The fuzzy based approach does not provide any feedback mechanism in order to fine tune the parameters, in other words there is no learning mechanism for the client hosts.

3 Proposed Technique

We have tackled shortcomings of techniques mentioned in Section 2 by employing sophisticated mechanism at middleware layer:

- The component which is providing a service will be the ideal to judge load on its system. We proposed to use a load monitor module incorporated within service which can monitor the load on the server with minimum overhead. This approach was also utilized by [5].
- Client can learn the best policy by employing reinforcement based learning technique [2]. Reinforcement based learning is an un-supervised learning, in which agents learn through trial and error interactions with environment.

3.1 Reinforcement Learning for Load Balancing

Distributed systems are inherently difficult to manage. The parameters are dynamic and cannot be treated as static [1]. In this paper, we have proposed to use *"Reinforcement Learning Technique"* to enforce load balancing mechanism. It is highly used in those environments where the response time prior to the execution is unknown and a static plan cannot be devised [8]. It has been used in solving problems of allocating resources to a grid [2] and task scheduling problem in parallel processor systems [3].

Reinforcement learning is the problem faced by an agent that learns behavior through trial-and-error interactions with a dynamic environment. The goal of reinforcement learning is to learn an optimal policy $\pi: S \rightarrow A$ that specifies which action $'a'$ to choose for every state $'s'$ in the environment to best achieve the goal or reward $'r'$. A model of reinforcement learning consists of a discrete set of environment states ($s \; \varepsilon \; S$), a discrete set of agent actions ($a \; \varepsilon \; S$) and a set of scalar reinforcement signals ($r \; \varepsilon \; R$). The agent's job is to find a policy, i.e. a mapping from states to actions, which maximizes rewards.

Common reinforcement learning methods are structured around estimating value functions $V(s)$ for every state. One way to learn optimal policy is to use the evaluation function $Q(s \, , \, a)$ defined as the maximum discounted cumulative award that can be reached by starting in state $'s'$ and taking action $'a'$ as first action.

$$Q(s,a) = r(s,a) + \gamma V * (\delta(s,a)) \tag{1}$$

Where γ is the discount factor, $r(s, a)$ is expected reward by taking action 'a' at state 's', $\delta(s, a)$ is the Markov function that takes the agent into next state and $V*(\ )$ is the optimal value function.

3.2 Training Phase

Unlike approach in [10], there is no centralized mechanism for load balancing. In the training phase, clients request for specific service from lookup registrar. Clients request for the current load condition on service providers. In order to estimate load on the service provider, we have incorporated a load monitoring module [5]. This module monitors current load on the service provider and predicts the future load. Clients submit their requests to perform tasks and wait for the response. We have utilized reciprocal of response time as a measure of reward. The *Q-Learning* algorithm is iterative in nature. It has been found in experimentation (refer to Section 5) that after some iteration QValues become saturated and change is very minimal. Thus Δ_i given in equation (2) is used as a condition for breaking the iteration.

$$\Delta_i = |Q_i(s,a) - Q_{i-1}(s,a)|^2 \tag{2}$$

3.3 Load Prediction

We have used a statistical sampling approach to obtain aggregate load on each service provider. The simple exponential smoothing method is based on a weighted average of current and past observations, with most weight to the current observation and declining weights to past observations. The formula for exponential moving average is given by equation (3):

$$\tau_{n+1} = \alpha L_n + (1-\alpha)\tau_n \tag{3}$$

Where $0 \leq \alpha \leq 1$ is know as gain parameter, L_n is the most recent load, τ_n stores the past history and τ_{n+1} is the predicted value of load. We maintained two exponentially-weighted moving averages with different gain parameters. A slow moving average ($\alpha \to 0$) is used to produce a smooth, stable estimate. A fast moving average ($\alpha \to 1$) adapts quickly to changes in work load. The maximum of these two values are used as an account for current load on the service provider.

4 Proposed Architecture

In order to support and facilitate Q-Learning process, we need to modify architecture of service providers and client hosts. In contrast with fuzzy based load balancing [10], there are no specific services for load balancing.

4.1 Service Provider Architecture

Following are the chief modules incorporated in service provider architecture.
- **Service Monitor:** This component monitors the status of service queue and predicts load (length of queue) as explained in Section 3.3.

- **Service Queue:** A local queue is maintained within each service provider to store client requests.
- **Scheduler:** Scheduler selects client request from local queue based on first come first serve basis and submits it to the service module.
- **Service:** Jobs are served without any preemption. We have employed delays for simulation and experimentation purposes.
- **Jini Related Modules:** These comprises of *discovery manager, join manager* and *lease manager* which are required to support distributed computing within the framework of Jini [9].
- **Service Interface:** Each service provider specifies a standard service interface to be utilized by the clients.

4.2 Client Architecture

In client hosts, we proposed to use the following modules.

- **Jini Related Modules:** It includes some key modules such as *discovery module* (to search for specific services), and *lease management module* (to receive remote events from lookup services), etc…
- **Service Requester:** This module interacts with users or utilizes pre stored search template and provides it to Jini modules to search for the services.
- **QLearning Module:** This module implements the reinforcement learning procedure as described in Section 3.1. It maintains a database to store QValues at various states of server.
- **Decision Making Module:** After Q-Learning phase, decision making module selects those service proxies which will maximize the reward. Decisions are made on the basis of current state of service providers. After the selection of service provider, it also updates the QValue it receives as a consequence of selecting a particular service provider.

5   Simulation and Experimental Results

For experimentation and simulation purposes, we employed Jini 2.0 version. The proposed architecture was implemented in Java 2.0. In our experimentation, we employed 8 machines as server, 2 machines for generating client request and 1 machine to run a lookup service. The configurations of machines are shown in table 1. In order to simulate services, we employed a pre-defined delay for each server machine. During the experimentation, clients and service providers do not know IP addresses or names of each other. They discover lookup service dynamically and thus proceed to accomplish the protocol specified in Jini specs 2.0. Clients train themselves during bootstrap process as explained in section 3.2. Round robin and random selections were used as a benchmark.

Fig. 1 demonstrates *QValues* variation for different epochs. In case of server state < 5, *QValues* are very close to each other. This is expected as for lightly loaded

Table 1. Configuration of machines used in simulation

Type	Jini Generated IDs	Processor	Ram
Service1	b15de466-c132-41d6-9d60-bd663585c09c	Pentium 4 2.00 GHz	512 MB
Service2	187de788-30ee-46c8-be0c-93c3cf4a4aab	Pentium 4 2.00 GHz	512 MB
Service3	bbb34b1c-1e44-4b2c-8e7d-aa908bac6f12	Pentium 4 2.00 GHz	512 MB
Service4	59eb92ea-04c4-4642-99f1-e4f4675dedd0	Pentium 4 2.00 GHz	512 MB
Service5	ff76839c-54b6-496e-b615-96eed63d2b76	Pentium 3 750 MHz	256 MB
Service6	6837acd8-7bb1-422d-baa5-a1252526d5f6	Pentium 3 750 MHz	256 MB
Service7	8766560a-4234-4a17-b524-87a7618a1b19	Pentium 3 750 MHz	256 MB
Service8	83eca5fc-e2d1-4a82-8c49-a2e4012988d5	Pentium 3 750 MHz	256 MB
Lookup Service	41e05d1a-a9bd-4e86-925b-ed94b0c84e8a	Xeon dual processor 1.7 GHz	1 GB
Client1	f58509f0-3213-4091-8c32-f749c27b0490	Xeon dual processor 1.7 GHz	1 GB
Client2	678c146f-7a6e-4c04-8223-b1176d9a7640	Xeon dual processor 1.7 GHz	1 GB

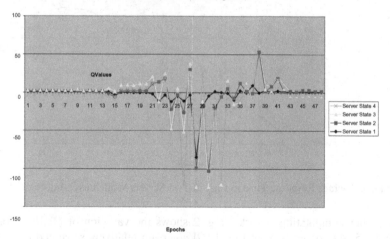

Fig. 1. QValues in Case of Server State < 5

servers there is not much variation in terms of response time especially for fast servers. Peaks represent variation in response time; this may happen due to increase in network traffic, servers running some background applications, clients busy in doing

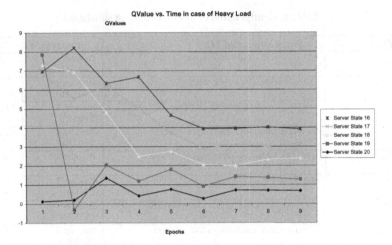

Fig. 2. QValues in Case of Server State > 15

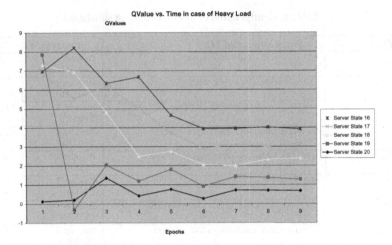

Fig. 3. Average Response Time in Case of Two Servers While Increasing No. of Clients

some other computational work. Fig. 2 shows the variation of *QValues* for server state > 15. As compared with Fig. 1, *QValues* are relatively separated and after few epochs there is not much variation in *QValues*. Similarly it is quite visible that *QValues* decrease as load is increased on service provider.

The average client response time of proposed approach is compared with benchmarks keeping number of servers constant. The Fig. 3-6 shows simulation results. We have configured to simulate these experiments for slow and fast service providers. Random strategy may select slow service provider which is represented by many peaks. While in round robin strategy there is not much peak as compared with

Av. Response Time vs. No. of Clients (Servers=4)

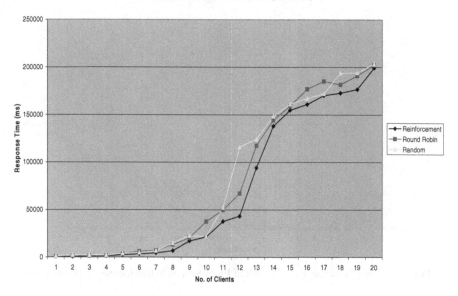

Fig. 4. Average Response Time in Case of Four Servers While Increasing No. of Clients

Av. Response Time vs. No. of Clients (Servers =6)

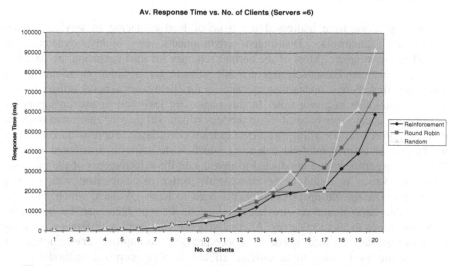

Fig. 5. Average Response Time in Case of Six Servers While Increasing No. of Clients

random strategy. On the other hand proposed strategy produces a smoother curve and provides response time smaller than two benchmarks. When no. of clients is equal or less than service providers then all strategies behave in similar fashion. With the increase in no. of clients, proposed strategy provides reduce response time. It should be noted that, random strategy may provide better response time at some instant but it is not consistent and it may be followed by long spike.

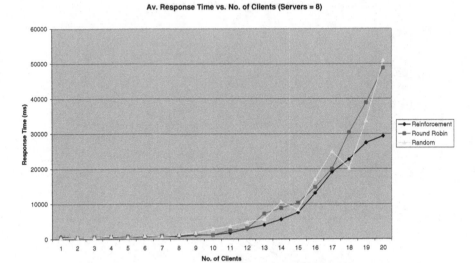

Fig. 6. Average Response Time in Case of Eight Servers While Increasing No. of Clients

6 Conclusion

In this paper, we have addressed the issue of load balancing in service oriented middleware framework. Distributed environments are highly dynamic and unpredictable in nature. Most of the current schemes for load balancing are based on static information. These schemes are not suitable for dynamic environments. In addition to that, there is no learning mechanism for client hosts to better utilize services so as to minimize response time. In this paper, we proposed to use un-supervised learning for client hosts to avail those services which will provide minimum response time. Reinforcement learning is utilized to train client hosts. There is no centralized mechanism or control for load balancing which is desirable in distributed systems. Extensive experiments are conducted to investigate the effectiveness of the proposed technique, which is found to be consistently better in comparison with existing techniques. During startup process, clients need to learn QValues, which may take considerable time if servers are heavily loaded. This problem can be solved by allowing clients to share QValues. Alternatively we may employ different scheduling algorithm within each local queue of service providers to improve service utilization. In our future work, we will investigate effectiveness of proposed methodology by considering different scheduling algorithm within local queues.

Acknowledgments

We would like to thank King Fahd University of Petroleum and Minerals (KFUPM) for supporting this research work and providing the computing facilities. Special thanks to anonymous reviewers for their valuable comments on this paper.

References

1. Andrew J. Page, Thomas J. Naughton: Dynamic task scheduling using genetic algorithms for heterogeneous distributed computing. 8th International Workshop on Nature Inspired Distributed Computing, IPDPS, Denver, Colorado, USA, April (2005).
2. Aram Galstyan, Karl Czajkowski, Kristina Lerman: Resource Allocation in the Grid Using Reinforcement Learning. AAMAS'04, ACM (2004).
3. C.A. Waldspurger et al: Spawn. A Distributed Computational Economy. IEEE Trans. Software Eng., Vol. 18, No. 2, Feb. (1992), pp. 103–117.
4. IONA Technologies: Orbix 2000. http://www.iona.com/products/orbix2000/home.htm.
5. Octavian Ciuhandu, John Murphy: A Modular QoS-enabled Load Management Framework for Component-Based Middleware. OOPSLA'03, October 26–30, 2003, Anaheim, California, USA.
6. Ossama Othman, Jaiganesh: The Design of an Adaptive Middleware Load Balancing Service. IEEE Distributed Systems Online, Volume 2, Number 4, April, (2001).
7. P. Krueger, N.G. Shivaratri: Adaptive Location Policies for Global Scheduling,. IEEE Trans. Software Eng., Vol. 20, No. 6, June (1994), pp. 432–444.
8. Russell, Norvig: Artificial Intelligence. A Modern Approach. 2nd Ed. (2003)
9. www.jini.org (Jini Technology).
10. Yu-Kwong Kwok Lap-Sun Cheung: A new fuzzy-decision based load balancing system for distributed object computing. J. Parallel Distributed Computing 64 (2004) 238–253 Science Direct.

VWMAC: An Efficient MAC Protocol for Resolving Intra-flow Contention in Wireless Ad Hoc Networks

Wanrong Yu[1,2], Jiannong Cao[1], Xingming Zhou[2], Xiaodong Wang[2],
Keith C.C. Chan[1], Alvin T.S. Chan[1], and H.V. Leong[1]

[1] Department of Computing, Hong Kong Polytechnic University, Hong Kong
[2] School of Computer, National University of Defense Technology, Changsha, China

Abstract. In wireless ad hoc networks, the performance of the media access control (MAC) protocol has significant impact on the overall network performance. Although the popular IEEE 802.11 DCF mechanism still works under multi-hop scenarios, its efficiency is unacceptable. Many efforts have been made to enhance the mechanism in various aspects. In this paper, a novel MAC protocol, called MAC with Voluntary Waiting (VWMAC), is proposed to solve the intra-flow contention problem in multi-hop ad hoc networks. Through voluntary waiting by mobile hosts according to the length of DATA packet transmitted, VWMAC uses a very simple strategy to achieve great performance enhancement. Our simulation results show that VWMAC outperforms IEEE 802.11 and existing approaches in terms of throughput, transmission delay and energy efficiency.

1 Introduction

A wireless ad hoc network is a network temporarily and spontaneously established by wireless communication nodes without requiring any infrastructure or central control. Management of and communications in such a network are typically performed in a distributed manner. The media access control (MAC) protocol is needed to allocate the communication resources efficiently and fairly among all nodes in the wireless networks.

Due to the lack of centralized control in wireless ad hoc networks, researchers have mainly focused on contention based MAC protocols in this area. Carrier Sense Medium Access (CSMA) is one of the earliest mechanisms adopted for ad hoc networks. In CSMA, a transmitter will first sense the wireless channel in the vicinity and refrain itself from transmission if the channel is already in use.

Based on the mechanism of CSMA, many protocols have been proposed, such as MACA [1], MACAW [2] and IEEE 802.11 [3]. The IEEE 802.11 scheme has gained its popularity rapidly for its simplicity and ease of implementation. Although the Distributed Coordination Function (DCF) mechanism in IEEE 802.11 supports multi-hop networks, its performance does not meet the requirements [4]. Many works have been done to improvement the performance of IEEE 802.11 in various aspects.

However, most of existing works do not consider the "intra-flow contention problem" in wireless ad hoc networks. As illustrated in Figure 1, the continuous flow is from node N0 to node N5, and nodes N1, N2, N3, and N4 are forwarding nodes on

Y.-C. Chung and J.E. Moreira (Eds.): GPC 2006, LNCS 3947, pp. 498–508, 2006.

the route. After node N0 successfully transmits a packet to node N1, it still needs to continually contend for the radio channel because it still has packets to send in its transmitting queue. While at this moment, node N1 also has packet to forward and thus will contend with node N0. Similarly, node N2 will contend with node N0 after it has received packet from node N1. We call this phenomenon the "intra-flow contention problem", which refers to that the neighboring nodes on the route of a given multi-hop flow content with each other when trying to fulfill the flow.

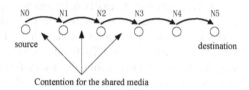

Contention for the shared media

Fig. 1. Illustration of intra-flow contention

Based on the above observations, we propose a novel MAC protocol, called *MAC with Voluntary Waiting* (*VWMAC*), which effectively solves the intra-flow contention problem in wireless ad hoc networks. In VWMAC, after sending a packet, a node voluntarily waits for a period of time before contending for the channel again. Also, during this period, the voluntary waiting node can safely switch to sleep mode and awake later in time. Thus, VWMAC saves the scarce battery power of mobile nodes. Simulation results show that VWMAC greatly outperforms IEEE 802.11 and existing schemes in terms of throughout, delay and energy consumption under multi-hop scenarios.

The remainder of this paper is organized as follows. In Section 2, we discuss the related works, focusing on the enhancements of the 802.11 scheme. The design of VWMAC is detailed in Section 3. Section 4 presents simulation results that indicate the great improvement in performance achieved by the VWMAC. Finally, Section 5 concludes the paper with our future work.

2 Related Works

The DCF mechanism defined in IEEE 802.11 is based on CSMA/CA (Carrier Sense Multiple Access with Collision Avoidance), with extensions to allow for the exchange of RTS/CTS packets between the transmitter and the receiver before the actual transmission of DATA packet. However, as pointed out in [4], the performance of IEEE 802.11 DCF under multi-hop scenario is far away from the optimized utilization of channel bandwidth. Many research efforts have been made to improve the performance of IEEE 802.11 DCF.

Generally speaking, existing MAC layer approaches enhance the IEEE 802.11 DCF using one or more of the following methods: (1) adjusting various intervals defined in IEEE 802.11, such as the inter-frame spacing (IFS) [5] and the contention window (CW) [5, 6]; (2) adjusting the carrier sense range to leverage spatial reuse [7, 8];

(3) enhancing the spatial reuse through the transmission power control (TPC) technology [9, 10].

However, all above works don't consider the intra-flow contention problem. This problem is first addressed in [11]. The author argues to solve intra-flow contention through adaptive pacing. When one node finds the average number of its retries goes beyond the pre-defined threshold, it further back-off an additional packet transmission time in addition to its current deferral period. However, as detailed later, other than the heavy contention indicated by the large number of retries, it is necessary for a node to defer transmission even when there exists only one multiple hops flow in the network. In [12], a fast-forward mechanism is proposed to solve this problem. After a packet is received, the receiving node determines the next-hop of the received packet and uses the MAC layer ACK as an implicit RTS for the next hop transmission. The solution in [13] is based on a similar idea, although in a different way. In [13], the receiver is assigned higher priority of channel access by using a smaller back-off timer. However, as illustrated later in this paper, delaying for one additional packet transmission time is not enough for completely solving the intra-flow contention problem. More importantly, these works have not explored the potential opportunity for energy saving during the deferral period. In fact, if a node knows that it should avoid occupying the channel for a certain period of time, it can switch to the sleep mode during this period so as to conserve the precious battery power of the node.

3   Description of Proposed VWMAC Protocol

In the design of the VWMAC protocol, we make the following assumptions. First, we assume that most flows in the network are multiple hops and the average number of hops of a flow is larger than 3. Second, a flow is assumed to be continuous from the source to the destination for a period of time. That is to say, the source is saturated during this period of time. In a moderate or large scale wireless ad hoc network, both assumptions are easy to keep. In addition, the first assumption can be relaxed as shown later. Third, we assume that the data transmission rate is identical for all the nodes in the network. So the time needed to transmit a packet of a certain size is proportional to the packet length and is the same to all nodes. Multi-rate is not considered in this paper.

To solve the intra-flow contention problem and improve the network performance, the key is that a node should not send next packet until the previous one is out of its interference range. Suppose the interference range equals twice of the space between neighboring nodes. In the idealized situation, the transmission schedule for the example shown in Figure 1 should be that as plotted in Figure 2. In the figure, T stands for the transmitter and R stands for the receiver.

Due to the random factor introduced by the random back-off of IEEE 802.11 MAC protocol, it is difficult, if not impossible, to achieve the ideal result. However, we can approach as close as possible to the ideal. The strategy used in VWMAC is that each node voluntarily waits for a period of time after sending out a packet. This strategy is so simple that the only issue needed to address is how long a node should wait for before attempting to send the next packet. Obviously, the length of Voluntary

	N0	N1	N2	N3	N4	N5
slot1	T	R				
slot2		T	R			
slot3			T	R		
slot4				T	R	
slot5	T	R			T	R
slot6		T	R			
slot7			T	R		
slot8				T	R	
slot9	T	R			T	R
		T	R			

Time ↓

Fig. 2. Idealized transmission schedule of Figure 1

Waiting Time (VWT) should be dependent on the length of DATA packet just transmitted.

In [14], the author suggests to always have the RTS/CTS activated to obtain a near best performance, while at the same time to save the complex work of designing and implementing a dynamic RTS_Threshold adjustment mechanism. In designing the VWMAC, we consider the RTS/CTS mechanism to be used for any size of DATA packets. Then, for a packet to be forwarded one hop away along the given path, the minimum time required is given by:

$$T_{required} = T_{RTS} + T_{CTS} + T_{DATA} + T_{ACK} + 3T_{SIFS} + T_{DIFS} + T_{backoff} \qquad (1)$$

In equation (1), T_{DATA} is decided by the size of DATA packet and $T_{backoff}$ is random. Other parts are all definite and common to all nodes. To avoid the effect of any random factor, we set the one-hop VWT slot T_{slot} to be:

$$T_{slot} = T_{required} - T_{backoff} \qquad (2)$$

T_{slot} is long enough for the next hop node to occupy the channel and nearly finish forwarding the received packet. If only sleeps for one T_{slot} time, the previous sending node may wake up a little earlier before the next sending node finishes transmitting. This is exactly the result we want, because the sleeping node will never be too late to contend for the channel again. Due to the existence of the carrier sense and back-off mechanism, the probability for the previous node that wakes up earlier to interfere with the next sending node is very small. Figure 2 also shows that the source node should wait for one more slot than the intermediate nodes, because it need not to receive DATA packets from any other node before transmission. But at the MAC layer, a node has no way to know whether it is the source node of a flow or not. Therefore, we use the same rule for all nodes to determine the length of the waiting period. Another benefit of this simplification is that it makes the action of all the nodes consistent.

Because the interference range is always larger than the transmission range, it is not enough for one node to wait for just one T_{slot} time. In fact, the node should wait for a period several times T_{slot}, and the specific number of times is called Number of Waiting Slots (NWS) in this paper. The value of NWS is determined by the interference range (R_i) and the average distance between neighboring communication nodes (D_n).

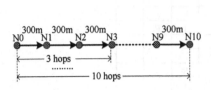

Fig. 3. String Topology

Fig. 4. Delay of various NWS

$$NWS = \left\lfloor \frac{Ri}{Dn} \right\rfloor \tag{3}$$

Here, $\lfloor x \rfloor$ means the floor of x.

We validate equation (3) by using Figure 3 where there are 11 nodes in sequence. The distances between neighboring nodes are the same and equal to 300m. Supposing the interference range, transmission range are 800m and 400m respectively, NWS should be set to 2 according to equation (3). Simulation results of CBR flow with 2K packets from node N0 to N10 is illustrated in Figure 4. Obviously, VWMAC achieves its best performance when NWS equals 2. This fits the computation of NWS perfectly. When the distances between neighboring nodes increase to 350m, the optimal value of NWS remains to be 2, as illustrated in Figure 4.

For a given R_i, if we can decide the value of D_n, the value of NWS will be known according to equation (3). Thus, in order to compute the optimal value of NWS, we only need to determine the value of D_n. Under general mini-hop based routing protocol such as AODV [15], the bound of D_n is easy to obtain. Denoting the transmission range by R_t, we have the following relationship between D_n and R_t: $R_t/2 < D_n \leq R_t$. Based on this relationship, we can obtain the bound of NWS accordingly. Because the interference range R_i is generally twice of R_t or even a little more, the optimal value of NWS resides in the range [2, 4]. Since the goal of a mini-hop routing protocol is to minimize the number of hops between the source and destination, the value of D_n is generally closer to R_t, rather than $R_t/2$. Thus, in designing VWMAC, we choose 2 to be the optimal value for NWS. Of course, according to equation (3), when the value of D_n is small enough, 2 is not the optimal value for NWS. So our choice may be a little conservative, but it achieves satisfying performance as shown by the simulation results even when D_n is small. Furthermore, it is very expensive and difficult for nodes in the MANETs to obtain the exact value of D_n dynamically. Under this consideration, without the accurate knowledge of D_n, we think that a conservative strategy is better.

Obviously, if the hop number between the source and the destination is 1, then it is not necessary for the nodes to wait. If we want to achieve performance improvement under VWMAC, the minimum hop number between the source and the destination should be 4 when NWS equals 2. From Figure 2, we can conclude that the exact value of the lower bounder of hop number is (NWS+2). This is the reason why we make the assumption that the hop number is large than 3. Now we consider it further. Recall that VWMAC only changes the behavior of a transmitting node but does not distinguish the source node and other forwarding nodes. In fact, if the hop number is 2, then it is not necessary for the nodes to wait for any additional time. If the hop number is 3, 1 is enough for NWS. So, to make VWMAC flexible, the value of NWS should be adjusted according to the number of hops between the source and destination. As explained before, the optimal value of NWS has been set to 2 in VWMAC, so the possible values for NWS are 0, 1 and 2. When the hop number is 1 or 2, the value of NWS is set to 0. Under this condition, VWMAC becomes the standard IEEE 802.11 DCF. When the hop number is 3, the value of NWS is set to 1. For those cases with the hop number large than 3, the value of NWS is set to 2.

However, at the MAC layer, there is no way for a node on the route to know the number of hops between the source and destination. Thus, to determine the actual value of NWS, VWMAC needs some information from the routing layer. Fortunately, general mini-hop based routing protocols such as AODV record the hop count in the source node, so it is very easy for the nodes to get the needed information at the MAC layer.

4 Performance Evaluation

To evaluate the effectiveness of the proposed waiting strategy, we conducted simulations using different flow models under various topologies. We implemented the VWMAC protocol in the GloMoSim [16] simulator and compared its performance with that of the IEEE 802.11 scheme and existing approaches.

The performance of a MAC protocol can be evaluated using the following metrics: *throughput*, *average end-to-end delay*, and *energy_goodput*. Energy_goodput means the power consumption per unit data received successfully by the destination, similar to the metric defined in [17].

To simulate power consumption by VWMAC, we use the same energy model implemented in GloMoSim. Because VWMAC only put those nodes that participate in transmitting data packets into sleep, we just need to collect the consumed power of these nodes when we compute total energy consumed. For other nodes that do not participate in communication, the energy consumption is the same as the IEEE 802.11 and thus is not included. Also, we ignore the energy consumption by state switching because it is insignificant compared with the energy consumed by communications. The parameters used in the simulations are listed in Table 1.

Table 1. Simulation parameters

Data packet size	2KB,1KB,500B	Transmit State	1200mW
Transmit power	30mW(15dBm)	Receive State	900mW
Transmission range(R_t)	400m	Idle State	900mW
Interference range(R_i)	800m	Sleep State	50mW

4.1 Line Topology

To highlight the performance improvement made by VWMAC, we first simulate a network with a line topology similar to that in Figure 3. Here, the distance between neighboring nodes are same and set to 250m. When the hop number is 1 or 2,

VWMAC equals IEEE 802.11, so we start from 3 for the value of hop number. The source node is N0 and the destination is N3 for 3 hops, N4 for 4 hops and so on, up to node N10 for 10 hops.

We use data packets of various sizes (2KB, 1KB, and 0.5KB) to measure the impact of the data packet length on the performance of VWMAC. When the hop number is near the lower bound of the required value, the throughput of VWMAC is similar to IEEE 802.11, but VWMAC still outperforms the 802.11 on energy_goodput and delay, as plotted in Figure 5. Here, the performance of IEEE 802.11 is used as the baseline. With the increase of hop number, increasing performance improvement is observed on throughput, energy_goodput, and delay. The improvement reaches a relative stable level when the number of hops is large enough. Through voluntary waiting, VWMAC improves the throughput and energy_goodput of the network by a factor of 40% and 60% respectively, while the average delay reduces to only 40% of IEEE 802.11. The results in Figure 5 also indicate that the bigger the size of DATA packet is, the greater the improvement can be made. Obviously, the bigger the DATA packet size, the longer a node will sleep. Thus, the probability for collision is decreased more compared with IEEE 802.11, because the size of DATA packet determines the average duration of collision in the network.

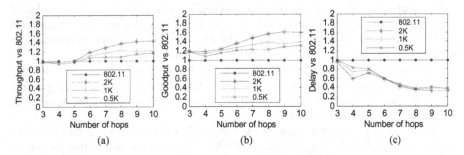

Fig. 5. Performance of VWMAC vs 802.11

The existing methods proposed for adaptive pacing [11] or fast forwarding [12] make the node to wait for one T_{slot} time under the best condition, so their best performance is always worse than the case where NWS equals 1. To compare VWMAC with exiting approaches, we use the case where NWS is set to 1 to represent the best performance of existing solutions for the metrics of throughput and delay. Again, the performance of IEEE 802.11 is used as the baseline. For existing approaches that do not sleep wireless nodes, their energy_goodput is nearly the same as 802.11 DCF. We conducted simulations using the line topology with 2K DATA packet and plot the results on throughput and delay in Figure 6. We conclude that VWMAC and the existing methods under the best condition (i.e., when NWS equal to 1) perform equally well for the cases where the hop number is 3, 4, 5. With increasing hop number, the performance of the existing methods under the best condition (i.e., when NWS equals 1) is poorer than VWMAC, though both outperform the IEEE 802.11 scheme greatly.

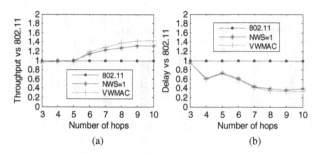

Fig. 6. Performance comparison of VWMAC, 802.11 and existing approaches

4.2 Grid Topology

We also evaluated the performance of VWMAC under a grid topology, which is more general. We consider an area of dimensions 2000*2000 (in meters). 81 nodes are placed uniformly. Thus, the whole area is split into 64 small equal-sized square areas, each with the edge of 250m. Under such a topology, we simulated two types of flows. One is that of two cross multi-hop flows, as illustrated in Figure 7(a). In this scenario, the two flows interfere with each other in the vicinity of cross point.

The simulation results demonstrate that VWMAC has better performance than IEEE 802.11 and the existing methods, as shown in Figure 8. The reason is that voluntary waiting greatly decreases the probability for collision. Similar to simulations with the line topology, the size of DATA packet is still a key factor that determines how much performance improvement can be achieved. Smaller DATA packet means fewer enhancements to the performance in terms of throughput and average delay, but both VWMAC and existing approaches outperform IEEE 802.11 greatly at various sizes, as we can see from part (a) and (b) of Figure 8. Because existing approaches do not sleep nodes, their good_put is similar to IEEE 802.11. To compare with VWMAC, we also produce the energy_goodput for the case with NSW=1. The result shows that VWMAC consumes the least power to transmit unit data and saves energy greatly, as illustrated in part (c) of Figure 8.

The second type of flows we considered is cluster flows which often occur in real wireless ad hoc networks such as wireless sensor networks. Suppose four nodes at different corners of the whole area send packets to the central node at the same time,

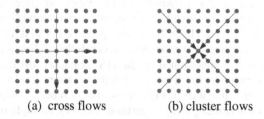

(a) cross flows   (b) cluster flows

Fig. 7. Two kinds of flows in the grid topology

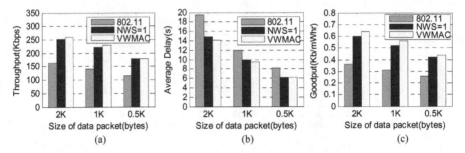

Fig. 8. Performance of cross flows under grid topology

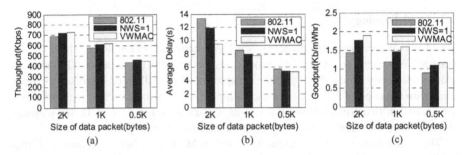

Fig. 9. Performance of cluster flows under grid topology

as illustrated in part (b) of Figure 7. Since the number of hops (of only 4) is not large enough to achieve obvious improvement on throughput, the throughput of VWMAC and the existing approaches are similar to IEEE 802.11, as plotted in part (a) of Figure 9. However, even under this condition, the average delay of packets is decreased and energy_goodput is increased greatly compared with IEEE 802.11, as we can see from parts (b) and (c) of Figure 9. Also, we can conclude that the performance of VWMAC is still sensible to the size of DATA packet under this scenario. Larger size packets achieves greater performance enhancement.

5   Conclusion

Intra-flow contention is one of the main factors that cause the failure of transmission in multi-hop wireless ad hoc networks. In this paper, we propose a novel strategy, called voluntary waiting, to solve the intra-flow contention problem and improve the performance of IEEE 802.11 DCF. In the proposed VWMAC protocol, a node voluntarily waits for a period of time after successfully sending a DATA packet. The length of time to wait is determined by the DATA packet just transmitted. Also, for the first time, we propose that a node can safely change to sleep mode during the waiting period. Our simulation results show that VWMAC outperforms the IEEE 802.11 and existing schemes greatly in terms of network throughput, packet delay and energy consumption.

Besides considering more complex topologies and traffic patterns, our future work also includes studying the influence of sleep on the performance of network and considering more types of contentions in wireless ad hoc networks. Other than the intro-flow contention, different flows in the network may interfere with each other if some of the nodes on their routes are close enough. This can be called inter-flow contention, which will be taken into consideration in our future work.

Acknowledgements

This work is supported in part by the Hong Kong Polytechnic Universities under the ICRG grant A-PF77 and 4-6941, and by the National Natural Science Foundation of China under Grant No. 60273068.

References

[1] Phil Karn, "MACA - A new channel access method for packet radio", ARRL/CRRL Amateur Radio 9th computer Networking Conference, 1990, pp. 134 – 140.

[2] Vaduvur Bharghavan, Alan Demers, Scott Shenker, Lixia Zhang, "MACAW: a media access protocol for wireless LAN's", Proceedings of the conference on Communications architectures, protocols and applications, 1994, pp. 210 – 225.

[3] IEEE, ANSI/IEEE std 802.11, 1999 Edition (R2003), Part 11: Wireless LAN Medium Access Control (MAC) and Physical Layer (PHY) Specifications.

[4] Shugong Xu and Tarek Saadawi, "Does the IEEE 802.11 MAC protocol work well in multihop wireless ad hoc networks?", IEEE Communications Magazine, Vol. 39, No. 6, pp. 130 - 137, 2001.

[5] S.-T. Sheu and T.-F. Sheu. "A bandwidth allocation/sharing/extension protocol for multimedia over IEEE 802.11 ad hoc wireless LANs". IEEE JSAC, 19(10):2065–2080, October 2001.

[6] F. Cali, M. Conti, and E. Gregori. "IEEE 802.11: Design and Performance Evaluation of an Adaptive Backoff Mechanism". IEEE JSAC, 18(9), September 2000.

[7] F. Ye, S. Yi, and B. Sikdar, "Improving spatial reuse of IEEE 802.11 based ad hoc networks," in IEEE Global Telecommunications Conference, San Francisco, CA, USA, December 1-5 2003.

[8] Jing Zhu, Xingang Guo, et al, "Adapting physical carrier sensing to maximize spatial reuse in 802.11 mesh networks", Wireless Communications and Mobile Computing , 4(8): 933-946, 2004.

[9] A. Muqattash and M. Krunz. "Power controlled dual channel (PCDC) medium access protocol for wireless ad hoc networks". In Proceedings of the IEEE INFOCOM Conference, pages 470–480, 2003.

[10] J. Deng and Z. Haas, "Dual busy tone multiple access (DBTMA)- a multiple access control scheme for ad hoc networks", IEEE Transactions on Communications, Volume 50, Issue 6, June 2002.

[11] Fu Z, Zerfos P, Luo H, Lu S, Zhang L, Gerla M. "The Impact of multihop wireless channel on TCP throughput and loss". Proc. of INFOCOM 03. San Francisco: IEEE Press, 2003. 1733-1753.

[12] Zhenqiang Ye, Dan Berger, Prasun Sinha, Srikanth V. Krishnamurthy, Michalis Faloutsos, Satish K. Tripathi, "On Alleviating MAC Layer Self-Contention in Ad-hoc Networks" Poster, MobiCom 2003.

[13] H. Zhai, X. Chen and Y. Fang. "Alleviating intra-flow and inter-flow contentions for reliable service in mobile as hoc networks". In Proc. of IEEE Milcom'04, Monterey, California, Nov. 2004.

[14] Shiann-Tsong Sheu, Tobias Chen, Jenhui Chen, Fun Ye. "The Impact of RTS Threshold on IEEE 802.11 MAC Protocol", ICPADS, 2002.

[15] http://www.ietf.org/internet-drafts/draft-ietf-manet-aodv-13.txt

[16] GloMoSim, http://pcl.cs.ucla.edu/projects/glomosim/.

[17] Rong Zheng and Robin Kravets, "On-demand Power Management for Ad Hoc Network", Elsevier Ad Hoc Journal, 2005

A Coloring Based Backbone Construction Algorithm in Wireless Ad Hoc Network*

Zhiwei Lin[1], Li Xu[1], Dajin Wang[2], and Jianliang Gao[1]

[1] School of Mathematics and Computer Science,
Fujian Normal University, Fuzhou, 350007, P.R. China
{lw, xuli}@fjnu.edu.cn
[2] Montclair State University,
Upper Montclair, NJ 07043, USA
wang@pegasus.montclair.edu

Abstract. A wireless ad hoc network consists of many mobile hosts communicating with each other without any infrastructure. Virtual backbone plays a key role in a wireless ad hoc network for routing optimization, energy conservation and resource allocation. To construct virtual backbones efficiently, a new distributed method based on coloring algorithm is proposed in this paper. Because the proposed algorithm uses only 1-hop neighbors information, it is proven that this coloring based method can cluster into groups with $O(\triangle)$ time complexity and $O(n\triangle^2)$ message complexity, which are better than referenced work in this paper.

1 Introduction

A wireless ad hoc network is a multi-hop wireless network composed of mobile nodes communicating with each other through wireless links. It is very different from traditional wireless environments, such as cellular networks or wireless LANs. In a wireless ad hoc network, mobile nodes equipped with limited energy are self-organizing and self-configuring. There does not exist a permanent center node for the system. So only distributed algorithms are feasible. The dynamic topology due to the node mobility causes frequent route failure. To enable the network to route efficiently and conserve the energy of mobile nodes, virtual backbone mechanism has been proposed. Mobile backbone is a collection of mobile clusterheads and gateways to maintain the connectivity of the network and guarantee the full coverage. A clusterhead set is a *dominating set* in graph theory that covers all other nodes in a graph. To connect all clusterheads in the dominating set, gateway nodes are introduced. Clusterheads and gateway nodes together make the ad hoc network's virtual backbone, which is a *connected dominating set*, or CDS for short.

It has been proven that the problem of finding a minimum connected dominating set (MCDS for short) is NP-complete, because it needs globally complete information about the topology. Some heuristic centralized methods [4,6] have been proposed, but all these cannot be applied to ad hoc networks whose topology constantly changes.

---

* Partially supported by National Natural Science Foundation of China (No. 60502047), Natural Science Foundation of Fujian Province of China (No.A0440001).

Y.-C. Chung and J.E. Moreira (Eds.): GPC 2006, LNCS 3947, pp. 509–516, 2006.

Therefore, the task of distributedly generating MCDS in an ad hoc network is even more challenging and harder because of the absence of global network topology.

Recently, many different distributed algorithms have been proposed to generate the dominating set and find gateways, and eventually construct the CDS. These so-called white-gray-back distributed algorithms can be characterized as global, quasi-global, quasi-local and local [2,5,8,9]. The global MCDS algorithm requires the global information to determine which node has the maximum degree, while the quasi-global method, proposed by Wan *et al*, is based on a spanning tree, rooted at an arbitrary node. Based on the lowest ID, Lee and Gerla proposed the local method, in which the node with the lowest ID becomes a clusterhead and colors itself black. Quasi-local clustering algorithm proposed by Wu requires 2-hop neighbors connectivity information and the result cannot guarantee minimum because of redundancy.

In this paper, a new distributed clustering algorithm is proposed with the idea of coloring in graph theory. This coloring-based algorithm only requires 1-hop information and can rapidly cluster into groups with less complexity of time and message. The rest of this paper is organized as follows. Section 2 reviews some representative dominating set methods in recent years and compares their performance. Section 3 describes the basic mathematical assumptions in this paper. In Section 4, the new distributed, coloring-based backbone construction algorithm (CBCA for short) is proposed to construct the maximum independent set. The set is proved to be a minimum dominating set. The node that is not in the minimum dominating set can determine whether it is a gateway according to CBCA. Section 5 analyzes CBCA's performance. Finally in Section 6, the main contribution of this paper is summarized.

2 Related Works

As mentioned in the previous section, recently existing algorithms take a white-gray-black progressing approach, in which all nodes are initially colored white and finally colored black. These algorithms can be characterized into four categories [2,5,8,9]. The global approach proposed by Sivakumar and Das is based on the maximum node-degree. In the 1st step, if a node has the maximum degree in the network, it first announces itself as a root and is colored black and all its neighbors are colored gray. The algorithm then selects a gray node that has the maximum white neighbors. This gray node is colored black and all its 1-hop neighbors are colored gray. The preceding step is repeated until no white node is left. The resulting set of black nodes dominates the network.

Wan and Alzoubi proposed a quasi-global method aimed at finding a minimum connected dominating set. This spanning tree based approach consists of 4 phases. In the first phase, a spanning tree is constructed according to a distributed leader election strategy. In the 2nd phase, every node will determine its level in the spanning tree. Accordingly, with the level-based spanning tree, a maximal independent set, that is a minimum dominating set, is formed and the nodes in the set are connected in the next 2 phases. The connected nodes form a MCDS. We point out that these 4 steps cannot be applied to the mobile ad hoc network due to its mobility.

The local approach is also a lowest-ID based algorithm. Lee and Gerla divided this approach into the following 2 steps: (1) A node colors itself black if all its neighbors'

IDs are higher than its ID. (2) All neighbors of the black node color themselves gray and join the cluster. These two steps are repeated until there is no white node left. This problem with this ID-based approach is that the node with minimal ID will be forced to act as a dominating node, which will rapidly run out its energy.

In [9], Wu and Li proposed that the set in which every node has two unconnected neighbors forms a connected dominating set. Because the set obtained with this method is not minimal, they have to prune some redundant nodes. Obviously, this quasi-local algorithm requires 2-hop connectivity information.

Based on these 4 representative methods, some new modified algorithms [3,7,10] were proposed but they are quite similar to these 4 methods. In this paper we will present a new MCDS algorithm based on coloring algorithm. We assume each node has the same transmission power and our target is to find a MCDS with a lower cost than that of previously proposed.

3 Preliminaries and Notations

A wireless ad hoc network is usually modeled as a unit disk graph (UDG), in which nodes are assumed to have the same transmission range. The construction of mobile backbone in a wireless ad hoc network is then the same as forming MCDS in UDG, which is shown to be NP-hard Clark *et al* [1].

Given a unit disk graph $G=(V,E)$, a subset S is a dominating set if and only if every node in $G-S$ is connected to at least one node in S. If the dominating set S is connected, S is called connected dominating set (CDS). A CDS with a minimum size is called MCDS.

A subset S is an independent set (IS) if and only if $\forall u,v \in S, (u,v) \notin E$. S is maximal if $\forall u \in V-S$, u has a neighbor in S; S is also called maximum independent set (MIS) or dominating independent set (DIS).

Lemma 3.1. *An MIS is a minimum dominating set (MDS).*

Proof: Assume that S is MIS but not a minimum dominating set. The subset $S-\{x\}$, where x belongs to S, is not an MIS. That means that $S-\{x\}$ cannot fully dominate the other vertices. This contradicts the definition of MIS. So S is a minimum dominating set.

Lemma 3.2. *Any node in an MIS can find at most one or two nodes to connect one of the other closest nodes in the MIS (means two or three hops away from its neighbor in the MIS).* [8]

Proof: Suppose that a node x in an MIS has to find at least 3 nodes a, b and c to connect another closest node y in the MIS and a, b and c do not belong to MIS (x-a-b-c-y). Since b does not belong to the MIS, then it must be adjacent to at least one of the nodes z in the MIS, which means that there exists another closest node z in the MIS such that x-a-b-z. This contradicts our assumption.

A *coloring* of an undirected graph $G = (V, E)$ is a function $C: V \rightarrow N$ such that for all $u,v \in V$, if $C(u) = C(v)$, then $(u,v) \notin E$; that is, no adjacent vertices have the same color. The set in which all nodes are the same color will be called a coloring division. The statement in the following Lemma is obviously true.

Lemma 3.3. *All the nodes colored with the same color form an independent set in the graph; or in other words, a coloring division set is an IS.*

Based on coloring divisions, we can generate an MIS, which can dominate the network. If a coloring algorithm can be modified to color the network in a distributed manner, then we can distributedly construct an MIS. Further more, according to lemma 3.2, if we want to minimize the size of MCDS, we must guarantee that an MIS member is only 2-hop away from its MIS neighbor after the coloring algorithm.

For reader's convenience, the terms and variables used in the rest of this paper are summarized in Table 1.

Table 1. Notations & Variants

MDS	The Minimum Dominating Set
MCDS	The Minimum Connected Dominating Set
Gateway	The Vertex that connects at least 2 clusterheads
$N(i)$	The Set of 1-hop neighbors of node i
c	The Color Value
$i.c$	The Color number of node i
$Color\_1\_ID$	The node ID whose color number is 1.
$Timer$	The node shot time-slot that can expire
$i.T$	The initial Timer value of node i
V_i	The vertex set in which node color number is i

4   The CBCA Algorithm

The CBCA algorithm to establish backbone for an ad hoc network is based on coloring. In the algorithm, every node has a color number variable C, initialized to 0. To enable the algorithm to run in an asynchronous manner, we assign a shot time-slot to every node, which is denoted by T and *Timer*. Every node uses equation (1) to compute the value of T.

$$T = random(degree \times ID) \tag{1}$$

Equation (1) guarantees that all nodes are different from each other by using random number, which belongs to [0,1]. The degree in (1) represents the number of the node's neighbors.

After the distributed algorithm, one of the coloring divisions is an MIS, such that the member of the MIS is 2-hop away from one of its MIS neighbors. And based on the color number information of its neighbors, the connected node will be determined. To achieve this goal, an arbitrary node is selected to start the backbone construction algorithm and this node is colored number "1". After coloring, the root node scatters its color number to its neighbor. When receiving a color number from its neighbor, a node runs the following algorithm to determine its color:

```
Clusterhead Election Algorithm:
1    A neighbor m receives c value sent by node n(n.c).
2    m.Timer=m.T;
3    Start m.Timer and waiting for Timer expiration.
4    Color_1_ID=0;
5    Color=0;
6    For(∀i∈N(m)) do {
7         If(i.c>color) then
8              Color=i.c;
9         If(i.c=1) then
10             Color_1_ID=i;
11   }
12   If (Color_1_ID=0) then
13             m.c=1;
14   Else
15             m.c=Color+1;
16   If(m.c>1) then
17        Compute T=random(m.c * degree * ID)
18   Send the color of itself to its neighbors
```

Theorem 4.1. *All nodes with color number "1" form an MIS. We call it the division set V_1.*

Proof: Initially, a node n is colored by number 1 and all its neighbors $N(n)$ will be colored by other numbers. According to the algorithm, every node will first search the information of its neighbors before it determines its color number. If there are no neighbors colored by number 1, then the node will first color itself number 1. That is, the algorithm guarantees that the number of nodes colored by number 1 is maximal. Thus, V_1 is an MIS.

Theorem 4.2. *The shortest-hop path between any two complementary subsets A and B of set V_1 is of two-hop distance.*

Proof: Let us assume that the shortest-hop path is 3-hop distance. Then there exist two nodes (x and y) that connect A and B, but do not belong to V_1. From Figure 1, we can see that a-x-y-b is the shortest path. The algorithm begins from one node (without loss of generality, assume that this beginning node is now in set A) and is scattered over the network. That means that before node b is colored by number 1, the node y has already been colored by 1. This contradicts the assumption.

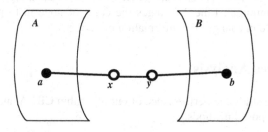

Fig. 1. The Assumption Model

Theorem 4.2 shows that the distributed algorithm needs much fewer inter-nodes to connect the nodes colored by number 1. From Theorem 4.2, we can easily draw the following conclusions:

Lemma 4.2.1. *Every node dominated by 2 nodes in V_1 is a **gateway candidate**.*

Lemma 4.2.2. *A node in the MIS needs only one node to connect to neighboring nodes in the MIS.*

Lemma 4.2.3. *The algorithm needs only $|V_1|-1$ gateway nodes.*

So far, all proposed methods to compute MCDS proceed with at least 2 steps, because they have to produce MDS before determining the gateways. This may not be necessary, and may not adapt to the fast mobile environment, where a clusterhead may have left before the gateway is generated. In our algorithm, the gateway nodes are determined in the process of computing MDS. The network elects gateways according to the following algorithm. It combines both election of gateway candidates and election of clusterheads.

```
Gateway Election Algorithm - Gateway Candidates:
1    As soon as a gateway candidate finds that it has
     been dominated by two clusterheads, then it imme-
     diately starts the Timer.
2    m.Timer=m.T;
3    Start m.Timer and waiting for Timer expiration.
4    m.c=1;
5    Send m.c value and its dominating nodes informa-
     tion to its clusterhead neighbors to announce it-
     self as a gateway

Gateway Election Algorithm - Clusterheads:
1    A clusterhead m receives c value(c=1) sent from
     its dominated node n.
2    If(m.degree=1) then
3            m.c=n.c
4    Change the information of node n and itself and
     broadcast the information to its neighbor to tell
     the gateway candidate to be a normal dominated
     node.
```

If a dominating node has only 1 degree, then it must be dominated by a gateway-clusterhead node. So line 2 is to prune itself from the dominating set and guarantee that the CDS is minimal. Line 3 changes the color of node m to previous color of node n before node m changes the information of node n.

5 Performance Analysis

In this section, we study the performance of our algorithm CBCA and compare it with the previously proposed methods.

Lemma 5.1. *The size of the MIS is at most $4\times opt+1$, where **opt** is the size of optimal MCDS.* [1]

Lemma 5.1 claims that the optimal MIS has ratio at most 4. According to Lemma 4.2.3, the size of the MCDS is $2|V_1|-1$. We can reach the following conclusions.

Theorem 5.1. *The size of the MCDS is at most $8 \times opt+1$.*

Proof: V_1 is a MIS. Since $|MIS| \leq 4 \times opt+1$, and $|MCDS|=2|V_1|-1$, we have $|MCDS| \leq 8 \times opt+1$. So our algorithm has a performance ratio of at most 8.

Theorem 5.2. *The time complexity of the algorithm is $O(\triangle)$, where $\triangle$ is the maximum degree and the message complexity is $O(n\triangle^2)$, where n is the number of nodes .*

Proof: The main part that decides the time complexity is the one that the node checks the color information of its neighbors. In our implementation, a node has to search the color values of its neighbors before coloring itself (line 6~11), so the time complexity of the algorithm is $O(\triangle)$.

The whole algorithm consists of 3 elemental messages: (1) a node broadcasts at most $\triangle$ messages to its neighbors to tell them its color value; (2) a gateway candidate broadcasts at most $\triangle$ messages to its dominators to announce itself as a MCDS member; (3) When the announcement arrives, the dominators have to broadcast the announcement and change information to its neighbors, so all these 2 steps messages are $\triangle^2$. We can conclude that the message complexity is $O(n\triangle^2)$.

Theorems 5.1 and 5.2 give a performance analysis of the algorithm on size ratio, time complexity, and message complexity. Table 2 compares our method with previously proposed methods. From the table, we can see that our method with only 1-hop local information is better than other methods at time and message complexity.

Table 2. Comparisons of the algorithms. *m* denotes the number of the edges in the network.

	Ratio	Time	Message	Information need
[2]	$\Theta (log\ n)$	$O(n^2)$	$O(n^2)$	global
[5]	$O(n)$	$O(n^2)$	$O(n)$	1-hop
[8]	$8opt-2$	$O(n)$	$O(nlog\ n)$	quasi-global
[9]	$O(n)$	$O(n\triangle^3)$	$\Theta (m)$	2-hop
CBCA	$8opt+1$	$O(\triangle)$	$O(n\triangle^2)$	1-hop

6 Conclusion

In this paper, we have studied the problem of constructing MCDS in a wireless ad hoc network. We have proposed a localized, coloring-based, and one-step distributed MCDS construction algorithm. Our method has a performance ratio of at most 8. The main reason we can get a less time and message complexity than other methods is that we only require 1-hop neighbors knowledge. In our future work, we will continue to study the maintenance of MCDS in a mobile environment. We will also investigate MCDS's performance in routing.

References

1. B.N. Clark, C. J. Colbourn and D. S. Johnson, Unit Disk Graphs, Discrete Mathematics, 86(1990) 165-177
2. B. Das and V. Bharghavan, Routing in Ad-Hoc Networks Using Minimum Connected Dominating Sets, International Conference on Communications, Montreal, Canada, June 1997
3. M. Min, Fe. Wang, D. –Z. Du and P. M. Pardalos, A Reliable Virtual Backbone Scheme in Mobile Ad-Hoc Networks, Proceedings of the 1st IEEE International conference on Mobile Ad Hoc and Sensor Systems , Oct., 2004, FL, USA
4. S. Guha and S. Khuller, Approximation algorithms for connected dominating sets, Algorithmica, 20(4), April (1998) 374-387
5. C. R. Lin and M. Gerla, Adaptive Clustering for Mobile Wireless Networks. IEEE Journal on Selected Areas in Communications, 15(7), Sep, (1997) 1265-1275
6. M. V. Marathe, et al., Simple heuristics for unit disk graphs, Networks, vol. 25, (1995) 59-68
7. I. Stojmenovic, M. Seddigh, Dominating Sets and Neighbor Elimination Based Broadcasting Algorithms in Wireless Networks, IEEE Transactions on Parallel and Distributed Systems, 13(1), (2002) 14-25
8. P, -j. Wan, K.M. Alzoubi and O. Frieder, Distributed Construction of Connected Dominating Sets in Wireless Ad Hoc Networks, IEEE INFOCOM,2002
9. J. Wu and H. Li, On calculating Connected Dominating Set for Efficient Routing in Ad Hoc Wireless Networks, Proc. Of the 3 International Workshop on Discrete Algorithms and Methods for Mobile Computing and Communications, August (1999) 7-14
10. J. Wu and H. Li, Domination and its Applications in Ad Hoc Wireless Networks with Unidirectional Links, Proc. of International Conference on Parallel Processing , Aug. (2000) 189-200

Route Error Reporting Schemes for On-Demand Routing in 6LoWPAN

Won-Do Jung[1], Shafique Ahmad Chaudhry[1],
Young-Ho Sohn[2], and Ki-Hyung Kim[1,*]

[1] Graduate School of Information and Communication,
Ajou University, Suwon, Korea
{yarang, shafique, kkim86}@ajou.ac.kr
[2] Dept. of Computer Engineering,
Yeungnam University, Gyungsan, Korea
sohn@yumail.ac.kr

Abstract. Due to their rapid growth and new paradigm applications, wireless sensor networks are morphing into low power personal area networks (LoWPANs), which are envisioned to grow radically. To achieve higher degrees of pervasiveness these LoWPANs must be connected to the wired networks where most of information resources reside. Integration of IPv6 with LoWPANs poses many challenges; the hardest of them, probably, is the difference in packet size. Solution to this problem demands new packet format definition, packet header compression, and a fragmentation and reassembly layer. Header compression techniques suggest different schemes including removal of source node's address from the packet header. In this paper we analyze the effects of eliminating the source address from the packet header and then propose solutions to propagate the route error message (RERR) to the source even without having the source address. We make use of MAC layer address for sending the RERR to the previous hop node, back tracking the route hop by hop, eventually to the source. The simulation results show that the proposed solutions deliver RERRs to the source even without the source address.

1 Introduction

Wireless sensor networks are being utilized in wide variety of embedded applications. These applications include consumer appliances, home automation, monitoring and control in industrial environments, personal area networks (PANs), and environmental monitoring and sensing. As a new paradigm PANs are morphing into low power personal area networks (LoWPANs). Valuable efforts are underway to consider the outreach of LoWPAN to peer networks and contemporary standardization activities.

The wireless standard IEEE 802.15.4 [1] describes the specifications for LoWPANs. The standard defines the transmission and reception on the physical radio channel (PHY), and the channel access, the PAN (personal area network)

---

* Corresponding author.

Y.-C. Chung and J.E. Moreira (Eds.): GPC 2006, LNCS 3947, pp. 517–526, 2006.
© Springer-Verlag Berlin Heidelberg 2006

maintenance, and reliable data delivery (MAC). LoWPANs are low power, low bandwidth, and low cost networks. LoWPANs have small packet size. The maximum physical layer frame size is 127 octets. They support IEEE 64-bit extended as well as 16-bit short media access control address. Devices in a LoWPAN are deployed in ad-hoc fashion and support star and mesh topologies.

While IEEE 802.15.4 provides specifications for physical and link layers, ZigBee [2] is striving for defining the upper layers over IEEE 802.15.4 especially for sensor networks. Meanwhile 6LoWPAN [4], a working group of the IETF [3], standardizes the use of IPv6 over IEEE 802.15.4. The internet draft [5] describes the overview of 6LoWPAN. It portrays the problems, assumptions and goals for transmitting IPv6 over IEEE 802.15.4 networks. It defines two main goals: first, the provision of the fragmentation and reassembly in the adaptation layer below the IP layer (i.e. sub-IP layer) and second, the header compression for IPv6 over IEEE 802.15.4. To achieve the above mentioned goals, a frame format for IPv6 transmission over IEEE 802.15.4 networks is presented in [6]. This work shows the forming of IPv6 link-local addresses and statelessly auto-configured addresses on IEEE 802.15.4 networks. It also describes a simple header compression scheme for IEEE 802.15.4. One interesting thing is that the working group is considering the use of source addresses in the adaptation layer as optional.

For the routing aspects, LOAD [10] has been proposed in 6LoWPAN. As a simplified version of AODV [7], LOAD enables multi-hop routing between IEEE 802.15.4 devices to establish and maintain routes in 6LoWPAN. However, it does not mention any mechanism for sending the route error (RERR) message to the originator in case of a link failure.

In this paper we analyze the effect of omitting the source address from the adaptation header and propose back-propagation mechanisms to propagate RERR messages to the originator. We make use of the MAC layer address for the previous hop node and use it to send RERR messages, back tracking the route hop by hop, eventually to the originator. Our mechanism can also be used, with minimum modifications, to propagate the RERR to all the affected nodes in the network. We analyze how data rates and transmission patterns affect the RERR propagation when originator's address is not known. Results show that our proposed mechanisms work well as compared to the existing mechanisms for the RERR delivery where the source address is present in the packet header.

Rest of the paper is organized as follows. We summarize the related work in section 2. In Section 3 we will elaborate the problem by discussing the issues involved in transmission of IPv6 over LoWPAN and the effects of not having the source address in IPv6 packets over IEEE 802.15.4. We propose our solutions in Section 4 followed by some evaluation results in Section 5. We mention future research directions and conclude in Section 6.

2 Related Work

We state that there is not much published work in this area. However in this section we summarize the available significant efforts for routing in 6LoWPAN.

The Ad hoc On-Demand Distance Vector (AODV) [7] is the most widely used routing protocol for mobile ad-hoc networks. It has been considered as a strong candidate for 6LowPAN because of its simplicity for finding routes. It is a loop-free protocol that conveys the route failure errors to the affected nodes so that nodes can mark the lost link as invalid. Another important feature is the use of the destination sequence number for each route entry which helps the node to select the better path, in case there are multiple routes to the same destination.

Slimmer versions of AODV have also been proposed. AODVjr, a trimmed version of AODV, has been proposed in [8]. This version removes sequence numbers, hello messages, gratuitous request reply, hop count, RERR and precursor lists from original AODV. AODVjr is much lighter than AODV yet gives performance comparable to AODV. TinyAODV [9] is another example of such work.

LOAD is a simplification of AODV for IEEE 802.15.4. The mesh is established by layering routing capability underneath IP layer that enables it to create a mesh underneath and unbeknownst to IP. The simplification suggestions include support of only those AODV control message types i.e. RREQ, RREP and RERR, and elimination of hello packets. LOAD assumes the use of either one of the two different addresses for routing: the EUI-64 address and the 16-bit short address of the 6LoWPAN device. The format of RERR is simplified to include only one unreachable destination while the RERR of AODV may include multiple ones. LOAD assumes to have originator's address and does not discuss the situation where RERR reporting could be done without having originator address.

3 Problem Description

The integration of IPv6 with IEEE 802.15.4 networks brings some challenges. The most important issue probably is the difference in packet sizes in the two technologies. The maximum transmission unit for IPv6 is at least 1280 octets and it therefore cannot be mapped onto IEEE 802.15.4 frame which has a maximum frame size of 127 octets at physical layer. This size includes the MAC layer header of 25 octets that gives a frame size equal to 102 octets at MAC layer which in turn may include a maximum of 21 bytes for security, at link layer level, leaving the minimum frame size of 81 octets at higher layers. Adding more to the irony, IPv6 header is 40 octets that leaves 41 octets for upper layer protocols, say UDP. UDP uses 8 bytes header that would leave only 33 octets for application data. This situation demands for definition of packet formats to be transmitted over IEEE 802.15.4, Header compression mechanisms and mechanisms for packet delivery in link-layer mesh.

The document [6] describes transmission of IPv6 over LoWPAN. Taking this document into account lets consider two different scenarios for the single-hop and the multi-hop packet transmission. In the single-hop packet transmission(the destination and the source node are in one-hop), the destination and source IP addresses in IPv6 header can be compressed and decompressed by utilizing the layer 2 destination and source addresses (EUI-64). In the multi-hop packet transmission, the layer 2 destination and source addresses cannot be utilized for the compression and decompression because they are just hop-by-hop destination and source, not the

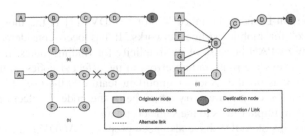

Fig. 1. Routing scenarios

originator and the final destination. This is why final destination field should be included in the adaptation layer. By utilizing the final destination field (which does not change hop-by-hop manner), the destination IP address can be compressed in the IPv6 header. In addition, the routing could happen at the adaptation layer, not in the IP layer.

The case of the originator address is quite attention-grabbing. Because the working group is now considering the originator address as optional in adaptation layer. Notice that the layer 2 source address is not the originator address, but the previous hop node's address. If, in case of link failure, route error message is not sent to the originator it may keep sending the packets without realizing that packets are being dropped. This situation can degrade the overall network performance and throughput.

Consider the scenario shown in figure 1(a). In this scenario A is the originator and E is the destination, and route includes nodes B, C and D i.e. $A \text{ --> } B \text{ --> } C \text{ --> } D \text{ --> } E$. In case, the link between C and D is broken as shown in figure 1(b), C could not report the broken link to the originator by utilizing Route Error message (in AODV) as the data packet does not have the originator address at the adaptation layer.

The route error message reporting to the originator is necessary in the Mesh routing because it might incur some performance drops in communication. The originator might send multiple packets through the broken route without being notified of the error. If the error is never reported to the originator the packets will be discarded and originator will never know that they are not being delivered.

Route error reporting can easily be made possible by adding the *originator address* in the adaptation layer. This is the originator's 64 bit link-layer address. It can be considered that the originator address is retrieved from the IPv6 source address at the IPv6 layer. If the packet is unfragmented, the adaptation layer could extract the originator address from the IPv6 source address. However if the packet is fragmented, interior fragments does not have the IPv6 header as a payload. The extraction of the IPv6 source address at the IPv6 layer could not be possible in that case. Certain provisions can be made to accommodate or support 16-bit short addresses as well.

4   Back Propagation of Route Errors

We contend that the route error can be sent to the originator even without having the originator address in the adaptation layer. We propose three schemes, to propagate the RERR message to the originator, named unicast back propagation, broadcast back propagation and routing table aware propagation.

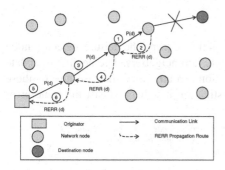

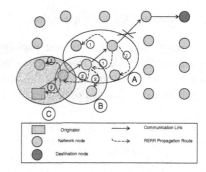

Fig. 2. Unicast back propagation   **Fig. 3.** Broadcast back propagation

4.1 Unicast Back Propagation

The main idea is to propagate the route error message using the hop-by-hop backward traversal. The node which finds a link break must notify its predecessor node about the link failure. The predecessor deletes that route entry from its routing table and notifies its preceding node when it receives next data packet for the same destination. Thus the route error will be propagated back to the originator. If there are n hops between the originator and the node that first detects the link breakage, it will take n steps to notify the originator. The propagation process is shown in Fig. 2. We assume that the communication path between the originator and the node noticing a link failure remain intact during the propagation process. Simulation results confirm that it shows almost similar performance to the case where the sources address is available. The basic algorithm is depicted in Fig. 4.

```
Legend:   P(p,d)   :  Data packet P, received from previous hop node 'p' for the destination 'd'
          E(d,n)   :  Route entry for destination node 'd' , node 'n' is the next hop node
          RERR(d):  Route error message notifying a link failure for node 'd'

Begin Proc
    If a node receives P(p,d)
        If there is an E(d,n) in Routing Table
            Send  P(d) to n
            If a link failure was notified by MAC Layer
                //Initiate the RERR reporting procedure
                Unicast RERR(d) to p
                Discard P(d)
            End If
        Else //there is no E(d,n) in Routing Table
            Unicast RERR (d) to p
        End if
    End if
    If a node receives RERR(d)
        Discard RERR(d)
    End If
End Proc
```

Fig. 4. Unicast-back propagation algorithm

4.2 Broadcast Back Propagation

It works similar to the unicast back propagation except the failure detector node broadcasts the route error message to its single hop neighbors. The neighbors update their routing tables by deleting this destination's route entry. In case any of these neighbors receives a packet for the very destination it will broadcast the route error

```
Legend:  P (p,d)  : Data packet P, received from previous hop node 'p' for the destination 'd'
         E(d,n)   : Route entry for destination node 'd' , node 'n' is the next hop node
         RERR(d): Route error message notifying link failure for node 'd'

Begin Proc
     If a node receives P(p,d)
          If there is an E(d,n) in Routing Table
               Send  P(d) to n
               If a link failure was notified by MAC Layer
                    //Initiate the RERR reporting procedure
                    Broadcast RERR(d) in one hop
                    Discard P(d)
               End If
          Else //there is no E(d,n)
               Broadcast RERR(d) in one hop
          End If
     End if
     If a node receives RERR(d)
          Delete E(d,k) from Routing Table
     End If
End Proc
```

Fig. 5. Broadcast back propagation algorithm

```
Legend:   P (p,d)    : Data packet P, received from the previous hop node 'p' for the destination 'd'
          E(d,n)     : Route entry for the destination node 'd' , node 'n' is the next hop node
          RERR(d,h) :Route error message notifying a link failure for the destination 'd' where 'h' is
                       the hop count from the node initiating the RERR to 'd'
          HC(n,d)    :Hop count from  node 'n' to the destination 'd'
Begin Proc
     If a node receives P(p,d)
          If there is an E(d,n) in Routing Table
               Send P(d) to n
               If a link failure was notified by the MAC Layer
                    //Initiate the RERR reporting procedure
                    Broadcast RERR(d,h) in one hop
                    Discard P(d)
               Else //there is no entry E(d,n) in Routing Table
                    Broadcast RERR(d,h) in one hop
               End if
          End if
     End if
     If a node receives RERR(d,h)
          If (there is an E(d,n) in Routing Table) AND ( HC(n,d) > h )
               Delete E(d,k) from RT
               Broadcast RERR(d,h) in one hop
          Else
               Discard RERR(d,h)
          End If
     End if
End Proc
```

Fig. 6. Routing table-aware back propagation algorithm

message and thus the route error will be propagated back. The process is depicted in Fig.3 and the algorithm is presented in Fig. 5. It may take the same time as the unicast back propagation mechanism to notify the originator but it generates more traffic. This scheme works well in the situation where multiple nodes are forwarding data through the same link. Such a scenario is shown in Fig. 1(c) where nodes A, F, G and B are the originators and E is the destination. In such case, the broadcast of route errors from B can stop any further packet loss for nodes A, F, G and H.

4.3 Routing Table Aware Propagation

This technique tries to exploit the conviction that if route error is propagated to all the potentially affected nodes then the future packet loss, which could occur by sending packets on failed link, can be saved. Fig. 7 shows that when a node finds a link failure it broadcasts the route error message to its single hop neighbors. All the nodes that have the route entry for the destination, upon receiving this route error message, will delete the route entry for this specific destination and broadcast the message again towards the nodes closer to the originator. The algorithm is described in Fig. 6.

5 Simulation and Evaluation

We have evaluated our propagation schemes using ns-2 simulations. We have modified AODV to incorporate our schemes. Though simpler versions of AODV have been suggested for 6LoWPAN but we use the original version because the relevant parts of AODV and its slimmer versions are similar. We have simulated our schemes for a scenario of one hundred 6LoWPAN nodes. The simulation setup details are given in Table 1. We have examined many metrics including delivery ratio, throughput, end-to-end average delivery time, and number of route error messages in order to analyze the impact of the back propagation. The results show that our algorithms improve the throughput and packet delivery ratio as compared to the situation when there is no provision for RERR propagation, in case of route failures, when a source address is not present. However, the use of these schemes is a tradeoff between putting a source address in the packet header and the system performance.

5.1 Delivery Ratio

It is defined as the percentage of packets delivered to the destination over total packets transmitted. Fig. 7 shows the effectiveness of our schemes, especially unicast back-propagation mechanism. It shows that the performance of unicast back propagation is close to that of AODV. Packet delivery ratio improves with the use of back propagation as compared to the case where no mechanism for propagating the route error message is present. This improvement can be explained by the fact that RERR message delivery to the originator stops further packet loss and thus improves the delivery ratio.

Table 1. Simulation setup

PARAMETER	Measurements
Area	117m * 117m
Total number of nodes in simulation	100
Total time of simulation	100s
Node's transmission range	15m
Protocol	AODV
Traffic type	CBR
RREQ packet size	36
RREP packet size	40
Inter-packet transmission delay	0.05 ~ 0.5s
Node transmission power	0.28J

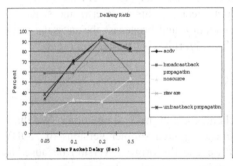

Fig. 7. Packet delivery ratio   **Fig. 8.** Throughput

5.2 Throughput

Throughput is the total number of packets delivered to the destination during the simulation time. Our schemes show almost same performance as AODV when the data rate is low. The performance of back propagation deteriorates a little when the transmission rate is high. It can be explained by the fact that there can be more data packets in the queue which are not delivered when a link failure occurs, and throughput decreases. Fig. 8 shows that unicast back propagation gives better performance than other propagation schemes. The main reason is that it generates less RERR traffic. The routing table-aware back propagation shows the lowest throughput because it generates the highest RERR traffic. However, the throughput is always better than having no mechanism for RERR notification.

5.3 End to End Average Delivery Time

Average end-to-end delivery time for our schemes is higher than AODV for low data rates, but the performance improves for higher data rates. When data rate is low, the propagation of RERR takes more time because each notification to the previous nodes needs more time, which increases the recovery time, especially in the absence of

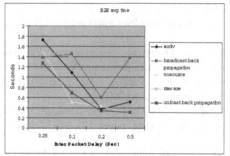

Fig. 9. End-to-end average delay

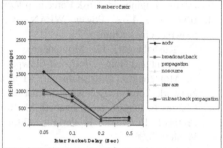

Fig. 10. Number of RERR messages

originator address. This increase in recovery time increases the average delivery time. Fig. 9 shows the end-to-end average delivery time results.

5.4 Number of RERR Messages

Routing table-aware back propagation generates the highest number of RERR messages. This scheme works well in certain static network environment where the link states do not change dynamically and thus routing tables maintain their state for a longer time span. In that case, once a change occurs, all the routing tables are pretty consistent and this can reduce the further packet loss. However, in highly dynamic environments it causes a great traffic overhead. Fig. 10 shows that number of RERR messages generated by the unicast back propagation is lower than AODV. The reason is that this scheme uses only unicast that generates less traffic of RERR messages. It shows that the unicast back propagation scheme has very low overhead in terms of control traffic generation.

6 Conclusion

Rapid growth of low power personal area networks has initiated a new paradigm to integrate IPv6 with IEEE 802.15.4. Transmission of IPv6 over LoWPAN has many advantages as well as challenges ahead. Definition of new packet formats and header compression are the core issues in 6LowPAN. We have analyzed the situation in which originator address is not provided in the packet header and thus no RERR message is delivered to the source. We have proposed back propagation mechanisms to propagate RERR message without having source address. The simulation results show that unicast back propagation mechanism shows performance almost equal to the AODV. Other mechanisms, however, show better performance in specific scenarios. Finally, our mechanisms improve the packet delivery and throughput by a considerable margin.

References

1. IEEE LoWPAN Standard 802.15.4-2003 http://standards.ieee.org/getieee802/ 802.15.html
2. ZigBee Alliance http://www.zigbee.org

3. Internet Engineering Task Force http://www.ietf.org/
4. IPv6 over Low Power WPAN Working Group http://www.ietf.org/html.charters/6lowpan-charter.html
5. N. Kushalnagar, G. Montenegro, "6LoWPAN: Overview, Assumptions, Problem Statement and Goals", draft-ietf-6lowpan-problem-01 (work in progress), Oct 2005
6. G. Montenegro, N.Kushalnagar, "Transmission of IPv6 Packets over IEEE 802.15.4 Networks",draft-ietf-6lowpan-format-01 (work in progress), Oct 2005
7. Charles E. Perkins and Elizabeth M. Royer, "The Ad hoc On-Demand Distance Vector Protocol" In Charles E. Perkins, editor, Ad hoc Networking, pages 173–219. Addison-Wesley, 2000.
8. Chakeres, Ian and Klein-Berndt, Luke, "AODVjr, AODV Simplified", ACM SIGMOBILE Mobile Computing and Communications Review pp. 100-101, July 2002.
9. TinyAODV Implementation, TinyOS Source Code Repository http://cvs.sourceforge.net/viewcvs.py/tinyos/tinyos-1.x/contrib/hsn/.
10. K. Kim, S.D. Park, G. Montenegro, S. Yoo,"6lowpan Ad Hoc On-demand Distance Vector Routing (LOAD) ", draft-danial-6lowpan-load-adhoc-routing-01 (work in progress) July 2005.

Are Low PANs a PAN or an Internet of PANs?

Ki-Hyung Kim* and Ali Hammad Akbar

Graduate School of Information and Communication, Ajou University, Suwon, Korea
{kkim86, hammad}@ajou.ac.kr

Abstract. ZigBee has recently emerged as a widely recognized forum that is formalizing IEEE802.15.4 devices for interoperability and compatibility amongst a number of vendors and designers. Under the auspices of IETF working group of 6lowPAN, efforts are underway to provide interconnectivity between low powered IEEE802.15.4 devices and wired IPv6 domain. Besides a plethora of interoperability issues, routing stands out as a challenging consideration. In this paper, we have discussed the routing approaches adopted in current ZigBee device specifications and existing work under the 6lowPAN charter. We describe, through a protocol, how to involve gateways in routing functionality in 6lowPAN networks. Through NS2-based simulation study, our performance analysis amenably supports the applicability of our protocol.

1 Introduction

Sensor devices are increasingly being used for monitoring and control applications in industrial environments by forming networks. Wireless sensor networks have been found to be of unprecedented applicability both in consumer electronics as well as home automation.

A relatively fresh wave in sensors-associated technologies has heralded even wider industrial applications. Efforts such as IEEE802.15.4 standard are geared to reduce costs, provide device customizability for diverse applications, and make room for inter-operability. Aimed at low data rate applications, industrial research is exploring possibilities of reaching at consensus and uniformity under the name and brand of ZigBee. A substantial cut is already being experienced in capital and recurrent costs of industrial systems by deploying IEEE802.15.4 devices that are ZigBee ready in a broader spectrum of environments [1].

While IEEE802.15.4 devices are considered for internet connectivity, Internet Protocol version 6.0 had emerged as a more powerful candidate. The merger of two networking paradigms gives rise to unprecedented issues and challenges. From address assignment to address management; from device discovery to network management, and from definition of packet formats to routing considerations, there are so many issues demanding to be researched into.

In this paper, we focus on the routing considerations in ZigBee and 6lowPAN. We discuss ZigBee's support for mesh routing. We also present notable efforts in routing

---

* Corresponding author.

Y.-C. Chung and J.E. Moreira (Eds.): GPC 2006, LNCS 3947, pp. 527–536, 2006.
© Springer-Verlag Berlin Heidelberg 2006

protocol design for 6lowPANs. This leads to our proposal for a gateway assisted routing framework and suggested enhancements in very recent 6lowPAN routing scheme proposed by the same author.

The remainder of the paper is as the following. In section 2, we summarize the work reported so far on IEEE802.15.4, and its inherent support for intra-PAN mesh routing. In the same section, we present a run-down of 6lowPAN and compare it with ZigBee. In section 3, we present an application scenario that forms the basis of inter-PAN routing. Section 4 presents a simple yet efficient scheme for augmenting routing framework of 6lowPAN through gateways. Section 5 presents gateway assisted routing protocol. In section 6, we present the performance result. Finally in section 7, we conclude our work and suggest future directions.

2 Related Work

This section describes the building blocks that form 6lowPAN and the 6lowPAN issues and considerations. Their respective support for mesh routing and upcoming challenges in inter-PAN routing are also discussed.

2.1 IPv6

In order to understand the basis of forming an odd combination between IEEE802.15.4 and IPv6, it is appropriate to consider motivations and envisioned service areas that have led to the selection of IPv6. The following is a listing of justifications for IPv6 suitability:

Extremely large address space: IEEE802.15.4 devices are expected to be abundant and pervasive. For retrieving and sharing contexts and information, these devices must have access to internet. An exceedingly large address space of Valid IP addresses can be provided only through IPv6 addressing scheme.

NAT devices obviated: Table driven translation to/from network addresses to local addresses is no more needed since each device has a unique IPv6 address. It is an immediate relief for sensor network designers and financiers.

Statelessness mandated in IPv6: Due to abundance and limited lifetime of low cost IEEE802.15.4 devices, it is a valid assumption that nodes shall not be manually configured. Similarly, maintaining a robust and extremely scalable configuration service is not a cost-effective proposition. IPv6 provides an all-encompassing solution through stateless address auto configuration.

Provision for location aware addressing: In IPv6 classless addressing scheme, there is greater freedom to tweak address space according to user and network needs. For example, location aware addressing can be tailored using IPv6 addresses.

2.2 IEEE802.15.4 and ZigBee

ZigBee Alliance is developing a very low-cost, very low power consumption, two-way, wireless communications standard. The ZigBee stack architecture builds on top

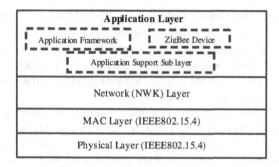

Fig. 1. Architecture of ZigBee stack built on IEEE802.15.4 layered model

of the 802.15.4-2003 layers as shown in Fig. 1. The alliance provides the network (NWK) layer and the framework for the application layer. It includes the application framework sub layer, ZigBee device object sub layer, and the application support sub-layer (APS).

IEEE 802.15.4-2003 has two PHY layers that operate in two separate frequency ranges: 868/915 MHz and 2.4 GHz. The IEEE 802.15.4-2003 MAC sub-layer controls access to the radio channel. Its responsibilities may also include transmitting beacon frames, synchronization and providing a reliable transmission mechanism. NWK layer includes functionalities for joining and leaving a network etc. In addition, the discovery and maintenance of routes between devices are done at the NWK layer too. Detailed functionalities of each layer is given in [3].

2.3 6lowPAN

IEEE802.15.4 devices that are implementing the ZigBee stack will form networks that allow devices to share services within the PAN environment. However, neither of the documents on IEEE802.15.4 and ZigBee specifies the details for cross-PAN communication.

In [2], Montenegro defines the frame format that will be used for transmission of IPv6 packets on top of IEEE 802.15.4 networks.

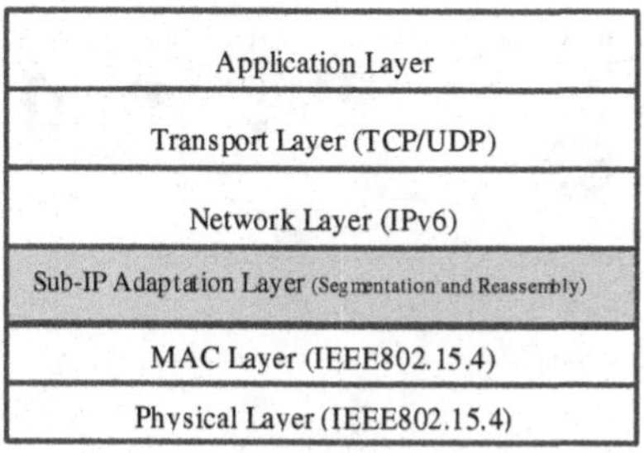

Application Layer
Transport Layer (TCP/UDP)
Network Layer (IPv6)
Sub-IP Adaptation Layer (Segmentation and Reassembly)
MAC Layer (IEEE802.15.4)
Physical Layer (IEEE802.15.4)

Fig. 2. Incorporated Sub-IP layer in IPv6 stack

A minimum IPv6 Maximum Transmission Unit (MTU) is 1280 Bytes. On the contrary, in the IEEE802.15.4 domain, a payload as low as 81 bytes is available. As shown in Fig. 2, Montenegro introduces a sub-IP layer that serves as an adaptation layer in IPv6 stack. This document however stops short of giving any description of inter-PAN routing. The following is a summary of other important issues that require being resolved for realizing a 6lowPAN.

Unique Interface Identifier: Since the native addressing schemes in IPv6 domain and IEEE802.15.4 domain are different, a unique inter-face identifier is signified that provides mapping to IPv6 addressing scheme. Similarly, a need is highlighted to infer PAN id from IPv6 prefix such that one PAN maps to a unique IPv6 link.

Header compression schemes: Montenegro in [2] suggests compression schemes with and without the usage of preliminary context exchange. In order to fully exploit compression, encoding of IPv6 header fields is also specified.

3 Multi-hop Routing Scenario for 6lowPAN

The motivation of the following scenario is to signify the fact that 6lowPAN routing needs the concept of routing to extend from intra-PAN to inter-PAN.

Fig. 3 shows an air-condition management system that regulates the temperature of a building through a 6lowPAN enabled controller. The controller accesses through the internet, the meteorological station such as www.ncds.noaa.gov for latest weather forecast. It adjusts the temperature and humidity of the entire building accordingly. Now, imagine a user, a flu-stricken person approaching room 'A'. His preferences are spelled out in his PDA that is part of his PAN, viz. the PAN 3. The prescribed settings include different HVAC settings as to those in place. However, PAN 3 cannot access the air-condition system in PAN 1 directly. There is a need to discover routes to PAN 1. As shown in Fig. 3, a route is only possible through PAN 2. A route is discovered and selected for PAN 1-PAN 3 routing. Finally, inter-PAN communication follows and user preferences are applied for room A.

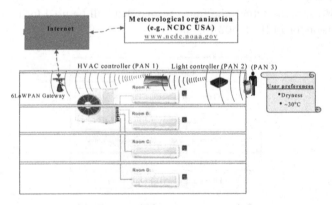

Fig. 3. Inter-PAN and cross-PAN communication scenario

3.1 Routing Support in 6lowPAN and ZigBee

In 6lowPAN environments, limited processing capability, battery constraints, and low data rate make the choice from existing pool of routing schemes very limited. AODV [4] has been identified to be a viable choice in reactive routing protocols for such networks. Basic modifications required for adapting Ad hoc On Demand Distance Vector Routing (AODV) protocol for 6lowPAN are described in [5].

LOAD [6] and all the routing protocols proposed so far assume no role, whatsoever, of gateways in routing and data delivery within the 6lowPAN environment. In this paper, we argue through scenarios that gateways can be utilized for the same purpose.

In the next section, we state the literal role of gateways in context to the realization of 6lowPAN; connectivity with global IPv6 network. Subsequently, we look at the scenarios where the role of gateways may be extended. We finally move onto interesting application scenarios.

4 Usage of Gateways for 6lowPAN

Can the gateways be used for 6lowPAN routing and data delivery as shown in Fig. 4? An alternate path to all-the-way-wireless path is available as source>Gateway X>Gateway Y>Gateway Z>Destination 1, that offers better routing metric. It is unbeknownst to the source. Such a scenario poses an interesting question; Are Low PANs a PAN or An Internet of PANs?

In the next sections, we propose modifications to the basic functionality of gateways. These allow the gateways to be part of routing activity and data delivery within the lowPAN, thereby increasing routing performance of 6lowPANs.

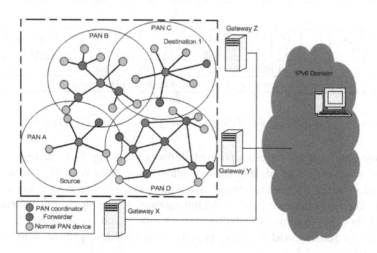

Fig. 4. Overlapping PANs with multiple gateways

5 Gateway-Assisted Inter-PAN Routing for 6lowPANs

As described in section 4, utilizing gateways for inter-PAN routing is expected to yield paths that are robust and have better network parameters. In this section, we present a routing protocol that makes gateways usable for hypothesized routing functionality.

Gateways usually comprise multi-board systems with unlimited power supply. They are connected through usually a high-speed wired network to IPv6 domain. Equipped with enough memory size and processing capability, gateways can afford to implement larger code spaces than IEEE802.15.4 devices. As a precondition, we assume that multiple gateways are deployed across 6lowPAN for load balancing.

We propose a simple operational strategy that allows a gateway to exhibit desired functionality.

5.1 Operation

The central idea of gateway-assisted routing pivots around modification to RREQ packet format used for route discovery. We propose to modify the RREQ packet to incorporate the hop count from the RREQ source to the default gateway. Any existing routing protocol can be enhanced to incorporate our functionality that we propose. For the scope of this paper, we modify RREQ packet format of LOAD [6] as shown in Fig. 5 (a) to the packet format shown in Fig. 5 (b).

Type (8)	R (1)	D (1)	O (1)	Reserved (5)	RREQ ID (8)	Route cost (8)
Link layer destination address (16 or 64)						
Link layer originator address (16 or 64)						

(a)

Type (8)	R (1)	D (1)	O (1)	HopstoG twy (5)	RREQ ID (8)	Route cost (8)
Link layer destination address (16 or 64)						
Link layer originator address (16 or 64)						

(b)

Fig. 5. Original and modified RREQ packet formats for LOAD

Table 1 summarizes the description of all the fields in Fig. 5 (a) and (b).

The additional field of HopstoGtwy allows originator of RREQ to notify the destination about its distance from its default gateway. The destination of RREQ already knows its distance from its default gateway. On receipt of this information, it can decide either to form a usual all-the-way wireless path or form a path through the gateway by sending RREP either through the all-wireless path or wireless-wired-wired path.

Table 1. Description of fields of Fig. 5

Field	Description
Type	1 for indicating a RREQ message
R	1 Local Repair
D	1 for the 16 bit address of the destination 0 for the EUI-64 address of the destination.
O	1 for the 16 bit address of the destination 0 for the EUI-64 address of the destination.
Reserved	Unused
RREQ ID	A sequence number uniquely identifying the particular RREQ when taken in conjunction with the originator
Route cost	The accumulated link cost of the reverse route from he originator to the sender of the RREQ
Link layer destination address	The 16 bit short or EUI-64 link layer address of the destination for which a route is supplied
Link layer Originator Address	The 16 bit short or EUI-64 link layer address of the node which originated the Route Request
HopstoGtwy	Hop distance of the node to default gateway (Each bit can represent either one hop or a prespecified range of hops)

5.2 Implications on HopstoGtwy

In our proposal, we are exploiting the presence of 5 reserved bits in RREQ packet format. This allows us to encode information upto 32 hops if each 5-bit code point represents a hop. This code-point represents per se fails to encode hop count that may go up to 128. Nonetheless, this anomaly can be addressed by making the code-point representation more flexible, e.g., each bit can represent a range of hops. An intuitive relationship between code-point representation and number of gateways can be established using Table 2. Network designers can define code-point representation in a flexible way by utilizing known information such as network diameter in number of hops and the total number of gateways they plan to deploy.

Table 2. Flexible code-point representation scheme

Number of deployed gateways	Code-point representation (Per code point)	HopstoGtwy representation (in hops)
2	4	128
3	3	96
4	2	64
>4	1	32

5.2.1 Advertisement-Based Gateway Selection for PAN Registration

Since, there are multiple gateways, nodes can select either of the gateways to be default. Default gateways make RREQ processing both at the sender and receiver more efficient. We propose the gateways to use announcements to advertise their presence. Announcements help IEEE802.15.4 devices to discover and identify gateways through their IDs. The scope of gateway advertisement message can be controlled by specifying the time to live (TTL) field. For two gateways deployment scenario, we simulate (in later section) for the advertisement scope to be half the network diameter, measured in number of hops. More specifically, if the network has a maximum diameter of n hops, advertisement message shall be broadcast to $(n+1)/2$. This also justifies the relationship between $RouteCost_{Max}$ of 256 bits and $HopstoGtwy_{Max}$ of 128 bits.

Incase, a node receives more than one advertisement, we propose that node choose gateways that are at the closest hop distance to them. Usually, the gateway closer to the PAN shall be nominated as the default. The information about default gateway can be as short as gateway-ID in the neighbour table [3].

6 Performance Evaluation

We have implemented our routing protocol in network simulator [NS-2] by modifying the AODV implementation by University of Uppsala. Table 3 shows the list and values of parameters we have adopted to adjust.

Table 3. List of parameters for simulation

Parameter	Values
Area size of simulation:	380m * 60m
Total number of nodes in simulation:	3hop : 15 30hop : 150
Total time of simulation:	100s
Node's transmission range:	15m
Packet or frame error rate:	Relative delivery rate
Data rate:	Decide by graph
Data packet size:	70 Bytes
Traffic type:	Constant bit rate
RREQ packet size:	36
RREP packet size:	40
Inter-packet transmission delay:	Decide by graph
Node transmission power:	0.28J

When a link fails to respond to a data packet (i.e., a node does not generate link layer acknowledgement), a RERR message is generated. Fig. 6 shows the total number of RERR messages generated during the simulation time. Gateway-assisted routing offers robust paths with better link qualities as compared to all-the-way wireless routes, therefore a significant difference is observed in the count of RERR messages.

Fig. 7 shows delivery ratio as the total number of packets delivered to the total number of packets transmitted. Gateway assisted routing shows considerable

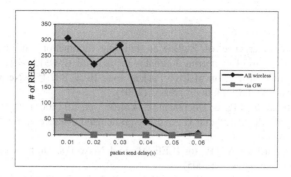

Fig. 6. Number of RERRs generated due to link failures

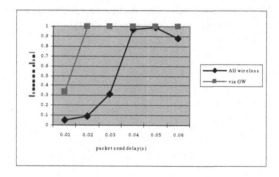

Fig. 7. Delivery ratio of data packets

performance gain at higher data rates because collisions are more common at higher data rates in wireless domain reducing overall throughput. At lower data rates, i.e., when the inter-packet delay increases, the performance of both the schemes seems to equalize.

7 Conclusion

In this paper, we have presented the considerations, issues, and challenges in routing over 6lowPAN domain. We have presented previous work on mesh routing in ZigBee and 6lowPAN for intra-PAN communication. We present work done in the form of LOAD, a light weight version of AODV for 6lowPAN. We ascertain that lowPANs form an internet of PANs instead of forming a single PAN due to the inherent working of underlying physical and datalink layers.

We then move on to discuss the role of gateways in cross 6lowPAN routing, and determine its feasibility for intra-PAN routing by proposing our scheme. We have simulated the purported protocol and analyzed the results to support the hypothesis.

References

1. Egan, D.: The emergence of ZigBee in building automation and industrial control. Computing and Control Engineering Journal. vol. 16, iss. 2, (2005) 14-19.
2. Montenegro, G.: Transmission of IPv6 Packets over IEEE 802.15.4 Networks. Draft-ietf-6lowpan-format-00.txt, (work in progress). (2005).
3. ZigBee Specifications, ZigBee Document 053474r06. ver. 1.0 (2005). ZigBee Alliance.
4. Charles, P. Elizabeth B. R. Samir D.: Ad hoc on-demand distance vector (AODV) routing. (2003). IETF Internet RFC 356.
5. Gabriel, M. Nandu, K.: AODV for IEEE 802.15.4 Networks. Draft-montenegro- lowpan-aodv-00, (work in progress). (2005).
6. Kim, K, H. Park, S, D.: Gabriel, M. Yoo, S. 6LowPAN Ad Hoc On-demand Distance Vector Routing (LOAD). Draft-daniel-6lowpan-load-adhoc-routing-01.txt, (work in progress). (2005).
7. Kim, K, H. Yoo, S. Kim H. Park, S, D. Lee, J.: Interoperability of 6LowPAN. Draft-daniel-6lowpan-interoperability-01.txt, (work in progress). (2005).

Ensuring Secure and Robust Grid Applications – From a Formal Method Point of View*

Ke Xu, Yuexuan Wang, and Cheng Wu

Department of Automation, Tsinghua University, Beijing, China, 100084
xk02@mails.tsinghua.edu.cn,
{wangyuexuan, wuc}@tsinghua.edu.cn

Abstract. Ensuring the reliability and robustness of complex scientific grid applications is a critical issue for managing and sharing expensive scientific instruments. However, guaranteeing the correct processing of grid applications under all circumstances is difficult and not fully addressed by existing grid infrastructure. Hidden flaws in the applications including unexpected internal behaviors, dissatisfaction of real-time constraints, incompatibility in service interactions, etc may lead to subtle failures in grid systems. This work tries to enhance the trustworthiness of grid applications by investigating existing formal techniques and their extensions. A formal framework based on extensions of Pi calculus is proposed which also integrates formal techniques of model checking and bisimulation analysis to enable the reasoning of grid applications from three perspectives: data, time and behavior. In addition, both application examples and our current implementation architecture are also concluded.

1 Introduction

Grid computing is becoming a key infrastructure to manage and share geographically distributed resources to collaborate on solution of complex scientific and engineering problems[1]. Consequently, building reliable grid applications, which is regarded as the realization of pre-planed scientific experiments by the cooperative composition of grid services, is a critical issue for the efficient large scale sharing of expensive grid resources. However, compared to the existing works on grid "enabling" techniques including grid workflow enactment, job scheduling etc, much less efforts have been made to the grid "ensuring" techniques that ensure the robustness of the developed grid applications and probe their hidden flaws that can lead to subtle failures in grid systems. However, special characteristics of grid systems impose additional challenges in modeling and analyzing grid applications: (1) *Service oriented:* In order to guarantee the trustworthiness of a grid application, not only the complex and dynamic interactions among services need to be precisely captured, but also these interactions should be asserted to follow expected behavioral constraints; (2) *State / action hybrid:* This feature is best explained by the WSRF specification with a motivation addressed in [2]. The introduction of stateful resources enables the life cycle management of resource states, and consequently the connections between system actions and states

---

* Supported by China "211 project" "15" construct project (CERS-219899004).

now need to be considered for grid application reasoning. (3) *Dynamic evolution:* The selection of underlying physical services for specific tasks may constantly evolve over time from run to run of a same grid application.

In this work, a Pi calculus[3] based framework integrating existing formal modeling and verification approaches and their extensions is proposed to address the above problem for grid application development. The main contribution of the work can be concluded as follows: (1) Based on the conclusion of existing reliability issues that are not fully addressed in current grid infrastructures, we show how existing formal techniques can be integrated to provide them an effective solution; (2) Pi Calculus and its possible extensions are evaluated and applied to model and reason grid applications from data, time and behavior perspectives. A unified formal framework is also formed to provide a theoretical foundation for our solution; (3) Example applications and our current implementation prototype is demonstrated to show how our formal framework can be applied to enhance the trustworthiness of grid applications.

The rest of the paper is organized as follows. Section 2 advocates the application of Pi calculus in grid application reasoning. In section 3, useful extensions of Pi calculus and existing formal verification techniques are integrated in a formal framework to reason about different reliability and consistency aspects in a grid application with example scenarios. Section 4 shows our current prototype implementation based on the framework. Section 5 concludes the paper.

2 Why Pi Calculus

Nowadays few will challenge the necessity of providing a formal foundation for complex software systems to clarify its ambiguity and facilitate its reasoning. In grid computing, [4] first successfully provides a precise formal definition of grid system to unambiguously identify its essential characterizes that differs to traditional distributed computing systems. In [5], the formalization of a grid workflow enactment model is proposed with Gamma calculus as a basis for its realization. In this work we choose and advocate the use of (polyadic) Pi calculus[3] as the formal basis for grid applications. Pi calculus is reputed for its compositionability and mobility and has already been accepted as one promising candidate for modeling and reasoning traditional business processes [6]. By compositionability, it means there is a natural mechanism in Pi calculus for building system/service by the composition of its sub-components /sub-services. By mobility, it means Pi calculus is capable of modeling dynamic evolving systems like grid with its name passing and renaming capability. The dynamic selection of underlying physical service to fulfill a specific task in grid applications and the constant changing of interactions among grid services are typical *mobility* issues[3] that Pi Calculus addresses. As a matter of fact, there have already been existing works that argue the suitability of Pi calculus as a component composition language[7] and appeals its application in the describing and reasoning of web service coordination[8]. The complete syntax and transition semantics of Pi calculus can be found in [3]. We will introduce in the next two sections how extensions of Pi calculus, together with existing formal techniques including model checking[9] and bisimulation analysis can be applied and integrated to reason about the reliability of grid applications according to the three perspectives in figure 1.

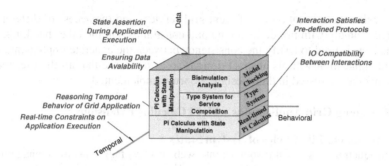

Fig. 1. A Fomal Framework for Reasoning Grid Applications

3 Formal Framework for Ensuring Reliable Grid Applications

3.1 An Overview

In figure 1, our formal solution framework based on Pi calculus extensions and the integration of existing formal verification techniques is proposed to address the ensuring aspects that are not yet fully analyzed in existing grid middlewares in three perspectives (data, behavioral and temporal). Data perspective ensures that in specific execution step of the application (e.g. when certain service is invoked or finished), indispensable states are well preserved (e.g. necessary data in specific format have been staged in). Behavioral perspective concerns whether the interaction among services follows desired protocols in a grid application, e.g. whether the inputs of a service can be provided in a pre-defined order by all its preceding services. In temporal perspective, we consider the necessary temporal constraints put on the global behavior of a grid application, e.g. certain resource must be always accessible within some time intervals or before specific operations. Although the aspects concluded in figure 1 may not be complete, in our experience we consider them as most common requirements in building reliable grid applications that are out of the concern of existing grid middleware. Correspondingly in the framework, the internal behavior of grid applications and its interconnection with system states and data is precisely captured with state operators that are extended into original Pi calculus. In addition, existing works on timed Pi calculus and type systems for component composition are also integrated to handle the analysis of real time behavior of grid applications and the reasoning of the correct composition of grid services.

After a specific grid application is formally modeled with the extensions of Pi calculus foundations, all possible behaviors and interactions in grid application can be deducted into a transition system with also the encoding of related information of data, time and resource states. The deduction ensures that expected states will always hold in specific execution steps of the grid application and the access of grid resources through service invocation is following expected protocol since these correctness requirements have been encoded in the semantics of Pi calculus models. Besides, it is based on the deducted transition system that other formal verification techniques including model checking and bisimulation analysis can further be integrated to analyze the global property of the grid applications. Model checking approach is applied to verify that the invocation of different grid services and the access of different grid resources comply with pre-defined temporal constraints. On the other hand, bisimulation analysis is used to testify the consistency between the concrete implementation of the grid application with its abstract designs so as to ensure that all the user requirements that are addressed in their designs are truly implemented.

3.2 Reasoning Grid Applications with Pi Calculus Extensions

3.2.1 Managing Life Cycles of System States

The introduction of stateful resources into web services facilitates the management of dynamic interactions among grid services. Figure 2 shows an example of typical states that are considered in a grid service. Enabling the management of system states imposes more challenges in reasoning about the composition of services in grid since historical state information is now accessible to instruct the behavior of service interaction. In Pi calculus, the life cycle management of system states can be modeled by extending specific operators for state creation, insertion and destruction.

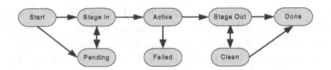

Fig. 2. State Transitions for Services in Grid Systems

A system state is defined as the valuation of a set of variables, $S: V \rightarrow D$, where V is the set of system variables and D defines the universe in which V range over. Therefore, input/output actions π in Pi calculus can be further equipped with a pair $\{Op, S\}$, where Op indicates a specific state operator and S indicates the new state value that is to be operated on the current system state. In order to enable the life cycle management of system states, at least two types of state operations are needed, that is, state creation (+) and state destruction (-). An additional state update operator can also be defined by the sequential combination of state destruction and creation (destroy first and then create). Without loss of generality, we assume the *state* associated with an action has only one variable v and the current system state is $SS:\{v_1,...,v_n\} \rightarrow D$. Their formal semantics can thus be defined as follows.

$$CREATE \quad \frac{SS:\{v_1,...,v_n\} \rightarrow D \quad v \neq v_i \ (i=1,...,n)}{+S=\{v_1,.......,v_n,v\}} \qquad UPDATE \quad \frac{SS:\{v_1,......,v_n\} \rightarrow D \quad v=v_i \ (i \in \{1,...,n\})}{+S=++S=\{v_1,...,v_{i-1},v_{i+1},...,v_n,v\}}$$

$$DESTRUCT \quad \frac{SS:\{v_1,......,v_n\} \rightarrow D \quad v=v_i \ (i \in \{1,...,n\})}{-S=\{v_1,...,v_{i-1},v_{i+1},v_n\}}$$

With this extension, a service in grid can be formalized as:

$Service(start, invoke, \overline{stagein}, stageout, clean, done, exceptionIn, \overline{exceptionOut}) = new \ ack($

$start\{+, s = pending\}.(\prod_{i=1}^{n} stagein_i \{++, s = StagingIn\}.\overline{ack} \mid ack\{++, s = Pending\}.....ack.new \ t \ f($

$invoke <t, f>\{++, s = Active\} \mid t.(\overline{stageout}\{++, s = StagingOut\}.\overline{ack} \mid clean\{++, s = Cleaning\}.\overline{ack} \mid$

$ack.ack.\overline{done}\{++, s = Finish\}) + f\{++, s = Failed\}.\prod exceptionOut)) + exceptionIn.\prod \overline{exceptionOut})$

The implementation of *Service* models the state transitions in figure 2 with a variable *s*. A service is either entered properly via *start* or an exception is received via *exceptioIn* and propagated out to its successors to cancel their execution. It can be invoked to generate its output when all needed inputs are provided. An advantage of modeling both service behavior and states is that it is easy to assert secure service executions in each step of the grid application. For example, suppose the above *Service* needs to stage in and stage out data from the same data storage resource. It is required whenever *Service* gets its needed data from the storage, the finished result of *Service* should always be sent to the storage so that users can be aware of this information. This pseudo application can be implemented as follows with an assertion clause for ensuring that the variable *GotResult* is true whenever the process of *Service* transits to 0 (empty process) indicating the finishing of the service.

PseudoApp = new stagein, stageout(Service(......, stagein, stageout, ...) | Storage(stagein, stageout))

where   Storage(stagein, stageout) = stagein_1. .... .stagein_n{+, GotResult = false}.

$$stageout\{++, GotResult = true\}.Storage(stagein, stageout)$$

Assert *GotResult = true* Whenever *Service* → 0

The *PseudoApp* fails to satisfy such assertion since the interaction of action *stageout* may be missed when the execution of *Service* is *Failed*. This reminds us that in order to build a reliable grid application satisfying this assertion, the service must also send out a failure notice to the data storage when its invocation is failed so that user can be aware of the failure by revising its implementation to:

$$Service(......, \overline{stageout}, ..., exceptionIn, \overline{exceptionOut}) = ... + f\{++, s = Failed\}.\overline{stageout}. \prod \overline{(exceptionOut)}) + ...)$$

3.2.2 Type System for Reasoning Grid Service Composition

Reasoning about the complex interactions among different services is critical for the assurance of service compatibility with desired I/O type, amount and quality (e.g. precision, size) during their composition. Type system for Pi Calculus is a natural answer to this issue. The type system introduced here is similar to [8], which is designed for the replacement and composition of service components, only except that ours is built upon the state extension in 3.2.1. By introducing type signatures in Pi calculus, an output $\overline{a} < y : t, s(post) >$ indicates sending a value *y* of type *t* via port *a*, while an input $a(x : t, s(pre))$ indicates receiving a value of type *t* via port *a*. A post / pre-condition *s(post) / s(pre)* is associated with an output / input action respectively. These conditions are formulated as a range of the valuation of system states defined in 3.2.1. Consequently, the following rule ensures that in service composition, the input of a service must be satisfied by the output of other services with the same type signature and the constraints imposed on the inputs should be less strict than those on the outputs. The disobeying of this rule is called a type mismatch. We call $Type(t_{11}, t_{12}, ..., t_{1n}, s(post))$ is a sub-type of $Type(t_{21}, t_{22}, ..., t_{2n}, s(pre))$ if $t_{1i} = t_{2i}$ (i=1,2,..,n) & *s(post)* → *s(pre)*. A grid application is thus well-typed if the interaction between service input/output always forms a type pre-order during the deduction of its model.

$$TYPE-COMM \quad \frac{P \xrightarrow{a(x:t_1, s(pre))} P' \quad Q \xrightarrow{\overline{a} < y:t_2, s(post)>} Q'}{P \mid Q \xrightarrow{\tau} \{y:t_2 / x:t_1\}P' \mid Q'} \quad t_1 = t_2, s(post) \rightarrow s(pre)$$

To illustrate the use of the type system, recall the service implementation in 3.2.1. Suppose there are two workstations A and B with different CPU powers to provide the same computation services (as denoted by a same service entrance of *start*). The requested task, however, must be selected to run under predefined hardware conditions in order to ensure its performance. This can be formalized as:

$Service_A(start, invoke_A, \overrightarrow{stagein_A}, stageout, ...) = new\ ack(start(CPU < 1.5G)\{+, \{s = pending, CPU = 2G\}\}.......$

$Service_B(start, invoke_B, \overrightarrow{stagein_B}, stageout, ...)$ is exactly the same as $Service......$

$ServiceSel(request, start) = request.start(CPU > 3G)$

$ServiceSelection = new\ start\ Service_A(start, invoke_A, \overrightarrow{stagein_A}, stageout, ...) |$

$\qquad Service_B(start, , invoke_B, \overrightarrow{stagein_B}, stageout, ...) | ServiceSel(request, start)$

The *ServiceSelection* now automatically ignores the alternative path for delivering the *request* to $Service_A$ since its CPU is 2GMhz and only runs applications requesting less than 1.5GMhz CPU frequency, which does not satisfy the requirement.

3.2.4   Modeling and Reasoning Time in Grid Applications

When real time aspects need to be considered in grid applications, a timed version of Pi calculus can be extended to capture the semantics. The typical need for modeling time in the grid applications includes the reasoning of execution time-out when specific deadline is imposed. In our previous work[10], a real timed Pi calculus is proposed which is able to block process execution when time-out signals are detected. In [10], time information associated with actions in Pi calculus is modeled as $a^{\{c, dd\}}[d]$, where d indicates the duration of the action, dd for additional deadline imposed on the action and c indicates an implicit local clock recording the current system time (which can also be implicitly associated with a process, denoted by $P^{\{c\}}$). Now recall the previously modeled *PseudoApp*. With the integration of real-timed semantics, time information can further be encoded and analyzed in the model.

$Storage(stagein, stageout) = stagein[0]\{+, GotResult = false\}.stageout^{\{c+6\}}[1]\{+, GotResult = true\}.$

$\qquad Storage(stagein, stageout)$

$PseudoApp = new\ stagein, stageout(Service(..., \overrightarrow{stagein}, stageout, ...)^{\{c\}} | Storage(stagein, stageout)^{\{c\}})$
Assert $GotResult = true$ Whenever $Service \rightarrow 0$

The action of *stagein* is transient since its execution time is 0. The missing specification of *{c, dd}* indicates there is no deadline requirement and the value of the local clock is implicitly computed with time elapses. The action of *stageout* costs 1 time frame and before it is started, the local clock of process *Storage* implicitly advances at least 0 time frames because of the execution of *stagein*. Most importantly, it is required by the deadline specification that *stageout* must be finished within 6 time frames after *stagein* is finished. This demands that not only the *Storage* must always get the result of the *Service* when it is done, but also the *Service* must generate the result within 6 time frames during its interaction with *Storage*. Since otherwise the process will be blocked from execution and an error for deadlock will be reported.

3.3   Reasoning Global Behavior of Grid Applications

3.3.1   An Application Example

The above work shows how grid applications can be formally modeled to reason about their reliability issues including state assertion, type compatibility and time-out alarms. In this section, we further consider formal verification techniques including model checking and bisimulation analysis to reason about the global behavior of grid applications. Before introducing the two techniques, an example scenario of studying material rupture characteristics in our equipment grid[11] is first illustrated. The rectangles in figure 3 indicate different service activities which perform specific tasks by accessing the expensive resources in grid. Each service activity is guarded by its input pins (denoted by columns). When a service activity is finished, its output pins are simultaneously generated. The formal implementation of this application can be quickly built based on the result in the previous section. The detailed implementation of each service activity can be referred in section 3.2 and is thus omitted here.

Invoking resources including including Scan Electron Microscope, high volume data storage and graphical processors via service interfaces

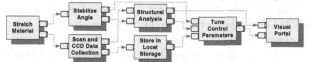

$MaterialAnalysis = Stretch \mid Outpins(doneSch, Stch2Stab, Stch2Scan) \mid Inpins(Stch2Stab, startStab) \mid Stabilize \mid$

$\qquad Outpins(doneStab, Stab2Struc, Stab2Tune) \mid Inpins(Stch2Scan, startScan) \mid Scan \mid Outpins(doneScan, Scan2Struc,$

$\qquad Scan2Store) \mid Inpins(Stab2Struc, Scan2Struc, startStruc) \mid StructuralAnalysis \mid Outpins(doneStruc, Struc2Tune,$

$\qquad Struc2vis) \mid Inpins(Scan2Store, startStore) \mid Store \mid Outpins(doneStore, Store2Tune) \mid InPins(Struc2Tune, Store2Tune,$

$\qquad Stab2Tune, startTune) \mid TunePara \mid Outpins(soneTune, Tune2Vis) \mid Inpins(Tune2Vis, Struc2vis, startVis) \mid VisualPortal$

$InPins(in_1, in_2, ...in_n, start) = new\ ack(in_1.\overline{ack} \mid in_2.\overline{ack} \mid ...... \mid in_n.\overline{ack} \mid \underbrace{\overline{ack}.....\overline{ack}}_{n}.start)$

$OutPins(done, out_1, out_2, ...out_n) = done.(\overline{out_1} \mid \overline{out_2} \mid ... \mid \overline{out_n})$

Fig. 3. An Example Grid Application for Studying dynamic Material Characteristics

3.3.2   Model Checking Temporal Constraints and Validating Grid Application

Model checking is an automatic verification technique which has been successfully applied in checking hardware/software designs. Its idea is to search system state space and verify its compliance with pre-defined properties which are usually specified with temporal logics[9] like CTL, LTL, etc. Consequently, desired behavior in grid applications can be encoded into logical property and be automatically verified to ensure its satisfaction. For example, in the previous application, it is expected that the final result of material studying must always be reachable to the users through the visual portal. Besides the service of *"Store in Local Storage"* must be invoked strictly after when the angle is stabilized and the CCD data are collected in order to ensure the quality of the final stored graphical data. Note that although the example seems to be trivial, complex implementation details of each service activity under their simple notations can still make manual reasoning an infeasible solution. Here LTL is used to capture the above requirement into two logical formulas:

G (StretchStatus=Active --> F VisualPortalStatus=Active)   /* **Formula 1: Result Reachability**
G (StoreStatus!=Active) | (StoreStatus!=Active U StabilizeStatus=Active) &
    (StoreStatus!=Active U ScanStatus=Active)   /***Formula 2: Execution Sequencing**

The automatic deduction of the Pi calculus model for the application results in a small state space of 898 states and 1929 transitions. Model checking result shows that both the two properties are failed. The counter-example generated for *Formula 1* tells us that it is possible for *"VisualPortal"* to skip its execution if any of its previous service activity throws an exception. The counter-example for *Formula 2* shows that *"Store in Local Storage"* can be actually activated before *"Stabilize Angle"*. This reminds us to fix the application by, e.g. adding a control relation between *"Store in Local Storage"* and *"Stabilize Angle"* so as to ensure their precedence relation.

Moreover, in a typical scenario of building grid applications, an abstract process with no physical implementation details is usually designed first to capture functional requirements in the application[12]. This abstract model is then refined into a concrete executable one to implement the application. However, a serious issue here is how to ensure the consistency or equivalence between the abstract design and its concrete implementation. In other words, how to make sure that our implementation really "implements" what we wanted? Bisimulation analysis is an important tool in process algebra to verify the equivalence between different models, which is a natural solution to the above concern. Without detailed consideration of service implementation, dynamic service selection, service interaction and real time constraints, the abstract requirement model of the example application can be simply formalized as follows:

$$MaterialAnalysisAbstract = new\ ack1\ ack2\ ack3\ invokeStretch.((invokeStabilize.(\overline{ack1}\,|\,\overline{ack2})+\tau)\,|$$

$$(invokeScan.(invokeStore.\overline{ack1}\,|\,\overline{ack2}+\tau)+\tau)\,|\,(ack2.ack2.(invokeStruct.(\overline{ack1}\,|\,\overline{ack3})+\tau))\,|$$

$$(ack1.ack1.ack1.(invokeTune.\overline{ack3}+\tau))\,|\,(ack3.ack3.(invokeVisual+\tau)))+\tau$$

On the other hand, the concrete implementation of the application is formalized in *MaterialAnalysis* in 3.3.1. The bisimulation test can be run directly on the two Pi calculus processes and the result shows that the application implementation in section 3.3.1 is truly consistent with this abstract specification (without state information).

4 Application and Current Implementation

Based on the above formal framework, a prototype (*GridPiAnalyzer*), which is itself encapsulated as a grid service, has been implemented to enable the automatic analysis of grid application reliabilities. *GridPiAnalyzer* takes the service flow script of either a user designed abstract workflow for specific task or a refined concrete grid workflow with detailed service information as its input. Figure 4 provides its architecture with the 6 main components. Considering that existing grid workflows have their own input scripts, the *Transformation Adapter* provides a set of standard model transformation interface and a transform engine to enable their automatic mapping to the input models that *GridPiAnalyzer* accepts (BPEL4WS extended for WSRF); The *Pi Formalizer* then automatically generates the formal semantics of these inputs based on the result in 3.2; The *Design Validator* receives Pi calculus models directly from *Pi Formalizer* and tests their equivalence based on bisimulation relations. Note this capability is provided by the integration of MobilityWorkBench[13] in our current implementation and hence the equivalency test is now only carried out when no state, type or time information is considered. The **GridPi Deductor** automatically deduces the results of *Pi Formalizer* into finite state machines based on different Pi calculus semantics in 3.2, during which the *State Assertion, Type-mismatch Checking* or *Timeout Detection* are also checked whenever necessary. The **Property Specifier** solves the issue of reducing the complexity of formula specification for temporal reasoning of grid applications by replacing the rigid temporal operators with natural languages (in IEEE standard of PSL[14]) and the Property Patterns[15]. For example, instead of writing the logical formulas manually in 3.3.2 (which is unreasonable for end-users), they can now be expressed as the combination of *GloballyResponse* and *GloballyPrcedence* property patterns respectively. *Property Specifier* will be responsible for automatically interpreting their underlying logical formulas. Once the state space for grid application and desired properties are generated, the **GridPiVerifier** assembles the two into the acceptable format of NuSMV2[16] engine for the temporal reasoning of grid application. Besides, *GridPiVerifier* also filters the trace of counter-examples so as to make this information directly understandable by end users.

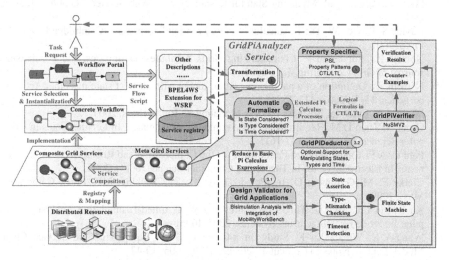

Fig. 4. Implementation Architecture of *GridPiAnalyzer* Service

The advantage of *GridPiAnalyzer* is its automaticity and intuitiveness. That is, the whole grid application analysis requires little user intervention and expertise knowledge since *GridPiAnalyzer* effectively hides the complexity of formal methods from end-users. We have applied our prototype in the equipment grid for studying material rupture structures[11]. In our experience with different problem scales, the analysis can be finished for applications of size 10^2 to 10^3 services (state space scales from 1000 to over 180000) within a reasonable time (from seconds to 10 minutes) on a Pentium4 1.5G RAM machine. This performance is acceptable for us since in our project the management of equipment sharing for material structure studying demands no strict need for real time service responses and equipment accessing.

5 Conclusion

This work investigates the serious issue of ensuring the reliability and robustness of grid application development from a formal method perspective. The Pi calculus with its different extensions and existing model checking and bisimulation analysis are investigated and integrated to address different reliability issues in grid application development. A formal framework is also proposed based on which our prototype of *GridPiAnalyzer* for the reasoning and verification of grid applications is implemented. Although *GridPiAnalyzer* enjoys the advantage of automaticity and intuitiveness, our future work still needs focusing on its performance tuning and testifying its effectiveness in more different grid applications so as to make it a more sophisticated solution.

References

1. Hai J, Yuan P.P., Shi K. Grid Copmuting2. Publishing House of Electronics Industry. 2004.
2. Foster I, Frey J, et al. Modeling Stateful Resources with Web Services, Globus Alliance, 2004.
3. Davide S, Davide W. The Pi-calculus: a theory of mobile processes, Cambridge University Press, 2001.
4. Németh Zs, Sunderam V. Characterizing Grids Attributes, Definitions, and Formalisms, Journal of Grid Computing, 1(1), 2003: 9-23.
5. Németh Zs. Definition of a parallel execution model with abstract state machine, Acta Cybernetica, 15(3), 2002: 417-455.
6. Michael H. Essential Business Process Modeling, O'Reilly Press, 2005.
7. Oscar N, Theo D.M. Requirements for a composition language, In Lecture Notes in Computer Science, 924, 1995: 147-161.
8. Pahl C. A Pi-Calculus based Framework for the Composition and Replacement of Components, In Electronic Notes in Theoretical Computer Science, 66(4), 2002.
9. Clarke E. M, Grumberg O, Jr., Peled, D. A. Model Checking. MIT Press, Cambridge, Mass, 1999.
10. Xu K, Liu L.C., Wu C. Time Pi Calculus and Weak-timed Bisimulation Analysis, Computer Integrated Manufacturing Systems, 2005, In Press.
11. Wang Y.X, Wu C, Xu K. Study on π-Calculus Based Equipment Grid Service Chain Model. Lecture Notes in Computer Science, 3779, 2005: 40-47.
12. Thomas F, Jun Q, Stefan H. Specification of Grid Workflow Applications with AGWL: An Abstract Grid Workflow Language, IEEE International Symposium on Cluster Computing and the Grid, 2005.
13. Victor, B. A verification tool for the polyadic Pi calculus. Ph.D. Thesis, Uppsala University, Sweden, 1994.
14. Geist D. The PSL/Sugar specification language for all seasons, Lecture Notes in Computer Science, 2800, 2003: 3.
15. Property Specification Patterns, 2005, http://patterns.projects.cis.ksu.edu.
16. Cimatti A, Clarke E, et al. NuSMV 2: an OpenSource tool for symbolic model checking. Lecture Notes in Computer Science, 2404, 2002: 359-364.

Supporting the OpenMP Programming Interface on Teamster-G

Tyng-Yeu Liang[1], Shih-Hsien Wang[2], Jyh-Biau Chang[2], and Ce-Kuen Shieh[2]

[1] Department of Electrical Engineering, National Kaohsiung University of Applied Sciences,
No.415, Chien-Kung Road, Kaohsiung, Taiwan, R.O.C
lty@mail.ee.kuas.edu.tw
[2] Department of Electrical Engineering, National Cheng Kung University,
No. 1, Ta-Hsueh Road, Tainan, Taiwan, R.O.C
{sanwangx, andrew, shieh}@hpds.ee.ncku.edu.tw

Abstract. An easy programming interface is a key factor to affect user's desire to exploit distributed resources for resolving their problems. Recently, much effort has been put into enabling MPI, RPC, and RMI for grid computing. However, these programming interfaces are not as easy as shared memory. To simplify the programming on the grid environment, we recently have developed a grid-enabled software DSM system called Teamster-G. However, users still must be familiar with the multithreaded programming toolkit and aware of the adopted consistency protocol. To further minimize user's programming load, we are devoted to supporting the OpenMP programming interface on Teamster-G in this study. Furthermore, we propose a novel loop scheduling algorithm called *Profiled Multiprocessor Scheduling (PMS)* for addressing the problem of load balance. We will describe the design and implementation of the OpenMP interface on Teamster-G, and discuss the preliminary performance of the OpenMP programs in this paper.

1 Introduction

OpenMP [1] is a standard of the shared memory programming interface. It provides a set of directives including parallel region, work sharing, and synchronization, and several data scope attribute clauses such as private or shared in conjunction with directives to explicitly direct the shared memory parallelism. When users want to parallelize their problems, they only need to add proper directives and clauses at the front of the program blocks which must be parallelized. Using the OpenMP compiler, the sequential programs can be automatically transferred to the C source codes composed of the OpenMP run time functions, and then the transferred sources codes can be compiled by the gcc compiler to be the multithreaded execution files with linking the OpenMP run time library. Therefore, users can easily develop the multithreaded programs on SMP machines by exploiting the OpenMP interface.

In recent years, computational grid has successfully provides a novel method for distributed computing. Such a system integrates geographically-distributed resources on wide area network to form a single unified resource, and provides users with a

Y.-C. Chung and J.E. Moreira (Eds.): GPC 2006, LNCS 3947, pp. 547–556, 2006.

uniform and cost-effective way to share and aggregate resources for solving their problems without caring about the problems of resource discovery and allocation. Many projects [2][3] have provided a core infrastructure for easily building a computational grid. Furthermore, several high level problem-solving environments [4][5] have been developed based on these core infrastructures. On the other hand, many studies [6][7][8] were dedicated to the grid-enabled implementation of Message Passing Interface (MPI), Java or Remote Procedure Call (RPC) to provide a familiar programming interface for users to develop applications on computational grids. Currently, computational grids have been applied to data-intensive, high performance or high throughput computing.

However, the growth of grid-computing applications is slow although computational grids have many advantages. The main reason is that the existing programming toolkits are not easy enough since they require programmers to explicitly use function calls for data communication. In contrast, software distributed shared memory (DSM) [9] allows users to exploit share variables to write parallel programs in the distributed environment. When processes/threads access the same shared variables on different nodes, data consistency will be automatically maintained by the DSM library. As a result, users can put attention on the development of program algorithm but data communication. However, for performance consideration, most of modern software DSM systems adopt the weaken consistency protocols [10][11]. Users must be aware of the consistency protocol and properly set data synchronization points in their programs, otherwise they may get wrong results. As to this problem, supporting the OpenMP programming interface on software DSM systems to hide these problems is a promised solution.

As previously discussed, we have developed a grid-enabled software DSM system called Teamster-G in our previous study. To further minimize the programming load of users, the main goal of this study is to support the OpenMP programming interface on Teamster-G. We have developed an OpenMP compiler and an OpenMP run time library for Teamster-G based on the Omni compiler and its run time library. In addition, we have developed a user-level thread library called *Distributed Pth* to minimize the overhead of parallelization. On the other hand, we also propose a loop scheduling algorithm called *Profiled Multiprocessor Scheduling* (PMS) to address the load balance problem for the OpenMP programs.

The rest of this paper is organized as follows. Section 2 is the background related to Teamster-G and the Omni compiler. Section 3 and Section 4 detail the design considerations and implementation of the OpenMP programming interface on Teamster-G, respectively. Section 5 discusses our experimental results of performance evaluation. Section 6 is the related work, and Section 7 gives the conclusions of this paper and our future work.

2 Background

The goal of this study is to enable the OpenMP programming interface on Teamster-G for grid computing. To simplify our work, we adopt the Omni compiler and the Omni run time library to be a basis of our implementation. Teamster-G [12] is a grid-enabled software DSM system which extends the library of Teamster to exploit the services provided by the Globus toolkit. This system supports users with not only a shared memory programming interface but also a transparent service of resource allocation to resolve their problems in the grid environment. Basically, Teamster-G is composed of three main components, i.e., TGrun, TGRB (Teamster-G Resource Borker), and TGCM (Teamster-G Cluster Manager). TGrun provides an interface for users to submit and monitor their programs to remote resources for execution. TGRB is responsible for allocating user applications onto remote resources for execution by cooperating with the gatekeeper of each cluster, i.e., GRAM. TGCM manages the resource of a cluster, and distribute the work of remote programs onto the local nodes. When a user wants to submit his programs through TGrun, TGRB will organize a virtual cluster for each user according to the resource demand of the user. After resource allocation, users can consecutively submit their programs to their own virtual dedicated clusters for execution. In addition, Teamster-G adopts a two-level consistency protocol to minimize the cost of maintaining data-consistency over WAN.

The Omni compiler [13] is a part of RWCP Omni compiler that is developed to allow the researchers to build the code transformer. This compiler is used to transform the OpenMP programs into the multi-threaded programs with the Omni run time library called OMP. Basically, the OpenMP programs are first translated into X-object codes, and then the transformed X-object codes are translated back to the C source codes by the Exc Java toolkit using the OpenMP run time functions to carry out the OpenMP directives. The next step is to compile the C source code to be the executable binary codes by using the gcc compiler and linking the OMP library which is implemented based on the kernel-level POSIX thread.

3 Considerations

Source Compatibility and program performance are two main considerations in our work. When source compatibility is maintained, users can easily port their OpenMP applications from SMPs to computer clusters without any source code modification. On the other hand, to prevent performance gradation, it is necessary to minimize the cost of program parallelization. Furthermore, the computational power of processors in a computer cluster is not promised to be as identical as that in a SMP machine. Therefore, dynamic load balance is essential to obtain a good program performance in a cluster.

3.1 Source Compatibility

To maintain source compatibility, there are three problems that must be addressed. The first is that the memory allocation of global variables. In SMPs, global variables declared in user programs are shared between threads even when they are not assigned with an initial value by programmers. However, Teamster-G allocates the global variables without initial values into the private space. Consequently, these global variables will be impossible to be shared among threads on different nodes. The second is the function of memory allocation. In SMPs, users can call the function, i.e, malloc() to allocate a block of shared memory for data communication between threads. However, this function allocates memory at the private space in Teamster-G.

Therefore, in order to allow users to allocate memory at the shared memory address, the memory allocation function must be modified or replaced. The third is the functions of the OMP library. For examples, omp_get_num_threads is used to return the total number of threads in a program. In Teamster-G, this function must be modified to summate the number of threads allocated at each one of the execution nodes, and then return the summation value. That implies that it is necessary to develop an OMP library dedicated for Teamster-G.

3.2 Program Performance

The OMP run time library is originally implemented based on the kernel-level Pthread. However, in order to minimize the cost of program parallelization and support thread migration or resource reallocation, using a user-level thread to implement the OMP library is necessary. For the sake of compatibility, we choose GNU Pth [14] that is a portable thread package supporting the UNIX-compatible systems. However, this thread package does not support the distributed systems. Therefore, it is necessary to develop a Pth library dedicated for Teamster-G.

Recently, Y. Sakae [15] proposed a loop partition algorithm called profiled scheduling to address the load balance problem of loop applications. The main concept of this algorithm is to assign a same amount of iterations in a loop structure to program threads for execution, and then profile the execution time of threads. According to the profiled thread execution time, the execution time of each node can be estimated by Equation (1), and the amount of iterations distributed to each node can be decided by Equation (2). After loop re-partition, the threads located at the same node will evenly share the iterations distributed to their execution node.

$$T_x = \frac{\sum_{y \in S_x} T_{yx}}{N_x},$$ (1)

where T_x is the execution time of node x , S_x is the set of threads located at node x , T_{yx} is the execution time of thread y on node x, and N_x is the number of threads located at node x.

$$W_x = \frac{\frac{1}{T_x}}{\sum_{x=1}^{n} \frac{1}{T_x}} \times I ,$$ (2)

where W_x is the number of iterations distributed to node x, n is the number of execution nodes, and I is the total number of iterations in a loop structure.

Compared to the scheduling methods based on thread migration [16], the cost of the profiled scheduling is cheaper. However, the profiled scheduling algorithm may make a mistake in the estimation of the execution times of execution nodes when the number of threads assigned to a node is more than that of processors of the node. Therefore, Equation (1) must be revised by simultaneously considering both of thread number and processor number per node.

4 Implementation

According to the previous considerations, the work of our implementation consists of the modification of the Omni compiler, the development of a distributed OMP library, a user-level distributed Pth thread library and a load balance mechanism.

4.1 Modification of the Omni Compiler

After tracking the compiling process, we find that the Omni compiler uses Ident objects and XobjectsDef objects to be the descriptors of data variables in user programs. The Ident object is used to describe the type, name and address of a variable. If a variable is not initialized, the field of XobjectDef will be filled with a NULL value; otherwise the field will be filled with an initial value. According to this observation, we modify the Omni compiler to automatically set an initial value in the XobjectDef field of each variable that is not initialized by programmers. As a result, all the variables in the transformed C source codes will be initialized, and then these variables will be allocated by Teamster-G at the shared memory space.

On the other hand, Teamster-G provides a function called pRelease_new() for memory allocation. In order to achieve source compatibility, we define a macro, i.e., #define malloc pRelease_new, in the omp.h head file. Since all the OpenMP programs originally must include this head file, the malloc() function will be automatically be replaced by the pRelease_new() function without any modification in source codes.

4.2 Distributed OMP Library

We have developed a distributed version of the OMP library for Teamster-G. For example, the parallel directive is mapped to the _ompc_do_parallel() function. When the parallel directive is put at the front of a program block, the program block will be replaced with the _ompc_do_parallel() function after the OpenMP program is transformed by the Omni compiler. The replaced program block will be packed into a working function. The name of the working function will be the parameter of the _ompc_do_parallel() function. When the _ompc_do_parallel() function is performed during the execution of the program, the function will fork a number of threads to execute the same working function with assigning a different working data set. In order to parallelize the OpenMP programs on a cluster, the _ompc_do_parallel() function is modified to broadcast the name of the working function to the other nodes. Each node forks a number of threads and then binds these threads with the working function to share the work of the parallel region according to the received function name.

4.3 Distributed Pth Library

The Distributed Pth library mainly consists of the functions of thread management and thread synchronization. In our implementation, five scheduling queues including *new, ready, waiting, suspend* and *dead* for each processor at a node. Threads forked in a parallel region are evenly distributed to the ready queues of processors, and then each thread scheduler fetches the threads from its ready queue for execution. If the ready queue is empty, the scheduler will fetch threads from the other queues in the same node. In addition, the global thread scheduler that manages all of program threads uses a data structure called *LoadMap* to store the information of threads, including thread state, and returned value, the identifier of the execution node, and the address of thread control block. When the master thread of a user program intends to join a slave thread, the identifier of the slave thread will be sent to the global scheduler. If the state of the slave thread is THREAD_TERMINATED, the return values of the salve thread is sent back to the main thread, and the main thread can continue its work; otherwise, the main thread will be blocked, and the state of the slave thread will be marked as THREAD_JOIN, and store the location of the main thread, and the TCB address of the main thread. After the slave thread finished its work, its identifier will be sent to the global scheduler, and its return value will be sent to the main thread and then the main thread is resumed to continue its work. However, if the state of a slave thread is not marked as THREAD_JOIN, the global scheduler only updates the state of the slave thread as THREAD_TERMINATED, and stores the return value in LoadMap. On the other hand, the lock and barrier of the Pth library is mapped to distributed-queue lock and hierarchical barrier in Teamster-G.

4.4 Load Balance Mechanism

We proposed a novel loop scheduling algorithm called *Profiled Multiprocessor Scheduling* (PMS) to address the load balance problem for user applications executed on the grid environment. The PMS algorithm is similar to the profiled scheduling algorithm while it uses the following equation to evaluate the execution time of each node. Since this equation simultaneously considers the number of processors and the number of threads in each node, it can prevent the error happening in the profiled scheduling algorithm.

$$T_x = \frac{\sum_{y \in S_x} T_{yx}}{N_x} \times \left\lceil \frac{N_x}{P_x} \right\rceil, \tag{3}$$

where P_x is the number of processors in node x.

We have implemented a load balancing mechanism in Teamster-G based on the PMS algorithm. When a thread starts to work for one iteration, the thread scheduler will record the start time of this thread. Until the thread arrives at the end of the iteration such as a barrier, the thread scheduler will record the arrival time and calculate the escaplsed time between the start time and the arrival time. All the calculation results made by each node will be sent to the root node. The root node will estimate the execution time of each node by using Equation 3, and calculate a new loop partition pattern. After broadcasting the new loop partition pattern, each node will receive the number of iterations it must work for, and evenly distribute the appending iterations to its local threads for parallel execution by adjusting the start iteration variable and the end iteration variable of the working function binding to each thread.

5 Performance

We have implemented a set of test applications to evaluate the efficiency of the modified Omni compiler and the PMS algorithm. The parameters of the test applications and our experimental environment are shown in Table 1.

Table 1. The parameters of the test applications and the experimental environment

Application		Cluster I	Cluster II
N-body	EP	Node(0,1,2,3)	Node(4,5)
8192 particles 200 loops	Class C	Pentium III Xeon 500Mhz * 4 512 MB SDRAM 100Mps Fast Ethernet	Pentium III Xeon 700Mhz * 4 512 MB SDRAM 100Mps 100Mps Fast Ethernet

5.1 Effectiveness of the Modified OpenMP Compiler

We use both of the programming interfaces of Pthread and OpenMP to implement the test applications in order to evaluate the effectiveness of the modified Omni compiler. We ran the applications in Cluster I. Table 2 shows that the performance of the test applications implemented by OpenMP is very close to that of the same applications implemented by Pthread. This implies that the modified OpenMP compiler can effectively translate the OpenMP programs.

Table 2. Effectiveness of the modified OpenMP compiler

	Pthread			OpenMP		
N-Body	N = 1	N = 2	N = 4	N = 1	N = 2	N = 4
Exec. Time(sec)	1084.904	545.320	280.611	1082.898	544.918	281.926
Speed up	1	1.989	3.866	1	1.987	3.841
EP	N = 1	N = 2	N = 4	N = 1	N = 2	N = 4
Exec. Time(sec)	1759.850	881.439	442.048	1760.953	882.428	443.563
Speed up	1	1.997	3.970	1	1.996	3.970

5.2 Effectiveness of Load Balancing

When we evaluated the performance of loop scheduling algorithms on load balance, we used two different thread mapping patterns to run the test applications. The first mapping pattern is to assign only one thread onto each processor while the second one is to assign two threads onto the first processor of the first node, and one thread onto the other processors. In addition, we use two nodes located at Cluster I and two nodes located at Cluster II to execute the test applications. In this performance evaluation, the work of the test applications is initially and evenly distributed to program threads, i.e., static scheduling. After profiling the information necessary for load balancing, two different scheduling algorithms including profiled and PMS are applied to re-partition the work of the test applications to program threads.

Fig.1 shows that both of the profiled scheduling algorithm and the PMS algorithm can effectively minimize the cost of load imbalance in both of the test applications no matter which thread mapping is applied. In addition, the profiled algorithm is as effective as the PMS algorithm when the first thread mapping pattern is used. That is because the first mapping of program threads to processors is one-to-one, and the profiled algorithm can estimate the execution time of a node as precisely as the PMS scheduling. However, the PMS algorithm is more effective than the profiled algorithm in load balancing when the second thread mapping pattern is used. The reason is that the PMS algorithm considers simultaneously the number of threads and the number of processors during the estimation of node execution time. Therefore, it can prevent the mistake made by the profiled algorithm, and significantly improve the performance of the test applications.

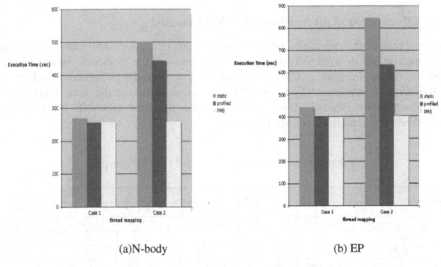

(a)N-body   (b) EP

Fig. 1. Effectiveness of load balancing

6   Related Work

Several past work also were dedicated to the implementation of the OpenMP programming interface on software DSM system such as TreaMarks [17], SCASH[18], JIAJIA [19], and COMPaS[20]. The implementation of TreadMarks is similar to our work. However, TreadMarks does not provide completed source compatibility for the OpenMP programs that are originally written on the SMP platform. SCASH exploits the Exec Java toolkit to translate the OpenMP programs into the multithreading programs. In addition to the support of the OpenMP interface, it also provides a set of extended OpenMP directives for co-allocating shared data in the same data pages to minimize the cost of data consistency maintenance. However, this will result in the

programs are not compatible since these directives are not the standards of OpenMP. JIAJIA implements a compiler called AutoPar to analyze the correctness of parallel programs, and automatically adjust computation granularity to make a compromise between parallelism and parallelization cost. Compared to the previous DSM systems, COMPaS exploits the Omni compiler to insert the message passing calls into source programs for maintaining data consistency instead of using the DSM library.

Compared with the previous work, our work in this paper is focused on a computational grid but a computational cluster. Our work can provides completed source compatibility for the applications developed on SMPs. In addition, the previous work usually implemented the OMP library based on the kernel-level Pthread while we develop a user-level distributed POSIX thread library for the implementation of the OMP library. On the other hand, thread migration was a common method adopted by the previous DSM work for load balancing. However, we exploit loop repartition instead of thread migration to achieve load balance in order for the minimization of overhead.

7 Conclusions and Future Work

In this paper, we have successfully implemented the OpenMP programming interface on Teamster-G for grid computing. The complexity of programming on the grid environment is effectively reduced by our work. Since source compatibility is maintained in our implementation, users can seamlessly apply their OpenMP programs that are developed on SMPs to the grid environment. As a result, the kinds of grid-computing applications will be enriched rapidly. Furthermore, we proposed a novel loop scheduling algorithm, i.e., PMS to address the problem of load balance for user applications executed on the grid environment. Our experimental results show that the proposed scheduling algorithm is more effective for improving the performance of user applications than the other algorithms.

Grid resource is dynamic and non-dedicated. That implies that it is difficult to promise an amount of available resources for grid users. Therefore, reconfiguring the resource allocated for user applications is essential to obtain a good program performance in the grid environment. We will develop an effective reconfiguration scheme for the OpenMP programs in future.

References

1. Mitsuhisa Sato, OpenMP: Parallel Programming API for Shared Memory Multiprocessors and On-Chip Multiprocessors, Proceedings of the 15th International symposium on System Synthesis (ISSS '02), (2002) 109-111.
2. I. Foster. "Globus Toolkit Version 4: Software for Service-Oriented Systems". IFIP International Conference on Network and Parallel Computing, LNCS 3779, (2005), 2-13.
3. Rajkumar Buyya and Srikumar Venugopal, "The Gridbus Toolkit for Service Oriented Grid and Utility Computing: An Overview and Status Report", Proceedings of the First IEEE International Workshop on Grid Economics and Business Models, (2004), 19-36.

4. Frey J., Tannenbaum T., Livny M., Foster I., Tuecke S., "Condor-G: A Computation Management Agent for Multi-Institutional Grids", Proceedings of 10th IEEE International Symposium on High Performance Distributed Computing, (2001) 55-63.
5. David Abramson, Rajkumar Buyya, and Jonathan Giddy, "A Computational Economy for Grid Computing and its Implementation in the Nimrod-G Resource Broker", Future Generation Computer Systems (FGCS) Journal, Volume 18, Issue 8, (2002), 1061-1074.
6. Nicholas T. Karonis, Brian R. Toonen, Ian. Foster, "MPICH-G2: A Grid-enabled implementation of the Message Passing Interface". Journal of. Parallel Distributed. Computing, 63(5), (2003), 551-563.
7. K. Seymour, H. Nakada, S. Matsuoka, D. Dongarra, C. Lee, and H. Casanova, "GridRPC: A Remote Procedure Call API for Grid computing". ICL Technical Report ICL-UT-02-06, Innovative Computing Laboratory, Department of Computer Science, University of Tennessee, (2002).
8. Von Laszewski, G., Foster, I., Gawor, J., Smith, W., and Tuecke, S., "CoG Kits: A Bridge between High Performance Grids Computing and High Performance Grids", ACM 2000 Grade Conference, (2000). http://www/globus.org
9. K. Li. "IVY: A Shared Virtual Memory System for Parallel Computing". Proceedings of the 1988 International Conference on Parallel Processing (ICPP'88), (1988), 94-101.
10. C. Amza, A.L. Cox, S. Dwarkadas, P. Keleher, H. Lu, R. Rajamony, W. Yu, W. Zwaenepoel, "TreadMarks: Shared Memory Computing on Networks of Workstations". IEEE Computer, 29 (2), (1996), 18-28.
11. Brian N.Bershad,Matthew J.Zekauskas,and Wayne A.Sawdon, "Midway: Shared Memory Parallel Programming with Entry Consistency for Distributed Memory Multiprocessors", Tech.Report, CMU-CS-91-170, Carnegie-Mellon University, (1991).
12. Tyng-Yeu Liang, Chun-Yi Wu, Jyh-Biau Chang, and Ce-Kuen Shieh, "Teamster-G : A Grid-enabled Software DSM System", Proceedings of DSM2005 included in CCGRID2005, vol. 2, (2005), 905-912.
13. Kazuhiro Kusano, Shigehisa Satoh, Mitsuhisa Sato: Performance Evaluation of the Omni OpenMP Compiler. ISHPC 2000, (2000), 403-414.
14. Ralf S. Engelschall. GNU Pth - The GNU Portable Threads. http://www.gnu.org/software/pth/
15. Y. Sakae, S. Matsuoka, M. Sato and H. Harada. "Preliminary Evaluation of Dynamic Load Balancing Using Loop Re-partitioning on Omni/SCASH". Proceedings of the 3th IEE/ACM International Symposium on Cluster Computing and the Grid/DSM (DSM2003: Distributed Shared Memory on clusters workshop in CCGRID), (2003), 463-470.
16. Kritchalach Thitikamol and Pete Keleher, Thread Migration and Communication Minimization in DSM systems, Proceedings of the IEEE, volume: 87, (1999), 487-497.
17. C. Amza, A. L. Cox, S. Dwarkadas, P. Keleher, H. Lu, R. Rajamony, W. Yu, and W. Zwaenepoel. "TreadMarks: Shared Memory Computing on Networks of Workstations". IEEE Computer, 29 (2), (1996), 18-28.
18. Y. Ojima, M. Sato, H. Harada and Y. Ishikawa, "Performance of Cluster-enabled OpenMP for the SCASH Software Distributed Shared Memory System", Proceedings. of the 3rd IEEE/ACM International Symposium on Cluster Computing and the Grid (CCGRID'03).
19. Z Feng, C Guoliang, Z Zhaoqing, "OpenMP on Networks of Workstations for software DSMs", Journal of Computer Science and Technology, vol.17, Issue 1, (2002), 90-100.
20. Y.Tanaka, M. Matsuda, M. Ando, K. Kazuto and M. Sato, "COMPaS: A Pentium Pro PC-based SMP Cluster and its Experience". IPPS Workshop on Personal Computer Based Networks of Workstations, LNCS 1388, (1998), 486-497.

Key Techniques of Software Sharing
for on Demand Service-Oriented Computing*

Xiaoshe Dong, Yinfeng Wang, Fang Zheng, Zhongsheng Qin,
Hua Guo, and Guofu Feng

School of Electronics and Information Engineering, Xi'an Jiaotong University,
Xi'an, 710049, China
wangyf@mailst.xjtu.edu.cn

Abstract. In this paper a software sharing system is developed in the grid environment to enforce On Demand Computing policy and maximize the usage of
both hardware and software resources. The system adopts the constellation
model for resource management and combines the sharing and scheduling of
both hardware and software license resources to address the ever-increasing
demands of software resource sharing in Grid and for Service-oriented computing. The system's ability to sustain the software's legacy GUI helps reduce the
complexity of system integration and enhance usability.

1 Introduction

On Demand strategies claims that IT resources will be delivered dynamically to users
according to their demands. In this fashion, any computing devices, networks and data
can be conveniently shared and exchanged. Utility Computing also adopts the "a pay-
as-you-use" model. On Demand can satisfy user's requests of resources flexibly and is
a feature of Service-oriented computing (SOC) [1].

At present, three notable technologies, Web Service, P2P, and Grid, all show their
own advantages in implementing On Demand SOC. Web Service defines the interface
by which applications can interoperate with each other. Heterogeneous resources can
be encapsulated as standard services to provide uniform resource abstraction and
facilitate resource management. P2P has good flexibility, scalability, and self-
management functionality in specific fields such as file sharing and mutual-benefit
service. Members connect with each other as peers and can use each member's computing power, storage, network and other services.

Grid provides users the ability to get access to potentially unlimited amount of
computing and storage resources from a single point, and is capable of constructing
dynamic virtual organizations (VOs) to meet various requests of service. Open Grid
Services Architecture (OGSA) and Web Service Resource Framework (WSRF) are
the building block of grid computing. As infrastructure abstraction level [1], the grid
can be regarded as the infrastructure of SOC.

---

* This research is supported by the"863" project, "CNGI" and "211"project of China.

Y.-C. Chung and J.E. Moreira (Eds.): GPC 2006, LNCS 3947, pp. 557–566, 2006.

On Demand SOC can maximize the value of IT resources to users. Resources are valued neither by how powerful computing and storage capabilities they could provide, nor by whether they implement a beautiful User Interface or complicated function, but by whether their services can satisfy users' real demands and help them to succeed.

This paper proposes a software sharing system in the Grid environment, by which software and hardware resources can be shared to the maximum degree. By sharing software licenses and hardware resources, the system lets users transparently use the computing facilities in Grid. By efficiently scheduling both software license and computing resources, the system ensures users' QoS requests and achieve the goal of quick response and on demand computing. This paper analyzes the major existing models of software licensing, proposes a licensee-based resource scheduling mechanism and approaches of dynamically organizing resources, and discusses some challenges confronted by software sharing.

2 Key Issues in Software Sharing

From the perspective of On Demand SOC, software sharing should achieve the following goals:

1) Utility: Make full use of software licenses and hardware resources;
2) Heterogeneity: Implement resource sharing and interoperating among a broad range of distributed, heterogeneous high performance computing platform and various license models;
3) Transparency: Automatically discover, schedule and reserve both software and hardware resources for users;
4) Minimum Overhead: Integrate software into the Grid without modifying the software and provide support for software's legacy user interface to save user's time in studying new interface.

To achieve those goals the following key issues must be addressed:

2.1 Eliminate the Bottleneck of License Management

Existing License Management systems, such as FLEXlm [2], iFOR/LS [3] and LSF License Scheduler [4], adopt the Client/Server architecture. The computers that run application software are treated as the clients and the License Management (LM) system as the server. Licenses are shared among clients under centralized control of LM systems. These LM systems work well in a small/medium scale environment (e.g. within an enterprise). But in Grid, the license sharing system is required to manage much more licenses than in an enterprise, and respond to thousands of concurrent requests of licenses. The complexity, heterogeneous and dynamic nature of Grid is much more intensive to satisfy by the traditional, centralized-control LM systems. Therefore, a reliable resource management model is needed so as to efficiently implement organizing resources dynamically.

2.2 Hardware and Software Combined Scheduling

Existing LM systems can only manage software licenses, but does not take computing environments as manageable objects in which users have valid licenses to run applications. In this way, users can login and choose which hardware environment to run their applications. This approach of resource selection, which is nontransparent to users, makes well-known powerful hardware heavily loaded and the entire system in poor load balance. To accelerate task processing and improve resource usage, hardware resource should be combined with software license sharing for scheduling, ensure provide better service and speedup response time.

2.3 Sustaining Software's Original User Interface

To hide the details of resource allocation to users, the Web-based user interface is adopted by most license sharing systems. However, the application's user interface is typically re-implemented in a Web-based way as well. It not only introduces burdensome and inefficient work but isn't adaptive to the increment of software resources in grid.

2.4 General Interface of Software Sharing

Software sharing system includes not only software registration, discovery and execution management, but also software license management. A flexible description of software resources is necessary and the platform-independent language XML is a suitable tool. However, there is no open standard or protocol for license management at this time. The license management and control model including user-lock, node-lock, site-lock and the floating license [5]. These mechanisms should be abstracted to a series of standard interfaces to support different operations.

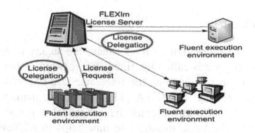

Fig. 1. Execution process of the floating license software

As shown in figure 1 [6], the Fluent execution software can generally execute on any computing platform. Therefore, the goal of software sharing system is to combine the sharing of software license and hardware resource, and to implement the dynamic binding of software license and the hardware resources at runtime. The system makes full use of resources in the grid environment and maintains the applications' original GUI in a more efficient way. Ultimate goal is achieve on-demand computing.

3   The Key Technologies of the System

The typical architectures involve hierarchy, P2P and hybrid. Meanwhile, in VOs, sharing relationship among participants is peer-to-peer in nature [7][8], how would the grid concept benefits from the P2P technology to provide the dynamic VO, open & standard interface and QoS assurance [9] is very important.

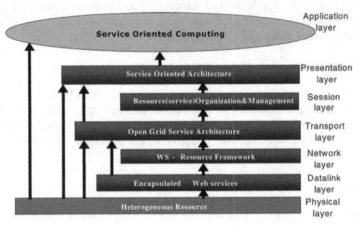

Fig. 2. Layered Service-oriented Computing Architecture

Service is not lonely for it originates from resource. We purpose the layered SOC architecture depicts in figure 2 and use Constellation model [10] for Resource (service) organization and management. Map the constellation model to the Session layer for providing QoS guarantee of the application service.

3.1   Constellation Model

We consider that in the Constellation model there are steady nodes that can provide reliable services. Such node is called the fixed star, to which other nodes can register their services. The connections among the fixed stars are P2P alike, but are different from hybrid architecture (e.g. the JXTA [11]). The basic manageable unit in other architecture is service; while in the constellation model it is the solar system [10]. Using solar system as the basic manageable unit helps to address the instability of QoS aroused by the conflicts between different organization policies, and security issues in the dynamic resources organization.

Different from the dynamic characteristics of P2P system, grid is essentially from the closed communities that require resource organization in grid conforms to the local management policy. In the Constellation Model, the local resources are organized into different solar systems according to their positions. Furthermore, according to the requirements of applications, the solar systems are dynamically organized into Professional Application constellation [12]. In the software sharing system, after the information service centers are organized into Professional Application constellations, they negotiate through the SLA protocol and route the jobs.

3.2 Information Service Center and Job Management

Figure 3 depict that the user commits request through Portal. After the user management module does the user authentication, Information Service (IS) Center estimates whether the license request can be satisfied in local environment. If can be, it notices the License Server to reserve corresponding number of licenses.

If the request cannot be satisfied, it begins to discovery in the whole grid environment [13]. When the selected execution environment needs license authorization to execute software; checkout the reserved license from the known License Server and start the application software.

Job scheduler distributes the jobs according to the information of local resources. Once jobs cannot execute locally because of the conflicts among execution environments, the Job queue route queued jobs to the execution environments managed by other Information Service Centers to execute.

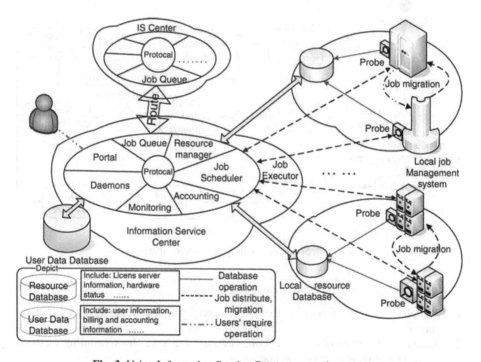

Fig. 3. Using Information Service Center to organize resources

3.3 Scheduling

The first step in the software sharing system for resource scheduling is the scheduling of license resources .The second step is the scheduling of execution environment in order to speed up user jobs execution and increase the resources utilization.

The process of scheduling is exampled as follows:

Assume the set of user jobs is A={a_1 ,..., a_M}, and there are M jobs. The execution environments are depicted as S = { s_1 ,..., s_N }, while the number is N. As the result, the number of possible ways for scheduling of resources is N^M .

One limitation condition is that r_i - the requirement for licenses should less than the current available licenses:

$$r_i \leq License^{available} \quad i = 1,...,M \tag{1}$$

And for assurance of the requirement for the execution environment, such as the CPU, I/O and bandwidth, it should satisfy that the hardware resources of execution environment s_j are no less than the requirement:

$$Hardware_j \geq \sum(a_i @ s_j) \quad j = 1,...,N , a_i \in A \tag{2}$$

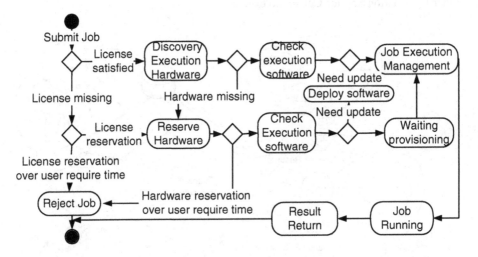

Fig. 4. Scheduling policy of software sharing

The policy for execution environment scheduling is:

1) Search the static information to find resources which can satisfy user's requirements;
2) Based on the 1) results, related constellations will give the scheduling methods according to their current load and so on.

After comparison among different scheduling methods, system will get the best one.

3.4 Sustaining Legacy GUI

X window is the traditional way for users to remotely use the GUI of application installed on the specified HPC server. This approach is considered unsafe, and more and more grid systems now provide Web-based interface to users [6]. The Web-based interface avoids the direct interaction between users and servers, therefore, the server's account is unnecessary and security is enhanced as well; lets the internal system take charge of resource selection, which makes users unaware of the underlying details and helps to implement load balance.

The Web-based interface, however, has a great difficulty in integrating the software's original GUI due to the users' indirect access to the application. The current method is to re-implement the GUI of the application in Web pages, which isn't adaptive to the increment of software resources in grid.

The details of software sharing system maintaining the GUI of applications are showed in the Figure 5. The system queries IS Center for corresponding resources as user request. After obtaining licenses and selecting the execution environment, the system establishes the link between the license server and the execution environment. The execution environment fetches licenses from license server and startups the Fluent software.

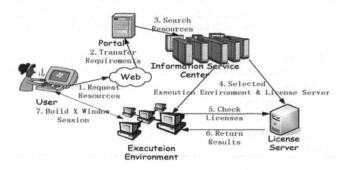

Fig. 5. Workflow of maintain the GUI

By starting Fluent software with the command-line option "-display user's local IP:0", an X window session between the Fluent software running on the execution environment and X Server on user's local machine (e.g. X11 or Exceed) is created. Hence, users can use Fluent's own GUI.

4 Tests and Evaluation

4.1 Test Environment

We constructed a testbed using the hardware resources of National High Performance Computing Center (Xi'an) and software GOS2 (http://www.cngrid.org). Each cluster uses OpenPBS as its job management system. The ANSYS software is deployed on all these clusters. Three workstations are equipped with ANSYS License server software and each of them can provide at most 5 floating licenses. An IBM Xeon server is used as GOS2 portal and provides a Web-based interface for users to submit jobs.

We use an automated load-testing tool to complete this test. Traditional batch mode does not use license sharing scheduling, while web online mode schedule the

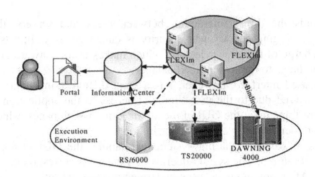

Fig. 6. Testing Environment

Table 1. User scenarios

Step	Traditional mode	Web mode
1	Randomly choose a server for computing, and login to it	Login to the Web portal
2	Randomly choose a license server	Submit the job
3	Initialize the execution environment	Wait for the result of the job
4	Submit the job	Download the result
5	If encountered an error, wait 90s ~ 145s. Then go to 3	Logout
6	Process the result	/
7	Logout	/

job among the resources based on the workload and software sharing policy. We defined 100 virtual users for each mode. These users concurrently access the servers. The behavior of a single user in each mode is defined in table 1.

4.2 Test Result and Analysis

In this test, successful job submission means that the license request of the job can be satisfied, while a job submission failure occurs when there aren't enough licenses to meet the job's license request. The purpose of the test is mainly to determine the rate of successful submission in the two different modes.

Fig.7 (next page) depicts the number of the virtual users who has already logged on the server. From the left figure, all these users have logged on the server, and randomly choose one of three license servers to checkout license resource. Supposed when a user successful submitted a job only occupied one license. There are only five vacant licenses on each license server, the user cannot forecast when and which license server has vacant licenses, so, user has to try to submit job again after a short interval. The interval value is set between 90s and 145s. When the license is enough, the user only submits once, and then it can successfully execute. But when the license is insufficient, the user even has to re-submit 34 times for a successful execution.

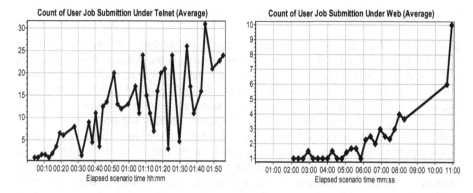

Fig. 7. Counts of User job submission of traditional (left) and web (right) mode

As the right figure 7 shows the average count of the total submitting action of each web online user of the 100 virtual users in a short interval, considered the status of the network and the job expiration, the average count of the submitting action is mostly below 4 times.

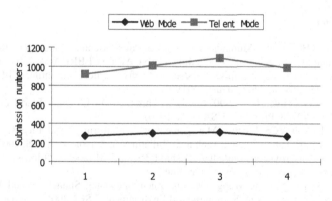

Fig. 8. Group test result

After 4-group test, the results show traditional mode affecting the usage of the re-sources and compelling the user has to re-submit job more times. In reality, once the server always denies users, the latter will not keep trying. This will lead to another poor load balance result: many resources are available later but no one knows. Using software-sharing system, it can gather many heterogenic resources, and allow the user to login the system from any portal and access all these resources if he is allowed.

The software-sharing system has all the advantages such as increases the usage of the resource and avoids some disadvantage of the traditional mode. But because the system has to schedule the jobs, execute, and return the result instead of the users, the time of executing small-scale jobs is less than the traditional mode's. In contrast, the load balancing can be achieved so the large-scale job will benefit from this software-sharing system.

5 Conclusion and Future work

Based on the characteristics of current License Management (LM) system, grid and SOC, we propose a software sharing system to solve some disadvantages of current LM systems, including poor scalability and lack management of hardware resources. Additionally, the system is compatible with software's original interfaces. Software sharing systems is a means not only to force software vendors to migrate to On Demand SOC, but also to provide a "Win-Win" resource sharing solution.

Most software has a life cycle of only a few years, and requires frequent upgrades, which makes users wonder whether they can virtually benefit from their investment on software licenses or not. Therefore, On Demand SOC is inevitable. It can drive vendors to migrate to On Demand SOC that includes the customer demands, the market pressure and open source community support as well.

The software sharing system is compatible with current LM systems' C/S architecture, and adopts Constellation Model to organize resources and obtain good scalability. Taking hardware resources as the object to share speeds up the processing of users' tasks and provides better QoS, as well as improves resource usage.

Future work includes 1) study the security and failure recovery mechanisms within software sharing system; 2) optimize system performance.

References

1. Michael N.Huhns and Munindar P. Singh: Service-Oriented Computing: Key Concepts and Principles. IEEE Internet Computing, (JANUARY • FEBRUARY 2005), pp.75-81
2. http://www.macrovision.com/services/support/software_licensing.shtml, "FLEXlm End User Guide" version 9.5, (August 2004)
3. http://docs.hp.com/en/B3782-90716/ch05s12.html, "iFOR/LS Quick Start Guide", HP Part No. B2355-90108, Printed in USA (June 1996)
4. "Policy Driven VCS License Management with Platform Global License Broke", The Synopsys Verification Avenue Technical Bulletin Vol. 3, issue 1, (March 2003)
5. http://www.macrovision.com/pdfs/art1.shtml Richard Mirabella, "License Management: How developers control software licensing"
6. Xiaoshe Dong, Yinfeng Wang, Guohua, Zhengfang,Yang Shuncheng and Wu Weiguo. "Floating License Sharing System in Grid Environment. " SKG2005, Beijing, pp857-863.
7. Domenico Talia and Paolo Trunfio: Toward a Synergy Between P2P and Grids. IEEE Internet Computing, (JULY•AUGUST 2003), pp.94-96
8. J. Joseph, M. Ernest, C. Fellenstein: Evolution of grid computing architecture and grid adoption models, IBM SYSTEMS JOURNAL, VOL 43, NO. 4, (2004), pp.624-645
9. I.Foster. What is the Grid? A three Point Checklist. GRIDToday 1(6), July 21,2002
10. Yinfeng Wang, Xiaoshe Dong et al.A Constellation Model for Grid Resource Management.APPT2005, LNCS 3756, pp. 263-272
11. Bernard Traversat, et al.: Project JXTA 2.0 Super-Peer Virtual Network. (May 25, 2003)
12. Xiaoshe Dong, Yinfeng Wang et al.: The Campus Resource Management Based on Constellation Model in the ChinaGrid. ISPA Workshops 2005, LNCS 3759, pp. 249-256
13. Yinfeng Wang, Xiaoshe Dong et al.: A Constellation Resource Discovery Model Based on Scalable Multi-tape Universal Turing Machine. GCC 2005, LNCS 3795, pp. 633-644

Embedding a Middleware for Networked Hardware and Software Objects*

David Villa, Felix Jesús Villanueva, Francisco Moya, Fernando Rincón,
Jesús Barba, and Juan Carlos López

Dept. of Technology and Information Systems,
University of Castilla-La Mancha,
School of Computer Science. 13071 - Ciudad Real. Spain
{David.Villa, FelixJesus.Villanueva, Francisco.Moya,
Fernando.Rincon, Jesus.Barba, JuanCarlos.Lopez}@uclm.es

Abstract. In this paper we present a novel approach to the design of
ubiquitous computing environments based on an ultra low-cost implementation of standard distributed object middlewares suitable for networked hardware and software components of the system.

We prove the feasibility of our approach with a set of prototypes supporting basic interoperability with CORBA and ZeroC ICE. In some
cases, the resulting embedded prototypes are two orders of magnitude
smaller than previous implementations of small objects. They are suitable for embedding into the smallest microcontrollers in the market, or in
the tiniest embedded Java virtual machines, or even in a low-end FPGA.

1 Introduction

A useful ubiquitous computing environment must be able to perceive stimuli
from the physical world and react on them. The perceived value of an ubiquitous system is mainly due to its ability to create and to support end-user
services, based on information from the environment. In this paper we face the
problem of developing effective communication mechanisms among a large set
of heterogeneous devices including, but not limited to, desktop computers, embedded computers, small microcontrollers, customized FPGA devices, etc. We
are mainly concerned with the implementation of minimum cost devices able to
support the large variety of device and network technologies currently deployed
in the target environments.

Our approach departs from many previous heterogenous device network architectures by requiring each device to be autonomous, in the sense that our
devices and basic services will work even when all available service gateways
fail. We believe this is the easiest way to achieve better robustness, reliability and fault tolerance at a minimum cost. Intermediate elements such as the
gateways advocated by e.g. OMG Smart Transducers [3] or OSGi [6] should be

---

* This research is supported by FEDER and JCCM, under Grant PBC-05-009-1, and
  by Spanish Ministry of Education, under Grant TIN2005-08719.

Y.-C. Chung and J.E. Moreira (Eds.): GPC 2006, LNCS 3947, pp. 567–576, 2006.

avoided in most applications. It should be possible to implement autonomous services whose correct operation does not depend on the correct operation of any gateway.

Therefore our main goal is to allow embedded devices to offer their capabilities as standard distributed objects. These objects should be able to hide the heterogeneity of underlying technologies such as transport protocols and network architecture.

The seamless communication of heterogeneous distributed components is usually approached in software environments by using a unifying element, the communication middleware. Unfortunately, current implementations of standard object oriented middlewares (DCOM, Java RMI, Jini, EJB, CORBA, Web Services, .NET Remoting, ZeroC ICE [26], etc.) require too much computing resources for many of our target devices.

2   Related Work

Many previous initiatives have been oriented towards the miniaturization of existing middlewares. Indeed, the Object Management Group [1] published the MinimumCORBA specification [8], a lightweight version of its popular CORBA architecture [2]. MinimumCORBA removes the most expensive features of the communication engine keeping a good degree of interoperability with standard CORBA objects.

As stated in [17] there are three main approaches to the minimization of distributed object implementations: 1) Remove costly features but keep genericity, 2) adapt the middleware to specific devices, 3) use proxies.

The first approach is used in dynamicTAO [10] and its descendants: LegORB [12] and UIC-CORBA [9]. LegORB is a modularized ORB with the ability to be dynamically configured. The monolithic library of TAO [7] is decomposed in a set of independent functional components that may be omitted from the target application. It is reported that a client-only CORBA application under 20 KB may be built on a HP Jornada 680 running Windows CE, and a 6 KB client-only may be built on a PalmPilot running PalmOS 3.0 (see [13]).

UIC (*Universally Interoperable Core*) define a component based middleware skeleton. Each component encapsulate a small set of features and may be dynamically loaded depending on the running platform, device and network used. UIC, as its name states, may be used to implement communication engines for different middlewares besides CORBA, such as Java RMI or DCOM. A CORBA static server is reported to be 35 KB on a SH3 running Windows CE.

A similar commercial product is e*ORB [14], a modular communication engine with real-time features able to run on a HP iPAQ or a Texas Instruments TMS320C64X DSP.

Another representative of the first approach to the development of small communication engines is MicroQoSCORBA [11]. A customized communication engine may be generated from a set of predefined pieces in order to implement servers and clients suited to a specific application and device (it has been tested on SaJe [24] and TINI [23]).

nORB [15] implements a set of pluggable transport protocols, including some environment-specific protocols (ESIOP in CORBA terminology). It borrows many ideas from MicroQoSCORBA, such as the simplified version of the GIOP standard protocol, called GIOPLite.

A representative of the second approach to the development of small footprint middlewares is TINIORB [18], a MinimumCORBA communication engine customized for the TINI device from Dallas Semiconductor. PalmORB [19] is another example of this approach.

The third alternative requires a mediating host to allow interoperability with objects in a standard middleware. This is the approach used in UORB [17] and one of the integration alternatives proposed in SENDA [21].

Another interesting proposal of the same type is [22]. This work shows how a set of small 8 bit microcontrollers may be published as a set of CORBA objects. The host runs a proxy object for each connected device and communications between each device and a the mediating host use a specialized protocol.

All these previous works follow the same basic rules: Remove dynamic invocation and dynamic instantiation features, simplify the interface definition language (OMG IDL in the case of CORBA) removing complex or variable length data types, remove some fields from the communication protocol, remove or simplify the types of messages used in the protocol, do not support indirect references, do not support common services, modularize the communication engine and instantiate only those components that are actually used.

It should be noted that the above mentioned communication engines require a lot of support utilities: data type marshalling, communication primitives, operating system, etc. Therefore, the actual resource requirements may be orders of magnitude larger than cited.

Even the smallest of the previous distributed object implementations is much larger than feasible on our target environment. Requiring a TINI (around 30 euro) for each device in the ubiquitous system would lead to astronomical prices for useful systems. Just thinking of a RMI-enabled Java virtual machine for each bulb or switch in a building is reserved to millionaires.

We need something much smaller, self-contained, and specially much cheaper, but with a similar set of features.

3   The Smallest Object

Instead of reducing the features provided by the middleware even more, let's think the other way. We will define the smallest implementation of a distributed object. From that point we will consider the overhead introduced for each additional feature when the application constraints allow them.

From the perspective of the ubiquitous system it is important that each device looks like a distributed object. But it is not essential that they are actual distributed objects. If devices are able to generate coherent replies when they receive predefined request messages then the system will work as expected. For a given communication middleware these request an reply messages are completely specified by the communication protocol (GIOP in the case of CORBA).

If the device is just an application-specific GIOP server it will be seen as a normal object from the rest of the network but there is a huge advantage for resource savings. The object may get rid of the whole communication engine and its API. There is no need for object adapters, marshalling routines, etc. We just need to implement the message handling code for those messages whose destination is an object placed at the device. Therefore we propose a generated ad-hoc implementation for each device.

In this paper we proposed PicoObjects as a materialization of the above implementation strategy. In summary PicoObjects provide a toolset for the automated generation of code able to replace a standard communication engine in low-end computing resources.

Code generation must be performed with careful consideration of the constraints imposed by the target platform. Generated code is obviously different for each platform but it will also differ for servers with a different set of objects, even when the platform and the interfaces of the objects are the same.

It is worth to note that a server implemented using this technique will only reply to messages directed to its resident objects. Messages handled by the communication middleware (such as object location in CORBA) will be silently discarded. It is always possible to include these messages as the methods of a special object if needed.

A communication middleware will usually expose two different interfaces to access every service in the system: At a programming level it provides a standardized application programming interface. It abstracts communication details, protocols, etc. At a network level it provides a common protocol (GIOP in the case of CORBA) allowing seamless communication among communication engines running on different machines.

A picoObject lacks a local communication engine. The server program must include code to perform communication primitives and manage its registered objects. Nonetheless for the rest of the network a picoObject behaves as an usual object. It provides a network level interface without significative differences with respect to a standard object. We may say that a picoObject implements a virtual communication engine.

Although it is already implicit in the context, it is worthy to note that a picoObject implement only the server-side of the communication middleware. This is consistent with the idea of developing remote interfaces for each device. The devices behave as small servers.

4   Functionality Scaling

The main goal of picoObjects is the implementation of the essential features needed for a device to expose a standard object behaviour in the network. From this point we intend to define and develop mechanisms to scale the functionality of the device depending on the constraints imposed by the target platform. Our initial targets range from an eight bit microcontroller to a standard PC.

Although the proposed model allows an implementation at almost any conceivable scale, our main targets were the smallest available computing devices. It may be argued that generating the message handling code for a whole communication middleware do not offer any particular advantage over a stantard middleware. Even in this case there may be constraints in the target system that make our approach more advisable (reliability, real-time constraints, security, etc.).

We define the minimum set of features using the considerations of section 2, adding a few additional constraints: a) On one hand we always follow the standard message format for the communication protocol. Using modified protocols (such as GIOPLite in the case of MicroQoSCORBA) implies the need for a mediating element (bridge) responsible for the transformation of messages to allow seamless interoperability. This would contradict our intention to make devices immediately available on the network. b) We will only support the simplest protocol version whenever interoperability is not compromised. c) Resident objects are *always on*. There is no way to activate or deactivate objects.

5   A Strategy for Small Objects

The simplest way to achieve a coherent behaviour for each picoObject is by means of message matching automata. In this context, the allowed message set for a given object constitute a BNF grammar defined by: a) The message format for the middleware communication protocol. b) The object identity, that is to say, object identifiers. It should be noted that several object identities may be backed by a single piece of code. This technique is usually called *default servant* in CORBA parlance. c) Concrete interfaces or set of interfaces provided by the object. It includes name, arguments and return value for each method. d) The marshalling procedure (CDR in case of CORBA). e) Standard interfaces inherited from the communication engine (CORBA::Object in case of CORBA). And f) Constraints of the target platform.

We first define the set of lexical elements (tokens): compulsory fields in each message with a known format and size, object names, method names, interface names. Then we generate the rules describing how these tokens may be combined together (the BNF grammar). This information is enough to automatically generate a complete functional parser. The whole development flow is shown in figure 1.

Every picoObject must include a set of user procedures (object method implementations) that must be filled by hand (as in any traditional middleware). When the grammar parser of a PicoObject identifies a whole request message the corresponding user procedure is automatically invoked and a reply message is generated. If the parser fails to identify a valid method request then the message is discarded and the picoObject looks for a new syncronization point.

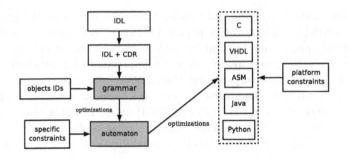

Fig. 1. Development flow of a picoObject

Input and output messages may be handled on-the-fly using a custom byte-stream processor. This is a very convenient solution for devices with severe memory constraints (just a few hundreds of program memory words and a dozen of general purpose registers). In this scenario there is no room to even store the incoming message. The request message is processed as the bytes arrive and the reply message is also generated partially from replication of the incoming data. The last part of the reply message is generated by the user procedure for each method.

In order to lower the memory requirements for token parsing we reduce them using a digital signature, a CRC code or just a checksum. Therefore, even when tokens may be arbitrarily long, the picoObject compiler substitutes it by a length and a single byte checksum. When the picoObject is parsing a request it may just incrementally calculate the input message checksum and check it when the length matches. Actually we do not need to check at every token boundary whether calculated and stored checksums match. If we arrange the set of implemented messages for a given object as a lexical tree then we just need to check at every forking point in order to decide the branch to follow.

Our strategy is quite different with respect to previous middleware minimization approaches such as MicroQoSCORBA. MicroQoSCORBA tries coarse grain code minimization by building a custom implementation from predefined libraries. PicoObjects use a finer grain code minimization strategy by completely generating the message parsing code for each application.

The above approach has been applied to a pair of existing middlewares: CORBA and ZeroC ICE, leading to picoCORBA and picoICE respectively. The constraints imposed by each particular middleware lead to slightly different design decisions. As illustration of the applicability of this work we will summarize in the following sections the features and design decisions of each prototype.

Both prototypes were developed in Microchip PIC assembler, Java on a standard embedded PC, Java on an embedded Dallas Semiconductors TINI device, C on a standard embedded PC, and VHDL on a Xilinx Virtex E FPGA.

6   PicoCORBA

CORBA is now a mature distributed object architecture and a lot of effort has been devoted to embedded CORBA implementations. Most of this previous work is influenced by MinimumCORBA, a reduced footprint specification which removes complex CORBA features keeping a good degree of interoperability with standard CORBA. MinimumCORBA objects are completely standard compliant and they may also be built on full CORBA engines. PicoCORBA goes much further with respect to removing features. PicoCORBA objects are not portable at all since they are usually implemented using a specific assembler language. Even if we use C or any other low level programming language there is no enforcement of any standard mapping since there is no need to link against a common library. The picoCORBA prototype is able to parse a byte stream coming from the network and generate a response. The transport protocol may range from TCP over Ethernet, through SLIP, SNAP, LonTalk, or any other reliable transport protocol.

As described above, there are two key points in which we should check the calculated checksum against the expected checksum: when we receive the object identity and when we must choose among the implemented methods. In order to simplify this procedure even further, we assume that the length of the identity string (`object_key` field) of every picoObject is exactly the same. This assumption do not introduce interoperability problems at all. Object identities will appear in the generated object references and clients are required to use it without modifications when sending requests.

CORBA standard mandates the implementation of GIOP communication protocol to ensure interoperability across the network. PicoCORBA is currenly GIOP 1.0 conformant. This does not introduce interoperability problems since the CORBA standard dictates that any updated GIOP protocol must be backwards compatible.

GIOP dictates that peers which initiate a connection determine the byte order used. With GIOP 1.0 the client is always the initiator and therefore the server is required to adapt to the requested byte order. PicoObjects are supposed to stay in a controlled environment and therefore implementing a single byte order may be acceptable. If this simplification cannot be afforded then picoCORBA objects must implement little endian and big endian versions of all the messages, virtually doubling the resources needed.

Any CORBA object implements a standard interface called CORBA::Object defining a set of common methods. Fortunately some of these methods are already handled by the remote proxy or by the communication engine at the client side. Therefore there is no need to implement all of them as possible GIOP messages. We identified the bare minimum set of common methods to non_existent and is_a. The former allows the client to know whether the object is willing to answer requests. The latter offers minimal introspection capabilities. Both of them are implicitly implemented in every generated picoObject even when no explicitly stated.

Table 1. Size of a small server on embedded middlewares

Embedded middleware	Minimal server
TAO	1738 KB
nORB	567 KB
UIC/CORBA	35 KB
JacORB (Java)	243 KB
ZEN (Java)	53 KB
MicroQoSCORBA (TINI)	21 KB
picoCORBA (C)	7 KB
picoCORBA (Java)	5 KB
picoCORBA (TINI)	4 KB
picoCORBA (PIC12C509)	415 words

A few limitations apply to the set of implemented messages. Experimental results show that interoperability is not compromised against all tested implementations of CORBA (TAO, OmniORB, MICO, JacORB, JDK1.4, ORBit2). We ignore the contents of the field `requesting_principal` for every incoming message which is already deprecated. Reply messages reproduce two fields from their matching request messages: `service_context` which encapsulates engine specific data and `request_id` which matches requests and replies. Field `reply_status` always contains `NO_EXCEPTION` since picoCORBA does not currently support exceptions or indirect proxies (location forward). We ignore *cancel request* messages. This is explicitly allowed by the CORBA specification. PicoCORBA does not implement *Locate request* or *Close connection* messages. Locate requests may be used by the client to optimize bandwidth when using indirect proxies. PicoCORBA objects are "always on". Therefore there is no need to ever generate *Close connection* messages. Finally PicoCORBA ignores any unhandled message. In particular it ignores any malformed messages and error reporting messages.

An implementation of a fully operative servant, able to handle method invocations for a set of 64 X10 objects fits on 415 program memory words of a Microchip PIC12f675 and requires less than 16 eight-bit registers. That is two orders of magnitude smaller than any other previous implementation of small embedded middlewares (see table 1).

7   PicoICE

ZeroC, Inc. developed a high quality distributed object framework called ICE (Internet Communication Engine) built upon the experience of CORBA but free of legacy or bureaucracy constraints. It implements a feature set unparalleled in any other distributed object platform (object persistence, object migration, authentication, security, replication, deployment services, firewall gateways, etc.). A summary of the differences between ICE and CORBA is available at the ICE home page [26].

Despite the current lack of support for embedded platforms, ICE offers a few advantages over CORBA to reduce resource comsumption even further. ICE protocol is simpler than GIOP for a number of design decisions: 1) messages are always little endian so we do not need to care about byte ordering, 2) there is support for unreliable transports such as UDP (much easier to implement in a low cost embedded device), 3) there are less types of messages and some of them may not be implemented without compromising interoperability, 4) unprocessed message fields may easily be skipped because they are usually preceded by the field total length, 5) there are no data alignment requirements for messages on-the-wire.

The picoICE prototype is fully conformant with the ICE protocol specification for connection-oriented transports and connection-less transports. Any reliable or unreliable transport protocol may be used in combination of picoICE objects. An implementation of a fully operative servant, able to handle method invocations for a set of 64 objects fits on 478 words of program memory in a Microchip PIC12f675 microcontroller and needs less than 16 eight bit registers. That is three orders of magnitude smaller than the ZeroC ICE implementation, and two orders of magnitude smaller than the ZeroC Embedded ICE implementation. Currently we support TCP and UDP transports over Ethernet or WiFi through a Lantronix XPort device. A picoObject may also be connected to SLIP (serial line IP) serial port.

As in the case of CORBA, ICE requires that every object implement a set of common methods. The picoICE prototype supports ice_ping, ice_id, ice_ids and ice_isA. These methods add minimal introspection capabilities and the ability to remotely test the existence of an object. These features may be removed if not needed.

8   Conclusions and Future Research

In this paper we propose an alternative implementation of distributed objects for low cost embedded devices such as eight bit microcontrollers or FPGAs. Results show that resource consumption is two orders of magnitude than previously published data on small middlewares implementation.

As they are currently implemented, picoObjects exhibit ultra-low latency, since the reply messages are composed on the fly while the object is still receiving the request. This makes them specially suitable for real-time operation even on low bit-rate networks. Exact figures of latency depend on the transport protocol used, which is currently independent of the picoObjects.

As the basic prototypes still evolve, we are now developing high level tools to deploy a picoObject network. We are also extending the concept to support other middlewares.

PicoObjects are being used as major components of SENDA, a middleware-based infrastructure for modeling, development, and deploying of next generation home services [21].

References

1. OMG (*Object Management Group*), http://www.omg.org/
2. Object Management Group, *The Common Object Request Broker: Architecture and Specification*, ed. 2.3, June 1999. Available in http://www.omg.org/, document id: 98-12-01.
3. Object Management Group, *Smart Transducers Interface Specification*, ed. 1.0, January 2003. Available in http://www.omg.org/, document id: 03-01-01.
4. OMG, *General Inter-ORB Protocol 2.3*, Available in http://www.omg.org/ (Document id: 98-12-01), June 1999.
5. Sun Microsystems, *Jini Architecture Specification*, ed. 1.2, available online at http://www.sun.com/.
6. Open Services Gateway Initiative, *OSGi Service Platform*, ed. 2.0, October 2001, available online at http://www.osgi.org/.
7. The ACE ORB, available online at http://www.theaceorb.com/.
8. Object Management Group, *Minimum CORBA Specification*, ed. 2.3, August 2002, available online at http://www.omg.org/, document id: 02-08-01.
9. M. Román, Fabio Kon, Roy H. Campbell, *Reflective Middleware: From Your Desk to Your Hand*, 2001.
10. Fabio Kon, F. Costa, G. Blair, Roy Campbell. *The Case for Reflective Middleware*.
11. Haugan, Olav. *Configuration and Code Generation Tools for Middleware Targeting Small, Embedded Devices*, M.S. Thesis, Dec 2001.
12. Manuel Roman, M. Dennis, Mickunas, Fabio Kon and Roy Campell. *LegORB and Ubiquitous CORBA*, Feb 2000.
13. LegORB, available online at http://choices.cs.uiuc.edu/2k/LegORB/.
14. OpenFusion e*ORB, available online at http://www.prismtechnologies.com/.
15. V. Subramonian, G. Xiang. *Middleware Specification for Memory-Constrained Networked Embedded Systems*, 2003.
16. C. Gill, V. Subramonian. *ORB Middleware Evolution for Networked Embedded Systems*, 2003.
17. Rodrigues, G., Ferraz, C., *A CORBA-Based Surrogate Model on IP Networks*, 2001.
18. J. Morena, F. Moya, J.C. López. *Implementación de un ORB para Dispositivos Empotrados*, Sep 2002.
19. M. Roman, A. Singhai, *Integrating PDAs into Distributed Systems: 2K and PalmORB*, HUC 1999.
20. M. Connolly, *CORBA Middleware for a Palm Operating System*, Sep 2001.
21. F. Moya, J.C. López. *SENDA: an alternative to OSGi for large-scale domotics*, Networks, The Proceedings of the Joint International Conference on Wireless LANs and Home Networks (ICWLHN 2002) and Networking (ICN 2002), World Scientific Publishing, pp 165-176, Aug, 2002.
22. W. Nagel, N. Anderson. *A Protocol for Representing Individual Hardware Devices as Objects in a CORBA Networt*, July 2002.
23. Tiny Internet Interface. Available online at http://www.ibutton.com/TINI/index.html
24. SaJe, Real-Time Native Java Execution. Available online at http://saje.systronix.com/.
25. E. Gamma, R.H., R. Johnson, J. Vlissides, *Design Pattens, Elements of Object-Oriented Software*. 1995, Addison-Wesley.
26. ZeroC, Inc., *ICE Home Page*, available online at http://www.zeroc.com/.

Mechanism of Authenticating a MAP in Hierarchical MIPv6[*]

Jonghyoun Choi and Youngsong Mun

School of Computing, Soongsil University,
Sangdo 5 Dong, Dongjak Gu, Seoul, Korea
wide@sunny.ssu.ac.kr, mun@computing.ssu.ac.kr

Abstract. In Mobile IPv6, when a Mobile Node (MN) moves from home net-work to the foreign network, it configures a new Care-of-Address (CoA) and requests the Home Agent (HA) to update its binding. This binding process requires high signaling load. Thus, Hierarchical Mobile IPv6 (HMIPv6) has been proposed to accommodate frequent mobility of the MN and reduce the signaling load in the Internet. A Mobility Anchor Point (MAP) is a router located in a network visited by the MN. The MN uses the MAP as a local HA. The absence of any protections between MN and MAP may lead to malicious MNs impersonating other legitimate ones, impersonating a MAP. In this paper, we propose a mechanism of authenticating MAP and MN in HMIPv6. The performance analysis and the numerical results presented in this paper show that our proposal has almost same as the performance of the HMIPv6 without security in spite of security process load.

1 Introduction

The Internet users desire high quality of service at anywhere. Mobile device users have increased by growing of mobile device and wireless techniques. Mobile IPv6 [1] proposed by Internet Engineering Task Force (IETF) provides a basic host mobility management scheme. Mobile IPv6 specifies routing support to permit IPv6 hosts to move between IP subnetworks while maintaining session continuity. whenever an MN moves from home network to the foreign network, it configures a new Care-of-Address (CoA) and requests the HA to update it's binding. This binding allows an MN to maintain connectivity with the Internet as it moves between subnets. However, binding process requires high signaling load. Thus, HMIPv6 has been proposed [3] to accommodate frequent mobility of the MN and reduce the signaling load in the Internet. In HMIPv6, when an MN moves into new Access Router (AR) domain, the MN may perform one or two types of binding update procedures: either the global binding update and the local binding update (intra-MAP) or the local binding update (Inter-MAP). A Mobility Anchor Point (MAP) is a router located in a network visited by the MN. The MN uses the MAP as a local HA. One or more MAPs can exist within a

---

[*] This research was supported by the MIC(Ministry of Information and Communication), Korea, under the ITRC(Information Technology Research Center) support program supervised by the IITA(Institute of Information Technology Assessment).

Y.-C. Chung and J.E. Moreira (Eds.): GPC 2006, LNCS 3947, pp. 577–586, 2006.
© Springer-Verlag Berlin Heidelberg 2006

visited network. The absence of any protections between MN and MAP may lead to malicious MNs impersonating other legitimate ones, impersonating a MAP. Any of these attacks will undoubtedly cause undesirable impacts to the MN's communication with all correspondent nodes [2]. In this paper, we propose a mechanism of authenticating MAP and MN in HMIPv6.

2   Overview of Hierarchical Mobile IPv6 system

The HMIPv6 protocol separates mobility management into intra-domain mobility and inter-domain mobility. A MAP in HMIPv6 treats the mobility management inside a domain. Thus, when an MN moves around the sub-networks within a single domain, the MN sends a BU message only to the current MAP. When the MN moves out of the domain or moves into another domain, Mobile IPv6 is invoked to handle the mobility.

The basic operation of the HMIPv6 can be summarized as follows [8].

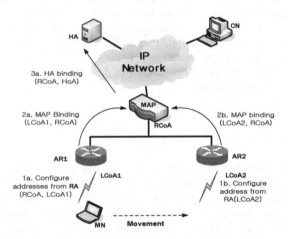

Fig. 1. The basic Operation of the HMIPv6

In HMIPv6, the MN has two addresses, a Regional CoA (RCoA) on the MAP's link and an on-link CoA (LCoA). When an MN moves into a new MAP domain, it needs to configure two CoAs: an RCoA and an LCoA. After forming the RCoA based on the prefix received in the MAP option, the MN sends a local BU to the MAP. This BU procedure will bind the MN's RCoA to its LCoA. The MAP then acts as an HA. Following a successful registration with the MAP, a bi-directional tunnel between the MN and the MAP is established. After registering with the MAP, the MN registers its new RCoA with it's HA by sending a BU that specifies the binding (RCoA, Home Address) as in Mobile IPv6. When the MN moves within the same MAP domain, it should only register its new LCoA to its MAP. In this case, the RCoA remains unchanged.

3 Mechanism of Authenticating MAP

In this paper, we propose mechanism of authenticating MAP without handicap of security processing cost. In order to authenticate MAP or MN, each other, [2] recommend IPsec with IKE. Fig.2 shows message flow of general HMIPv6.

When an MN moves into new AR domain without changing MAP, an MN needs not to perform both IKE phase 1 and Global BU. IKE phase 1 consists of the exchange of three sets of two messages and IKE phase 2 consists of one sets of two messages and one message from initiator to responder.

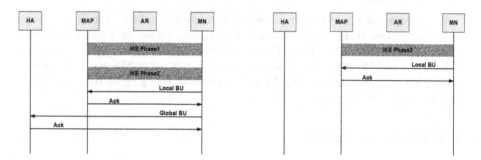

Fig. 2. Message flow of general HMIPv6. The left figure shows message flow of Inter-MAP movement and the right figure shows message flow of Intra-MAP movement.

In this paper, we propose new mechanism of authenticating MAP. We assume that two links of HA-MAP and HA-MN are secure and the HA has already known an MN's public key. Fig.3 shows message flow of proposed mechanism. Our proposed mechanism is similar to RSA system. However, our proposed system must obtain peer's public key from Certificated Agent (CA). Thus HA acts as CA in our proposed system.

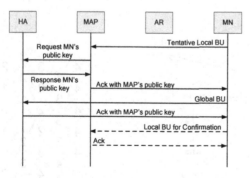

Fig. 3. Message flow of proposed mechanism

When an MN moves into new MAP domain, our proposed system operates as follows:

1. An MN detects movement by receiving router advertisement message from New AR.
2. An MN configures LCoA and RCoA.

3. An MN sends a local BU with Home Address (HoA) to the MAP for binding new LCoA to new RCoA.
4. A MAP sends request MN's public key to HA and obtain MN's public key
5. A MAP sends Ack. message together with MAP's public key and digital signature encrypted by MN's public key obtained from HA.
6. An MN sends a global BU with MAP's address to the HA for binding new RCoA to HoA.
7. An MN receives Ack. message with MAP's public key.
8. An MN sends Local BU together with digital signature encrypted by MAP's public key obtained from HA.

We recommend 5 second as the lifetime of tentative Local BU. The Second Local BU can extend the lifetime. If a MAP could not receive the second Local BU within 5 second, lifetime of tentative Local Binding shall be expired. After step 5, a MAP can authenticate an MN. After step 8, a trust relationship between MN and MAP is contracted. When an MN moves new AR domain without changing MAP, the proposed system operates just step 8.

4 Performance Analysis

4.1 Mobility Model

In this paper, we use hexagonal cellular network model, as shown in Fig. 5. Each MAP domain is assumed to consist of the same number of range rings, R. Each range ring r ($r \geq 0$) consists of 6r cells. The center cell is innermost cell 0. The cells labeled by 1 formed the first range ring around cell "0," the cells labeled by 2 formed the second range ring around cell 1 and so on. Therefore, the number of cells up to ring R, N(R) is calculated in Eq.(1).

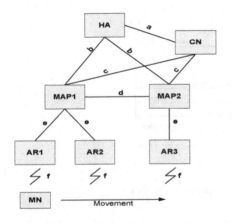

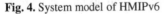

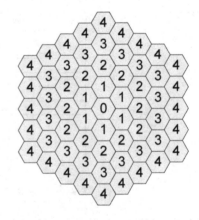

Fig. 4. System model of HMIPv6   **Fig. 5.** Hexagonal cellular network architecture

In terms of user mobility model, random-walk mobility model is taken into consideration as commonly used mobility model. The random-walk model is appropriate for pedestrian movements where mobility is generally confined to a limited geographical area such as residential and business buildings [4].

$$N(R) = \sum_{r=1}^{R} 6r + 1 = \frac{6R(R+1)}{2} + 1 \tag{1}$$

In terms of random-walk mobility model, we consider the two-dimensional Markov chain model used in [5]. In this model, the next position of an MN is equal to the previous position plus a random variable whose value is drawn independently from an arbitrary distribution [5]. In addition, an MN moves to another cell area with a probability of $1-q$ and remains in the current cell with probability q. In the cellular architecture shown in Fig. 5, if an MN is located in a cell of range ring r ($r > 0$), the probabilities of movement resulted in an increase or a decrease in the distance from the center cell are given by

$$p^+(r) = \frac{1}{3} + \frac{1}{6r} \quad \text{and} \quad p^-(r) = \frac{1}{3} - \frac{1}{6r} \tag{2}$$

We define the state r of a Markov chain as the distance between the current cell of the MN and the center cell. This state is equivalent to the index of a range ring where the MN is located. As a result, the MN is said to be in state r if it is currently residing in range ring r. The transition probabilities $\alpha_{r,r+1}$ and $\beta_{r,r-1}$ represent the probabilities of the distance of the MN from the center cell increasing or decreasing, respectively. They are given as follows:

$$\alpha_{r,r+1} = \begin{cases} (1-q) & \text{if } r = 0 \\ (1-q)p^+(r) & \text{if } 1 \leq r \leq R \end{cases} \tag{3}$$

$$\beta_{r,r-1} = (1-q)p^-(r) \quad \text{if } 1 \leq r \leq R \tag{4}$$

where q is the probability that an MN remains in the current cell.

Let $P_{r,R}$ be the steady-state probability of state r within a MAP domain consisting of R range rings. As Eq.(3) and Eq.(4), $P_{r,R}$ can be expressed in terms of the steady state probability $P_{0,R}$ as follows:

$$P_{r,R} = P_{0,R} \prod_{i=0}^{r-1} \frac{\alpha_{i,i+1}}{\beta_{i+1,i}} \quad \text{for } 1 \leq r \leq R \tag{5}$$

With the requirement $\sum_{r=0}^{R} P_{r,R} = 1$, $P_{r,R}$ can be expressed by

$$P_{0,R} = \frac{1}{1 + \sum_{r=1}^{R} \prod_{i=0}^{r-1} \frac{\alpha_{i,i+1}}{\beta_{i+1,i}}} \tag{6}$$

where $\alpha_{r,r+1}$ and $\beta_{r,r-1}$ are obtained from Eq.(3) and Eq.(4).

4.2 Cost Functions

In order to analyze the performance of HMIPv6 [2] and proposed mechanism, the total cost, consisting of security association(SA) establishment cost, location update cost and paging cost, should be considered. In normal HMIPv6, we divide the total cost into SA establishment cost, location update cost and packet delivery cost. In proposed mechanism, we divide total cost into new SA establishment cost, location update and packet delivery cost. C_{SA}, C_{new-SA}, $C_{location}$ and C_{packet} denote new SA establishment cost, location update and packet delivery cost, respectively. Then, the total cost of HMIPv6 (C_{total}), the total cost of HMIPv6 without any security (C_{total_nosec}) and proposed mechanism ($C_{new-total}$) can be obtained as follows:

$$C_{total} = C_{SA} + C_{location} + C_{packet} \tag{7}$$

$$C_{new-total} = C_{new-SA} + C_{location} + C_{packet} \tag{8}$$

$$C_{total\_no\,sec} = C_{location} + C_{packet} \tag{9}$$

4.2.1 Location Update Cost

C_g and C_l denote the signaling costs in the global binding update, the global binding update of proposed mechanism and the local binding update, respectively. In the IP networks, the signaling cost is proportional to the distance of two network entities. C_g and C_l can be obtained from the below equations.

$$C_g = 2 \cdot (\kappa \cdot f + \tau \cdot (b+e)) + 2 \cdot N_{CN} \cdot (\kappa \cdot f + \tau \cdot (b+c)) \tag{10}$$
$$+ PC_{HA} + N_{CN} \cdot PC_{CN} + PC_{MAP}$$

$$C_l = 2 \cdot (\kappa \cdot f + \tau \cdot e) + PC_{MAP} \tag{11}$$

where τ and κ are the unit transmission costs in a wired and a wireless link, respectively. As Fig. 4, b, c, e and f are the hop distance between nodes. PC_{HA}, PC_{CN} and PC_{MAP} are the processing costs for binding update procedures at the HA, the CN and the MAP, respectively. N_{CN} denotes the number of CNs that is communicating with the MN.

In terms of the random walk mobility model, the probability that an MN performs a global binding update is $p_{RR} \cdot \alpha_{r,H}$. Specifically, if an MN is located in range ring R, then the boundary ring of a MAP domain composed of R range rings and performs a movement from range ring R to range ring R + 1. The MN then performs the global binding update procedure. In other cases, except this movement, the MN only performs a local binding update procedure. Hence, the location update cost of normal and proposed mechanism per unit time can be expressed as follows:

$$C_{location} = \frac{p_{RR} \cdot \alpha_{R,R+1} \cdot C_g + (1 - p_{RR} \cdot \alpha_{R,R+1}) \cdot C_l}{T} \tag{12}$$

where T is the average cell residence time.

4.2.2 Packet Delivery Cost

The packet delivery cost, C_{packet}, in HMIPv6 can then be calculated as follows:

$$C_{packet} = C_{MAP} + C_{HA} + C_{CN-MN} \tag{13}$$

In Eq.(13), C_{MAP} and C_{HA} denote the processing costs for packet delivery at the MAP and the HA, respectively. C_{CN-MN} denotes the packet transmission cost from the CN to the MN.

In HMIPv6, a MAP maintains a mapping table for translation between RCoA and LCoA. The mapping table is similar to that of the HA and it is used to track the current locations (LCoA) of the MNs. All packets directed to the MN will be received by the MAP and tunneled to the MN's LCoA using the mapping table. Therefore, the lookup time required for the mapping table also needs to be considered. Specifically, when a packet arrives at the MAP, the MAP selects the current LCoA of the destination MN from the mapping table and the packet is then routed to the MN. Therefore, the processing cost at the MAP is divided into the lookup cost (C_{lookup}) and the routing cost ($C_{routing}$). The lookup cost is proportional to the size of the mapping table. The size of the mapping table is proportional to the number of MNs located in the coverage of a MAP domain [4]. On the other hand, the routing cost is proportional to the logarithm of the number of ARs belonging to a particular MAP domain [4]. Therefore, the processing cost at the MAP can be expressed as Eq.(15). In Eq.(15), λs denotes the session arrival rate and S denotes the average session size in the unit of packet. α and β are the weighting factors.

Let N_{MN} be the total number of users located in a MAP domain. In this paper, we assume that the average number of users located in the coverage of an AR is K. Therefore, the total number of users can be obtained as follows:

$$N_{MN} = N_{AR} \times K \tag{14}$$

$$
\begin{aligned}
C_{MAP} &= \lambda_s \cdot S \cdot (C_{lookup} + C_{routing}) \\
&= \lambda_s \cdot S \cdot (\alpha N_{MN} + \beta \log(N_{AR}))
\end{aligned} \tag{15}
$$

In MIPv6, using the route optimization, only the first packet of a session transmits the HA. Subsequently, all successive packets of the session are directly routed to the MN. The processing cost at the HA can be calculated as follows:

$$C_{HA} = \lambda_s \cdot \theta_{HA} \tag{16}$$

where θ_{HA} refers to a unit packet processing cost at the HA.

Since HMIPv6 supports the route optimization, the transmission cost in HMIPv6 can be obtained using Eq.(17). As mentioned before, τ and κ denote the unit transmission costs in a wired and a wireless link, respectively.

$$C_{CN-MN} = \tau \cdot \lambda_s \cdot ((S-1) \cdot (c+e) + (a+b+e)) + \kappa \cdot \lambda_s \cdot S \tag{17}$$

4.2.3 SA Establishment Cost

In Fig.2, general MIPv6 system operates IKE procedure before Local BU. IKE procedure consists of two phases. Thus, SA establishment cost of general MIPv6, C_{SA}, can be calculated as follows:

$$C_{SA} = \frac{p_{R,R} \cdot \alpha_{R,R+1} \cdot C_{SA\_g} + (1 - p_{R,R} \cdot \alpha_{R,R+1}) \cdot C_{SA\_l}}{T} \tag{18}$$

C_{SA_g} denotes SA establishment cost of Inter-MAP movement and C_{SA_l} denotes SA establishment cost of Intra-MAP movement. C_{SA_g} and C_{SA_l} can be calculated as follows:

$$C_{SA\_g} = 3 \cdot 2 \cdot (\kappa \cdot f + \tau \cdot e) + 7 \cdot PC_{SA} + (2 \cdot (\kappa \cdot f + \tau \cdot e) + (\kappa \cdot f + \tau \cdot e)) + 3 \cdot PC_{SA} \tag{19}$$
$$= 9 \cdot (\kappa \cdot f + \tau \cdot e) + 10 \cdot PC_{SA}$$

$$C_{SA\_l} = 2 \cdot (\kappa \cdot f + \tau \cdot e) + (\kappa \cdot f + \tau \cdot e) + 3 \cdot PC_{SA} \tag{20}$$
$$= 3 \cdot (\kappa \cdot f + \tau \cdot e) + 3 \cdot PC_{SA}$$

In Fig. 4, e and f are the hop distance between nodes. PC_{SA} are the processing costs for security parameters calculation.

In proposed mechanism, as Fig.3, an additional message for SA establishment is only one pair between MAP and HA. Local BU for confirmation message does not influent proposed system to perform handoff. Therefore, C_{new_SA} and $C_{new\_SA\_g}$ can be obtained as follows:

$$C_{new\_SA} = \frac{p_{R,R} \cdot \alpha_{R,R+1} \cdot C_{new\_SA\_g}}{T} \tag{21}$$

$$C_{SA\_g} = 2 \cdot (\kappa \cdot b) + 2 \cdot PC_{SA} \tag{22}$$

Is Fig. 4, b is the hop distance between nodes. PC_{SA} are the processing costs for calculating security parameters.

5 Numerical Results

This section presents performance analysis of proposed mechanism as compared with general HMIPv6 and HMIPv6 without security. The parameter values for the analysis were referenced from [4], [6] and [7]. They are shown in Table 1.

Table 1. Numerical simulation parameter for performance analysis

parameter	α	β	γ	θ_{HA}	τ	κ	a	b	c
value	0.1	0.2	0.05	20	1	2	6	6	4
parameter	d	e	f	N_{CN}	PC_{HA}	PC_{MAP}	PC_{CN}	PC_{SA}	
Value	1	2	1	2	24	12	6	24	

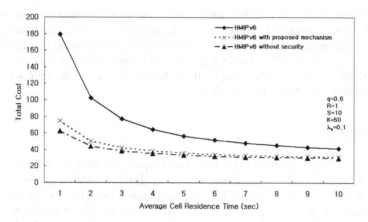

Fig. 6. Total cost as a function of average cell residence time (T) of MN

Fig.6 shows the variation in the total cost as the average cell residence time is changed in the random-walk model. The total cost becomes less as the average cell residence time increases. This must be true because an MN becomes static by residing in a cell longer, the frequency of location update to HA become reduced. To compare with HMIPv6, proposed mechanism reduces the total cost by from 58% to 25% approximately. To compare with HMIPv6 without security, our proposed mechanism just gains the total cost by from 4% to 20% approximately.

In HMIPv6, the MAP needs to lookup the destination MN on mapping table and to calculate security parameters. The cost for this lookup and calculating procedure depends on the number of MNs in a MAP domain. Therefore, the packet delivery cost increases as the number of MN in the MAP domain increases. In Eq.(14), the number of MN is $N_{AR} \times K$.

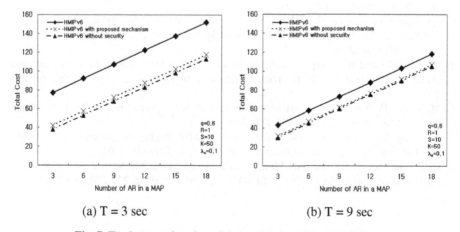

(a) T = 3 sec   (b) T = 9 sec

Fig. 7. Total cost as function of the number of AR in a MAP domain

Fig. 7 shows the impact of the number of AR per a MAP domain on the total cost in a random-walk model. As shown in Fig. 7, the total cost increases linearly as the number of AR increases. To compare with HMIPv6, our proposed mechanism reduces the total cost by 32% (T=3sec) and 16% (T=9sec) approximately. To compare with HMIPv6 without security, proposed mechanism just gains the total cost by 6% (T=3sec) and 2% (T=9sec) approximately.

6 Conclusions

HMIPv6 has been proposed to accommodate frequent mobility of the MNs and reduce the signaling load in the Internet. However, HMIPv6 focused on the intra-MAP domain handoff, not on the inter-MAP domain handoff [4]. The absence of any protections between MN and MAP may lead to malicious MNs impersonating other legitimate ones, impersonating a MAP. In this paper, we propose mechanism of authenticating MAP in HMIPv6. The performance analysis and the numerical results presented in this paper shows that our proposal has nearly same performance of the HMIPv6 without security in spite of security process load. To compare with HMIPv6, our proposed mechanism reduces the total cost by 32% (T=3sec) and 16% (T=9sec) approximately. To compare with HMIPv6 without security, proposed mechanism just gains the total cost by 6% (T=3sec) and 2% (T=9sec) approximately.

References

1. D. B. Johnson and C. E. Perkins, "Mobility support in IPv6," IETF RFC 3775, June, 2004.
2. Hsham Soliman, Claude Castelluccia, Karim El-Malki and Ludovic Bellier, "Hierarchical MIPv6 mobility management," IETF Internet draft, draft-ietf-mipshop-hmipv6-04.txt (work in progress), Dec. 2004.
3. IETF MIPv6 Signaling and Handoff Optimization (mipshop) WG: http://www.ietf.org/html.charters/mipshop-charter.html
4. Sangheon Pack and Yanghee Choi, "A study on performance of hierarchical mobile IPv6 in IP-based cellular networks," IEICE Transactions on Communications, vol. E87-B no. 3 pp.462-469, Mar. 2004.
5. I.F. Akyildiz and W. Wang, "A dynamic location management scheme for next-generation multitier PCS systems," IEEE Trans. Wireless Commun., vol.1, no.1, pp.178–189, Jan. 2002.
6. M. Woo, "Performance analysis of mobile IP regional registration," IEICE Trans. Commun., vol.E86-B, no.2, pp.472–478, Feb. 2003.
7. X. Zhang, J.G. Castellanos, and A.T. Capbell, "P-MIP: Paging extensions for mobile IP," ACM Mobile Networks and Applications, vol.7, no.2, pp.127–141, 2002.
8. Jonghyoun choi and Youngsong Mun, "An Efficient Handoff Mechanism with Web Proxy MAP in Hierarchical Mobile IPv6," ICCSA2005, LNCS 3480, pp. 271-280, May 2005.

Reducing Binding Updates in High Speed Movement Environment Based on HMIPv6

Dae Won Lee [1], Kwang Sik Jung [2,*], Sung-Ju Roh [3],
KwangHee Choi [3], and Heon Chang Yu [1]

[1]Dept. of Computer Science Education, Korea Univ.,
1, 5-ka, Anam-dong Sungbuk-gu, Seoul, Korea
{daelee, yuhc}@comedu.korea.ac.kr
[2]Dept. of Computer Science, Korea National Open Univ., Seoul, Korea
kchung0825@knou.ac.kr
[3]Dept. of Computer Science and Engineering, Korea Univ., Seoul, Korea
{loadroh, khee}@korea.ac.kr

Abstract. In this paper, we propose a new mobile host protocol that is opti-mized to provide access to a Mobile IP enabled internet in support of fast mov-ing wireless hosts. Actually, for fast moving wireless hosts, we need certain environment for seamless mobile computing that internet mobile users have to sit down or put laptop computer on some place, and so on. It could be using ve-hicles: automobile, train, subway, train express (TGV), etc. To address this, we define high speed movement environment. Then, we make up high speed movement environment to virtual organization (VO). Finally, we propose opti-mized hierarchical protocol in high speed movement environment that classifies global mobility into VO mobility (within a VO) and global mobility manage-ment. Handoffs in VO are locally managed and transparent to corresponding host (CH) while global mobility is managed with Mobile IPv6. Our proposed protocol improves handoff performance and significantly reduces signaling overhead for fast moving wireless hosts.

1 Introduction

By improved internet technique, wireless internet users are rapidly increased mobile IPv6. Mobile IPv6 (MIPv6) is designed to manage mobile nodes' movements be-tween wireless IPv6 networks by IETF. Using MIPv6, nodes are possible to access wireless IPv6 networks without changing their IP address. However, if mobile host (MH) moves frequently, MIPv6 results in high handoff latency and high signaling costs to update the MH's location [1]. Thus, many mobility management protocols [2, 3, 4, 5, 6] have been proposed to improve handoff performance and reduce signaling overhead. Conventional protocols [2, 3, 4, 5, 6] separate local mobility (within do-main) from global mobility (across domain) management. However, these protocols have no consideration about moving pattern within reality. Actually, laptop users access wireless internet in some fixed place such as home, school, library, etc. But pedestrians with PDA couldn't keep up using wireless internet. Usually, they stop walking to access wireless internet, and then walk again. It is just using wireless

---

* Corresponding author.

Y.-C. Chung and J.E. Moreira (Eds.): GPC 2006, LNCS 3947, pp. 587–596, 2006.
© Springer-Verlag Berlin Heidelberg 2006

internet, not moving with using wireless internet. The case of moving with wireless internet is a movement through vehicles such as automobile, train, subway, high speed train (eg. TGV). Using vehicle, it provides certain place to sit down or put laptop computer on.

In this paper, we define high speed movement environment based on two factors: user group movement and fixed movement path. Then, we propose virtual organization (VO). A high speed movement environment is organized by VOs that consist of domains. By VO, we separate VO mobility (within VO) from global mobility management. The VO is connected to the rest of internet via one or several interconnection domains that we call virtual mobility anchor point (VMAP). We design hierarchical architecture and protocol that minimizes signaling overhead by continual binding update (BU). Also we show our proposed protocol improves handoff performance and reduces packet loss by handoff latency.

This paper is organized as follows: section 2 reviews the MIPv6 protocol and HMIPv6 protocol. Section 3 explains hierarchical architecture of high speed movement environment. Section 4 describes our proposed protocol. And then section 5 shows comparison between HMIPv6 and proposed protocol. Finally, section 6 concludes this paper.

2 Related Works

The Mobile IPv6 protocol is specified by the IETF IP Routing for wireless/mobile hosts working group [1]. When an MH moves from one domain to another, it gets new care-of-address (CoA). Then, it registers its binding update (BU) with its home agent (HA) and corresponding hosts (CHs). BU is a mapping between MH's home address and MH's CoA. And HA records BU in its Binding Cache. If any packets address to the MH, HA intercepts and tunnels them to MH's CoA using IPv6 encapsulation. If CH receives BU, CH can send packets directly to MH's CoA. MIPv6 suffers from several well known weaknesses such as handoff latency or signaling overhead, that have led to macro/micro mobility, FastMIPv6, and BETH [2, 3, 4, 5, 6]. Thus, many mobility management protocols [2, 3, 4, 5, 6] have been proposed to improve handoff performance and reduce signaling overhead.

HMIPv6 presents an n-level hierarchical mobility management architecture for IPv6. HMIPv6 defines a domain as the highest level of hierarchical architecture. A domain is an arbitrary structure, as ISP network, campus network, or a single LAN. A domain is connected to the rest of internet via one or several interconnection routers that is called mobility anchor point (MAP). [2] separates local mobility (within domain) from global mobility (across domain) management. Using n-level hierarchical architecture, HMIPv6 improves handoff performance that becomes reducing packet loss and signaling overhead. It doesn't fix anything on router and it is flexible and scalable [2].

Actually, we can see wireless internet user who is moving by train. But [2] has no consideration about moving pattern within reality. If we assume that train moves at 60km/h, an MH moves rapidly across many domains that are the highest hierarchy in HMIPv6 architecture. It causes macro handoff continuously. HMIPv6 has better performance than MIPv6, but it can't tolerate this condition. Therefore, our research need to study high speed movement by vehicles such as automobile, train, subway or train express (TGV).

3 Design of Hierarchical Structure in High Speed Movement Environment

Within reality, laptop users access wireless internet at some fixed place such as home, school, library, etc. And, in case of PDA and cellular phone, pedestrians couldn't keep up using wireless internet. Usually, they stop walking to access wireless internet and then resume walking again. It just means usage of wireless internet and doesn't move with usage of wireless internet.

But easily we can see users who use wireless internet in automobile, train, subway, high speed train (eg. TGV). Using wireless internet within reality, we need certain environment for seamless mobile computing that internet mobile users have to sit down or put laptop computer on some place, and so on. It could be using vehicles: automobile, train, subway, high speed train (eg. TGV), etc. Previous MIP protocols [2, 3, 4, 5, 6] don't consider high speed movement such as automobile, train, subway, train express (TGV). There are two factors about moving with vehicle. They are static route and group movement that are occurred in high speed movement environment. In this paper, we define high speed movement environment as follows:

Definition 1. *High Speed Movement Environment*
High speed movement environment has group movement on a fixed route. It is a movement by vehicles such as automobile, train, subway, high speed train, etc. Thus, the high speed movement environment is wireless computing environment in which vehicles move on a fixed route.   ■

The high speed movement environment has a fixed route and it is physically connected. But from the point of network view, it is moving fast from a domain to another domain. Conventional mobility management protocols [2, 3, 4, 5, 6] are proposed to improve handoff performance and to reduce signaling overhead for pedestrians. Thus they can not be adopted into high speed movement environment.

In this paper, we construct virtual organization (VO) that consists of domains. We organize physically distributed domains into one logical VO. Therefore, an MH that is moving within VO, is in physical domain i, but it is logically in VO.

[2] defines a domain as the highest level of hierarchical architecture. It separates local mobility (within domain) from global mobility (across domain) management. Local mobility does not require binding update signaling to HA. It is managed by mobility anchor point (MAP), and minimizes handoff delay. Global mobility requires binding update signaling to HA as MIPv6.

In this paper, we separate VO mobility (within VO) from global mobility management using VO. And we define a VO as the logical highest level of hierarchical architecture. VO mobility doesn't require binding update signaling to HA. It is managed by VMAP, and minimizes handoff delay on high speed movement environment. Global mobility requires binding update signaling to HA as HMIPv6. We extend [2]'s hierarchical architecture and propose VMAP (virtual mobility anchor point) for extending hierarchical architecture. A VMAP is a set of MAPs that makes VO, and also it is logically on MAP. Fig. 1 is an example of hierarchical architecture of VO.

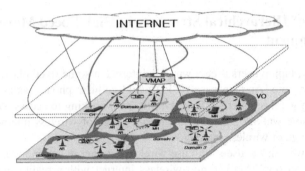

Fig. 1. Example of hierarchical architecture of VO

4 Design of Hierarchical Protocol in High Speed Movement Environment

4.1 Overview

In this paper, we separates VO mobility (within VO) from global mobility (across domain) management. VO consists of domains in high speed movement environment. And VO is connected to rests of internet via one or several interconnection domains that we call virtual mobility anchor point (VMAP). The main operations of the proposed protocol are the following:

● **Global mobility:** When an MH enters into a new domain, it gets two CoAs: LCoA which is a CoA on the link and a GCoA which is a CoA in domain. If visited domain is in VO, it gets one more CoA: a virtual care-of-address (VCoA) which is a CoA in VO. Then, the MH sends the following BUs:

In general
• a BU that specifies the binding between its GCoA and its LCoA to the domain MAP. If the request is accepted, an acknowledgement is sent back to the MH. • a BU that specifies the binding between its *home address* and its GCoA to its HA and each of its external CHs that are outside the domain. • a BU that specifies that binding between its *home address* and its LCoA to each of its local CHs that are within the domain.
In VO
• a BU that specifies the binding between its GCoA and its LCoA to the domain MAP. If the request is accepted, an acknowledgement is sent back to the MH. • a BU that specifies the binding between its VCoA and its GCoA to the VMAP. • a BU that specifies the binding between its *home address* and its VCoA to its HA and each of its external CHs that are outside the VO. • a BU that specifies that binding between its *home address* and its GCoA to each of its local CHs that are within the VO.

As a result, send/receive operation is as follows:

In general
• An external CH that sends packets to the MH, uses its GCoA. Packets are intercepted by MAP and forwarded to the current LCoA of the MH.

• A local CH that sends packets to the MH, uses its LCoA. Packets are directly delivered to the MH.
In VO
• An external CH that sends packets to the MH, uses its VCoA. Packets are intercepted by VMAP and forwarded to the current GCoA of the MH. And packets are intercepted by MAP and forwarded to the current LCoA of the MH. • A CH that sends packets to the MH, uses its GCoA. Packets are intercepted by MAP and forwarded to the current LCoA of the MH. • A local CH that sends packets to the MH, uses its LCoA. Packets are directly delivered to the MH.

● **VO mobility:** When an MH moves within the VO, it gets new GCoA on its new domain. The VCoA remains constantly as long as the MH is roaming locally. Then, the MH sends the following BUs:

In VO [proposed]
• a BU that specifies the binding between its VCoA and its new GCoA to the VMAP. • a BU that specifies that binding between its *home address* and its GCoA to each of its local CHs that are within the VO. An external CH that sends packets to the MH, uses its GCoA. Packets are intercepted by MAP and forwarded to the current LCoA of the MH.

4.2 Extended Protocol

4.2.1 Registration Phase
An MH gets several CoAs (LCoA, GCoA, VCoA) and registers each of them with VMAP, MAP, HA, CH. This registration phase differs in VO mobility and global mobility.

● **VO mobility:** When an MH moves within the VO, the MH must find the lowest domain and find a domain MAP. The MH performs the following operations.

VO mobility
•It gets a new GCoA in each domain from $domain_1$ to $domain_N$, •It gets a new LCoA on the link, •It registers the (VCoA, GCoA) binding with VMAP, •It registers the (GCoA, LCoA) binding with MAP, •It registers the (*home address*, GCoA) binding with its CH in VO.

An MH can move anywhere in VO. The packet is delivered to a VMAP that is the highest hierarchy, and it is directly forwarded to the MH.

● **Global mobility:** When an MH moves globally, the MH performs the following operations.

Global mobility
• It gets a new GCoA in each domain from $domain_1$ to $domain_N$, • It gets a new LCoA, • It gets a VCoA, if it enters by VO, • It registers the $(GCoA_1, GCoA_N)$ binding with MAP for i going from 1 to N, • It registers the $(VCoA, GCoA_N)$ binding with MAP, • It registers the $(GCoA_N, LCoA)$ binding with MAP, • It registers the (*home address*, $GCoA_N$) binding with its CH in VO, • It registers the (*home address*, VCoA) binding with its external CH and HA.

BUs are only sent outside the domain (HA and external CH), when an MH moves from one domain to another. Therefore, our protocol using VMAP reduces signaling overhead on global mobility.

4.2.2 Virtual Organization and Virtual Mobility Anchor Point Discovery

To perform the registration operation in section 4.2.1, an MH needs the following information: the prefix of the domain the depth of the hierarchy, the network prefix of MAP, the domain in VO or Not. This information is advertised by a new option that we extended in the router advertisement message of the IPv6 neighbor discovery [5]. Fig. 2 shows an extended router advertisement message format.

ICMP Fields:

O   1-bit "Virtual Organization" flag. When set, MHs use to notice what the domain is in VO.

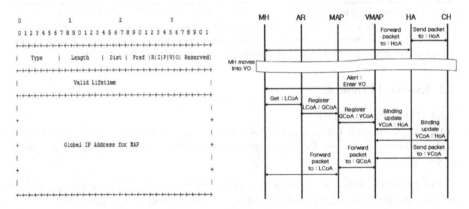

Fig. 2. Extended RA message format   **Fig. 3.** Call-flow of proposed protocol

4.2.3 Packet Delivery

When a CH sends packets to an MH, the CH uses its VCoA. VMAP intercepts packets and encapsulates packets to MH's GCoA. Then MAP intercepts packets and encapsulates packets to MH's LCoA. Then, packets are forwarded to the MH. When an MH sends packet, it sets the source field of IP header to its LCoA whether a CH is local, in VO, or external. And using home address option, it specifies its home address. Fig. 3 shows the call-flow of proposed protocol.

5   Comparison Between HMIPv6 and Proposed Protocol

In this section, we compare the MIP, HMIPv6 with our proposed protocol respect to the context described in previous section.

5.1   Handoff Comparison Parameters

We investigate the handoff management on the basic of the simple network in fig. 4 with respect to:

- *handoff management parameters:* the interaction with the radio layer, initiator of the handoff management mechanism, use of traffic bicasting, etc.,
- *handoff latency:* the time needed to complete the handoff inside the network,
- *potential packet losses:* the amount of lost packets due to the handoff process,
- *involved stations:* the amount of MA involved in the handoff management, i.e. that must update their routing data or process message in the handover mechanism.

For this comparison, we assume here that n_{gate} is an average number of hops between an MH and a gateway. The delay between these two hosts is t_{gate} *msec*. Similarly, n_{prev} is the number of hops between an MH and its domain (delay: t_{prev} *msec*). t_{cross} is the average delay between the MH and the so-called *crossover node* for a given handoff. This node is the first common network entity located in a path between the new domain and the old domain and in the path between the new domain and the gateway. For example, in a four levels hierarchy in Hierarchical Mobile IPv6, n_{gate} would be equal to four. In general, we can assume that $t_{gate} \geq t_{prev} \geq t_{cross}$. t_{HA} is the average time needed to reach the HA with the classical Mobile IP registration mechanism.

When investigating performance of handoff mechanisms in micro mobility, we must consider the important point of movement detection. We have already seen that the micro mobility approach reduces the registration latency as most of the registrations are limited inside the current domain. Moreover, proposed protocol reduces the registration latency since most of the registrations are limited to VMAP. However, detection of the occurrence of a handoff is another important source of delay for real time application. And, the IP handover management mechanism is useless, if the movements of the MH are detected too late and packets are already lost. In Mobile IP, the movement detection is made via two algorithms described in [1]. These algorithms are based on the ICMP router discovery messages. Handoff is detected when receiving a Mobility Agent Advertisement with a source address located in another network or when the lifetime expires for the last Mobility Agent Advertisement received. With the first algorithm, generally the detection occurs after the time between two Agent Advertisements. With the second algorithm, it occurs after the lifetime of the Agent Advertisement. The values of these parameters must be tuned to be adapted

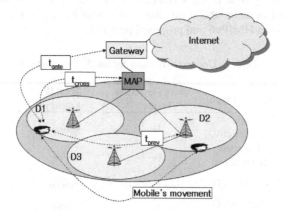

Fig. 4. Simple model to compare handoff mechanisms

to the local network (their default values are 30 min. for the lifetime and 7-10 min. for the rate of Agent Advertisement [7]). We will call this latency t_{mip}.

5.2 Handoff Comparison

Hierarchical Mobile IPv6 handoff mechanisms are designed to limit the handoff management at a "local" level while an MH remains in the same hierarchy. When changing of domain, the MH must issue a registration request. This registration request must only reach the first MAP with an existing binding for this MH. This MAP is obviously the crossover node and the time to reach it is thus $t_{MH-MAP}(t_{cross})$. When receiving a regional registration request for an MH for which it already has an entry in its visitor's list, the crossover node must send a binding update with a zero lifetime to the previous address of this MH to remove the old route: this is called deregistration. As t_{MH-MAP} is the average time to reach the crossover, the total time to reach the crossover node and to remove the old route is $2t_{MH-MAP}$. When changing of hierarchy, the MH must perform a classical Mobile IP registration with its HA, the latency is thus $2t_{HA}$. The uncertainty time is $t_{mip} + t_{MH-MAP}$ in the first case. In the case of a registration with the home agent, it is more difficult to evaluate this time interval. Indeed, Hierarchical Mobile IPv6 allows to use the soft handoff mechanisms to ensure that the losses occur only during the time needed to reach the previous AP. If we assume a handoff between two hierarchies belonging to the same domain, the uncertainty time is $t_{mip} + t_{prev}$.

Proposed protocol tries to reduce the handoff latency by using VO to detect the mobile movements. And our handoff mechanisms are designed to extend handoff management at "local" level while the MH remains in VO. When changing of domains in VO, the MH must issue a registration request. This registration requests must only reach the VMAP with an existing binding for the MH. This VMAP is obviously the crossover node and the time to reach it is thus $t_{MH-VMAP}(t_{cross})$. When receiving a regional registration request for an MH for which it already has an entry in its visitor's list. As $t_{MH-VMAP}$ is the average time to reach the VMAP, the total time to reach the VMAP and to remove the old route is $2t_{MH-VMAP}$. When an MH moves out VO, the MH must perform a classical Mobile IP registration with its HA, the latency is thus $2t_{HA}$. The uncertainty time is $t_{mip} + t_{MH-VMAP}$ in the first case. If we assume a handoff between VO and domain, the uncertainty time will be $t_{mip} + t_{prev}$. Table 1 shows comparison between HMIPv6 and proposed protocol.

Table 1. Comparative chart for handoff parameters

Protocol	Handoff type	Move Detection Latency	Total IP Latency	Uncertainty Time
Hierarchical Mobile IPv6	Inside a hierarchy	t_{mip}	$2t_{MH-MAP}$	$t_{mip} + t_{MH-MAP}$
	Between hierarchies	t_{mip}	$2t_{HA}$	$t_{mip} + t_{prev}$
Proposed Protocol	Inside a VO	$t_{mip} + t_{VMAP}$	$2t_{MH-VMAP}$	$t_{mip} + t_{VMAP} + t_{MH-VMAP}$
	Outside VO	t_{mip}	$2t_{HA}$	$t_{mip} + t_{prev}$

Table 2. Comparative chart for high speed movement in VO (n domains)

Protocol	Handoff type	Move in VO Latency	Total IP Latency	Uncertainty Time
Hierarchical Mobile IPv6	Between hierarchies	t_{mip}	$2t_{HA} \times n$	$(t_{mip} + t_{prev}) \times n$
Proposed Protocol	Inside a VO	$t_{mip} + t_{VMAP}$	$2t_{MH\text{-}VMAP} \times n$	$(t_{mip} + t_{VMAP} + t_{MH\text{-}VMAP}) \times n$

Table 3. Performance analysis parameter

t_{mip}	t_{HA}	$t_{MH\text{-}VMAP}$	t_{VMAP}
15	40	20	02-10

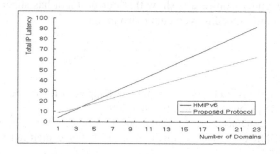

Fig. 5. Effect of Domains in VO on Total IP Latency

For comparison between HMIPv6 and proposed protocol, we assume that an MH moves fast within VO that consists of n domains. If the MH moves in VO, the proposed protocol doesn't require any registration to HA/CN. Table 2 shows each parameter for high speed movement environment. For performance comparison, we demonstrate some numerical results. Table 3 shows parameters used in our performance analysis [9].

As shown in fig. 5, the total IP latency for HMIPv6 increases as the number of domains in VO increases. For small number of domains in VO, the performance of the HMIPv6 is better than that of the proposed protocol. These results are expected since proposed protocol reduces BU to HA when fast movement occurs among domains. Based on the above analysis, our proposed protocol tried to reduce the number of BUs using VO. Therefore, proposed protocol has better performance than HMIPv6 when fast movement and group movement occur among domains in high speed movement environment. We conclude that proposed protocol achieves performance improvements by eliminating unnecessary BU to HA when MHs move within VO.

6 Conclusion

This paper proposes a new mobile host protocol that is optimized to provide access to a Mobile IP enabled internet in support of high speed mobile hosts. Actually (With reality), for fast moving wireless hosts, we need certain environment for seamless mobile computing that internet mobile users have to sit down or put laptop computer on some place, and so on. It could be using vehicles: automobile, train, subway, train express (TGV), etc. To address this, we define high speed movement environment. Then, we make up high speed movement environment to Virtual Organization (VO) to separate global mobility into VO mobility (within a VO) and global mobility management. By global mobility, we proposed improved hierarchical protocol in high speed movement environment. Proposed protocol has two advantages. First, it improves handoff performance, since VO handoffs are performed locally. This increases the handoff speed and minimizes packet loss during transition. Second, it reduces the signaling overhead from BU on internet since the signaling messages corresponding to local mobility do not cross the whole internet. It means that HA/CH doesn't know that the MH moves or not. From the point of HA/CH view, the MH stays in VO. To construct VO, Also, it does not require any modification to the router, therefore it is easy to exploit. Comparison results show that our protocol has superior performance to the HMIPv6 in high speed movement environment.

References

1. D. Johnson, C. Perkins, and J. Arkko, "Mobility Support in IPv6", Internet draft (work in progress), draft-ietf-mobileip-ipv6-24.txt, June 2003.
2. H. Soliman, C. Castelluccia, K. E. Malki, and L. Bellier, "Hierarchical MIPv6 mobility management (HMIPv6)", Internet Engineering Task Force draft-ietf-mobileip-HMIPv6-04.txt, July 2001.
3. R. Ramjee, T. La Porta, S. Thuel, K. Varadhan, L. Salgarelli, "HAWAII: a domain-based approach for supporting mobility in wide-area wireless networks", IEEE/ACM Trans. Networking, vol. 10, pp. 396-410, June 2002.
4. A. T. Campbell, J. Gomez, S. Kim, Z. Turanyi, C-Y. Wan, A. Valko, "Cellular IP", Internet Engineering Task Force, draft-ietf-mobileip -cellularip-00.txt, January 2000.
5. C. Williams, "Localized Mobility Management Requireme-nts', Internet Engineering Task Force draft-ietf-mobileip-lmm-requirements-04.txt, October 2003.
6. J. Kempf, "Leveraging Fast Handover Protocols to Support Localized Mobility Management in Mobile IP", Internet Engineering Task Force draft-kempf- mobileip-fastho -lmm-00.txt, June 2003.
7. Narten, T., Nordmark, E., and Simpson, W., "Neighbor Discovery for IP Version6. (IPv6)", RFC 2461, December 1998.
8. R. Chakravorty and I. Pratt. "Performance issues with general packet radio service", Journal of Communications and Networks, 4(2), December 2002.
9. Jiang Xie, Akyildiz, I.F. "A novel distributed dynamic location management scheme for minimizing signaling costs in Mobile IP", IEEE Transactions on Mobile Computing, (3), pp. 163-175, 2002.

A Low-Overhead Non-block Checkpointing Algorithm for Mobile Computing Environment

Bidyut Gupta, Shahram Rahimi, Rishad A. Rias, and Guru. Bangalore

Computer Science Department, Southern Illinois University,
Milcode 4511, Carbondale, IL 62901-4511, USA
{bidyut, Rahimi, rrias, gbangal}@cs.siu.edu

Abstract. In this paper, we have proposed a new approach toward designing a low-overhead non-blocking single phase synchronous checkpointing algorithm suitable for distributed mobile computing environment. The algorithm produces a reduced number of checkpoints. To achieve this reduction in the number of the checkpoints we have used very simple data structure. Each process independently takes its decision whether to take a checkpoint or not. It makes the algorithm simple, fast, and efficient. The algorithm has been shown to be suitable for distributed mobile computing environment.

1 Introduction

Checkpointing / rollback-recovery strategy has been an attractive approach for providing fault-tolerance to distributed applications [1]-[6]. A checkpoint is a snapshot of the local state of a process, saved on local nonvolatile storage to survive process failures. A global checkpoint of an n-process distributed system consists of n checkpoints (local) such that each of these n checkpoints corresponds uniquely to one of the n processes. A global checkpoint M is defined as a consistent global checkpoint if no message is sent after a checkpoint of M and received before another checkpoint of M [1]. The checkpoints belonging to a consistent global checkpoint are called globally consistent checkpoints (GCCs).

There are two fundamental approaches for checkpointing and recovery. One is the asynchronous approach and the other one is the synchronous approach [2]. In the asynchronous approach, processes take their checkpoints independently. So, taking checkpoints is very simple as there is no coordination needed among the processes while taking the checkpoints. After a failure occurs, a procedure for rollback-recovery attempts to build a consistent global checkpoint [2]. However, in this approach because of the absence of any coordination among the processes there may not exist a recent consistent global checkpoint which may cause a rollback of the computation. This is known as domino effect. In the worst case of the domino effect, after the system recovers from a failure all processes may have to rollback to their respective initial states to restart their computation again.

Synchronous checkpointing approach assumes that a single process other than the application processes invokes the checkpointing algorithm periodically to determine a consistent global checkpoint. This process is known as initiator process. It asks

Y.-C. Chung and J.E. Moreira (Eds.): GPC 2006, LNCS 3947, pp. 597–608, 2006.
© Springer-Verlag Berlin Heidelberg 2006

periodically all application processes to take checkpoints in a coordinated way. The coordination is done in a way so that the checkpoints taken by the application processes always form a consistent global checkpoint of the system. This coordination is actually achieved through the exchange of additional (control) messages. It causes some delay (known as synchronization delay) during normal operation. This is the main drawback of this method. However, the main advantage is that the set of the checkpoints taken periodically by the different processes always represents a consistent global checkpoint. So, after the system recovers from a failure, each process knows where to rollback for restarting its computation again. In fact, the restarting state will always be the most recent consistent global checkpoint. Therefore, recovery is very simple. On the other hand, if failures rarely occur between successive checkpoints, then the synchronous approach places unnecessary burden on the system in the form of additional messages and delay. Hence, compared to the asynchronous approach, taking checkpoints is more complex while recovery is much simpler. Observe that synchronous approach is free from any domino effect.

In this work, we have presented a non-blocking synchronous checkpointing algorithm to determine the GCCs. In this approach, application processes are not suspended during checkpointing. There exist some efficient non blocking algorithms [7]-[9]; however they require significant number of control (system) messages to determine a consistent global checkpoint of the system. In the present work, the proposed non-blocking algorithm does not require that all processes take their checkpoints; rather only those processes that have sent some message(s) after their last checkpoints will take checkpoints during checkpointing. In [7], the authors have proposed a very efficient non-blocking coordinated checkpointing scheme that offers minimum number of checkpoints. We have shown in this paper that our algorithm outperforms the one in [7] mainly from the viewpoint of using much less number of system (control) messages. It may be noted that the ideas of non-blocking checkpointing, reduction in the number of checkpoints to be taken, and using less number of system messages may offer significant advantage particularly in case of mobile computing, because it helps in the efficient use of the limited resources of mobile computing environment, viz. limited wireless bandwidth, and mobile hosts' limited battery power and memory.

This paper is organized as follows: in Sections 2 and 3 we have stated the system model and the necessary data structures respectively. In Section 4, using an example we have explained the main idea about when a process needs to take a checkpoint by using some very simple data structures. We have stated some simple observations necessary to design the algorithm. In Section 5 we have presented the non blocking checkpointing algorithm along with its performance and discussed its suitability for mobile computing systems. Section 6 draws the conclusion.

2   System Model

The distributed system has the following characteristics [3], [4], [10]:

1. Processes do not share memory and communicate via messages sent through channels.

2. Channels can lose messages. However, they are made virtually lossless and order of the messages is preserved by some end-to-end transmission protocol. Message sequence numbers may be used to preserve the order.

3. When a process fails, all other processes are notified of the failure in finite time. We also assume that no further processor (process) failures occur during the execution of the algorithm. In fact, the algorithm may be restarted if there are further failures.

4. Processes are piecewise deterministic in the sense that from the same state, if given the same inputs, a process executes the same sequence of instructions.

3 Data Structures

Let us consider a set of n processes, $\{P_0, P_1, \ldots, P_{n-1}\}$ involved in the execution of a distributed algorithm. Each process P_i maintains a Boolean flag c_i. The flag is initially set at zero. It is set at 1 only when process P_i sends its first application message after its latest checkpoint. It is reset to 0 again when process P_i takes a checkpoint. Flag c_i is stored in local RAM of the processor running process P_i. A message sent by P_i will be denoted as m_i.

As in the classical synchronous approach [2], we assume that an initiator process initiates the checkpointing algorithm. It helps the n processes to take their individual checkpoints synchronously, i.e. the checkpoints taken will be globally consistent checkpoints. We further assume that any process in the system can initiate the checkpointing algorithm. This can be done in a round-robin way among the processes. To implement it, each process P_i maintains a variable CLK_i initialized at 0. It also maintains a variable, $counter_i$ which is initially set to 0 and is incremented by 1 each time process P_i initiates the algorithm. In addition, process P_i maintains an integer variable N_i which is initially set at 0 and is incremented by 1 each time the algorithm is invoked. Note the difference between the variables $counter_i$ and N_i. A control (request) message M_c is broadcasted by a process initiating the checkpointing algorithm to the other (n-1) processes asking them to take checkpoints if necessary.

In the next section, we explain with an illustration the idea we have applied to reduce the number of checkpoints to be created in the non blocking synchronous checkpointing scheme proposed in the paper.

4 An Illustration

In synchronous checkpointing scheme, all involved processes take checkpoints periodically which are mutually consistent. However, in reality, not all the processes may need to take checkpoints to determine a set of the GCCs.

The main objective of this work is to design a simple scheme that helps the n processes to decide easily and independently whether to take a checkpoint when the checkpointing algorithm is invoked. If a process decides that it does not need to take a checkpoint, it can resume its computation immediately. This results in faster execution of the distributed algorithm. Below we illustrate with an example how a process decides whether to take a checkpoint or not.

Consider the following scenario of a distributed system of two processes P_i and P_j only. It is shown in Fig. 1. Assume that their initial checkpoints are C_i^0 and C_j^0 respectively. According to the synchronous approach, P_i and P_j have to take checkpoints periodically. Suppose that the time period is T. Before time T, P_i has sent an application message m_1 to P_j. Now at time T, an initiator process sends the message M_c asking both P_i and P_j to take their checkpoints, which must have to be consistent.

Process P_i checks its flag and finds that $c_i = 1$. Therefore P_i decides to take its checkpoint C_i^1. Thus because of the presence of C_i^1, message m_1 can never be an orphan. Also, at the same time P_j checks if its flag $c_j = 1$. Since it is not, therefore process P_j decides that it does not need to take any checkpoint. The reason is obvious. This illustrates the basic idea about how to reduce the number of checkpoints to be taken. Now we observe that checkpoints C_j^0 and C_i^1 are mutually consistent.

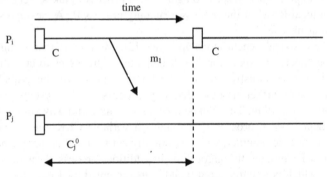

Fig. 1. C_i^1 and C_j^0 are mutually consistent

The above discussion shows the simplicity involved in taking a decision about whether to take a checkpoint or not. Note that the decision taken by a process P_j whether it needs to take a checkpoint is independent of the similar decision taken by the other process. It may be noted that keeping a copy of each of the flags c_i and c_j in the respective local RAMs of the processors running P_i and P_j can save some time as it is more time consuming to fetch them if they are stored in stable storage than to fetch them from the respective local RAMs.

Below, we state some simple but important observations used in the proposed algorithm.

Theorem 1: Consider a system of n processes. If $c_j = 1$, where C_j^k is the latest checkpoint of process P_j , then some message(s) sent by P_j to other processes may become orphan.

Proof: The flag c_j is reset to 0 at every checkpoint. It can have the value 1 only between two successive checkpoints of any process P_j if and only if process P_j sends at least one message m between the checkpoints. Therefore, $c_j = 1$ means that P_j is yet to take its next checkpoint following C_j^k. Therefore, the message (s) sent by P_j after its latest checkpoint C_j^k are not yet recorded. Now if some process P_m receives one or more of these messages sent by P_j and then takes its latest checkpoint before process P_j takes its next checkpoint C_j^{k+1}, then these received messages will become orphan. Hence the proof follows. ∎

Theorem 2: If at any given time t, $c_j = 0$ for process P_j with C_j^{k+1} being its latest checkpoint, then none of the messages sent by P_j remains an orphan at time t.

Proof: Flag c_j can have the value 1 between two successive checkpoints, say C_j^k and C_j^{k+1}, of a process P_j if and only if process P_j has sent at least one message m between these two checkpoints. It can also be 1 if P_j has sent at least a message after taking its latest checkpoint. It is reset to 0 at each checkpoint. On the other hand, it will have the value 0 either between two successive checkpoints, say C_j^k and C_j^{k+1}, if process P_j has not sent any message between these checkpoints, or P_j has not sent any message after its latest checkpoint. Therefore, $c_j = 0$ at time t means either of the following two: (i) $c_j = 0$ at C_j^{k+1} and this checkpoint has been taken at time t. It means that any message m sent by P_j (if any) to any other process P_m between C_j^k and C_j^{k+1} must have been recorded by the sending process P_j at the checkpoint C_j^{k+1}. So the message m can not be an orphan. (ii) $c_j = 0$ at time t and P_j has taken its latest checkpoint C_j^{k+1} before time t. It means that process P_j has not sent any message after its latest checkpoint C_j^{k+1} till time t. Hence at time t there does not exist any orphan message sent by P_j after its latest checkpoint.

5 Problems Associated with Non-blocking Approach

We explain first the problems associated with non-blocking approach. After that we will state a solution. The following discussion although considers only two processes, still the arguments given are valid for any number of processes. Consider a system of two processes P_i and P_j as shown in Fig. 2. Assume that the checkpointing algorithm has been initiated by process P_i and it has sent the request message M_c to P_j asking it to take a checkpoint if necessary. As pointed earlier that both processes will act independently, therefore P_i takes its checkpoint C_i^1 because its flag $c_i = 1$. Let us assume that P_i now immediately sends an application message m_i to P_j. Suppose at time $(T + \epsilon)$, where ϵ is very small with respect to T, P_j receives m_i. Still P_j has not received M_c from the initiator process. So, P_j processes the message. Now the request message M_c from P_i arrives at P_j. Process P_j finds that its $c_j = 1$. So it decides to take a checkpoint C_j^1. We find that message m_i has become an orphan due to the checkpoint C_j^1. Hence, C_i^1 and C_j^1 cannot be consistent.

5.1 Solution

To solve this problem, we propose that a process be allowed to send both piggybacked and non–piggybacked application messages. We explain the idea below.

Each process P_i maintains an integer variable N_i, initially set at 0 and is incremented by 1 each time process P_i receives the request message M_c from the initiator process. In the event that process P_i itself is the initiator, then also it increments N_i by 1 immediately after the initiation of the algorithm. That is, the variable N_i represents how many times the checkpointing algorithm has been executed including the current one (according to the knowledge of the process P_i). Note that at any given time t, for any two processes P_i and P_j, their corresponding variables N_i and N_j may not have the same values. It depends on which process has received the request message M_c first. However it is obvious that $| N_i - N_j |$ is either 0 or 1.

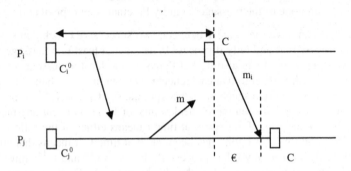

Fig. 2. C_i^1 and C_j^1 are not mutually consistent

Below we state the solution for a two process system. The idea used in this solution is similarly applicable for an n process system as well.

Consider a distributed system of two processes P_i and P_j only. Without any loss of generality assume that P_i initiates the algorithm by sending the message M_c to process P_j and it is the the kth execution of the algorithm, that is, $N_i = k$. We also assume that process P_i now has taken its decision whether to take a checkpoint or not, and then has taken appropriate action to implement its decision. Suppose P_i now wants to send an application message m_i for the first time to P_j after it has finished participating in the kth execution of the checkpointing algorithm. Observe that P_i has no idea whether P_j has received the message M_c corresponding to this k^{th} execution of the algorithm and has already implemented its checkpointing decision or not. To make sure that the message m_i can never be an orphan, P_i piggybacks m_i with the variable N_i. Process P_j receives the piggybacked message $<m_i , N_i >$ from P_i. We now explain below why the message m_i can never been an orphan. Note that $N_i = k$; i.e. it is the kth execution of the algorithm that process P_i has last been involved with. It means the following to the receiver P_j of this message:

(1) Process Pi has already received Mc from the initiator process for the kth execution of the algorithm,
(2) Pi has taken a decision whether to take a checkpoint or not and has taken appropriate action to implement its decision,
(3) Pi has resumed its normal operation and then has sent this piggybacked application message mi.
(4) The sending event of message m_i has not yet been recorded by P_i.

Since the message contains the variable N_i, process P_j compares N_i and N_j to determine if it has to wait to receive the request message M_c. Based on the results of the comparison process P_j takes one of the following three actions (so that no message received by it is an orphan), as stated below in the form of the following three observations:

Observation 1: If $N_i (= k) > N_j (= k-1)$, process P_j now knows that the kth execution of the checkpointing algorithm has already begun and so very soon it will also receive the message M_c from the initiator process associated with this execution. So instead of waiting for M_c to arrive, it decides if it needs to take a checkpoint and implements its decision, and then processes the message m_i. After a little while when it receives the message M_c it just ignores it. Therefore, message m_i can never be an orphan.

Observation 2: If $N_i = N_j = k$, like process P_i, process P_j also has received already the message M_c associated with the latest execution (k^{th}) of the checkpointing algorithm and has taken its checkpointing decision and has already implemented that decision. Therefore, process P_j now processes the message m_i. It ensures that message m_i can never be an orphan, because both the sending and the receiving events of message m_i have not been recorded by the sender P_i and the receiver P_j respectively.

Observation 3: Process P_i does no more need to piggyback any application message to P_j till the $(k+1)^{th}$ invocation (next) of the algorithm. The reason is that after receiving the piggybacked message $<m_i, N_i>$, P_j has already implemented its decision whether to take a checkpoint or not before processing the message m_i. If it has taken a checkpoint, then all messages it receives from P_i starting with the message m_i can not be orphan. So it processes the received messages. Also if P_j did not need to take a checkpoint during the kth execution of the algorithm, then obviously the messages sent by P_i to P_j staring with the message m_i till the next invocation of the algorithm can not be orphan. So it processes the messages.

Therefore, for an n process distributed system, a process P_i piggybacks only its first application message sent (after it has implemented its checkpointing decision for the current execution of the algorithm and before its next participation in the algorithm) to a process P_j, where $j \neq i$, and $0 \leq j \leq n-1$.

5.2 Algorithm Non-blocking

Below we describe the algorithm. It is a single phase algorithm since an initiator process interacts with the other processes only once via the control message M_c.

At each process P_i $(1 \leq i \leq n)$

    if $CLK_i = (i+ (counter_i * n)) * T$ *//when its turn to initiate the checkpointing procedure*

        $counter_i = counter_i + 1$;
        $N_i = N_i + 1$;
        broadcasts M_c to (n-1) other processes;

        if $c_i = 1$ *// at least one message it has sent after its last checkpoint*
            takes checkpoint C_i;
            $c_i = 0$;
            continues its normal operation;

        else *// if it decides not to take a checkpoint*
            continues its normal operation;

else if P_i receives M_c
  $N_i = N_i + 1$;
  if $c_i = 1$ // *at least one message it has sent after its last checkpoint*
   takes checkpoint C_i;
   $c_i = 0$;
   continues its normal operation;
  else
   continues its normal operation;

else if P_i receives a piggybacked message $<m_j, N_j>$ && P_i has not yet received M_c for the current execution of the checkpointing procedure

  $N_i = N_i + 1$;
  if $c_i = 1$ // *at least one message it has sent after its last checkpoint*
   $c_i = 0$;
   takes checkpoint C_i without waiting for M_c;
   processes the received message m_j;
   continues its normal operation and ignores M_c, when received for the current execution of the checkpointing procedure;

  else
   processes any received message m_j;
   continues its normal operation and ignores M_c, when received for the current execution of the checkpointing procedure;
 else
   continues its normal operation;

Proof of Correctness: In the first 'if else' and 'else if' blocks of the pseudo code, each process P_i decides based on the value of its flag c_i whether it needs to take a checkpoint. If it has to take a checkpoint, it resets c_i to 0. Therefore, in other words, each process P_i makes sure using the logic of Theorem 2 that none of the messages, if any, it has sent since its last checkpoint can be an orphan. On the other hand, if P_i does not take a checkpoint, it means that it has not sent any message since its previous checkpoint.

In the second 'else if' block each process P_i follows the logic of Observations 1, 2, and 3, which ever is appropriate for a particular situation so that any application message (piggybacked or not) received by P_i before it receives the request message M_c can not be an orphan. Besides none of its sent messages, if any, since its last checkpoint can be an orphan as well (following the logic of Theorems 1 and 2).

Since Theorem 2, and Observations 1, 2, and 3 guarantee that no sent or received message by any process P_i since its previous checkpoint can be an orphan and since it is true for all participating processes, therefore, the algorithm guarantees that the latest checkpoints taken during the current execution of the algorithm and the previous checkpoints (if any) of those processes that did not need to take checkpoints during the current execution of the algorithm are globally consistent checkpoints.

5.3 Performance

We use the following notations (and some of the analysis from [7]) to compare our algorithm with some of the most notable algorithms in this area of research, namely [3], [7], and [8]. The analytical comparison is given in Table 1. In this Table:

C_{air} is cost of sending a message from one process to another process;
C_{broad} is cost of broadcasting a message to all processes;
n_{min} is the number of processes that need to take checkpoints.
n is the total number of processes in the system;
n_{dep} is the average number of processes on which a process depends;
T_{ch} is the checkpointing time.

Table 1. System performance

Algorithm	Blocking time	Messages	Distributed
Koo-Toueg [3]	$n_{min} * T_{ch}$	$3 * n_{min} * n_{dep} * C_{air}$	Yes
Elnozahy [8]	0	$2 * C_{broad} + n * C_{air}$	No
Cao-Singhal [7]	0	$\approx 2 * n_{min} * C_{air} +$ $min(n_{min} * C_{air}, C_{broad})$	Yes
Our Algorithm	0	C_{broad}	Yes

Figs. 3 and 4 illustrate how the number of control messages (system messages) sent and received by processes is affected by the increase in the number of the processes in the system. In Fig. 3, n_{dep} factor is considered being 5% of the total number of processes in the system and C_{broad} is equal to C_{air} (assuming that special hardware is used to facilitate broadcasting – which is not the case most of the times). As Fig. 3 shows, the number of messages does not increase with the increase of the number of the processes in our approach unlike other approaches. In Fig. 4, we have considered absence of any special hardware for broadcasting and therefore assumed C_{broad} to be equal to $n * C_{air}$. In this case, although the number of messages does increase in our approach, but it stays smaller compared to other approaches when the number of the processes is higher than 7 (which is the case most of the time).

5.4 Suitability for Mobile Computing Environment

Consider a distributed mobile computing environment. In such an environment, only limited wireless bandwidth is available for communication among the computing processes. Besides, the mobile hosts (MH) have limited battery power and limited memory. Therefore, it is required that, any distributed application P running in such an environment must make efficient use of the limited wireless bandwidth, and mobile hosts' limited battery power and memory. Below we show that the proposed algorithm satisfies all the above three requirements.

▶ The first requirement about the efficient use of the bandwidth is satisfied by our checkpointing algorithm, because the presented algorithm is a single phase algorithm unlike any other existing algorithms [3], [6]-[9]. That is, the initiator process requests any other process to take a checkpoint by broadcasting only the control message (M_c) during any invocation of the algorithm. There is no other control message used. So our algorithm ensures effective utilization of the limited wireless bandwidth. In this context, it may be noted that our algorithm needs much less number of the system messages than in [3], [7], [8], [11].

▶ The second requirement about the efficient use of the mobile host's battery power is satisfied, because (1) each MH is interrupted only once by the control message M_c, as our algorithm is a single phase one. It saves time since interrupt handling time can not be ignored. Note that in other approaches [7], [11] it is more than one; and (2) each process P_i only checks if its $c_i = 1$ in order to decide if it needs to take a checkpoint. This is the only computation that an MH is involved with while participating in the algorithm.

▶ The third requirement about the efficient use of the mobile host's memory is satisfied, because the data structure used in our algorithm is very simple. Only four variables are needed by each process P_i. These are: three integer variables, viz. N_i, $counter_i$, CLK_i, and one Boolean variable c_i. The amount of data structures stated above is much less than the same in the related works [7], [11].

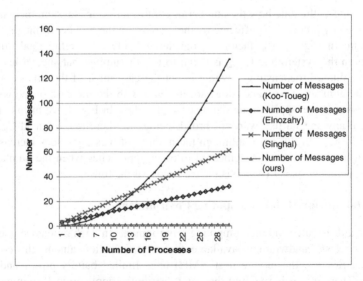

Fig. 3. Number of messages vs. number of processes for four different approaches when $C_{broad} = C_{air}$

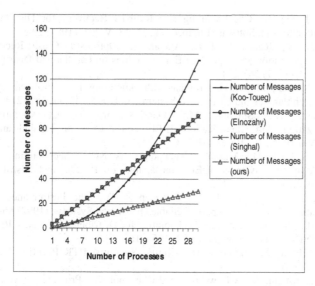

Fig. 4. Number of messages vs. number of processes for four different approaches when $C_{broad} = n * C_{air}$

6   Conclusions

In this work, we have presented a non-blocking synchronous checkpointing approach to determine globally consistent checkpoints. In the present work only those processes that have sent some message(s) after their last checkpoints, take checkpoints during checkpointing; thereby reducing the number of checkpoints to be taken. This approach offers advantage particularly in case of mobile computing where both non-block checkpointing and reduction in the number of checkpoints help in the efficient use of the limited resources of mobile computing environment. Besides, the presented non-blocking approach uses minimum interaction (only once) between the initiator process and the system of n processes and there is no synchronization delay. This is particularly useful for mobile computing environment because of less number of interrupts caused by the initiator process to mobile processes, which results in better utilization of the limited resources (limited battery power of mobile machines and wireless bandwidth) of mobile environment. To achieve this we have used very simple data structures, viz., three integer variables and one Boolean variable per process. Another advantage of the proposed algorithm is that each process takes its checkpointing decision independently which may become helpful for mobile computing. The advantages mentioned above make the proposed algorithms simple, efficient, and suitable for mobile computing environment.

References

1. Wang, Y.-M.: Consistent Global Checkpoints that Contain a Given Set of Local Checkpoints. IEEE Transactions on Computers, Vol. 46, No.4, (1997) 456-468
2. Singhal, M. , Shivaratri, N.-G.: Advanced Concepts in Operating Systems. McGraw-Hill, (1994)

3. Koo, R., Toueg, S.: Checkpointing and Rollback-Recovery for Distributed Systems. IEEE Transactions on Software Engineering, SE-13, Vol. 1, (1987) 23-31
4. Venkatesan, S., Juang, T. T-Y., Alagar, S.: Optimistic Crash Recovery without Changing Application Messages. IEEE Transactions on Parallel and Distributed Systems, Vol. 8, No. 3, (1997) 263-271
5. Cao, G., Singhal, M.: On Coordinated Checkpointing in Distributed Systems, IEEE ransactions on Parallel and Distributed Systems, Vol. 9, No.12, (1998) 1213-1225
6. Manivannan, D., Singhal, M.: Quasi-Synchronous Checkpointing: Models, Characterization, and Classification. IEEE Transactions on Parallel and Distributed Systems, Vol.10, No.7, (1999) 703-713
7. Cao, G., Singhal, M.: Mutable Checkpoints: A New Checkpointing Approach for Mobile Computing Systems. IEEE Transactions on Parallel and Distributed systems, Vol.12, No. 2, (2001) 157 – 172
8. Elnozahy, E. N., Johnson, D. B., Zwaenepoel, W.: The Performance of Consistent Checkpointing. Proc. 11th Symp. on Reliable Distributed Systems, (1992) 86-95
9. Silva, L. M., Silva, J. G.: Global Checkpointing for Distributed Programs. Proc. 11th Symp. on Reliable Distributed Systems, (1992) 155 – 162
10. Jalote, P.: Fault Tolerance in Distributed Systems. PTR Prentice Hall, Addison-Wesley, (1998)
11. Ahmed, R., Khaliq, A.: A Low-Overhead Checkpointing Protocol for Mobile Networks. IEEE CCECE 2003, Vol. 3, (2003) 4 – 7

Applying Dynamic Handoff to Increase System Performance on Wireless Cellular Networks

Chow-Sing Lin and Cheng-Chi Lu

Department of Information Management
Southern Taiwan University of Technology
Tainan Shien, Taiwan, R.O.C.
{mikelin, cclu}@msrg.mis.stut.edu.tw

Abstract. With the rapid advance in wireless network communication, multimedia presentation has become more applicable. However, since Mobile Hosts (MHs) are free to move around a wireless network, workloads among cells tend to be imbalanced, leading to higher call dropping probability (CDP) and call blocking probability (CBP). How to balance the workloads among cells to provide better quality of service (QoS) has become an important issue to be addressed. In this paper, we propose a novel dynamic handoff adjustment (DHA) scheme to balance workloads among cells. The DHA scheme dynamically hands over MHs to neighbor cells based on the workloads of cells. With well-balanced workloads of cells, a cell can have more available bandwidth to serve more MHs. Our simulation experiments show that the DHA scheme has lower CDP and better bandwidth utilization (BU) than other existing schemes.

1 Introduction

In recent years, the demand for data access on mobile networks has been greatly increased. In addition to delivering plain text, the evolution of computing and wireless networking technologies has made ubiquitous multimedia communication such as audio, video, and data [1][2][3][4] become feasible. These multimedia services normally require guarantee of Quality-of-Service (QoS), and cannot be disrupted during the service time. How to continuously provide a mobile host (MH) moving around a wireless network with services without hiccups is an important issue to be addressed.

In this paper, we assume services are provided on wireless cellular networks. A wireless cellular network consists of a group of hexagonal cells, which constructs large coverage [5] for communication services. Each cell has a base station (BS) to communicate with MHs in the cell, and a MH is free to move across cells. In order to avoid disrupting connections during the migration of MHs among cells, a seamless wireless cellular network [6] must be constructed . In the seamless wireless network, there is an overlapping area between two cells. A MH receives multiple signals from neighbor cells in the overlapping area [6][7][8][9], as shown in Fig. 1. In general, when a MH is handed over to a neighbor cell is based on received signal strength (RSS). When the RSS of a neighboring cell reaches a certain threshold, the MH is handed over to the target cell. The process of handing over a MH from a cell to another cell is called *handoff* which normally happens in the overlapping area, or so called handoff zone. There are

Y.-C. Chung and J.E. Moreira (Eds.): GPC 2006, LNCS 3947, pp. 609–619, 2006.
© Springer-Verlag Berlin Heidelberg 2006

two types of handoffs, *hard handoff* and *soft handoff*. Hard handoff is a break-before-make method, where a new channel is set up after the release of the old channel. On the other hand, soft handoff is a make-before-break method, where a new channel is set up before the release of the old channel. Therefore, the transient dropping time of soft handoff is much shorter than that of hard handoff which is almost imperceivable by users[5][6][10].

Nowadays, MHs request various types of services. Each service may require different quality-of-service (QoS). How to maintain QoS guarantee of a MH without being affected by its movement becomes a difficult challenge [1][2][11]. Moreover, the coverage area of a cell now tends to be shrunk [12] in order to increase service throughput, such as the number of servable MHs, but this inevitably increases the frequency of handoffs on the cellular network. As a result, the utilization of cell bandwidth may be greatly varied from time to time, and some of cells become hot spots so that MHs short of desired bandwidth are dropped. From above observations, we conclude that in order to approach the maximum system performance in terms of bandwidth utilization and dropping/blocking rate of MHs, it is extremely important that the workload of cells should be balanced.

With soft handoff, we may divide the overlapping area into two areas based on the signal strengths received from the original cell and the target cell. One is called *early-Handoff area*, in which the RSS from original cell is greater than that from the target cell, and MHs in this area use the resource of original cell. The other is called *lateHandoff area*, in which the RSS from original cell is less than that from the target cell, and MHs in this area use the resource of target cell. But, the fact is that a MH can receive signals from both original cell and the target cell in the overlapping area, as shown in Fig. 1. Therefore, as long as the received signals from both cells is strong enough to provide acceptable bandwidth, we may dynamically adjust the number of MHs in these two areas to balance the workloads of original and target cells.

In this paper, we propose the dynamic handoff adjustment (DHA) scheme, which dynamically hands over MHs based on the workload of original cell and target cell to balance their workloads. With soft handoff, a MH receives signals from both original cell and target cell in the overlapping area. In this handoff zone, a MH can be selected to stay in the current cell or to be directly handed over to the target cell to continue services. In general, a normal handoff happens when the RSS of resided cell begins to be less than that of target cell. In the paper, the proposed DHA defines that a handoff is called *early handoff* if the RSS of target cell is less than that of original cell when handoffing, and a handoff is called *late handoff* if the RSS of original cell is less than that of target cell when handoffing. When the workload of original cell is heavy, the original cell can attempt to early hand over (*early handoff*) MHs to other lightly loaded target cells. On the other hand, if the workload of target cell is heavier than that of original cell, the handoff can be delayed (*late handoff*). We can apply these two handoff strategies to dynamically change servicing base stations of MHs in a handoff zone to balance the workloads of cells.

On the wireless cellular network, there are two important QoS parameters: call blocking probability (CBP) of new call and call dropping probability (CDP) of handoff call. Due to the limited resource of a cell, decreasing CDP inevitably leads to the

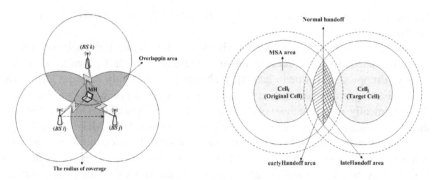

Fig. 1. Signal receiving in the overlapping area   **Fig. 2.** The model of signal overlapping of an original cell and a target cell

increase of CBP, and vice versa. From a user's perspective, a connection terminated in the middle of a call is far more annoying than having a new call attempt blocked [3]. Therefore, in the paper, like most of other research works, we focus on lowering the CDP while still keeping the CBP within an acceptable range.

The rest of this paper is organized as follows. In Section 2 we describe the analysis of the related research works. In Section 3 the wireless communication signal and coverage is introduced. The proposed DHA scheme is presented in Section 4. In Section 5, we present the experiment results of extensive simulations. Finally, we conclude the paper in Section 6.

2   Related Works

Recently, there are many research interests in increasing system performance which use the characteristic of overlapping area on wireless cellular networks. In [13], Eklundh proposed directed retry (DR) method. In DR method, new call can use the available channels of neighbor cells in the overlapping area when the initial cell has no available channel. Because the DR only applies to new calls in the overlapping area, the performance improvement is not effective when either the overlapping area is small or a lot of new calls are not in the overlapping area. In [14], Kim and Kang proposed adaptive soft handover algorithm (ASHA) scheme. In ASHA scheme, a set of parameters is broadcasted to alter the regular soft handoff process, and then the notified MHs are early handed over to neighbor cells regardless of the workload of neighbor cell. In this way, MHs handed over to neighbor cells may be dropped when the neighbor cell is heavily loaded. As a result, the ASHA cannot guarantee the QoS of MHs. In [15], Paik et al. proposed integrated call control (ICC) strategy. In ICC strategy, each cell reserves a certain number of channels for handoff calls and sets the upper threshold for the number of service connections. The MH performs the quick soft handoff process to hand over to neighbor cell when the number of service connections in the residing cell exceeds the threshold. The ICC strategy has two drawbacks. First, reserved fixed channels as guard channels results in inefficient bandwidth utilization. Second, the MH, which has been handed over to neighbor cell, may be dropped when neighbor cell has no adequate bandwidth.

To conclude the aforementioned analysis, we propose the DHA scheme, which utilizes the characteristic of received signal strength in overlapping area to overcome the issue of dropping MHs due to inadequate bandwidth. Not only does the DHA take the same advantages of relocating new connections in overlapping area to neighbor cells for dynamically adjusting the workload as DR does, compared to ASHA, it also applies the *earlyHandoff* algorithm which periodically hands off the MHs which have been successfully reserved bandwidths in the target cells to balance the workloads of cells whenever is necessary. When the available bandwidth in the target cell is inadequate, ICC directly drops the handoff calls. However, in the DHA we also propose *lateHandoff* to delay handing off MHs to target cells as long as possible to further reduce the dropping probability.

3   Wireless Communication Signal and Coverage

In the paper, we assume the system has several service types. Each requires different bandwidth and different signal strengths to maintain the quality of service, and consequently, the effective coverage (EC) of each service type is also different. Within the EC, each MH can obtain desired bandwidth and guarantee its QoS. Let ρ and σ denote the signal power and the noise of a channel, respectively. The signal-to-noise rate, ς, can be expressed as (1). According to Hartley-Shannon Law, the maximum transmission rate of a channel, C, can be expressed as (2) when bit error rate is zero, where B represents the available frequency of a channel. The required RSS^{EC} on the boundary of EC can be represented as (3).

$$\varsigma = \frac{\rho}{\sigma} \tag{1}$$

$$C = B \log_2(1 + \varsigma) \tag{2}$$

$$RSS^{EC} = \delta\left(2^{\frac{C}{B}} - 1\right) \tag{3}$$

The Received Signal Strength, RSS, is influenced by three factors [14]: path loss, shadow fading, and multipath fading, and it can be expressed as (4), where μ denotes the transmission power of a base station, γ is the path-loss exponent, $Z(d)$ denotes the signal attenuation function, and d denotes the distance of MH from the base station.

$$RSS = \mu - \gamma \log_{10}(d) + Z(d) \tag{4}$$

In this paper, the RSS of a MH is based on the following assumptions. First, by passing a low-pass filter, the multipath fading of the RSS is averaged out. Second, shadow fading is nearly constant over any short period of time [14][15]. As a result, the path-loss is the main factor that affects the RSS. Therefore, (4) can be reduced to (5).

$$RSS = \mu - \gamma \log_{10}(d) \tag{5}$$

When a MH is not resided in any overlapping area, it must be serviced by the original cell. In the paper, we define such an area as Master Service Area (MSA). Assume that R denotes the signal radius of a cell and α denotes the signal overlapping area of two cells, then we can derive the RSS on the boundary of MSA, RSS^{MSA}, from (3) and (5) as (6).

$$RSS^{MSA} = \mu - \gamma \log_{10}(2R(1 - \alpha) - 10^{\frac{\mu - \delta(2^{\frac{C}{B}} - 1)}{\gamma}}) \tag{6}$$

4 Dynamic Handoff Adjustment

The DHA scheme consists of two components, *earlyHandoff* and *lateHandoff*. The objective of earlyHandoff is to reduce the CBP by distributing connections with inadequate bandwidth to neighbor cells. The earlyHandoff early hands over MHs whose bandwidth in the target cell is already reserved to the target cell. On the other hand, the goal of late-Handoff is to delay the hand off of a MH who has failed to reserve bandwidth in the target cell until either it leaves the EC or there is sufficient bandwidth in the target cell. In a sense, we dynamically adjust the number of MHs in the overlapping area served by original cell and target cell to balance the workloads. As a result, there are no hot-spot cell and the workload of each is well balanced. Consequently, the CDP and CBP can be further reduced, and bandwidth utilization is therefore increased.

4.1 Description of DHA Scheme

In the seamlessly wireless cellular network, there is a given ratio of the overlapping area between two cells [16]. In this overlapping area a MH can continue its service by switching the servicing station from original cell to target cell without being dropped. Figure 2 shows the model of signal overlapping of an original cell and target cell. The outer most dotted line represents the boundary of signal coverage of a cell. The inner most solid line represents the boundary of MSA. MHs inside the MSA are served by the resided cell. The middle solid line represents the boundary of EC. The resided cell can provide adequate signal strength for MHs inside the EC. MHs outside the EC cannot be served by the resided cell and must be served by the target cell even though it is still within the signal coverage of the resided cell. The shaded area in the middle is the overlapping area, or so-called handoff zone. The *normal handoff* happens in the middle of the area where the received signal strengths from the original cell and target cell are the same. Handoffs happening in the left part and the right part of the shaded area are called *earlyHandoff* and *lateHandoff*, respectively.

When a MH leaves the MSA area of the original cell, it issues a bandwidth reservation request to the target cell. In the paper, we assume that the target cell can be precisely predicted by applying the approaches proposed by [17][18] where the Global-Positioning-System (GPS) is applied to predict the movement of a MH on a highway. If the target cell has sufficient bandwidth, it reserves the requested bandwidth for the MH and adds it to the set of reservation success , $S^{rv\_success}$, of the target cell. On the other hand, if the target cell does not have adequate bandwidth, we insert the request into the queue of reservation failure, $Q^{rv-failure}$ based on its priority. Assume that w_1 denotes the relative weight of speed priority, VP, w_2 denotes the relative weight of RSS from the target cell, and w_3 denotes the relative weight of the priority of service type, CP. We use (7) to calculate the priority of a request.

$$RequestPriority = [w_1 \times (VP) + w_2 \times (RSS) + w_3 \times (CP)] \tag{7}$$

4.2 earlyHandoff Algorithm

In DHA scheme the earlyHandoff algorithm is performed periodically. At each interval, we compare the workload of original cell and target cell. If the workload of original cell is greater than that of target cell, we handoff those MHs who are in earlyHandoff area and already successfully reserved bandwidth in the target cell to the target cell. In this way, the reserved bandwidth in the target cell is utilized immediately and the bandwidth allocated to handoffed MHs is released to reduce the workload of original cell. This approach not only favors the reduction of CDP and CBP in the original cell but also the increase of bandwidth utilization in the target cell.

Assume that in cell i, $BwAvail_i$ denotes the available bandwidth, $BwRv_i$ denotes the total reserved bandwidth, and $BwTotal_i$ denotes the total bandwidth. Then, we can compute the workload of cell i by (8). Figure 3 shows the pseudo code of earlyHandoff process.

$$WorkLoad_i = \frac{BwTotal_i - BwAvail_i - BwRv_i}{BwTotal_i} \tag{8}$$

---

earlyHandoff()

$Cell_i$: original Cell;
$Cell_j$: Target Cell;
$BwReq_x$: the required Bandwidth of MH_x ;

1. FOR EACH MH_x in $Cell_i$
2.   IF MH_x in $S_j^{rv\_success}$ THEN
3.   IF $WorkLoad_i \geq WorkLoad_j$ THEN
4.   Issue MH_x's handoff request to $Cell_j$;
6.   Release $BwReq_x$ in $Cell_i$;
7.   Update $BwAvail_i$;
8.   Update $WorkLoad_i$;
9.   Bandwidth_Adjustment();

Fig. 3. earlyHandoff algorithm

---

lateHandoff()

$Cell_i$: original Cell;
$Cell_j$: Target Cell;

1. IF $RSS_i^x \leq RSS_j^x$ and $RSS_j^x < RSS_j^{MSA}$ and MH_x not in $MH_j^{rv\_success}$ THEN
2.   Send MH_x's lateHandoff request to $Cell_j$;
3. ELSE IF MH_x in $S_j^{rv\_success}$ THEN
4.   Send MH_x's handoff request to $Cell_j$;
5.   Release $BwReq_x$ in $Cell_j$;
6.   Update $BwAvail_i$;
7. ELSE IF $RSS_j^x \geq RSS_j^{MSA}$ THEN
8.   Issue MH_x's handoff request to $Cell_j$;
9.   Release $BwReq_x$ in $Cell_i$;
10. Update $BwAavail_i$;
11. Bandwidth_Adjustment();

Fig. 4. lateHandoff algorithm

4.3   lateHandoff Algorithm

When the workload of a cell is lighter than its neighboring cells, the MHs in the earlyHandoff area are not early handed off to target cells. As a MH moves to the center of overlapping area, a normal handoff is triggered. At this time, if previously the target cell fails to reserve the requested bandwidth for the MH and also it still cannot provide adequate bandwidth for the MH, rather than directly dropping the MH, we apply the lateHandoff to delay the handoff process and expect some bandwidth will be released to satisfy the request during the extra time. MHs who failed to reserve bandwidth in the target cell then are moved from $Q^{rv-failure}$ queue to the $Q^{late\_handoff}$ queue. MHs in the $Q^{late\_handoff}$ queue are all in the lateHandoff area and thus are more close to target cells. They are more urgent to obtain adequate bandwidths from target cells to avoid being dropped. Therefore, MHs in the $Q^{late\_handoff}$ queue should have higher priorities to get the released bandwidth than those in the $Q^{rv-failure}$ queue. The lateHandoff algorithm is described in Fig. 4.

4.4   Bandwidth Adjustment

The bandwidth adjustment scheme suitably allocates released bandwidth to MHs in $Q_i^{late\_handoff}$ and $Q_i^{rv-failure}$ according to both CBP and CDP of the cell. The pseudocode of bandwidth adjustment scheme is presented in Fig. 5. In order to avoid dropping MHs, our bandwidth adjustment scheme first allocates the released bandwidth to MHs in $Q_i^{late\_handoff}$ and then MHs in $Q_i^{rv-failure}$, based on the thresholds of CBP_{th} and CDP_{th}. If CDP is greater than CDP_{th} and CBP is smaller than CBP_{th}, the remaining released bandwidth is allocated to MHs in $Q_i^{rv-failure}$; otherwise, it returns to base station for serving new calls.

Bandwidth_Adjustment()

$Cell_i$: original Cell;
$Cell_j$: Target Cell;

1. WHILE $Q_i^{late\_handoff}$ is not empty
2.   MH = $DeQueue(Q_i^{late\_handoff})$;
3.   Allocate bandwidth to MH;
4.   Update $BwAvail_i$;
5. IF CDP≥CDP_{th} or CBP≤CBP_{th} THEN
6.   WHILE $Q_i^{rv-failure}$ is not empty
7.   MH = $DeQueue(Q_i^{rv-failure})$;
8.   Allocate bandwidth to MH;
9.   Update $BwRv_i$;
10.   Update $BwAavail_i$;

Fig. 5. Bandwidth adjustment algorithm

Table 1. The priority of speed

Average Velocity	Practical Example	Velocity Priority (VP)
<20cm/s	Almost static	0
1m/s	Walking	0.2
10m/s	Normal driving	0.4
20m/s	Fast car	0.7
>30m/s	Super fast	1

Table 2. Multimedia service types

Class No.	Bandwidth Requirement	Average Holding Time	Class Priority (CP)
1	5Mbps	10min.	0.3
2	3Mbps	5min.	0.6
3	1Mbps	3min.	1.0

5 Simulation Results

In this section, we present the performance results for our proposed scheme. The simulation model is a wireless cellular network, which comprises 100 cells. Each cell, represented by a hexagon, has six neighboring cells. The arrival of MHs is modeled by Poisson distribution and the generated MHs are evenly distributed to cells. Each MH randomly selects a moving speed of 1 m/s, 10 m/s, and 20 m/s whose priorities are listed on Table 1. The service types of requests are listed on Table 2. The holding time of a MH complies with Exponential distribution. The detailed simulation parameters are shown in Table 3.

Table 3. Simulation parameters

Parameter	Description	Value
$Cell_i$	Wireless Cell	100
Bw_i^{all}	The total bandwidth of $Cell_i$	60Mbps
Bw_x^{req}	The required bandwidth of MH_x	5Mbps, 3Mbps, 1Mbps
B	The available frequency of channel	4MHz
$Cell\_ms$	The diameter of each Cell	1000m
$T_{interval}$	The interval time of earlyHandoff algorithm	10sec
α	The ratio of overlapping area	0.4
δ	Noise power	1Watts
μ	Transmit power	81
γ	Path-loss exponent	30
ν	The speed of MH	1m/s, 10m/s, 20m/s
CDP_{th}	CDP threshold	0.3
CBP_{th}	CBP threshold	0.3

In this simulation, we investigate the performance of DHA in terms of the call blocking probability, the call dropping probability, and the bandwidth utilization by comparing it with NR (No Reservation), RR (Reservation Resource), and ASHA schemes. In NR and ASHA scheme, no bandwidth is reserved for handoff connections. Therefore, a handoff connection is equivalent to a new connection, which is accepted only if the cell has sufficient available bandwidth. In RR scheme, we assume that a MH move in a fixed direction which is randomly selected when generated throughout its life span. The target cell reserves bandwidth for a MH if it has sufficient available bandwidth. A request is issued to the target cell for bandwidth reservation once a MH moves into a new cell. Both DHA and RR need to reserve bandwidth in the target cell. However, the two schemes specify different moments when bandwidth reservation requests are issued. In DHA scheme, a MH issues a request for bandwidth reservation to target cell when it leaves the MSA area. On the other hand, in RR scheme, a MH issues the request for bandwidth reservation to the target cell when it moves into a cell. A MH is dropped when the request of bandwidth reservation to the target cell fails.

Figure 6 shows the CBP of DHA, NR, RR and ASHA with respect to the increase of call arrival rate. The CBPs of DHA, NR, RR ,and ASHA increase as the call arrival increases. The CBP of our proposed DHA scheme is similar to the RR scheme with

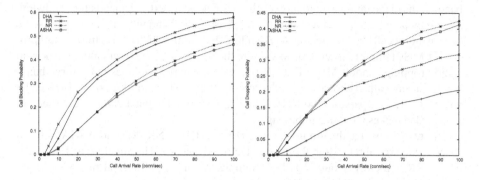

Fig. 6. Call Blocking Probability   **Fig. 7.** Call Dropping Probability

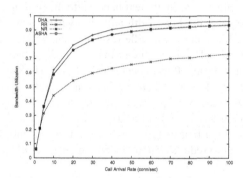

Fig. 8. Bandwidth Utilization

the increase of call arrival rate. This is because the ratio of overlapping area is set to be 0.4 and thus the MSA is relatively small. Most MHs are not initially in the MSA so that when they are generated, they issue requests of bandwidth reservation to their target cells immediately. This kind of situation is similar to the RR. When the wireless cellular network is saturated, if both CBP and CDP are smaller than their thresholds, the released bandwidths are preferentially allocated to MHs in $Q^{rv-failure}$. As a result, the CBP of DHA is increased. As shown in the Fig. 6, the NR and ASHA perform almost equally well, and they always have the lowest CBP. This is because NR and ASHA have no reserved bandwidth in target cells. Without the idle bandwidth for reservation, the available bandwidth for new connections are increased so that the CBP is reduced.

Figure 7 shows the CDP of DHA, NR, RR and ASHA with respect to the increase of call arrival rate. The CDPs of DHA, RR, NR and ASHA increase as the call arrival increases. The DHA has the lowest CDP at all different arrival rates. The CDP of our proposed DHA obviously offers more improvement on RR , NR and ASHA. When the call arrival rate is 100 connections/second, the CDP of our proposed DHA offers as much as 38%, 52%, and 50% improvement with respect to that of RR, NR, and ASHA. This is because the released bandwidth by the earlyhandoff algorithm is designed to be first allocated to MHs in the $Q^{late\_handoff}$ and then MHs in the $Q^{rv-failure}$ rather than serving new calls. This kind of early handing off MHs, who successfully reserve bandwidths in the target cell, to target cell does not incurs extra demands for bandwidth since they are already reserved, but it can release more bandwidth in advance to serve more handoff calls. Moreover, the lateHandoff algorithm, which delays the handoff process of MHs failing to reserve bandwidth in the target cell, also offers more chances to avoid dropping handoff MHs. The NR treats calls equally and does not reserve bandwidth for any call. Although it has the lowest CBP as shown in Fig. 6, it also has the highest CDP. Compared to the DHA scheme, the inflexible bandwidth reservation approach also makes CDP inevitably higher.

Figure 8 shows bandwidth utilizations (BU) of DHA, NR, RR and ASHA with respect to call arrival rate. Both the BUs of DHA, NR, and ASHA are close to 100%, and that of RR is merely about 72%. For example, when the call arrival rate is 100 connections/second, the BU of the DHA offers as much as 32% improvement with respect to RR. Due to the idle reserved bandwidth, the RR cannot fully utilize bandwidth to serve more MHs, which leads to inefficient bandwidth utilization. On the contrast, NR and ASHA do not reserve any bandwidth and take whatever bandwidth left to serve as more MHs as possible. There is no idle reserved bandwidth, and thus they can efficiently utilize bandwidth. However, due to the lack of load balancing scheme, some cells may become hot spots and thus unnecessarily drop MHs. This phenomenon leads to the conclusion that the BUs of NR and ASHA are slightly less than that of DHA. Although the DHA also reserves bandwidth in the target cell, it early hands off MHs who has successfully reserved bandwidths to the target cell when the workload of the resided cell is heavier than that of target cell. Again, it not only favors the reducing workload of resided cell to reduce CDP and CDP but also the BU of target cell.

6   Conclusion

With increasing demands for mobile multimedia services, the QoS guarantee is more difficult and the load is non-balance between cells in virtue of both mobility of MH and limited bandwidth of cell. The imbalanced loads increases the probabilities of dropping handoff calls and blocking new calls. In this paper, we propose the DHA scheme, which utilizes earlyHandoff and lateHandoff algorithms to balance the loads among cells to improve service performance. Our simulation results show that the DHA scheme achieves better system performance than NR, RR, and ASHA in terms of CDP and BU. In the future, we plan to relax the limitations stated in the paper to provide a more general mechanism in the system model such as dynamic bandwidth reservation, mobility prediction, multiple classes of services. The performance of DHA under this more general system model will be reported in our future publications.

References

1. El-Kadi, M., Olariu, S., Abdel-Wahab, H.: A rate-based borrowing scheme for qos provisioning in multimedia wireless networks. In: IEEE Transactions, Parallel and Distributed Systems. Volume 13. (2002) 156–166
2. Epstein, B.M., Schwartz, M.: Predictive qos-based admission control for multiclass traffic in cellular wireless networks. IEEE Journal, Selected Areas in Communications **18**(3) (2000) 523–534

3. Mlla, A., El-Kadi, M., Olariu, S., Todorova, P.: A fair resource allocation protocol for multimedia wireless networks. IEEE Transactions, Parallel and Distributed Systems **14**(1) (2003) 63–71

4. Oliverira, C., Kim, J.B., Suda, T.: An adaptive bandwidth reservation scheme for high-speed multimedia wireless networks. IEEE Journal, Selected Areas in Communications **16**(6) (1998) 858–874

5. Harte, L., Kikta, R., Levine, R.: 3G wireless Demystified. 1st edn. McGraw-Hill (2002)

6. Kim, D.K., Sung, D.K.: Characterization of soft handoff in cdma systems. IEEE Transactions, Vehicular Technology **48**(4) (1999) 1195–1202

7. Gilhousen, K.S., Jacobs, I.M., Padovani, R., Viterbi, A.J., Weaver, L.A., Jr., C. E. Wheatley, I.: On the capacity of a cellular cdma system. IEEE Transactions, Vehicular Technology **40**(2) (1991) 303–312

8. Lee, W.C.Y.: Overview of cellular cdma. IEEE Transactions, Vehicular Technology **40**(2) (1991) 291–302

9. Viterbi, A.J.: CDMA-Principles of Spread Spectrum Communication. Addison-Wesley (1995)

10. Das, S., Sen, S., Jayaram, R.: A dynamic load balancing strategy for channel assignment using selective borrowing in cellular mobile environment. Wireless Networks **3**(5) (1997) 333–347

11. Chiu, M., Bassiouni, M.: Predictive scheme for handoff prioritization in cellular networks based on mobile positioning. IEEE Journal, Selected Areas in Communications **18**(3) (2000) 510–522

12. Hanzo, L.: Bandwidth-efficient wireless communications. IEEE, Proceeding **86**(7) (1998) 1342–1380

13. Eklundh, B.: Channel utilization and blocking probability in a cellular mobile telephone system with directed retry. IEEE Transactions, Communications **34**(4) (1986) 329–337

14. Kim, W., Kang, C.: An adaptive soft handover algorithm for traffic-load shedding in the wcdma mobile communication system. In: IEEE Wireless Communications and Networking. Volume 2. (2003) 1213–1217

15. Paik, C., Jin, G., Ahn, H., Teha, D.: Integrated call control in a cdma cellular system. IEEE Transactions, Vehicular Technology **55**(1) (2001) 97–108

16. Lee, D., Cho, D.: Channel-borrowing handoff scheme based on user mobility in cdma cellular systems. In: IEEE International Conference, Communications. Volume 2. (2000) 685–689

17. Lee, W.C.Y., Yeh, Y.S.: On the estimation of the second-order statistics of log normal fading in mobile radio environment. IEEE Transactions, Communications **22**(6) (1974) 869–873

18. Lee, D., Hsueh, Y.: Bandwidth-reservation scheme based on road information for next-generation cellular networks. IEEE Transactions on Vechicular Technology **53**(1) (2004) 243–252

A Paradigm of a Pervasive Multimodal Multimedia Computing System for the Visually-Impaired Users[*]

Ali Awde[1], Manolo Dulva Hina[1,2], Chakib Tadj[1],
Amar Ramdane-Cherif[2], and Yacine Bellik[3]

[1] LATIS Laboratory, Université du Québec, École de technologie superieure,
1100, rue Notre-Dame Ouest, Montréal, Québec H3C 1K3, Canada
{ali.awde.1, manolo-dulva.hina.1}@ens.etsmtl.ca,
ctadj@ele.etsmtl.ca
[2] PRISM Laboratory CRNS, Université de Versailles-Saint-Quentin-en-Yvelines,
45, avenue des Etats-Unis, 78035 Versailles Cedex, France
rca@prism.uvsq.fr
[3] LIMSI-CRNS, Université de Paris-Sud,
B.P. 133, 91043 Orsay, France
yacine.bellik@limsi.fr

Abstract. Incorporating multimodality in a computing system makes computing more accessible to a wide range of users, including those with impairments. This work presents a paradigm of a multimodal multimedia computing system to make informatics accessible to visually-impaired users. The system's infrastructure determines the suitable applications to be used. The user's context and user data type are considered in determining the types of applications, media and modalities that are appropriate to use. The system design is pervasive, fault-tolerant and capable of self-adaptation under varying conditions (e.g. missing or defective components). It uses machine learning so that the system would behave in a pre-defined manner given a pre-conceived scenario. Incremental learning is adapted for added machine knowledge acquisition. A simulation of system's behaviour, using a test case scenario, is presented in this paper. This work is our original contribution to an ongoing research to make informatics more accessible to handicapped users.

1 Introduction

A MULTIMODAL interface allows user to do computing with more than one mode of interaction. Incorporating *multimodality* into a computing system makes it more accessible to a wider range of users, including those with disabilities. A multimodal multimedia (MM) computing system [1] allows combining two different types of data – one from a multimodal source, usually demonstrated by human action (e.g. speech) and another from the usual media (e.g. keyboard) – and their fusion produces a new data which has a new meaning to the system. The fused data could be treated, among others, the same or complementary, depending on the time the two data are generated. We in this paper, however, are not into the fusion of data; rather, we treat multimodal

---

[*] This work has been made possible the funding awarded by the Natural Sciences and Engineering Research Council (NSERC) of Canada.

and multimedia processing separately. A computing system is pervasive [2] if the user could access data and process his task anytime and anywhere. The system must be self-adapting and self-evolving. A pervasive MM computing system intended for the blind makes such computing possible by associating applications, modalities and media to the user context and the types of data to be used.

In this system, there is an association that maps data types (e.g. .doc, .txt) to certain applications (e.g. text editor, web browser). Once an application, chosen in order of priority, is selected, the supplier of the application is also selected based on the user's preferences as indicated in his user profile. Finally, the media and modality to be used to input or receive data are selected based on the user's context.

In a pervasive computing environment (CE), the user context is used as a parameter to deduce the applications and tools to be accorded to the user. Given a context, a *scenario* is a situation that is to be taken into account. In this system, *machine learning* (ML) [3] is adapted, and knowledge acquisition is based on scenarios. A *precondition scenario* is a condition that requires a reaction, preferably intelligent, from the system. The reaction itself is called the *post-condition scenario*. In general, the ML component detects the pre-condition scenario, and then applies the corresponding post-condition scenario. An *incremental ML* [4] allows continuous knowledge acquisition for as long as there is something new (i.e. new scenario) to learn. The concept of ML suits well on the assumption of a correct post-condition scenario, that is, the devices are both present and functional. If it is not (e.g. a component is missing), instead of allowing exception error, one that could potentially cause the system to stall or crash, the system would instead find replacement to the missing component. This process of finding replacement to a failed component so that the system remains fault-tolerant does constitute the incremental ML of the system. The concepts of *pervasive computing*, *multimodal multimedia computing*, and *machine learning* are put together to produce a computing system that suits the needs of the visually impaired users. The system, although not physically constructed, is designed so that it resembles real-life scenarios; its components are designed in a way that they behave as if they really do exist in a real, functioning environment.

2 Related Work

Lately, there have been techniques developed to make computing more accessible to visually-impaired users. Speech synthesis and the Braille terminal are just a few examples. Using the method in [5], the blind could work independently on a few applications. For accessing data, software like GUIB [6] and vOICe [7] translate visual information into speech. For web browsing, BrailleSurf [8] and WebbIE [9] could convert text into either speech or Braille. Mathematical software like VICKIE [10] and AudioMath [11] could transfer data in LaTex or MathML format into another form (i.e. Braille or speech). This collection of software is important to the visually handicapped, hence we intend to use them as applications suppliers in our work.

An *agent* is some software that senses its environment and is capable of reaction, proactivity, and social interaction, a group of which forms a Multi-Agent System (MAS) [12]. Significant works in agency for the blind include Tyflos [13] which could help a user to be partially independent, able to walk, and work in a 3-D dynamic environment. Our work, in contrast, uses agents to detect user context, and other data in order to assist the system to determine the appropriate media and modalities. Other important works on multimodality for the blind include [14] and [15]. In concept, multimodality encourages system adaptation to various computing situations and user profiles. Having multimedia and multimodality in the system makes it possible to include devices that could replace those that cannot be used by handicapped users. For example, instead of regular screen that is inappropriate for blind users, a system could be designed with speech recognition system or with Braille terminal.

A *user profile* is important in determining the most appropriate method for the user to send/receive data to/from the system. For pervasive computing, the transfer of data, usually incompatible in size, from one environment to another, usually incompatible in resources, the technique proposed in [16] collects user profile from execution traces on geographically distributed computing resources. In [17], user data is created for virtual home environment management, representing information describing the network and personalized environments related to a roaming user; after analysis, a user profile is built. In [16], there exist many user profiles everywhere in the system which is costly, while in [17], the user profile is so big that it is inappropriate to use when computing device (e.g. PDA) has limited resources. Our work, in contrast, uses a single user profile that follows the user wherever he goes and adapts accordingly to the user's computing device.

Learning is the acquisition of knowledge. Knowledge could be given *a priori* or gained by *experience*. A machine has learned *positively* if it has acquired data or behavior that improves its future performance. In [18], a ML method is used in collecting data for conversational agent model. In [19], the ML is used in the dynamic reconfiguration of the system architecture. Compared with [18], the scope of ML applied to our work is limited; hence, the a priori training set already covers a large portion of possible scenarios. In [19], the ML is dependent on user context alone whereas in our work, it is dependent on user context, data types, computing device, and modalities; the design itself is suited for visually-impaired users. Indeed, our work is unique and different in many ways yet similar in objective of finding means to make computing more accessible to the visually-impaired users.

3 Paradigm of a Pervasive MM Computing System

3.1 Architectural Framework

Figure 1 shows the architectural framework of our pervasive MM computing system. A typical user could be a blind person who has some tasks to do. A *task* is a name used to describe a computing work (e.g. homework). The accomplishment of such task requires the user to utilize one or more applications, each of which has its own *quality of service* (QoS) parameters. For the system to be pervasive, it is essential that the user could continue working on his task anytime, anywhere. It follows that the user profile and information would have to "follow" the user wherever he goes. The intended user needs a set of media and modality that are different from those used by regular users. The components of the system and their functionalities are as follows:

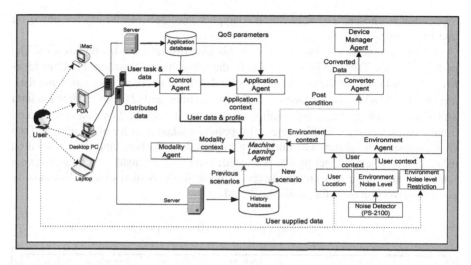

Fig. 1. The architectural framework of a pervasive MM computing system for visually-impaired users

(1) The *Control Agent (CA)* – is tasked to get user application's data, files and user profile; (2) The *Application Agent (AA)* – it manages user's task by instantiating the applications with appropriate suppliers and QoS service parameters; (3) The *Environment Agent (EA)* – it determines user's context by getting the noise level in the environment and the input from the user on user location and the noise constraints imposed in the user's location; (4) The *Modality Agent (MA)* – it manages and decides the modalities that are appropriate to use given the application data type and the context of the user; (5) The *Converter Agent (ConvA)* – it is responsible for conversion, if necessary, of data from one form to another (e.g. text to speech); (6) The *Device Manager Agent (DMA)* – it selects media suited for user's needs and context; and (7) The *Machine Learning Agent (MLA)* – responsible for machine's acquisition of knowledge which is based on user scenarios.

3.2 The User Task and User Profile

Figure 1 also illustrates the different possibilities for the user to connect to the distributed data. These data contains the user's profile, and up-to-date data and task registry. For a visually-impaired user, the applications' data types, for the time being, are fewer than those for the regular users, namely: *text*, *audio* and *video* files. The applications are also limited, namely: *web browser*, *text editor*, and *video player*. There is a mapping between a data type and different applications, and each application to different suppliers. There are pre-defined applications to use with respect to the data type. The applications themselves are ranked by priority. We have done the ranking based on our knowledge and experience concerning the applications that are most often associated with data type. By default, the highest ranked application is instantiated for the given data type. If the application itself is missing, the second-ranked application is chosen. The application's supplier and QoS parameters are based on user preferences.

The *user profile* is a record of the user, his identification and his preferences. The user profile (see Table 1 (Top)) consists of the following information: (1) *User identity* – this part contains the username, password, and the list of all computers and their identity (i.e. IP address) that the user could use anytime; and (2) *User application data preferences* – this contains information concerning the applications the user would usually invoke, along with his preferred suppliers, ranked in order of priority, and the QoS parameters he prefer. The ranking of preferred application suppliers is based on user's choice when his user profile is created; and (3) *User modality data preferences* – this contains the user's preferred type of voice for TTS (text-to-speech) modality and the conversion table for Braille keyboard.

Table 1. (Top) A sample of a user profile, and (Bottom) a sample of a task registry

Identity		Application data preferences		Modality data preferences	
Username:	\<username>	\<application 1> *(e.g. text editor)*		Text to Speech : Voice	
Password :	\<password>	*Preferred supplier* 1. \<supplier 1> 2. \<supplier 2> 3. \<supplier 3>	*QoS Parameter* Volume audio=x	*Gender* (Masculine | Feminine)	*Age* Young Adult
Computer 1	\<Computer1, IP address= \<t1.x1.y1.z1> ...>				
		\<application 2> *(e.g. audio)*		Text to Braille	
Computer 2	\<Computer2, IP address= \<t2.x2.y2.z2>, ...>	*Preferred supplier* 1. \<supplier 1> 2. \<supplier 2> 3. \<supplier 3>	*QoS Parameter* Volume audio=x	*Notation* (Marburg | French Braille | Nemeth)	
		\<application n>		Modality n	
Computer n	\<Computer n, IP address= \<tn.xn.yn.zn>...>	*Preferred supplier* 1. \<supplier 1> 2. \<supplier 2> 3. \<supplier 3>	*QoS Parameter* Volume audio=x		

Application 1		Application 2		Application n	
Last update	\<date x>	Last update	\<date y>	Last update	\<date z>
1. File 1	\<filename 1> \<supplier 1> \< date 1 last modified >	1. File a	\<filename a> \<supplier a> \< date a last modified >	1. File u	\<filename u> \<supplier u> \< date u last modified >
2. File 2	\<filename 2> \<supplier 2> \< date 2 last modified >	2. File b	\<filename b> \<supplier b> \< date b last modified >	2. File v	\<filename v> \<supplier v> \< date v last modified >
m. File m	\<filename m> \<supplier m> \< date m last modified>	i. File i	\<filename i> \<supplier i> \< date i last modified >	w. File w	\<filename w> \<supplier w> \< date w last modified >

A *new* user profile is created by network administration when a new user is added to the system. The user profile is *private*, but the user could modify it anytime he wants. The data profile is presented in generic form in Table 1 to accommodate all possible values of a certain item. The *task registry* (see Table 1 (Bottom)) is a table of all the applications the user had used recently. In our work, when a user logs onto a computing system with no resource restriction (e.g. no RAM restriction, etc.) such as with PC or laptop, then the last file for each application will be instantiated automatically, with user's desired QoS parameter values. For one with limited resources, such as PDA, then only the most recent applications will be instantiated (i.e. based on assumption that the user will continue working on his latest task) depending if there are sufficient available resources; without such resources, there will be no instantiation of application. When the user logs out, the task registry is updated to include the applications used by the user in such session. The diagram in Table 1 is, again, in a generic format in order to accommodate all possible values of certain parameters.

3.3 The User Context

The *user context* is dependent upon three variables, namely (1) the *user's location* (i.e. whether the user is at home, at work or on the go), (2) *the noise level of environment*, and (3) *the noise restriction imposed by environment* (e.g. silence required in a library, silence is optional in a park). Figure 1 (Right-side) also shows how user context is obtained. The user supplies the information about his present location. This is implemented by creating a voice-activated pop-up menu where the user would select his current location from a given list of his previous whereabouts. The list keeps growing each time he includes new places into the list. By default, the last whereabouts of the user is chosen. If his current location is different from the default location, he simply has to state his current location when the pop-up menu is activated. The noise level imposed by the environment is also manually entered by the user. The user chooses one from the two choices: either that the user is obliged to maintain silence (as in the library) or not (as is the case in a cafeteria, for example).

The noise level of the environment is detected by a sensor. The noise level is important in whether to invoke speech recognition or not. In this work, we opt for *PASPORT PS 2100 noise detector* [20] which can be connected to a computer's USB port. In concept, the EA takes *n noise samples per unit of time*. Taking 1 sample per minute, and 5 total samples are adequate to detect the environment noise level.

The unit of noise intensity is decibel (dB). At this stage, we consider that 40 dB or less makes the environment "*quiet*", 41 to 50 dB is considered as "*acceptable*" and 51 dB or more is "*noisy*". This range could be modified by the user based on his perception of noise. In general, in a quiet or acceptable noise-leveled environment, a speech recognition modality is effective; it is less effective in a noisy environment; hence, the system opts for alternative modality that is effective in a noisy setting.

3.4 The Data Types, Applications and Application Suppliers

Table 2 provides the data types that can be created or retrieved by the user. The applications associated with each data type are determined a priori. The priority is based upon the usual application used to open up the data type, as observed from the choices of the majority in such a situation. Also shown is the list of the suppliers that support the application. For example, a *.txt* data is usually browsed by a user using a text editor. However, if a text editor is missing (a remote possibility) from the current system, then a web browser would be invoked as alternative application. The supplier which instantiates an application totally depends on the user's supplier preference. The same concept applies to all other data types listed in Table 2. The list is not exhaustive yet; we intend to update it from time to time. The table's data forms part of the AA's knowledge. It means that only the AA has jurisdiction over this file. Recall that the AA determines data type and instantiates application using user's preferred supplier and QoS parameters, all of which are available in user's profile (see Table 1).

Table 2. List of software applications ranked in priority, for selected data types, and selected suppliers for different applications

Data type			Software Application appropriate for the data	
.txt	.doc		1. Text Editor	2. Web Browser
.pdf	.html	.xml	1. Web Browser	2. Text Editor
.wav	.mp3	.wma	1. Audio Player	
.wmv	.avi	.mpg	1. Video Player	2. Audio Player
...				

Application	Supplier
Text editor	Ms Word, Word Pad, Note Pad, Latex, Acrobat Reader, Meditor.
Web Browser	Explorer, Netscape, Opera, FireFox, BrailleSurf, Simply Web 2000.
Audio Player	Media Player, Real One Player, Winamp, JetAudio, BsPlayer.
Video Player	Media Player, Real One Player, JetAudio, PowerDVD.

3.5 Machine Learning

Machine Learning (ML) concerns about development of techniques allowing computer to acquire knowledge. In *supervised learning*, the system generates a function that maps inputs to some desired outputs. There exists a function f, the function to be learned and h, the hypothesis about the function. There is a set of vector-valued input $X = \{x_1, x_2, ..., x_n\}$ with n components. Hypothesis h is implemented with X as an input and $h(X)$ as the output. A hypothesis denoted as $h(x1) = 100\%$ means that such possible action merits implementation. A hypothesis denoted as $h(x1) = 0\%$ means the action being considered lacks merit and will not be implemented. In this system, X is a set of the parameters being considered in a pre-condition scenario, namely: (i) *computing device used to login* (e.g. laptop, PDA), (ii) *application used* (e.g. text, video), (iii) *modality* (e.g. Braille, speech), (iv) *noise level* (e.g. quiet, noisy), and (v) *environment noise restraint* (e.g. silence required). Hence, X_i = a set of pre-condition scenarios, for $i = 1$ to n. There is a mapping from set X to set Y = a set of post-condition scenarios, denoted by $f: X \rightarrow Y$. The post-condition set Y_j = a set of post-condition scenarios, for $j = 1$ to m.

The *a priori* training set is the machine's initial knowledge. The machine's capacity to react to a computing situation is initially based on this training set. However, the possibility of the system stall or crash is real if a situation that is not available in the training set arises. Indeed, for the system to adapt to its changing environment, the system must continue to learn. This is the rational for adapting incremental ML.

In the *a priori training set*, we can have one *image* (i.e. a post-condition scenario) for one or more *ranges* (i.e. pre-condition scenarios). For example, the pre-conditions 1 and 2 have a common post-condition scenario in Table 3 which illustrates the a priori training of the ML system. Here, to avoid repetitive long names, we use the following abbreviations: *KB=Keyboard, OKB=Overlay Keyboard, SRQ=Silence required, SOP=Silence Optional, SP=Speech, BR=Braille, BRT=Braille Terminal, HST=Headsets, SPK=Speakers, Mic=Microphone, WMP=Windows Media Player.*

Table 3. A priori training set

Scenario No.	Computing	Application	Modality	Noise level	Environment restriction	Supplier	Medias Activated						Medias deactivated	
1	PC	Audio/Player	KB/SP/BR	Quiet	SRQ	Real Player	KB	HST	OKB				Mic	SPK
2	PC	Audio/Player	KB/SP/BR	Acceptable	SRQ		KB	HST	OKB					
3	PC	Audio/Player	KB/SP/BR	Quiet	SOP	Real Player	KB	HST	OKB					
4	PC	-	-	-	-	-	-	-	-	-	-	-	-	-
-	PC	-	-	-	-	-	-	-	-	-	-	-	-	-
-	PC	-	-	-	-	-	-	-	-	-	-	-	-	-
i	PC	Text editor	KB/SP/BR	Quiet	SRQ	Notepad	KB	HST	OKB			BRT	Mic	SPK
i+1	PC	Text editor	KB/SP/BR	Acceptable	SOP	Notepad	KB	HST	OKB	Mic	SPK	BRT		
-	PC	Text editor	-	-	-	-	-	-	-	-	-	-	-	-
-	PC	Text editor	-	-	-	-	-	-	-	-	-	-	-	-
j	PC	Text editor	KB/SP	Noise	SOP	Word	KB	HST			SPK		Mic	
j+1	PC	Text editor	KB/SP	Acceptable	SRQ	Word	KB	HST					Mic	SPK
-							-	-	-	-	-	-	-	-
k	PDA	Video/Player	KB/SP	Quiet	SRQ	Movie Player	KB	HST					Mic	SPK
k+1	PDA	Video/Player	KB/SP	Quiet	SOP	Movie Player	KB	HST		Mic	SPK			
-	-	-	-	-	-	-	-	-	-	-	-	-	-	-
l	Laptop	Audio/Player	KB/SP/BR	Acceptable	SRQ	WMP	KB	HST	OKB				Mic	SPK
l+1	Laptop	Audio/Player	KB/SP/BR	Acceptable	SOP	WMP	KB	HST	OKB	Mic	SPK			
-	Laptop	-	-	-	-	-	-	-	-	-	-	-	-	-
-	Laptop	-	-	-	-	-	-	-	-	-	-	-	-	-
m	Laptop	-	KB/SP	Quiet	SRQ	Real Player	KB	HST					Mic	SPK
m+1	Laptop	-	KB/SP	Quiet	SOP	Real Player	KB	HST		Mic	SPK			
-	-	-	-	-	-	-	-	-	-	-	-	-	-	-
n	Laptop	Web Browser	KB/SP/BR	Noise	SOP	Braille Surf	KB	HST	OKB	Mic	SPK	BRT		
n+1	Laptop	-	-	-	-	-	-	-	-	-	-	-	-	-

As stated in [4], a learning task is incremental if the training examples used to solve it become available overtime, usually one at a time. The main characteristics of an incremental learning task are: (i) *examples are not available a priori but become available over time, usually one at a time,* and (ii) *learning may need to go on indefinitely.* A learning algorithm is *incremental* if for any given training sample $e_1, e_2, \ldots e_n$, it produces a sequence of hypothesis $h_1, h_2, \ldots, h_n$ such that h_{i+1} depends only on h_i and the current example e_i.

In this paper, the incremental ML process (see its algorithm in Figure 2) happens when the system is set to implement the post-condition scenario but is unable of doing so because of missing components. In such a situation, an exception error is produced that could cause the system to stall or to crash. To deal with it, system stall or crash can be prevented by invoking incremental ML. When a component is missing or defective, a replacement is automatically selected. When the replacement selection is empty (i.e. incremental ML is still null), the system delivers the choice selection to the user who then interacts with the system; the user choice is then considered as *alternative1* (Figure 2). This is the first training for the machine. This new knowledge is added into the *knowledge database* (KD) for actual and future use. When this scenario occurs again in the future, the system then knows how to react correctly. Now, imagine that such scenario happens again and *alternative1* is also found missing or defective. The system will be trained for the second time on this scenario, this time the system asks the user to intervene in selecting *alternative2*. As before, this new knowledge is then appended into the KD. If necessary, the ML system could be trained as many times as possible. When trainings have been done, the system becomes fault-tolerant and could react accordingly with no or very little intervention.

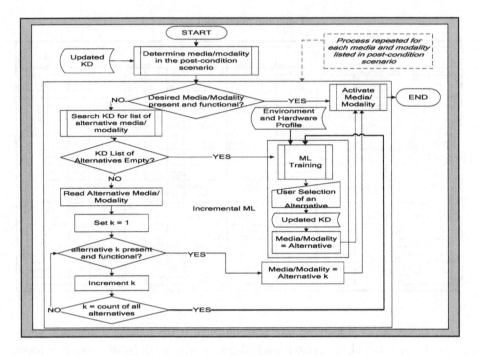

Fig. 2. The incremental machine learning process

3.6 Device and Modality Selection

While the MLA gets involved in determining the post-condition scenario of the user and the AA instantiates the application with the supplier and QoS preferred by the user, the CA itself finds the way to convert the user data from one form to another (e.g. text to speech) depending on the calculated/pre-determined post-condition scenario. Sometimes, there may not even be a need for data conversion (e.g. speech to speech). The CA yields an output data file that has to be delivered to the user via one or more output devices. The output of CA is sent to DMA which would activate selected output media and deactivate some others. This is demonstrated in the example scenario (Figure 4) later on. In general, the DMA has a complete knowledge of the media devices that are currently available in the CE. Its decision what media and modality to activate or deactivate depends entirely on the pre-determined post-condition scenario. The techniques used by the CA in its task of data conversion are patterned from various techniques already mentioned.

4 Formal Specification and Sample Simulation

A *formal specification* is a mathematical description of software, hardware or system that may be used to develop an implementation. It describes *what* the system should do, but *not how* the system should do it. Even without actual implementation, one could determine the overall system behaviour via formal specification. Petri Net is an appropriate formal specification for us since it could demonstrate the system's dynamism, and the demonstration of variations in the user's CE. We use HPSim [21] for Petri Net specification shown in Figure 3.

4.1 Formal Specification Using Petri Net

The *Petri Net* was defined by Carl Adam Petri in 1962. It extends the concept of state machine to include concurrency. Petri Net is a formal, graphical, executable technique for the specification and analysis of a concurrent, discrete-event *dynamic* system. It is represented by an ellipse called *place* (basically a state), a rectangle called *transition* (basically a process) and an arc representing *input for a transition to take place* (either from a place to a transition, or from a transition to a place). Places can contain *tokens*; the current state of the modeled system (the marking) is given by the number of tokens (and type, if they are distinguishable) in each place. When the transition fires, it removes tokens from its input places and adds some to all its output places. The number of tokens removed/added depends on the cardinality of each arc.

A marking of a Petri Net is reachable if, starting in the initial marking, a sequence of transition firings exist that produces it. A Petri Net is bounded if there is a maximum to the number of tokens in its reachable markings. Petri Net specification can be defined as a quadruple *(P, T, F, B)*, where *P* = a non-empty set of places, *T* = a non-empty set of transitions, F: P x T $\rightarrow$ N is the forward incidence function, *B: P x T $\rightarrow$ N* is the backward incidence function and **N** = the set of integers $\geq$ 0. *"Firing"* of any transition changes the marking of the Petri Net. The system's Petri Net specification is shown in Figure 3.

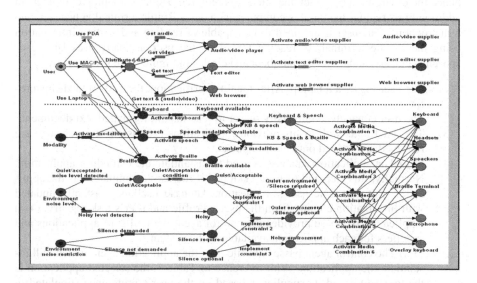

Fig. 3. Formal specification depicting different pre-condition scenarios and their resulting post-condition scenarios using Petri Net

As depicted in Figure 3, there are 4 places that are all activated simultaneously, namely the user which logs in a particular computing device, and the modality activated by the system, the level of noise in the environment and the noise restraint imposed by the environment. The topmost place yields the activation of three applications (i.e. audio/video player, text editor, and web browser). The supplier and QoS parameters used to instantiate the application are based on user's preferences found in the user profile. The modality place yields a final output that combines keyboard and speech, and a trio combination of keyboard, speech and Braille. The environment noise level produces a final output which is either quiet/acceptable, or noisy. The noise restraint imposed by the environment could only be silence required or silence optional. As per Petri Net specification, a final output is produced only after all the values of the 4 parameters are taken into account. Briefly, the output of the Petri Net is the activation of software applications and the selection of a set of media and modalities for activation as the appropriate input-output devices or modalities for such a context combination. Petri Net specification illustrates all possible variations of the 4 input parameters and depending on these inputs, the simulation produces every possible output in the media and devices that are activated by the system.

4.2 Sample Scenario Simulation

We present a scenario that demonstrates how each component of the system interacts with other components. Scenarios are based on some real-life situations in which the visually impaired user would usually do computing.

The Scenario

Assumptions: The user is a visually-impaired student. He is in a university library, hence the environment is quiet and silence is required. He uses a laptop computer. In addition to its regular media, this computer includes a Braille terminal, a headset, and a microphone. The user is assumed to be capable of reading and writing information using the Braille terminal. In reading text data, the user normally uses Braille or speech synthesis modality. The numbers and circles in Figure 4 are given below:

(1)   The user logs via a laptop. After identity verification, the system loads his profile.

(2)   The user connects to university server to read his .txt formatted text document.

(3)   The .txt file as well as his previous applications (via user's task registry) are retrieved and loaded onto his computer.

(4)   (4-a) The application database is used to instantiate the text editor application. Normally, this step and (4-b) are skipped if the user's computer has the application software. The user's application database itself is constantly updated with information coming from the user's profile and user's task registry. (4-b) Application database provides the control agent with a list of applications and suppliers for each application available in the system.

(5)   (5-a) The control agent passes .txt file onto the application agent which will instantiate the application. With reference to Table 3, the selected application is the text editor and its supplier is based on the user's preference stipulated in the user profile. (5-b) Default quality of service parameter of the selected application is supplied to the application agent. QoS parameter is derived from the user profile.

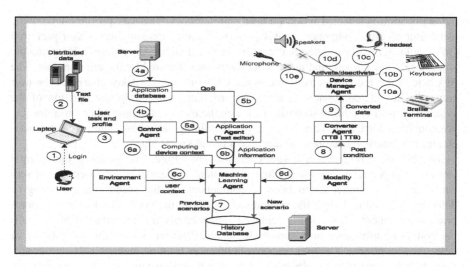

Fig. 4. A sample scenario simulation

(6)   (6-a) The user's computing device is made known to the MLA through CA. (6-b) The application used by the AA is also conveyed to the MLA. (6-c) The EA passes the user context to the MLA. The environment noise level is decided by sample readings from the sensor (i.e. PASPORT PS 2100) while the other context data are supplied by the user. (6-d) The MA informs the MLA which modalities are currently available in the system. In this example, the Braille, speech recognition system and keyboard are all available.

(7)   The MLA retrieves the previous scenarios (i.e. previous knowledge) from the KD. In this example, we assume that there is a similar scenario found in the KD. Hence, a new calculation has been evaded, and the system would simply implement the post-condition scenario stated in the record read from the KD.

(8)   The post-condition scenario is to be implemented. With reference to the user profile and context, the CA would convert text into Braille and speech.

(9)   Converted data is received by DMA. DMA would then decide which available media have to be activated /deactivated.

(10)   (10-a) Braille terminal is activated. (10-b) Keyboard is also activated. (10-c) The headset is activated. (10-d) The speaker is completely inappropriate to use for the setting so it is deactivated. (10-e) The microphone is obviously a no choice in a library so it is also deactivated.

5   Conclusion

This paper demonstrates the paradigm of a pervasive MM computing system that supports the needs of visually-impaired users. The infrastructure makes user's profile, data files and the machine's knowledge omnipresent, making them accessible to the user whenever and wherever he may be. A selected set of data types is part of the AA's knowledge base. Application software is mapped with data type; the supplier of the application is selected based on user's preferences. The user profile contains the usual user identity component + user preferred application suppliers + user preferred QoS parameter values. The user context is decided based on user's location, the workplace's noise level, and noise level restriction imposed by the environment. The MA detects the modalities available in the CE while the EA takes charge of the user context. The ML component is aimed at providing the appropriate reaction of the system (i.e. post-condition scenario) based on the user context and other variables (i.e. pre-condition scenario). There is an a priori training set whose data (pre- and post-condition scenarios) becomes the machine's initial knowledge.

The ML is incremental if it keeps learning over time. The system's incremental learning component is activated when the system realizes that a post-condition scenario cannot be implemented because components in the scenario are missing or defective. Instead of letting the system stall or crash, the system looks for the appropriate replacements. If the list of replacements is empty (i.e. incremental ML is null) the system requires user intervention; he chooses the replacement to the missing or defective component. The user response is taken as training number 1. If similar scenario happens again and replacement 1 is also found missing or defective, then the ML component is subjected to training number 2; the replacement is called replacement2. This process is repeated for knowledge acquisition for the replacements of other components. The more training the machine is subjected to, the more it becomes smarter, making it more fault-tolerant. Incremental ML is also important because new media and modality could be introduced to the system with very little user intervention.

Future works include the dynamic reconfiguration of the system architecture when there are cascaded failures of components. Also, we intend to mention the exceptions and errors that are manifested by different media and modality under different conditions. The resource management in the PDA is a concern as we try to transfer data and files from a laptop, for example, to a PDA. The *dynamic software architecture* [23] and the system's ability to be *autonomic* [24] are also part of our future works.

References

1. Djenidi, H., et al *"Generic Multimedia Multimodal Agents Paradigms and their Dynamic Reconfiguration at the Architectural Level"*, EURASIP Journal on Applied Signal Processing, Vol. 2004, No. 11, Sept. 2004.
2. McCullough, M. *"Digital Ground: Architecture, Pervasive Computing, and Environmental Knowing"*, Cambridge, Mass., USA, MIT Press, © 2004. ISBN 0262134357.
3. Mitchell, T. M., *"Machine Learning"*, McGraw-Hill, USA, 1997, ISBN. 0-07-042807-7.
4. Giraud-Carrier, C. *"A Note on the Utility of Incremental Learning"*, AI Communications, v 13, n 4, 2000, pp. 215-223.
5. Ross, D.A. *"Cyber Crumbs for Successful Aging with Vision Loss"*, IEEE Pervasive Computing, Vol. 3, Issue 2, April-June 2004, pp. 30 – 35.
6. Royal Natl Institute of the Blind, *"Final Report of the TIDE"*, UK, 1995, (website: http://www.rnib.org.uk)
7. Meijer,P., *"The vOICe: Vision Technology for the Totally Blind"*, 2005, (website: www.seeingwithsound.com/voice.htm)

8. Archambault, D., *"BrailleSurf: An HTML Browser for Visually Handicapped People"*, CSUN Conf., Los Angeles, USA, 1999.
9. King, A., et al *"WebbIE, A Web Browser for Visually Impaired People"*, 2nd CWUAAT Workshop, Cambridge, UK, 2004.
10. Moço, V. and Archambault, D. *"Automatic Conversions of Mathematical Braille: A Survey of Main Difficulties in Different Languages"*, ICCHP Conference, Paris, France, 2004.
11. Ferreira, H. and Freitas, D., *"Enhancing the Accessibility of Mathematics for Blind People: the AudioMath Project"*, ICCHP Conference, Paris, France, 2004.
12. Wooldridge, M., *"An Introduction to Multi-agent Systems"*, Wiley, Chichester, UK, 2001.
13. Bourbakis, N.G., et al *"An Intelligent Assistant for Navigation of Visually Impaired People"*, 2nd IEEE Intl Symposium on Bioinformatics and Bioengineering Conference, 2001.
14. Edwards, A., *"MATHS, Mathematical Access for TecHnology and Science"*, UK, 1997. (www.cs.york.ac.uk/maths)
15. Bellik Y., «*Interfaces multimodales : concepts, modèles et architectures* », Ph.D. Thesis, Université d'Orsay, Paris, 1995.
16. Antoniol, G., et al *"A Distributed Architecture for Dynamic Analyses on User-profile Data"*, 8th European Conference on Software Maintenance and Reengineering, 2004.
17. Bougant, F., Delmond, F., Pageot-Millet, C., *"The User Profile for the Virtual Home Environment"*, IEEE Communications Magazine, Vol. 41, Issue 1, Jan. 2003, pp. 93 – 98.
18. Okamoto, M., *"Design and Application of Learning Conversational Agents"*, Ph.D. Thesis, Department of Social Informatics, Kyoto University, 2003.
19. Hina, M.D., et al *"A Ubiquitous Context-sensitive Multimodal Multimedia Computing and Its Machine-Learning Assisted Reconfiguration at the Architectural Level"*, Workshop on Multimedia Information Proc. and Retrieval, 7th IEEE Intl Symp. on Multimedia, 2005.
20. http://www.pasco.com/products/
21. http://www.winpesim.de/petrinet/
22. Herbordt, W., et al *"Noise-Robust Hands-Free Speech Recognition on PDA's Using Microphone Array Technology"*, Autumn Meeting of the Acous. Society of Japan, 2005.
23. Han, T., et al *"Structure Analysis for Dynamic Software Architecture"*, 6th Intl. Conf. on Software Eng., Artificial Int., Net. and Parallel/Dist. Comp., May, 2005.
24. Horn, P., *"Autonomic Computing: IBM's Perspective on the State of Information Technology"*, IBM Research, 2001.

Context-Aware Adaptation for Media Delivery in Pervasive Computing Environment[*]

Wenzhe Zhang, Haibing Guan, Minglu Li, Min-You Wu,
Chongqing Zhang, and Feilong Tang

Department of CSE, Shanghai Jiaotong University,
1954# Huashan Road, Shanghai, China
wzzhang@sjtu.edu.cn

Abstract. A robust solution for context-aware multimedia delivery in the pervasive computing environment remains a challenging problem. Its heterogeneous and dynamic nature demands a more flexible and intelligent framework than Internet does. We propose an adaptive middleware solution to address this issue. The system responds to the condition of the network to offer extensibility and efficiency. Furthermore, we propose an active controlling scheme, in which the multimedia delivery is able to adapt to the environment variation in a timely fashion. In addition, we describe an application scenario of our framework, which opens out a wide prospect.

1 Introduction

Over the last decade, there has been a dramatic increase in the use of computer embedded devices, such as PDA, to perform control tasks and access the Internet or other information sources. Furthermore, emerging standards in wireless communications enable embedded devices to inter-communicate and pervasively access information. These trends have led to a change from the traditional computer- centered to a future human-centered information access mode. The resulting change in our view of computers and their use by humans is the subject of the field known as Pervasive Computing [1]. As users are beginning to rely more heavily on pervasive devices, there is a growing need for applications to bring information to the devices. However, as for the Internet and other applications that make use of various types of multimedia data, such as Video-On-Demand, most multimedia content was designed and organized with desktop computers and high-speed networks in mind. They usually contain rich media data such as images, audio, and video, which are not suitable for those pervasive devices with limited display capability, process power and network bandwidth. Therefore, the quality of media information often needs to be adjusted according to the network bandwidth and the capabilities of pervasive devices [2]. As a result, some challenging research issues were proposed to eliminate the mismatch between the rich multimedia content and the limited network conditions.

---

[*] This research was supported partially by Natural Science Foundation of Shanghai Grant (No.05ZR14081).

Y.-C. Chung and J.E. Moreira (Eds.): GPC 2006, LNCS 3947, pp. 634–643, 2006.

Context-aware Adaptation for Media Delivery can solve this problem by adapting media content to the specific capabilities of the network environment. In order to realize it, many issues from different aspects must be addressed and integrated [2]. These issues include:

- Multimedia content description model that supports the description of resource requirements of multimedia objects.
- Management and selection of different versions of multimedia objects to adapt to client capabilities, network bandwidth and user preference.
- General and extensible mechanisms that describe and exchange the information of the client devices' capabilities, such as the display size, screen color depth, audio, video display capabilities, storage space, processing power, network access bandwidth, and so forth.
- Methods for manipulating, transcoding and summarizing multimedia objects.
- A framework that integrates all of the above technologies together.

Our main goals while developing the architecture were to investigate how context information could be integrated with a multimedia delivery system, what types of context information would be most suitable to support useful functions in context-aware applications and to provide an architecture for organizing data in a pervasive environment. The implementation and further experience with the system will help us to better understand how multimedia delivery system must be changed to accommodate the unique characteristics of pervasive computing.

1.1 Previous Work

Context-aware pervasive computing emphasizes on using context of users, devices, etc. to provide services appropriate to particular person, space, and time. Since it was proposed about a decade ago, many researchers have studied this topic and built several context-aware applications to demonstrate the usefulness of this new technology. However, context is application-dependent. Schilit divides context into three categories [3]: *Computing context*, such as network connectivity, communication costs, and communication bandwidth, and nearby resources such as printers, displays, and workstations, *User context*, such as the user's profile, location, people nearby, even the current social situation and *Physical context*, such as lighting, noise levels, traffic conditions, and temperature. G. Chen[4] generally defines two kinds of context as active context and passive context, which are critical or relevant but not critical respectively. G. Xu [6] presents QoSTalk, a unified QoS (Quality-of-Service) programming environment for pervasive multimedia applications.

Here we try to formally define context as "any information that can be used to characterize the situation of an entity. An entity is a person, place, or object that is considered relevant to the interaction between a user and an application, including the user and applications themselves". Due to the merits of video programs, real-time video distribution in the pervasive environment has become one of the most important applications. But the pervasive infrastructure is vulnerable and dynamic, the Quality-of-service can't be guaranteed.

In our previous paper [13], we focused on the traditional uni-cast environment, and proposed a Layered transmission solution over the dynamic communication environment. In this paper, we would like to propose a universal architecture for context-aware media delivery.

1.2 Paper Organization

The paper is organized as follows. In section 2 we present different media content description models that support the description of resource requirements of multimedia objects. In section 3 we illustrate the context abstracted for multimedia delivery in pervasive environment and context modeling. Section 4 presents the framework of adaptive delivery and its application scenario. After analyzing the effectiveness of scheme proposed, we conclude the paper with section 5.

2 Different Media Models

Media information exists in various types, such as text, images, video, and audio. In addition, each type may have different representations. For example, an image can be saved in JPEG, GIF, or BMP formats. To describe a real object, we can use different media types, at different levels of quality or detail. For example, to introduce a new movie, we can use text in different languages to give a brief introduction about the story, use images to introduce the actors, use video and audio clips from the movie to attract the audience, etc. Here, we will briefly discuss several existing standards and data models for media information [7].

The Hyper-Text Markup Language: HTML is based on SGML (Standard Generalized Markup Language) and is designed to specify the logical organization of a document. It defines syntax to enrich text pages with structural information using SGML elements. It is also possible to include various kinds of media elements into a HTML document. Although HTML is the most common choice for current web pages, it does not offer any mechanism to specify adaptation of a document to user preferences and technical infrastructure. Dynamic HTML (DHTML) describes the abstract concept of breaking up a web page into processable elements, and exposing those elements to a scripting language. Such scripts first determine the user or system profile, and then change the structure of the HTML according to the profile. With DHTML, page modifications appear immediately following a trigger, such as a user selection at the client side. Since the author must code and know all adaptation alternatives at authoring time, this kind of adaptation is static. In addition, since DHTML can only modify the currently loaded page, it does not reduce document size and transmission load.

MHEG-5 and MHEG-6: MHEG is an ISO/IEC international standard that specifies a coded representation of final-form multimedia/hypermedia information objects, for their interchange within or across systems. MHEG part 5 was created to allow the development of a MHEG interpreter which fits in a device with minimal resource. MHEG-6 extends MHEG-5 by adding data processing and communication functions with the external environment, such as servers, and local devices. In MHEG-6, the MHEG engine could call a Java program that retrieves the actual values for a given profile and then sets the variables of the document. So, with the use of MHEG-6, adaptation of a presentation to user interests or technical infrastructure is possible.

Since all adaptation alternatives must be specified within a document at authoring time, this is static adaptation.

SMIL: The SMIL (Synchronized Multimedia Integration Language) is a W3C standard that aims at synchronized multimedia presentations on the Web. An interesting feature of SMIL is the "switch" element, which is a simple means for modeling alternatives and quality of a presentation. With the help of switch elements, an author can specify different presentation alternatives among which one is chosen at presentation time due to external parameters. Thus, the switch element allows for static adaptation. The selection of the alternatives is guided by simple predicts which include parameters set outside the SMIL document. These parameters are predefined by the standard and describe mainly technical features, like the available bandwidth. This allows adapting a SMIL document to the technical infrastructure.

MPEG-7: MPEG-7 is an ISO/IEC standard developed by MPEG (Moving Picture Experts Group). MPEG-7, formally named "Multimedia Content Description Interface", aims to create a standard for describing the multimedia content. MPEG-7 Multimedia Description Schemes define a set of Data types and Description Schemes, which can describe the visual as well as the aural content of a single AV document. Among all Description Schemes, the Variations DS is used to specify variations of audio-visual data. The variations may be, in general, generated in a number of different ways, or reflect revisions of the original data. The quality of the variation compared to the original is given by a fidelity value.

These approaches are mostly concerned with document layout, structure, interaction and synchronization, and only have a limited ability to support static adaptation. Besides, several multimedia information models have been also proposed by different research groups [7].

3 Contexts for Media Delivery

In this section, we introduce the context we abstract. "Primary" contexts, including location, entity, activity and time, act as indices into other sources of contextual information [5]. Combining several context values may generate a more powerful understanding of the current situation. For example, knowing the current location and current time, together with the user's calendar, the application will have a pretty good idea of the user's current social situation, such as having a meeting, sitting in the class, waiting in the airport, and so on [10]. In this paper we take advantage of both location and time context as well as network bandwidth. Context history is generally believed to be useful, so we'll discuss it successively.

3.1 Context Acquisition

Location: Since the location is an important context that changes whenever the user moves, a reliable location-tracking system is critical to many context-aware applications. It is easy to gather such location information if the user is willing to (and always remembers to) supply her location context to the system. Typical techniques include user sliding her badge or pressing a fingerprint reader before entering and leaving (ideally) a room. The system can also watch which workstation the user logged in. These methods, however, need user's explicit cooperation and only provide coarse granularity and low accuracy (if the user forgets to let system know when she leaves the room). The obvious choice for automatic location sensing techniques is the Global Positioning System (GPS). Recently, the US Government turned off degradation of the civil GPS signal to allow an accuracy of 10 to 20 meters, which is 10 times more accurate than before. Automobile navigation systems instantly benefit from this new policy, and we can certainly imagine many other applications will become possible, such as PDA's user location [11].

Time: This contextual information is not difficult to obtain, of course, from the built-in clock of the computer. Many applications correlate the location information with timestamp. Though there are other forms of time context, such as day of the week, day of the month, month of the year, season of the year, time zone, and so forth, only time-of day information has been used as far as we know. Also, time context tends to be used together with schedule information, while in our scheme it is used to reflect the user's activity.

Network bandwidth: As stated before, network bandwidth is also an important computational context in our scheme. Underlying system support is a usual way for applications to adapt to the bandwidth changes. Implemented as a user-level module, system provides API calls by which applications can be notified when the network bandwidth changes. In our opinion, we indicate the media receiver report network condition to the sender actively.

High-level contexts: In addition to the raw contextual information such as location, time and bandwidth, we are also interested in high-level context information such as the user's "current activity". It is, however, a big challenge to sense complex social contexts. One approach is to consult the user's calendar directly to find out what the user is supposed to do at certain time. The user, however, is not always willing or able to put her activities in the calendar and she may not always follow the calendar. Another method is to use Artificial Intelligence techniques to recognize complex context by combining several simple low-level contexts.

3.2 Modeling the Context

Similarly the models developed for context aware applications are often opportunistic and strongly related to the technologies deployed. In our understanding the following properties of context are central:

- ♦ Each context is anchored in an entity.
- ♦ Context-awareness is always related to an entity.

An entity is a place, a subject, a device, an application, another context, or a group of these. When creating sensing systems that supply context about an entity the domain knowledge that is available on the entity can be exploited [11].

To illustrate the concept consider the contexts described in Table. 1. It can be observed that these contexts of single entity are greatly independent on the general

Table 1. Examples of Entries with Typical Contexts assigned

Type of entity	Entity	Examples of typical context	Contexts relations in examples
Place	location	Workroom, Smart kitchen, Driving simulator, Living room, Conference room	Non-exclusive
Time	time	Daytime, Night	Exclusive
Subject	bandwidth	<10Mbps, 10-100Mbps, >100Mbps	Exclusive

situation of use, so on this level there is no difference whether the bandwidth is based on cable, infrared or fiber communication. Relating situations and tasks to objects and properties is a bottom-up approach to understanding and modeling context [8].

4 Context-Aware Adaptation for Media Delivery

Based on the introduction of context abstraction, in this section we propose a universal context-aware framework for multimedia delivery in pervasive computing environment.

4.1 Location-Aware System

Mobility is the most characteristic of devices in pervasive computing environment [1]. The ability to use implicit situational information, or context, is crucial to the development of "intelligent" mobile applications. Instead of relying on the explicit user inputs, context-aware applications are capable of providing tailored services and information by exploiting user context (e.g., location context, social context and computing context). For applications to perceive context, sensors are used to acquire various contextual information in the environment [16], and inference procedures are employed to aggregate contextual knowledge from raw data [14], [15]. Contextual information is inherently distributed and heterogeneous. Individual context-aware applications, in particular ones that operate under resource-limited mobile devices, have limited capability to acquire contextual information and to reason about context. To overcome these problems, firstly we are prototyping a location-aware system as a middleware infrastructure to enable context-awareness in mobile applications. This will provide support for acknowledge integration, knowledge consistency, and spatial and temporal reasoning.

The architecture of basic location aware system is shown as fig.1. The hardware includes a portable PC, a GPS receiver, a CDPD modem. Message Engine embedded in Client's PDA packs GPS data and sends to Server via CDPD Modem. Thus we can acquire the client's location and figure out its position in the virtual map at Server.

4.2 Context-Aware Framework for Media Delivery

We propose an adaptive framework to solve the sender-receiver adaptation in multimedia delivery. Adaptation performed at receivers is only fixed layer rates and

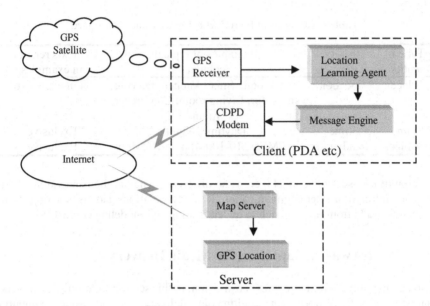

Fig. 1. Location aware System

limited num of layers. Adaptation at sender is how to acquire the user's bandwidth, location and current time, abstract high-level context and regulate the coding and transmission according to the context.

Here we introduce User Profile Server (UPS) to support this adaptive mechanism. UPS works as the partner of media server, storing personal information for each user, including individual setting, specialized QoS policy, and their current states during the service etc. The data can be fetched from it in case of application loading or user login. Combining them with the application prerequisites, the media server will get the overall specifications, thus provide the QoS-Enabled service without sacrificing the individual interests.

The user's profile in USP is the overall description of user's demanding. It includes device setting, user preference, context profile, network condition and Qos specification. So adaptation at USP including:

Device setting adaptation: Current pervasive devices vary widely in their features such as screen size, resolution, color depth, computing power, storage and software. To ensure that a requested content is properly rendered on the user's device, it is essential to include the capabilities and characteristics of the device into the content personalization process. Information about the rendering device may include the hardware characteristics of the device, such as the device type, processor speed, processor load, screen resolution, color depth, available memory, number of speakers, and display size.

User preference adaptation: The user's profile captures the personal properties and preferences of the user, such as the preferred audio and video receiving/sending qualities (frame rate, resolution, audio quality...). Other preferences can also be related

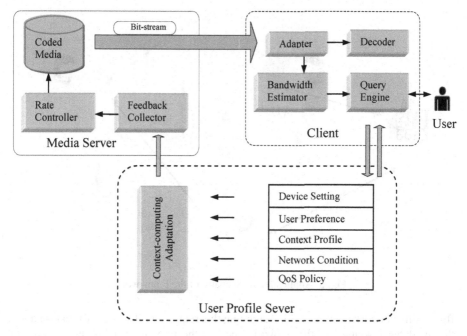

Fig. 2. The Framework of adaptive Media Delivery

to the quality of each media types for communication with a particular person or group of persons. The user's profile may also hold the user's policies for application adaptations, such as the preference of the user to drop the audio quality of a sport clip before degrading the video quality when resources are limited. Some other information in the user profile might include also the user's authorization, authentication and accounting information.

Context profile adaptation: A context profile would include any dynamic information that is part of the context or current status of the user. Context information may include physical (e.g. location, weather, temperature), social (e.g. sitting for dinner), or organizational information (e.g. acting senior manager). Some context information, such as the role or task of the user, can be manually keyed in by the user, while other information, such as location, time of the day, weather condition, can be easily gathered using sensing devices. Some other information, such as the current status of the user, can be gathered from other sources such as the calendar of the user or from a meeting attendees list.

Network condition adaptation: Streaming multimedia content over a network poses a number of technical challenges due to the strict QoS requirements of multimedia contents, such as low delay, low jitter, and high throughput. Failing to meet these requirements may lead to a bad experience of the user. With a large variety of wired and wireless network connectivity, it is necessary to include the network characteristics into content personalization and to dynamically adapt the multimedia content to the

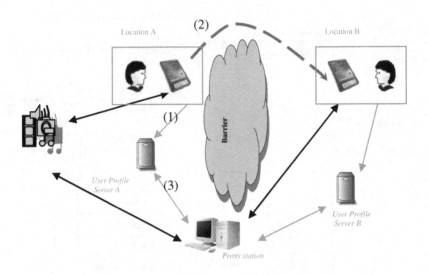

Fig. 3. Application of Scenario of the Framework

fluctuating network resources [6]. Achieving this requires collecting information about the available resources in the network, such as the maximum delay, error rate, and available throughput on every link over the content delivery path.

QOS specification adaptation: For a specific multimedia presentation, individual users may have different requirements on the level of details or some other parameters. For example, given a medical tele-learning system, both a professor and a student are interested in a surgery, but the professor wants to get the in-depth multimedia material for his lecture, while the student only needs an abstraction of the same material to pass the upcoming exam.

The proposed framework supports media coding and transmission adaptation according to the receiver's temporal, spatial, and communicational conditions. So it can serve the user with acceptable video quality even in the poor bandwidth. An application of scenario is shown as follows in Fig. 3. At Location A, the user enjoys the video from the Media Server. Location of the user has been detected and reported to UPS A. When the user moves to Location B passing by Barrier, the communication is blocked. Fortunately, the video can be transmitted successively by Proxy Station. But the bandwidth of Proxy Station may be lower than that of the user needs. With the media adaptation of architecture, the user can continue to enjoy his video on the acceptable level.

5 Conclusion and Future Work

In this paper, we present different media content description models. Successively we illustrate the context abstracted for multimedia delivery in pervasive environment and propose an active controlling framework for media delivery. Our main contribution is a formal study on the context-based media adaptation and its framework, which preserves user-centric philosophy of pervasive computing. As we present context-aware application scenario, we will be able to determine what types of different applications are best supported in pervasive environment. After the usability tests, we will improve the system based on the evaluation of system performance and user's satisfaction. Future work will also involve the development of automatically launched applications based on context.

References

1. M. Weiser, the Computer for the 21st Century. Scientific American, 1991,265(3): pp.94-104
2. M. Satyanarayanan, Pervasive Computing: Vision and Challenges, IEEE Personal Communications, vol.8, pp.10-17, Aug 2001.
3. Bill Schilit, Norman Adams, and Roy Want, Context-aware computing applications, IEEE Workshop on Mobile Computing Systems and Applications, pp. 85-90, December 1994.
4. G. Chen and D. Kotz, A Survey of Context-aware Mobile Computing Research, Technical Report TR 2000-381, Dartmouth Computer Science, 2000.
5. Anind K. Dey and Gregory D. Abowd, Towards a Better Understanding of context and context-awareness, Technical Report GIT-GVU-99-22, Georgia Institute of Technology, College of Computing, June 1999.
6. Xiaohui Gu, Duangdao Wichadakul, Klara Nahrstedt, Visual QoS Programming Environment for Pervasive Multimedia Services, Proceedings of IEEE International Conference on Multimedia and Expo 2001(ICME2001), Aug 2001.
7. Z. Lei, ND Georganas, Context-based media adaptation for pervasive computing, Proceedings of Canadian, Conference on Electrical and Computer Engineering. Toronto, May 2001.
8. Hopper, A., "Sentient Computing", The Clifford Paterson Lecture, Phil. Trans. R. Soc. Lond A (2000) 358, pp. 2349-2358, 1999.
9. Guang-You XU, Uuan-Chun SHI, and Wei-Kai XIE, Pervasive/ Pervasive Computing, Chinese Journal of Computers, Vol. 26 No. 9, pp.1042-1050, Sept. 2003 (in Chinese).
10. Sumi Helal, Wiliam Mann, Hicham El-Zabadani etc. The Gator Tech Smart House: a Programmable Pervasive Space, IEEE Computer Society, Computer 0018-9162 pp.50-60 2005.
11. Albrecht Schmidt, Pervasive Computing– Computing in Context, Ph.D. Thesis, Computing Department, Lancaster University, U.K. November, 2002.
12. J. Liu, B. Li, Y.-Q. Zhang, An End-to-End Adaptation Protocol for Layered Video Multicast Using Optimal Rate Allocation, IEEE Transactions on Multimedia, (6)7: 87-102, February 2004.
13. Wenzhe zhang, Minglu li, Chongqing Zhang, CSMD: Context-based Scheme for Multimedia Delivery for Ubiquitous Environment, In the Proceedings of workshop on Modeling and Security in Ubiquitous System of ICESS'05, pp. 565-569, December 2005.
14. H. Chen and S. Tolia, Steps towards creating a context-aware agent system. Technical Report HPL-2001-194, Hewlett-Packard Labs, Palo Alto, CA, U.S.A., 2001.
15. J. McCarthy, Notes on formalizing contexts. In Tom Kehler and Stan Rosenschein, editors, Proceedings of the Fifth National Conference on Artificial Intelligence, pages 555-560, Los Altos, California, 1986. Morgan Kaufmann.
16. D. Salber, A. Dey, and G. Abowd. The context toolkit: Aiding the development of context-enabled applications. In CHI, pages 434-441, 1999.

CAMPS: A Middleware for Providing Context-Aware Services for Smart Space*

Weijun Qin, Yue Suo, and Yuanchun Shi

Key Laboratory of Pervasive Computing, Ministry of Education,
Department of Computer Science and Technology,
Tsinghua University, Beijing 100084, China
{qinweijun99, suoy}@mails.tsinghua.edu.cn, shiyc@tsinghua.edu.cn

Abstract. Context-awareness enhances intelligent behaviors in pervasive computing environments, although it is still a great challenge to enable context-awareness due to lack of effective infrastructure to support context-aware applications. In this paper, we present an agent-based middleware called CAMPS for providing context-aware services for Smart Space in order to afford effective supports for context acquisition, representation, interpretation, and utilization to applications. In CAMPS, a formal context model, which combines First Order Probabilistic Logic with OWL ontologies, has been investigated to facilitate context modeling and reasoning about imperfect and ambiguous contextual information and to enable context knowledge sharing and reuse. A context inference mechanism based on an extended Bayesian Network approach has been studied to enable automated reactive and deductive reasoning. In addition, we implement a prototype and study on our experience in smart classroom application.

1 Introduction

It's widely acknowledged that Smart Space is a typical open, distributed and heterogeneous pervasive computing system, which aims at creating a ubiquitous, human-centric environment with embedded computers, information appliances, and multimodal sensors that facilitates human to achieve task efficiently by offering abundant information and assistance from computers. A prominent characteristic of Smart Space for supporting human-centric computing is that it senses and reacts to context, information sensed to characterize the situation of the people, activities, physical environment, and computing entities that is considered relevant to the interaction between user and application [1].

Researchers have been investigating on many research issues of context-aware computing, e.g. context modeling, representation, context inference and knowledge sharing, etc. and developing tools and architecture that make efforts to investigate a number of effective and powerful ways to acquire, represent, and

---

* This work has been funded by Program for New Century Excellent Talents in University of China (NCET-04-0079).

Y.-C. Chung and J.E. Moreira (Eds.): GPC 2006, LNCS 3947, pp. 644–653, 2006.

make use of sensed and inferred data for providing context-aware services to applications. However, developing context-aware middleware to enable computer applications to make use of contextual information and to enhance human's task is still a great challenge. To address these issues above, we have built a middleware called CAMPS which provides context-aware services to allow applications in a smart space environment to be context-sensitive. Some of the key features of CAMPS are:

- An agent-based, loose-coupling middleware that enables the gathering and management of contextual information from various sensors and software entities, and provides appropriate context-aware services for applications.
- A formal context model that describes and represents various kinds of contextual entities(e.g. person, location, activity, environment, platform, etc.) in a smart space environment.
- A context inference mechanism that supports the deduction new and relevant high-level contextual information to the use of the applications from low-level sensed context data.

The rest of the paper will be organized as the following: Section 2 gives an application scenario and presents the features of contextual information in Smart Space. The ontology-based context model is investigated in Section 3. Section 4 describes the system architecture of CAMPS middleware and Section 5 describes context inference mechanism. A case study on making use of context-aware services is on discussion in Section 6. Section 7 gives related works which encourage our approach, and finally Section 8 makes a conclusion.

2 Context-Awareness in Smart Space

Ongoing research on building context-aware application for Smart Space has been more and more significant and compelling. We discuss the *Smart Cameraman* application in our Smart Classroom system [2] in order to illustrate the nature of context-awareness required by applications in Smart Space, and then return to this application scenario throughout the paper in order to illustrate our middleware architecture for supporting context-aware service.

Ross is giving a lesson in Smart Classroom. A remote student Joey is watching the live-video of overview of the classroom on his laptop computer, while another remote student Monica is watching it via her PDA. Ross posts a question on the Blackboard (shared whiteboard). At that moment the live-video on Joey's laptop turns to the close-up of the "Blackboard" while Monica's PDA displays only the question written on Blackboard. After that, Ross asks Chandler, a local student in the classroom, to answer the question. Chandler stands up and gives his answer. At that moment, the live-video on both Joey and Monica's display screen turns to the close-up of Chandler's posture.

From the description of a context-aware application above, it's obvious that there are many different types of contextual information that can be used by applications in a smart space environment, including physical contexts (e.g. time, location), personal contexts (e.g. identity, preference, mood), device contexts (e.g. display size, power), activity contexts (e.g. class, meeting schedule). Besides those, other types of information are still considered as crucial context in a smart space environment which may be invisible to the participants e.g. systematic contexts (e.g. CPU power, network bandwidth), and application contexts (e.g. agents, services), environmental contexts (e.g. light, temperature), etc.

In order to distinguish the specific properties or attributes of different contextual information, we consider that contexts can be classified as three categories: *Sensed Context, Profiled Context,* and *Derived Context. Sensed Contexts,* which are usually captured from the physical sensors in the real world, e.g. RFID, location tracker, are a type of temporal sensitive, imperfect and ambiguous information. *Profile Contexts,* which are usually predefined from user or environment profile information, e.g. user profile, are more static but incomplete. *Derived Contexts,* which are usually deduced from the other basic information, are imprecise with inaccuracy.

3   The Context Model

It's acknowledged that a well-designed context model plays an important role to access the context in any context-aware system [3]. In our approach, the basic structure of context is represented as first-order probabilistic logic in order to measure the ambiguity of contexts, which combines the expressive power of first-order logic with the uncertainty handling of probabilistic theory [4]. Referred as a sharing understanding of specific domains, ontology is a formal explicit description of concepts and relationships [5]. In our approach, we adopt an ontology approach to model conceptual contexts in a smart space environment for the following reasons: i) ontologies with fully expressive power allow context representation semantically and explicitly; ii) a common ontology enables entities in Smart Space, e.g. agents, devices, to share, reuse and interoperate context knowledge; iii) ontologies provide various complex efficient inference mechanism to deduce high-level context from low-level, raw context data, and to check inconsistent contextual information due to imperfect sensing [6].

3.1   The Basic Structure of Context

In our model, First Order Probabilistic Logic (FOPL) is adopted to represent the basic structure of context which follows the notion of combining first order logic and probabilistic models in machine learning community [4]. Before representing the basic structure of context, we first introduce several definitions of terminology *Field, Predicate, ContextAtom* and *ContextLiteral.*

- *Field*$\in F^*$, where a *Field* is a set of individuals belong to the same class, e.g., *Person* = {*Ross, Joey, Chandler*}, *Room* = {*Room*526, *Room*527}.
- *Predict*$\in V^*$, where a *Predict* indicates the relationship among the entities or the properties of an entity, e.g. *location, coLocate.*

- $ContextAtom \in A^*$, where $ContextAtom$ is represented as the form of $predicate(term, term, ...)$ in which a $term$ is a constant symbol, a variable symbol, or a function followed by a parenthesized list of $terms$ separated by the commas, and a $predicate$ acts on $terms$. For example, $location(Ross)$ indicates $Ross'$ location.
- $ContextLiteral \in L^*$, where $ContextLiteral$ is represented as the form of $contextAtom = v$ in which $contextAtom$ is the instance of $ContextAtom$ and v indicates the status of $contextAtom$ or the value of the $terms$. For example, $location(Ross) = Room527$ indicates that $Ross'$ location is $Room527$.

The structures and properties of this basic model are described in an ontology language in order to define the conceptual contexts in rich semantic level. In our approach, we propose to represent basic context structure in Web Ontology Language (OWL) [7]. Influenced by Ding's approach of representing probabilities in OWL [8], we define two OWL classes: $PriorProb$, $CondProb$. A prior probability $Pr(L_1)$ of a context literal L_1 is defined as the instance of class $PriorProb$, which has two mandatory properties: $hasContextLiteral$ and $hasProbValue$. A conditional probability $Pr(L_1|L)$ of a context literal L_1 is defined as the instance of class $CondProb$, which has three mandatory properties: $hasContextLiteral$, $hasProbValue$ and $hasCondition$.

3.2   The Context Ontology

In our model, we divide context ontology into two sets: core context ontology for general conceptual entities in Smart Space and extended context ontology for domain-specific environment, e.g. classroom domain. The core context ontology attempts to define very general concepts for context in Smart Space that are universal and sharable for building context-aware applications. The extended context ontology attempts to define additional concepts and vocabularies for supporting various types of domain-specific applications.

The core context ontology investigate seven basic concepts of user, location, time, activity, service, environment, and platform, which are considered as the basic and general entities existed in Smart Space as shown in Figure 1. Part of the core context ontology is adopted from several different widely-accepted consensus ontologies, e.g. DAML-Time [9], OWL-S [10], etc. The instance of Smart Space consists of classes of $User$, $Location$, $Time$, $Activity$, $Service$, $Environment$ and $Platform$.

- $User$: As user plays an important and centric role in the smart space applications, this ontology defines the vocabularies to represent profile information, contact information, user preference and mood which are sensitive to user's current activity or task.
- $Location$, $Time$ and $Activity$: Note that the relevancy among location, time, and user's activity facilitates the validation of inconsistent contextual information because these contexts might be sensed by various sensors with different accuracies.

– *Platform* and *Service:* The platform ontology defines descriptions and vocabularies of hardware devices or sensors, and software infrastructure in a smart space. The service ontology defines the multi-level service specifications that platform provides in order to support service discovery and composition.
– *Environment:* The environment ontology defines the context specification of physical environment conditions that user interacts with, such noise level, light condition, humidity and temperature, etc.

The extended context ontology extends the core context ontology, and defines the details and additional vocabularies of which apply to various different domains. The advantage of extended context ontology is that the separation of domain reduces the scale of context knowledge and burdens of context processing for pervasive computing applications, and facilitates the effective context inference with the limited complexity [5].

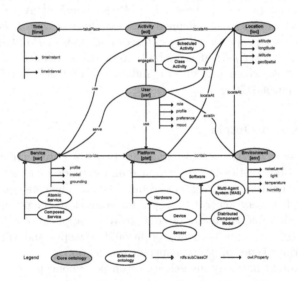

Fig. 1. Context ontology of Smart Space

4   The CAMPS Architecture

The CAMPS is an agent-based context-aware middleware that provides supports for applications to make use of contextual information in a smart space environment. The CAMPS middleware consist of several individual, collaborating agents as depicted in Figure 2.

– *Context Wrapper(CW) Agent.* The *CW Agent* acquires various types of raw context data from different sensors, devices, profiles and software agents.
– *Context Provider(CP) Agent.* The *CP Agent* abstracts context data from heterogeneous source via different types of *CW Agent*, and represents contextual information using ontologies for knowledge sharing and reuse.

- *Inference Engine(IE) Agent.* The *IE Agent* provides inference mechanism including reactive method, first order probabilistic logic and bayesian networks, to infer high-level context from low-level data.
- *Knowledge Base(KB) Agent.* The *KB Agent* stores inference rules, observed facts, and ontologies for context data management and maintenance.
- *Query Filter(QF) Agent.* The *QF Agent* provides query interface to upper applications to query or subscribe the context-aware services with support of system-level coordination mechanism using formal query language.

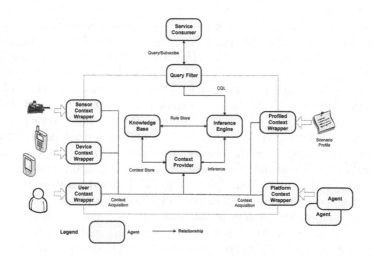

Fig. 2. The CAMPS middleware architecture

The most important considerations of our design architecture for providing context-aware services are mainly relied on some considerations below:

- *Loose coupling.* Contextual Information in a smart space environment is very dynamic and heterogeneous. From the benefits of loose coupling feature, the system can adopt suitable plug-in module to meet different demands of context-aware applications for modeling and reasoning with different types of context knowledge with the least cost of system integration.
- *Scalability.* The middleware architecture with component abstraction and encapsulation provides an easy way to enable context-aware services scalable. By customizing the scenario profile and deploying various types of sensors, *CW Agent* can capture abundant contextual information from different sources to be more adaptive to the real smart space environment.
- *Invisibility.* With notion of the separation of application procedure and underlying services, the middleware provides *QF Agent* module for enabling underlying system functionalities(e.g. context data storage, sensor distribution, inference engine) invisible to the upper applications.

5   Context Inference Mechanism

The inference mechanism of supporting context-aware reasoning is *ContextLogic* that follows the idea of Knowledge-Based Model Construction (KBMC), which is considered as a formal inferential system based on first order probabilistic logic. It consists of formal representation of context knowledge and rules, and the upper inosculation and inference to the knowledge. In this section, we introduce the design approach of *KB Agent* and *IE Agent* which extends Bayesian Network (BN) reasoning arithmetic with restriction of syntax and semantic hypotheses in order to enable the complexity of context reasoning within the acceptable restricted range.

The *KB Agent* takes charges of context persistence, maintenance and management. The construction of *KB Agent* consists of *Field Definition, Predicate Definition, Observed Facts* and *Rule Definition*. Context rules are the form of $Pr(L_h|L_{b_1}, L_{b_2}, \ldots) = c : -L_{C_1}, L_{C_2}, L_{C_3}, \ldots$, which means that in the constraints of $L_{C_1}, L_{C_2}, L_{C_3}$, etc. and under the condition of L_{b_1}, L_{b_2}, the probability of L_h is the value of c. Note that L_{C_i} denotes only context fact and others denote arbitrary *ContextLiteral*, e.g. the statement $Pr(TeacherStatus(Teacher) = talking|Speaking(Student) = false) = 0.7 : -IsBlackboardTouched(Room527)$ denotes the rules that when the blackboard of *Room527* has not been touched, the probability value of that the teacher is talking equals 0.7 under the condition of that the student is silent. We propose XML-based database to store and manage all the definition and information of *Knowledge Base*.

The *IE Agent* takes charges of inferring high semantic context knowledge from low-level context facts with restricted constrains and deductive rules. For example, from the rule of $Pr(Speaking(Joey) = true|Speaking(Ross) = true) = 0 : -status(Roos527) = onMeeting$, we can deduce that while *Ross* is speaking on the meeting in the *Room527*, it's impossible that *Joey* is also speaking. In CAMPS, We develop a inference module called *ContextLogic* for converting the context description in *Knowledge Base* into BN's DAG and to calculating the probabilistic distribution. In order to reduce the scale of BN's DAG, we investigate an approach to build DAG according to the context query's content. To achieve the above goal, several constrains are involved, including valid rule of the syntax, the independence hypothesis of causal set that extends definition of causal independence in [11], the hypothesis of average distribution of residual probability, and the conditional independence hypothesis, in order to avoid generating unnecessary node of the net so as to minimize the scale of BN's DAG and ascertain exclusively the distribution of the answer. Therefore, with the help of the constraints and hypothesis, the complexity of inference on BN's DAG is under control within acceptable limited range.

The *QF Agent* classifies the input query into two categories: i) query for context facts. In this case, no complex inference mechanism is involved, but a reactive mapping approach is adopted to provide the answer to the query; ii) query for context knowledge. In this case, the above inference approach is adopted to infer the answer. We defined the basic formal of context query language (CQL) as $?L_{C_1}, L_{C_2}, \ldots$, where L_{C_i} can have either *Field Variable (FV)* or *Field Element (FE)*. The advantage of defining a well-formalization CQL is that we can use it to query in *Context Base* in a uniform way, and the distribution and storage structure of data and the complicated inferential process are transparent to the upper applications and users.

6   Case Study

As depicted in the application scenario, a *Smart Cameraman* module is designed to change the live-video scene adapted to situational context initiatively according to the clue of class activity in local classroom by switching an array of cameras. Distinct with previous version applied in Smart Classroom project [2], we adopt Smart Platform [12], a software infrastructure of Smart Space with multi-agent architecture, as a supporting platform to the middleware CAMPS for providing reliable data communication and module coordination mechanism.

In this case, context-awareness that CAMPS provides embody two aspects: i) CAMPS capture the contextual information relevant to user's activity and provide the clue of class activity to *Smart Cameraman* module. ii) CAMPS deliver various customized video respectively to remote student individuals with different quality due to different capabilities of computers or devices, e.g. size of display screen, network bandwidth.

To demonstrate Smart Cameraman scenario, we define several context rules for this module and develop case generator to simulate a variety of situations as Figure 3(d) shows:

Fig. 3. Different scenes delivered to remote students according to the class context: (a)teacher writing on MediaBoard; (b)teacher showing a model; (c)teacher having a discussion with local students; (d)Case generator module

- *Teacher writing on the MediaBoard.* When the teacher is writing comments on the MediaBoard, the module may select a close-up view of the board, as Figure 3(a) shows.
- *Teacher showing a model.* When the teacher holds up a model, the model may zoom in on it, as Figure 3(b) shows.

- *Remote student speaking.* When a remote student is speaking, live video of the student may be delivered to other remote students.
- *Other.* In all the other situations, the module may select the overview of the classroom, as Figure 3(c) shows.

Compared with the previous version of *Smart Cameraman* in Smart Classroom project, several great systematic improvements have been done with the supports of context-aware middleware CAMPS as depicted in Table 1. The enhanced *Smart Cameraman* module has better scalability and adaptability performance, more expressive power of context representation, inference and discovery, and much easier to maintain and upgrade for the independence relationship among the components.

Table 1. Comparison on systematic improvements of *Smart Cameraman* module

Smart Cameraman Module	Module Deployment	Context Model	Inference Mechanism	Query Interface
Previous Version	Toolkit	XML-based Event Description	IF-THEN-ELSE Statement	Ad hoc Manner
Enhanced Version	Agent-based Component	Ontology	FOPL Bayesian Network	Formal Context Query Language

7   Related Works

Over the past few years, a number of works have been done in the area of context-aware computing. Significant work has been done by Dey, et al. in defining the concepts of context and context-awareness, identifying categories of context and features of context-aware applications and developing a conceptual framework for supporting rapid prototyping of context-aware applications [1].

Chen et al. introduce the Semantic Web technologies and ontologies in building an architecture for supporting context-aware systems, investigate the Standard Ontology for Ubiquitous and Pervasive Applications (SOUPA) that uses OWL to represent the entities in a smart space environment, and develop the Context Broker Architecture (CoBrA) that is an agent-based context-aware framework to support ubiquitous agents, services and devices [13].

Gu et al. investigate a Bayesian approach for dealing with uncertain contexts that proposes a probabilistic extension to an ontology-based model for representing uncertain contexts, and use Bayesian Network to reason about uncertainty. A serviced-oriented context-aware middleware has been investigated in order to enable building and rapid prototyping of context-aware services [6].

8 Conclusion

In a conclusion, we have presented a middleware for providing context-aware services for Smart Space. The middleware supports the high-level abstraction of context data with the power of formal context model which combine with first-order probabilistic logic and ontologies, and allows context inference based on extended Bayesian Network to provide more precise context information adapted to changing, heterogeneous smart space environment. Our ongoing research is investigating description logic approaches with more expressive power to make middleware robust and extensible.

References

1. Dey, A.K., Salber, D., Abowd, G.D.: A conceptual framework and a toolkit for supporting the rapid prototyping of context-aware applications. Human Computer Interaction (HCI) Journal - Special Issue on Context-aware Computing 4(2-4) (2001) 97–166
2. Shi, Y.C., Xie, W.K., Xu, G.Y., Shi, Y.T., Chen, E.Y., Mao, Y.H., Liu, F.: The smart classroom: Merging technologies for seamless tele-education. IEEE Pervasive Computing Magazine 2(2) (2003) 47–55
3. Strang, T., Linnhoff-Popien, C.: A context modeling survey. In: Proc. UbiComp workshop on Advanced Context Modeling, Reasoning and Management. (2004)
4. Poole, D.: First-order probabilistic inference. In: Proc. IJCAI. (2003) 985–991
5. Guarino, N.: Formal ontology and information systems. In: Proc. FOIS. (1998) 3–15
6. Gu, T., Pung, H.K., Zhang, D.Q.: A service-oriented middleware for building context-aware services. Journal of Network and Computer Applications 28(1) (2005) 1–18
7. OWL Web Ontology Language Guide, http://www.w3.org/TR/owl-guide/.
8. Ding, Z.L., Peng, Y., Pan, R.: Bayesowl: Uncertainty modeling in semantic web ontologies. Soft Computing in Ontologies and Semantic Web (2005) 27
9. DAML-Time, http://www.cs.rochester.edu/ ferguson/daml/
10. OWL-S: Semantic Markup for Web Services, http://www.daml.org/services/owl-s/1.1/
11. Rish, I., Dechter, R.: On the impact of causal independence. In: Stanford Spring Symposium on Interactive and Mixed-Initiative Decision Theoretic Systems. (1998) 101–108
12. Xie, W.K., Shi, Y.C., Xu, G.Y., Mao, Y.H.: Smart platform - a software infrastructure for smart space (siss). In: Proc. ICMI. (2002) 429–436
13. Chen, H., Finin, T., Joshi, A.: An ontology for context-aware pervasive computing environments. Knowledge Engineering Review - Special Issue on Ontologies for Distributed Systems 18(3) (2004) 197–207

A Novel Power Management Scheme for E-Textiles

Nenggan Zheng, Zhaohui Wu, Zhigang Gao, and Yanfie Liu

College of Computer Science &Technology, Zhejiang Univ., Hangzhou, China
{zng, wzh, gaozhigang, yliu}@cs.zju.edu.cn

Abstract. As battery-driven systems, e-textiles need battery-efficient power management schemes for increasing the time of the operations. We present a novel power management scheme for e-textiles, which focuses on a battery selection model based on the dependable infrastructures of the token grid communication networks and the flexible power networks (FPN). In the FPN, a power consuming node (PCN) can attain power energy from one of the multiple battery nodes, while the PCNs are interconnected into the e-textile token grid network able to preserve the full-connectivity in the case of faults. By decomposing the battery-efficient model into the Transaction Efficiency for each battery selection transaction, the selection model proposed in this paper aims to achieve high Transaction Efficiency to extend the lifetime of the e-textile applications. Simulation results show that significant lifetime extensions can be obtained with respect to conventional sequential discharge policy.

1 Introduction

With the current new computing paradigm of pervasive computing, microprocessors are embedded into wearable objects such as glasses, wrist-watches and even fabrics. Electronic textiles (e-textiles) are emerging new computing substrates, which combine the advantages of electronic modules and textiles into one [1]. Potential applications for e-textiles include medical monitoring, military uniforms and sensor networks [2]. Researchers in materials and textiles have presented new fibers, which function as speakers, durable wires and batteries [3]; new packaging technologies for electronic circuits give permission to manufacture practical electronic textiles [4]. Several prototypes are documented in the papers and websites available [5-6].

Applications based on e-textiles may be deployed in inaccessible terrains or be tailored as garments, isolated from permanent power sources. Similar to the portable computing devices, e-textiles are battery-driven and restricted by the limited capacity of the batteries. When the fabrics are tailored as a wearable garment or when the applications are in use, tear and wear are highly frequent, which potentially introduce some short- or open-circuit faults into the electric networks of e-textiles. While the open-circuit faults will make some electronic components have to stop their work due to the disconnection form the power sources, the short-circuit faults can result in the rapid leakage of the limited charge stored in the corresponding batteries.

From the point of view of the battery-driven and failure-prone systems, e-textiles need battery-efficient power management schemes for prolonging the lifetime of the operations. The paper presents a novel power management scheme to meet this demand, which is based on the dependable infrastructures of the electric networks [7]

Y.-C. Chung and J.E. Moreira (Eds.): GPC 2006, LNCS 3947, pp. 654–663, 2006.

and the communication networks [8] [9]. The fault-tolerant electric networks, the Flexible Power Networks (FPN), can protect the battery from being discharged by short-circuit faults and prevent the power consuming components from being disabled by open-circuit faults. The power consuming nodes in the e-textiles can attain power energy form one of the multiple choices of batteries in FPN, instead of a "fixed" one in conventional electric networks. In addition, the power consuming nodes can also communicate with each other by the e-textile token grid network that can provide full-connectivity in the case of the faults [8]. The main part of our power management is the load assignment modules running in every active power consuming node of the FPN, which can "schedule" the discharge of the battery nodes by implementing the battery selection model. This module aims to make use of the dependable and flexible characteristics of the FPN and the data communication networks to maximize the lifetime of the system. When a battery selection transaction is requested for some reasons, the battery selection model considers the electrochemical characteristics of the batteries and selects the right one of the highest Transaction Efficiency in the choices of the battery nodes available.

The remainder of this paper is organized as follows: Section 2 surveys the related works on the dependable infrastructure of e-textiles and power management policies in battery-driven systems. In section 3, the battery selection model designed for every active power-consuming node is illustrated. Next, section 4 describes the results of simulation experiments, which gives the evidence to verify the effectiveness of the new power management scheme. Finally, Section 5 concludes the paper and mentions the future work.

2 Related Work

The main areas related to this paper range from the dependable infrastructure of the electric networks and the token grid networks for e-textiles to the power management policies for battery-driven systems, especially for multiple battery systems.

Electric networks embroidered on the fabrics are the infrastructure of the power management policies for e-textiles. The research on the electric networks of the e-textiles is in its infancy phase, without specialized documents reported. In the papers on power management of e-textiles published before, the majority of these works have the assumption that the elements get power energy from a fixed battery [5] [6] [11] [12]. When implementing, previous prototypes base their power management policies on the "fixed-relation" electric networks in which the inter-connecting relations between the power consuming nodes and the batteries are "one to one". That is, a power consuming node is connected to one battery or one group of battery cells. This relation is determined in the phase of manufacturing and can not be changed dynamically in use. Due to wear and tear or the depletion of energy resources in this "fixed-interconnection" electric networks, power consuming nodes in the loops will be disabled in a high frequency. And the power energy stored in the batteries is potentially wasted for the open- or short-circuit faults introduced by some factors. Tanwir Sheikh et al conducts simulations and experiments on such an electric network to search the dependable power management schemes with some performance versus system lifetime tradeoff when some faults are introduced [6]. Another research group also proposes a novel concept of *dynamic fault-tolerance management* (DFTM) for e-textiles with the "fixed" electric networks [11]. To enhance reliability of the e-textiles systems, we introduce the "dynamic-changeable links" between the power consuming nodes and the batteries into our electric network, the Flexible Power Network (FPN) for e-textiles [7]. Consequently, we realize the idea of routing the power energy in the dynamic changeable electric networks, which is listed as an open issue in the paper [6].

Since each PCN owns several battery channels to obtain power energy in the new electric network, the battery selection algorithm for scheduling the discharging of the batteries in the power consuming node may like those in the multi-battery portable systems [13] [14]. Sequential discharge is the basic discharging schemes in existing products, which means that the discharging order of batteries are fixing and determined during system design [10]. Q. Wu models the battery efficiency as the ratio of actual capacity to theoretical capacity and designs an interleaved battery power supply to minimize the discharge delay product. Benini et al also propose an alternative approach for scheduling multiple batteries, referred as *virtual parallel with proportional current steering*.

Although from the point of the power consuming node, a power consuming node and its several battery choices are formed to a multiple battery system, the electric system of e-textiles have two explicit differences from the portable multi-battery systems. One difference is that in portable multiple battery systems, there is only one power consuming devices, while e-textiles are distributed systems and large numbers of power consuming nodes may drain energy simultaneously from the different power supply. It may bring forth some synchronous problems. On the other hand, as the result of the faults introduce into the FPN, a power-consuming node may be unable to obtain energy from part of its battery choices. For the virtual parallel policy has an assumption that the connection between the batteries and the power supply in the system are stable, the virtual parallel does not allow for the cases in the e-textiles.

3 The Battery-Efficient Power Management Scheme

The implementation of requires some support of the electric networks and the communication networks for e-textiles. Our FPN proposed in [7] has the ability to realize the dynamic routing of the power energy in runtime and provide multiple battery channels for every power consuming node. In the FPN, the nodes (the power consuming nodes or the battery nodes) can change the topology of the interconnection according to the runtime situations that may introduce some faults (open-circuit or short-circuit faults) into the e-textiles. A power consuming node (PCN) can attain power energy from one of the choices of the batteries nodes. The PCN has been connected to several battery nodes. And its battery selector can fulfill the battery channel switch when some faults occur or the current battery channel is exhausted. With the FPN for e-textiles, it is more flexible to implement the power-aware and dependable power supply policies for e-textiles.

On the other hand, the Token Grid Network for e-textiles in [5] [8] provides the fault-tolerant infrastructure of data communication network. While the power consuming nodes and the battery nodes are interconnected into the dependable FPN, all the PCNs communicating with each other by the e-textile token grid network. By parsing the information encapsulated in the token, a PCN can get the information it required, such as the number of PCNs in the ring, the ID of the current master of the token, the states of each PCNs in the ring and the path of the data transmitted. In this paper, we utilize these protocols to perform potential concurrent battery selection transactions.

The kernel of our battery-efficient power management scheme is the load assignment module running in every active PCN. The module provides two transactions (Update and Selection) to implement the power management scheme, which we will discuss in section 3.2. Considering the electrochemical characteristics of the batteries, we develop a battery selection model to select the right battery node that can achieve the highest battery efficiency. With the battery selection model, the load assignment module has the ability to determine which BN is the battery-efficient choice. Then the module can require the FPN to perform the battery switch, while necessary parameters of the battery selection transaction are sent to other PCNs in the token grid to update relevant parameters.

In the rest of this section, we will relate the battery selection model allowing for extending the lifetime by increasing the battery efficiency. The load schedule model of each active power consuming node implements the battery selection model to assign the load to the selected battery and thus schedule the discharge of the battery nodes.

3.1 The Battery Selection Model

The chemical energy stored in a battery may not be extracted as power energy to full extent (i.e., the ideal capacity) for some electrochemical reasons. Like other battery-driven systems, it is necessary to implement battery-efficient schemes to extend the system service time for e-textiles. Here, we based our work on the model of battery efficiency proposed by Massoud Pedram and Qing Wu [14]. Let μ denote the efficiency factor of a battery, I represent the output current required by the discharge circuit. If C_0 is the actual capacity that can be used by the discharge circuit and C is the ideal battery capacity, there is an equation as follows:

$$C_0 = C \cdot \mu \tag{1}$$

The efficiency factor of a battery is a monotonic-decreasing function of I :

$$\mu(I) \mid_{(\beta, \alpha)} = 1 - \beta \cdot I^{\alpha} \tag{2}$$

where both β and α are positive factor constant numbers and can be obtained from the datasheet of the battery. Higher rate discharge can result in more dramatic waste of the chemical energy stored in the battery, which is equivalent to the μ of a smaller magnitude. In the following paragraphs, we derive the battery selection model for the e-textiles. There are two kinds of parameters as the input of the model.

Static parameters: The input to our battery selection model is the battery profile of the BN set in the FPN, described by the following several sets: the set of the rated currents $S_{Ir} = \{I_{I_k} \mid k = 0,1,...,m-1\}$, the set of the factor constants $S_{\beta} = \{(\beta,\alpha)_k \mid k = 0,1,...,m-1\}$ and the set of ideal capacity at a new battery $S_c = \{C_k \mid k = 0,1,...,m-1\}$. For $0 \le k < m$, the pair $< I_k, C_k >$ corresponds to the rated discharge current and the ideal capacity of the BN k. Each PCN in the electric network stores the pairs of every BN that is connected to it. Let $\Gamma \subseteq \{< I_{I_k}, C_k > \mid 0 \le k < m\}$ denote this ideal parameters pair subset for a PCN with m battery channels.

Runtime parameters: When the system is powered on, the active PCNs in the FPN are consuming the energy stored in the BNs. Despite the ideal parameters pair subset, each active PCN (the subscript i denotes the index of the PCN) also keeps the runtime battery profiles which is a linear list of the parameters pair $< I_{run}, C_{run} >$ for every BN interconnected to the PCN, where I_{run} is the discharge current and C_{run} is the remaining capacity of the BN. In the FPN, many PCNs may drain the power energy from the same BN and the discharge current of the BN k is the sum of current in all these PCNs. A linear list of nodes of the parameters $< P_{cn}ID, \Delta I, T_{st} >$ follows the correspondent list head of battery runtime parameters pair $< I_{run_k}, C_{run_k} >$ for BN k, where $P_{cn}ID$ is the global ID for one of these PCN, ΔI is the discharge current of the PCN $P_{cn}ID$ and T_{st} is the start time stamp of the PCN drained the energy from the BN k. Consequently, a PCN keep the same number of such linear lists as the number of its choices of BNs.

To utilize the energy stored in the multiple batteries in the FPN effectively, our objective is to maximize the combined amount of actual energy extracted from all batteries in the electric network. Given an e-textile system with n BNs, let

$$C_{total} = \sum_{k=1}^{n} C_k \cdot \mu_k(I_k) \qquad (3)$$

Intuitively, C_{total} is the actual charge that can be used in the discharge circuit with n batteries in the system. We use C_{total} as our cost function to be maximized in every switch task performed by the PCN.

We model all the BNs in the FPN as a *virtual* battery of the total capacity, formulated in equation (3), and define the Transaction Efficiency of a battery selection transaction requested by a PCN as equation (4), which is a ratio of the necessary actual capacity TC_{actual} to the ideal capacity TC_{ideal} consumed by the selection transaction.

$$TE = TC_{actual} / TC_{ideal} \qquad (4)$$

Each battery switch transaction is regarded as an increment of the load attached to the virtual battery. For a PCN of the current load ΔI, the actual necessary capacity TC_{actual} is determined by the product of the switch interval and the current of the PCN (if we do not consider the dynamic voltage scaling approaches). Consequently, we can decompose the goal of maximizing the cost function in equation (3) to achieve the highest Transaction Efficiency of every battery switch transaction.

If the selection model attaches the PCN of index i to the BN of index k, the affect resulted from the selection transaction is twofold: (a) the incremental load ΔI will increase the load of BN from I_{run_k} to $I_{run_k} + \Delta I$, thus decrease the efficiency factor of the corresponding battery; (b) the lower efficiency factor will also affect the behavior of previous load I_{run_k} on the battery node k. As a result, the evaluation of TC_{ideal} should considers both sides. To achieve the highest efficiency as the PCN i can get, the computing model should search the runtime battery profile of PCN i with the static set of the factor constants S_β. Considering the twofold affect of the incremental load ΔI, we derive equation (5) from equation (3) and (4), evaluating the Transaction Efficiency of the battery selection transaction for PCN i.

$$TE_i = \max_{1 \le k \le n} \{ \frac{\mu_k(I_{run_k} + \Delta I) \cdot \mu_k(I_{run_k}) \cdot \Delta I}{\mu_k(I_{run_k}) \cdot (I_{run_k} + \Delta I) - \mu_k(I_{run_k} + \Delta I) I_{run_k}} \} \tag{5}$$

Especially, when μ is a linear function of I, i.e., $\alpha = 1$, we can get the following equation:

$$TE_i = \max_{0 \le k \le n} \{ \mu_k(I_{run_k} + \Delta I) \cdot \mu_k(I_{run_k}) \} \tag{6}$$

Based on equation (5), the battery selection model searches the runtime battery profile of PCN i and get the BN k with Transaction Efficiency TE_i. Then, the load assignment module implementing the battery selection model performs the battery switch transaction and attaches the PCN i to an appropriate BN.

3.2 Transactions Load Assignment Module

There are two kinds of transactions in the load assignment module to update the parameters and perform the battery selection. One is the battery selection; the other is the update of the battery runtime profiles. Of the two, the latter has a high priority.

Update: The update transaction is conducted locally in parameter tables of every active PCN, which is to update the runtime battery profiles. Since the runtime parameters are the input of the selection model, these parameters should reflect the dynamic changes of the capacity and the current load during the discharging of the batteries. It is necessary to update these runtime parameters in an appropriate interval of a few seconds. The tokens traversing the grid check the state of every PCN and the interconnection topology of the PCNs. While some PCNs are isolated for tear and wear, the token traversing the grid will advertise the information to every interconnected PCN in the grid that will update its own runtime battery profiles in the next update transaction. And for a PCN isolated, what it has to do is to halt its own running and disconnect itself from the corresponding BN.

The update transaction also predicts the remaining discharge time of the battery which is the current power source. If it is coming to be exhausted (that is, the

Fig. 1. Basic flow chart for battery selection transaction

remaining discharge time is lower than a threshold), a request of the battery selection transaction is called.

Battery selection: There are some occasions on which a request of the battery selection transaction will be called. When the battery schedule slice is due, or some faults are introduced into the circuits or the load of the PCN is changed to a new state, the PCN has to request a battery selection transaction to select an appropriate power supply in accordance to the battery selection model. It works as follows: Firstly, the PCN running the battery selection transaction has to wait for the switch token which is traversing in the grid or is captured by some PCN requesting the battery selection transaction earlier. Then, after the PCN gets the switch token, the Transaction Efficiency is evaluated to search the BN k of the highest value in the runtime battery profile of the PCN. Finally, the PCN performs the channel switching from previous battery to the BN k. and then sends the select packet (i.e., the update token) encapsulating the PCN ID, the incremental load ΔI, the current index of the BN, the index k of the Selected BN and the Start time. Each active node updates its runtime battery tables from the update token traversing in the grid. When the update token with the flags of all row and column set return to the PCN that is performing the battery selection, the transaction is fulfilled. Fig.1 is the basic flow chart of the battery selection transaction.

4   Experiments

Firstly, we use PSPICE simulation tools and experimental electronic nodes to get the load profiles as the input data for the experiments, which are designed to verify our scheme described in the previous sections.

The experiment consists of evaluating a real-life workload extracted from an acoustic beam-forming system [5]. The system simulated in the Ptolemy II is designed for detecting the direction of the moving vehicles, which runs a beam forming algorithm and is based on the e-textiles with many sensitive microphones. In the simulation environment, an accurate battery model is implemented to simulate the behavior of the batteries [15]. Two kinds of power management schemes are simulated to explore the advantages offered by the new battery selection introduced in this paper. One is the existing sequential discharging policy which discharges the BNs in the ascending order of the battery index in the case of same batteries or in the descending order of the battery voltage, and the other is our battery selection model. The power consuming nodes in the system have an alternate sequence of actions (sampling acoustic signals, running the beam-forming algorithm, sending token package and receiving token package) and sleep intervals. We have taken some usage traces of the real beam-forming e-textile applications to get the typical current load of one node in these states, listed in Table 1. The load profile is used as a lookup table in the

Table 1. A Power Consuming Node Load Profile Summary (the unit of current is μA). SMP:sampling, BMFM: beam-forming, S/R: Sending/Receiving, SLP: Sleep.

Node	SMP	BMFM	S/R	SLP
I	17520	21250	13350	1.5
II	8100	9215	7541	2.7
III	1139	1574	1293	8.6
IV	19618	21584	17982	10.4

Table 2. Efiicient factor Functions and Ideal Capacity of the Batteries in the System

Battery	Ideal Capacity(mAh)	Efficient Factor Functions
I	1400	$1 - 0.0007 \cdot I^{1.3}$
II	2500	$1 - 0.000018 \cdot I^{1.4}$
III	1200	$1 - 0.00004 \cdot I^{1.2}$
IV	16000	$1 - 0.0000085 \cdot I^{1.9}$

evaluation of the Task Efficiency in the battery selection model. The battery efficient factor functions μ in Table 2 are obtained from the discharge curves from datasheets of various batteries in Sony Lithium-Ion Rechargeable Battery Catalog. We conducted three groups of experiments:

Experiment 1. Four instances of Node I and four instances of Battery I
Experiment 2. one instance of every PCN type and four instances of Battery I
Experiment 3. one instance of every PCN type and one instances of every Battery type.

Each group of the experiments has five task modes: SMP (Sampling), BMFM (beamforming), S/R (Sending/Receiving), SLP (Sleeping) and the real working mode of an acyclic sequence of these four states. Fig.2 plots the percentage of lifetime increase for three groups of experiments over the counterpart of the sequence policy.

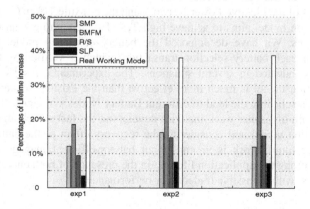

Fig. 2. Lifetime increase over the sequential discharge policy grouped by the Experiments

It can see from the plot that the proposed battery selection model has significant improvements on the lifetime of the multiple battery systems. Note that all the results are the lifetime increase percentages, not the absolute values of the lifetime. There are also some distinguishing features shown in the plot. Firstly, we notice how the lifetime extensions increase with the average value of the current load. In the results of single experiments such as Exp1, the increase tends to be larger for workloads with higher current load (i.e., higher load and larger increase). While the battery efficiency is lower in the case of higher current load, in Experiment 1, the PCN nodes of type 1 in the real-working mode achieves a lifetime increase five times larger than that of the same node in the sleeping state. This matches the feature that the proposed battery selection model splits the load to different batteries while the sequential policy attaches the entire load on a single BN. For lower load, the batteries tend to behave as ideal battery models and thus the lifetime increase is inferior. It is apparent that, as the current load goes to zero, the battery selection model and the sequential discharge policy will have the same battery service lifetime.

When comparing the results of Exp1 with those of Exp2, the battery selection model in the latter case achieves a higher lifetime incensement percentages with deferent types of power consuming nodes. Due to the higher Task Efficient factor in the case of Exp2, the variance of the discharge current has lower influence on the battery selection model which tends to assign the incremental load to the BNs with lighter load. Similarly, we can get the same results comparing the results of Exp1 with those of Exp3, which can be attributed to the same reasons.

In Exp3, there are four kinds of BNs and each BN has different pairs of the factor constants (β, α), while in Exp2, four BNs have the same type of Battery I. However, when we compare the lifetime increases obtained in Exp2 with those obtained in Exp3, it is not remarkable and has no definite tendency, which is also consistent with cost function.

5 Conclusion and Future Work

In this paper, we present a novel power management scheme for efficiently utilizing the ideal capacity of the batteries embroidered into e-textiles. Based on the dependable infrastructures of the Flexible Power Network and the e-textile Token Grid Network, the battery selection model aims to achieve high Task Efficiency to extend the lifetime of the applications. We have decomposed the battery efficiency model into the Task Efficiency for each battery selection transaction, which is verified by the simulation experiments conducted in several situations. The experimental results show that the battery selection model is much more effective than the existing sequential discharge policy and can schedule the load to different Battery Nodes symmetrically.

Our program of further work includes developing the fast search algorithm for the battery selection model and considering the recovery effect of the batteries. The objective of the future work is to implement battery-efficient management modules, which can prolong the application lifetime in the presence of both energy and reliability constraints, with a possible tradeoff for performance.

References

1. Diana Marculescu, et al, "Electronic Textiles: A Platform for Pervasive Computing", Proceedings of the IEEE, VOL. 91, NO. 12, 1995-2018, December 2003.
2. Mark Jones, et al, "Analyzing the Use of E-textiles to Improve Application Performance", IEEE Vehicular Technology Conference 2003, Symposium on Wireless Ad hoc, Sensor, and Wearable Networks (VTC 2003)(extended abstract), October 2003.
3. Power Paper ®, "Power Paper website" (2004), [Online].Available: www. owerpaper.com.
4. Jung, S. Lauterbach, C., and Weber, W. "IntegratedMicroelectronics for Smart Textiles," Workshop on Modeling, Analysis, and Middleware Support for Electronic Textiles, October, 2002.
5. Zahi Nakad, Architecture for e-Textiles. PhD thesis, Bradley Department of Electrical and Computing Engineering, Virginia Tech, 2003.
6. Tanwir Sheikh, Modeling of Power Consumption and Fault Tolerance for Electronic Textiles, Bradley Department of Electrical and Computing Engineering, Virginia Tech, Sep.2003.
7. N. Zheng, Z. Wu, M. Lin, M. Zhao, "A Dependable Infrastructure of the Electric Network for E-textiles", to appear in the Proc. of the 20th International Parallel and Distributed Processing Symposium.
8. Zahi Nakad, Mark Jones, and Thomas Martin, "Fault-Tolerant Networks for Electronic Textiles", in the Proc. Of the 2004 International Conference on Communications in Computing, Las Vegas,pp. 51-56 June 2004.
9. T.D. Todd and E.L. Hahne, "Multiaccess Mesh (Multimesh) Networks," IEEE/ACM Transactions on Networking vol. 5, pp. 181-189, 1997.
10. HP OmniBook 500 (2000). [Online]. Available:
www.hp.com/notebooks/us/eng/products/professional/ultra_portable/index.htm.
11. P.Stanley-Marbell, D.Marculescu, "Dynamic fault-tolerance and metrics for battery powered, failure-prone systems", in the Proc. Of International Conference on the Computer Aided Design, page(s):633 – 640, 2003.
12. Thomas Martin, et al, "Modeling and Simulating Electronic Textile Applications", In Proceedings of the Proceedings of the 2004 ACM SIGPLAN/SIGBED conference on Languages, compilers, and tools, pages 10-19,LCTES2004,June 2004.
13. L. Benini et al., "Discharge Current Steering for Battery Lifetime Optimization," Proc.2002 Int'l Symp.Low-Power Electronics and Design, pp. 118-123, 2002.
14. Q. Wu, Q. Qiu, and M. Pedram, "An Interleaved Dual-Battery Power Supply for Battery-Operated Electronics," Proc. 2000 Conf. Asia and South Pacific Design Automation, IEEE Press, pp. 387-390, 2000.
15. L. Benini, et al, "Discrete-time battery models for system-level low-power design", IEEE Transactions on Very Large Scale Integration (VLSI) Systems, Volume 9, Issue 5, Oct. 2001 Page(s):630 – 640.

Author Index

Lecture Notes in Computer Science

For information about Vols. 1–3852

please contact your bookseller or Springer

Vol. 3904: M. Baldoni, U. Endriss, A. Omicini, P. Torroni (Eds.), Declarative Agent Languages and Technologies III. XII, 245 pages. 2006. (Sublibrary LNAI).

Vol. 3903: K. Chen, R. Deng, X. Lai, J. Zhou (Eds.), Information Security Practice and Experience. XIV, 392 pages. 2006.

Vol. 3901: P.M. Hill (Ed.), Logic Based Program Synthesis and Transformation. X, 179 pages. 2006.

Vol. 3899: S. Frintrop, VOCUS: A Visual Attention System for Object Detection and Goal-Directed Search. XIV, 216 pages. 2006. (Sublibrary LNAI).

Vol. 3898: K. Tuyls, P.J. 't Hoen, K. Verbeeck, S. Sen (Eds.), Learning and Adaption in Multi-Agent Systems. X, 217 pages. 2006. (Sublibrary LNAI).

Vol. 3897: B. Preneel, S. Tavares (Eds.), Selected Areas in Cryptography. XI, 371 pages. 2006.

Vol. 3896: Y. Ioannidis, M.H. Scholl, J.W. Schmidt, F. Matthes, M. Hatzopoulos, K. Boehm, A. Kemper, T. Grust, C. Boehm (Eds.), Advances in Database Technology - EDBT 2006. XIV, 1208 pages. 2006.

Vol. 3895: O. Goldreich, A.L. Rosenberg, A.L. Selman (Eds.), Theoretical Computer Science. XII, 399 pages. 2006.

Vol. 3894: W. Grass, B. Sick, K. Waldschmidt (Eds.), Architecture of Computing Systems - ARCS 2006. XII, 496 pages. 2006.

Vol. 3893: L. Atzori, D.D. Giusto, R. Leonardi, F. Pereira (Eds.), Visual Content Processing and Representation. IX, 224 pages. 2006.

Vol. 3891: J.S. Sichman, L. Antunes (Eds.), Multi-Agent-Based Simulation VI. X, 191 pages. 2006. (Sublibrary LNAI).

Vol. 3890: S.G. Thompson, R. Ghanea-Hercock (Eds.), Defence Applications of Multi-Agent Systems. XII, 141 pages. 2006. (Sublibrary LNAI).

Vol. 3889: J. Rosca, D. Erdogmus, J.C. Príncipe, S. Haykin (Eds.), Independent Component Analysis and Blind Signal Separation. XXI, 980 pages. 2006.

Vol. 3888: D. Draheim, G. Weber (Eds.), Trends in Enterprise Application Architecture. IX, 145 pages. 2006.

Vol. 3887: J.R. Correa, A. Hevia, M. Kiwi (Eds.), LATIN 2006: Theoretical Informatics. XVI, 814 pages. 2006.

Vol. 3886: E.G. Bremer, J. Hakenberg, E.-H.(S.) Han, D. Berrar, W. Dubitzky (Eds.), Knowledge Discovery in Life Science Literature. XIV, 147 pages. 2006. (Sublibrary LNBI).

Vol. 3885: V. Torra, Y. Narukawa, A. Valls, J. Domingo-Ferrer (Eds.), Modeling Decisions for Artificial Intelligence. XII, 374 pages. 2006. (Sublibrary LNAI).

Vol. 3884: B. Durand, W. Thomas (Eds.), STACS 2006. XIV, 714 pages. 2006.

Vol. 3882: M.L. Lee, K.-L. Tan, V. Wuwongse (Eds.), Database Systems for Advanced Applications. XIX, 923 pages. 2006.

Vol. 3881: S. Gibet, N. Courty, J.-F. Kamp (Eds.), Gesture in Human-Computer Interaction and Simulation. XIII, 344 pages. 2006. (Sublibrary LNAI).

Vol. 3880: A. Rashid, M. Aksit (Eds.), Transactions on Aspect-Oriented Software Development I. IX, 335 pages. 2006.

Vol. 3879: T. Erlebach, G. Persinao (Eds.), Approximation and Online Algorithms. X, 349 pages. 2006.

Vol. 3878: A. Gelbukh (Ed.), Computational Linguistics and Intelligent Text Processing. XVII, 589 pages. 2006.

Vol. 3877: M. Detyniecki, J.M. Jose, A. Nürnberger, C. J. '. van Rijsbergen (Eds.), Adaptive Multimedia Retrieval: User, Context, and Feedback. XI, 279 pages. 2006.

Vol. 3876: S. Halevi, T. Rabin (Eds.), Theory of Cryptography. XI, 617 pages. 2006.

Vol. 3875: S. Ur, E. Bin, Y. Wolfsthal (Eds.), Hardware and Software, Verification and Testing. X, 265 pages. 2006.

Vol. 3874: R. Missaoui, J. Schmidt (Eds.), Formal Concept Analysis. X, 309 pages. 2006. (Sublibrary LNAI).

Vol. 3873: L. Maicher, J. Park (Eds.), Charting the Topic Maps Research and Applications Landscape. VIII, 281 pages. 2006. (Sublibrary LNAI).

Vol. 3872: H. Bunke, A. L. Spitz (Eds.), Document Analysis Systems VII. XIII, 630 pages. 2006.

Vol. 3871: E.-G. Talbi, P. Liardet, P. Collet, E. Lutton, M. Schoenauer (Eds.), Artificial Evolution. XI, 310 pages. 2006.

Vol. 3870: S. Spaccapietra, P. Atzeni, W.W. Chu, T. Catarci, K.P. Sycara (Eds.), Journal on Data Semantics V. XIII, 237 pages. 2006.

Vol. 3869: S. Renals, S. Bengio (Eds.), Machine Learning for Multimodal Interaction. XIII, 490 pages. 2006.

Vol. 3868: K. Römer, H. Karl, F. Mattern (Eds.), Wireless Sensor Networks. XI, 342 pages. 2006.

Vol. 3866: T. Dimitrakos, F. Martinelli, P.Y.A. Ryan, S. Schneider (Eds.), Formal Aspects in Security and Trust. X, 259 pages. 2006.

Vol. 3865: W. Shen, K.-M. Chao, Z. Lin, J.-P.A. Barthès, A. James (Eds.), Computer Supported Cooperative Work in Design II. XII, 659 pages. 2006.

Vol. 3863: M. Kohlhase (Ed.), Mathematical Knowledge Management. XI, 405 pages. 2006. (Sublibrary LNAI).

Vol. 3862: R.H. Bordini, M. Dastani, J. Dix, A.E.F. Seghrouchni (Eds.), Programming Multi-Agent Systems. XIV, 267 pages. 2006. (Sublibrary LNAI).

Vol. 3861: J. Dix, S.J. Hegner (Eds.), Foundations of Information and Knowledge Systems. X, 331 pages. 2006.

Vol. 3860: D. Pointcheval (Ed.), Topics in Cryptology – CT-RSA 2006. XI, 365 pages. 2006.

Vol. 3858: A. Valdes, D. Zamboni (Eds.), Recent Advances in Intrusion Detection. X, 351 pages. 2006.

Vol. 3857: M.P.C. Fossorier, H. Imai, S. Lin, A. Poli (Eds.), Applied Algebra, Algebraic Algorithms and Error-Correcting Codes. XI, 350 pages. 2006.

Vol. 3855: E. A. Emerson, K.S. Namjoshi (Eds.), Verification, Model Checking, and Abstract Interpretation. XI, 443 pages. 2005.

Vol. 3854: I. Stavrakakis, M. Smirnov (Eds.), Autonomic Communication. XIII, 303 pages. 2006.

Vol. 3853: A.J. Ijspeert, T. Masuzawa, S. Kusumoto (Eds.), Biologically Inspired Approaches to Advanced Information Technology. XIV, 388 pages. 2006.